P9-DNT-878

SECRETS

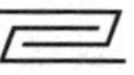

SECR

SECRETS

A Memoir of Vietnam and the Pentagon Papers

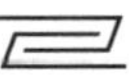

DANIEL ELLSBERG

VIKING

VIKING
Published by the Penguin Group
Penguin Putnam Inc., 375 Hudson Street, New York, New York 10014, U.S.A.
Penguin Books Ltd, 80 Strand, London WC2R 0RL, England
Penguin Books Australia Ltd, 250 Camberwell Road, Camberwell, Victoria 3124, Australia
Penguin Books Canada Ltd, 10 Alcorn Avenue, Toronto, Ontario, Canada M4V 3B2
Penguin Books India (P) Ltd, 11 Community Centre, Panchsheel Park, New Delhi–110 017, India
Penguin Books (N.Z.) Ltd, Cnr Rosedale and Airborne Roads, Albany, Auckland, New Zealand
Penguin Books (South Africa) (Pty) Ltd, 24 Sturdee Avenue, Rosebank, Johannesburg 2196, South Africa

Penguin Books Ltd, Registered Offices:
Harmondsworth, Middlesex, England

First published in 2002 by Viking Penguin,
a member of Penguin Putnam Inc.

10 9 8 7 6 5 4 3 2 1

PHOTO INSERT CREDITS: p. 5, bottom: courtesy of Randy Kehler; p. 7, top: *New York Times;* p. 7, bottom: photograph by Cary Wolinsky, from the author's collection; p. 8, top and bottom: Bettmann/Corbis. All others from the author's collection.

LIBRARY OF CONGRESS CATALOGING-IN-PUBLICATION DATA

Ellsberg, Daniel.
Secrets : a memoir of Vietnam and the Pentagon Papers / Daniel Ellsberg.
p. cm.
ISBN 0-670-03030-9
1. Vietnamese Conflict, 1961–1975—United States. 2. Pentagon Papers. 3. Ellsberg, Daniel. I. Title.
DS558 .E44 2002
959.704'3373—dc21 2002016874

This book is printed on acid-free paper. ♾

Printed in the United States of America
Set in Adobe Garamond with Nofret display
Designed by Carla Bolte

To my children, Robert, Mary, and Michael,

my grandchildren, Julio, Nicholas, Ana, Catherine, and Christina,

my brother, Harry,

and the love of my life, Patricia

PREFACE

On the evening of October 1, 1969, I walked out past the guards' desk at the Rand Corporation in Santa Monica, carrying a briefcase filled with top secret documents, which I planned to photocopy that night. The documents were part of a 7,000-page top secret study of U.S. decision making in Vietnam, later known as the Pentagon Papers. The rest of the study was in a safe in my office. I had decided to copy it all and make it public, perhaps through Senate hearings or the press, if necessary. I believed this course, especially the latter possibility, would probably put me in prison for the rest of my life. How I came to do this is the focus of this memoir.

For eleven years, from mid-1964 to the end of the war in May 1975, I was, like a great many other Americans, preoccupied with our involvement in Vietnam. In the course of that time I saw it first as a problem, next as a stalemate, then as a moral and political disaster, a crime. The first three parts of this book correspond roughly to these emerging perceptions. My own personal commitment and subsequent actions evolved along with these changing perspectives. When I saw the conflict as a problem, I tried to help solve it; when I saw it as a stalemate, to help us extricate ourselves, without harm to other national interests; when I saw it as a crime, to expose and resist it, and to try to end it immediately. Throughout all these phases, even the first, I sought in various ways to avoid further escalation of the conflict. But as late as early 1973, as I entered a federal criminal trial for my actions starting in late 1969, I would have said that *none* of these aims or efforts—neither my own nor anyone else's—had met with any success. Efforts to end the conflict—whether it was seen as a failed test, a quagmire, or a moral misadventure—seemed no more to have been rewarded than efforts to win it. Why?

As I saw it then, the war not only needed to be resisted but remained to be understood. Thirty years later I still believe that to be true. This book represents my continuing effort—far from complete—to understand my country's war on Vietnam, and my own part in it, and why it took so long to end both of those.

For three years starting in mid-1964, with the highest civil service grade, I had helped prosecute a war I believed at the outset to be doomed. Working in Washington under top decision makers in 1964–65, I watched them secretly maneuver the country into a full-scale war with no real promise of success. My pessimism during those years was not unbroken, and for about a year—from the spring of 1965 to the spring of 1966—I hoped for and worked toward some sort of success. That was after the president, despite many misgivings, including his own, had committed us to war. Once we were fully committed, I volunteered in mid-1965 to serve in Vietnam as a State Department civilian. My job came to be evaluating "pacification" in the countryside. In this I drew on my earlier training as a marine infantry commander to observe the war up close. Whether we had a *right*—any more than the French before us—to pursue by fire and steel in Indochina the objectives our leaders had chosen was a question that never occurred to me. But during two years in Vietnam, its people and plight became real to me, as real as the U.S. troops I walked with, as real as my own hands, in a way that made continuing the hopeless war intolerable.

Knocked out of the field with hepatitis and back in the United States in mid-1967, I began to do everything I could imagine to help free our country from the war. For two years I did this as an insider, briefing high officials, advising presidential candidates, and eventually, in early 1969, helping the president's national security adviser, Henry Kissinger, discover uncertainties and alternatives. But later that same year I felt called on to go beyond this approach and so to end my career as a government insider.

One of these actions risked my own freedom. In 1969 and 1970, with the help of my friend Anthony Russo, a former Rand associate, I secretly photocopied the entire forty-seven-volume Pentagon Papers, a top secret study of U.S. decision making in Vietnam from 1945 to 1968, which were then in my authorized possession, and gave them to Senator William Fulbright, chairman of the Senate Foreign Relations Committee. In 1971 I also gave copies to the *New York Times,* to the *Washington Post,* and ultimately, in the face of four unprecedented federal injunctions, to some seventeen other newspapers, all of which defied the government in printing them for the public to read.

I wasn't wrong about the personal risks. Shortly thereafter I was indicted in a federal court, with Russo later joining me in a second, superseding indictment. Eventually I faced twelve federal felony charges totaling a possible 115 years in prison, with the prospect of several further trials for me beyond that first one. But I was not wrong, either, to hope that exposing secrets five presidents had withheld and the lies they told might have benefits for our democracy that were worthy of the risks. This truth telling set in motion a train of events, including criminal White House efforts to silence or incapacitate me, that led to dismissal of the charges against me and my codefendant. Much more important, these particular Oval Office crimes helped topple the president, an act that was crucial to ending the war.

This is the story of the greatest change in my life, which began well after my return from Vietnam. The disillusionment of the brief hopes that I experienced in Vietnam and the skepticism toward the war that I brought back in mid-1967 were not really new for me. On the contrary, they were a return to the pessimism that I had acquired on a first trip to Vietnam in 1961 and that had been reinforced in my first year in the Pentagon from mid-1964. By 1967 this skeptical mood was widely shared inside the government, perhaps even more than in the public. This was a time when my general desire to see the war ended did not distinguish me from almost any of my colleagues in the government or government-sponsored research, whether or not they had served in Vietnam. An entire generation of Vietnam-era insiders had become just as disillusioned as I with a war they saw as hopeless and interminable. I was like them in most respects, no different in character or values, no less committed to the cold war, to anticommunism, to secrecy, and to the presidency. By 1968, if not earlier, they all wanted, as I did, to see us out of this war. Indeed this poses a question that I have worked at understanding ever since: How could it be, under these circumstances, that after the massive disillusionment of the Tet offensive in early 1968 the war still had seven years to go?

The heart of this memoir tells the story of how it was that starting from this common insiders' position critical of our policy, I eventually came to go beyond efforts to stop the war from within the executive branch, to be willing, instead, to give up clearances and political access, the chance of serving future presidents, my whole career, and to accept the prospect of a life behind bars. It focuses on what in my experience made it possible for me to do in 1969 through 1972 what I now wish I (or others) had done in 1964 or 1965: *go to Congress and the press and tell the truth, with documents.*

It's easy to say that the idea of doing this simply didn't occur to me at the time, any more than it did to others. The question remains why it didn't. Like so many, I put personal loyalty to the president (and to my career, my access to inside information and influence, however I idealized my purposes) above all else. Above loyalty to the Constitution. Above obligation to truth, to fellow Americans, and to other human lives. It was the face-to-face example, for which I will always be grateful, of young Americans who were choosing to go to prison rather than to take part in a war they knew was wrong that awakened me to these higher loyalties.

I hope to pass on such lessons to future officials in similar circumstances and to all the citizens who should hold them accountable. And another, happier lesson (described in Part IV) that emerged toward the end of our trial and after it: that telling the truth, revealing wrongly kept secrets, can have a surprisingly strong, unforeseeable power to help end a wrong and save lives.

CONTENTS

PART III

PART IV

SECRETS

PART I

SECRETS

Prologue: Vietnam 1961

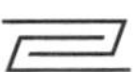

In the fall of 1961 it didn't take very long to discover in Vietnam that we weren't likely to be successful there. It took me less than a week, on my first visit. With the right access, talking to the right people, you could get the picture pretty quickly. You didn't have to speak Vietnamese, or know Asian history or philosophy or culture, to learn that nothing we were trying to do was working or was likely to get better. I read somewhere you don't have to be an ichthyologist to know when a fish stinks.

It helped that I was part of a high-level Pentagon task force, visiting the Military Assistance Advisory Group (MAAG) in Vietnam with a "go anywhere, see anything" kind of clearance. The chief of MAAG, General Lionel McGarr, told his staff members to help us any way they could and to speak frankly. One colonel in particular whom I talked to was near the end of his tour and inclined to pass on what he had learned in-country to someone who might have the ear of folks in Washington. He opened MAAG's files to me and pulled out piles of folders, and I stayed up half the night several nights in a row reading plans and reports and analyses of our programs in Vietnam and their prospects. The smell of rot, of failure, lay all over them, and my colonel friend made no attempt to pretend otherwise.

He told me—and the documents and what I heard from his colleagues supported it—that under President Ngo Dinh Diem, the dictatorial leader we had essentially chosen for South Vietnam seven years earlier, the Communists would almost surely take power eventually, probably within a year or two. If Diem was deposed in a coup—one had almost succeeded the year before—the Communists would probably win even faster. His reasoning was informed and complex; my notes of our discussions are filled with diagrams of "vicious circles," a whole network of them. It was persuasive.

Most of the MAAG officers agreed with him, and with many Vietnamese officials, that the only thing that would change this prospect in the short run would be American combat forces on a large scale. (The Geneva Accords of 1954 permitted only some 350 American military "advisers" in the country, although by various subterfuges some 700 were present, none in American combat units.) But even American divisions, this colonel believed, would only postpone the same outcome. The Communists would govern soon after our forces left, whenever that might be.

This was not good news to me. I was a dedicated cold warrior, in fact a professional one. I had been anti-Soviet since the Czech coup and the Berlin blockade in 1948, my last year of high school, and the Korean War while I was a student at Harvard a couple of years later. For my military service I had chosen the Marine Corps and spent three years as an infantry officer. After the Marines I returned to Harvard as a graduate fellow and then went to the Rand Corporation, a nonprofit research organization whose entire focus was the military aspects of the cold war. My own work up to 1961 had been mainly on deterring a surprise nuclear attack from the Soviet Union. I should have liked nothing better than to hear that South Vietnam was a place where Soviet-backed Communists were going to be defeated, with our help. But the colonel's arguments persuaded me that this was not that place.

When I got back to Rand the next month, my informal message to my bosses was that they would be well advised to keep clear of Vietnam, stay away from counterinsurgency research, in Vietnam at least. We were on a losing course there, I said, that was very unlikely to be changed, and all associated with it would only be frustrated and tarred by failure. They would suffer the fate of those who had worked on the Bay of Pigs, just a few months earlier. I privately decided to have nothing to do with it.

But the Kennedy administration didn't have that luxury in the short run. Just weeks after I returned from Vietnam a White House team under two top presidential advisers, General Maxwell Taylor and Walt W. Rostow, headed out to Saigon to assess the situation for the president. In particular, they were to judge the necessity for sending U.S. ground forces. Soon after their return a month later the White House announced an increase in our involvement in Vietnam. In mid-November President Kennedy launched a steadily growing increase in the number of U.S. military personnel in Vietnam, breaking through the ceiling set by the Geneva Accords in 1954. He doubled the number of military advisers in the last two months of 1961 and accompanied them with support units for the Vietnamese armed forces: helicopter companies and specialists in communications, transportation, logistics, and intelligence.

I wasn't really surprised by this. I was glad that contrary to press speculation over the previous weeks, he sent no U.S. ground combat units. Nevertheless, I thought the increased involvement went in the wrong direction. (U.S. presence had increased to twelve thousand "advisers" by the time President Kennedy died in 1963, and some U.S. support was being supplied covertly, but still no ground combat units.) It was what I had feared was likely to happen; that was why I'd made a conscious decision not to be part of it.

I kept that resolution for the next three years.

1

The Tonkin Gulf: August 1964

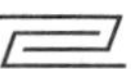

On Tuesday morning, August 4, 1964, my first full day on my new job in the Pentagon, a courier came into the outer office with an urgent cable for my boss. He'd been running. The secretaries told him Assistant Secretary John McNaughton was out of the office; he was down the hall with Secretary of Defense Robert McNamara. They pointed him to me, his new special assistant. The courier handed me the cable and left. It was easy to see, as I read it, why he had been running.

It was from Captain John J. Herrick, the commodore of a two-destroyer flotilla in the Tonkin Gulf, off North Vietnam in the South China Sea. He said he was under attack by North Vietnamese patrol boats and had opened fire on them. He was in international waters, over sixty miles off the coast of North Vietnam. One torpedo had been heard by the sonarman on his command ship, the USS *Maddox,* and another had just passed by the other destroyer, the *Turner Joy.*

As soon as he gave me the cable, the courier returned to the message center of our department in the Pentagon, International Security Affairs (ISA), part of the Office of the Secretary of Defense, the civilian part of the Department of Defense. Within ten minutes he was back to me with another one in the same series: "Am under continuous torpedo attack."

A few minutes later Herrick reported another torpedo had run by him, and two more were in the water. His ships were firing at the attackers and might already have destroyed one of them. They were firing by radar, without visual contact. The encounter was taking place in total darkness, on an overcast night without moon or stars, in the hours close to midnight.

This was no ordinary event. It was exactly the second attack on a U.S. Navy vessel since World War II. But the first had been less than three days earlier. That was on Sunday, August 2, also on Herrick's ship, the USS *Maddox,* on patrol in the Tonkin Gulf. In broad daylight in the middle of the afternoon, twenty-eight miles out to sea, three North Vietnamese PT boats had attacked and launched torpedoes at the *Maddox.* All the torpedoes had missed, and there was no damage to the destroyer, except for a single 14.5-mm bullet that lodged in one of its stacks. The boats were driven off, all damaged, by fire from the *Maddox* and from navy planes from the carrier *Ticonderoga* nearby.

Since there had been no American casualties or significant damage, President Johnson had decided to take no further action, except to add another destroyer, the *Turner Joy,* to the mission. The two destroyers were directed to continue what was described publicly as a routine patrol in order to assert U.S. rights to navigate freely in international waters. But the president also announced on Monday his orders that in case of any further attacks, the attacking boats were to be not only repulsed but destroyed. He had sent a formal protest to Hanoi, warning that "any further unprovoked offensive military action against United States forces" would "inevitably" result in "grave consequences." All this, except for the latest announcement, I'd read in the Monday morning newspapers. That afternoon, reading classified accounts of the episode, I'd learned a good deal more.

Now, as each new message came in, I looked at the date-time group, the six-digit number (followed by a letter indicating the time zone, then the month) at the upper-left-hand corner of the cables. The first two digits indicated the day of the month; the next four, in military time (2400 for midnight), the exact time the message had been transmitted. The first cable had been transmitted from Herrick's command ship at 10:42 A.M. Washington time (9:42 P.M. in the Tonkin Gulf). I compared the time of transmission with the clock on the wall of my office in the Pentagon, which showed, as I recall, that it was about half an hour later, an extremely short time in this precomputer age for this message to reach me. The same was true for the second, sent at 10:52 A.M. Washington time and handed to me about 11:20, and for the others that kept arriving every few minutes. Herrick was giving them "Flash" priority, the highest priority for message handling, so they were taking precedence at every terminal for handling, retransmission, and distribution.

But twenty or thirty minutes was a long duration for an action like this. The whole exchange on Sunday, surface and air, had lasted thirty-seven minutes. It could have been all over, on the other side of the world, by the time I read the first message, or the latest one. Or a destroyer might have been hit, might already be sinking, while we were reading about its evasive maneuvers or its success at destroying an attacker. But there was no way for anyone in Washington to know that as he read these.

There was then no CNN on which to watch live action half a world away. There was not even any direct voice contact between Washington and destroyers in the western Pacific. The closest to it was radio and telephone contact with Admiral Ulysses S. G. Sharp, commander in chief Pacific (CINCPAC), at his command post in Hawaii, as far away from the Tonkin Gulf as Washington was from Hawaii. CINCPAC cables, and many others, were now adding to the pile on my desk, but they weren't arriving as frequently or as fast as the flash cables from the destroyers. Following Captain Herrick's stream of messages, we weren't really watching the action in real time, but they were coming in such quick sequence that it felt as if we were.

The messages were vivid. Herrick must have been dictating them from the bridge in between giving orders, as his two ships swerved to avoid torpedoes picked up on the sonar of the *Maddox* and fired in the darkness at targets shown on the radar of the *Turner Joy*. "Torpedoes missed. Another fired at us. Four torpedoes in water. And five torpedoes in water. . . . Have . . . successfully avoided at least six torpedoes."

Nine torpedoes had been fired at his ships, fourteen, twenty-six. More attacking boats had been hit; at least one sunk. This action wasn't ending after forty minutes or an hour. It was going on, ships dodging and firing in choppy seas, planes overhead firing rockets at locations given them by the *Turner Joy*'s radar, for an incredible two hours before the stream of continuous combat updates finally ended. Then, suddenly, an hour later, full stop. A message arrived that took back not quite all of it, but enough to put everything earlier in question.

The courier came in with another single cable, running again, after an hour of relative quiet in which he had walked in intermittently at a normal pace with batches of cables from CINCPAC and the Seventh Fleet and analyses from the State Department and the CIA and other parts of the Pentagon. I was sitting at my desk—I remember the moment—trying to put this patchwork of information in some order for McNaughton on his return, when the courier handed me the following flash cable from Herrick: "Review of action makes many reported contacts and torpedoes fired appear doubtful. Freak weather effects on radar and overeager sonarmen may have accounted for many reports. No actual visual sightings by *Maddox*. Suggest complete evaluation before any further action taken."

It was a little after 2:00 P.M. The message had been sent at 1:27 P.M. Washington time. Half an hour later another message from Herrick, summarizing positive and negative evidence for an attack, concluded: "Entire action leaves many doubts except for apparent attempted ambush at beginning. Suggest thorough reconnaissance in daylight by aircraft." The reconnaissance in daylight, still three or four hours away in the gulf, would search for oil slicks and wreckage from the boats supposedly hit, indications that an attack, not just a fight with radar ghosts, had actually taken place.

In my mind, these messages erased the impact of the two-hour-long "live" drama that we'd been following. This new information was a cold bath. Around three o'clock, in response to frantic requests for confirmation, Herrick cabled, "Details of action present a confusing picture although certain that original ambush was bona fide." But how could he be "certain" of that, or why should anyone else be, when he had seemed equally confident, an hour earlier, of all the succeeding reports up till now? Herrick continued to assert at 6:00 P.M. Washington time (5:00 A.M. in the gulf) that "the first boat to close the *Maddox* probably fired a torpedo at the *Maddox* which was heard but not seen. All subsequent *Maddox* torpedo reports are doubtful in that it is suspected that sonarman was hearing ship's own propeller beat." But his acknowledgment that all the other vivid reports he had been sending were unreliable undercut his assertion of continued confidence in his initial messages and the first torpedo. As negative evidence accumulated, within a few days it came to seem less likely that any attack had occurred on August 4; by 1967 it seemed almost certain there had been no second attack, and by 1971 I was convinced of that beyond reasonable doubt. (In 1966 credible testimony from captured North Vietnamese officers who had participated in the August 2 attack refuted any attack on August 4. In late 1970 journalist Anthony Austin discovered and gave me evidence that intercepted North Vietnamese cables supposedly confirming an August 4 attack actually referred to the attack on August 2. Finally, in 1981 journalist Robert Scheer convinced Herrick—with new evidence from his ship's log—that his long-held belief in the first torpedo report was unfounded.) However, on August 4, given Herrick's repeated assurances and those of a number of seamen over the next few hours, I concluded that afternoon, along with everyone else I spoke to, that there probably had been an attack of some sort. At the same time, there was clearly a good chance that there had been none. In that light, Herrick's recommendation to pause and investigate before reacting seemed prudent, to say the very least: Reverse engines, stop the presses! But that was not how things were moving in Washington that Tuesday afternoon.

Herrick's new cables didn't slow for a moment the preparations in Washington and in the Pacific for a retaliatory air strike as quickly as possible, preferably at first light in the Tonkin Gulf. What they did stimulate was a flurry of probes for evidence and witness testimony that would support his earlier descriptions of the attack or at least confirm the fact that some attack had occurred.

As these were arriving in Washington, the president was meeting with the National Security Council (NSC) basically to inform it of the planned actions. Next he briefed congressional leaders. Carriers were moving into position to launch their planes at first light or as early in the morning as possible. In Washington time that could be anywhere from six o'clock in the evening to nearly midnight. But the president was determined to tell the American people of the U.S. attacks more or less as they were happening. He didn't want them to hear about the strikes in the morning news the next day, hours after they had taken place and after the rest of the world, in earlier time zones, had already heard.

The navy was concerned, on the other hand, not to have the president's public announcement warn Vietnamese antiaircraft gunners that an attack was coming before the planes had entered North Vietnamese radar. The president undertook not to do that. He asked for airtime for 7:00 P.M., which shifted to 8:00, then to 9:00, because the carrier *Constellation* had still not reached its launching station or finished briefing its pilots. The president was determined to speak no later than 11:30 P.M. After that his entire audience on the eastern seaboard would be in bed. Through McNamara to CINCPAC (Admiral Sharp, in Hawaii), he was pressing to see if he could make his announcement before the planes were over their targets, perhaps when the first ones started to launch. Would they be picked up immediately on radar, he asked, so that it wouldn't be his announcement then that broke the news to Hanoi? The answer was yes, but Hanoi wouldn't know where the planes were heading, so he should take numbers and types of targets off the TelePrompTer.

At this point in the evening I was sitting with John McNaughton in his office along with his director of Far Eastern affairs and other members of his staff, reading cables from the carriers and CINCPAC on progress toward the launch and trying to help answer questions from McNamara or the White House. The large TV in McNaughton's office was on continuously, with the sound turned down, in case the president decided to break in on the programming.

Word came in that planes had taken off, then word that they had not; requests arrived that the announcement be delayed till the planes were on enemy radar, but it was too late for that. Admiral Sharp (CINCPAC) told McNamara at 11:20 P.M. that the *Ticonderoga* had launched its planes, and the president went on TV at 11:37. He announced that "air action is now in execution," though in fact the *Constellation* had not yet launched its planes and no other planes had as yet reached the coast of North Vietnam or entered its radar. So the announcement did give Hanoi warning, which it passed down quickly. Our navy concluded from the results that surprise had been sacrificed.

McNamara gave a press conference at the Pentagon after midnight. We were up all night in the office following the raids, to prepare for another McNamara press conference the next day. My first full day in the Pentagon had been over twenty-four hours long.

The president's announcement and McNamara's press conference late in the evening of August 4 informed the American public that the North Vietnamese, for the second time in two days, had attacked U.S. warships on "routine patrol in international waters"; that this was clearly a "deliberate" pattern of "naked aggression"; that the evidence for the second attack, like the first, was "unequivocal"; that the attack had been "unprovoked"; and that the United States, by responding in order to deter any repetition, intended no wider war.

By midnight on the fourth, or within a day or two, I knew that each one of these assurances was false.

"Unequivocal"? In the president's initial public announcement and in every official statement afterward, it was implicit that the August 4 attack on our ships, which had triggered our retaliatory strikes, was a simple fact. There was no official hint, either to Congress or to the public, that in the minds of various experienced navy operators and intelligence analysts at the time of our retaliation, as well as earlier and later, doubt adhered to every single piece of evidence that an attack had occurred at all on August 4.

A *"routine patrol in international waters"*? The two destroyers were on a secret intelligence mission, code-named DeSoto patrols, penetrating well within what the North Vietnamese regarded as their territorial waters. We assumed, correctly, that the North Vietnamese claimed the same limits as other Communist nations, twelve miles from their coastline and from their islands. The United States did not officially "recognize" this extended limit; nevertheless U.S. Navy ships were prudently directed to keep at least fifteen miles out from the Chinese islands or mainland. But before the August 2 incident the *Maddox* had been frequently eight miles from the North Vietnamese mainland and four miles from their islands. The purpose of this was not merely to demonstrate that we rejected their claims of limits on our "freedom of the seas" but to provoke them into turning on coast defense radar so that our destroyers could plot their defenses, in preparation for possible air or sea attacks. Thus it was true that the August 2 attack had been twenty-eight miles out to sea, but that was because a warning of attack when the *Maddox* was just ten miles from the coast had led the skipper to change course and to head out to sea, with torpedo boats in pursuit.

"Unprovoked"? Hanoi had claimed that "puppet" forces of the Americans had shelled two of its coastal islands, Hon Me and Hon Nieu, on the night of July 30–31. In public releases, the State Department denied any knowledge of any such attacks, as did McNamara in his press conferences on August 4 and 5. In top secret testimony to congressional committees in closed hearings over the next two days, Secretary of State Dean Rusk and McNamara acknowledged such attacks but insisted that they could not realistically be considered U.S. provocations that justified or were intended to evoke North Vietnamese counterattacks because they were entirely "South Vietnamese" operations, run by the South Vietnamese navy, aimed at stopping infiltration from the North. The United States supported them and knew about them in general terms but, Rusk claimed, not in detail; there was little knowledge of them in Washington. They had no relationship at all with our destroyer patrols, they were in no way coordinated, and in fact the commander on the destroyers knew nothing of them at all. It was implicit in this testimony, and not challenged, that in any case no such raids were taking place in the context of the second attack or since July 31. The resolution that Congress was being asked to pass quickly and as nearly unanimously as possible was nothing other than a gesture of support for the president's action, to demonstrate solidarity to Hanoi and to deter future attacks on our forces. Each of these assertions was false.

In my new job I was reading the daily transcripts of this secret testimony, and at the same time I was learning from cables, reports, and discussion in the Pentagon the background that gave the lie to virtually everything told both to the public and, more elaborately, to Congress in secret session. Within days I knew that the commander of the destroyers not only knew of the covert raids but had requested that his patrol be curtailed or terminated after the first attack on August 2 because he expected retaliatory attacks on his vessels as a result of the raids. His request was denied. Moreover, I learned, these weren't South Vietnamese operations at all, not even joint operations. They were entirely U.S. operations, code-named 34A ops. The anti-infiltration operations by South Vietnamese junks that McNamara described in some detail to Congress were entirely separate and different, as he knew. For the raids against North Vietnam, of which Hanoi had publicly complained, the United States owned the fast patrol boats known as Nastys (which the CIA had purchased from Norway), hired the crews, and controlled every aspect of the operations. The CIA ran the training, with help from the U.S. Navy, and recruited the crews; some of them were recruited, as individuals, from the South Vietnamese navy, but others were CIA "assets" from Taiwan and elsewhere in Asia, along with mercenaries from around the world. The operations had been run originally by the CIA but now were jointly controlled by the CIA and Military Assistance Command, Vietnam (MACV), in coordination with the navy. Despite the use of foreign personnel, to provide "plausible deniability" if captured, the 34A operations were exactly as much American operations as were the U.S. Navy DeSoto patrols of the destroyers. Moreover, the North Vietnamese were not mistaken to believe that the two types of American operations were coordinated at various levels. For one thing, the DeSoto missions in that particular area were timed to take advantage, in their plotting of coastal radars and interception of communications, of the heightened activity that was triggered in North Vietnamese coastal defenses by the 34A raids.

As for Washington knowledge of them, top officials read and signed off personally on schedules for them in advance, based on incredibly detailed descriptions of the planned actions. I soon knew this because I came later that month to be the courier who carried these highly secret plans around Washington from one to another of these officials for their signatures. These included Deputy Secretary of Defense Cyrus Vance, Deputy Secretary of State Llewellyn Thompson, and finally, National Security Adviser McGeorge Bundy in the White House. They were among the members of the 303 Committee, which oversaw and approved all covert operations for the president. While they read the documents, I sat in their offices, along with a colonel from the covert operations branch of the Joint Chiefs of Staff (JCS) who had initially brought the file to me.

The contrast between what the senators had been told by the secretaries in a secret joint session of the Senate Foreign Relations and Armed Services committees, as I read the testimony, and what I soon knew as a first-week staffer in the Pentagon was striking. Pressed by Senator Frank Church to acknowledge that "our government which supplied these boats" (supposedly, as he had just been told, to the South Vietnamese) did know that they would be used for attacks on North Vietnam, Secretary Rusk replied, "In the larger sense, that is so, but as far as any particular detail is concerned we don't from Washington follow that in great detail."

In contrast with this disclaimer, as I knew very well, it would have been more accurate to say that *every particular detail* of these operations was known and approved by the highest authorities in Washington, both military and civilian. The monthly plan for September 1964, the month following the August raids, which I carried over to the State Department to be read and initialed by Mr. Rusk's deputy and then to McGeorge Bundy in the White House, included the following scheduled actions:

> Two junk capture missions; remove captives for 36–48 hours interrogation; booby trap junk with antidisturbance devices and release; captives returned after interrogation; timing depends upon sea conditions and current intelligence; . . . Demolition of Route 1 bridge by infiltrated team accompanied by fire support teams, place short-delay charges against spans and caissons, place antipersonnel mines on road approaches; . . . Bombard Cape Mui Dao observation post with 81 MM mortars and 40 MM guns from two PTFs; . . . Destruction of section of Hanoi–Vinh railroad by infiltrated demolition team supported by two VN [Vietnam] marine squads, by rubber boats from PTFs, place short-delay charges and anti-personnel mines around area. . . .

Some of these operational details, such as the placement of antipersonnel weapons and 81-mm mortar rounds, might have seemed rather petty to be occupying the attention of these officials, but this was the only war we had. Of course it was precisely the "sensitive" nature of the operations—their illegality, the danger both of exposure and of escalation, and their covertness, defined as "plausible deniability"—that required such high-level officials to lie to the Senate if questions were raised and therefore to need such detailed prior awareness and control of what it was they would have to lie about.

This wasn't the end of the coordination in Washington. After a monthly program like this was approved, General William Westmoreland, U.S. military commander in Vietnam, requested approval for execution of each individual maritime mission, and I again carried these around for approval. When an attack that had earlier been approved in Washington for the following month actually took place—the exact timing would depend on weather and sea conditions—that fact and its results were reported back to Washington before another attack was approved by Washington. On August 2, during the Sunday morning meeting in which President Johnson was told of the daylight attack on the *Maddox,* there was discussion of the results of the July 31 covert attacks on the islands, and the president personally approved the next proposed covert raids, for the nights of August 3 and August 5.

On the evening of the fourth, at an NSC meeting when the president asked, "Do they want war by attacking our ships in the middle of the Gulf of Tonkin?" Director of Central Intelligence John McCone answered: "No. The North Vietnamese are reacting defensively to our [*sic*] attack on their off-shore islands. They are responding out of pride and on the basis of defense considerations." He was referring to the July 31 raids, but his answer covered the supposed attack that morning, since there had been another raid, this time on the North Vietnamese mainland, the night before. This estimate did not prevent the president from saying, in his message as he urged Congress to pass the resolution days later: "We have answered their unprovoked aggression. . . ."

On August 7 Congress approved the Tonkin Gulf Resolution, which reads: "Congress approves and supports the determination of the President, as Commander in Chief, *to take all necessary measures* to repel any armed attack against the forces of the United States *and to prevent further aggression*. . . . The United States is . . . prepared, *as the President determines,* to take all necessary steps, including the use of armed force, to assist any member or protocol state of the Southeast Asia Collective Defense Treaty requesting assistance in defense of its freedom" [emphasis added].

There was some unease expressed regarding the unusually vague and open-ended scope of the resolution drafted by the administration. Senator Wayne Morse called it a predated declaration of war. Senator Gaylord Nelson offered an amendment expressing a sense in Congress that "[o]ur continuing policy is to limit our role to the provision of aid, training assistance, and military advice," and "we should continue to attempt to avoid a direct military involvement in the Southeast Asian conflict." Senator Fulbright, who managed passage of the resolution in the Senate, said he believed this amendment was "unobjectionable" as "an accurate reflection of what I believe is the President's policy." He rejected it only because (as Johnson had stressed to him in private) the delay in passage to resolve differences in language between the House and Senate versions would weaken the image of unified national support for the president's recent actions. At this moment it was announced that the House had passed the resolution 416 to 0 after forty minutes of debate. Fulbright hoped the Senate would approach that unanimity. Soon after this the Senate voted 88 to 2, with only Senators Morse and Ernest Gruening voting against it.

Several senators, including George McGovern, Frank Church, Albert Gore, and the Republican John Sherman Cooper, had expressed the same concern as Nelson. Fulbright acknowledged that the language was broad enough to permit the president to launch direct combat involvement, including U.S. infantry divisions, which was what worried them. But they accepted Fulbright's assurances—reflecting his talks with officials including the president—that there was no consideration in the administration of using the resolution as an authorization for changing the American role in the war. He had "no doubt that the president will consult with Congress in case a major change in present policy becomes necessary." Most of the Democrats saw the resolution mainly as a way to get a strong expression of bipartisan support for the president's forceful action, undercutting Goldwater's campaign claim that Johnson was uncertain in foreign affairs and indecisive in Vietnam. By thus helping to defeat Goldwater, they saw their support for the resolution as a way of *avoiding* escalation in Vietnam, which only Goldwater was promising.

But Fulbright's assurances, all of them, were as unfounded as those of Johnson, Rusk, and McNamara. The difference was that he didn't know it. He had been deceived, and in turn, unwittingly, he misled the Senate. Of all the week's deceptions, these were by far the most significant.

We seek no wider war? But the president that summer was secretly and explicitly *threatening* the Hanoi regime with a wider war against North Vietnam itself, unless its leaders took steps to end the conflict that no one in the administration thought they were likely to take. Johnson's messages to Ho Chi Minh, through a Canadian intermediary, amounted to a secret promise by the president of the United States to the leaders in Hanoi to widen the war unless they called it off.

The warnings were being delivered to North Vietnam by Blair Seaborn, the Canadian member of the International Control Commission (ICC), set up to monitor observance with the 1954 and 1962 Geneva Accords. In his first meeting in Hanoi on June 18, he had met privately with Prime Minister Pham Van Dong. Seaborn had relayed the warning, drafted by U.S. officials and coordinated with the Canadians, that "U.S. public and official patience with North Vietnamese aggression is growing extremely thin," and that if the conflict should escalate, "the greatest devastation would of course result for the DRV [Democratic Republic of Vietnam, or North Vietnam] itself."

Among those who had advocated these threats—virtually all of the president's civilian and military advisers—no one regarded them as bluffs. The Joint Chiefs of Staff had been directed to make detailed plans for air attacks on North Vietnam. By the end of May it had completed studies and preparations, down to target folders for a recommended list of ninety-four targets. The targets for retaliation selected so quickly on August 5 had simply been drawn from this ninety-four-target list. Both this planning and the warning by a Canadian intermediary figured in detailed scenarios coordinated within the government since March and April—most recently on May 23—leading up to a "D-Day" air assault on North Vietnam, to continue until "terrorism, armed attacks, and armed resistance to pacification efforts in the South stop." Another key element, scheduled for D-20 (twenty days before the attacks began), was: "Obtain joint resolution [from Congress] approving past actions and authorizing whatever is necessary with respect to Vietnam."

Although the detailed thirty-day scenario approach was shelved by the president's top advisers in late May, they recommended to him as separate items that month nearly all of its pre–D-Day elements, including those above. They also recommended an initial strike against North Vietnam to underline the secret warning. This followed a proposal by Ambassador Henry Cabot Lodge in Saigon, a strong advocate of attacks on the North who had earlier in the spring introduced the notion of the warning through Canada. On May 15, in a message to the president, he suggested:

> If prior to the Canadian's trip to Hanoi there has been a terroristic act of the proper magnitude, then I suggest that a specific target in North Vietnam be considered as a prelude to his arrival. . . .

This had not occurred prior to Seaborn's first visit to Hanoi in June. But his second visit was scheduled for August 10. The events of August 2–7 allowed the United States to point out, in case of any doubt in Hanoi, just what that warning meant in concrete terms. Moreover, the second discussion would allow the administration to make clear what it felt entitled to do with the authority granted by the Tonkin Gulf Resolution, lest Hanoi had been misled by the interpretation Senator Fulbright had given to his fellow Democrats.

To these ends my new boss, John McNaughton, was asked to draft instructions for Seaborn's August 10 session. That was why McNaughton chose to tell me about and to show me a file on the threat process, describing it as one of the most closely held secrets in the administration. He told me that I must not hint of the existence of this process to anyone, including any of his own deputies. One reason for the extreme secrecy of the information McNaughton gave me was that it was a very dubious role for an ICC commissioner to be conveying U.S. threats to Hanoi. (An intermediary was needed because the United States had no formal representation or contact with the Hanoi regime.) That role could not be known to the other members of the ICC, Poland and India, or to the Canadian Parliament or public, which would not be as quick to accept it as Canadian Prime Minister Lester Pearson. But what was most "sensitive" about this information was that this official warning by the president to the heads of an adversary state came very close to committing him to the course of action that his Republican opponent, Senator Goldwater, was advocating and that President Johnson was opposing and describing in his campaign as dangerously reckless. Moreover, it put the administration's intentions with respect to the Tonkin Gulf Resolution in an entirely different light from what Congress was being told. Indeed, on August 7, as Congress was voting on the Tonkin Gulf Resolution, John McNaughton was drafting instructions on the message Seaborn should (and later did) deliver that precisely reversed the emphasis on the two key clauses in the resolution that Senator Fulbright had been encouraged by the administration to convey to his fellow senators. His draft, which was adopted by the administration and followed by the Canadians, told Seaborn to conclude his comments with the points:

> a. That the events of the past few days should add credibility to the statement made last time, that "U.S. public and official patience with North Vietnamese aggression is growing extremely thin."
>
> b. That the congressional resolution was passed with near unanimity, strongly reaffirming the unity and determination of the U.S. government and people not only with respect to any further attacks on U.S. military forces but more broadly to continue to oppose firmly, by all necessary means, DRV efforts to subvert and conquer South Vietnam and Laos.
>
> c. That the U.S. has come to the view that the DRV role in South Vietnam and Laos is critical. If the DRV persists in its present course, it can expect . . . to suffer the consequences.

Pham Van Dong's reaction on August 13, as a State Department report described it, was "extremely angry" and cold. And unyielding, as on the first visit (when the exchange had been friendlier, despite the threat). Then he had said that the prospect for the United States and its friends in South

Vietnam was *"sans issue":* no way out, a dead end. Now, in the aftermath of the American raids, he said that the United States had found "it is necessary to carry the war to the North in order to find a way out of the impasse . . . in the South."

He had gotten the message. (It remained a secret from the American electorate, and from Congress, for the next eight months.) A wider war was on the way.

2

Cold Warrior, Secret Keeper

After my discouraging introduction to the Vietnam problem in 1961, I had successfully dodged the issue as a defense consultant for the next three years. That was easy. The focus of my work as a Rand Corporation analyst and Washington consultant remained what it had been for three years before that: avoidance of general nuclear war, within the context of the cold war. The brief trip to Southeast Asia had been related to that too. It was part of a study of research and development on conventional weapons in limited wars, to escape from the Eisenhower administration's focus on nuclear weapons for all conflicts. But for me that was an unwonted distraction from the problems that preoccupied me and to which I returned, of deterring a Soviet surprise nuclear attack and avoiding accidental eruption of nuclear war. Although I was invited to kibitz or poked my head into policy discussions in a wide range of government offices in Washington, all on the subject of nuclear weapons and deterrence, no one asked for my thoughts or a helping hand on Vietnam policy. It was out of my line, and I was glad to keep it that way.

Yet in mid-1964 I had accepted an offer to leave Rand to join the Defense Department to assist a high official primarily on his Vietnam policy-making responsibilities. That takes some explaining. I had no newly acquired interest in Vietnam, nor had I gained a more hopeful attitude about our prospects there. Quite the contrary; within weeks on my new job, everything I was reading in the secret cables from our embassy in Saigon confirmed my worst suspicions about the situation, and that came as no surprise. Why, of all possible desks in the government, had I chosen one with these particular, depressing cables coming across it? What brought the stinking fish to my plate?

It was, from my point of view, research. Though it wasn't obvious on the surface, it was research addressed to the same end as that of the previous six years, avoiding nuclear war. Certainly I would not have predicted that three years after my trip to Vietnam I would be working seventy hours a week in the Pentagon to help sneak the country into a war there. What I was doing over six years *before* that trip, working on preparations for general nuclear war, was just as bizarre in terms of my own background. The intense irony of my doing such work was rooted in my revulsion—ever since I was a child during World War II—at the bombing of civilians and my extreme abhorrence of nuclear weapons like the bombs that were dropped at the end of the war. Those attitudes, which figured in my eventual response to the Vietnam War, have been virtual constants in my life, not matters of midlife conversion.

I was born in 1931 in Chicago, where my father was out of work as a structural engineer. We moved to Springfield, Illinois, when I was five, and to Detroit a few years later. I remember vividly the radio announcement of the attack on our warships at Pearl Harbor when I was ten, after which my father spent the war years designing factories to build bombers. I remember just as vividly films and radio reports of bombing, largely of civilians, for two years before that. Newsreels of the Nazi bombing of Warsaw, Stukas strafing and dive-bombing refugee families with children on the roads, the total destruction of the city center of Rotterdam, and above all, the London blitz represented for me the essence of Nazism. Nothing else, not German aggression, blitzkrieg, the prewar persecution of the Jews (I knew nothing of the extermination program during the war), seemed so purely, incomprehensibly evil as the deliberate bombing of women and children. Not even the concentration camps that I knew would already have engulfed my own family if we had been in Germany. (Though both my parents were born in America and grew up in Denver in nonreligious households, all my grandparents were Jews who had emigrated from Russia in the late 1880s. My mother had become a Christian Scientist before marrying my father, a widower she had known as a child in Denver, and my father had joined her devotedly in that religion before I was born. As my father told me, we were Jews, though "not in religion." I was raised as a Christian, in an extremely devout Christian Scientist household, but that didn't make us less Jewish in the eyes of my parents or, I knew, the Nazis.)

In grade school after Pearl Harbor we had air-raid drills. One day the teacher showed us a film on the London blitz and handed out a model of a short, slim silver-colored incendiary bomb that was used to start and spread fires. We were told it was a magnesium bomb, whose blaze couldn't be extinguished by water. It had to be covered with sand, to keep oxygen from getting to it. In every room in our school there was a large bucket filled with sand for this purpose. I take it that this was a way of making us identify with the war effort, like the blackout curtains on every window and the air-raid watchers and wardens on each block, since the likelihood of German or Japanese bombers' penetrating to Detroit seems small in retrospect. But the notion of the magnesium bomb made a very strong impression on me. It was uncanny to think of humans designing and dropping on other humans a flaming substance that couldn't easily be extinguished, a particle of which, we were told, would burn through flesh to the bone and wouldn't stop burning even then. It was hard for me to understand people who were willing to burn children like that. It still is.

Later the newsreels were of American and British bombers bravely flying through flak to drop their loads on targets in Germany. I wasn't aware that they were often dropping incendiary bombs of the same kind we had handled in model form in school or with substances with similar characteristics of clinging to flesh and burning inextinguishably, white phosphorus and later napalm. We didn't see films of what was happening to people on the ground under our bombers or in the firestorms in Hamburg, Dresden, or Tokyo. We believed what we were told: that our daylight precision bombing with the Norden bombsight was aimed only at war factories and military targets, though some civilians were inevitably hit by accident. British leaders were telling their own public the same thing about British nighttime "area" bombing, though that was a total lie. Official secrecy and lies concealed a deliberate British campaign of terror bombing targeted directly on population, in which the United States joined in the later years of bombing Germany and throughout the bombing of Japan.

I wasn't aware, in short, how thoroughly we were imitating Nazi bombing practices, especially in the firebombing of Japanese cities. But it was not by accident that in later years I studied the history of strategic bombing, including the U.S. Strategic Bombing Survey in considerable detail. I've found convincing the conclusions of many critics at the time that neither the terror bombing nor the "precision" bombing of factories had contributed at all, on balance, to shortening the war, while the former had been by all previous standards a clear-cut war crime, committed by us as by the

Nazis. Even before that the unmistakable targeting of civilians in Hiroshima and Nagasaki left me at the end of the war with deeply ambivalent feelings about our possession of atomic weapons, which appeared to be, above all, instruments of terror bombing. That continued study taught me enduring skepticism about the claims of strategic bombing advocates, in Vietnam and elsewhere. Yet fifteen years later I found myself drafting guidance for war plans that included the possibility of launching retaliatory attacks with thermonuclear weapons against cities.

One element that underlies that paradox, as it does my passage to Vietnam, is that I had become in my late teens, along with many other Americans, a cold warrior. This was not because I had grown up as a conservative, like my father. I was a cold war Democrat, a liberal Democrat, who revered Franklin Roosevelt for his role in the New Deal and in World War II and who believed in the causes of unions and of civil rights. I got the latter interests initially from my half brother, Harry, eleven years older than I was, who had been radicalized in the Depression. During my junior year in high school he gave me an economics textbook for Christmas and interested me in the labor struggle. I was at the time a student on full scholarship at Cranbrook School in Bloomfield Hills, where many of the parents were executives in Detroit automobile corporations, who had been on the other side in that struggle; but when I graduated in June 1948, my hero was Walter Reuther, and I was eager to join his United Auto Workers and work in an auto plant that summer before I went to college. I needed my father's authorization to join the union at seventeen. He was a Republican and rather antiunion, but he gave permission, and I operated a punch press on the night shift and went to union meetings. I had won a four-year full scholarship awarded by the Pepsi-Cola Company to a college of my choice, and I chose Harvard because I'd heard it had a good economics department. I majored in economics at Harvard with a specialty in labor, with the intention of becoming a labor organizer or a union economist.

My awareness of postwar foreign policy began at about the same time as my interest in economics and labor, with the Truman Doctrine announced in the spring of my junior year of high school, 1947. As I followed the news in subsequent years about the Communist coup in Czechoslovakia, the Stalinist regimes and political trials in Russia and Eastern Europe, the Berlin blockade, and later the North Korean attack and the uprisings in Eastern Europe, I came gradually to accept all the cold war premises and attitudes. These went beyond abhorrence of Stalinist repressive regimes, which I've never lost, whether in the Soviet Union and Eastern Europe, China, North

Korea, Cuba, or Vietnam. Problematically, in retrospect, these premises linked nearly every "crisis" ultimately to our confrontation with the Soviet Union and identified that with the challenge we had faced before and during World War II. Perhaps the basic premise was an equation of Stalin with Hitler, not only in their internal totalitarian controls (where there was a valid analogy) but in their threat to freedom worldwide and directly to Western Europe and America, the danger they posed of military aggression, and the need to confront them with military preparedness, vigilance, and a readiness for collective defense. In particular, fatefully, the equation of Stalin with Hitler ruled out attempting meaningful negotiations with Communist regimes for the resolution of conflicts or arms control.

I was beginning to see myself, as I did for many years afterward, as a Truman Democrat: liberal on domestic matters, but realistic and tough, though measured, in confronting the Soviet Union. A liberal cold warrior, prolabor and anti-Communist, like Senators Hubert Humphrey and (later) Henry Jackson or Walter Reuther himself. I admired Truman's action in sending bombers filled with coal and food to resupply the people in Berlin and his response to what looked like naked aggression in Korea. I also admired his decision to keep Korea a limited war, rejecting General Douglas MacArthur's recommendations to expand the war to China and to use nuclear weapons. Believing in the policy, I was prepared to go to Korea myself, though I had no eagerness for it. I had gotten engaged in the fall of my junior year at Harvard, to Carol Cummings, a Radcliffe sophomore who was nineteen, my age. It was about the same time that marines were surrounded at the Chosin Reservoir and fought their way out. (I was eventually privileged to work directly under a marine hero of that operation, the Medal of Honor winner Major William Barber.) Because I expected to be called up by the draft no later than the end of the school year, over Christmas vacation I proposed to Carol that we get married between terms, so we would have a few months together before I went.

A month after our marriage, in February 1951, a draft exam was instituted that permitted me and all our friends to be deferred till we finished college. I was glad to take advantage of that, and when I won a Woodrow Wilson fellowship for a year of graduate study at Cambridge University, I got a further deferment. But I took it for granted that I wouldn't try to extend my deferment beyond that year. Others, presumably, had had to go in my place and the Korean emergency was still on; when I returned from England, I thought it was time for me to do my duty.

Still, most of my friends and professors were very surprised when I applied for the officer candidates' course (OCC) in the Marine Corps. I didn't seem the type. My interests were almost entirely intellectual, and I wasn't any kind of an athlete. One of my professors, Wassily Leontief, offered to get me a commission in the air force in the new mathematical field of linear programming, but that sounded too much like the academic work in economics I expected to be doing for the rest of my life. The Marines would be something different, a lot different. More important for me, the corps didn't bomb cities; in the Pacific and Korea, it fought soldiers, not civilians.

The corps also was alone in offering a reserve officer's tour of just two years, which was an incentive, but nobody joins the Marines just because it has a shorter tour. Another motive was a special one. My wife's father was a career marine colonel who had retired after the war with the rank of brigadier general. She had fond memories of growing up on marine bases; her older brother had left Yale to enlist in the Marines and been killed on Guadalcanal on his nineteenth birthday. I wanted to surprise her with my choice; I thought it would make her happy to go back to a marine base. It did.

I applied to the marine officer candidates' course when I returned from Cambridge in the summer of 1953, but it didn't have an opening till the spring of 1954, so I went to graduate school in economics at Harvard for a term and a half. Since I'd taken most of the required graduate courses as an undergraduate, I took my Ph.D. oral exams the day before I left for training at Quantico. A few weeks later—on May 8, 1954—we were standing on the drill field in the early morning when our drill instructor told us, "Your rifles had better be clean, because Dien Bien Phu just fell."

We hadn't seen a newspaper during our first month of boot camp, so that didn't mean a lot to us. Anyway, our rifles were always clean. I hadn't noticed President Eisenhower's famous announcement of the domino theory—predicting the fall of most of Asia to communism if North Vietnam was "lost"—on my twenty-third birthday, April 7, 1954, just before I left for Quantico. We'd all missed Vice President Richard Nixon's trial balloon the day after our training started, April 16, when he said that because "the Vietnamese lack[ed] the ability to conduct a war or govern themselves," the United States might have to send troops there to prevent a French defeat: "[I]f the government cannot avoid it, the Administration must face up to the situation and dispatch forces."

There had been a strong outcry to Nixon's speech, with thousands of letters and telegrams to the White House opposing U.S. intervention in support of French colonialism, for all that the nationalist forces were led by Communists. Democratic Senator Edwin Johnson said on the Senate floor:

"I am against sending American GI's into the mud and muck of Indochina on a blood-letting spree to perpetuate colonialism and white man's exploitation in Asia." More important, the Senate majority leader, Lyndon Johnson, influenced by his mentor Senator Richard Russell, convinced President Eisenhower that there must be no unilateral U.S. action, without British participation. Prime Minister Winston Churchill and his foreign minister, Anthony Eden, failed to rise to President Eisenhower's appeal to regard the challenge posed by Ho Chi Minh as equivalent to that of Hitler in the Rhineland or Munich. So my officer class missed an American invasion of Indochina that would have meant a much fiercer war in the North than we ever did experience in South Vietnam and probably the use of nuclear weapons against China (both of which Vice President Nixon supported). Eisenhower and Secretary of State John Foster Dulles returned the compliment to Eden three years later, when they refused to apply the same analogy—Eden, now prime minister, was comparing Hitler to Egypt's President Gamal Abdel Nasser—in the Suez crisis, when my marine battalion was on duty with the Sixth Fleet. We missed that colonial war too.

I didn't know any of this at the time, at Quantico. Our sergeant was just telling us what we did know, that we marines were the ready force, the president's guard. There may well have been marines in amphibious ships off Indochina at that time. That was what we had joined up for. As soon as our training permitted, I would have been glad to go. All the more if I'd thought that our going in might serve to make use of nuclear weapons unnecessary. A year or so later, when I was a platoon leader in Camp Lejeune, North Carolina, I was proud to read testimony by the Marine Corps commandant before Congress that "the Marine Corps had three divisions to sacrifice to prevent having to go to nuclear war." That was my idea of a good reason to serve.

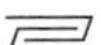

After a rocky beginning in OCC, from which I almost washed out, I had learned to become a good marine infantry officer. I enjoyed the work of a rifle platoon leader and, above all, the opportunity—unusual for a first lieutenant in peacetime—to command a rifle company in the Second Marine Division. I would have been tempted to remain in the Marines as a career if it could have meant a lifetime of troop commands that satisfying. In preparation for leaving active service in the summer of 1956, I had to give up my company. But I was looking forward to going back to Harvard. Our son, Robert Boyd, had just been born, and I had been awarded a three-year junior fellowship at Harvard. My battalion was due to go to the Mediterranean for six months as the duty battalion afloat with the Sixth Fleet, something I didn't regret missing.

However, just at this time there were almost daily warnings of a possible Middle East war arising out of the nationalization of the Suez Canal by Nasser. Our battalion received a classified briefing on its possible involvement in hostilities. I couldn't stand the thought that men I'd commanded might be called on to put their training to the test while I watched their performance and fate from Cambridge, Massachusetts. I wired the commandant of the Marine Corps requesting an extension of my active service till my battalion was released from duty in the Mediterranean, and when this was granted, I informed the Society of Fellows of my decision.

A few months later I was handling top secret documents for the first time. I had hastily been granted a top secret clearance, so that I could draw up operational landing plans for our battalion based on the top secret contingency war plans of the Sixth Fleet. At the moment it was unclear to my superiors in the battalion and in the Sixth Fleet whether we might be operating against Egypt or Israel. (The British and French hadn't yet emerged as belligerents, though there were ominous intelligence indications.) While our troopship steamed on orders toward the southeastern corner of the Mediterranean as the crisis heated up, I was assigned to draw up an amphibious landing plan for Haifa, while at the next desk the other assistant battalion operations officer made one for Alexandria. In terms of the opposition we would face, it would have gone much worse for us, we supposed, if we'd had to use mine. (In the end we used neither; even so, our troopship evacuated more than a thousand American civilians from Alexandria, while British and French planes hovered to bomb the port as we cleared the harbor.) But what's most noteworthy for me to recall is how ready I was to see either of those plans implemented, whichever the president chose. I would have been glad to use my marine training wherever he directed, quite apart from any sense of the rights and wrongs of the conflict.

It so happened that I had come to the conclusion that our allies were very much in the wrong in this case. My battalion commander had asked me to prepare a briefing for our officers on the background of the situation. I read intelligence analyses that had come to our flagship over the summer and did research on the history of the canal and the relations of Egypt and Britain in the ship's library, which contained several encyclopedias. To my surprise, in view of the outrage the British were expressing about Nasser's act, it seemed that the Egyptian government had an unquestionable right to nationalize the canal and that any military action to retake possession of it would be clear-cut aggression, a simple reassertion of colonialism. That was the conclusion I briefed to the officers on our ship, and they found it so interesting that I was sent from ship to ship to repeat the lecture to other contingents. But that didn't answer the uncertainty, for any of my hearers or for me, of what U.S. policy would turn out to be and what role we might be ordered to play. Nor do I remember any of us, including me, being very concerned about that.

It was hard to imagine, despite what I had learned for my briefing, that the United States would choose to oppose its NATO allies. In cold war terms, it seemed unthinkable; it would mean in effect taking the same position on the merits as the Soviets, who were supplying arms to the Egyptians and had just made a deal to supplant the United States in financing the Aswan Dam. When President Eisenhower chose to do exactly that, forcing the British and French to end their Suez adventure, I was surprised and proud as an American. Nothing could have confirmed for me more dramatically that my country was committed on principle to uphold international law against aggression, no matter by whom, even against our closest allies. That was what I believed had been involved in our defense of South Korea; it was why I'd felt called on to fulfill my military obligation during the Korean emergency; it was why I was in the service. When I picked up European magazines and saw photos of what our allies' bombing planes had done to the city of Port Said at the head of the canal, I felt glad the Americans didn't have to look at pictures like that as our work.

Though I was pleased at the president's decision to oppose a colonialist policy, I would have carried out his orders in a different direction with full commitment. At that time in my life, I cared a great deal about how well we fought, but very much less about whom we fought, or why. That was for the president to decide. That widely held attitude, a legacy of World War II and the cold war, stayed with me for another decade. When I finally lost it in 1969, my life changed abruptly.

I came back to Harvard to do independent research, as a junior fellow in the Society of Fellows, in the area that had most interested me since my senior year in college (when, at the advice of my faculty adviser, I had switched my special field from labor to economic theory). I had became fascinated with the new field of decision theory, the abstract analysis of decision making under uncertainty. My degree was in economics, and I had written my senior economics honors thesis and was later to write a Ph.D. thesis on the question of how to describe and understand, and perhaps to improve, the way people make choices when they are uncertain of the consequences of their actions. That included situations of conflict in which the uncertainty partly pertained to the choices of an adversary, the subject of so-called game theory or bargaining theory.

All this had obvious relevance to military decisions, along with others. Partly for that reason, one institution that had shown a special interest in the field was the Rand Corporation, where mathematicians had made basic contributions. That in turn attracted my own attention to Rand, a nonprofit research organization in Santa Monica, California, founded in 1947 to do both basic research and classified analysis for the Defense Department, mainly the air force. After visiting briefly in late summer 1957, I sought and accepted an invitation from Rand's Economics Department to spend the summer of 1958 there as a consultant during my graduate study at Harvard. My three years in the Marines had left me with respect for the military, an interest in strategy, and a greater readiness to apply intellectual concepts to military problems than I would have felt otherwise. Nevertheless, prior to coming to Rand I expected to pursue an academic career as an economic theorist. I was twenty-seven.

As it happened, just after my exploratory visit to Santa Monica in 1957, the Soviets sent *Sputnik* into orbit, demonstrating an ability to launch ballistic missiles of intercontinental range (ICBMs) earlier than the United States could do so. The summer I arrived at Rand was the high point of secret intelligence predictions of an imminent vast Soviet superiority in deployed ICBMs, the "missile gap." Even before those predictions, top secret Rand studies of the previous four years had concluded that the ability of the Strategic Air Command (SAC) to retaliate with its strategic bombers to a Soviet surprise attack well designed to destroy them was very far from reliable. To my new Rand colleagues, the projected Soviet buildup looked unmistakably like an urgent effort, with a startlingly high chance of success, to acquire the capability to disarm the ability of SAC to retaliate. Such a Soviet capability, and even the costly crash effort to achieve it, destroyed the basis for confidence in nuclear deterrence. At least it did for anyone reading these studies who shared the widely accepted cold war premise that the Soviets aimed ultimately at world domination.

Within weeks of my arrival I found myself immersed in what seemed the most urgent concrete problem of uncertainty and decision that humanity had ever had to face: averting a nuclear exchange between the Soviet Union and the United States. In the last years of the decade, nearly all the departments and individual analysts at Rand were obsessed with solving the single problem, which looked both more difficult and more pressing than almost anyone outside Rand seemed able to imagine, of deterring a Soviet nuclear attack on U.S. retaliatory forces and society in the next few years and beyond, by assuring that a U.S. ability to retaliate with nuclear weapons would survive any such attack.

When I entered the Economics Department at Rand as a permanent employee the next summer, I joined this effort wholeheartedly, even with a sense of privilege and dedication, despite my intense personal aversion to nuclear weapons. In view of my strong feelings against indiscriminate bombing of cities by both sides in World War II, there was, as I've said, a terrible irony to my working for the air force on studies aimed at threatening the Russians with the ultimate in terror bombing if they should attack us. But there was a consistent logic to it. I had come to believe, from the Rand analyses, that this was the best, indeed the only, way of increasing the chance that there would be no nuclear war at all in the immediate future.

In the circumstances described by the highest-level national intelligence estimates, the logic of deterrence seemed irrefutable. According to these top secret estimates, we faced a powerful enemy making very costly efforts to exploit the potential of nuclear weapons to disarm us totally and to gain unchallenged global dominance. No nonnuclear U.S. military capability could promise to survive such an attack and respond to it on a scale that would reliably deter an enemy so determined and ruthless. Nothing could do so other than a reliable capability for devastating nuclear retaliation, a capability that could assuredly survive a well-designed nuclear first strike, a nuclear Pearl Harbor attack.

For my own contribution, I chose to specialize in a subject that seemed up to this point understudied in relation to its importance, the command and control of nuclear retaliatory forces by senior military officers and especially by the president. Most of my colleagues were studying how to reduce the vulnerability of nuclear weapons, bases, and vehicles. I joined some others who were examining the survivability and reliability of the military's nervous system. It was widely accepted that the decision on whether and when to launch U.S. nuclear forces against the Soviet Union under any circumstances should be made by the president or highest surviving authority. This concrete problem exemplified and drew on everything I had learned in my graduate study of decision making under uncertainty. Since the warning and evidence bearing on his decision would inevitably be equivocal, it would be the transcendent, and conceivably the last, decision under uncertainty ever made by a national leader.

But the ability of the president, or even of any high-level commanders, to make this decision wisely or at all was threatened both by their own vulnerability to nuclear attack in Washington and all other command posts, along with that of communications networks and information systems, and by the tendency of these warning and intelligence systems to generate ambiguous signals and false alarms. No military secrets were more tightly guarded than the details of how, by whom, and under what circumstances decisions to execute nuclear war plans would really be arrived at and implemented. A study of the problems of nuclear command and control of CINCPAC, to which I was lent by Rand, gave me knowledge of some of the most highly protected and closely held secrets in our military structure. These included military plans for general nuclear war that were generally inaccessible even to the highest civilian authorities.

I learned, for example, the secret that contrary to all public declarations, President Eisenhower had delegated to major theater commanders the authority to initiate nuclear attacks under certain circumstances, such as outage of communications with Washington—an almost daily occurrence in those days—or presidential incapacitation (twice suffered by President Eisenhower). This delegation was unknown to President Kennedy's assistant for national security, McGeorge Bundy—and thus to the president—in early 1961, after nearly a month in office, when I briefed him on the issue. Kennedy secretly continued the authorization, as did President Johnson. (Johnson falsely implied the opposite during his campaign against Senator Goldwater in 1964, in which broad delegation, advocated by Goldwater, was a major issue.) I also reported to Bundy that this delegation to four-star theater commanders had, in the Pacific Command, been imitated by comparable delegation to subordinate commanders (apparently without knowledge or authorization of the president), giving an indefinite but large number of fingers authorized access to the nuclear button. Such arrangements, and a number of others that put the U.S. nuclear forces on a dangerous hair trigger, reflected intelligence estimates of both Soviet intentions and capabilities that made the acceptance of such risks appear necessary to deter a Soviet surprise attack.

However, in the fall of 1961 a highly secret, dramatically revised national intelligence estimate turned the strategic world that had preoccupied me for three years upside down. The missile gap favoring the Soviets had been a fantasy. There was a gap, all right, but it was currently ten to one in our favor. Our 40 Atlas and Titan ICBMs were matched by 4 Soviet SS-6 ICBMs at one launching site at Plesetsk, not by 120, as in the latest national estimate in June, or by the SAC commander's estimate of 1,000 I had heard of at SAC headquarters in August. The specter of a deliberate Soviet surprise attack suddenly appeared, with the new estimates, to have been a chimera.

For me, reading this estimate in late 1961 had the same shocking effect on my professional worldview as, in a much more restricted context, reading the Herrick cable did three years later. Like that, it might appropriately have signaled throughout the government's national security apparatus: Stop engines! Investigate in daylight! Reconsider best course! But it didn't. Like the Herrick cable, the new estimate was kept effectively secret (by me, among others) from Congress, the press, and the public, and it had a comparably imperceptible effect on military programs. It was after this secret recognition that the Soviets had deployed four liquid-fueled ICBMs to our forty that the Kennedy administration decided, in the late fall of 1961, on the appropriate size for the projected force of U.S. solid-fueled Minuteman missiles: one thousand. That was less than the sixteen hundred to six thousand that the air force had earlier requested, but it was down only to the level that Secretary McNamara had earlier decided on *before* the new estimate.

Not only was the missile buildup going into high gear, eventually on both sides, but our high state of alert continued. In my work I had uncovered a number of pitfalls in the U.S. command and control process and the hair-trigger preparations for nuclear war that raised a real danger of an all-out nuclear war started inadvertently, triggered by a false alarm. The danger of nuclear war, possibly U.S.-initiated, continued to be very real for me, perhaps resulting from an accident, unauthorized action, the interaction of alerts or feints in a crisis, a false alarm, or misunderstood commands.

My knowledge of these phenomena and how the presence of Soviet missiles on Cuba might affect them led my friend and former Rand colleague Harry Rowen, now a deputy assistant secretary of defense, to call me to Washington to participate in working groups staffing the ExComm (Executive Committee of the NSC) during the Cuban missile crisis in 1962. That experience left me with a vivid sense of how thermonuclear warfare might actually come about in a crisis, not only by the failures of high-level control I had begun to foresee—which were exhibited on both sides in this confrontation—but as a result of major miscalculations at the highest levels and of prior commitments made without any adequate sense of where they were likely to lead. Each side had grossly misunderstood the other, wrongly estimated its behavior, failed to understand actions of the other as responses to interpretations of the combination of their own words and actions. There had been "failures of communication" of a sort risking the most dangerous of consequences.

With the two most elaborate intelligence apparatuses in human history, each of them focused almost entirely on the superpower adversary, President Kennedy had failed to foresee that Soviet Premier Nikita Khrushchev would try to deploy medium- and intermediate-range ballistic missiles on Cuba within range of the United States, and Khrushchev had failed to foresee Kennedy's response to this move. Recent revelations from the former Soviets have disclosed a much larger number of their troops on the island than we realized at the time, armed—unknown to us—with tactical nuclear weapons the control of which Khrushchev had delegated to local commanders. In light of this information, it has become clear that nearly everyone in the U.S. government had seriously underestimated at the time the danger of all-out nuclear war resulting from the two prior failures of foresight. That was true for me as well. But the dangers I saw then were frightening enough.

I spent the first half of 1964 in Washington, as a Rand researcher working on a project that reflected my concerns arising out of the missile crisis. I proposed to explore dangerous patterns in governmental decision making and "communications"—explicit or tacit and inadvertent—between governments in nuclear crises. I was not a historian, and I had no interest in producing detailed case histories of particular incidents. I knew that such histories existed, on a highly classified basis, within various branches of the government. What I wanted, and what I got, was access to an array of these, covering a range of crises, so that I could do comparative analyses. I was looking for problematic patterns that might improve the president's understanding and control of his own bureaucracy and its interactions with an opposing one, in ways that could help him reduce the likelihood of disaster.

I had conceived this project in 1963, expecting it to keep me in Washington only temporarily. But at the beginning of 1964, after thirteen years of marriage, my wife asked for a divorce. I stayed on the Rand payroll, but I moved to Washington to pursue this research, returning to California after that mainly to visit my two children, Robert and Mary, then eight and five.

An interagency panel consisting of officials just below the highest level in State, Defense, the CIA, and the Joint Chiefs of Staff was convened for me by Walt Rostow, chairman of the policy planning staff in the State Department, to sponsor my research. Each had undertaken to facilitate my access to classified studies in his respective agency, dealing with such past international events as the missile crisis, Berlin, Suez, Lebanon, the Taiwan Strait crises, the U-2 shootdown, and Laos. Some of these studies were classified higher than top secret, and I was granted special clearances so I could see them. Six months into this research, drawing in particular on a number of detailed studies of the Cuban missile crisis, I had arrived at what I thought were some important tentative conclusions. I made a partial report to Rostow's interagency discussion group, but what I learned in this period, along with what I had learned in the previous six years, most of it little known to the public, is a long story that remains to be told elsewhere. Meanwhile I was looking forward to at least another six months of investigation, working out of Pentagon offices, on the Rand payroll.

Then, in July, the assistant secretary of defense for international security affairs, John T. McNaughton, called me into his office and proposed that I become his special assistant. He was a former Harvard law professor who had earlier been general counsel for the Defense Department. I'd had several discussions with him over the past couple of years, largely on nuclear arms control, that had left us with a good deal of mutual respect. McNaughton told me that Secretary of Defense McNamara was managing Vietnam for the president, and McNamara had asked him to be his principal assistant on it. I would in turn be his personal assistant in that area. He was spending as much as 70 percent of his time on Vietnam, and he would want me to devote 90 percent of my attention to it. In a year or less that would probably lead to a job for me at the deputy assistant secretary level.

Neither part of that prospect attracted me very much. It wasn't my ambition or calling to be a bureaucrat; at any level Rand was the perfect home for me. I would have been glad to stay there for the rest of my life; in fact I looked forward to it. Rand allowed me, with great freedom and very loose supervision, to pick my own problems, to investigate and learn deeply about particular issues that especially concerned me, centered on the dangers of nuclear war. Moreover, flying frequently from Rand's Santa Monica offices to Washington to take part in working groups or act as an individual consultant to policy staffs and officials in the Pentagon, at State, or in the Executive Office Building, I was able to feel I could actually contribute to reducing those dangers. I could also limit my participation to those areas in which I'd earned a sense of expertise. I've never had any ambition or desire to be a government official with responsibilities over a variety of matters about which I might personally know little and care less. Vietnam policy was a perfect example of such an issue. In fact after my brief visit there it looked to me like a trap. I didn't want to know more about it than I did.

I'd discussed my crisis research with McNaughton before, and I told him that I was finding it fascinating and extremely worthwhile. It had taken a good deal of time to set it up, and that effort was paying off. I thought I could make my best contribution by continuing it. But McNaughton said he was offering me the chance to observe a crisis from the inside, while it was going on. "Vietnam is one crisis after another; it's one long crisis." Histories of past crises could tell me only so much, not really what one needed to know. If I wanted to know how crises arose, how mistakes got made, and what crises were really about, I had to get the feel of government operations as an insider, not as a researcher or a consultant. He said I could continue to work on my crisis study, as time allowed. But in effect, as I saw what he was offering me, Vietnam would be added to my list of cases. I wouldn't be writing a history of it. I would be living the history of it. I finally accepted.

I knew the value of rank, within the building and the other agencies. I asked for the highest civil service "supergrade," GS-18, which had the same pay and status as a deputy assistant secretary, the civilian equivalent of a military rank between lieutenant general and major general. That would be a very unusual rank for a special assistant to an assistant secretary, but McNaughton said he would argue that I needed it as his "alter ego" on Vietnam, so that I could represent him, as his deputy assistant secretaries did, at interagency meetings.

The most important assurance McNaughton gave me was that I would see everything he saw on Vietnam or any other matter he assigned me. In fact I would see most of it even before he did. A major part of my job would be to screen the immense amount of information available on Vietnam and help decide (along with his military aides and his deputies) what needed to be brought to his attention. As his assistant I would be seeing memos and cables that were routed directly to him, "for his eyes only," not to be shared even with his deputies. My discretion would be as crucial a part of my job as any other qualification. That seemed to be no problem. When it came to sensitive secret keeping, I'd already had plenty of opportunity to demonstrate a talent for discretion, as he knew.

I was in some other managerial respects not very well suited to what he wanted from me. That wasn't well defined, except for his saying that he hoped I would "double his efficiency and his productivity." Given his phenomenal energy and intelligence, that would have been a tall order for anyone, but I'm sure that many others, more organized than I've ever been, would have come a lot closer. Still, he amply carried out his promise to me of a uniquely placed learning experience, a window on policy making with few rivals outside the White House or Secretary McNamara's personal office.

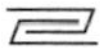

In the afternoon of Monday, August 3, 1964, I came into the assistant secretary's suite of offices ready to start learning my new job. McNaughton's office was a very large, high-ceilinged room with windows looking out over the Jefferson Memorial and, on the other side of the Tidal Basin, the Washington Monument. I would have the same view, from a single window in a cubbyhole just wide enough for a desk, with one chair for a visitor, a small bookcase, and two four-drawer top secret safes for files. The advantage of my location was that it was just a few yards from the door to McNaughton's office. One secretary had a desk in between us, just outside his door. Two more had desks in the open space on the other side of his door, in the room one entered from the Pentagon corridor. McNaughton's military aide, who managed the office, and his aide's assistant, Major Harry Harris, had cubbyholes adjoining mine. We were in the E-ring near the River Entrance on the third floor, a coveted location in the Pentagon because it was just down the hall from Secretary McNamara's suite.

Once I moved into my own small office, I told the military aide that I wanted to see everything that came in on Vietnam or from Vietnam. He asked me, "Everything? The whole take?"

"That's what I said. All of it."

The next morning when I came in, between my desk and the window behind it were two neatly stacked columns of paper, about the same height, each slightly taller than I am. I'm five feet ten and a half inches tall. I took an armload of paper off the top of one pile, being careful not to knock over the stack, and moved it to the desk. I began to shuffle through it. There were no single sheets. This was a pile of multipage stapled reports, memos, queries, messages, almost no original copies, all copies of documents sent to someone else or some division of International Security Affairs (ISA). A lot of it was sent pro forma to the deputy assistant secretary of defense, ISA, among other addressees, but was clearly not meant for his own attention; the message center distributed copies to the bureaus that managed that particular subject matter or handled queries from that sender. Most of these, I soon learned, wouldn't normally be sent to the assistant secretary's office initially; the message center would rely on the bureau to send that document, or a summary or commentary reflecting it, upward if it seemed to merit higher attention. That was how the greater part of what I'd understood to be part of my job, selecting material for McNaughton's personal attention, got done, by many other people with specific responsibilities. But I'd asked to see "everything," and here it was. The bureaucracy did what it was told.

On the other side of the desk was what I was informed was a burn bag, a huge paper sack that came up to my waist, heavy brown paper stiff enough to stand up by itself, top edges folded back, to take classified trash paper, anything I discarded. I didn't need to reroute anything to anyone other than McNaughton; the people who might need to see it would have their own copies already. Virtually everything was classified. Very little was confidential, the lowest level of secrecy; these were mostly routine weekly reports from low-level commands in the Pentagon, requests for logistic support or replies, and they went into the bag quickly. Most was secret or top secret. They were cables from the embassy in Saigon or from the Military Assistance Command, Vietnam (MACV) or different parts of each, from other agencies in the mission in Vietnam, from bureaus in State or all over the Pentagon, intelligence estimates from the CIA or the Defense Intelligence Agency (DIA) or Intelligence and Research (INR) in State—those looked interesting—and plans, weekly or monthly reports, and queries and responses.

For the first half hour I was diffident about discarding secret documents, but before long I was throwing them into the bag with abandon. The bag had been filled by midday, was taken away to be burned somewhere in the basement and replaced by two more. The load was impossible. Even to glance at each one of these documents took more time than I had in a twelve-hour day (since a few of them did attract more than a glance). I don't remember if I got through both stacks by the evening, but I can't believe I did. Moreover, the next day, when I came in, there were two new stacks, that morning's take, which had arrived at the center the afternoon or night before. Twelve more feet of paper. Much of it came from Vietnam, generated during its daytime hours, twelve time zones ahead of us. And as fast as I looked at it, new batches came in during the day, from Vietnam and Washington.

By the third morning it was obvious that I had to change my request. Eventually I managed to cut down the daily traffic that I looked at to two piles on my desk, each about two and a half feet high—from twelve feet of paper down to five. I did this by asking to see only documents that were top secret, certain specific regular reports and estimates, and messages that were eyes only, NoDis, ExDis, LimDis. These last referred to State Department designators on cables or reports, apart from classification, that specified limited distribution—not routine distribution to all interested bureaus—or executive distribution, a still more limited and specific list of recipients, or no distribution, meant strictly for the specific high-level office to which it was addressed. NoDis, referring to an office or offices specified, corresponded to eyes only for an individual or a set of individuals, supposed to be seen "only by the eyes of" the addressees named. The point was to control and direct who knew—and shouldn't know—in an elaborate hierarchy of responsibility and secrecy.

I was never a person named in the list of addressees of an eyes only message, nor, for that matter, was John McNaughton usually on the list. When I saw that stamp or heading, I was looking at a copy of a document that in principle, according to the designator, wasn't supposed to be copied at all, or to be seen by me or my boss. Nor was International Security Affairs or its assistant secretary (let alone his special assistant) very often among the addressees of a NoDis State dispatch. Usually no one in the Pentagon, even the secretary, was listed for receiving one of these relatively infrequent messages, which tended to be addressed to the secretary of state or the president. But there it was, in front of me, from the message center. Obviously, NoDis and eyes only were, in practice, relative terms, intended (one had to assume that the senders knew this, from their own experience) to cut the number of people who saw a particular secret or top secret message from thousands or hundreds down to scores or even dozens (apart from secretaries or couriers or special assistants).

To get below even that, senders sometimes put rather desperate warnings in the heading, in capitals, "Literally Eyes Only of the Secretary" or "the President." I was aware of this of course because I was reading it, and I hadn't stolen it, nor had I made the copy that I was reading. But that was fairly rare, and I was aware that it was a privilege for me—or, for that matter, for John—to be reading it. It was a privilege John was risking by letting me see it in his office, a privilege I would lose fast if I let anyone else, even one of his deputies, know that it existed or that I had seen it. That applied to certain other categories as well; one had to develop a feel for it.

I learned this by almost being fired for a particular mistake after a couple of weeks in the office. I'd been talking on the phone to Mike Forrestal, who had been the coordinator of interagency Vietnam affairs from the White House. As I understood it, he now had a similar job in State. I quoted to him from a cable in front of me on my desk from the ambassador in Saigon, NoDis and eyes only for the secretary of state and the president. He was struck by the quote and said he hadn't seen it. I was surprised. I gave him the cable number and mentioned that it was from a new series of weekly reports the ambassador was sending personally. It had a special slug, or code word, to designate the series, limiting the distribution, presumably very severely. But I was getting my own copy, as was McNaughton. I told Forrestal these were very interesting, and he should make sure he got on the list.

Within hours I was called into McNaughton's office. He was as agitated as I ever saw him. He asked me, "Did you have anything to do with telling Mike Forrestal about the new series from the embassy?"

I said, "Certainly. He didn't seem to know about it, and it was obvious he needed to see these."

John looked at me for a long time and said, "I don't know if I can keep you in this job. I've been told to fire you. I'm in real trouble on this." He looked away and thought, tapping the desk. I was thinking: I couldn't share a State Department message with Mike Forrestal? The man who was, as far as I knew, in charge of coordinating all the civilian affairs on Vietnam in Washington? Son of the first secretary of defense, a well-known confidant of President Kennedy's on Vietnam? Granted, there was a new president, but Forrestal still had at least one foot in the White House. How could it make sense to exclude him from a weekly communication that got over to us? (The only sense I could make subsequently of the sensitivity on this was that the code word list must have been devised at Ambassador Maxwell Taylor's request—for some personal reason that I never learned—to allow him to communicate to his two bosses in private, specifically keeping the information from his former White House colleague Forrestal.)

Finally John said, "Well, you're new on the job. My father used to say, 'Every dog gets one bite.' You've had yours. Really, Dan, watch out after this." Meanwhile he paid a continuing price for my error. This particular set of messages was no longer sent to his office. Only one copy of these came to the Pentagon, to Secretary McNamara's office. McNaughton had to go there to read the copies, on a clipboard from which he couldn't remove them.

That's how you learn. I did keep my job after that. I wasn't a beginner, when it came to discretion, after years of moving among various warring offices in the Pentagon as a Rand consultant. But McNaughton was right when he'd held out the new post to me as a learning experience; I had a lot left to learn about what it actually meant to be inside one of these agencies as a full-time, trusted employee at a high level, responsible to a boss. McNaughton was in the same position, of course, as this particular example demonstrated. I learned a lot just from watching him in interagency meetings at which he was representing McNamara's views, with which I knew he sometimes didn't agree.

Once at lunch a State Department official who obviously didn't know John very well told me that my boss was the most straightforward man in Washington. I told that to John after lunch and assured him, "I defended your reputation. I told him you were the most devious man in town." John smiled warmly and said, "Thank you."

I often watched McNaughton with reporters, because he called me into his office whenever he had to give an interview. This was a way of covering himself—it may even have been a requirement in the department—so he could have a witness confirm that he was not the source of any classified or sensitive information in the ensuing story. I watched and marveled. John was great at this. As he got into areas where he had to be especially untruthful or elusive, his Pekin, Illinois, accent got broader till he sounded like someone discussing corn at a country fair or standing at the rail of a riverboat. You looked for hayseed in his cuffs. He simply didn't mind looking and sounding like a hick in the interests of dissimulation. My future boss in Vietnam, Edward Lansdale, had the same willingness to appear simple-minded when he wanted to be opaque, as he did with most outsiders. In both cases it was very effective. Reporters would tell me how "open" my boss was, compared with others they ran into, this after I had listened to an hour of whoppers. It became clear to me that journalists had no idea, no clue, even the best of them, just how often and how egregiously they were lied to.

The lies themselves didn't bother me, but there were several cases that year when I thought a false story was so likely to be found out that it made me nervous. My worry was nearly always misplaced; the cover story held surprisingly long. Only once did I actually have a cautionary influence.

One phone on John's desk was an open line from McNamara. When the buzzer sounded and the light flashed on that phone, John picked it up immediately, in the middle of a sentence if he was talking to someone else, and said crisply, "Yes, Bob." He either took a note or was out the door of his inner office and the outer office in a flash, his long legs scissoring down the E-ring corridor to the secretary's office just below the level of a run. He didn't want to be seen by military officers actually running down the hallway.

One morning just before eight o'clock John came back from McNamara's office minutes after he'd gotten a call and dashed out. He said to me, "A Blue Springs drone has gone down in China. Bob is seeing the press at eight-thirty. We have ten minutes to write six alternative lies for him."

It was the only time I remember the actual word "lies" being used. Blue

Springs was the code name for an espionage program of reconnaissance photographic flights by unmanned drone planes. John threw me a yellow pad, and I pulled up a chair to the opposite side of his desk. We sat across from each other and wrote as fast as we could for ten minutes. There was no time to exchange thoughts, to avoid overlap. The first ones were obvious, probably the same for each of us. If the Chinese had already announced the incident, one, we had no idea whose plane it was; it wasn't one of ours. Two, it was a Chinese Nationalist plane. I asked as we scribbled, "Does it have U.S. markings on it?"

"Who knows?" John didn't look up. Three, it was an experimental drone, off course. Four, it was taking weather readings when it went off course. I remembered that one from Gary Powers's U-2, which went down in Russia in 1960. That cover story hadn't worked so well because the Soviets had captured the pilot live and Khrushchev hadn't told us at first. This didn't have any pilot, but what if the Chinese could display U.S. cameras? I had to think harder for the next couple of stories. McNaughton looked at the clock, ten minutes, grabbed my pad and started to run out, looking down at my six entries. As he was leaving the outer office, I called after him, "Why doesn't he just say 'No comment'?"

John said over his shoulder, "Bob won't say 'No comment' to the press."

A few minutes later he was back and waved me down to his desk again. He tore off the pages we'd written on and pushed one of the pads back to me. He said, "Bob liked these. He wants four more. We have five minutes."

We wrote fast again. I had thought of another one while he was away, but the rest took more imagination than before. I can't remember them. As he tore off the new pages after exactly five minutes, I said, "Look, really, I think he ought to give serious consideration to 'No comment' on this one." I'd been thinking about it while John was out of the office. "The Chinese probably have enough wreckage that they can prove any of these stories are lies. The reporters understand about intelligence gathering, and they're sick of being lied to. I think they'd rather be told we won't talk about it."

In his hurry John listened intently, as always, and he nodded. "I don't think he'll do it, but I'll tell him what you said." He was gone. It was eight twenty-five.

A little after nine o'clock John came back from the press conference. I asked him how it had gone. He said, "I was amazed. Somebody brought up the Chinese report, and he actually used your line. He said, 'I have no comment on that,' and took the next question. I never thought he would."

"How'd it go over?"

"They actually seemed to like it! They didn't press him at all." A few minutes later one of the regular Pentagon reporters dropped into our outer office after leaving McNamara's conference room. I was standing there, and he said to me, "Listen, tell your boss that that 'No comment' in there was very refreshing. I didn't think McNamara had it in him." Actually, what had made that line usable, as I had suspected, was that it pointed toward an area of covert intelligence collection whose secrecy our own reporters would almost surely respect without trying to penetrate further. That wasn't generally true. You couldn't say "no comment" when you needed to discourage follow-up questions, which was most of the time. Then there was no substitute for what the uninitiated would call a lie. In those days it almost always worked.

Even within the executive branch, self-discipline in sharing information—lack of a "need to tell"—and a capability for dissimulation in the interests of discretion were fundamental requirements for a great many jobs. There was an abundance of people who, like John and me, could and did meet those requirements adequately. The result was an apparatus of secrecy, built on effective procedures, practices, and career incentives, that permitted the president to arrive at and execute a secret foreign policy, to a degree that went far beyond what even relatively informed outsiders, including journalists and members of Congress, could imagine.

It is a commonplace that "you can't keep secrets in Washington" or "in a democracy," that "no matter how sensitive the secret, you're likely to read it the next day in the *New York Times*." These truisms are flatly false. They are in fact cover stories, ways of flattering and misleading journalists and their readers, part of the process of keeping secrets well. Of course eventually many secrets do get out that wouldn't in a fully totalitarian society. Bureaucratic rivalries, especially over budget shares, lead to leaks. Moreover, to a certain extent the ability to keep a secret for a given amount of time diminishes with the number of people who know it. As secret keepers like to say, "Three people can keep a secret if two of them are dead." But the fact is that the overwhelming majority of secrets do not leak to the American public. This is true even when the information withheld is well known to an enemy and when it is clearly essential to the functioning of the congressional war power and to any democratic control of foreign policy. The reality unknown to the public and to most members of Congress and the press is that secrets that would be of the greatest import to many of them can be kept from them reliably for decades by the executive branch, even though they are known to thousands of insiders. (See chapter 3.)

As one of those insiders I had no particular objection to this. I shared the universal ethos of the executive branch, at least of my part of it: that for the Congress, the press, and the public to know much about what the president was doing for them, with our help, was at best unnecessary and irrelevant. At worst, it was an encouragement to uninformed (uncleared), short-sighted, and parochial individuals and institutions to intervene in matters that were too complicated for them to understand, and to muck them up. This sounds paternalistic to the point of being antidemocratic, and so it was. (And is: I doubt that this has ever changed.) But we're talking foreign policy here, and national security matters, in which we didn't see that people without clearances had any really useful role to play in the nuclear cold war era. It was in the national interest, as we saw it, simply to tell them whatever would best serve to free the president from their interference.

Even when I regarded the administration's policy as inadequate or misguided, as I often did on nuclear matters, I saw little hope for improvement by Congress, with its committees generally headed by conservative southerners. Once I was inside the government, my awareness of how easily and pervasively Congress, the public, and journalists were fooled and misled contributed to a lack of respect for them and their potential contribution to better policy. That in turn made it easier to accept, to participate in, to keep quiet about practices of secrecy and deception that fooled them further and kept them ignorant of the real issues that were occupying and dividing inside policy makers. Their resulting ignorance made it all the more obvious that they must leave these problems to us.

There was one more feature of our environment within the executive branch that contributed to a disregard of the opinions or criticisms of outsiders, that made it hard to listen to or learn from them. Perhaps the most startling discovery on entering the government at this level from having been a consultant was the unrelenting pace of the work. I've already described the almost inconceivable amount of information and demands for information pressing on you. A high official had to protect himself with an elaborate array of filters; I was just one of many such filters for McNaughton. As my friend Alain Enthoven put it, after he had left Rand to become assistant secretary of defense for systems analysis, it was "like drinking from a fire hose."

And not just one hose. Another revelation was the breadth of responsibilities for an assistant secretary or even a deputy. The twelve feet of daily paper I had looked at was only for Vietnam. But that was only one region and one set of problems for which McNaughton had responsibility, out of dozens or scores, albeit one to which McNamara wanted him to give his special attention. McNaughton encouraged me to look at anything to do with Vietnam that was placed on his desk by his military aides or his deputies. But that would be only one or two or three piles or file baskets of papers out of eight or nine stacked on his large desk at a time, dealing with Europe, or NATO, or elsewhere in Asia or the world, with military aid programs or hearings or proposed speeches or testimony by the secretary or the president on one or another subject of the day.

McNaughton, who as a law school professor had written a standard textbook on evidence, had extreme powers of concentration. So did I, for that matter, but I was used to focusing for long periods, not just hours but days and months, on a particular subject area. What I saw McNaughton have to do was to refocus that concentration regularly, at not very long intervals, from intense consideration of a pile of files dealing with one particular problem to another representing entirely different subject matter in another part of the world.

He had a ritual that I saw him do hundreds of times; I think it was not just a joke but a self-focusing device that was more than symbolic. After taking the thirty-five minutes he had explicitly allotted to look at a pile of papers on a particular problem that had been "staffed out" for his attention and decision—tabbed for background papers, relevant cables and estimates, and alternative options and analyses of them for his choice—signing off on an option or checking off an "Agree" or "No" box listed for him by a deputy or bureau head, or asking for more work or information, he would look up at the clock and push that pile away from him on the desk. Next he would put his hands, fingers extended, on either side of his head, pause for a moment, then with a decisive motion of his forearms swivel his head to face another pile on which he had to concentrate next, on another part of the desk. Sometimes he would look up and grin at me after he did this, but I often saw him doing it, through the doorway, when there was no one else in the office. It was his way of deleting from his mind, his short-term storage, what he had just been focusing on and turning his full attention to an entirely different subject that demanded the next twenty-seven minutes.

I saw the same pressure in every office at that level: Alain Enthoven's Office of Systems Analysis, or Adam Yarmolinsky's as assistant to McNamara, or McGeorge Bundy's in the White House. Everyone had his personal way of dealing with the stress. McNaughton would clench his nails into his hands fiercely, his knuckles white. Some cracked their knuckles repetitively. Alain had a spectacular habit, when he was thinking hard and fast, of flipping a sharpened pencil end over end, somehow catching it without looking. As an amateur magician and tyro juggler myself, I could never grasp how he did that. It was hard to think of anything while you were watching him. I heard it drove four-star admirals crazy when he did that while he was talking to them.

Everything was a crisis. Everything had a deadline: a speech that had to be delivered, testimony before Congress or a scheduled press conference, a proposal or request from a head of state that had to be answered immediately, all requiring a determination of policy, which in turn had to be coordinated beforehand with other departments and the White House. I'd felt the pressure of the Cuban missile crisis as a consultant in ISA, several nights sleeping a few hours on the very leather sofa in what was now John's office (then Paul Nitze's). But what I was learning now was that crises came every day, and usually several overlapped at a time. In one forty-eight-hour period in mid-October 1964, the Chinese tested a nuclear warhead for the first time, Khrushchev was ousted as leader of the Soviet Union, and the Conservative government in Britain was replaced by the Labour party. Yet these world-shaking events were not what was occupying our highest officials on those particular days. I represented McNaughton at an interagency meeting at the State Department discussing the implications of the first two events (the second of which had been totally unforeseen). My boss wasn't there because, as I recall, he and Secretary McNamara, with Secretary Rusk, were at meetings discussing if and how the United States should support an imminent French-Belgian covert operation in the Congo. Meanwhile, as recently released White House tapes reveal, President Johnson was preoccupied on those days with containing a sex scandal involving his closest aide, Walter Jenkins, which threatened his political campaign. Now I could understand what I'd heard from several participants in the missile crisis: that it was almost relaxing to have a crisis so important that you could concentrate all your attention on nothing but that one for thirteen whole days.

All this was exciting. Both the incredible pace and the inside dope made you feel important, fully engaged, on an adrenaline high much of the time. Clearly it was addictive. People clung to these jobs despite seventy-hour weeks and no family lives. If they left, with a change of administration or for financial or personal reasons, most of them took care to keep themselves looking available for a return: to the cables, the clearances, the crises. When you saw them after they'd left, "outside," at nongovernmental meetings or on the street, they often looked unplugged. John McNaughton, inside, throve on it. Once, as I listened to him make a quick series of phone calls trying to figure out how to undo, or to further, what had just happened at a meeting he had attended, he looked over at me with a big grin, covered the phone with his hand, and said, "You know, I couldn't stand doing this if I didn't love it so much."

It was easy to reassure ourselves—I suspect this is true for every administration—that whatever our limitations and errors, we were doing our very best and that no other team in the running to replace us was likely to deal with all these challenges much better than we could.

The image that often came to my mind as I watched John or (occasionally) a master operator like McGeorge Bundy move from one caller to another on the phone, one crisis to another, was that of the juggler in a circus who keeps a dozen plates spinning in the air at once on the ends of long, flexible poles, moving from one to another deftly as a plate begins to wobble and threatens to fall, giving another spin to the pole, just enough to set the plate whirling while he moves down the line to another that is going out of control. It was an art form, it was amazing, it took unusual talent and energy and discipline to do as well as they did, with as few mistakes (often managing to catch the plate, when it fell, before it shattered), but . . . I asked myself more than once: Can they really get away with decision making like this? With all these simultaneous problems (whose range reflected America's postwar sense of its "responsibilities," its power, its entitlements), or even for any one of them, can they this way devise or choose adequate policies without setting up disastrous failures? Can men even as brilliant and adroit as these—and for sheer brainpower and energy, the Kennedy crew that Johnson inherited could not easily be bettered—manage safely and wisely so many challenges at once, with so little time to acquire more than a shallow understanding of any one? Can you really run the world this way?

Within a few years Vietnam would provide the answer.

3

The Road to Escalation

The day I started working on Vietnam ended with the president's televised assurance "We still seek no wider war." Soon that became a major theme of his electoral campaign. But every official I dealt with in Washington that summer and fall expected a wider war under President Johnson no later than the start of the new year.

To a man, administration insiders had agreed since the spring of 1964 that the present course of U.S. policy in Vietnam, which limited our overt involvement to funding, equipment, and advisers in the South, was failing, rapidly. Unless the United States broadened its role to include direct participation in combat, either by air and naval attacks on the North or by ground units in the South, or both, Communist-led forces would take over South Vietnam within months. This would come about by some combination of Communist military victory, collapse of the anti-Communist regime or army, or negotiations among the Vietnamese. On this point no one in internal government discussions disagreed with Senator Goldwater or his Republican colleagues. Nor was there anyone, so far as I could tell, who departed from the internal consensus that defeat could be averted, even in the relatively short run, *only* by a direct U.S. combat role. The sole internal controversy throughout 1964 involved when and on what initial scale it must begin and exactly what form it should take.

Except for their chairman, Maxwell Taylor, the Joint Chiefs of Staff favored starting a large-scale bombing program up to the border of China immediately, along with mining North Vietnamese ports and waterways.

General Taylor, who became ambassador to Saigon in midyear, disagreed tactically on this. Like a number of civilians, he preferred a more gradual approach, to begin later, in hopes that the government of Vietnam (GVN) would achieve some stability beforehand. (The generals who had overthrown President Ngo Dinh Diem in November had themselves been displaced in a coup by General Nguyen Khanh early in 1964.)

Johnson had not yet decided these issues of timing and tactics. For that matter, he had not made a definite decision on the basic question of escalation versus extrication. But there was little doubt in the Pentagon, or any other place I visited in Washington, what his decision would be between those last alternatives. He had made clear within the government two days after he had taken office that he was determined not to accept failure or defeat in Vietnam, not to be "the President who saw Southeast Asia go the way China went." His secretaries of state and defense, along with the JCS, shared that commitment. Moreover, since both the Joint Chiefs and Secretary of Defense McNamara were strongly convinced that some form of bombing campaign against the North was essential to avoid defeat, it was taken for granted in the Pentagon that the president would come to accept that conclusion.

However, the president was clearly very anxious not to make this decision or act on it before the election in November. He wanted not just to beat Goldwater—all polls showed that was virtually a foregone conclusion—but to win by the largest possible margin, preferably by the largest landslide in history. That would erase the notion that he was an "accidental president." He wanted a strong mandate for his Great Society programs. Along with many of his fellow Democrats, he also hoped to smash the Republican right wing supporting the Goldwater candidacy. He intended to run as the reasonable, moderate "peace" candidate, emphasizing domestic issues, while painting his opponent as a dangerous, unbalanced extremist, eager to escalate to full-scale war in Vietnam. At the same time, he needed to answer Goldwater's charge that he was indecisive and weak in foreign policy.

The one-shot "restrained reprisal" on August 5 fitted his campaign needs incredibly well. He shot up in the polls, and bipartisan support for his action and the resolution took the issue of Vietnam out of the campaign, except as a negative for Goldwater. But after the Tonkin Gulf reprisals Johnson strongly hoped to avoid any further major military moves before the election and to conceal the pressures for escalation within his own administration. He was campaigning in large part against Goldwater's proposals for Vietnam, which ironically were identical to those of Johnson's own Joint Chiefs of Staff. That last fact was a well-kept secret during the campaign.

On September 25 the president criticized "those that say you ought to go north and drop bombs, to try to wipe out the supply lines." Three days later he was more specific: "Some of our people—Mr. Nixon, Mr. Rockefeller, Mr. Scranton and Mr. Goldwater—have all, at some time or other, suggested the possible wisdom of going north in Vietnam." Neither then nor at any other time did he mention that the people who said this included all of his own principal military advisers, the JCS and his secretary of defense, Robert McNamara. It's true that the president was not committed before the election to following their specific advice, and certainly he had not yet made an official determination to do so, but they, and those of us working for them, knew that he disagreed as sharply as any of the Republicans mentioned with "some who say we ought to go south and get out and come home." Given the views of his top advisers in the Pentagon, insiders understood that to mean that bombing lay ahead for North Vietnam no later than early 1965, whichever candidate was elected.

It didn't mean that there was no difference at all on this issue between the two candidates. Johnson was not likely to begin bombing in the precise way that Goldwater almost surely would. That was the way of the four service chiefs, starting out very big with a "hard knock," hitting targets close to Hanoi and to China at the outset, and pursuing the destruction of North Vietnam to full victory. But it was even less likely that Johnson would not be bombing the North at all in the spring of 1965. There was scarcely any chance that the U.S. role by then would still be within the limits observed from 1945 to 1964.

Yet that was what most voters thought Johnson was projecting with his campaign slogan "We seek no wider war." It was what an overwhelming majority of them believed they were voting for on election day, November 3. No one I knew within the administration voted under that particular illusion. I don't remember having time to vote that day myself, and I doubt if McNaughton did. We both were attending the first meeting at the State Department of an interagency working group addressing the best way to widen the war.

The group had been set up by the president under Assistant Secretary of State William P. Bundy the day before. It hadn't started a week earlier because its focus might have leaked to the voters. That could have considerably lessened the landslide victory for Johnson, which reflected an exaggerated view of the difference on the war between the two candidates. Moreover, we didn't start the work a day or week later, after the votes had been cast, because there was no time to waste. It seemed urgent to arrive at an internal consensus on how to avert a Communist victory in South Vietnam by expanding the war. Except for a status quo option, a straw man, all the alternatives we considered called for escalation. On the day the electorate, as expected in polls, was voting in unprecedented numbers against bombing North Vietnam or otherwise escalating the war, we were working to set such a policy in motion.

How could we possibly have justified doing this? We served the president and our immediate bosses. It was our understanding that it was the president's job to make foreign policy, with the advice of our bosses, not, in any serious sense, with the advice of Congress. It didn't matter that much to us what the public thought.

After all, it didn't make much difference what we ourselves thought. I soon learned from John McNaughton that Lyndon Johnson was skeptical about the value of a systematic bombing campaign against the North. I myself was more than skeptical, and so was McNaughton. But our boss, McNamara, was not, and we worked for him. In the fall of 1964 McNaughton began to accompany McNamara to regular White House meetings on Vietnam with the president. Some of these were cabinet level meetings at which John was the only assistant secretary in the room. If he had time to debrief me when he came back from the White House, he did, and at those moments I heard things about the personal perspectives of the players I could never have read in cables or memos. This was a running course for me on bureaucratic behavior, a subject of endless fascination for McNaughton.

John would mention what someone had said, and then he would give his interpretation about why he had said that at that moment and in just that way: how it related to his agency's interests and the relationships he was trying to protect and serve. Or he would comment on what some had not said, what they had been silent about and why. That applied to John himself. He told me he said very little at these meetings, never volunteering anything, commenting only when McNamara asked him something. One reason for that was his junior position. McNamara was the only one who could get away with bringing an assistant with him. John felt very privileged to hear what the big boys and especially the president were thinking—it was precious to us in our work; it was bureaucratic gold—and he knew his position there was precarious. He didn't want to jeopardize it by being intrusive and perhaps stepping on anyone's toes.

Another reason was that at this time he often privately disagreed with what he was hearing McNamara say to the president. The secretary of defense was pressing for the necessity of a bombing campaign against the North, which McNaughton didn't believe in, any more than I did. These meetings gave him the chance to learn that the president was dubious about it too. That was vital information of a sort that McNaughton would get only by being in the room with them. McNamara wouldn't have been likely to tell him about the president's doubts and questions, at least with any concreteness and vividness.

Those reports gave me a good impression of Johnson. For once McNamara seemed off base to me; I couldn't figure out why. The president sounded like the only sensible adult in the room. That gave me some hope that fall that things would turn out all right. (What I didn't know at the time—and I don't think John knew either—was that LBJ's own preference was to put troops in South Vietnam rather than bomb the North.) To hear from John that the president, in speaking to McNamara, regularly referred to "your bombing bullshit" made me think that Johnson was reluctant to undertake escalation of any kind and perhaps therefore open-minded about extricating us altogether.

McNaughton told me that McNamara would say of bombing, "It's something you can stop. It's a bargaining chip." When someone criticized it, as not being likely to get good results or to be all that easy to stop, he challenged him: "Well, what's your alternative?" Answering McNamara's question by saying, "Getting out, withdrawing, negotiating out," would have amounted to saying, "My alternative is quitting. Losing." Given the president's views, that was an answer no one in these meetings, which were in effect preparatory to discussions in front of the president, was willing to advance. It was a nonoption. As a result, McNamara's challenge and his proposed policy (which was far from his alone) looked less crazy than they really were.

McNaughton's fear, he told me one afternoon when he had just come back from the White House, was that one day the president would turn to him and ask him what he thought about bombing. In a memoir written years later, NSC aide Chester Cooper describes having had a comparable fantasy more than once. The president would be going around the table, asking if everyone agreed with his decision, and he imagined himself saying when it came to his turn, "No, Mr. President, I do not agree!" As he was contemplating this thought, he would notice the president's eyes turning to him and he would hear himself saying, as he nodded yes, "I agree, Mr. President."

McNaughton told me, "I've asked myself what I would do." Then he paused and looked at me. "I would have to follow McNamara's lead. I'd have to say something along the same lines as McNamara. I couldn't contradict McNamara or undercut him in front of the president." I didn't say anything. He went on: "You know, my family owns a newspaper in Illinois. We don't have much to do with running it; that's for the editor. The main thing we have to do is pick the editor. And when we pick an editor, well, there're a number of things you look for, but my father taught me that the number one thing you look for is loyalty."

He continued to look at me, and I continued to listen. I knew why he was telling me this. He didn't define what he meant by loyalty, but it was clear enough from his story: Do what's good for your boss, the man who hired you; put that above what you think is best for the country, above giving the president or the secretary of defense your best advice if that would embarrass your boss. I heard it, but I didn't accept it. Actually I was shocked. Lie to the president? Deprive him of your own best judgment, when he was asking you for it, on a matter of war and peace? Or lie to McNamara, the secretary of defense, if I was in the room with him and McNaughton and he asked me for my own thoughts? That was the real point of this story. Never, I thought. I didn't say anything to John, and the situation never arose.

I did have a chance earlier in the fall to argue outside our offices against initiating air strikes against the North at all. Walt Rostow, the chairman of the policy planning staff at State, circulated a paper proposing that we seek to change, by both declaration and action, the prevailing "common law" rules of the game in international relations. These limited our military responses to what he called "covert aggression" such as what we all believed to be North Vietnam's covert direction and support of the National Liberation Front (NLF) in South Vietnam. Rostow had argued since 1961 for the legitimacy and necessity of American bombing of North Vietnam. McNaughton asked various parts of his staff to contribute to a detailed critique of "the Rostow thesis that covert aggression justifies and must be fought by attacks on the source of the aggression." I wrote a section of our very critical response, which was circulated to all the relevant agencies, on the costs and risks of applying the thesis:

> Given present attitudes, application of the Rostow approach risks domestic and international opposition ranging from anxiety and protest to condemnation, efforts to disassociate from U.S. policies or alliances, or even strong

> countermeasures. . . . Currently, then, it is the Rostow approach, rather than the measures it counters, that would be seen generally as an "unstabilizing" change in the rules of the game, an escalation of conflict, an increasing of shared international risks, and quite possibly, as an open aggression demanding condemnation. . . .

This is one of the very few passages in the surviving drafts or official documents of that period in which I can recognize my own words. On rereading it now, I'm struck by two things. First, so far as I know, it is the *only* use of the word "aggression" applied to a possible action of the United States in the entire official documentation of that era. Second, I note that I took care to tender that word not as a compelling, objective judgment or as my own. It expressed how our bombing a country that had made no overt armed attack against us or anyone else would possibly be "seen" and condemned by *others*. There was no other way to get such a thought into official discussion internally even once and remain employed. I'm sure that's still true. The same holds for the words "criminal" and "immoral" applied to a policy that one's agency or the president might favor or has adopted.

These three taboo words would have been widely used by others, including our allies, if the Joint Chiefs' preferred program had ever been implemented. Yet the same words, only a little less obviously, could apply to the plan for "graduated pressure on the DRV [Hanoi regime]" that McNaughton had fashioned for McNamara. He drafted this on September 3, three weeks after he had drafted instructions for Seaborn's threat to Hanoi and about the same time I was criticizing Rostow's proposal. In his "Plan for Action for South Vietnam," John listed several classes of actions that "should cause apprehension, ideally increasing apprehension, in the DRV," and "should be likely at some point to provoke a military DRV response" that would

> provide good grounds for us to escalate if we wished . . . to commence a crescendo of GVN-U.S. military actions against the DRV. The escalating actions might be . . . mining of harbors . . . air strikes against North Vietnam moving from southern to northern targets, from targets associated with infiltration . . . to targets of military then industrial importance. . . . The possibility that such actions would escalate further, perhaps bringing China into the war, would have to be faced.

Aside from the issue of aggression involved in planning for provocation, I believed, as McNaughton did privately, that this graduated approach to bombing was not a whole lot better than the JCS plan for an initial full-scale attack. I thought it was likely to come to the same thing eventually. Still, given that some form of bombing seemed inevitable, McNaughton's proposal slowed the progression toward the most destructive and dangerous forms. Its other supposed advantage was flexibility and control. "The timing and crescendo should be under our control, with the scenario capable of being turned off at any time." In a later formulation for the Bundy group, McNaughton wrote that the scenario "would be designed to give the U.S. the option at any point to proceed or not, to escalate or not and to quicken the pace or not."

But was such controllability real? Did John himself believe in it? In *The Best and the Brightest* (1972) journalist David Halberstam answers the latter question. He describes McNaughton as having shared with Michael Forrestal, then at the White House, as early as the spring of 1964 all his doubts about the GVN, bombing, and the war that I heard from him when I joined him months later. Evidently quoting Forrestal as his source, Halberstam says Michael "was not yet as pessimistic as McNaughton." He didn't think entrapment was inevitable.

> He was sure that it could be avoided somehow, that there were options, that good intelligent men in Washington could control decisions and avoid the great entanglement. McNaughton was not sure. "The trouble with you, Forrestal," he once said, "is that you always think we can turn this thing off, and that we can get off of it whenever we want. But I wonder. I think it gets harder every day, each day we lose a little control, each decision that we make wrong, or don't make at all, makes the next decision a little harder because if we haven't stopped it today, then the reasons for not stopping it will still exist tomorrow, and we'll be in even deeper."

That was the John McNaughton I knew in private. It was how he spoke to me, and he told me it was what he said to McNamara when they were alone together. But it was not what he drafted for McNamara's use as talking papers or memos to others or what he said in meetings, speaking for his boss. None of that seems so wise. Whether McNamara himself really felt differently or not, I don't know. He worked directly for the president. That means his written memos to the president or others, often drafted by McNaughton, might misrepresent his most private thinking as much as John's did his own. It's more than possible that his positions in meetings or in writing, like McNaughton's, often represented his boss's beliefs and priorities, with which he didn't agree. But the written record can't answer that. Unless

McNamara chooses to clarify more than he has how his perspective differed from those of his two presidents, I don't think his own behavior, or the history of that era, can be adequately understood.

Meanwhile John was giving him what he wanted. Subsequent accounts based on documents from the Pentagon tend to credit, or blame, McNaughton as a driving force in the promotion of bombing, particularly as it was actually conducted (against the instincts of the JCS). In those memos, my boss appeared constantly to be making recommendations to bomb, as well as how to do it, when and what and why to bomb, in what sequence and to what effect. He didn't believe any of it. That is, he didn't believe any of it was necessary or to the advantage of the United States or the Vietnamese, except that it was preferable to—less disastrous than—what the JCS wanted to do. His attitude, like mine, was that bombing the North was absurd and dangerous, that it would not achieve anything positive but would only bring us into the war in a heavier way.

Even more than I, considerably more, McNaughton was committed to the view that we should stop what we were already doing in Vietnam and get out on almost any basis. He was not impressed with the arguments that our efforts up till then had created a serious national interest, that we were being tested in some significant way, that withdrawal would lose us prestige, or that important alliances would suffer along with our influence in world affairs. On the contrary, he believed that we would suffer more in every one of these dimensions by our prolonged involvement than by our withdrawal. Moreover, even if by means of massive military intervention we could in some sense be successful, he didn't believe the benefits in terms of our national interest could measure up to the costs or to the harm we would inflict on the Vietnamese. There is scarcely a hint of any of these attitudes in any piece of paper he drafted or signed in the last years of his life, from 1964 to 1967. Yet that is what he did believe. Where we disagreed on these assessments, he was right; I was wrong.

Personally I thought he underrated the cost to our influence and our ability to confront communism elsewhere that would result from a U.S. failure in Vietnam. Sometimes I wondered if he might be less of a cold warrior than I was. I thought our retreat from Vietnam would cause us more trouble in our worldwide conflict with communism than John seemed to believe. It would, I believed, embolden the Soviets and Chinese and insurgents worldwide and discourage our clients and allies. On that point I could agree, contrary to John, with Secretary of State Rusk and the JCS. But whereas the true Vietnam hawks believed that was a sufficient reason for expanding our involvement and generally thought they knew a way to succeed at it, I did not. I agreed with John's private opinion that we would be even worse off, on balance, if we tried to keep a doomed effort going, and still worse if we escalated. Vietnam was not the place to plant our flag. So we would just have to deal as best we could with the problems that would arise if we left. Far more than I knew at the time, that attitude was shared by a number of officials, cold warriors all, just below the top levels.

But not by any of their bosses. It was not what the president had in mind or Secretary of State Rusk, or the secretary of defense. Given my admiration for Robert McNamara, I could never understand why he wanted to set out on this path of provocation and escalation at all, however "gradually." It was steadily more perplexing and disturbing for me to know that he was among the strong proponents of bombing the North.

That was especially paradoxical for me because of my strong confidence that McNamara shared some of my deepest values, particularly my abhorrence of nuclear war. This feeling had its roots in my earlier work as a Rand consultant to the Office of the Secretary of Defense on nuclear war plans and command and control of nuclear weapons. Like a number of my Rand colleagues, including Harry Rowen and Morton H. Halperin, a young consultant on arms control, I believed that to initiate limited or general nuclear war under any circumstances would be catastrophic. We felt strongly about this, though it was a position that contradicted U.S. defense policy and strategy in NATO. That rested openly on U.S. readiness to carry out its threat and preparations for a nuclear first-use strike against a Soviet conventional attack. Our personal opinions also contradicted the doctrine of the air force, for which we worked at Rand. Nevertheless, I believed that McNamara agreed with us.

I had inferred his position from the way he talked with me in a private lunch at his desk in 1961. I had written papers that had gone to him but had never met him before. He impressed me strongly and positively that day with his conviction that under no circumstances must there be a first use of U.S. nuclear weapons in Europe. It would be totally disastrous even if it did not lead to an all-out war between the United States and the USSR, as he believed it surely would. Even before that, "It would be total war, total annihilation, for the Europeans!" He said this with great passion, belying his reputation as a cold, computerlike efficiency expert. Moreover, he thought it was absurd to suppose that a "limited use" would remain confined to Europe, that it would not immediately trigger general nuclear war.

I had recently drafted, and he had approved, the top secret secretary-of-defense guidance to the Joint Chiefs of Staff for a new version of the operational plans for general nuclear war. It was in that context that he had invited me to lunch. At the request of his deputy secretary of defense, Roswell Gilpatric, I had drafted a number of questions on the Eisenhower-era war plans, which were still current. Gilpatric had sent these to the JCS for their response. When I showed the draft list to Robert Komer of the NSC staff, he picked out one of the questions and sent it to the chiefs as a presidential query. The question was: "If existing general war plans were carried out as planned, how many people would be killed in the Soviet Union and China alone?"

During our discussion over lunch, I told McNamara that the JCS supplied the White House with an answer almost immediately, within a day or two. It was classified top secret—for the president's eyes only—but since I had drafted the question, Komer called me over to the NSC offices to look at it. The answer was in the form of a straight-line graph, a rising line that related fatalities on the vertical axis, in millions of deaths, against time on the horizontal axis, in months from the time of attack. The number rose to reflect delayed radiation deaths from fallout after the attacks. (I had asked only for fatalities, not for casualties, which would have included wounded and sick.) The lowest point of the graph, starting at the left-hand side of the chart, gave the number that would die in the first few days of our attacks. The highest number, at the right-hand side of the chart, showed the cumulative number killed by our attacks within six months of the execution of the plans.

The lower number was 275 million dead. The higher number was 325 million.

This was for the Soviet Union and China alone, all that I had asked for. I drafted a follow-up question for Komer covering areas contiguous to the Sino-Soviet bloc, and the staff provided comprehensive estimates with equal dispatch. Another hundred million or so would die from our attacks on targets in the Eastern European satellite countries. Moreover, fallout from our surface explosions on the Soviet Union, the satellites, and China would decimate the populations of the neutral nations bordering these countries—such as Finland, Sweden, Austria, and Afghanistan—as well as Japan and Pakistan. The Finns, for example, would be virtually exterminated by the fallout from surface bursts on Soviet submarine pens near their borders. These fatalities from U.S. attacks, up to another hundred million depending on wind conditions, would occur without a single American warhead landing on the territories of these neutral countries.

Fallout fatalities inside our NATO allies from U.S. attacks against the

Warsaw Pact could be up to a hundred million allied deaths from our attacks, "depending on which way the wind blows," as a general testifying before Congress had recently put it. All this was without considering the effects of Soviet nuclear attacks on the United States, Western Europe, and U.S. bases elsewhere, retaliating for the U.S. first strike that these JCS calculations presumed. Nor did it include the effects of U.S. tactical nuclear weapons, the point that McNamara had just made to me passionately.

The total death toll from our own attacks, in the estimates supplied by the JCS, was in the neighborhood of five to six hundred million. These would be almost entirely civilians. A hundred Holocausts. The greater part would be inflicted in a day or two, the rest over six months, about a third in allied or neutral countries.

This was not a hypothetical calculation of what was needed to deter a Soviet nuclear attack on the United States or its allies (as such it would still have been obscenely absurd). It was the JCS's best estimate of the actual results, in terms of human fatalities, of our setting into motion the existing machinery for implementing the current operational plans of the JCS for general war. Current U.S. plans for "any armed conflict" with conventional forces of the Soviet Union, anywhere, arising under any circumstances—Berlin, uprisings in East Germany, Soviet attacks on Iran or Yugoslavia—presumed that the president would initiate general nuclear war, with these consequences outside the United States.

I still remember holding that graph in my hand and looking at it in an office of the White House annex in the Executive Office Building on a spring day in 1961. I was thinking: This piece of paper, what this piece of paper represents, should not exist. It should never in the course of human history have come into existence.

I didn't say that to the secretary. From the tone of our conversation I didn't think I had to. I've never had a stronger sense in another person of a kindred awareness of this situation and of the intensity of his concern to change it. Thirty years later McNamara revealed in his memoir *In Retrospect* that he had secretly advised President Kennedy, and after him President Johnson, that under no circumstances should they ever initiate nuclear war. He didn't tell me that, but it was implicit in everything he had said. There is no doubt in my mind that he did give that advice and that it was the right advice. Yet it directly contradicted the U.S. "assurances" on U.S. readiness for first use he felt compelled to give repeatedly to NATO officials throughout his years in office. (NATO retains a first-use policy to this day, as does the United States outside the NATO area—perhaps now with a new degree of sincerity, indicated by the first-use premises of the Bush administration's nuclear policy review leaked in March 2002.) McNamara's private advice also contradicted the long-term assumptions in U.S. limited-war planning for necessary first use of nuclear weapons in a conflict with large Chinese forces in Asia.

McNamara's assistant Adam Yarmolinsky had joined us for the last part of the lunch. After we left McNamara's office, Adam took me into his small adjoining room and said, "You must tell no one outside this room what Secretary McNamara has told you."

I asked if he was referring to fears of the reaction from Congress and the JCS (I could have added "NATO"), and he said, "Exactly. This could lead to his impeachment." I told him I understood. He went on to emphasize the seriousness of not telling anyone. "By no one," he said, "I mean, not Harry Rowen, not anybody." Evidently he knew that Harry was my closest friend and confidant, the colleague with whom I normally would have shared even such highly sensitive information. I got the message and respected his way of putting it. I never did tell anyone what McNamara had said, even Rowen, though Harry would have found it as heartening as I did. But I did ask Adam, "As far as you know, is the president's thinking on these subjects different from the secretary's?" He said, "Not an iota."

I left the secretary's suite thinking that Robert McNamara was someone worthy of my greatest loyalty and trust. He had, as I saw it, the right perspective on the greatest dangers in the world and the power and determination to reduce them. Also, he and his assistant had the street savvy to know that if he wanted to achieve that, he had to keep his cards very close to his chest. I felt that extreme loyalty over the next three years, and I brought it with me when I came to work full-time in the Pentagon. It was a sense that McNamara and his trusted lieutenants were men with my values and concerns trying to tame powerful and irrational institutional forces—largely, though not all, within the same building—that threatened to steer us toward nuclear disaster. I felt privileged to try to help them.

Thus I gave McNamara great benefit of the doubt even when, as now, I couldn't understand his choices. Uneasy as I was about the policy of escalation he had us working on, there was no question in my mind that it was, at least in the short run, far less likely to trigger nuclear war with China than the Goldwater approach that the JCS was urging. If anything, Johnson seemed even more concerned about that risk. So my loyalty attached itself to Johnson as well. I wanted to see him reelected with as big a mandate as possible, and I don't recall that the dissimulation to that end bothered me very much. It was important not only to keep men like Johnson, McNamara, and McNaughton in office but to enhance their power relative to the Joint Chiefs. We were staving off pressure for a course that appeared considerably more dangerous.

The same objective justified the efforts of my boss and me in the NSC working group starting on election day. Our job, as McNaughton framed it, was not to keep alive the withdrawal option, which either of us would personally have regarded at that time as the least bad of a bad lot. It was to work to achieve a consensus for McNamara's preferred bombing strategy, "gradual pressure," and a rejection of the Joint Chiefs' "hard knock." The latter called for hitting all the targets on the chiefs' ninety-four-target list as nearly simultaneously as possible, for maximum surprise and shock. First to be hit were the MiG base at Phuc Yen on the outskirts of Hanoi and oil storage sites in the same populated area.

Nearly every policy recommendation from the Joint Chiefs reiterated: ". . . the United States should seek through military actions to accomplish the destruction of the North Vietnamese will and capabilities as necessary to compel the [Hanoi regime] to cease providing support to the insurgencies in South Vietnam and Laos." The key words in this objective, as the chiefs emphasized in distinguishing it from alternative aims of influencing, coercing, or persuading, were "destruction," "compel," and "capabilities." To this end they recommended a list of specific proposals, recited so regularly from early 1964 through 1968 that it was almost a litany. These included mining Haiphong Harbor and waterways within North Vietnam, blockading the seacoast of Vietnam up to China, bombing land, water, and rail communications between China and North Vietnam, and eliminating any air support from China, along with unrestricted air attacks against military and industrial targets throughout North Vietnam up to the Chinese border. The idea was to cut off the flow of supplies from the Sino-Soviet bloc that came through China and by sea, thus isolating North Vietnam and the NLF in the South from their Communist suppliers, and, by the unrestricted air campaign, to pound the leaders and people of North Vietnam into submission.

Moreover, the army and marines believed it was essential to cut off the infiltration of both troops and supplies from the North to the NLF by divisions of U.S. ground troops across the infiltration routes in Laos and Cambodia and/or U.S. divisions within or on the coast of South Vietnam. This part of their victory strategy surfaced only occasionally in interagency discussions in 1964. It was submerged not only because of the election campaign but because Maxwell Taylor and Robert McNamara both opposed it until April 1965. Nevertheless, planning for ground deployments within army and marine staffs was going on throughout that period. From the logic of the situation it was no surprise to me when pressure for it became explicit and urgent in early 1965.

From my study of bombing in World War II and Korea, I agreed with the civilian intelligence analysts of the CIA and the State Department that conventional bombing would simply fail either to cut off the relatively small flow of infiltration needed to sustain the guerrilla war in the South or to induce the Hanoi leadership or its people to give up the armed struggle. Nor did these intelligence analysts expect ground operations in the highlands or border areas to "isolate the battlefield" in the South, as the army hoped. Even if they did, they wouldn't have a decisive effect in the largely indigenous conflict in the South. But once the United States had so committed itself and taken heavy casualties, I foresaw very strong tendencies to try to recoup early failures and break out of a stalemate by expanding the war still further. This would likely take two forms. First, although the chiefs and the air force disclaimed any intention to target cities or population per se, as in World War II and Korea, I doubted that restraint would long survive a failure to destroy the "capability" of the North to persist in the war. Going after their "will" decisively would mean both city bombing, whether admitted or not, and destroying the Red River dikes in the North, threatening a million deaths from famine.

The other response to a failure to end the North's support to the war in the South would be our army's extending the efforts to block infiltration in Laos and Cambodia to an invasion of the southern part of North Vietnam. That in turn, in failing to end the war, would encourage full invasion of the North, meaning a far bloodier replay of the French war, up to the border of China. This was very likely to bring in Chinese troops, if earlier moves had not. Our war planners had long presumed that we would initiate nuclear war against China in that case.

It was popularly understood that the legacy of the Korean stalemate was a "never again" club in the U.S. Army, meaning "Never again a land war in Asia." I knew from my earlier work on war planning that the real meaning of that motto was "Never again a land war with China *without nuclear weapons.*" The files I read in McNaughton's office made it clear that lesson was still doctrine. And not only (though mainly) among the military. Secretary of State Dean Rusk (who had been assistant secretary for the Far East during the first two years of the Korean War) could not have agreed more. In a conference with Ambassador Henry Cabot Lodge in Saigon in mid-April 1964, he had recited the formula in so many words: "[W]e are not going to take on the masses of Red China with our limited manpower in a conventional war."

In a Honolulu conference on June 2, 1964, General Taylor spoke of the real possibility that air attacks on the North—which all present favored—would bring in Chinese Communist ground forces. Secretary McNamara said we had to be prepared for this eventuality, even if it was not probable; this led to

> a serious question of having to use nuclear weapons at some point. Admiral [Harry D.] Felt (CINCPAC) responded emphatically that there was no possible way to hold off the communists on the ground without the use of tactical nuclear weapons, and that it was essential that the commanders be given the freedom to use these as had been assumed [in] the various plans.

Talk of commanders' "freedom to use" tactical nuclear weapons bore on the most dramatic issue of the electoral campaign in its preliminary stages that month: Senator Goldwater's advocacy of using nuclear weapons in Vietnam, and even of delegating authority to use tactical nuclear weapons to field commanders. This position was Goldwater's greatest vulnerability in the campaign. (President Johnson's secret delegation of authority under some circumstances, such as failure of communications with Washington, was carefully concealed from the public and Congress, and it was considerably more limited than the delegation Goldwater proposed with the secret support of General Curtis LeMay, Admiral Felt, and many others among Johnson's top military men.) Goldwater's supposedly extreme stand lay behind the most devastating TV political ad ever: a little girl plucking petals off a daisy while a voice in the background counted down "Ten, nine, eight . . ." Nevertheless, though from my knowledge of him McNamara could not have agreed with either Felt or Rusk, the record of the Honolulu conference shows no argument with their position from any of the civilian officials of the Johnson administration present.

Nor was this official discussion—which would have gotten a good deal of attention if leaked to Congress or the public that campaign summer—confined to private talks among American officials. In talking with South Vietnamese General Nguyen Khanh (who was then premier) in Saigon on May 30, 1964, just before the Honolulu conference, Rusk brought up the subject, along with a reference to somewhat earlier discussions with other Asian leaders. He informed the department in a cable that he had told Khanh:

> U.S. would never again get involved in a land war in Asia limited to conventional forces. Our population was 190,000,000. Mainland China had at least 700,000,000. We would not allow ourselves to be bled white fighting them with conventional weapons.
>
> . . . This meant that if escalation brought about major Chinese attack, it would also involve use of nuclear arms. Many free world leaders would oppose this. Chiang Kai-Shek had told him fervently he did, and so did [UN Secretary-General] U Thant. Many Asians seemed to see an element of racial discrimination in use of nuclear arms; something we would do to Asians but not to Westerners. Khanh replied he certainly had no quarrel with American use of nuclear arms, noted that decisive use of atomic bombs on Japan had in ending war saved not only American but also Japanese lives. One must use the force one had; if Chinese used masses of humanity, we would use superior fire power.

From January 1964 through 1968, the JCS continuously favored the immediate implementation of certain military measures—air, land, and sea—each of which, it acknowledged, posed tangible risks of war with China. No civilian quarreled explicitly with its assertion that such a war, if it resulted, must be nuclear. The differences between the civilians (with whom Maxwell Taylor tended to side) and the JCS on the scale of these risks, and on the importance of averting nuclear war with China, were large and significant. To a very great extent these differences shaped the strategy President Johnson chose and how he chose to describe it and conceal it, because he urgently desired to prevent these differences from being made public and debated. Yet although it was the favored proposals of the JCS that raised the prospect of nuclear war with China most immediately and acutely, all the proposals that the civilian leaders took seriously also involved clear risks of such a war eventually. The JCS was inviting the administration to play with nuclear fire. And whatever their reasons and reservations, the top civilian officials were not refusing to play.

4

Planning Provocation

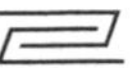

From early September 1964 U.S. "retaliatory" capability against North Vietnam was a cocked pistol. Officials just below the president were waiting for something to retaliate to and increasingly ready to provoke an excuse for attack if necessary. Six days after John McNaughton's September 3 plan "to provoke a military DRV response and to be in a good position to seize on that response . . . to commence a crescendo of GVN-U.S. military actions against the DRV," the highest officials forwarded the proposal to the president for his decision. After recommending the immediate resumption of DeSoto patrols off the coast of North Vietnam and the resumption of 34A actions, both suspended since August 5, they added: "The main further question is the extent to which we should add elements to the above actions that would tend deliberately to provoke a DRV reaction, and consequent retaliation by us. Examples of actions to be considered would be running U.S. naval patrols increasingly close to the North Vietnamese coast and/or associating them with 34A operations."

I recall that these proposals excited a flurry of concrete suggestions by the JCS on how best to provoke an attack on U.S. forces by the North Vietnamese if it proved hard to get a rise out of them. Along with running a U.S. destroyer increasingly close to beaching on their coast, U-2 reconnaissance planes over North Vietnam could be supplemented by low-level reconnaissance jets flying progressively lower over populated areas. This could culminate, if necessary, in a supersonic flight that would break every window in Hanoi with a sonic boom.

But nothing so spectacular proved to be necessary. On the night of October 31 there was an attack on U.S. forces, killing five Americans, wounding thirty, and destroying or badly damaging eighteen of the B-57 jet bombers that had been deployed to Bien Hoa air base in South Vietnam as part of a buildup rationalized by the Tonkin Gulf incidents. Having moved through heavily populated areas up to and within the American air base near Saigon without giving warning, the VC guerrillas didn't rely on advanced weaponry from the Soviet bloc to accomplish this destruction. They simply used 81-mm mortars and satchel charges. Again Taylor and the JCS strongly demanded retaliation, this time urging plausibly that to fail to respond would show weakness. The JCS proposed initial attacks in Laos and North Vietnam, to be followed by a night attack by B-52s on Phuc Yen airfield near Hanoi and a dawn strike by tactical fighters on other airfields and oil storage in the area of Hanoi and Haiphong. But the VC attack was three days before the election, and the pistol stayed cocked by decision of the candidate in the White House.

On January 27, though I didn't know it at the time, McNamara and McGeorge Bundy argued forcefully to the president that the time had come "to use our military power in the Far East and to force a change of Communist policy." He was no longer inclined to wait passively for an excuse for a "retaliatory" strike on the North. On January 28 DeSoto patrols, with the mission of provoking an attack, were ordered back into the Tonkin Gulf for the first time in five months. Naval retaliatory forces were to be in position before the patrols commenced on February 3. If the Communist attackers didn't come to our troops on land, as they had at Bien Hoa, we would go to them by sea, as close as necessary to get them to attack. The American public, in the dark about the administration's objectives and sense of commitment in Vietnam, still needed to be given a plausible reason for dropping bombs on North Vietnam. But it shouldn't take long now for one to come around. Bundy recalled later that it was like waiting for a streetcar.

As it had been once before, in late July 1964, the American pistol aimed at North Vietnam was not merely cocked but on a hair trigger. This time, with no election campaign pending, it was loaded for more than a single shot.

The attack came by land. On February 7 a U.S. helicopter base and barracks in Pleiku in the Central Highlands was attacked. Eight Americans were killed, and 126 wounded; ten planes were destroyed, and many others damaged. At this point the president ordered a reprisal raid against North Vietnam, the first such strike since the retaliation for Tonkin Gulf in August. It was code-named Flaming Dart. The White House announcement called it an "appropriate reprisal action," like the Tonkin Gulf reaction, and stated once again, "We seek no wider war."

Prior plans had already existed for such a raid, and targets had been picked. As on my first day in the Pentagon, I was up all night monitoring the strike and its results to help the ISA staff prepare a report for McNamara and the president the next morning. McNaughton was in Vietnam at the time on a trip with McGeorge Bundy, and they visited Pleiku the morning after the attack. They had already drafted before the attack a memo of recommendations from their trip. In fact it was largely drafted even before they left Washington for Vietnam; on the way back they just modified it to include references to Pleiku, which they said had "created an ideal opportunity" for the prompt execution of a policy they had already decided to recommend to the president. They called it a policy of sustained reprisal, meaning a long-term systematic bombing campaign against the North, which would be rationalized at first as reprisals to "acts of relatively high visibility such as the Pleiku incident," but gradually, in order to be sustained, related merely to the ongoing level of VC activity in the South. Early reactions might be to "'spectacular' outrages" like Pleiku, but:

> Once a program of reprisals is clearly under way, it should not be necessary to connect each specific act against North Vietnam to a particular outrage in the South. It should be possible, for example, to publish weekly lists of outrages in the South and to have it clearly understood that these outrages are the cause of such action against the North as may be occurring in the current period.

But neither on the seventh nor on the eighth, when Bundy and McNaughton returned to argue for their memo in Washington, was Johnson ready yet to go beyond a reprisal raid to launch a sustained program. But the day after the raid, McNamara asked the JCS to give him its recommendations for an eight-week bombing campaign against infiltration-associated targets in southern North Vietnam as a sustained reply to the next provocation. The president had not yet committed himself to such a program, but he did order the withdrawal of U.S. dependents from South Vietnam.

On the night of February 10 there was a second VC attack on Americans, this time on an American advisory compound in Qui Nhon, also in the Central Highlands. Again Americans had been killed and injured, though we didn't yet have details on just what had happened. The president rejected the immediate JCS recommendation to begin the eight-week program, ordering only another one-shot raid. This attack carried out the next day with 130 planes was code-named Flaming Dart II.

Rather than having me monitor this raid as before, McNaughton, just back from McNamara's office, told me urgently to gather "atrocity" details regarding the VC attack on Qui Nhon and a list of other terrorist actions in recent weeks. That was for the explicit purpose, he told me, of helping McNamara convince LBJ that the time had come to go beyond a tit-for-tat retaliation—which was all the president had permitted two days earlier after the attack on Pleiku and all he had yet authorized for this attack—and launch systematic bombing. He also wanted, as the Bundy-McNaughton memo suggested, to get away from relating our strikes only to attacks on Americans.

For the first time I was being drawn into the process of directly persuading the president on a course I considered disastrous. Usually I just helped McNaughton clarify memos he was writing for McNamara's use, whatever that use might be. Now I was asked to gather data directly for McNamara for a use I deplored. But I didn't have time to reflect on that. I had until eight the next morning, when the secretary would be leaving for the White House. I needed to get started right away. An order from McNamara to McNaughton for fast action was like an order from God; it wasn't an occasion for John to express reservations or show hesitation. He passed it on to me with the same expectation. I didn't disappoint him. I had no doubts or hesitation as I went down to the Joint War Room to do my best. That's the memory I have to deal with.

I went to the Joint War Room in the offices of the Joint Chiefs of Staff in the Pentagon because direct communications with MACV headquarters in Saigon were there. The duty officer gave me a desk with a phone line to Saigon, and I sat there all night with an open line. I told the colonel at the other end that I was representing the secretary of defense, as John had told me to do, and I had, it seemed, a whole staff at MACV headquarters collecting data for me. Briefly I told the colonel I needed details of atrocities by the VC anywhere in Vietnam, especially over the last week or the last month or the day before. Above all, I wanted gory details of the injuries to Americans at Pleiku and especially at Qui Nhon. I told the colonel, "I need blood."

It was early morning in Vietnam when we started, and it was a working day at MACV headquarters as I talked through the night from the Pentagon, so it was relatively easy for his staffers to collect data. They were calling province representatives and division advisers all over Vietnam. We always talked a lot about VC terrorism and atrocities, but weekly reports mentioned only individual incidents. No one had collected statistics on them. The Vietnamese province officials, it turned out, did keep an accounting of incidents, province by province, but they didn't tend to be reported from the provinces to MACV headquarters, and no one put them all together countrywide. Also, the data even at the province level, collected from districts and hamlets, tended to be a month behind the actual occurrences. Still, it was possible to get information on some incidents from the last week or two: a bus blown up by a mine; a district chief killed.

I asked for graphic details, to make it more concrete, more dramatic. How many had been killed in the bus? Who were they? Where were they going? How many children? Was it a pressure mine, which might not have been intended for a civilian vehicle, or a wire-detonated mine, which had to be detonated deliberately under the bus?

Most of the reports didn't go into such details, but some of them did. The district chief had been disemboweled in front of the whole village, and his family, his wife and four children, had been killed too. "Great! That's what I want to know! That's what we need! More of that. Can you find other stories like that?"

With my encouragement, the staff in Saigon was working hard, on phones and radios. There was no fax in those days; detailed paper reports were being brought in from provinces by helicopter. Most of them had to be translated. They were working under heavy pressure from me. I told them it all had to be in, for the president, by 7:00 A.M. my time so I could put it together by 8:00 with the help of a couple of secretaries.

While I was on an open line all night to MACV in Saigon, staff members there were on an open line to Qui Nhon throughout the day, trying to find out just what had happened. It was chaotic there. It had been hit just the night before, and MACV still didn't have a complete picture of what exactly had happened, which was coming in during the day. What I needed was not the military details but the human interest, the horror and the terroristic aspects. "Terrorism" wasn't exactly the right word, since this was an attack on a military base during a war, but it was an attack on sleeping soldiers in a barracks. Also, these were Americans, advisers, helpers; the United States wasn't even at war as far as the public had been told. It was not unlike an unprovoked attack on our destroyers, on routine patrol on the high seas. It was a challenge to our honor, to the safety of our troops in the face of our direct warnings. It was exactly the sort of thing the Tonkin Gulf Resolution, passed nearly unanimously by Congress, had been intended to prevent, the sort of thing that called for direct reprisal against North Vietnam, like our raids of August 5. This, after the attacks at Bien Hoa and Pleiku, had exhausted American patience. At least it would after the president and the public learned the concrete details of what had been done at Qui Nhon, which I was in the process of gathering.

About four in the morning, afternoon in Vietnam, I got what I was looking for. In hushed tones, haltingly, the colonel told me that they had just gotten information that two American advisers—a major and a lieutenant, as I remember—in an advisory compound that had been overrun the night before appeared to have been captured and killed. For all that this was a terrible story to tell and to hear, the colonel had a clear idea by this time of what I was hunting for, and he knew, we both knew, that he had come up with what I needed. There were puncture wounds in the bodies of the two officers, not from bullets or fragmentation. I pressed for details.

Half an hour later there was a little more. Their bodies showed signs of having been dragged across the courtyard of the compound, perhaps by chains. This might have been after they had died. It wasn't clear whether the mutilation occurred before or after they had been killed or was a result of their being dragged, before or after death, or tortured.

This sounded like a first in the war. As far as I knew, there was not a single American prisoner of war at that point or one American who had been killed point-blank rather than by impersonal explosions or weapons at a distance. American bodies mutilated, either alive or dead, officers captured and murdered. This was what John had sent me down to get for McNamara. I was exultant. As I was writing down the details, I was telling the colonel, "Good. Good. More like that. Wow. Jesus! This is it. Anything else? Anything like this anywhere else?" The count on American dead and injured at Qui Nhon kept going up, but all the rest were from mortars. This was the only incident of the kind found—it may have been the only one in Vietnam in the war up to that point—but one was enough for my report. At 6:30 A.M. I wrapped it up. I thanked the colonel emphatically and asked him to thank his whole crew.

I gathered my notes and went back up to my office in ISA to put it all together for McNamara: in the preceding month so many minings of buses, schools and district offices blown up, hamlet, village, and district officials assassinated; American deaths in the last three days at Pleiku and Qui Nhon, a detailed, graphic account of the condition of the bodies of the two American advisers. I did not encourage releasing this last information to the public. On the contrary, I noted that the White House would probably want to withhold it, not only out of respect for the families of the two men but because it might be too inflammatory. Public outrage might compel the president to respond in ways that went beyond where he and McNamara wanted to go. But with an eye to where I knew the secretary wanted the president to go, I mentioned that there was a good chance that these gory details would leak to the press (from military circles, in their understandable outrage and in their desire to see an all-out response; I wasn't hinting at a deliberate leak by McNamara or his immediate subordinates). That could seriously embarrass the administration if there were no response at all against North Vietnam, as there had been none in November after the attack on Bien Hoa, or even if the response continued to be as limited as the recent reprisal for Pleiku. The hawk columnist Joe Alsop could then be counted on, if he got this information, to attack the White House both for craven inaction and for a deliberate cover-up to that end.

I was handing pages of my draft, partly handwritten and partly typed, to one of two secretaries who had come in early for this. The other was typing John's paper, written that morning, arguing the case for a bombing campaign to begin now. With McNaughton standing over her, my typist pulled the last page out of the typewriter, clipped it together with the others, and John raced down the hall to hand our two papers to McNamara to read in his limousine on the way to the White House. A little after nine McNamara came back and told John to thank me for my input. It was exactly what he had needed. He said that it had had a significant influence on the president.

I saw one result quickly. Rather than relating the strikes specifically to the Qui Nhon attack on Americans, the White House announcement on the raids that day issued my list of VC incidents and attacks since February 8, describing them as "continued acts of aggression." The statement actually avoided the words "reprisal" and "retaliation," describing our attacks simply as a "response" to "further direct provocations by the Hanoi regime." That followed Bundy's rationale for an ongoing bombing program. Since most of the data I had collected were on unspectacular VC actions of the sort that occurred daily, this press release paved the way for a systematic campaign without actually announcing it. The president accepted the recommendation for such a campaign several days later. The campaign, code-named Rolling Thunder, began on March 2. In the same period, U.S. jets began overt missions within South Vietnam for the first time. U.S. bombing within and beyond the borders of South Vietnam continued for eight more years.

Given my foreboding about that bombing campaign, I have never been able to explain to myself—so I can't explain to anyone else—why I stayed in my Pentagon job after the bombing started. Simple careerism isn't an adequate explanation; I wasn't wedded to that role or to more research from the inside; I'd learned as much as I needed to. That night's work was the worst thing I've ever done.

What came just after was part of that. Most accounts give February 13 as the date when the president finally decided on what became the Rolling Thunder campaign. The campaign didn't really get under way, because of weather, till March. It could conceivably have been rejected during those weeks. Even afterward, the raids were still presented as reprisal raids for days and weeks; it would have been relatively easy to cancel the program, since its ambitious internal objectives had not yet been made public. But during this period I was doing my bit to keep it moving forward. I was given the job of instituting a reporting system in South Vietnam for collecting and distributing data on weekly VC atrocities, to justify our raids. This was precisely one of the action recommendations in the Bundy-McNaughton memo a week earlier: "We should develop and refine a running catalog of Viet Cong offenses which can be published regularly and related clearly to our own reprisals." The "weekly lists of outrages." Now I was selling the policy, though I didn't think of it that way. I thought of what I was doing as a kind of research.

Not all of the VC violence, directed at militia or military posts, was properly called terrorism or atrocities, but a great deal of it was. Buses were mined, civilians kidnapped, railways and bridges sabotaged, hamlet chiefs, sometimes with their families, assassinated or kidnapped. My first report, in a series designated Fishnet for purposes of data collection and distribution, was headed "Viet Cong Acts of Violence 11–15 February." It listed sixty-seven separate incidents, by day of occurrence. At first my weekly reports were internal, classified confidential, but they were eventually issued to the public. They were extremely popular with the bureaucracy in their dealings with the press. Everybody wanted a copy of them because they were psychologically reassuring. At last they seemed to provide a justification for our actions, precisely Bundy's intention. Before long I had more statistics and vivid details of VC atrocities and terrorist actions in my files and even in my head than almost anyone else around, which colored my thinking about the VC to some degree permanently. It was a real and relevant part of the situation, but to think that I provided data used to justify and promote what we came to do from the air, and increasingly on the ground, is not a happy memory. Nor is the fact that it didn't bother me at the time.

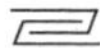

Six days after the first Rolling Thunder raid, two battalions of marines arrived at Da Nang, one by air and one over the beach, to provide base security for the airfield there. Ambassador Taylor and Secretary McNamara, the two top advisers who strongly opposed sending U.S. ground combat forces to Vietnam, were very reluctant to approve this deployment. However, they couldn't ignore urgent warnings, after the Bien Hoa attack, that the Army of the Republic of Vietnam (ARVN) simply couldn't be relied on to provide adequate security for our air operations out of the base. Nevertheless, Taylor and McNamara were determined to keep this from being a first step toward taking over the ground war, or even participating in it.

So was my own boss. I remember the moment—on the morning of March 2, the record shows—when I heard John cry out as he looked at the last-minute orders, "Oh my God! We're '*sending in the marines*'! That means we'll never get out! 'The marines have landed!' It says we're going to take care of this, we're going in to win, on the ground. Can't it be anything but the marines?" He went into a frenzy of coordinating a message that directed that the 173d Airborne Brigade, based in Okinawa, be sent instead of the marines, who were already on the way. He didn't reveal the basis for his apparently capricious impulse to screw up all the contingency plans of the JCS and CINCPAC—which got his directive reversed by the next day—so this brief crisis in civil-military relations has remained unexplained in historical accounts, until now.

As far as the ambassador and the secretary were concerned, it was not just for public relations that the mission orders read "The U.S. Marine Force will not, repeat will not, engage in day to day actions against the Viet Cong." That restriction held good for three weeks. On April 1 the president authorized the marines to expand their mission beyond their announced function of providing base security and defending airfields, to include limited offensive operations. McGeorge Bundy's April 6 action memorandum to the secretaries of state and defense and the director of central intelligence on the president's decisions ended by admonishing them that with respect to the force increase and the change in mission, "The President desires that . . . premature publicity be avoided by all possible precautions. The actions themselves should be taken as rapidly as practicable, but in ways that should minimize any appearance of sudden changes in policy. . . . The President's desire is that these movements and changes should be understood as being gradual and wholly consistent with existing policy." With this, the eight-year U.S. ground combat role in Vietnam began as stealthily as the bombing campaign.

One Saturday morning in 1965 I had my first date with Patricia Marx. It's easy for me to check out the date, April 17, 1965, because it's in all the histories of the period. It was the day of the first big Students for a Democratic Society (SDS) march to protest the Vietnam War. She was going, so I went with her.

It wasn't the way I would have chosen to spend my first Saturday off since I had joined the government. Friday morning, the day before, my boss, McNaughton, told me that McNamara was going to the LBJ ranch in Texas for the weekend and McNaughton wasn't coming in to the office, so I could take the weekend off. I had worked a full day, twelve hours, every Saturday since I had started working for John eight months earlier and at least half a day every Sunday. So this was a big deal. Moreover, because I knew about it a day in advance, I could make a date. Usually I couldn't leave the office in the evening before McNaughton, who didn't leave before McNamara did, and that was almost never before eight o'clock, but you couldn't predict exactly. It might be eight-thirty or nine-thirty. So there was no way to make a date with anyone in advance, and there weren't many people you could call up at nine, or eight, for that matter. I had been a bachelor for more than a year (my former wife and I were in divorce proceedings), but these hours didn't allow a social life.

As soon as I heard I had the next day off, I called up Patricia Marx to go out with me to see the cherry blossoms. I had met her briefly at a party given for her by Dan Jacobs, an old Harvard friend of mine, about a year earlier. She had impressed me at the party as a beautiful girl (we didn't say "young woman" then), very self-assured and intelligent. She had a weekly syndicated program, "Patricia Marx Interviews," on public radio. But I assumed she mostly went out with the kind of men she interviewed on her show, like Ted Sorensen and Carl Sagan. She was out of my league. She asked me what I was doing and asked for suggestions on whom she might interview in Washington, but I didn't expect her to show any interest in interviewing me, and she never did. I was then a Rand analyst doing research in the Pentagon that I couldn't say much about.

Patricia had been away in New York most of the time since, and I hadn't thought much about her, but toward the end of March she had called me out of the blue and invited me to a dinner her sister was giving in Washington for Jonas Salk. It wasn't for a Sunday night, so I explained that I would have to come from the office and couldn't say exactly when I could get there, but she said that was all right. I got there late, and she met me at the door, but she wasn't sitting next to me, and I didn't see much of her.

April 16, when I called her from the Pentagon, was just past the height of the cherry blossoms, which I hadn't had a chance to see yet. I suggested that we take the day to go look at them. She said that she was going to a demonstration the next day at the Washington Monument and a march around the White House to protest the war. I pointed out that I couldn't very well take part in that, since I was helping to run the war being protested. I asked if she couldn't get away from it in the middle of the day for a picnic. She said no, she was going to be doing interviews in the crowd and taping the speeches.

I said, "You can't ask me to go to an antiwar rally on the first day I've had off from the war, the one day I've had off from the Pentagon in eight months!"

She said, "Well, that's where I'll be. You're welcome to come."

My day off was less than twenty-four hours away, and I did want to see her. I made a deal. My weekend off was starting that afternoon at six, another first. If she would go out to dinner with me that night and then come see the blossoms with me on Sunday, I would spend Saturday at her rally. She agreed.

For the first time in almost a year it was light when I left the Pentagon on a Friday. I picked her up at an apartment she was renting in Georgetown, on O Street just across from a park, and we walked past Wisconsin to a college hangout called King George's Tavern. It was crowded with college kids drinking beer, and when I asked if there was a quieter table, I was told we could sit in a disco upstairs called Queen Victoria's that wasn't really open that evening. It was a small dark room with candles, walls painted black, with a spotlight on a huge portrait of Queen Victoria. A table was set for us, and we had the room to ourselves. As we ate and I told her guardedly about what I was doing, I saw that she had marvelous eyes, green and slightly tilted, pointed at the corners like a cougar's. Eyes were always what I mainly noticed. Hers were strange and entrancing. I've never gotten over them.

Since it was a disco, there was a small dance floor. Somehow there was a tape playing slow music, the only kind I could dance to. Maybe I had asked for it. I danced with her very slowly, very close, the only way I knew how to dance. No one came up the stairs. We were alone the whole time, dancing under the eyes of Queen Victoria. By the end of the evening I was very glad I was going to see her the next day, and the day after that.

On Saturday morning I went with her to the Washington Monument. I carried her heavy professional Uher tape recorder for her interviews; she carried a big mike attached to it by a cord. Back in December, just after the election and before the bombing had started, the SDS had called the march for April 17. There had been a controversy whether to focus the rally on Vietnam or on domestic matters, since it looked as though the issue of the war had been settled by the landslide vote against Goldwater's platform of widening it. When the group decided on the war as the issue anyway, it had no reason to expect a large turnout. But when the bombing started in February, the SDS could see that it might draw more than it had expected, maybe five or ten thousand people. In March the marines went into Da Nang, ostensibly to protect the security of the air base. That Saturday morning in mid-April there were twenty-five thousand people at the Washington Monument.

It was a beautiful day, blue skies over the cherry blossoms and the antiwar banners. At one point we set out for the White House, and we walked all the way around it. There were a lot of TV cameras moving with us, and I was carrying Patricia's Uher and hoping that none of my colleagues in the Pentagon was watching this if it was being broadcast live. I didn't know just how I would explain it if I was recognized in any of the pictures.

We walked through Lafayette Park, most people chanting antiwar slogans; I was carrying the tape recorder and not saying anything while Patricia held the microphone up to catch the chanting. We were walking with two friends of Patricia's, Marty and Ruth Garbus, who had just gotten married. They were very much against the war, like the speakers and everyone else there, except, I suppose, for me. Actually I was ambivalent. In fact I could agree with most of what I was hearing. My reservations about being there were not so much about what the speakers were saying—it seemed to me they were on solid ground even if they didn't have inside information—as about possibly having my picture taken. I would have been glad if all this could have had enough influence to get the bombing stopped and put a lid on our involvement. But Patricia and her friends didn't know any of that.

We sat on the grass at the monument and heard speeches by SDS President Paul Potter, political commentator I. F. Stone, and Senator Ernest Gruening and songs by Joan Baez, with the Uher on the grass and Patricia recording it all. At the end I felt I had to go back to the Pentagon to see if anything big was happening, even though I had the weekend off, and Patricia went off to dinner with the Garbuses. Patricia told me the next day that Marty had asked her incredulously how she could be going out with someone from the Pentagon.

Sunday morning I picked her up in my white Triumph Spitfire with the top down, and we drove out to Kenwood, where the streets were lined with cherry trees heavy with blossoms. I have pictures of her in the Triumph, her arm resting on the side of the car, heart-shaped face under reddish hair framed under cherry blossoms, green eyes, strange-shaped eyes, looking at me. We walked and drove through cherry blossoms and pear blossoms and magnolias. Then we went to a park for a picnic.

We were all alone, sitting on the grass, by a big gnarled, thick-trunked tree. I had a wicker picnic basket that just fit behind the seat of the Triumph, and I had brought French cheese and pâté and a baguette and—this impressed Patricia a lot, on a picnic—two big-bellied crystal glasses with fragile stems for our wine. After we had eaten and drunk a bottle of wine I sat with my back against the tree, her head on my lap, and we talked and smelled the grass and the blossoms, and for a long time, she says, I didn't kiss her. That impressed her too, she remembers; it got her impatient and more than ready by the time I finally did bend down. We didn't stay all that long in the park, then, before we got back in the car and drove to her apartment on O Street.

By the next morning, as I drove on the Rock Creek Parkway toward the Pentagon, I realized I was falling in love.

In Washington the cherry blossoms were followed by plums, azaleas, dogwoods. I saw Patricia nearly every day. In the morning I left her town house in Georgetown and got on the Rock Creek Parkway to drive through blossoms and greenery toward the Pentagon. Almost to my surprise, a year after my separation, I found myself fairly committed.

Meanwhile the war was going badly, as it had for the last two years (really, the last twenty years). The theme of Westmoreland's cables was that the Vietcong were trying to cut South Vietnam in two, in attacks across the highlands to the coast. It was never clear just how significant militarily that would be, since the United States controlled the sea along the coast. But it had an ominous ring to it—"South Vietnam has been cut in two!"—and it was taken for granted that it would be psychologically disastrous, like Dien Bien Phu.

What these cables really reflected was Westmoreland's desire to get a lot more U.S. troops into Vietnam right away. I didn't have a strong opinion about this, given what we were already doing. I had strongly opposed the bombing of North Vietnam, privately to McNaughton, just as he did, privately to me. But once the bombing was under way in March, I felt our prestige had been staked. Therefore, I supported more than John did our putting some U.S. ground troops into Vietnam to secure air bases, ports, and major cities rather than risking their being overrun in the current NLF offensive. I don't recall, I'm sorry to say, having a limit in mind on how many troops to put in or how they should be employed.

In the course of April 1965, as the president sent more marine battalions and expanded their mission, there occurred a significant change in my attitude toward the war, and a new phase in my own relation to it (which lasted about a year, until the spring of 1966). As McNaughton had feared, the marines had landed, and the army was clearly on the way. For good or bad, the president now had planted our flag. We were at war. I would have preferred that we avoid this particular test of our competence and will, but it was too late for that. The war didn't look any more winnable to me, in any traditional or ambitious sense, than it had before. But it now seemed to me of major importance, in our worldwide cold war struggle with the Soviet Union, that we not accept what could generally be perceived as a military defeat. At the same, as we pursued some sort of moderate, achievable success, it was crucial that we not ignite a hot war with the Soviets or the Chinese. The escalating bombing of the North threatened that, so I hoped it could be curtailed in favor of an alternative political-military approach.

Up to mid-April, both McNamara and Ambassador Taylor had vigorously opposed the JCS recommendations for the large-scale deployment of ground troops in an offensive role. As late as April 14, Taylor was resisting the introduction of the 173d Airborne, which McNamara had approved the previous day. But McNamara had now changed his position, and on April 20 he met with the ambassador in Honolulu "to bring Taylor on board" (as John McNaughton, who went along, told me). The effort was successful. The next day, McNamara reported to the president that Taylor and he had now joined in a consensus for the deployment of sizable (though not yet unlimited) ground combat units: an increase in U.S. ground troops from 35,000 to more than 80,000, with more possible later. They had also agreed on a "plateau" in the air strikes against the North, avoiding the Hanoi–Haiphong–Phuc Yen areas for "at least six months, perhaps a year or more." McNamara reported a shared view that, as Ambassador Taylor put it, "it is important not to 'kill the hostage' by destroying the NVNese assets inside the 'Hanoi donut.' " The participants in Honolulu all saw a settlement coming "as much or more from VC failure in the South [hence the agreed need for more U.S. ground troops] as from DRV pain in the North."

I was relieved to read that, for the next six months to a year, the principal advisers were turning away from the rapid escalation of the air war up to the border of China. That inclined me not to be critical of what they saw as the alternative, an increase in our ground involvement, which I saw as less immediately dangerous. I was especially glad to hear that they had given up the mining and blockade of Haiphong for now; I had just coordinated a study for McNamara and McGeorge Bundy, done by intelligence and naval specialists, which had concluded that such an effort would pose considerable danger of direct conflict with the Soviet Union and China, without having any promise whatever of decreasing, except very briefly, the trickle of supplies needed in the South from the North and China.

McNaughton kept next to his desk a bookstand with a row of his most frequently referred to and most sensitive directives, cables, estimates, and memoranda compiled into separate binders and three-ring notebooks. It was on rollers, so that when he left late each evening it could be easily moved from his desk into the closet-size, floor-to-ceiling safe that lined the outer wall of his room, along with the library shelves of classified documents stored there. Each morning before he arrived, his military aide unlocked the safe, which had a top secret combination lock, and wheeled his stand of personal reading materials over to his desk, so that he could reach a reference file easily from his chair.

I had access to the materials on this shelf, as I did to anything in the piles of paper on John's desk. But since he wanted instant access to these when he was at his desk, I rarely, if ever, took one of these binders out of his office into my cubbyhole a few steps away. I had copies of most of these same materials in my own safe. But if I needed to refer to something on his personal shelf, I would walk into his office—if he didn't have a red light showing in the row of lights above his door—pull it out, and look at it, standing next to his desk, while he worked away. His power of concentration was such that this didn't bother him, if it was carried out quietly and without my saying anything to him. Even so, I generally did that when he wasn't in the office. Since I often worked later than he did, I had the combination to his closet safe, so I could wheel the stand back into it when I was ready to leave the office. As far as I knew, the only others who had that combination, apart from John, were his military aides.

One day in the late spring his chief military aide abruptly left the office. I never heard an explanation for his apparent firing, but the first sign was that his assistant, the junior military aide, gave me a new combination to McNaughton's office safe. It had been changed that morning, the day of the colonel's departure. Sometime before that, though I hadn't made any connection at the time, John had pointed out to me a large binder at the left-hand end of his personal shelf that he asked me not to look in. The label on it was something to the effect of "Vietnam, McNaughton Eyes Only." I could use anything else on the stand or in his files, but these were *really* for his eyes only. He told me it held papers that he had been directed not to share with anyone else at all, and in this case that included me.

I observed that rule for a long time, perhaps a month or more. But we were moving fast toward escalation that spring. Both McNamara and Ambassador Taylor, who had previously opposed the large-scale deployment of ground troops, had now joined a consensus for the deployment of sizable, though not yet unlimited, ground combat units. The issue that clearly lay ahead was whether to endorse the Joint Chiefs' recommendations for an open-ended commitment of hundreds of thousands of troops to take over the ground war. Neither McNamara nor Taylor had endorsed that, but neither they nor anyone else, so far as I read or heard, was directly opposing it. All I saw were arguments for it from MACV and the JCS.

As I've said, at this point I didn't have strong feelings on this question—not that my opinion on any of these large issues mattered at all to anyone but me. I wasn't in the remotest way involved in the policy-making process, except as a kind of clerk and sounding board for John's latest thoughts. He had his own opinions on these matters—except for the bombing, which we both opposed, he was more consistently opposed to every new form of engagement than I was—and I had little or no influence on them. Also, none of our personal views was reflected at all in what issued from his office. He worked for McNamara, and McNamara was pressing the president toward escalation, more now on the ground rather than in the air.

Meanwhile I had a very good window on the high-level policy process, but it was long past the time when my only interest in all this was as a case study of governmental crisis decision making. I was now involved. It was obvious that decisions of great historical importance were under way. I had no sense that I could influence them—I no longer even had a clear opinion on how they should go—but I had a passion to understand them.

I dealt with that bookstand, every other night, time after time, late in the evening, alone in the suite of offices. For a number of such nights, I didn't think of looking into the binder that was out of bounds. But John was asking me not to look at high-level policy papers, on Vietnam, in 1965, never to try to find out what was really going on among the "principals," what they were considering and proposing, what they were writing to one another, even when, it seemed, I could do so without anyone's knowing.

It was too much for me. There came a night—I can't remember how many weeks it was after John had directed my attention to this forbidden binder—when I did pull it out of the row of files and open it. I don't know the date, but I remember the moment. The office was dark; the light was coming from inside the closet. I was in the process of putting the rolling stand away for the night. I looked inside the thick binder and riffled through the contents. It was like opening the door on Ali Baba's treasure.

There was the distinctive typeface of White House directives and memoranda, a font we rarely saw in the Pentagon. There were memos from McNamara to the president that I had never seen. These too had a distinctive typeface that you could recognize immediately, just as you could recognize a memo originating in McNaughton's office, without having to look at the heading or the signature. There were some cables and reports I'd never seen, though I thought I'd seen everything on Vietnam. There were some transcripts of phone conversations and verbatim memoranda of meetings of the "principals" (the president, top NSC and CIA officers, cabinet secretaries, sometimes some assistant secretaries, sometimes the JCS or its chairman). There were personal memos by George Ball, an undersecretary of state, and McGeorge Bundy, signatures I almost never saw. At a glance I could see that what I held in my hand was precious. Reading just a few paragraphs here and there was, for me, like breathing pure oxygen. My heart was pounding. If it hadn't been so late, I would have sat down and read on immediately. But I was tired and I didn't.

Now that documents of those months, long concealed, have finally come to light, I can guess with high confidence the precise identity of some of the files in that binder and the tenor of much of the rest. It was the file of the official, "personal" *critiques* of the JCS and the McNamara recommendations, the latter shortly to be accepted by the president, and the description and recommendation of alternatives to that policy, that would extricate us from the conflict.

Two memos that were surely included in that file were by McGeorge

Bundy and George Ball, both written shortly before the night that I glanced at and failed to read them. (I first saw them when they were published seventeen years later.) Bundy's, dated June 30, 1965, was a detailed criticism of McNamara's recommendations of June 26 (drafted by McNaughton), more cogent and devastating than anything I read at the time. His summary response to McNamara's proposals: "My first reaction is that this program is rash to the point of folly."

A Ball memo of July 1, attacking the rationale for either the JCS or the McNamara-Johnson strategy and proposing a detailed alternative toward extrication, presented the president with extraordinarily prescient judgments:

> The South Vietnamese are losing the war to the Viet Cong. No one can assure you that we can beat the Viet Cong or even force them to the conference table on our terms no matter how many hundred thousand white foreign (U.S.) troops we deploy.
>
> No one has demonstrated that a white ground force of whatever size can win a guerrilla war—which is at the same time a civil war between Asians—in jungle terrain in the midst of a population that refuses cooperation to the white forces (and the SVN) and thus provides a great intelligence advantage to the other side. . . .
>
> [Such a war will be] almost certainly a protracted war involving an open-ended commitment of U.S. forces, mounting U.S. casualties, no assurance of a satisfactory solution, and a serious danger of escalation at the end of the road. . . .
>
> The decision you face now, therefore, is crucial. Once large numbers of U.S. troops are committed to direct combat they will begin to take heavy casualties in a war they are ill equipped to fight in a noncooperative if not downright hostile countryside.
>
> Once we suffer large casualties we will have started a well-nigh irreversible process. Our involvement will be so great that we cannot—without national humiliation—stop short of achieving our complete objectives. Of the two possibilities I think humiliation would be more likely than the achievement of our objectives—even after we had paid terrible costs.

Advice to the president in this same period from his vice president, Hubert Humphrey; from his chosen successor as Senate majority leader, Mike Mansfield; and above all, from the Senate mentor who had earlier chosen Johnson himself as majority leader, archconservative Senator Richard Russell, all turns out to have had the same tone and thrust as that of George Ball. Thus, Clark Clifford, one of Johnson's closest personal consultants, face-to-face with the president and Robert McNamara at Camp David, July 23, 1965:

> I don't believe we can win in South Vietnam. If we send in 100,000 men, the North Vietnamese will meet us. And when they run out of troops, the Chinese will send in "volunteers." Russia and China don't intend for us to win the war. If we lose 50,000 men there, it will be catastrophic in this country. Five years, billions of dollars, hundreds of thousands of men—this is not for us. . . . I can't see anything but catastrophe for our nation in this area.

Advice to a president, or foresight, doesn't come any better. The urgent counsel by all these men was not merely to avoid further escalation but to cut losses and extricate the United States entirely from the war. These exhortations to withdraw were coming from men who were both charter cold warriors and, in the case of the senators and Clifford, as sensitive to Democratic domestic politics as Johnson himself. The fact that the president enjoyed access to advice like this from men like these was the longest and best-kept secret of the Johnson Vietnam era.

It's clear to me now that throughout that era, supersecrecy—such as I came close to breaching that night—was attached above all to recommendations and analyses urging extrication. In 1967 none of these memos or notes of conversations was available to the working group on the McNamara study; not one, or anything like them, appears in the Pentagon Papers. This was so not just because of the charges of "weak on communism," "appeasement," and "defeatism" that could be expected if they leaked to the Republicans (or the JCS). Of more importance, such documents, if leaked, would reveal that a president strongly inclined to escalate had had a real choice, an alternative both to the JCS "victory" program and the McNamara escalating stalemate, an extrication option that was actually recommended by advisers of great authority. That revelation would burden the president with personal responsibility for all that followed from his decision to reject their alternative. Hence the need to keep this advice unusually secret from Congress, from the public, and even from people like me in his own bureaucracy.

To have read even one of these critiques in June or July of 1965 would have punctured, for me and for a lot of others like me, the spell of apparent unanimity of support by insiders for what seemed a crazy but consensual policy. In retrospect, if I had spent that night in the Pentagon reading through the whole file, it would almost surely have changed my life. For one thing, I would not have gone to Vietnam.

But it was very late, and despite my excitement, I put the binder back on the stand, closed the doors of the closet (which turned off the inside light automatically) and spun the combination lock. I intended to stay late the next night, and as many nights afterward as it took, to learn what it was about the ongoing policy debate that was knowable to the assistant secretary and so far unknown to me.

The next day I stayed in the office until my boss left, as usual, around eight o'clock. Since I expected to be up a long time, I left when he did to get something to eat, at a cafeteria in the Pentagon that stayed open for the many people working at night. I went back to the ISA suite of offices and went into John's large office, which was dark. I switched on a light and dialed the combination to his safe.

It didn't open. I tried it again, then a third time. There was no question of my having forgotten the combination. I had used it a hundred times. Sometime during that day the combination had been changed.

There were only two people that could have been directed against: Harry Harris, John's military aide, and me. We were the only ones besides John who had the combination. It could be that Harris was about to go the way of his predecessor a couple of months earlier, but that seemed very unlikely. It was too much of a coincidence that this had happened the day after I had disobeyed John's order and taken a small bite from the fruit of the forbidden tree of knowledge. Most of the apple was still there, now out of my reach, probably forever. It could still happen that Harris, or his successor as military aide, would come into my office the next morning and tell me the new combination, but I had a strong feeling that wasn't going to happen.

How had McNaughton picked this up so fast? One night, one quick look! He was a professor of criminal law, an expert on evidence. Maybe he had picked up some simple tradecraft somewhere: a loose scrap of paper tucked inside the file that would show displacement; a hair across the top of the binder that would be moved or broken if it was opened. I'd read about such tricks in one novel or another. He must have been taking that precaution—with *me* as his special assistant, with my interest in policy—from the time he'd been collecting in that one binder the items he had been ordered not to show anyone.

Why was his special assistant not to see these documents? It was not because he feared that I wasn't loyal to him, extremely discreet, ready and able to serve a policy even when I disagreed with it. He knew that I was, and I knew he knew it. It had to be there was something about this process or debate that was unusually "sensitive," something that had to be kept extraordinarily secret. That meant that knowledge of it, its existence, had to be held to the absolute minimum number of people.

What McNaughton had to fear was not so much that I would be so indiscreet as to tell the contents of what I might learn to someone who was not supposed to know them as that I would inadvertently give one of the people who had given him these documents some reason to suspect that McNaughton had allowed me to know of their existence or contents—that he had broken his assurance not to show them to anyone. Then he himself would be cut off from access immediately. It would be a replay of the incident with Mike Forrestal, but much worse. He could not risk having a special assistant who couldn't be absolutely relied on to obey such an order, not to try to find out or to understand better our policy in Vietnam, not to look at a certain policy document, even if it was lying there in front of him and there was no one else around. That was the kind of discretion I could not be absolutely trusted to exhibit. I did not have a need to tell—I was a trustworthy member of the secrecy system—but I did have an unusual personal need to understand.

If my guess was right and the changed combination meant that I had just lost access to that safe, what did that mean for my job? I couldn't do a job as special assistant if I couldn't go into his office when he wasn't there during the day.

I didn't anguish too much about this. While I was in no hurry to leave, I felt I had learned pretty much everything I could at that level, and there were lots of other types of work, in the government or back at Rand, that would have been more congenial and satisfying to me. What I was suited for, enjoyed, and was good at was to be a research analyst or a consultant on matters I cared and knew a lot about. So the prospect of losing my job was not traumatic, though it would have been embarrassing to have had to acknowledge to John that I knew why he had shut me out of his safe.

Sure enough, in the morning one of McNaughton's secretaries told me that he wanted to see me as soon as I came in. John was totally friendly. He was as convincingly frank and open with me as he was with reporters. He told me that he had been feeling for some time that I was overqualified for this job. All it really called for was a younger, lower-rank person. (He could have said, a person in line to be a deputy assistant secretary—which I was obviously not equipped to be, temperamentally and in terms of executive skills—but he tactfully refrained from saying that.) I could continue to do some special projects for him from a different office, a private office in the ISA suite.

It was not in the E-ring, with windows to the outside, but it was a good-size room, and I would have it to myself. If it looked all right to me, I could start moving my files into it right that day. (I would keep my rank and salary, and he would find a title for me.) Nothing was said about the binder or the changed combination to the safe. Given that he said strongly that he wanted me to continue working with him, there was no need to bring that up; he just needed to get me out of his private office.

I had never been particularly suited for the special assistant job, or very good at it, except for the intellectual and policy exchanges that I'm sure he enjoyed but found distracting. He asked me what sorts of projects I might be interested in doing. I said I would think about it and discuss it with him later. He couldn't have been more cordial as I left his office. It hadn't been embarrassing at all.

Later that summer I said that there ought to be a working group looking at "long-range" problems in Vietnam, meaning six months ahead. I know that sounds odd to someone outside the bureaucracy, but the fact was that that was a very long time horizon in our kind of work. During the Cuban missile crisis I was a member of two of the working groups under the ExComm (Executive Committee of the NSC). One was the short-range group, which toward the end of the crisis was working on invasion plans two to three days away. The other, the long-range planning group, looked two weeks ahead. I used to say, when I mentioned the name of that group, that two weeks was "long-range" for our normal operations, not only for crises, and that wasn't just a joke.

I pointed out to John in the summer of 1965 that even though Berlin hadn't really been a crisis situation for more than two years, there was still a long-range planning subgroup within the Berlin working group inside ISA in 1961–62. However, there had never been a group that systematically looked at problems as far as six months ahead in Vietnam, though Vietnam could be said to have constituted an ongoing crisis since the summer of 1963. I said we ought to have such an operation, and I would be willing to head it.

John looked up at me from his desk and said, "You don't understand, Dan. I don't want us to *be* in Vietnam six months from now! I want out!"

He slapped the desk hard three times, something he'd never done before. "Out! Out! Out!"

I said, "Ah. Hmm. Yeah . . ."

I remembered an occasion in the late spring of 1965, when we had resumed bombing after a one-week "pause" in May. I was sitting next to John's desk in his office with a pile of papers on my lap, looking for a reference he had asked about for a memo he was writing. He mentioned that he had to leave earlier than usual because he had to pick his wife up for a formal dinner they were going to. He had almost never mentioned his wife or family to me. Close as we were for twelve hours a day, joking together a lot, he never asked anything about my personal life or invited me to his home or to meet his family. He told me early on that he didn't believe in socializing with anyone who worked for him. But since he had just mentioned his wife, something led me to ask him, "What does your wife think about what we're doing?"

Without any pause to reflect, he looked up from the paper he was marking with a pen and said, "She thinks we're out of our minds. She thinks what we're doing is insane." He didn't show any expression. He held the glance for a few seconds, then went back to his editing.

5

"Off the Diving Board": July 1965

In mid-July 1965 Secretary of Defense McNamara was in Saigon to assess General Westmoreland's request from a month earlier to send another 100,000 U.S. troops immediately. We now had about 75,000 men in Vietnam. Westmoreland's request was calculated to bring U.S. troops to a total of at least 175,000 by the end of the year. He wanted forty-four battalions—thirty-four American, nine South Korean, and one Australian. If the latter weren't available, all forty-four would be American, raising the total of U.S. troops in-country to 200,000.

McNamara had a long list of questions about the need for such an increase, its possible impact compared with alternatives, and the requirements for additional troops in 1966 if this request was granted. But on July 17, the day after he arrived in Vietnam, he got a message from Deputy Secretary of Defense Cy Vance that it was the president's "current intention" to approve Westmoreland's full request for thirty-four U.S. battalions. Johnson was also likely to call up reserves and extend tours of duty for certain soldiers, as the JCS had strongly recommended.

On that day or the next, back in Washington, I was told that McNamara would announce and explain the new deployments, as well as wartime measures, including mobilizing reserves, in a major speech that I was to draft for him. I started work right away. The next day, as background for my speechwriting, I started attending meetings that Vance began holding in his office every morning for the next week or so, with representatives of the Joint Chiefs and of the Office of the Assistant Secretary for Personnel. The meetings were to coordinate the mobilization of reserves and extension of service that, it was taken for granted, would be part of the program. These were working meetings, addressing how many reserves would have to be activated, which units, and under exactly what authority. They also dealt with the issues of funding the new programs and what requests for budget supplementals would have to be presented to Congress. I was there just to get a feel for the issues and the dimensions of the program that I would be describing and justifying in the speech.

In his remaining time in Saigon, McNamara focused on what more would be needed in 1966 after the thirty-four/forty-four-battalion level had been reached. In his memo to the president on July 21, the day he returned from Vietnam, the secretary recommended the increase to forty-four battalions. This was in line with what Vance had cabled him on Johnson's current intention, but McNamara had actually favored Westmoreland's request himself since mid-June.

Moreover, McNamara made clear that this was just a first installment of a buildup. He reported that Westmoreland regarded the 175,000 to 200,000 U.S. troops as enough for only through 1965; "it should be understood that more men (perhaps 100,000) may be necessary in early 1966, and that the deployment of additional forces thereafter is possible but will depend on developments."

In his June request Westmoreland had already warned that the forty-four-battalion U.S./third country force was enough only to "re-establish the military balance by the end of December"; "it will not per se cause the enemy to back off." He had signaled that "substantial" additional U.S. forces would be needed in 1966 to "maintain the military initiative." Now he had told McNamara that

> twenty-four more battalions in addition to the forty-four under consideration, plus more combat support and logistical troops[,] would put us in a position to begin the "win phase" of our strategy. That meant about 175,000 American troops at the start, followed by about 100,000. Yet, I warned that VC and North Vietnamese actions well might alter the figures [upward], which they did any number of times.

That pointed to a total of 300,000 troops (with the foreign battalions), 275,000 of them American, by mid-1966; that was what was needed just to stop losing and to be "in a position to begin the 'win phase.'" It would be close to a ceiling only if North Vietnam halted its infiltration, rather than maintained its pace or stepped it up (as happened and as everyone had foreseen as at least a strong possibility). McNamara also recommended that the president authorize the call-up of approximately 235,000 reserves and National Guard and that the regular forces be enlarged by about 375,000 men, by increasing recruitment and the draft and extending tours of duty.

Moreover, much more than numbers were involved. There was to be "an important change in mission for these troops—to search and destroy." The increased forces were to be used aggressively "to take the offensive—to take and hold the initiative . . . keeping the enemy at a disadvantage, maintaining a tempo such as to deny them time to recuperate or regain their balance, and pressing the fight against VC/DRV [Democratic Republic of Vietnam, or North Vietnam] main force units in South Vietnam to run them to ground and destroy them." This might result in a rise in the level of U.S. soldiers killed in action to "the vicinity of 500 a month" by the end of the year.

On his return from Saigon the morning of July 21, McNamara prepared a press release stating that the total immediate increase in U.S. forces with the latest approved add-ons would be about one hundred thousand. This was the figure he presented to the president that morning and briefed to the NSC, along with the other recommendations above. But his press release was not issued. Meanwhile I was writing the speech for him to deliver.

A final draft was completed the next day, July 22. Because this speech was so important, my draft was sent for approval not only to McNamara but to McGeorge Bundy at the White House and to Rusk, who was on a trip outside the country at the time. Each read it personally and approved it over the next day or two, with only Bundy making minor editorial changes. Such high-level approval for this expression of administration thinking and policy makes the draft worthy of close attention. The first substantive paragraph, after a page describing the purpose of McNamara's recent trip to Vietnam with General Earle Wheeler, chairman of the Joint Chiefs, presents the steps to be taken on the basis of their findings: "We shall be adding, in the near future, combat and support troops totaling about 100,000 to those already within South Vietnam. Our forces there will defend their own bases; they will assist in providing security in neighboring areas; and they will be available for more active combat missions when the Vietnamese Government and General Westmoreland agree that such active missions are needed, as they surely will be. To offset these additional deployments and to reconstitute the central reserve, we shall be calling up some reserve units, increasing our draft calls and extending some tours of duty."

The next paragraph began: "At this time, when we are calling for new burdens and sacrifices from the families and young men of this country, it is right that we should spell out once again why it is that these efforts are needed." The following nineteen pages were devoted to that subject. In explaining the challenge of the VC and why so many more U.S. troops were now needed in a combat role, I followed talks I had given at teach-ins on Vietnam at Antioch College, Harvard, and elsewhere and an earlier speech I'd written for McNaughton. But my earlier accounts had been in the context of a very limited deployment of U.S. troops, mainly for the defense of bases. The challenge now was to explain why such a large increase in U.S. forces was both needed and justified.

I knew, and my draft implied but didn't say explicitly, that the increase was open-ended, potentially huge. On the day my draft was completed, the president was meeting with his military advisers, all of whom were telling him that the additional two hundred thousand—at least one hundred thousand by the end of the year and another hundred thousand "in January" 1966—was just a beginning. It was enough to stop losing; many more, over a number of years, would be needed to win, along with greatly expanded air and naval operations against North Vietnam. McNaughton had summarized for me the same message from a meeting with the president that he'd attended the day before. He wasn't at the meeting with the full Joint Chiefs on the twenty-second, but he gave me a secondhand account. The following quotes are from official notes of the latter discussion, declassified much later (emphasis added).

The president asked: "Doesn't it really mean if we follow Westmoreland's request we are in a new war? *Isn't this going off the diving board?*"

McNamara's answer was essentially yes. "This is a major change in policy. We have relied on South Vietnam to carry the brunt. Now we would be responsible for satisfactory military outcome." That change in responsibility was what made this new course of escalation open-ended.

How far might it go? A few minutes later LBJ asked the group: "Are we starting something that in two or three years we simply can't finish?"

He got an answer, from General Wallace Greene, commandant of the Marine Corps; it wasn't the answer a president facing reelection in three years would want to hear, but he couldn't ask for a clearer one. Greene rephrased the question and answered it: "How long will it take? *Five years, plus 500,000 troops.*" He added, "I think the American people will back you."

No one around the table contradicted him or suggested a lower ceiling for troops. Actually, Greene preceded this answer by premising it explicitly on a very expansive and aggressive war policy, including a number of elements, like blockading Cambodia and hitting all targets in the North, that, it soon became apparent, LBJ was determined to resist. Yet without those, it was implicitly clear in Greene's response, his estimate of troops and time required would be higher and longer. Yes, we *are* proposing that we start something we simply can't finish in two or three years. Nor was this the first time Johnson had heard this estimate from the highest military authorities. As early as March 15, 1965, General Harold K. Johnson, chief of staff of the army, had reported to him personally, after a trip to Vietnam at the president's request, that to win the war could take *five hundred thousand U.S. troops and five years.* Now the president was hearing the same estimate from the commandant of the Marine Corps, only with "could" changed to "will."

This wasn't the highest figure for total U.S. troops mentioned that day. Johnson repeatedly stated that he had to take into account the possibility that "if we come in with hundreds of thousands of men," this could cause China to come in with many divisions. McNamara told him that if they brought in thirty-one divisions, which they could clearly sustain, we would require three hundred thousand more men in addition to "what we need to combat the VC."

Five hundred thousand plus three hundred thousand: That was getting close to a million, in the very real contingency of Chinese entry. But even without the Chinese involvement, figures in the neighborhood of a million had been mentioned earlier that summer. According to David Halberstam, the president asked General Wheeler in June what he thought it would take to do the job. Wheeler replied: "It all depends on what your definition of the job is, Mr. President. If you intend to drive the last Vietcong out of Vietnam it will take seven hundred, eight hundred thousand, a million men and about seven years." In a discussion with Clark Clifford and the president later that month, Wheeler used the figures of 750,000 and six or seven years.

For this same ambitious goal of driving all VC out of South Vietnam (our official goal through 1968), Senator Mansfield had come up with comparable estimates in a letter to Johnson: If the administration was planning to stay in Vietnam "until we or our Vietnamese military allies prevail everywhere south of the 17th parallel down to the smallest hamlet," then "we are talking in terms of years or decades, and upwards of a million American soldiers on the ground in South Vietnam, assuming that the Chinese do not become involved with men." Mansfield, who was a specialist on Asia, repeated that figure in another letter to Johnson on July 23, the day my draft was being read by McNamara and Rusk. Two hundred thousand to three hundred thousand men would not be enough to do the job, Mansfield wrote. "In my opinion, a figure of *one million,* if this situation continues to develop as it has, could be considered conservative."

The maximal outcome in Vietnam that Wheeler and Mansfield were describing, eliminating armed VC from South Vietnam, was no hyperbole or straw man, so far as official planning went; it was exactly what my boss John McNaughton invariably used to define U.S. "success," our basic objective, in 1964–65. His memos described anything short of that as a form of "compromise" or "inconclusive outcome."

Although the figure of a million U.S. troops did not come up in the July 22 meeting, no one was taking issue with Greene's estimate of half that, half a million men. Minutes after he said that, the president raised him a hundred thousand: "Do all of you think the Congress and the people will go along with 600,000 people and billions of dollars [being spent] 10,000 miles away?"

Secretary of the Army Stanley Resor responded (reiterating Greene's comment earlier that the American people would back this): "Gallup poll shows people are basically behind our commitment."

President: "But if you make a commitment to jump off a building and you find out how high it is, you may withdraw the commitment."

The president himself had just been told how high the building was. In my speech drafting that same day, I hadn't been told to pass on to the public the full height of the drop. But the figure I was given to use was impressive enough. A force level within months of 175,000—more than doubling our present force, with many more to come soon after that—would give the American public plenty to think about.

On July 26 I learned that McNamara would not be giving my speech after all. The president meant to announce the increases himself at a press conference on July 28, and there would be no call-up of reserves after all. On the twenty-eighth, a number of us on the ISA staff gathered to watch the president's statement on the large TV in McNaughton's office. It was the only time I can remember our doing this. We were standing in a semicircle around the set—with our boss sitting in front of it—waiting for the president to announce we were going to war. I was wondering how much of my draft he would use.

He didn't use any of it. Someone else had written his introductory comments on Vietnam, which recalled our solemn pledges and the lessons of Munich.

> We did not choose to be the guardians at the gate, but there is no one else. Nor would surrender in Vietnam bring peace, because we learned from Hitler at Munich that success only feeds the appetite of aggression. . . . Moreover, we are in Vietnam to fulfill one of the most solemn pledges of the American Nation. . . . We just cannot now dishonor our word. . . .

This scene appears in a biography of Supreme Court Justice Abe Fortas for two reasons. First, just the day before, "troubled by a difficult decision about whether to send more troops to Vietnam, Johnson met for two hours in the Oval Office" with Fortas. "More than just the decision itself, the problem of how to explain and justify it to the press and the American people troubled Johnson." Fortas always helped LBJ on just such matters of rationale. The second reason was that the president also used his opening statement to announce that Fortas would take the seat on the Supreme Court vacated a week earlier by Arthur Goldberg, who was going to the UN as U.S. ambassador.

In fact, the president intended his surprise announcement of this appointment to be the major news item coming out of the conference. That was not exactly what we were expecting. But so it worked out, since after his essentially familiar remarks about why we were involved in Vietnam, his announcement of the next steps to be taken there was low-key and, in light of earlier leaked predictions, reassuring:

> First, we intend to convince the Communists that we cannot be defeated by force of arms or by superior power. They are not easily convinced. In recent months they have greatly increased their fighting forces and their attacks and the number of incidents. I have asked the commanding general, General Westmoreland, what more he needs to meet this mounting aggression. He has told me. We will meet his needs.
>
> I have today ordered to Vietnam the Airmobile Division and certain other forces which will raise our fighting strength from 75,000 to 125,000 almost immediately. Additional forces will be needed later, and they will be sent as requested. This will make it necessary to increase our active fighting forces by raising the monthly draft call from 17,000 over a period of time to 35,000 per month, and for us to step up our campaign for voluntary enlistments.
>
> After this past week of deliberations, I have concluded that it is not essen-

> tial to order Reserve units into service now. If that necessity should later be indicated, I will give the matter most careful consideration and I will give the country due and adequate notice before taking such action, but only after full preparations.

As Johnson said the figure "125,000," we all gasped. I said to McNaughton, "What? What's that? Has he changed the decision?" McNaughton held up his hand to silence me, to wait till we'd heard out the statement.

As for the shift in strategy to search and destroy, the president was asked during the question period: "Does the fact that you are sending additional forces to Vietnam imply any change in the existing policy of relying mainly on the South Vietnamese to carry out offensive operations and using American forces to guard installations and to act as emergency backup?"

He replied, "It does not imply any change in policy whatever. It does not imply change of objective."

Johnson said nothing about the full increase to 175,000 or more by the end of the year. All he mentioned was an increase "from 75,000 to 125,000." He seemed clearly to have told the public that although further requests and increases were likely in the future, it was Westmoreland's judgment that no more than 50,000 additional men were necessary right now. No more than that would be sent until the general made further requests.

As far as any of us watching in the Pentagon knew up to that moment, this was untrue. But it was hard to believe he would just lie about *that.* It must mean that as in the case of the reserve call-up, he had changed his mind. Yet if that were so, some of us in that office, starting with our boss, should have heard that by now, before the broadcast. I repeated my question to McNaughton. "So? Did he decide not to send the hundred thousand?"

McNaughton told me, "You'd better find out."

I left the office at a fast clip and went down to the Joint Chiefs, where I found the general in charge of scheduling the deployments. I asked him if there'd been a last-minute change. He said no, Westmoreland's full request was on the way. I asked if he'd heard the president's press conference. He said he had. But there was no question, as far as the JCS was concerned, that the president's decision stood, to send one hundred thousand more men as fast as they could get over, without awaiting any further request from Westmoreland. I went back and told McNaughton.

A JCS memorandum forwarded two days later, July 30, reported the final Phase I package "approved for deployment" as forty-four maneuver battalions and a total strength of 193,887 U.S. fighting men in South Vietnam after all units had closed. The thirty-four U.S. battalions were in place within ten weeks of the president's press conference, and the third country units a month later, for a total fighting force of forty-four maneuver battalions. U.S. strength in South Vietnam at the end of 1965 was 184,314 men.

The press reported that most members of Congress were relieved by what they had heard at the press conference, especially by the fact that Johnson was not calling up the reserves and that the number of additional troops he had announced was half what had been leaked in advance. But the leaks in fact had been accurate.

The officers who had fought for mobilizing the reserves and a war footing for the nation and who had thought just days earlier they had the president's agreement had a different reaction. Vivid as my own memory of that press conference is, it's poignant for me to read, in Mark Perry's book on the Joint Chiefs of Staff, the reaction of some others who were watching their television sets at that same moment—in particular, General Johnson, the army's chief of staff, who was watching in another suite in the same building. Like the other chiefs, Johnson had regarded it as essential—furthermore, obligatory—to alert the public to the fact that the president's decision meant that a big and prolonged war lay ahead. The JCS saw the mobilization of reserves as indispensable to that message, which in turn was necessary to assure the public support that the military would need to see the effort through. As Chairman of the JCS Wheeler put it later, "We felt that it would be desirable to have a reserve call-up in order to make sure that the people of the U.S. knew that we were in a war and not engaged at some two-penny military adventure. Because we didn't think it was going to prove to be a two-penny military adventure by any manner of means."

The chiefs had already learned to their extreme regret, two days earlier, that this message would not be conveyed to the public and Congress by a reserve call-up. What they had just learned from the press conference was that the president was determined to mislead the public on this point, to conceal that he was taking the country into a major, prolonged war.

Not only did they think this was dangerous, from the point of view of public support and commitment, but some of them had a sense that this was unconstitutional and deeply wrong. One of these was General Bruce Palmer—then Harold Johnson's deputy for operations, later deputy chief of staff under Westmoreland—who has told me passionately of his own feelings at the time, shared by General Johnson. Palmer confirmed Perry's account of Johnson's reaction to the TV performance we all had just watched from another suite in the Pentagon:

> At the Pentagon, [General Harold] Johnson was almost desperate. After the speech, he closed the door of his office and put on his best dress uniform. When he emerged, he ordered his driver to get his car; he was going to talk to the president, he told his staff. On the way into Washington, Johnson reached up and unpinned the stars from his shoulders, holding them lightly in his hands. When the car arrived at the White House gates, he ordered his driver to stop. He stared down at his stars, shook his head, and pinned them back on. Years later he reflected on the incident, regretting his own decision. "I should have gone to see the president," he reportedly told one colleague. "I should have taken off my stars. I should have resigned. It was the worst, the most immoral decision I've ever made."

6

Joining the Foreign Legion

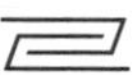

Something happened. I misunderstood (it appears from a later perspective) Patricia's unexpected burst of feeling for a radical German poet she had met at a conference at Princeton. When I learned of it, I lost confidence in her commitment to our being together. I found myself suddenly thinking about going to Vietnam. A week later there appeared a possible opportunity to serve in Vietnam in a hopeful capacity. I volunteered.

I had a regular Saturday-morning meeting of the Interagency Group on Vietnam to attend at the State Department. The meeting was chaired that morning by Bill Bundy, assistant secretary of state. I was representing the civilian part of the Department of Defense. There were representatives from the Joint Chiefs of Staff, the United States Information Agency (USIA), the Agency for International Development (AID), the CIA, the Vietnam desk at State, and all the other agencies that dealt with the war. We all knew one another from past meetings.

We'd been told on the agenda for the meeting that at the end of it General Ed Lansdale would be introduced to the group because President Johnson had just named him to go to Vietnam as head of an interagency group to do political work with the Vietnamese government. It wasn't clear from the notice what the makeup of the group or its mission would be, but I came to the meeting with a notion that I might say something to Lansdale afterward, depending on what I heard him say.

Lansdale was an air force major general, now retired, who had spent most of his government career working for the CIA. He was always described as a "legendary" figure in the field of counterinsurgency. I'd heard that he stressed the political as much as the military struggle against communism, constantly urging the need for political reform and democracy and an appeal to patriotism in confronting rebellion. This had been the key to his success in helping put down the Huk insurgency in the Philippines in the early fifties. He had been sent in 1954 to South Vietnam, where he had developed a close personal relationship with President Diem and had been crucial in persuading the U.S. government to maintain its support for him through an unpromising period in 1955. Unfortunately, as I'd observed in 1961, the lack of promise had been real, more than Lansdale could ever bring himself to acknowledge.

Unlike most American officials who dealt with Diem, Lansdale truly liked him. But I later came to suspect that Lansdale's hopes for what might be achieved with Diem had really been based on the premise that Diem would continue to follow his advice on political matters: to allow a relatively open politics, with a broad cabinet and a "loyal opposition" party. Diem had no actual impulse to do any of that. Lansdale's influence had subsequently declined relative to that of Diem's brother Ngo Dinh Nhu. Lansdale left Vietnam, and Diem and his brother were eventually assassinated in a U.S.-authorized coup, in which, ironically, Lansdale's former CIA team member Lucien Conein was the liaison between the coup plotters and the American ambassador, Henry Cabot Lodge, who strongly favored the coup.

Lansdale had made a good impression on me at a conference earlier that spring, by criticizing U.S. bombing and indiscriminate use of artillery and calling for political competition with the Communists. I had already been attracted by these themes of his in an article he had published in *Foreign Affairs* in October 1964: "The Communists have let loose a revolutionary idea in Viet Nam, and it will not die by being ignored, bombed, or smothered by us."

Now Lodge was going back to Vietnam again as ambassador, replacing General Taylor, and had asked Lansdale to accompany him. Lansdale was gathering some members of his old team, including Conein, who was with him at the State meeting.

After other business had been dealt with, just before Lansdale was about to be brought in, Bill Colby of the CIA said, "I want to make it clear to this group that Lansdale is not going over there for us. Lansdale was with CIA for a long time, but he's retired now and this is not one of our operations. He'll pick people from many of the agencies here, including some CIA people, but this will be an interagency group, and he won't be representing

CIA in heading it." Given the group he was speaking to and the way he said it, I didn't have any doubts that Colby was being candid. (Nor do I now.)

Lansdale made a short presentation on what he hoped to do in Vietnam. He would be taking mostly people who had worked with him before, in the Philippines or Vietnam. At the end of the meeting I stayed as the others were leaving and told him I should like him to consider taking me along as part of his team. I gave him a brief account of my background. He seemed intrigued by the fact that I had worked for McNamara but that I was critical of the bombing and the reliance on military operations. I told him I didn't have any credentials to be on the team he was describing except as an apprentice. I believed in the kind of political work they would be doing; I wanted to learn it from him and the others. I was eager to do that. I was willing to go at reduced rank, I said, even the lowest pay grade, as long as it covered my alimony payments.

Lansdale listened to me seriously and told me he would have to think about it. He asked me for the names of some people he should talk to about me. I told him to talk to McNaughton and some others. We shook hands, and I left to wait for his response. It seemed like a long shot that he would take me on, but I hoped it would work out. Patricia was very upset to hear that I had volunteered to go without discussing it with her, but in my mind I had made a commitment.

In a couple of weeks, Lansdale called me to say that he wanted me to come with him. He invited me to a gathering in Alexandria to meet the other members of the team, all old colleagues of his. For some reason, the bureaucracy determined that I should transfer from the Defense Department to the State Department. I would keep my same pay grade, with the rank of FSR-1 (Foreign Service Reserve-1).

Just at this time, my children arrived from California for a long-scheduled visit with me in Washington. In between briefings on Vietnam, paperwork on my transfer to State, shots, and visas, I took Robert and Mary to see the historical monuments, mostly at night. At the Lincoln Memorial I was struck by the passage from the second inaugural address inscribed on the wall. It seemed very relevant to the spirit and goals of the Lansdale team, as I understood them, in the war toward which I was heading (and which I privately took to be also a civil war):

> With malice toward none, with charity for all, with firmness in the right as God gives us to see the right, let us strive on to finish the work we are in, to bind up the nation's wounds, to care for him who shall have borne the battle

> and for his widow and his orphan, to do all which may achieve and cherish a just and lasting peace among ourselves and with all nations.

Robert, who was nine, had found a box of leaflets inside the memorial that reprinted these words, and as we were leaving, going down the steps in front of Lincoln's statue, I asked him to go back and grab a handful of them for me to take to Vietnam. I told him that I thought the people of South Vietnam might be encouraged to realize that we in America were united, free, and rich, although we had had a civil war ourselves. And Lincoln's thought "With malice toward none, with charity for all" might be important for some of them to hear.

With Lincoln's words in my luggage, I left for Vietnam.

7

Vietnam: The Lansdale Team

In a letter sent home to friends after my first month in Vietnam, I observed:

> *Arriving in Saigon, after a year of reading cables in Washington, it's difficult at first to overcome the sense of foreboding. Which of the newsboys, the cyclo drivers, the soup peddlers might be the enemy? Heavy concrete posts, three feet thick, close the approaches to the Embassy. Barbed-wire barricades stand behind them, and MPs with shotguns checked for passes. Before letting a car proceed they pass a mirror underneath affixed to a long pole to check for bombs. The incongruous presence everywhere of guns gives the French city the look of a frontier town. "All weapons must be cleared before entering," read frequent door signs. But before long one's alertness is dulled, because nothing happens, because people are friendly, and because the streets became increasingly familiar.*
>
> *I have fallen in love with the children of Vietnam. I have never seen any, anywhere in the world, so gay, so friendly and funny. They all remind me of my own. "It's funny," says an American, "you worry about people being anti-American; but when you walk through the villages, the way these kids come on with you . . . it's hard to believe that their parents could hate us, when they're so friendly." Again and again, a crowd of kids sees us approaching, on foot or in a car, and explodes into a chant, almost in unison: "Okay! Okay! Hallo! Hallo! Number one." They rush out with*

hysterical grins—and I remember Robert and Mary running out to climb over me at the end of the day, and my heart turns over.

In the hamlets, they want to hold your wrist, pluck the hair on your arms [they weren't used to seeing hairy arms]; if you try to catch them to lift them up, they dart just out of reach, till a brave one tries it, then they all want to be swung. "Chao em" *(Hello . . . to a child) brings thrilled looks, giggling consultation;* "Chao ba" *to an old lady splinters her old-apple face in a big grin, lips and teeth stained with betel nut. In a village, a province capital, or a hamlet, the children don't leave; they follow you around like a cloud of birds; as you walk, talking to someone, little hands slip into yours from behind; another hand may slap you impudently on the butt. They seem so pleased by your existence, by your own friendliness—it's head-spinning. I love them, and I don't want to leave them.*

The dozen members of General Edward Lansdale's senior liaison team all had worked with him in the past. They were funded by the various agencies from which the different individuals were drawn: CIA, USIA, AID, one from the army staff. Some were now retired, and some were private individuals. My own funding and my paycheck were from the State Department.

There was a great discrepancy between my high rank and pay and my lowly status on the Lansdale team. Not that any of us on the team, even Lansdale and the group as a whole, had very well defined responsibilities. But whereas all the others had had experience in working for Lansdale in something like the situation we were in, I was taken on in effect as an apprentice to Lansdale, to learn how to engage in political warfare as he understood it. Just why he took me on in this capacity, the only one not known to him personally earlier, he never told me. But as I came to realize how bitter Lansdale felt toward his former boss McNamara, who had never appreciated his point of view and had eventually forced him to retire, I suspected that a major reason Lansdale had decided to take me, a young, inexperienced outsider, with him was that he liked the idea of having won the loyalty of a high-ranking aide from the McNamara circle.

Several times I heard him tell about one of his first meetings with McNamara, perhaps his first in early 1961. The secretary of defense wanted a briefing on the situation in South Vietnam, and Lansdale, who was his acting assistant for special operations, had come in to give him an education. He brought with him a large bag of captured VC weapons, VC clothes, and rubber sandals he had gotten from an office in the Pentagon. He dumped them out of the bag onto the secretary's desk, he said, although I suppose he laid them out carefully so as not to scar the desktop. Even so, he said, the weapons hadn't been polished up; some of them still had dried mud on them, and they all looked homemade, as they were, except for an old French rifle. The grenades and mines looked especially homely, along with the blocks of wood with nails protruding, for penetrating boots along jungle trails. McNamara wasn't happy to see these dirty weapons on his clean desk. He said, "What's all this?"

Lansdale said, "Mr. Secretary, I thought you ought to see how the enemies we're fighting in South Vietnam are armed. You see, the troops we're advising and paying all have the latest American equipment. They have American rifles and uniforms; they have a lot of artillery; they even have tanks and airplanes. Their enemies don't have any of those things. They have old French weapons they've captured from our side; they make their own mortars and grenades and mines in the jungle. They wear black pajamas like these, and they make these rubber sandals they wear from truck tires. They're beating the shit out of us."

It didn't get through. McNamara never did grasp, Lansdale thought, what he was trying to tell him, that this was fundamentally a political conflict, in which technology and mass of firepower mattered less than whom and what the two sides thought they were fighting for and how much they cared about it. Anyway, this little theater at the outset didn't make a good impression on the secretary. He told Lansdale to take his props off his desk, and the briefing was over.

In his first days back in Saigon, high Vietnamese officials who met with General Lansdale regarded him warily but with awe because of his reputation as a kingmaker. They assumed he was there to pick out one of them to be the next Diem. For all I knew, they were right. I didn't have much idea what his secret charter from the president was or how he really saw his role. I'd heard what he had to say to us on the team, which wasn't a lot, but I didn't assume he was telling us, especially me, everything he knew or thought. I'd never really dealt with a clandestine operator before. There were several of them from the CIA on our team, and I assumed (correctly) they lived with a higher order of secrecy than even I was used to. But I'd been around secret keepers long enough not to appear too inquisitive about as-yet-unrevealed aspects of our mission. I kept my mouth shut and listened, waiting to learn whatever Ed chose to tell me.

But Lansdale's mystique among the Vietnamese was not something that the CIA station chief and political officer wanted to encourage. It threatened their prestige and influence, and they got the ambassador to agree that Lansdale wouldn't be encroaching on their bureaucratic territory. That didn't leave a lot of room for him, in terms of primary contacts with officials or responsibilities. I was surprised at how quickly my new boss seemed to have been outmaneuvered bureaucratically. I began to suspect what others who had known him longer confirmed for me. It wasn't just that Lansdale didn't like bureaucratic infighting; he wasn't very good at it.

Back in 1954 in Vietnam, and before that in the Philippines, as a lone operator wearing an air force uniform but carrying out strange missions that he defined for himself, his success had reflected the fact that he had the backing of the agency. He didn't have that anymore. He had no institution and in particular no budget behind him. In those earlier days he could bypass channels because he came to have the personal sponsorship of the head of central intelligence, Allen Dulles; his brother, John Foster Dulles, the secretary of state; and even their bosses in the White House, Eisenhower and Nixon (who, unlike most vice presidents, took an active interest in covert operations, particularly in Indochina and later in Cuba). Now, almost before we left Washington, it had become clear that Lyndon Johnson had appointed him only so that he could say he was trying everything, not merely military force. Lansdale had strongly preferred that his appointment not even be announced, so that he and his team could enter Saigon quietly, reestablish contacts, and feel out their possible role without much attention on them. But LBJ made a press conference announcement immediately on appointing him. Within days it seemed clear that this ended the president's interest in the mission; he had amortized that investment very quickly.

Ambassador Lodge awarded Lansdale a special role with respect to pacification, which General Westmoreland wasn't interested in and which was in limbo since the deaths of Diem and Nhu and the collapse of their strategic hamlet program. Lodge had pressed the notion that the GVN should be competing with the VC in propaganda terms and that the Communists should not be allowed to have a monopoly of the word "revolution." We too should be promising revolution, our own brand of revolution, better—more evolutionary, more democratic, more materially promising—than the Communists' sort. The Vietnamese officials who worked with us, nearly all former French collaborators, still used the French term "pacification." Lodge wanted to replace that word, of colonialist lineage, with "Revolutionary Development." This never appealed to "our" Vietnamese at all, partly because the Communists did have a monopoly on the word "revolution," and they meant it. The landowning elites that the Saigon regime represented regarded any sort of revolution as anathema and didn't want to publicize it at all, even as a hollow slogan. The simple solution was to give the ministry and the program a Vietnamese name that meant "Rural Construction," but that was translated for Americans as "Revolutionary Development."

The minister of rural construction, with Lansdale as his adviser, was an ARVN general named Thang, who was very tall and heavily built for a Vietnamese. In his olive green GI uniform, he looked like an American. He even joked that a little boy had come up to him on the road with his hand out, saying, "Hey, OK, you number one, give me cigarettes!" Thang said he gave him a tongue-lashing for begging, and the boy looked up at him in astonishment and said, "You speak Vietnamese?" General Thang did speak English well, so that he was qualified to get on with Americans and earn their confidence. Beyond that he was intelligent and energetic, and Lansdale, one could tell, began to have some hopes for him.

The high point of those hopes came less than a year later, when Thang was minister of the interior and had the responsibility for organizing elections for a Constituent Assembly, a concession to the Buddhist struggle movement of that spring. Since the Assembly was to have no power other than to draft a constitution, the generals were not too concerned about it, and there was a real chance that it would be relatively honest and free (except for ruling out NLF participation or parties proposing negotiations with the NLF). Lansdale was excited at the thought of offering Vietnamese their first experience of free elections. From the time he arrived in Vietnam he had hoped to see a return from military rule to a civilian regime, ideally an elected one with popular support. Many Americans thought that Lansdale was naive, but we believed it wouldn't take peasants long to pick up on the potential advantages of free elections. As a Vietnamese friend, Tran Ngoc Chau, told me, "Give villagers a way to get rid of a corrupt or abusive district chief other than having him killed by the VC, and they'll take to it very quickly."

I sat in for Lansdale at a meeting of the Mission Council, chaired weekly by Ambassador Lodge. Since Deputy Ambassador William Porter began the meeting with comments about Thang, Lansdale, and the upcoming elections, I took careful notes for my boss. Porter said that Thang had made some very interesting remarks to Lansdale the other day. Thang "is concerned with making the elections as well run and honest as possible. I recommend that Lansdale be requested to ask Thang just how we can be most helpful to him. . . . We are going to come in for a good deal of criticism on these elections—the newspapermen are watching very closely and they are quite critical already—and we want to come out as well as we can."

Lodge, who had been Nixon's vice presidential running mate in 1960, responded to this opening with a good deal of reserve, launching into a long commentary that put him on distinctly different ground from Thang, Porter, and Lansdale. He began: "When you talk about honest elections, you can mean two things: (1) lack of intimidation—this we must have; (2) the fear in some quarters—not, I think, in the highest quarters [i.e., LBJ]—that we won't be nice enough to the people who would like to tear the whole thing down." This last referred to concerns expressed in a cable in that morning from State about the prospect that Buddhists, who had been the major force demanding the elections and were suspected of wanting peace even if it meant negotiations with the NLF, would be excluded from the candidate lists. Lodge said this reminded him of a British song during World War II, "Don't Let's Be Beastly to the Germans."

Lodge continued with arresting statements: "You've got a gentleman in the White House right now [LBJ] who has spent most of his life rigging elections. I've spent most of my life rigging elections. I spent nine whole months rigging a Republican Convention to choose Ike as a candidate rather than Bob Taft. If that was bad . . .

"Nixon and I would have taken Chicago in 1960 if there had been an honest count. The Republican machine there was simply lazy; they didn't get out the vote, and they didn't have anyone watching the polls. But I don't blame Democrats for that, I blame the Republicans. There is just a limit to how naive or hypocritical we can afford to be out here." Lodge turned to Porter and said, "Is that responsive to your question?"

Porter, looking slightly taken aback, said, "I just thought General Lansdale should stay close to General Thang on the issue of elections."

Lodge replied, "Well, I want General Lansdale to stay close to Thang on the subject of elections; and I want General Lansdale to stay close to Thang on the subject of pacification, which I think is a great deal more important." Later he declared, "Get it across to the press that they shouldn't apply higher standards here in Vietnam than they do in the U.S." But in a cable responding to State's concerns that same morning, the ambassador had put it slightly differently: "The first steps for us in Saigon and in Washington are to make it clear to the press and to Congress that Vietnam should not be judged by American standards."

My report did not bode well for the support we could expect from Lodge for our current aspirations. But Lansdale saw a way he might yet change the ambassador's attitude. Soon after this Nixon himself passed through Saigon on a visit to the Far East. He stayed with Lodge, and he was scheduled to spend an afternoon with our team. Nixon thought highly of Lansdale, whom he knew from his vice presidential days in the fifties. If we could persuade Nixon of the importance of free elections in this context, Lansdale hoped that would carry weight with the man who had shared the ticket with him in 1960.

The opening moments of that visit often came back to me over the next decade, during three elections in South Vietnam and two in the United States. Nixon came up to the large room on the second floor of Lansdale's villa where the team members were gathered in a semicircle to greet him. I had never seen him before in person, and never did again. He was jet-lagged and rumpled, with the jowls and heavy five o'clock shadow of the Herblock cartoons. But in the long discussion that followed, he was alert and articulate. He went around the circle and shook hands with each of us. Then he joined Lansdale, standing in front of two armchairs side by side, and said, "Well, Ed, what are you up to?"

Getting right to business, Lansdale said, "Mr. Vice President, we want to help General Thang make this the most honest election that's ever been held in Vietnam."

"Oh, sure, honest, yes, honest, that's right"—Nixon was seating himself in an armchair next to Lansdale—*"so long as you win!"* With the last words he did three things in quick succession: winked, drove his elbow hard into Lansdale's arm, and, in a return motion, slapped his own knee. My colleagues turned to stone.

8

Travels with Vann

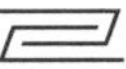

Before I left for Saigon, I had collected names of people to talk to. Within a week or two of arriving I had met them all, and started a process of learning from each of them that never ended for me while I was in Vietnam. They tended to share a greatly common point of view—much in harmony with Lansdale's—that seemed quickly to be confirmed for me in my own travels and observations. These people were far from being cool, detached problem solvers. Unlike other Americans, they mostly spoke Vietnamese, and they had close Vietnamese friends. They had grown to love Vietnam and its people and wanted to believe, and did believe, that our presence there could be helpful to them. I came to think of them as "the good guys." In the letter to friends I quoted earlier, I described certain common characteristics and problems they tended to have in their agencies:

> *Within a week, I know many Americans who are "involved." Fanatics, mavericks, non-team-players, fluent speakers of Vietnamese, old Vietnam hands who have hung on or gotten back, or have found a place on their own that keeps them in Vietnam. They are mostly distrusted or handled with great reserve by their organizations, because they care too much, because they are arrogant and contemptuous of the majority of uninvolved, not very highly motivated Americans who necessarily fill the ranks [and who, not speaking Vietnamese, knew nothing of the peasants and had no close Vietnamese acquaintances]. More and more I*

come to suspect that these men are essential: that we simply cannot succeed without them.

At the top of that list was John Paul Vann. David Halberstam had told me about him just before I left Washington, and I'd already read about him in David's book *The Making of a Quagmire.* Halberstam, like other reporters I talked to, spoke highly of Vann's honesty, candor, and nerve in 1962–63, when he had been a lieutenant colonel in the army, senior adviser to the ARVN Seventh Division in the delta. Now retired from the army, he was back in Vietnam as a civilian adviser in the Agency for International Development. AID, which was nervous about his famous candor, had stuck him for ten months as a province representative in Hau Nghia, a small, dusty, wholly insecure province west of Saigon that functioned mainly as a highway for Vietcong moving out of the adjacent Plain of Reeds.

After a phone call Vann came to visit me at my home in Saigon, in a tall, air-conditioned apartment building filled with American officials. For security, it had a guard at the door and a desk where visitors had to sign in. The first thing Vann said to me was, "You've got to get out of here. You have to be able to talk to all kinds of Vietnamese, and they won't come in here, past that desk." We spoke for several hours about our programs in Vietnam and why they weren't working, what could be done, what our prospects were. I would ask a question, and back would come an answer that was exactly to the point, a stream of relevant statistics—real, contrasted with phony official ones—and blunt opinions that sounded knowing and reliable and held nothing back. After a year of reading cables and estimates, talking to him was like breathing pure oxygen. I asked a lot of questions and took notes as fast as I could. He invited me to visit his province, and I arranged to do it as soon as I could.

On Sunday afternoon, October 17, 1965, Vann picked me up to drive me to Bao Trai, the provincial capital of Hau Nghia. He was driving an International Harvester Scout, a kind of utility vehicle with four-wheel drive that I ended up using a lot in the provinces. The American mission had a fleet of them, and I had one assigned to me. Over the next three days Vann drove me to each of the four districts of Hau Nghia, visiting hamlets, the district towns, subsector adviser posts, and several refugee relocation centers. We traveled on every road in the province that was not physically blocked.

Almost no one from the embassy traveled much outside the environs of Saigon alone in a car; everyone moved by chopper or sometimes in a convoy, especially in a place like Hau Nghia. I'd already heard that Vann drove places that no one else did. But he didn't do this without gathering information on what lay ahead and paying very close attention to signs of local dangers. As a colleague of his told me, "John doesn't take any risks he doesn't have to, short of abandoning the roads to the VC."

He and his assistant Doug Ramsey kept a map up-to-date in their office showing the latest status of the roads, marked in grease pencil as "passable—not hazardous"; as passable but "slightly," "moderately," or "extremely hazardous"; or as physically "impossible." Over long stretches of "moderately hazardous" road, Vann drove fairly fast, fifty to fifty-five miles per hour. On brief stretches of "extremely hazardous" road he drove very fast, fifty-five to seventy miles per hour, with one hand on an AR-15 (an automatic rifle that was the precursor to the M-16) pointed out the window, extra ammunition for it around his shoulder, and grenades in his belt. One of Vann's points was that generally the risks on the roads weren't nearly as high as people thought. But his own behavior in moments like this, while it showed discrimination and a certain amount of prudence, suggested that sometimes the risks were pretty high. (Vann would say, when I asked, that this was just a place to be "extra-careful.")

Over the next six weeks we drove together to every province capital in III Corps (the eleven provinces that included Saigon), some of which had not been visited by road for over a year. I listened, watched for what he told me to look out for, and followed his instructions on when to rest the weapon he had lent me on the open window of the car with my finger on the trigger, when just to hold it in my lap, and when I could put it on the floor and roll up the window against the dust.

Here are my notes on Vann's running comments on road security (details and quotations are from a report I wrote later for General Lansdale):

"The roads were generally clear from mines by ten or eleven in the morning; the VC had either blown them already or road-clearing details of RFs (Regional Force militia, operating in a district) have found them." However, at 3:00 P.M. that day, a mine killed five RF troops and wounded seven on a stretch of road we had driven over at 11:00 A.M. The mines were almost all wire-controlled, and the electric circuits had delays in them, so it was hard for the VC controller, who might be hundreds of yards away, to hit a vehicle moving fast. The VC preferred to wait for a convoy, so that they had the best chance of getting one vehicle. An informant had recently led Vann to a row of twenty 105-mm shells—supplied by the United States, bought or stolen from ARVN—controlled by a single wire. "Someday they may catch on that the way to get a single fast vehicle—like Ramsey or me—is to blow the mine just ahead of us. You're safest in a single, unmarked vehicle, driving fast at irregular times, during the day."

When we drove out from Saigon, Vann deliberately avoided joining the province chief's small convoy. But on the way back on Tuesday he gave in reluctantly to the chief's insistence that we ride with him in his car. Vann told me, "We're so much more likely to get our ass blown off in this convoy than in my Scout."

We came to a little fort behind barbed wire and a moat, an outpost of the Popular Forces (PFs), local, lightly trained and equipped militia operating in squads and platoons to "provide security" at the village level; a village consisted of several smaller hamlets. It had a sandbagged bunker and a concrete watchtower. PFs lying on top of the tower waved at us as we drove up. Vann said, "This PF outpost has an accommodation with the VC." How did he know that? "It hasn't reported any contact with the VC in months; no casualties, hasn't been attacked. Now, you see this wreck next to it?" We stopped, and he showed me a skeleton of a building, only part of the frame and a few sheets of roofing, in the same open field as the PF outpost. It was surrounded by brand-new barbed wire. Every section of the wire had been cut and trampled into the ground. "That's a PF training center we've been trying to build. The VC have torn it down five times. Last time was three nights ago. They ripped the boards and the roofing off, tore up the wire. It's exactly one hundred and seventeen paces to that post over there. But the PFs didn't hear anything, didn't see anything, didn't do anything." Some workers were lying nearby, taking a siesta. "Those are the construction workers. Some of them probably helped tear it down."

Might the PFs have just been nonalert, sleeping? "Hell, no. People tell us what happened. While those VC workers were out there, tearing up the building and making a hell of a racket, they're yelling right into this post: 'We're your brothers. Why are you working for the Americans and the traitors in Saigon?' And most of the time when these little deals are made, the PF leader or hamlet chief has talked face-to-face with the VC commissar."

When we drove by the post two days later, on the return to Saigon, the last sheets of roofing had been removed from the training center and the wire was further tangled.

Again and again we rode over patches where the road had been recently trenched and then filled in, or where a dirt wall had been built across it so that we had to drive around, or where a large mine hole had been filled. In nearly every case, there was a PF outpost fifty to one hundred yards away.

This was no coincidence, Vann explained. The VC were deliberately cutting and mining the road—with much hand labor, pick-and-shovel work that could probably be heard for half a mile—within eyesight and earshot of ARVN soldiers, PF posts, and even district towns with RF detachments. It made a clear-cut lesson for the villagers as to who controlled the area at night and how much protection from the NLF—if they should want any—they could count on from the GVN forces.

One of the ways I learned to read conditions of security along the roads in a few days of driving with Vann was to keep watching the state of barbed wire near the outposts or along the road. Had it been cut, and if so, how recently? Near one post he stopped to show me the ends of some cut wire not far from a post. The wire was old, but the cut parts were shiny, not rusted. "That might have been cut last night or a day or two ago. And look how they did it. They didn't just make a break through the fence. They cut every strand, all along. They were sending a message."

It was also pretty plain that one could find VC local guerrillas, if one wanted to, without going very far. The roads were being cut or mined, or ambushes laid, in exactly the same spots day after day. The American intelligence adviser at the MACV post in Bao Trai told me, "If I wanted to meet some guerrillas, I'd wait in the ditch any night next to the Sui Sau Bridge." He pointed on the map to the bridge, locally known as Sui Cide, on a one-and-one-quarter-mile stretch of road where eighteen people had been killed in the last month.

The day before, we had been driving at about seventy miles per hour on that stretch when we were stopped by some cars mired down where the road had been destroyed by VC two days earlier and badly repaired. We pulled one car loose with a towrope from our Scout, then got stuck ourselves and had to be pulled out with help from the others. Meanwhile five individuals had come up to tell us, in various languages and signs, to "leave quickly" because there were VC on both sides of the road. It was forty-five minutes before we could leave. It was the only time in two years I ever saw John Vann edgy.

Three months later, near that bridge, his assistant, Doug Ramsey, was ambushed and captured; if Doug had been driving himself, Vann felt sure, he would have driven through the ambush, but his Vietnamese driver slowed and then stopped at gunpoint. The driver was released, but Ramsey was a prisoner of the VC for more than seven years. (He spent much of that time in bamboo cages, three to four feet on a side—Ramsey was more than six feet tall—exposed to rain and sun, in jungles on both sides of the Cambodian border.)

We drove to Tan Hoa hamlet, which was now the seat of the village of Hiep Hoa, because Hiep Hoa hamlet had become too insecure. It was shown on the sector map of pacification as "black"—"undergoing securing"—because it had cadre in it in the daytime. But all these, including the village chief, moved to Dong Hoa every night, to the security of the sugar mill. We drove slowly along a canal to a dead end, then turned back. Vann said, "These people are pretty surprised to see us. They haven't seen anyone connected with the GVN poke down this street for a hell of a long time." They did look surprised. But when I waved, they smiled and waved back. At one point we passed a gathering of a dozen black-clad boys in their early twenties, draft age, but not in "our" army. Vann said, "There's little doubt you're looking at a VC squad," so I took a picture. They straightened up and smiled. Vann muttered, "The fact is, they look too clean-cut to be GVN."

Back at the marketplace, two blocks on, I got out to take some more pictures till Vann honked the horn. He said, "Let's move out of here; they're starting to move away from the car." There was now a noticeable empty space around the Scout. "We're safe for a little while because they didn't expect to see us and it takes them a few minutes to react. But eventually one of the people back there starts thinking about collecting the twenty-thousand-piaster reward the VC gives out for a dead American."

One road we didn't go down at all. At an intersection Vann pointed right and said, "If you want to meet VC with one hundred percent certainty, day or night, just go into that tree line, four hundred yards off. Some Polish journalists wanted to meet VC. They went into that tree line and met VC all right, who burned their jeep and kept them for three days. They got a good story."

I gradually got the picture that everywhere we went in both the hamlets and the countryside there were little signposts visible to all who knew the neighborhood that said "To find VC, turn left—about ten feet," "This bridge closed for mining, tonight and every night," "GVN not welcome here," or "GVN traffic on this road only between 7:00 A.M. and 6:00 P.M., at all other hours VC traffic only" (like streets in Washington, D.C., that were one way in opposite directions during the morning and evening rush hours).

Why this should be so, in a province so close to Saigon and with so many South Vietnamese units operating within it, was something I was only beginning to learn in the fall of 1965. But the answers I heard, from the contacts I was fortunate enough to make, were repeated over and over, across Vietnam, till I left in mid-1967. One of the earliest of these lessons looked, on the surface, like a purely military phenomenon (though like everything else in the conflict, I learned later, it had political roots). It was the paradox that in a province where the VC were so pervasive, it seemed strikingly hard for most GVN units to find them or make contact.

The first explanation for this paradox, the American advisers in Hau Nghia told me (and I later discovered repeatedly for myself), was that the reports of operations were false. The local militia did not move, ever, from their outposts at night. The same applied to the regional forces and the Twenty-fifth Division in Hau Nghia (as throughout Vietnam, I soon learned); most of the small-unit actions reported by ARVN and virtually all the alleged night actions were simply fictitious. The American advisers knew this and for various reasons did not report it upward. Second, when units, both small units and large-scale operations, did venture out, it was to go places where the VC were expected not to be; that was the end to which intelligence information was put, and the intelligence was good enough to assure it. Third, large-scale operations could be expected to be compromised in advance, the American advisers informed me, by VC penetrations of headquarters and supporting units and by nonexistent communications security by ARVN (i.e., they revealed their plans and movements over radio to VC listeners). Finally, the advisers to the Forty-ninth Regiment told me, "Nearly every regimental plan is changed by Twenty-fifth Division headquarters, and virtually every change—changing the axis of approach, removing the blocking force, leaving an open flank—is such as to reduce the chance of contact or to allow the VC an avenue of escape." The advisers told me that they urged "daily" that each of these patterns be changed, with what they describe as "zero" success.

These problems were not of recent origin. In 1962–63 President Diem feared that ARVN casualties would jeopardize his fragile base of support. Military command at all levels was based scarcely at all on competence but on corruption (promotion and placement based on bribes and regular kickbacks, financed in turn by various forms of extortion in the provinces and embezzlement of funds and resources furnished by the United States) and on loyalty to the regime in Saigon. Clearly none of this had changed under the military junta following Diem's assassination. Nor did it change when Harkins was replaced by Westmoreland, who put his trust in the American units that flooded in beginning in 1965 and who made almost no effort to reform ARVN promotion policy or operations.

Ultimately, of course, it was a matter of a political system, a social structure, that the U.S. government, for a variety of its own reasons, relied on in pursuit of the war and that it didn't want to destabilize.

Soon after my trip to Hau Nghia, John Vann told me about a Vietnamese officer who had had a major influence on his own thinking, Lieutenant Colonel Tran Ngoc Chau. Vann considered him the most knowledgeable Vietnamese on the subject of defeating Communist insurgency he had ever met, in part because of his firsthand experience with it. Unlike most of the military leaders whom we supported in Vietnam and who had fought on the side of the French, Chau had served first as a battalion commander and then as a regimental political officer in the Vietminh army against the French until 1950. He had joined the forces under Emperor Bao Dai at a time when he believed that the French were granting independence to Vietnam. Later he had been one of the first officers in the military academy in Vietnam and had come south in 1954 to serve in the army under Diem. Most of his family, including his brothers, had remained in the North. One of them was a North Vietnamese intelligence officer of the same rank.

What made him particularly interesting was that he had been the secretary of the National Security Council under Diem and then a province chief in Kien Hoa Province at the time of the Buddhist uprising in 1963. Chau was a devout Buddhist. He had been raised in his teens to be a monk together with Tri Quang, a leader of the Buddhist struggle movement in 1963. In Kien Hoa he had introduced a number of ideas reflecting his experience in the Vietminh, ways of competing with the Vietcong and shifting political support to the government. For instance, he set up what he called census grievance teams, which went from hamlet to hamlet, finding out about the local grievances of the people and the projects they wanted to support.

Vann took me out to meet Chau in Kien Hoa. In his strongly accented but fairly fluent English Chau made a strong impression on me, particularly because of his obvious nationalism as well as the respect he showed for many aspects of the Communist movement. In particular he cited the Communists' closeness to the rural population and concern for its welfare. For these qualities he felt the government had much to learn from the Communists. At the same time, his religious Buddhist commitment had led him away from the Communists, and he continued to think it was possible for the government of South Vietnam—with U.S. foreign aid—to offer his people a better alternative, freer and more respectful of Vietnamese religion and traditional culture.

Chau was a brave soldier as well as an intellectual. He had been decorated by both the Vietminh and Diem for bravery in combat. He was clearly committed to seeing the GVN improve in areas that unmistakably needed improvement, and despite his obvious respect for the courage, discipline, and patriotism of the Communists, he still believed that it was necessary to fight against them and if possible to prevent their dominating Vietnam. Like others who knew him, I found his commitment reassuring, insofar as it confirmed my belief at the time that we were present in Vietnam not simply to promote our own interests but to further the interests of the Vietnamese. Here was obviously a very thoughtful, brave, and dedicated Vietnamese who was happy to see American involvement.

As I had already learned, one of the things that prevented much progress in the war was the extremely poor quality of leadership in the South Vietnamese army. Most of the officers had either bought their positions or acquired them through nepotism. The problem wasn't the lack of good officer material but the refusal to promote the good leaders who actually did exist. The officers had to have rich and educated backgrounds; they were part of the landowning class, meaning that they had little empathy or experience with their own troops. The French had favored Catholics, a tradition that Diem and his successors had continued. Chau was one of only two officers of his rank or higher in the army who had had serious experience in the Vietminh. That background, as well as his Buddhism, made it extremely unlikely that he would rise to the rank of general, despite his extreme ability.

John Vann and Doug Ramsey believed that the major "problem" in the countryside was that "the present leaders, bureaucrats, and province and district officials do not come from, think like, know much about, or respond to the wishes of the rural population." In all these respects, they contrasted sharply with NLF officials. That was another part of the "problem."

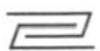

At the end of October Vann was promoted to civilian affairs adviser to the commanding general of U.S. forces in all of III Corps. He decided to "find out who owned what" in the area the way he was used to doing in Hau Nghia. He laid a schedule of weekend trips for driving to each provincial capital, and he invited me to go along with him. Every weekend my education continued. There were always new things to learn in each province, each district, though it was also true that it was already for me a matter of seeing and hearing many of the same things over and over again. I never stopped learning from John. We had a lot of time to talk on these trips. Mostly he answered my questions about Vietnam, but we also told each other a lot about our lives.

Vann's unique proclivity for driving had several bases. He firmly believed better-informed American influence on the South Vietnamese government could make a great difference in the situation. But knowing what needed to be done required an understanding of circumstances at the village and hamlet level no one could acquire sitting in a provincial capital or district town or peering down from helicopters. Not only did you miss a lot that way, flying high enough to avoid snipers, but more important, you visited many parts of the area only rarely. There just weren't that many helicopter flights.

Most of the officials and some of their advisers relied on written reports coming up through official channels. That meant living in ignorance, usually with gross optimism, compared with what could be learned from confidential talks face-to-face with lowest-level representatives or villagers on the spot. Being willing to go by car made it possible to inspect much more frequently and to go places that otherwise would not have been visited at all. Moreover, you could see things on the road that you could encounter no other way.

I heard Vann frequently give advice to the other Americans in the pacification program about the importance of finding out for themselves the conditions and problems in their areas. He urged them not to wait for convoys or helicopters but to drive out to the hamlets and see what was happening. It was physically risky. Neither of us thought you should give advice to other people on risks you thought they ought to take unless you had the feel of the risks yourself; we did what he (and later I) preached.

For me there was another tacit reason to drive the roads. In the first months especially, as someone relatively young, a civilian, and a person inexperienced in Vietnam, I would have been taken a good deal less seriously if I had arrived at a distant outpost by helicopter than when I got out of a dusty vehicle, accompanying John Vann. His presence, with his military background and reputation in Vietnam, protected me against any impression that I was callow or simply foolhardy to arrive by car. The majors and colonels we were visiting took it for granted that Vann must know what he was doing; he made his point that the visits were important and that the risks were worth taking. They all were clearly impressed.

The provinces we went to in the first weeks were those closest to Saigon.

John put off visiting two of the more distant provinces till the end of the list. He was a little less sure of what we would find on our trip to the next to last, Ham Tan, the capital of Binh Tuy Province, north of Saigon, on the coast. We couldn't go there directly. There were hardly any direct roads, and a VC base area lay between it and Saigon. We would have to make a long dogleg, for a total of about 140 miles, largely through forest and jungle. We would drive first to Xuan Loc, 60 miles northeast of Saigon, talk to the advisers there and have lunch, then drive about 80 miles east to Ham Tan. We would spend the night there and come back the same way Sunday. Vann had researched the route as well as he could, and he thought it could be done. But it was hard to tell because no one had driven from Saigon to Ham Tan for nearly a year.

The night before we left I mentioned the trip to one of the political field reporters under Phil Habib at the embassy, a friend of mine whom I'll call Victor. He was a young Foreign Service officer who spoke Vietnamese and was very bright and knowledgeable about Vietnam. Habib had been keeping him in Saigon doing political analysis, and it had been a long time since he'd traveled anywhere in Vietnam except by helicopter or plane. When he heard we were driving, he was eager to go with us, to get a sense of security conditions on the ground. Vann was happy to be able to give a tour to someone from the political section.

We had to leave early on Saturday morning so as to get to Ham Tan before dark. We picked up Victor and made our way through crowded streets in Saigon and the outlying neighborhoods. On the large highway to Bien Hoa there was heavy truck traffic to and from the big American base and airstrip there. As we turned to the northeast after passing Bien Hoa, the traffic got very much thinner. Before long our Scout was the only vehicle in sight. We were passing through rice fields, with the usual peasant women in conical straw hats bending over, planting shoots, and little boys riding on the backs of water buffalo. Some of them waved at us. Victor was excited to be outside Saigon again, on the road. He told us Habib was very conservative about what he would let his political officers do, in the way of taking risks. It limited Victor in doing the kind of job he wanted to do, as a political reporter in the provinces.

Victor was sitting on a little bench seat just behind Vann, who was driving. When we picked him up, John had offered him a weapon, but he declined. Nearly all civilians stationed outside Saigon, even in towns, had weapons in their offices or vehicles and kept them nearby when they were in the countryside, though they didn't carry them inside the towns or villages where they were based. But Victor had had no military training or experience with weapons.

We were now in open countryside, rather desolate. No other vehicles passed us in either direction. John gave his usual running commentary, pointing out especially for Victor what he had earlier taught me to notice: fence stakes with strands of cut barbed wire curling from them, nearby burned-out PF outposts, dirt strips across the asphalt where the VC had blown up the road and it had been filled in. At first Victor asked John a lot of questions and wrote notes. Then he was quiet for a stretch. Finally he said, "John, how would you describe the security along this road?"

John said, "Fair. Kind of average."

Victor was silent again. Then he said quietly, "John, the truth is that I'm not supposed to be doing this. Phil would have a fit if he knew I was out here with you. Political officers are not supposed to be out on the roads, in case we get captured. I think I'd better go back." Vann told him we didn't have time to drive him back, or we wouldn't be able to make Ham Tan during daylight. But there was an ARVN base up ahead where we could drop him off. On Saturday it was pretty sure to have a convoy going back to Saigon that could take him. An ARVN lieutenant at the base confirmed this, and Victor got out of the Scout and wished us luck on our trip. He said he wished he could go with us, he had really looked forward to it, and it had already been as interesting as he'd hoped, but he should have thought it through better before we had set out.

An hour later, after driving through large rubber plantations, we got to Xuan Loc. We got a big reaction from the American advisers as we drove into the provincial advisory compound. They hadn't seen a lone vehicle come in from Saigon for nearly a year. But they were expecting us because Victor had arrived there ahead of us and told them we were on the way. A helicopter had stopped at the ARVN base on its way to Xuan Loc, and Victor had decided to hitch a ride to come hear our briefing from the advisers there.

During lunch, after the briefing, we got a lot of questions about conditions along the road. The advisers were interested in our comparisons with the other nine provinces we'd visited in the last few weeks. There was a lot of head shaking and whistling when we said we were driving on to Ham Tan. They had never even seen much of that road from the air, flying over the double-canopy forest in helicopters. They gave us some extra grenades and ammunition and gathered around the Scout to see us off. Just as we were about to leave, Victor rapped on the door and opened it. He said, "To hell with it. I'm going with you." John said sure, and he climbed in.

We continued the conversation from lunch as we left for Ham Tan. Victor was a good companion, very smart and funny. He was sitting behind John again; I was in the passenger seat to the right. Very soon after we left Xuan Loc we entered a dense rain forest. It got dark almost immediately. It was a sunny day, but the sky had disappeared. I had heard about double- and triple-canopy forests before, but I'd never been in one. It meant there were several consecutive layers of foliage, corresponding to different types of trees of different heights, each layer interweaving like a separate ceiling. I saw what the advisers in Xuan Loc had meant when they said they'd never seen this road from above. The word "jungle" was used rather loosely in Vietnam for what often seemed better called forest or swamp, but this was a storybook jungle.

The road through it was narrow and winding, so we couldn't see very far ahead in the gloom. It was as if a tunnel had been cut through one large bush. I had never seen anything like this. During years of war this road hadn't been kept up, and the jungle had pressed in on it so that in most places it was just wide enough for a single vehicle. I wondered what we would do if we met one coming the other way, let alone if there was an ambush. I had the feeling in some patches that if I stuck my arm out the window into the tangle of foliage just outside, I wouldn't get it back. Not only were we closed in by green walls on either side, but there was usually one facing us about fifty yards ahead at a bend in the road. I was thinking that it would only take one person behind the foliage at one of those curves with an automatic weapon to stop a battalion on this one-way track. Choppers couldn't find him from above, and it would take a long time for infantry to outflank him, if they could get off the road at all.

Vines and branches were scraping and thumping against the sides of the Scout, and it was tempting to close the windows to keep them from probing inside. But about ten minutes into this, Vann, who couldn't drive very fast because of the bends in the road, had rested his M-16 on the windowsill with his left hand on the grip and the trigger while he drove with his right. When he did that, I did the same with my carbine on the right side. I kept a good grip on it to keep a stray branch from grabbing it backward as we drove. I opened one of the cardboard tubes of grenades we were carrying, two to a canister, and gave one to John, who laid it on the seat next to him. I put one in my lap.

This was a drill we'd gone through several times in the past month, usually when John was driving a good deal faster. John was talking to me matter-of-factly about something or other as we drove, hoping, I guessed, that these precautions would not make our passenger nervous. Victor wasn't saying anything. But after twenty minutes had gone by, Victor leaned forward and tapped Vann on the arm. He said, "John, what's the security like on this road?"

John said, "Bad."

Victor didn't hesitate long. He said, "John, I think I have to go back." John didn't say anything. It was obvious that we couldn't turn the Scout around just where we were. But after another hundred yards the road opened up a little, and with some backing and filling he was able to reverse direction. Going back to Xuan Loc the way we had just come, he put his weapon down and drove with both hands on the wheel, speeding up and taking the turns faster to compensate for the time we were losing. Victor didn't say anything as he got out back at the base. We waved good-bye, and Vann spun the Scout around and raced back. The sun was still fairly high, till we lost sight of it when we reentered the Enchanted Forest.

John slowed somewhat but kept going faster than the first time, till he put the M-16 on the sill again and went back to driving with one hand, at about the place where we had turned around. He'd said hardly anything since that time, back and forth, but all of a sudden at this point he shook his head and laughed. He said, "I really didn't think he'd do that a second time. I didn't think he had the guts."

I said, "Jesus, John, why did you have to say the security was bad?"

For a second he took both hands off the wheel, held them out, palms open, pointing to the vegetation scraping the sides of the car, and said, "What could I say? Look at it!"

It wasn't dark yet when we got to Ham Tan, but it was getting late. We went inside the advisory compound and introduced ourselves. An officer asked us when we'd arrived; he hadn't heard a chopper come in. We said we hadn't come by chopper. At that point he looked outside and saw our dirty, unfamiliar vehicle. He did a double take, and asked, "Did you guys drive here?" John said yes, from Saigon that morning, through Xuan Loc. Other advisers gathered around, looking at us as though we'd traveled through time. In a way we had. They said no one had arrived in a single vehicle for almost a year. Someone asked, "Is that road open?"

John said, "It was, today."

An infantry adviser in jungle fatigues asked, "Were there any good ambush locations along the route?"

John said, "Two. Saigon to Xuan Loc and Xuan Loc to Ham Tan."

After we got back to Saigon, we had one last trip. Vung Tau, the province on the seacoast nearest to Saigon, was generally believed by Americans to be extremely dangerous for them to try to get to by road. Vietnamese and French residents drove there all the time, on a relatively good highway, though they sometimes were "taxed" at Vietcong roadblocks. But the trip was thought to be sure death or capture for Americans.

John said he suspected, from his own information and for the psychological reason mentioned earlier, that this was overdrawn. Vung Tau was the one place outside Saigon that everyone wanted to go to on weekends because it had a beautiful beach. But helicopter space was limited. So Americans felt conflicted between their strong temptation to drive there or take a bus, like the Vietnamese or the French, and their disinclination, which they didn't like to acknowledge to themselves, to take any risk at all.

John thought that the universal belief among Americans that it was *impossibly* dangerous to try to drive there reflected their way of resolving this conflict without feeling cowardly. He didn't want to concede that the VC owned the approaches to one of the provinces in his area. By driving there, he hoped he could shame the province chief into more aggressive security operations, which would take away any basis for the reputation and make the province safer. But perhaps his strongest reason for going, I had a suspicion, was his personal desire to have visited every one of his eleven provinces by road. In any case, he had left this one till last.

As usual, John drove. He had brought some sandwiches to eat on the way. On this trip there was a good deal of traffic going our way. But after an hour we hit a line of stopped cars, trucks, and buses that stretched as far ahead as we could see. Vann decided to see what the problem was. There was just enough room between the highway and a ditch to the right for him to pull off the road and drive toward the head of the line of stalled cars. It turned out to be a couple of miles long. It was a hot day, and many of the drivers and passengers, including whole busloads of people, were standing on the road outside their vehicles. They'd been stopped for more than two hours. Little boys had come from somewhere to sell pop and sticks of pineapple. Some drivers told us there was a military blockade ahead.

When we finally got to the head of the line, an ARVN soldier stopped us. An ARVN lieutenant came over from a platoon of men lying on the grass and told us, in French, we couldn't go any farther. A thousand VC—*"mille VC"*—were crossing the road ahead. It was a striking announcement. That was a lot of VC. I'd never heard of that many in one operation. I thought, No wonder they say this road isn't safe. The lieutenant didn't know when the road would be clear. He was polite, but he was very firm that we would have to wait; we couldn't go on. That seemed obvious, from what he said. I translated for John, who didn't speak French.

John looked over at the platoon. Most of the men were napping; some were eating or smoking. He squinted up at an observation plane that was making lazy circles over the road about a mile ahead. Then he said, "Bullshit." He began to move the car back onto the highway, ahead of the other cars.

The lieutenant looked astonished, then furious. He ran in front of the car, with his hands out, palms forward, gesturing us to stop. He was saying, in French, "No! You cannot! It's absolutely forbidden." John waved him away and drove slowly forward.

The lieutenant did get to the side, but he pulled his revolver from his holster and started to level it at us. He was waving his other hand wildly and speaking French much faster than I could understand, though I got its tone. He shouted in Vietnamese to some of his troops, who began to get up. I expected John to stop, but he gave the lieutenant a hard look—which kept the barrel of his revolver pointed upward—and then turned his head forward and kept moving. As we picked up speed, I glanced back. The lieutenant looked both angry and genuinely alarmed at what we were doing, and that worried me.

John pushed the car as fast as it could go. We had weapons in the car, but he didn't bring his up to the window. The road was straight, and the countryside was level on either side. There was no vegetation, no cover. It was the opposite of the forest on the way to Ham Tan. But there was no one to be seen, no sign of VC, no ARVN either, no other vehicles. Mile after mile we had the road to ourselves.

After ten or twelve minutes I asked Vann why he'd been so sure the lieutenant was wrong. He said it didn't smell right. What gave him the clue? "Did you see those ARVN troops lying on the ground? They wouldn't have been lounging around if they really thought there were VC a mile up the road. They probably wouldn't have been there at all." He hadn't heard any artillery. He pointed to the little plane overhead, which had moved ahead of us along the road. "See how low it's flying and how slowly. It's not taking any fire from the ground. There aren't any VC along here or up ahead." Nevertheless, he kept driving fast through the empty fields. In a few minutes we came to another line of cars facing us on the other side of the road. It looked as long as the one we'd left behind in the other direction. There were ARVN soldiers at its head. They looked very startled to see us. As we drove past the vehicles, the drivers lying by the road all scrambled to get back in their cars and trucks and start their engines. John said, "They see us, they think the road's been opened. Well, I guess it has." We couldn't tell if the ARVN troops were letting them move, though. Our lane was empty, and we could make good time, driving by several miles of vehicles stopped bumper to bumper in the other lane.

When they were behind us, I asked John, "What do you think that was all about? That lieutenant really seemed worried about our going ahead."

John said, "He was worried that if we went through, he wouldn't have any excuse for lying around. He'd have to move out with his troops and find out if there really was anything in there."

"But why did they have the traffic stopped then? What was going on?"

John said, "Oh, there may have been a report of some VC, who knows, maybe a squad, crossing the road hours earlier."

"He said a thousand."

"Fat chance."

As usual, it turned out John knew what he was doing, though there had been some minutes after we passed the first roadblock when I wasn't so sure. We got to Vung Tau in good time and had discussions and dinner with the advisory group and the AID representatives there. The next morning John visited the province chief and congratulated him on how much safer his province was than last year, when we would never thought of driving there, as we had just done. The province chief listened to John's suggestions for making even more progress before waving us off as we drove back to Saigon.

9

Losing Hope

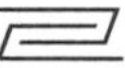

The experience I gained driving the roads, and the authority it gave me, paid off in an investigation I was asked to undertake in the spring of 1966. President Johnson had put in a request to the embassy for regular reporting on what he called officially the other war, the less military, more political side of the conflict over the allegiance of the peasants in the countryside, as distinct from the war of major combat units fighting North Vietnamese forces or VC main force units. This was to begin with a report to him on the "expected progress" to be made in Vietnam in pacification in 1966. On the basis of my earlier reporting, Deputy Ambassador William Porter asked for me to be assigned from Lansdale's team to gather data from the III Corps area surrounding Saigon for this study, independently of MACV, which would provide its own evaluations.

I drove again to every province in III Corps, this time mainly by myself, observing conditions along the roads and talking to every American adviser. I concentrated on them rather than the Vietnamese in this case because my report had to be done quickly. I brought back findings that I incorporated in a detailed March 31 draft on "progress" to be expected, which began: "In most of III Corps national priority area, odds are against achieving even modest goals for hamlet pacification in 1966. . . ."

I distributed, described, and defended this draft in a meeting of the Mission Council, the heads or their deputies of all the agencies under the ambassador, which was chaired by Deputy Ambassador Porter, in the presence of the major military representatives, including the general who was in charge of pacification for MACV. There was a representative from the CIA station and reps from all the other agencies in the mission. Robert Komer from the NSC staff in the White House, who later came to Vietnam to head the pacification effort under General Westmoreland, was at this meeting investigating progress for President Johnson. I remember the date of this meeting because it was my birthday, April 7, 1966.

I started by relating my remarks to the briefing, with charts, just preceding mine, by General Harris W. Hollis, who worked on pacification. He had given the military account of what progress was to be achieved in III Corps. He had done so by means of a map in which parts of III Corps colored red represented Vietcong control, contested areas were cross-hatched, and areas controlled by the GVN were in blue. His map was still displayed on a stand next to me as I spoke. In principle, these different areas were determined by an elaborate set of criteria. But in practical terms, I remarked, "GVN control" meant an area in which a village or district official, paid by the government of Vietnam or ultimately out of our own budget, could sleep overnight without bodyguards in a hamlet. That was a good test of an area controlled by the government. There were very few of those in III Corps, even in the blue areas. Furthermore, I had learned by dealing with officials that a contested area was one in which an official would not sleep overnight but could go into during the day with a squad or a platoon of guards to protect him. A red area, controlled by the VC, was a place where he wouldn't go without a company or two of troops, if at all.

Another way to look at this was that in a contested area, the GVN had pretty good access to the people on many of the days but essentially none of the nights. The VC had good access on some of the days, when there were no GVN troops there, and virtually all the nights. In effect, the GVN "ruled" by day, and the VC by night. That meant the VC could levy taxes regularly, conduct recruiting, hold indoctrination sessions, and even sleep there many nights. For practical purposes, they lived there; the others wouldn't inform on them, even to the government officials who visited by day, with a guard. The GVN might be able to enter it too during the day, to collect taxes (and rents), try to draft people, propagandize. The local guerrillas weren't so strong as to keep them out altogether unless they came as part of a military operation. But if VC units wanted to operate in that area, to move through or to ambush an RF or ARVN unit, they would have no trouble. They could count on the support they needed from locals and on the others' keeping their silence to ARVN. In short, we were deluding ourselves by calling these areas and hamlets contested. For most effective uses, they were controlled by the VC.

The map in front of the conference, I reminded the audience, was expressing, "Here is the way it is now in terms of colors, zones of control." Then there was an overlay in transparent acetate that said, in effect, "And here is the way it will be at the end of the year, after we have carried out our plans. We expect to report to the president then that there will be much more blue. We shall have expanded the blue area by this much."

I pointed to the map with the overlay on it and said: "The plan is that the blue area will expand from here to here. That is the plan. Now, what should we tell the president as to how he should bet on whether that plan will be achieved?

"He should bet that *none* of this expansion of blue will happen. There will be no progress made in this corps in 1966." The reason went beyond the lack of security from the VC; just as important was the villagers' lack of security or protection from *government* forces. To explain that, I told them of what I had witnessed in the last ten days of traveling on the roads within that area.

One of those sights was of a burning hamlet, near a bridge in Long An Province, not far from Saigon. The hamlet was still on fire when I came to it as I was driving south from Saigon one morning. I was told by a villager that it had been occupied peacefully by a Vietcong militia squad during the night. A short way from the village, a large bridge was very visible. It was less than a hundred yards away. I took a picture of it, which I passed around at the conference, from among the burning huts because only by standing there on the ground as I was or by seeing a photo that combined the bridge and the huts could you realize how close that bridge was to the hamlet.

The reason this mattered was that a regiment of the South Vietnamese army, the Forty-ninth Regiment of the Twenty-fifth Division, had its headquarters under the support buttresses of that bridge. There were two battalions of Vietnamese troops living in the immediate vicinity of the bridge, one to two hundred yards from the hamlet. The reason the hamlet was burning, it was explained to me both by the villagers and by the Vietnamese troops, was that when the Vietcong militia squad bunked down in the hamlet for the night, the Vietnamese units less than two hundred yards away fired rockets and mortars into the hamlet and set all the huts on fire. The huts were made of palm fronds, but now they were mostly smoking ash.

Not one squad or platoon had ventured forth from the bridge to challenge the presence of the Vietcong that had moved in. Just by walking into the hamlet to sleep, the VC had caused the South Vietnamese army to destroy the hamlet, their neighbors. Perhaps the VC had done this deliberately, to punish the villagers for some reason. Or they may have believed from past experience that there was an accommodation between them and the regiment, and it broke down on this night. Or perhaps the regimental commander had been in a mood to punish the villagers for some reason. Whatever the cause, it was the villagers who suffered. The VC squad, I was told, had gone away without any casualties when the firing started. Everyone agreed that ARVN troops had fired first.

I didn't know how many casualties there had been. I didn't think a great many rounds had been fired, just enough to set the fire moving from one to another of the huts, which were close together. In every square patch of earth where a hut had been, people and children were poking through the ashes, collecting fragments of pottery, and teakettles, a few toys, a burned piece of a photograph. I had taken pictures of some of these people, which I also passed around. The villagers looked very sad, except sometimes a kid brightened up when he found a plastic toy that hadn't been too badly burned.

It was the kind of scene you could encounter only by being on the road because you really didn't get that type of reporting from an adviser. In this case I checked ten days later to see if that incident had been reported by the adviser. It hadn't.

I went on to describe two other things I had observed in the last ten days. I had been inspecting schools that were being constructed as part of the pacification program. We provided cement for these schools through the AID program, as the nonmilitary part of what we were doing. What I saw spoke for itself. In a matter of days, in school after school, if you pressed your heel down on the floor, your heel pushed through what was called concrete. If you took a small coin out of your pocket and scraped the walls or the floor, they cratered or crumbled. In fact you could poke your finger through them. This was the nature of "concrete" that was mainly sand. The AID province rep said that about thirty bags of cement had been used per classroom, instead of the seventy-five needed and supplied by USAID. The rest had been diverted for his own profit by the district chief, to whom AID had given the cement, to be sold on the black market for private housing for the rich or for apartment buildings in Saigon. This was the common understanding of everyone. I quoted the province rep to the meeting: "These people know what concrete should look like; they know what they're getting, and they know where the rest of it is going. Just what are the political effects of a program run like this? Are they happy that they're getting anything? Or do the broken promises and the shoddy construction and the diversion and rake-offs make them madder at the government than if we had no program at all? We ought to try to find out."

Other advisers I talked to, I said, didn't think any further study was needed. They said the people were well aware of where the cement was going, instead of into schools for their children, and of the fact that the United States tolerated it, since it happened under our eyes. It made them furious at the governments of both Vietnam and the United States, and it encouraged their sons to enlist in the National Liberation Front. At the same time, it was true that some of the schools, if they stood up after they were built, were destroyed by the Vietcong. I saw those too, along the road and sometimes right beside Popular Forces outposts. But in many cases the VC didn't have to destroy them because they were simply disintegrating. Along with pictures of my own boot heel crunching into what was supposed to be a concrete floor, I passed out at the meeting photos I had taken of the sand castle classrooms. They showed thick whorls of sand drifting across the floor under a light breeze. Classrooms constructed in the last month, gifts from the United States, were dissolving before our eyes, blowing in the wind.

The third thing that I reported was in the village of Duc Lap, the hamlets of Duc Han A and Duc Han B. These were hamlets supposedly protected by the Thirty-eighth Rangers, independent Vietnamese battalions modeled on our own ranger battalions. What I observed were signs on the walls of the houses, which were scarred with bullet holes from the previous week. The signs in Vietnamese, which were translated for me, were very obscene slogans against what Americans called the RD (Revolutionary Development) cadre. The signs had been put up by the rangers, who were also responsible for the bullet holes. I was informed that a ranger platoon leader had ordered a girl cadre to sleep with him. When she refused, the cadre leader, to keep peace, asked her to comply. She still refused, and fighting broke out between the rangers and the cadre; the rangers then killed several members of the cadre. In the same period, perhaps in frustration over a VC attack on the battalion that had caught them without security, the ranger battalion had rampaged through the hamlets, holding up the villagers at gunpoint, stealing all objects of value from them, and raping a number of the women, including the cadre. The cadre had ceased staying in the hamlets because they were afraid of the rangers. On the morning of my visit,

March 27, word had just been received that villagers in those hamlets had been in contact with the VC, asking them to destroy the Thirty-eighth Rangers to get them off their backs.

I ended my report by saying that the president should be told that material support and money and equipment—like the cement for the schools or funding for Vietnamese forces like the ARVN regiment and the ranger battalion—would not result in any progress, in the sense of achievement of American goals or advantage to U.S. aims so long as practices like these could be expected to continue. Try as we might to change these things, and we should try—I made some recommendations on how to do that—the president should not expect any real progress in the year 1966—if ever.

As I recall this occasion, it is almost chilling to think of challenging this bluntly the assessments of the military who were present, in front of a direct representative of the president. But after my ten days on the road I just didn't give a shit. Also, thanks to my apprenticeship with Vann, I had one important card: I was the only one in that room who had been in the hamlets to see these things. No one else of my rank, civilian or military (except John), was in a position to report on such things from his own observation. Along with the sheer machismo of it, which counted for a lot in that company, that gave my conclusions an authority with which they just couldn't argue or flatly contradict.

To give them credit, I quickly had evidence that the reaction of some of the high-ranking officers there was less hostile to this presentation than I had reason to expect. One of the most experienced colonels there, someone I didn't know well, took me aside into an adjoining room after the meeting, sat down at a desk across from me, and said soberly, "What you have said is the truth. You have spoken the truth." Then he looked me in the eye, nodded, and said, "Good for you." I nodded, and we got up and rejoined the others, who were leaving.

After I spoke, the general who had given the briefing for MACV made one attempt to recover the earlier mood. He said that while much of what I had reported was true about the past, and even the present, the fact was that under American guidance some of the ARVN units, specifically the Fifth Division, were "improving."

That was the mantra that American (and, before them, French) advisers had been relying on for decades to deflect the concern of superiors. I had pointed out that there was some basis for saying that in some cases. "But the question that must be faced is: How fast are they improving, and how much? Is it more than the VC are improving? Will it be enough, by the end of this year, to change the projection that I claim should be given to the president, that there will be no net progress to report?" I said I thought not.

Seven years later, in April 1973, I found myself recounting my briefing that day to the jury in my trial. My lawyer had asked me to describe my experience in Vietnam, but I had found that the prosecutor successfully objected to anything I said if it took the form "I learned" or "I concluded," or if it referred to anything I had written that hadn't been presented in evidence. However, I noticed that when I testified that I had seen something or that I had reported orally, his objections weren't sustained. It occurred to me that I could recount this oral briefing, as a way of conveying what I had learned in Vietnam, what had changed me.

When I had described the smoking village, I paused, then said in a low voice, "It was a very bad scene." At this point, the trial transcript shows, I said, "Excuse me." I had trouble going on, for a minute. Then I recovered and continued for half an hour or so, going over the rest of my briefing to the conference. There was a break for lunch, and I went to the room assigned to the defense team and sat at the table by myself and cried for most of the lunch period.

The other members of the defense team left the room, leaving me alone. They didn't know why I was crying. Neither did the reporters who opened the door to the room several times to talk to one of my lawyers, saw me sobbing with my head in my hands, and closed the door hastily. It was the only time they saw me like that. At the end of the lunch hour I washed my face and went back to the courtroom and continued my testimony on the witness stand. Most people assumed my breakdown was simply from the tension of testifying.

I was crying because I was reliving that morning, the smoke rising from the burned sleeping mats, the blackened hearths, the old woman picking up a pink teacup from the ashes. I hadn't thought of that scene for seven years. I saw it again. I saw the pictures I'd taken and had shown to the generals and to Komer at the conference. I saw a little girl with a blackened plastic doll. I saw Vietnam.

In the spring of 1966 there was another major Buddhist uprising in I Corps, the northernmost provinces of South Vietnam, including the cities of Hue and Da Nang. Prior to this Hubert Humphrey had arrived in Saigon for a quick visit and to offer a public embrace of General Ky.

In the excitement of his strong U.S. backers, Ky decided to dispense with his greatest rival, General Nguyen Chanh Thi, perhaps the best military commander in ARVN. Though both Ky and Thi were Buddhists, Thi, who was in charge of I Corps near Da Nang, had closer relations to the Buddhists to the north. When Ky fired him, Thi refused to go and rallied the Buddhists to his support. They defied the administration in Saigon and joined forces with Thi, pressing for the replacement of the Ky regime by national elections.

At this point Lodge and MACV arranged to transport Vietnamese marines to Da Nang, along with tanks and air support, to put down the uprising. By this time monks, joined by women and children, had erected Buddhist altars in the streets and sat by them. The tanks of the ARVN First Division based in I Corps came up to the altars and stopped. They would not go through them. It appeared that ARVN tank crews were poised to join the Buddhist revolt. But on April 7, the day I was briefing the Mission Council, tanks transported by the United States from a different region rolled right through the altars. All the demonstrators, including the Buddhist monks, were arrested. Many Buddhists now went into the jungle to join the Vietcong, while others were arrested and tortured.

I noticed the impact of these events on my friend Chau. It seemed to me that by this point he had clearly lost hope that the GVN could be reformed. With Chau's disillusionment, my own hopes received a grave blow. Many of my closest associates and I had retained a sense of the legitimacy of this effort because of knowing a few Vietnamese like Chau, who had seemed to have faith in our mutual efforts. From then on I believed that we were just going through the motions. The most we could hope for was to moderate the worst atrocities of the war effort. We concentrated on trying to stop indiscriminate bombing and artillery shelling. We continued to give advice, but with less hope that it would be followed or would make all the difference if it were.

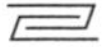

Later in the spring of 1966, during the Buddhist uprising, I was driving along a road between Da Nang and Hoi An in I Corps. The road had been blocked or cut every half mile or so—there were trenches across the road that we had to drive around on the shoulder or barbed-wire fences we had to cut through—not by the VC but by Buddhist ARVN troop units who were opposed to General Ky's regime in Saigon. In effect, both sides in this civil war within the war were being paid out of the U.S. budget.

Along the road was an unusual succession of abandoned fortifications, of varying constructions, that dated from different periods successively further back in time. There were recent Popular Force outposts. We had supplied the wages for the local militia that had built them and the cement, if there was any. But basically these were mud forts, very primitive little outposts along the road supposedly to protect local hamlets. They had been recently abandoned because of the regional nonviolent uprising against the Saigon regime, which had been paying the troops out of U.S. aid. Posts like these I'd seen all over Vietnam.

But next to one of them was a pillbox of another kind, better constructed and made out of concrete, a cylindrical box with narrow portholes. The interpreter driving with me, a young Vietnamese lieutenant, explained that this had been built by the French. I recognized that it looked like one of the smaller pillboxes I had seen in pictures of the French Maginot Line at the outset of the German invasion of France. We drove by several of these. Most were from the 1946–54 war by France to regain its colony, during which it had run a pacification program very similar to ours. But some of them, the lieutenant pointed out, went back much earlier, to the twenties and thirties (when the Maginot Line had been built) and even much earlier in the French pacification of Vietnam.

In the midst of these, along the road, were some pillboxes of a distinctly different sort, also concrete but rounded, like ovens. I recognized those from pictures of the Pacific island fighting by the marines in World War II. They were Japanese, built when the Japanese had pacified the area of what was now I Corps in their occupation of Vietnam during the war. Finally, we came to a massive knoll, overgrown with grass and studded with very old stones. I was told it was an ancient Chinese fort, constructed when the Chinese had pacified Vietnam, starting with what was now I Corps, over a period of a thousand years. When the interpreter told me that, I was reminded of what Tran Ngoc Chau had once said to me: "You must understand that we are a people who think of ourselves as having defeated the Chinese, though it took us a thousand years."

Driving this road was like time travel or visiting an archaeological dig that had brought strata from many historical epochs to the surface. It was a kind of open-air museum of successive efforts by foreigners to establish their authority and control over Vietnamese or at least to protect their own troops and collaborators from resisting locals. At this moment it was not secure for us, since the militia and ARVN paid by the GVN had left the countryside to the VC to demonstrate against the Saigon regime in Da Nang and other local towns. We drove fast, between the obstacles on the road, with our weapons at the ready. Even so, the children we passed, as always, were friendly to us. They waved and called out the only American words they knew: "Hallo! Number one! OK!," the same words that had so touched my heart when I heard them for the first time after my arrival in Vietnam.

The lieutenant driving with me remarked, when we heard some of these shouts, "When I was a little boy, their age, I used to shout hello at foreign soldiers too."

I said, "How did you say it? *Bonjour?*"

He said, *"Ohayo gozaimasu."* Good morning, in Japanese.

I knew we were following the French in Vietnam, who for all their colonialism were our allies in two world wars. But as someone who had grown up on movies of the war in the Pacific, and then on war stories in the Marines, I found it eerie to hear I was walking in the footsteps of Japanese invaders.

In the spring of 1966, I reported to General Lansdale on a plane ride accompanying a forward air observer calling in artillery and air attacks in a contested area in the vicinity of the Plain of Reeds, a desolate swamp near Saigon. I had seen some aspects of the war and our operations that could not be seen any other way—namely, the circumstances under which targets were selected, not by plan or order but by the man in the air who called in strikes, and how he chose what to direct them at, as well as the effect of our defoliation and herbicide programs on the countryside of Vietnam.

From the plane I photographed a particular region in a province bordering the Plain of Reeds, a province of dense green vegetation, very rich in rice fields, date palms, and other foliage. One color picture from the air made the point that I thought my boss should know about. There was a river in that province that, in one area, divided the region we regarded as controlled by the government—that is, by the Saigon regime, which we supported—from an area that we colored red on our military maps: Vietcong-controlled. The red side of the river had been defoliated from the air by planes that sprayed herbicides that killed the leaves and all kinds of vegetation.

Generally the colors on a political map don't correspond to anything you can see on the ground or from the air. But in this case the defoliation had taken place on one side of the river but not on the other, so from the air you saw a very spectacular contrast. On one side of the river, green, extremely lush countryside—in fact, as beautiful as I had ever seen—and on the other side, a desert. Dry, nothing living, no vegetation. In fact it was red, just like our maps; there must have been iron in the soil. As I reported to General Lansdale and my photographs showed, we had made a desert.

On the same trip we were fired at from the vicinity of a village. The pilot, who was experienced, had warned me that if fire came directly at our plane, we would be able to tell from the sound. We would hear a sharp crack, "like corn popping." (The following week an observer accompanying him in the same light observer plane was struck by a bullet coming up through the seat where I had been sitting.) He was right; the sound from the ground was very like popping corn, though we weren't hit. He called in an air strike on the village, by a flight of planes in the vicinity evidently waiting for him or another observer to give them targets. The lead plane fired rockets with white phosphorus warheads at the village, perhaps to mark the target for the others, which dropped bombs and napalm. One of the napalm canisters exploded short of the village, raising a hill of flame in a rice field. The other canisters, and the bombs, hit the village, which had looked unusually prosperous. Some of the houses had red tile roofs.

White phosphorus explodes like a blossom. It spreads out brilliant white petals, whiter than anything else, with crimson tips. It's a gorgeous sight. When white phosphorus touches flesh, however, it burns down to the bone; you can't put it out with water. In Vietnamese civilian hospitals Vann and I visited, I'd seen children who had been burned by it and others who had been burned by napalm, which leaves a different kind of scar. You can't put napalm out with water either. I'd seen both of these in the Marines, in demonstration exercises, and I know they're very effective weapons. We think of them as saving the lives of our troops, especially when we're the only side using them, as in Vietnam, but when I was a marine, I didn't want to be saved by them, any more than I wanted to be saved by nuclear weapons. And that was before I'd seen firsthand what they did to humans.

On our way back to his airstrip, flying over the Plain of Reeds, the pilot said to me over the intercom, "There's VC down there." The plane suddenly went into a steep dive. The pilot pointed down to the ground below us and said, "Vietcong." It was the first time I'd heard anyone say that about someone in sight in Vietnam. When we had set out that morning, he had asked me to bring a pistol along in case we were shot down, and when he said, "Vietcong," I reached for the pistol instinctively. I looked where he pointed and saw two figures in black pajama–type clothes, which were worn by guerrillas or militia of the Vietcong as well as by all the rural people in South Vietnam. They seemed to be running away from a boat nearby. The pilot picked up an M-16 and began firing it on automatic, one-handed, from the window next to his seat as we were diving. We were right over them, eventually only about a hundred feet above them, and it was clear they were unarmed. I mentioned this to him, and he said they had probably left their weapons in the boat. I felt foolish holding the pistol, and I put it back in the holster.

The pilot pulled up and did a sort of figure eight with the plane. Then he came back and dived down again, firing. When we dived down, the men lay down in the reeds, and it was hard to see them. But when he had flown over where we had last seen them and he pulled up and did another tight figure eight, I looked back and saw that they had got up and were running again. This happened several times. Whenever he dived, they lay down, then got up and ran after we had passed. They didn't seem to realize that we could see them through the back of the cabin and that they were visible when they ran. But there didn't seem to be much chance of hitting them from the plane anyway. This kept up for about fifteen minutes. I was getting somewhat sick from these tight loops we were making.

Finally the pilot put his M-16 away, picked up altitude, and flew back toward the base. I asked him, "Does this happen often?"

He said, "All the time. That's why I carry this."

I said, "Do you ever hit anyone this way?"

He said, "Not very often. It's hard to hit anybody from a plane with an M-16, but it scares the shit out of them. They will be pretty scared VC tonight."

I wasn't so sure about that. It seemed to me that there might be a lot of VC who were very proud of having confronted American machines and survived.

After we'd landed on a little dirt strip, the pilot of the observer plane commented to me, "Well, you've had a very well rounded trip. You got to see an air strike and some VC. . . ." I asked him how he had known they were VC, and he said, "There's nothing but VC in the Plain of Reeds." The Plain of Reeds was a "free-fire zone," which meant we had condemned to death anyone who might be found in it.

Back at the embassy I checked into what he had said. I was told, by John Vann, among others, that there were almost two thousand fishermen in the area who continued to fish in it despite our attacks. That didn't prove the pilot was wrong about the two we'd seen. But when I got back I told General Lansdale of my very great sense of unease at the thought that all over Vietnam humans were being hunted like animals from the air on the basis of where they were and what they were wearing.

In describing the day to Lansdale, I said that the most striking demonstration was how little it took for that village to get struck by American fighter-bombers. We had been fired at, all right, but by whom? What connection did they have to the village? Or to the people, and the children, in the burning houses? You could see a lot from six hundred feet—and this plane flew that low, or lower, except when we were fired at—but you couldn't see answers to those questions. Anyhow, whatever the answer was, how were we serving American purposes (it hadn't occurred to me yet to ask what was our right, our justification) in raining down punishment on the people in these houses from the sky? I didn't ask this question of the pilot, who was carrying out his job in a strikingly matter-of-fact way. I saved it for my boss, though it was a rhetorical question to pose to him. It was reading and hearing his judgment of the effect of air strikes against civilians in a war like this, in his *Foreign Affairs* article in October 1964, that had originally recruited me to his team: "The most urgent military need is to make it the number one priority for the military to protect and help the people. When the military opens fire at long range, whether by infantry weapons, artillery or air strike, on a reported Viet Cong concentration in a hamlet or village full of civilians, the Vietnamese officers who give those orders and the American advisers who let them 'get away with it' are helping defeat the cause of freedom. The civilian hatred of the military resulting from such actions is a powerful motive for joining the Viet Cong." By now I'd heard the same refrain from John Paul Vann dozens of times, but I'd heard it first from Lansdale—it was one reason Vann, like me, revered him—and he hadn't changed his mind.

In the summer of 1966, Patricia Marx arrived in Saigon for a second long-planned trip with me on my annual leave. When I had departed for Vietnam in 1965, on the heels of my misunderstanding of her feelings, it had been uncertain in my mind that we would ever be close again. But we began exchanging letters and sending tapes back and forth, and very swiftly I was falling in love once again. In December 1965, she had come to visit me in Saigon, and for my Christmas leave we had traveled together in Thailand, India, and Nepal. It was a marvelously romantic time. I found myself, almost to my surprise, thinking hard about remarrying. Meanwhile, we argued over

Vietnam, but I thought I was able to persuade her, or at least to raise the possibility in her mind, that we were engaged in a good cause, on the side of Vietnamese like Chau who were struggling to keep their country free of Communist rule. I gave her a book to read by Hoang Van Chi, *From Colonialism to Communism,* on the brutality of land reform in North Vietnam.

My one slight question about Patricia as a life partner was if she was adventurous enough. That was answered for me one early morning in Benares, when we went out on the Ganges in a small boat past the burning ghats where bodies were cremated. Off the piers and stairs leading to the river, people were bathing in the holy Ganges. At one point the boatman suggested that I bathe in the river myself. I asked if that would be acceptable to the other bathers, but he said no one would pay any attention, and that turned out to be true. I stripped down to my underwear and went over the side of the boat. I noticed some ash on the water floating by from one of the cremations upstream. Meanwhile, without hesitating, Patricia stripped off her jeans and waded out to me wearing her red shirt. I was impressed. I didn't think I knew many American girls who would have gotten into that water. (She says: "I was smitten. I was madly in love. Out of my mind.") In the river I asked her if she would marry me, and she said yes.

On our return to Saigon she had to go back, and I didn't see her for six months. Before she came out in June 1966, we had made plans to go together to Japan during my leave. But I told her I couldn't pass up the opportunity to give no-holds-barred recommendations to the Mission Council in an interagency study group on pacification. She took that in good stride and, while I was traveling a good deal for the project, set off to find work of her own. After meeting the journalist Frances FitzGerald, Patricia proposed they do an article together on the "other victims" in Vietnam, the refugees who had fled from the countryside to the areas of our control. The U.S. public relations line was that these people had "voted with their feet" against Vietcong terrorism by moving from their homes. Interviews with the refugees and talks with their representatives in the camps, however, showed very clearly that there was basically one and only one condition that had made them leave their fields, homes, family altars, and ancestral graves: the cumulative effect of American air attacks and artillery.

Patricia and Frankie set out to interview the GVN and American officials who were involved in caring for these refugees. They were quickly appalled at the complacency and indifference these officials, especially the Vietnamese, seemed to show toward the conditions of the refugees whose concentrations in the vicinity of Saigon they were visiting. With all my traveling in the countryside, I had never been to one of the camps near Saigon they were describing to me. At one point Patricia urged me to come along with them. It was during the rainy season. What I found was a small city of people living under rain tents in fields of mud and shit, indistinguishably mixed. The refugees would cross this swamp of fetid mud on a narrow plank from one tent to another. It was impossible, especially for a Westerner, not to tip over into the muck. You could see why it took bombs to get people to move into these places.

Patricia saw the war with different eyes from mine. There weren't many American women in Vietnam except for secretaries. One night in Cholon, the Chinese quarter, at dinner with eight or nine of my male friends, she happened to ask each of them their marital status. She observed to me later that all of them were either divorced or separated from their wives by more than distance. Nobody at the table had an ongoing marriage. It was her sense that they were desperate men, enamored of danger and the war, risk takers who didn't feel they had a lot to lose. She was ready to generalize that to the whole mission, the men she saw running the war in-country, though I wasn't sure that was fair.

I, on the other hand, was now engaged. But it seemed that my fiancée had come back to Vietnam reinfected with strong antiwar views. My previous efforts to inoculate her appeared to have worn off. Who had been indoctrinating her? I wondered. When I asked her, she pointed out that for years now television had been offering Americans at home daily scenes of combat and destruction in Vietnam that we weren't viewing at all in Saigon, where we didn't see stateside news shows. It wasn't that hard for her to see what was really going on in Vietnam when she was away from me. *I* was the one who had tried to indoctrinate her, she said. Also, her firsthand look at what Johnson and Humphrey called the other war hadn't helped me.

At a going-away party for Neil and Susan Sheehan, who were leaving Saigon after Neil's second tour for the *New York Times*, we met a commissioner on the International Control Commission (ICC) who had just arrived from Hanoi. I had never met anyone who had been in North Vietnam under our attacks. (Harrison Salisbury's reports for the *Times* six months later were the first accounts of civilian damage in the North that most Americans, including high officials, had read.) As we were leaving the party, just after hearing his description of civilian neighborhoods flattened by our bombing, Patricia turned to me and said in intense, accusing tones, "How *can* you be part of this?"

I felt despair. And anger. I hadn't liked what we'd just heard, any more than she did. I hated it. Didn't she know me well enough to know that? I had always *opposed* the bombing of the North, and right now I was doing my best, the most effective way I knew, to moderate it in the South. Granted, I wasn't getting anywhere. But I felt I was being held responsible for every aspect of the war, including the parts that I had never believed in and that I wanted to stop. We seemed to be back at June 1965. Privately I gave up on the engagement and the idea of marriage to someone who gave me so little benefit of the doubt. When we parted, I assumed that it was for good. It was, in fact, for three long years. I was joining the company of men she had met in Cholon. When I look back, her diagnosis of them fitted me pretty well for the remaining months of my time in Vietnam.

In October I returned to the States for leave. But in Washington I was ordered to turn around to accompany Nicholas Katzenbach, just made undersecretary of state, on an orientation trip to Vietnam. On McNamara's windowless KC-137, a converted tanker that could fly to Vietnam nonstop, I had the opportunity to show all the memos I'd brought from Saigon to my old boss, John McNaughton. I had the intense satisfaction of seeing John hand each one to McNamara as he finished it and watching them read it page by page. It was a long trip, and they didn't seem to have brought anything else to read. I always thought of that as the high point of my bureaucratic career. Normally you never know if a boss has really read what you've written, let alone shown it to his boss. At one point McNaughton took me aside and made two requests, for himself and the secretary: Could I give him an extra copy of my trip report from Hau Nghia, and would I mind refraining from showing that and certain others to General Wheeler, in the interest of civilian-military relations?

On the return flight to Washington a week later, as we got near the end of the journey, McNamara called me to the rear of the plane, where he was standing with Bob Komer, who was still special assistant to the president coordinating Washington efforts on pacification. McNamara said, "Dan, you're the one who can settle this. Komer here is saying that we've made a lot of progress in pacification. I say that things are *worse* than they were a year ago. What do you say?"

I said, "Well, Mr. Secretary, I'm most impressed with how much *the same* things are as they were a year ago. They were pretty bad then, but I wouldn't say it was worse now, just about the same."

McNamara said triumphantly, "That proves what I'm saying! We've put more than a hundred thousand more troops into the country over the last year, and there's been no improvement. Things aren't any better at all. That means the underlying situation is really *worse*! Isn't that right?"

I said, "Well, you could say that. It's an interesting way of seeing it."

Just then the plane began to go into a turn and the pilot announced, "Gentlemen, we are approaching Andrews Air Force Base. Please take your seats and fasten your seat belts."

Ten minutes later we were on the ground, and McNamara was descending the ladder with us behind him. It was a foggy morning, and there was an arc of television lights and cameras set up at the spot the plane had taxied to. In the center of the arc there was a podium covered with microphones. McNamara strode over to the mikes and said to the crowd of reporters, "Gentlemen, I've just come back from Vietnam, and I'm glad to be able to tell you that we're showing great progress in every dimension of our effort. I'm very encouraged by everything I've seen and heard on my trip. . . ."

10

Rach Kien

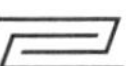

From late November 1966 until I left Vietnam in June of the following year, I was special assistant to Deputy Ambassador Porter, who was in charge of all U.S. civil field operations in Vietnam. My job was primarily to make field evaluations for him of programs and operations, particularly those that dealt with pacification and other joint military and civil operations. In late December I visited a newly "liberated" VC village named Rach Kien in Long An Province, south of Saigon in the Mekong Delta. No Saigon forces had tried to enter that area for a couple of years. To demonstrate that U.S. forces could take over and pacify a strongly VC-controlled district, the U.S. Twenty-fifth Division dropped in a reinforced battalion by helicopters near the village on December 22, 1966, the day before I arrived for a ten-day visit.

The main reason I had come was the skepticism of Ambassador Lodge and Deputy Ambassador Porter about the involvement of American troops in combat and pacification in the densely populated Mekong Delta. Lodge didn't usually interfere in military operations, but he had a strong, well-founded feeling that American artillery and air support would cause a lot of civilian casualties in the delta. He wanted a judgment from me on whether he should make an effort to restrain MACV from deploying American combat units in that area.

There had been little opposition the first day the battalion choppered in. The VC cadre that had been living with their families in the row of huts and offices with plaster walls and thatched roofs in the center of the village had fled quickly, leaving the huts to the Americans, who made them the battalion headquarters. I arrived the second day, by helicopter. The commanding officer, a lieutenant colonel, who had received a message from division headquarters that I was coming, was at the door of the helicopter to meet me when I got out. He grabbed my pack, with a sleeping bag, extra field clothes and boots, and ammunition, and carried it over to the headquarters huts. He was a few years older than I was, but as an FSR-1 I outranked him by several grades. He gave me a canvas cot next to his in the house next to his command post, both vacated the day before by the VC.

He told me that this was his first week in an infantry outfit, in all his years in the army, all of them spent as an artillery officer. He had wanted an infantry command for career purposes, but he had counted on being shown the ropes a little by his predecessor in command, who was being rotated into another assignment. Instead, he said in a tone of incredulity and some bitterness, the changeover process had consisted of a handshake under the blades of the helicopter that brought him into the previous base of the battalion. The previous commander had brought all his gear with him out to the helicopter, wished him good luck, shoved his gear in, climbed into the seat his successor had just left, and flew off. "He didn't even walk back with me to introduce me to his exec or any of the other officers!"

The new commander did better by me. He introduced me to his officers as we ran into them, having introduced himself to them the week before. I told him that the deputy ambassador wanted me to observe the operation here as a pilot American pacification project. I didn't tell him about the ambassador's misgivings about American firepower in the delta.

This battalion had been based near Saigon and had seen little or no action since arriving in Vietnam. According to the exec, a major who had been with them for several months, for most of these men their first sound of gunfire had been the scattered shots when they dropped in the day before. Despite the reputation of this area, he didn't really expect to encounter all that much more, with the firepower they had with them and the air support on call. As we spoke, heavy transport helicopters were bringing in artillery pieces and pallets of ammunition to the artillery base near the center of the village.

We were talking at a crossroads that marked the center of the village, and we could see a small group of men in American uniforms walking up one of the roads between the rice paddies toward us. They turned out to be the American advisory group, two officers and a sergeant, to an ARVN battalion that had come in on foot the day before in a combined operation with the U.S. battalion. They were based about a mile and a quarter up the road and had walked over to meet us, along with a squad of heavily armed ARVN troops to guard them. A lot of their troops and noncoms, they told us, were originally from this area, and they wanted to warn us that we were not in for an easy time. We should be constantly on guard.

"You'll be mortared tonight," the senior American adviser said. He was a young, stocky captain who had been an ARVN adviser for nearly a year. That was the main warning he had come to convey. He added, "Remember, they've been living a long time right where you're standing. They'll have all your positions taped."

"Are you kidding?" the exec said. "This is a reinforced American battalion, with artillery and air support. There won't be a VC for ten miles around tonight." The three Americans left a little while later, saying that they wanted to get off the road and back to their base "before dark." Before they left, they invited me to spend the next evening with them. Their Vietnamese battalion commander, who was Catholic, was giving a special Christmas Eve dinner in honor of the American advisers.

"Those guys have been with ARVN too long," the exec said to me. "Their outfit wouldn't even come into this district if we weren't around. But they're going to be safe tonight. You won't catch any VC getting within mortar range of us for the next month."

Most of the battalion was to do a sweep of the area the day after Christmas, three days away. Meanwhile they would be patrolling heavily, to familiarize themselves with the terrain. I could go along on anything I wanted. After supper there was a briefing for the officers on the next day's patrols in the hut that served as the command post.

There was a large-scale map of Rach Kien District on the wall, with the battalion perimeter and the positions of the different units marked on it with grease pencil. The hut, like all those in the row near the crossroads, was relatively solid, with plaster walls and corrugated tin roofing, probably reflecting pacification programs years before. Like the other huts we were occupying, there were Coleman lanterns, lit by gas, hanging from hooks. There was of course no electricity in the village.

On the way out after the briefing, I spoke a little with a young private with an M-16 who was guarding the command post. This was his first night in-country. He had arrived that morning at Tan Son Nhut Airport outside Saigon and had been sent immediately to Long An Province and then, in the late afternoon, to join this unit at Rach Kien. It had been a long day for him. In the hut next door I put up mosquito netting around the canvas cot the colonel had offered me and lay down in my clothes to go to sleep. The colonel put out the Coleman lantern and went to sleep in the cot next to me.

About two hours later we were awakened by sharp metallic explosions that seemed to be walking up the road toward us. "Whoomp, whoomp, whoomp!" We put on our boots in the darkness and rushed outside without lacing them. I followed the colonel to the command post next door, brushing past the sentry, who looked flustered.

The door had just closed behind us when another "Whoomp!" sounded just outside it and the walls shuddered. The Coleman lamp swung wildly on its hook, sending shadows spinning. One side of the corkboard holding the map came unstuck and crashed down on a field desk, and coffee spilled out of tin cups on the table. We all were staggering and bumping one another as the hut seemed to rock. Everyone scrambled for his helmet. I was suddenly sorry that I hadn't had one of my own to bring. I'd thought there would be no problem finding a helmet in a battalion headquarters when I needed it, but this was not the moment to try to borrow one.

As the lamp stopped swinging, someone came in with the word that the sentry outside, who had arrived from the States that morning, had been hit by the mortar that had just exploded outside the door. He was badly wounded. An evacuation helicopter took him away, along with some other wounded, but he died on the flight.

The radiomen in the next room were on their sets to the different elements of the battalion. The operations officer was matching reports to the map, trying to figure out where the mortar fire was coming from, so they could get countermortar fire on it. There were fifty-caliber machine guns firing on us too, from several positions not that far away. The adviser down the road had been right: The VC had our positions cold, and their mortars were very, very good. On their first volley they had walked a string of mortar shells right up the road, dropping one in each house along the way. They had missed only the command post, by a few yards, and apparently the hut where the colonel and I had been sleeping next door. We waited for the next volley of shells, but it didn't come. Patrols were sent out in the direction of the fifty-calibers, without much hope of finding anything. There were wounded in a number of the huts. After a while we returned to our hut and went to sleep.

The next morning someone noticed an unexploded 60-mm shell that I hadn't seen, lying in an indentation in the floor a few feet from my cot. It must have come in seconds after we ran out, since we hadn't heard it crash through the roof. All soldiers talk about the rounds that have their names on them. The thought that a round with my present address on it had just missed finding me in bed made me lose sight of the fact that it was still a live shell. I was snapping photos busily, moving around so I could get close-ups and dramatic shots of it in the same frame with the edge of my cot, when the demolition team came in. They saw a happy moron trampling around armed, unexploded ordnance and said, "For Christ's sake, that round is live!" They ordered me out somewhat brusquely. Not my most professional moment.

That afternoon a sobered battalion that had not had much sleep expanded the perimeter and prepared for another sleepless night on high alert. It was Christmas Eve. In the middle of the afternoon the adviser from down the road came to pick me up and take me back to his base. We walked a couple of miles, with his bodyguards looking unusually alert. They had heard the mortaring the night before.

I was carrying with me a fruitcake in a round tin box. Just before I left for Long An, Deputy Ambassador Porter had taken it off a table in his office and given it to me, to pass on to some deserving person in the field. Someone he didn't know, "to judge by her note, a little old lady," had sent it to the embassy for Christmas cheer. I figured this unexpected Christmas Eve banquet would be the perfect occasion.

It was very well received, though none of the Vietnamese officers had ever seen a fruitcake before. It didn't exactly go with the Vietnamese food and the *nuoc mam,* but it fit in all right with the other American contributions, the Chivas Regal and Rémy Martin that were dirt cheap at the PX in Saigon and made all advisers popular with their Vietnamese counterparts. There were about a dozen of us around a board table outside: four Americans, an interpreter, the battalion commander, his company commanders, and his executive officer. It was a hot, humid night, and along with the scotch and cognac and Vietnamese wine, a lot of Vietnamese "33"—*ba muoi ba*—beer went down.

The one who didn't hold it very well was the exec, a Vietnamese major. He had been around American liquor before, because he had had an advisory team with him when he had commanded the recon company in the same ARVN division, but evidently it didn't sit well with him, not in the amounts he was drinking. Actually it was Americans in Vietnam that didn't sit well with him. Something, probably not the fruitcake, seemed to be bringing that out in him. The captain who had invited me had been warned when he took the post that this major was somewhat notorious for his dislike of Americans. But it wasn't till later that evening that we learned that he had been transferred from his last command because he had shot at his advisers, missing them.

The exec did not take part in the dinner conversation, and he drank silently as the other Vietnamese officers sang some sentimental-sounding Vietnamese songs, interspersed with Christmas carols from the Americans. Then he started talking, throwing questions at the Americans in a low, bitter tone. The Vietnamese lieutenant who was interpreting told us, "He asks, 'Why are you Americans here? What do you think you have to teach the Vietnamese, in Vietnam?'" Then: "'Do you think we are not brave enough to fight the Communists?'"

The major was talking faster and louder. He wasn't waiting for the translation, and he didn't wait for any answers. Now he was talking to the Vietnamese, more loudly. They sat silently, looking embarrassed. The translator didn't interpret till we asked what he was saying. "He says, 'It is the Americans who are cowards.' He says—" The lieutenant looked hesitantly at the battalion commander, also a major.

"What does he say?"

"He thinks the major is . . . too friendly with Americans." It was clear the lieutenant wasn't willing to translate much of what the exec was now almost shouting. But when we pressed, he paraphrased it. Americans were arrogant, stupid, ignorant; it was a disgrace for Vietnamese to have to pretend to take advice from them. The commander was frowning but said nothing. Then abruptly he got up from the table, spoke sharply to the major, and left. Everyone got up except the exec, who slapped the table hard with his hand and reached for the cognac bottle.

The American captain took me off to show me where I would be sleeping, in the same hut with him. It was fairly late but still light. We were thinking of taking a walk around the battalion area before it got dark. But the Vietnamese lieutenant came by, for the battalion commander, to apologize about the major. "He is drunk," he said. We said we knew that. Still, I said, perhaps many Vietnamese felt as he did. It would be understandable.

The lieutenant said nothing. After a moment I asked him, carefully, what the other officers might have thought about what the major had said. He said quickly, "They were very sorry that he said these things in front of you. They did not agree with that. They are angry at him. But he is a major."

"But do they disagree with what he said?"

"The battalion commander does not agree at all." But the others?

He hesitated. "Well, they might agree with some things that he said, but not so strongly."

There was a loud shot, very close. We scrambled to find our weapons. The lieutenant had jumped slightly, as we all had, but he didn't look surprised. He waved his hand at us and said, "Don't worry. It's nothing."

"What do you mean, nothing? That was right outside!"

"It's nothing," he said. "It's all right. Don't worry." There was another shot, a little farther away. The lieutenant put both hands up, standing in front of the door, and urged us not to go outside just now.

"It's the major," he said. "But it's all right. He is very drunk and angry. He went to get his pistol. He is saying he is going to shoot the Americans. I thought to tell you, but I didn't want you to worry. There is no danger. But you should stay inside here tonight. You will be safe. The commander ordered soldiers to watch him, and they won't let him come near this house."

A third shot seemed to come from still farther away, perhaps a hundred yards. It sounded as though it could have been aimed in our direction.

"Who is he shooting at? Us? The soldiers?"

"Nobody. He is just firing in the air. He is drunk." The lieutenant told us to go to sleep, to sleep well, there was no need to worry. He said good night and left.

The captain and I looked at each other for a few minutes. Finally I asked, "Well, what do you think?"

He shrugged, put down the M-16 he had grabbed when we heard the first shot, and started to take off his pants. "Let's turn in," he said. "We're OK here. They won't let him near us. It would be embarrassing for them if they let him get us."

I thought for a while. In the silence we could hear shouting, apparently from the major. It got quiet. Then more yelling came from a different location. He seemed to be circling. Every now and then there was a single shot and more shouting.

It was dark now. With what I knew of ARVN attitudes about working at night, it didn't seem right to me to be putting our trust in ARVN nighttime security. This guy was after us. It might embarrass the commander if his exec slipped through those guards and shot us both while we were sleeping, but not as much as it would embarrass me. I told the captain that the only responsible thing for us to do was to stand watch ourselves. I would take the first watch, from ten to two. He didn't argue. Pretty soon he was snoring.

To help stay awake, I kept a candle burning. I lay on the canvas cot in my clothes, with my boots next to the cot. There was one more burst of muffled shouting, then no more. There were no more shots nearby. The major had fallen asleep. But I stayed awake. I lay on my back with my hands under my head, looking at the shadows from the candle. I tried putting my pistol on the edge of the cot, at arm's length so I could find it, but the cot was too narrow. On the ground it would be too hard to find quickly in the shadow of the cot. I laid it on my chest.

Around midnight a fifty-caliber machine gun rattled in the distance. A little later artillery fire sounded at the horizon. There was silence. Then the same dialogue. It was a few miles away, at Rach Kien. I decided not to wake the captain up for a watch, but I stayed awake till two anyway. The candle guttered down. I listened to the machine gun, like a cricket, far away, balanced the weight of the pistol on my chest, thought about my children back home, and felt lonely. I thought: This is a shitty way to spend Christmas Eve.

The Vietnamese major was still sleeping it off the next morning when I left the hut. The adviser walked me back to the American base at midday, along with some ARVN troops. We got back to Rach Kien just after a single mortar round had exploded, at noon, smack on the crossroads in the center of the village. Merry Christmas. Somebody out there had a nice dramatic touch, along with very good aim.

The American executive officer, the major who had observed on the first day that no VC would be found within ten miles of an American battalion, had been sitting on a four-holer latrine surrounded by canvas about ten yards from the crossroads when the mortar shell hit. But that must have been a coincidence. The VC couldn't have known he would be sitting there at that moment, and they hadn't overheard his comments two days before, standing at more or less the same spot. I didn't suppose he remembered what he had said, and I didn't remind him.

We were in time to share the turkey dinner that the United States manages to provide American troops in the field on Christmas and Thanksgiving. In the spirit of Christmas I spent the afternoon passing out piasters to peasants whose thatch huts had been blown down by the turbulence when helicopters landed near them. I had a large wad of piasters a USAID representative had given me for this purpose. No major operations were run that day, only patrols sent out to try to discourage the VC mortar squads from getting in too close.

The day after Christmas the operations officer sent out two companies to sweep, or walk through, areas not far from the village, and I went out with one of them. Since I was there as an observer, I didn't take a weapon. It hardly seemed necessary, in the midst of a couple of hundred armed men, no matter what we might run into. But this turned out to have a serious drawback. The men paid no particular attention to me as I joined a column on the march or moved across a rice paddy, after I had introduced myself to the platoon leader. They must have noticed I had no insignia on my field jacket and carried no weapon, but they understood I was some sort of civilian. Some of them assumed at first I was a journalist. If they asked me, I said I was from the embassy in Saigon, and they rarely showed much curiosity about what I was doing there.

But when the unit I was with came under fire, as happened after an hour of walking that first morning, I saw that the men near me seemed to feel a responsibility to look out for me. Apparently it was because I wasn't carrying a weapon, having a job that they understood didn't call for one, like a corpsman or a reporter. As soon as shots came roughly in our direction, they moved in closer to me and a little ahead of me, and I could see they were keeping one eye on my whereabouts, as though they had been given the job of taking care of me. It was as if my being unarmed made me more likely to be hit, or their weapons gave them a special ability to protect me from shooters we couldn't see.

Neither was true, any more than the magical notion that having weapons in their own hands made them safer from enemy fire. But soldiers tend to believe that, and what goes with it is that being unarmed under fire makes you seem more vulnerable. So my weaponless state drew attention to me and distracted them from what they were supposed to be doing. It was not an effect that I wanted to have. After a day and a half of this I started to carry the weapon I had brought with me.

It was a Swedish K submachine gun that a CIA province representative had given me out of his stores. The CIA men armed the counterterror teams they organized with it. Some Vietnamese and a few Americans who saw me with it were hip enough to assume as a result that I was CIA. It was distinctive-looking, impressively ugly and simple, with an air-cooled metal jacket around the barrel that looked like a piece of pipe with holes punched in it. After I started to carry it with the troops, the weapon itself attracted some attention, but I no longer did.

It still hadn't occurred to me that I would have occasion to fire it unless we were seriously ambushed. I had no desire to. I certainly didn't want to shoot anyone, and I didn't want to have to clean the weapon. I wasn't in any chain of command, subject to orders. I was in fact a civilian. In the back of my mind was a faint recollection that it was a violation of laws of war for a civilian to carry a weapon in a war zone, let alone to fire one. I never chose to ask anyone about this. Most American civilians from AID or the USIA or embassy political officers outside Saigon or the major towns routinely carried weapons if they were driving or walking in the countryside. But I didn't know any others who walked with troops in operations except Vann, and I'd never asked him what he did about firing his weapon.

However, it soon turned out that carrying a weapon that you didn't use if you were under fire was also a way of attracting unfavorable attention. A squad I was walking with was ordered to go on line and lead the platoon across a rice paddy. I went along with them, as I'd been doing for the last couple of days. Suddenly, as we were walking through waist-high rice, some shots came at us from the trees ahead, and without needing an order, the men on both sides of me began firing at the tree line. It didn't seem urgent for me to join them, since they were already answering a handful of shots with a dozen M-16s on full automatic, so I took out my camera and took some pictures of them and our tree line objective.

After we got to the tree line and the firing had stopped, a sergeant came over to me, looking agitated. First he asked me if I was a reporter. I said no, I was from the embassy. He looked pointedly at the camera still in my hand and the weapon hanging on my shoulder and began to get red in the face. He asked me incredulously, "Were you taking *personal photographs* in a *firefight*?"

"No," I said evenly. "I'm here observing for the deputy ambassador, and I'm taking pictures for him." He looked dubious, but he went off, and I made a quick decision. After that, when people around me were firing, I was too. It worked. From then on I was essentially invisible in the field.

In this guerrilla war in the delta all the attacks were turning out to be hit-and-run. Usually a few shots from snipers or one or two heavier volleys would come from a clump of trees and brush or a tree line or a patch of forest bordering a paddy. One or two of our troops, or none, would be hit. The men would get down, and the ones in front would return fire on the cover where they thought the shots were coming from. I didn't mind doing that. As soon as we were fired at as we were walking through a paddy, the platoon leader would call down artillery, or sometimes an air strike or a gunship, on the vegetation where the shots seemed to have come from. That took about ten minutes or more to arrive. If there were wounded, usually one or two from the first volley, the unit didn't move forward till a medical evacuation helicopter had arrived to carry the injured away. That took at least twenty minutes. Relying on external support, artillery or air, might minimize American casualties. Certainly quick medevac reduced U.S. killed in action. But to let both of these slow us up so much seemed to have real drawbacks when it came to having anything to show for the casualties we were taking. It would usually be about half an hour after taking enemy fire, even a shot or two, before a company started moving forward again. In most cases no more would be heard from that position after the initial burst. No one would have seen the guerrillas who were firing. No bodies would be found on the position when it was finally occupied. If there were any wounded or killed, the VC were taking them with them when they left, and they were probably moving out right after firing, screened by high rice or by tree lines. So a couple of snipers could routinely stop an American company for half an hour.

At the end of a day of getting fired at regularly by opponents you never saw, who had no hesitation about leaving positions abruptly for you to occupy—both of you knowing they would be firing at you from the same spots or others just like them the next day—it was hard to believe we were accomplishing anything at all. I heard no talk of body counts, perhaps because with all the fire we were pouring into various patches of foliage, there was not one enemy body to count. The only body encountered, other than an American, was that of an eighteen-year-old girl who had come down from Saigon, where she was attending a French school, to spend a day with her family. She was killed by a stray U.S. artillery shell. That didn't improve morale.

Among our men, along with growing frustration, there was growing admiration for their opponents. I often heard the comment "They've got more guts than brains." For soldiers, that was a compliment. On its face it spoke of daring that went to the point of recklessness, foolishness. But it wasn't even clear that was true. *We* were the only ones taking casualties, as far as we could tell. Without a single known enemy casualty at the end of twelve days, there were nine American dead and twenty-three wounded. A couple of those, radiomen, I was close to when they were hit. When I wasn't at the point, I often walked behind the radioman, following close on the unit leader, to whom he was often connected by a telephone cord. The radioman's tall whip antenna made him the first target of snipers. We lost four in the battalion while I was there.

The men were getting more and more angry at the lack of information we were getting from peasants in the huts we passed—mothers with their children, old people, never young men—as we chased in the direction of the people firing at us. It was obvious that these people must have seen the ones we were hunting, or who were hunting us, moving around and ahead of us. Our troops were resentful, and perplexed, that the villagers, who, as the troops understood it, we were in-country to protect, weren't cooperating with us by pointing out the hiding places of those ambushing us. From the comments I heard, I gathered that our men hadn't yet made the connection that the snipers firing at us were almost surely the missing young men from the same households. I didn't point it out.

Stopping and starting all day under a hot sun, the troops got tired and bored. Even occasionally coming under fire didn't keep their interest steady. Slogging through mud or rice paddies with water up to your knees was slow going, and it meant lying down in water or mud when you got fired at, with your head above the water carrying the weight of a helmet on your neck muscles and trying to keep your weapon out of the water and mud. It wore you down.

A day in the field, being fired at, quickly confirmed something you learn marking targets for shooters on a rifle range. It's easy to tell from the sound when bullets are coming directly at you. Sitting in a trench under one of a long line of canvas targets with the shooters a hundred to several hundred yards away, you find you can tell when the target a few feet over your head has been hit without looking at it, just from the sound of the shot. Out of a continuous drumroll of shooting from the firing line, the shot aimed precisely in your direction sounds distinctly different—a sharp, flat crack—from one fired at the next target just a few feet away, one side or the other. All these troops had had that experience, and as they got tired, they used that knowledge in ways that didn't do a lot of credit to their training or their leadership: When firing rang out, they wouldn't lower themselves to the ground, especially in a muddy paddy, unless the shots were coming right at them.

A lot of them who took to buckling their hot, heavy helmets on their packs or belts wouldn't bother to put them on their heads unless they were being directly fired at. So if shots were aimed at the platoon in the next field, maybe just fifteen or twenty yards away, easy to tell from the sound, the platoon that was not at that moment under fire continued to plod along, often without bothering to put their helmets on, until the fire shifted, if it did, to start coming directly at them. Of course that meant an increased chance that it would catch one of them standing up without a helmet on. Their sergeants and platoon leaders should have been keeping them better protected, at the cost of making them a little more tired and irritable, but that was a price most of the leaders didn't seem willing to pay. The short tours and frequent rotation policies, I came to learn, which sustained individual morale and officers' service records, affected the quality of leadership not only at the battalion level and higher but right down to the platoons. Just like the colonel, few of the lieutenants had had their units long or had much field experience. They didn't know their noncoms or men well, so they were nervous about riding them too hard.

One evening my hut mate, the battalion commander, said that he was hearing very good things about me from his company officers. "You handle yourself in the field very well; it's clear that you know what you're doing. They like having you along." I told him again that I had been a rifle company commander, and he told me again that he had not.

I asked him if it would be helpful to him for me to give him some thoughts on what I was seeing, and he was very eager to hear them. He was only slowly getting the feel of his officers, and he didn't have a chance to see them in the field. I was seeing all of them at work because as I came back to the base from a half day's operation with one company or platoon, I would peel off and hook up with another that was just setting out. I was going out on two operations a day and often on a platoon patrol at night. I spent about an hour every evening commenting to the battalion commander on what I'd seen during the day while he took notes.

After seventeen months in Vietnam I saw an unmistakable enemy for the first time on New Year's Day 1967. Four of us were walking point, about fifty yards ahead of the company, moving through tall rice, chest high, water about up to our knees. As I looked around, there wasn't much to see in the waving rice, but our eyes were mainly on the tree line ahead of us. Just as we climbed out of the paddy onto the dry ground among the trees, we heard firing very close behind us. We spun around, ready to fire, and I saw a kid about fourteen or fifteen with short, brushy black hair, wearing nothing but ragged black shorts, his back halfway to us, standing slightly crouched, firing an AK-47 at the rest of the troops. I could see him clearly in the swath we had opened behind us moving through the rice minutes before. To his right and to his left I could see two others, heads just below the top of the rice. They were firing too.

They must have been lying in the water a few feet from us as we went past. They must have seen, or maybe, heads down, heard and felt the splashes of our boots in the water and mud around the rice roots within a few feet or yards from their bodies. They had lain there, letting the four of us pass by so as to get a better shot at the main body of troops to our rear. We couldn't fire at them, because we would have been firing into our own platoon. But since our troops were the ones getting shot at, a lot of fire came back right at us. Dropping down and getting as close to the ground as I could, I watched this kid firing away for what seemed like ten seconds, twenty seconds, but may have been closer to five or six, till he crouched down and disappeared with his buddies into the rice. After a minute the platoon ceased fire in our direction, and we got up and moved on.

We had a lot to think about, as we crossed a patch of woods and dropped down into the water of the next paddy over. The platoon leader sent up three men to relieve the ones who were at the point with me, but they didn't need to be told what had just happened. They were very alert—I was too—as we walked through the rice, but you just couldn't see anything in the thick, high rice more than a few feet away. The other three and I had been alert enough before, and we could see now that the only way we could have found those guys was to have stepped on top of them. It was our job on point to draw fire—even if we couldn't spot the enemy ourselves—to warn the main body of troops behind us. But the enemy here didn't seem to feel any obligation to help us do our job. There could have been a platoon of VC hidden in one of those fields with us without our knowing it.

About an hour later exactly the same thing happened again. Firing came from the rice just behind us toward the troops to our rear. This time I didn't see anything but a glimpse of a black jersey through the rice. I was very, very impressed not only by their tactics but by their performance. One thing was clear: They were local boys. Wearing ragged shorts and rubber sandals—if they had anything on their feet at all under the rice water—they came from this village, probably this hamlet. So they had the advantage of knowing every ditch and dike, every tree and blade of rice and piece of cover in the area as if it were their own backyard, because it *was* their own backyard. No doubt (I thought later) that was why they had the nerve to pop up in the midst of an American reinforced battalion and fire away with U.S. troops on all sides of them. They thought that they were shooting at trespassers, foreign occupiers, that they had a right to be there and we didn't. This would have been a good moment for me to ask myself if they were really wrong about that and whether we had a good enough reason to be over there in their backyard to be fired at. But I don't think I faced that question squarely till I left Vietnam. When you're under fire, and armed, you don't think twice about firing back. The question of whether you had a right to be there to be shot at doesn't occur till later if it hasn't occurred before then.

This morning's work had sown in my guts a thought that had been only in my head before: These opponents were going to be very hard to beat. Or to put it another way, we were not going to defeat them.

And the long day wasn't half over.

We were taking a break on the slope of a berm when we saw troops ahead, just outside the edge of the forest on the other side of a shallow paddy, about seventy-five yards away. They were American or ARVN. You couldn't easily tell, since ARVN troops used American uniforms and equipment. They were in camouflage uniforms, and they were wearing web gear and helmets. Web gear was the heavy canvas straps that packs were strung on and the broad canvas belts with metal-edged holes for carrying canteens, pistols, and knives. VC guerrillas didn't wear it. They also didn't have helmets.

I could clearly see one of the men turned away from us holding a machine-gun tripod, standing in the bare rice paddy, a couple of yards in front of the tree line. Two others were bent over, moving around in the ferns just inside the bamboo, and for a moment I saw two or three others to the left in the darkness of the trees. They hadn't seen us. They were setting up a machine gun in the cover a few yards from the right corner of the paddy.

The platoon leader, with his radioman, had come up to join the four of us on the point during the break. He slumped down on the side of the berm, motioned the radioman to hand him the handset, and rang up the company headquarters behind us. He asked over the phone, "Who are the friendlies ahead of us? I thought we were supposed to be in the lead." He listened to the response. Then he said, "Yes, there are. We could see them clearly. They're wearing web gear and helmets." He waited again. Then he said, "Hunh."

"What do they say?"

"They say there are no friendlies ahead of us. They said those are not, repeat not, friendlies. I said they have web gear and helmets. They said, 'Golf Company to the rear of the battalion is in a heavy firefight with troops wearing web gear and helmets.'"

The platoon leader put his helmet back on and was tightening up his gear. I asked him, "What are you going to do?"

He said, "I guess we're going to find out who they are."

Some other troops had joined us. The platoon leader was going to have seven or eight of us crawl across the paddy and assault, while the rest of the platoon laid down a base of fire from the berm. For once, we weren't waiting to call in artillery or an air strike first. I looked around the terrain. The paddy was almost bare. The rice in it was very new, tender green shoots several inches apart, providing no cover in water that was only a few inches deep. There was a mound in the middle of the paddy that rose about four feet high, covered with grass. That was the only cover, about four or five feet wide, in a flat space about three-quarters the size of a football field.

"You going?" the platoon leader asked me. I nodded. I didn't know his name, and he didn't know mine, but he knew I had been up with the point all day.

"Do you realize what those troops are up ahead?" I said to the lieutenant, who would be staying behind on the berm to control the action. "Those have to be NVA [North Vietnamese army, regular army units from North Vietnam]." They were the only Communist troops, I thought, who wore regular uniforms and helmets. They had started infiltrating into the South two years before—that was when I tracked the first intelligence reports on them in a Pentagon study for McNamara—and by now they were regularly in large-scale combat in the northern sectors of South Vietnam, mainly I and II Corps. But I had never heard of NVA units south of Saigon, in the Mekong Delta, where we were. "As far as I know, these must be the first NVA troops south of Saigon. It's amazing our running into them," I told the platoon leader.

"How 'bout that?" he replied. He didn't seem as struck by that as I was.

The seven or eight of us who were going to make the assault spread out along the berm. I was on the right flank, right across from the machine gun we had seen them emplacing, with one man farther to my right. On command we slipped over the berm and started moving forward. While we were crawling, on line, across the paddy, our heads just above the few inches of water, the troops behind us began firing over our heads at the tree line. Holding our weapons in front of us in both hands above the water, we moved on our elbows and knees through the mud, keeping our butts low. Left knee forward, flat to the ground, left shoulder and elbow forward, straightening out the left leg, right knee forward, right shoulder and elbow forward, moving across the field like a crab, flat to the surface. I got into the rhythm of it, and several times I looked around and found that I had gotten ahead of the others. I waited for them.

Gunfire behind us had the flat, sharp crack of bullets aimed directly at us. So did the bullets coming from the tree line in front. But the fire from behind us, from our own troops, was like a sheet just over our heads, sizzling and whishing as though the sheet were being ripped. I didn't see how people in an assault generally survived the friendly fire from their rear. I couldn't see how we were going to survive it. You didn't need to be told to keep your ass down.

I could see the flashes of the machine gun right ahead of me. When I was about fifteen yards away, I took two grenades off my belt, pulled the pin on one, and, lying on my side, tossed it with a straight arm at the machine gun. I pulled the pin on the other one and threw it too. Both went off, and the machine gun stopped firing. At the same moment the fire behind us also stopped, and we got up and moved fast across the last few yards into trees, firing our weapons. As we got into the forest, I couldn't see anyone, but I could hear brush being trampled just ahead of us, ten or twenty yards away. They had taken the machine gun with them, and if there were any wounded or dead, they had taken those with them too, within the last minute or so. Very good soldiers.

It was important, I had been taught and passed on to my troops a decade earlier, to pursue the enemy hard, to move *through* the objective, not to stop on the forward edge or to mill around on top of it waiting to be mortared. At that moment I forgot my role, the lieutenant being far behind us, and I yelled out to the others to keep moving, keep after them. But they didn't seem to have been trained that way. They stopped and waited for the others to come up to us, and I shut up. I was standing where the machine gun had been; there was a large pile of empty cartridges at my feet. I didn't see any blood on the ground or the foliage. I picked up a handful of cartridges for souvenirs, bullets that had been fired directly at me, and they were so hot that they burned my hand and I dropped them. They hit water and hissed. They had been fired at us less than a minute before.

It took a while for the rest of the platoon to come up on the objective, and maybe fifteen or twenty minutes elapsed before we came to the other side of the little island of jungle and saw again the flat sea of paddy fields that surrounded it. As soon as we emerged, we were taking fire again. But it wasn't from the tree line a hundred yards ahead of us, where we presumed the troops we were chasing had retreated. It was coming from the right, diagonal to our advance, from a patch of trees beyond the paddy next to the one ahead of us, several hundred yards away. Could those troops have moved that far that fast? Or were there enemies in every patch of cover in this sea? Whatever, we shifted our axis of advance toward where the fire was coming from, and the platoon leader called down artillery from the base in the hamlet onto the patch of trees.

In another half hour, with a delay for a medevac of some wounded, we were on the objective, the tree patch, empty of enemy. We were under fire again, this time diagonally across the paddy field to our left front. Obediently we moved back toward those shots. This happened three or four times, taking fire and zigzagging toward it every half hour or so, during which it became pretty obvious what was going on. There were two groups of enemy troops, maybe no more than a squad each, who were working us back and forth between them as each retreated along parallel lines of paddy fields. As soon as we occupied the ground on which one team had been hidden, the other took us under fire while the first group escaped to the next position. Even though the pattern was becoming clear, each time we came under fire we moved predictably toward the shots fired at us, like a bull following the movements of a cape. Before we got to their position, they would move out; minutes later fire coming at us from the other direction would cover their retreat and get us to drop the pursuit and shift to another target, which was soon to recede. They were playing with us, a kind of leapfrog, and they were doing it very well, probably not for the first time.

By the end of the day our troops had the steps down and were getting tired of the dance. They had taken five or six wounded, and as usual, except for those of us at the point, they had seen no enemies, alive or dead. Whoever the units we were chasing were, they weren't all from the North or from north of Saigon either. There were local men with them, who knew these paddies. Maybe the same wild boys in black shorts who had run circles through us that morning, or their brothers.

As a matter of fact, I later learned that helmets and uniforms with webbing were available to what our intelligence called main force units, Vietcong regular forces, uniformed VC organized into regiments and divisions. That was apparently what we had run into that afternoon. There still were no signs of NVA in the delta, though it was rare to see even VC main force units in this region, so it was a bit of a historic day anyway. But our troops, including me, were ready for it to be over. Eventually, having swept through a large circle during the day, we could see the base camp several paddy fields ahead of us. There was just one thin line of coconut trees between us and the hamlet where our artillery and mortars and battalion headquarters were located.

The platoon leader, the latest one to lead the company advance, had called a short break, and the men had their helmets off, drinking from their canteens and eating, or licking, melted chocolate out of candy bar wrappers. The radioman, a wiry black kid who as usual looked too thin to be lugging a seventy-five-pound radio, was slouched back on his radio pack with the weight off his shoulders. As I thought about the day, it came to me to ask him something I had begun to ask myself that morning: "By any chance, do you ever feel like the redcoats?"

Without hesitating a beat he said, in a drawl, "I been thinking that . . .

all . . . day." You couldn't miss it if you'd gone to grade school in America. Foreign troops far from home, wearing helmets and uniforms and carrying heavy equipment, walking along dikes in formation and getting shot at every half hour mostly by ragged local irregulars firing from tree lines that bordered their homes.

The platoon leader grunted. He looked out over the quarter mile we had to go yet and said, "Well, that's it for today anyway." I asked him how he knew that. He said, "We're in sight of our base camp. We've got half a battalion behind us, and our artillery and mortars right over there. There's no cover between here and there, except for that tree line. And the VC aren't going to be crazy enough to get between us and all that."

The radioman, still lying back and looking up at the trees, said quietly, in a reflective, singsong drawl that started high and ended low and drawn out: *"I . . . wouldn't . . . be . . . so . . . sure. . . ."* As his voice trailed off, the entire tree line ahead of us, in between us and the base, exploded in a wave of fire.

Helmets went on fast; candy wrappers dropped; the men scrambled into positions and fired back, keeping down low. It was funny in its way, at least for the radioman and me. The lieutenant, on his stomach next to the radioman, called in an air strike on the tree line, since the range from the base was too short to use our artillery. But whoever it was had stopped firing after that one long, spectacular burst that seemed to come from the whole tree line at once. This time they hadn't even waited for us to step down into the paddy in the open. Maybe they just wanted to let us know they were there. A curtain call. Probably before the gunships arrived, they had moved off the scene along the line of trees, to wherever they were spending the night now that we were occupying their huts in the hamlet.

After the gunships had raked up and down the tree line a few times, we redcoats approached it, cautiously, without drawing fire anymore. We walked through it to the base.

On my last night in Rach Kien the operations officer showed me a spot on the map several miles from the village, at a bend in a river. "Every patrol that's come near that spot has drawn fire. There's heavy cover there and all along the riverbank, but there must be VC there all the time. I'm sending a company there tonight. We'll take them by surprise in the morning and clean it out."

I was planning to leave the next afternoon, but I decided to go along. It was the first time that a whole company had moved at night. They weren't planning a night attack. The idea was to move at night so they could get into position without being spotted, something that couldn't be done around here during daylight. The operations officer had planned a very circuitous route circling the VC ambush spot so we would be attacking from the side opposite our base, where they might not expect us early in the morning. A kind of counterambush. It would be a long walk in the darkness, starting after midnight.

I got together all my gear to leave the next afternoon, had a last dinner with the colonel, and lay down on the cot for a nap. Someone woke me up at 2:00 A.M. Moving at night, we could walk on the dikes, so we made good time and kept our feet dry. Even so, the planned route was so long and roundabout that it took several hours of walking. The men had done enough night patrolling by now that they had everything strapped down with their pockets empty, so there was no jingling. There were no twigs to snap on the dikes, and the dirt was soft. A company of men was surprisingly quiet.

It wasn't really dark. There was a full moon and no clouds. There was no breeze either, so the water in the paddies we were passing was still. Hour after hour the moon accompanied us, shining in the water we walked by. It was as clear and bright just below our feet in the fields next to us as when we looked up and saw it in the sky. But the moon below was shadowed by the silhouettes of black leaves rising from the water. It was incredibly beautiful.

We drifted along for hours. Sometimes we stopped briefly while the officers read their maps by the moon. Finally it set, and we walked in full darkness. Not long after that there was a halt, and the word came back, whispered man to man, to lie down and wait for orders, which would come before dawn. The lead platoon had reached the objective.

I made my way up the column to the platoon leader, and he offered to take me up and show me where we were supposed to attack. Moving as softly as we could, he led me up to the corner of a paddy that had water in it but no rice that I could see. With our eyes used to the darkness, even the starlight was enough to make out, just barely, that the field was cut diagonally in front of us by a dense grove of trees. That was our objective.

When we moved back, he told me that shortly before dawn he was going to deploy his men behind the dike along one side of the paddy, to make the assault. The third platoon, now behind us, would take up position at right angles, along the adjacent side of the paddy, to provide a base of fire to cover our assault soon after daybreak.

So far at Rach Kien I had never commented on any of the orders I had heard. It wasn't my job, and I didn't want to draw attention to myself. But as I thought about what I had just seen and heard, I felt uneasy about the plan to cross that open paddy in daylight, into an area that we felt sure had VC in it. For the first time I ventured to make a suggestion. I told the platoon leader that it might be a good idea to move his platoon across the paddy in darkness into the forward edge of those trees, not very far in, where they might get lost, but just inside the foliage. He said no, he was afraid he would lose control if he tried to deploy them anywhere but along that straight dike. That might have been true, but I still felt uneasy.

In half an hour it began to be light. Our platoon moved forward and spaced out behind the dike, trying to keep our heads below it, lying low in muddy water after being dry all night. Looking to the left, our eyes at the level of the water, we could see almost to the horizon, across flat paddies unobstructed by trees. Something astonishing was happening. The largest sun I've ever seen was beginning to rise from the edge of the earth. It was dark orange, as sharply defined as the full moon but enormously larger. It rose on a column of red light stretching across the flooded paddies.

At that moment helmeted figures carrying weapons emerged from the forest behind us and started to walk along the adjoining dike to the left, at right angles to ours. It was the third platoon, taking up its firing position. After walking all night on top of the dikes, their platoon leader had evidently forgotten that it wasn't dark anymore. They were walking across the rising sun.

My heart stopped. It was like watching a child step unknowingly into heavy traffic. My own infantry training was ten to twelve years old, but after the last dozen days in the rice fields I could feel its roots in my body, and none of these reached deeper than the rule, the vital instinct: Stay off the skyline in daylight; don't stand on the crest of a hill; don't ever be silhouetted against the sky. This wasn't the sky the men were outlined against. It was an orange sun. One by one each man was moving into the center of the biggest lit-up bull's-eye that had ever been seen. Before it rose off the earth, it was so broad that two to three men at a time were silhouetted against it.

It was a gorgeous sight, but it was not good soldiering. My whole body was tensed, waiting for a machine gun to open up from the trees in front of us to punish them. But for some reason the AK-47s—which were there, all right, just inside the branches touching the water in front of us—didn't open up until the third platoon got down behind the dike and stopped making targets of themselves and the signal came for the first platoon to move out. Right on cue, as we slid over the dike and into the water up to our thighs, the usual staccato rattle came at us from all across the tree line, as if they were responding to the same command as we were, as if they were drumming us on.

I muttered, "Shit," and hesitated for a second in front of the dike, waiting to get hit. So did everyone else. Then we all moved forward while the third platoon poured fire into the leaves. As I was walking through the water, firing ahead, I was thinking: I knew it wasn't a good idea to wait till daylight to cross this field. But then I had to admit that my suggestion of getting into the trees before dawn might not have worked out so well either. Were those guys already in the fringe of this foliage during the night? Had they known we were coming, or did they spend every night sitting in the water in their hunters' blind? Would meeting them hand to hand in the darkness, in the brush, have been even worse than this?

As usual, the VC, after the first couple of volleys, stopped firing and backed off. They had made their point, which seemed to be that they, not we, would continue to do the surprising, that we weren't going to catch them, that they knew these parts a lot better than we ever would, and that they would be here after we were gone. So they didn't need to stick around now.

For once we were ordered to maintain contact, to stay in pursuit. Inside the canopy of foliage we had entered was a tangle of vines hanging down into the water. Some of the men were slashing a way through with machetes. But it was slow going. And nearly every step we took the water got a little deeper, till it was up to our waists, sometimes our chests. Where was this taking us? How deep was the water going to get? And where were the guys we were pursuing? Evidently the river next to us overflowed its banks, maybe seasonally, and we were in a long stretch of water flooding the jungle vegetation that bordered the river. We had entered a deep swamp, with little or no current. At one point we stopped for a while, and in the silence we could distinctly hear low voices in Vietnamese. We got very quiet and could make out that they were about twenty yards away, to our right. They were next to us, but on the other side of the river. There were no friendlies operating in the area. We were actually listening to Vietcong talking to each other, in calm tones, closer to us than the platoon to our rear. They were probably not the ones we were chasing; they evidently didn't know we were near.

The platoon leader decided to call artillery down on them. It seemed pretty close to us to be doing this, but he had confidence in his map reading and compass. He whispered coordinates into the radio. The river right next to us, clearly marked on the map, may have helped the artillerymen place their rounds because the bursts did come on the other side, in the vicinity of the voices, which we stopped hearing. Seconds after each explosion there was a shower of particles on the surface of the water all around us, like the patter of rain. I couldn't tell if it was fragments from the shells or, more likely, bits of foliage scattered by the explosions.

Finally we moved left, away from the river and out of the water. The first platoon dropped back to the rear of the company, and the third and second platoons were moved on line for a sweep back to the base. It was my last afternoon with the battalion. The leader of the third platoon, a sallow, tough-talking young lieutenant from New Jersey, asked me to accompany them. I didn't much like him. He had been the joker who walked his platoon across the sun that morning. But for a while I walked with him.

The men were tired. They had been up all night, and the morning hadn't lived up to the operations officer's expectations, or anyone's. But it wasn't by their impulse—it was on a direct order from the lieutenant—that the point fired on the first hut we came to without having been fired on. The hut turned out to be deserted when we got up to it, though it had obviously been occupied that morning. There were warm ashes in a hearth, some food on a table, and crude toys on the floor.

I asked the lieutenant why he had told the point to start firing. He said it was "reconnaissance by fire." That was a familiar, controversial notion, anathema to Vann and many other infantrymen in this kind of war. It meant finding out if a particular location, either a building or vegetation, had enemies in it by shooting into it and seeing whether anyone shot back. It killed a lot of civilians. This was the first time I had actually seen it done. I could see that the point liked doing it because it undoubtedly did seem safer for them than walking into what might be an ambush and maybe because for once, they were given a clear target to shoot at. But it was also obvious in cases like this that they were firing at someone's house, and they didn't do it unless they were told to. I had the feeling that this particular lieutenant was ordering it as much because his troops liked it as for any other reason. I asked him what if there happened to be a family inside. He said, "Tough shit. They know we're operating in this area, they can hear us, and they ought to be in their bunker. I'm not taking any unnecessary chances with my men."

It was true that virtually every hut in the area had some kind of bunker for the occupants, sometimes an underground shelter outside the hut, sometimes just a pile of sandbags in one corner inside the hut. Apparently this was for protection against air strikes, since there hadn't been ground operations in this area for a long time. There were usually even trenches outside to shelter the water buffalo or the pigs, if the family had any. It was also true that the men regarded the area we were walking through as especially hostile, a VC hamlet, because of its nearness to the ambush site we had attacked that morning. But in reality that was no more or less true for these huts than for all the others in the district.

After another empty hut had been shot up, I left the lieutenant, whom I was coming to dislike more and more, and moved over to the second platoon, which was making a parallel sweep a hundred yards away. It was commanded by a lieutenant whom I respected for following the book. I found his men covering one another in turn as they cautiously approached a hut and explored inside. Their orders were obviously not to fire unless fired upon, the right orders for a populated area. The platoon leader asked me what all the noise was from the third platoon. I told him, and he said, "That guy's an asshole. He always does that. I won't work with him unless I have to. He doesn't give a shit."

Half an hour later we finally came to a hut that wasn't empty. There were three small children and a baby in it, huddled on the floor in one corner. If there was a bunker anywhere, they hadn't been in it. The platoon leader said to me as we moved on, "Do you know why those kids are alive? There's only one reason. Because it was this platoon that came up to that hootch, and not the third."

The intermittent firing was still going on a hundred yards away, but now something else was added. The third platoon was setting fire to the huts. I had heard the operations officer brief the company commanders ten days earlier that there was to be no burning of huts. A couple of days after that I had taken an odd photograph, of an American soldier bayoneting a canteen, stabbing it with a look of great anger on his face. The company commander had just been requested by the platoon leader to allow the troops to burn down a particular hut we had come to, on the grounds that it was a "Vietcong house." The only evidence of that was that it contained this canteen—which actually happened to be an American one, perhaps captured from ARVN—and a photograph of someone in a uniform that was not familiar to our troops. They believed this showed that there must have been Vietcong soldiers in the hut, and they wanted to burn it. Permission was denied. Directives were not to burn any houses or we would antagonize the population, which would help the Vietcong. There was much swearing and stamping at the refusal, and this soldier was punching holes in the "enemy" canteen in a mood of frustration.

But now two huts, about fifty yards apart, were blazing across from us like burning barns. In almost two years in Vietnam this was another first for me. Before I ever came to Vietnam I'd seen Morley Safer's pictures of a marine lighting up a thatch roof with a Zippo, up north in I Corps two years earlier. It had given me a sick feeling, especially because it was a marine.

We crossed a road that led back to the base, and I decided to join a company that was marching along it at that moment, coming back from another operation. We walked past the third platoon on the way, and its leader, the barn burner, saw me and waved good-bye. Behind him one of his squads was busy at work trying to light a third hut. It was taking a while to catch. If the jungle around the huts had been less damp, he would have started a forest fire. He jerked his thumb at his men with their palm torches and yelled, "These are VC huts. Tonight they'll have to hump it in the rain, same as us!"

The men near him laughed. Once again he had given an order his troops liked. After a day spent plowing the sea, they were glad to be allowed at least to mark their passage. It was silly to think that burning huts would have any useful effect on the war in Rach Kien District or Long An Province, but it was the first thing they had done in two weeks that had any visible effect at all. It was the only sign they were able to leave that they had ever been there.

As soon as I got back to the village, I went to find the operations officer. I asked him, "When did you change the orders not to burn huts?" He said he hadn't changed the orders. I said, "Well, look," and pointed back to the area where the operation was still going on. Seven pillars of smoke in a line were rising into the sky.

"I queried the company on the radio when I saw that," he said. "They told me they were burning the thatch off enemy bunkers."

"They haven't made contact once in that sweep," I told him. "The third platoon is burning every hut it comes to."

He said, "Jesus Christ," and went off to the command post.

I had been twelve days in Rach Kien. I was ready to go. I picked up my gear, said good-bye to the battalion commander and other officers I ran into, and got into a chopper that was about to leave. As it rose in the air, tilted over, and headed for Long An, I counted, again, the seven columns of smoke hanging over the flooded fields. Several of them had drifted and tangled together, before they faded in the blue sky.

I heard later in Saigon that the battalion terminated the operation after a few more weeks and moved out of Rach Kien. I never saw a report on their success or if Rach Kien District, or village, was counted as pacified.

But about a year later, when I was back in the States, I saw a long article in the *New York Times Magazine* describing the difficulties of pacifying a VC district, Rach Kien. At first I thought it was reporting the operation I had been in. But it was about a different battalion, eight months later. All the problems and experiences sounded very familiar. The article said that Rach Kien had always been a Vietcong district up till then, and this was the first time American troops had tried to operate there.

11

Leaving Vietnam

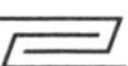

One night in mid-January 1967 Colonel Chau had me over to dinner at his house to meet his new boss at the Joint General Staff, General Ngo Dzu. That conversation too, following the practice General Lansdale had taught us, I reported to Deputy Ambassador Porter in a memo the next day. Dzu said that poor morale throughout ARVN stemmed from lack of confidence in and respect for top GVN leadership. Each level—from squad leader to division commander and above—saw that its superior officers were engaging in corrupt practices or political maneuverings and took this for license to do the same. Until there was reform at the top, the troops would continue to alienate the population by their practices of theft and maltreatment. These malpractices by both troops and officers, he said, reflected directly their feeling that "the long war, of which they have grown very tired, cannot be won by the type of national government and leadership now in place." I underlined that in my report, to express the intensity with which he said that, soberly, in the darkness at a candlelit table behind his house. Corruption, he went on, reflected this mood of despair. "When you see, from the nature of our leadership, that there is no hope of any progress, nothing you can achieve in your province or division, militarily or politically . . . you turn to doing what you can do, which is to take care of your family."

About a week later Colonel Chau came to my house to talk. I had just come back from observing an operation in the course of which I had explored a long VC tunnel. Evidently it was not empty, because at one point

I found smoking candle stubs, stuck into the fins of mortar shells, in which the wax was still liquid and hot. I decided not to go any farther. I brought the stubs back, along with some handwritten notes next to them that turned out to be love letters when I had them translated. I told Chau about the operation, and I said I had something to show him. I went up to my bedroom and brought down a pair of Ho Chi Minh sandals I had taken from the tunnel, the vulcanized rubber sandals with treaded soles cut from discarded truck tires, worn by the Vietcong and before them the Vietminh fighting the French.

His eyes lit up, and he took them from me. He held them in his hands and looked at them for a long time as if he were holding a baby. His face was soft, and when he spoke, it was in a tone I had never heard before. It was personal. He said, "I wore these for four years," meaning when he had been in the Vietminh in the late forties fighting the French. There was a long pause. I didn't say anything. He said, "They were the best years of my life."

After a while he put the sandals down and said, "You know, something I often ask myself is: I say that I left the Vietminh and joined Emperor Bao Dai and then President Diem because the Communists were too harsh, they didn't respect our religion or traditions, their way of development would be too hard for us, we needed help from the West. But is that really the truth? Or did I change sides because I was tired of living in tunnels and the jungle, I wanted to wear leather shoes and a good uniform and sleep in a bed, in a house? I often ask myself that."

I waited for him to go on, but he didn't say any more. I asked him, "What is your answer?"

He said, "I don't know."

In February I decided to make some inspection trips in the delta that I had been putting off over the last month. I visited several other provinces first, but what I was really looking forward to, the main purpose of my trip, was to go out with a unit from a Vietnamese division that, according to its American advisers, was carrying on an elaborate program of night patrols. I'd long since learned that no other unit did this, large or small, and it was a shortcoming fatal to any prospect of pacification. In the report of the roles and missions study the previous July, I'd written: "A particularly urgent need is for 'offensive' patrols and ambushes—i.e., located where intelligence indicates that contact is probable—*at night*. Unless RVNAF [Republic of Vietnam Armed Forces] night time operations begin at last to make it unsafe for the VC to move and enter hamlets at night, it is flatly impossible to sever their roots in the population and thence to destroy the guerrilla bands or reduce VC control."

"They've taken the night back from the Vietcong." That was the word about this division. I'd heard that line before, but people at MACV headquarters said this was the real thing; the advisory team had amazing rapport with an outstanding division commander, and this was really happening. I trusted the people who were saying this, the way they said it. I wanted to see it firsthand not because I had any doubts but because I wanted to find out how this miracle had come about and then spread the word.

Sure enough, at the division headquarters the colonel who was head of the advisory team had a large chart showing the number of night patrols sent out by each battalion in the division each week over the last several months. The numbers varied for the different battalions, and they fluctuated every week, but it was easy to see the trend that was summarized by curves on another chart. The number of patrols, starting at zero or close to it, had steadily climbed to where the division was putting out hundreds of patrols in a week, dozens every night. In two years in Vietnam I had never seen anything like it. The colonel was understandably proud. I wanted to hear the whole story of how he had brought this about, but that could wait till the next day. It was getting late in the afternoon, and I wanted to be sure I had time to get down to a battalion area where I could join a patrol that night. I went over to the large map where the patrolling zones were marked off with grease pencil for regiments and battalions, pointed to a particular regiment, and told the colonel my intention.

He seemed surprised at the idea, but I explained my background and my recent experience in Rach Kien. He could see that I was all ready, with all the gear I needed. He already knew my rank, and he didn't argue with me. But he said he wasn't sure it could be arranged on such short notice. It was all the better to do it so informally, I said. This wasn't an official inspection; it would just make a much more impressive story to be able to pick out one among dozens of patrols at random, go out with them, and then describe the difference it made in the countryside to have a Vietnamese division actually operating at night. I'd never heard of another Vietnamese unit where you could do that, and the sooner we got this story out, the better.

He saw the point, but he said that it wouldn't be convenient at this particular moment for me to visit the regiment I had picked out on the map. He was vague about the reasons. Maybe it would work out better to put this off till my next trip. But I wasn't sure when I could get down again, and I had been looking forward to this, a success story at last. I pressed him to let me go to another regiment, and after some calls on the radio he sent me off to a regimental command post a mile away.

There the regimental adviser had the same hesitations about sending me down to a battalion. I understood their reservations. For all I said that this wasn't an inspection, I was from the embassy, and no troop commander, or adviser, was going to feel entirely easy about an unwarned, unplanned-for observation of one of their units in action. Who could say what might happen, or what that one unit would look like on this particular night, or who might hear about it? So I wasn't surprised to be told again that it was too short notice, that it wasn't clear that it could be arranged, but I wasn't easily discouraged. I leaned on him with a clear conscience; I knew that I wasn't there to embarrass them. I didn't care about the quality of the operations. As far as I was concerned, the story was that they were taking place at all, that Vietnamese troops were walking out beyond the battalion perimeter at night.

There was in fact a problem with all this, as I eventually learned at the battalion command post, to which I was finally sent, arriving just as it was getting dark. The American, a major who advised a battalion, showed me a map with the actual routes of the patrols for that night. When he learned that I was there to go out on one of these, he told me that it wouldn't be possible. I asked why, and this time I got a straight answer. The patrols on the map weren't actually going to happen. There weren't really any night patrols. Not in that battalion and not, as far as the major knew, anywhere else in the division.

What about all the statistics and patrol zones and lists on all those charts at division and regimental headquarters? Made up. Under pressure from the division adviser and his Vietnamese counterpart, the general commanding the division, every battalion made patrol plans every single day and sent the reports and figures up the line, but they couldn't get the Vietnamese companies actually to send troops out to walk in the darkness in VC country. It wasn't clear if anyone had ever really tried to get them to do it.

The colonel at division got figures to put on his charts. Hundreds of patrols a week. Not one was taking place. Not ten, not fifty. Zero. There was nothing for me to accompany. I thanked the major for his candor, which was not uncommon at his level, though it could have got him into trouble. But I felt like an idiot. Got me again. I was like Charlie Brown the eleventh time he's kicked at empty air. I didn't think I was that easy to fool at this point in my life. What was it that had brought me all the way down here without a doubt in my mind till I heard the bad news from the major? It was the way people had said, "This is the real thing. This is really happening. For once it's not bullshit," as if they'd really known. Presumably they hadn't known; I didn't think they had consciously kidded me. What fooled them? It must have been the detail of the reporting, the effort that went into it.

Did the colonel know? I found I didn't care. A year earlier I would have felt it was my job to go back to the division HQ to inform him—if he really didn't know—or confront him, but that wasn't why I had come down this time. I sat up for a while talking with the major, slept on a cot he offered me, and the next day I drove back to Saigon.

I was tired of learning and reporting the same things time after time in forty-three separate provinces. I was tired of exposing lies about ARVN and pacification. I was pretty much free to decide what I did. What occurred to me to do was to go back to working with American troops, observing, the way I did at Rach Kien. I had an excuse to do it; there were plenty of different types of American operations and units to observe in line with my job of evaluating pacification for the deputy ambassador. I could start up at the DMZ in the north and work my way down the length of South Vietnam, observing one unit after another.

I started on this agenda in a week or two by an uneventful day with an ARVN unit in the north near the DMZ. A few days later, working south, I visited a program that sounded interesting near Da Nang. The adviser was a marine lieutenant colonel, William Corson, who had invented what he called CAPs, combined action platoons. They were squads of which two-thirds of the men were Vietnamese and one-third American marines. The squad leader was Vietnamese, with a marine deputy. The troops were supposed to learn enough of each other's language so that they could communicate with each other in a basic way.

It was, in the small, what LBJ had proposed in the way of combining Vietnamese and American units back in 1965. The army leadership had wanted no part of it then. It wanted American units to be able to operate independently of the Vietnamese, in whom it didn't put much stock. It assumed the Vietnamese units were all penetrated by Vietcong intelligence anyway, and it didn't want any American units parceled out in what it thought would be mainly a training role.

But Corson's idea, which he explained to me that afternoon, was that both sides would contribute strengths. The Vietnamese obviously knew the territory and the people. The marines would learn from them and would train their counterparts in tactical skills just by example. Their presence would assure the Vietnamese of good fire support, air and artillery, which the marines could call in from American bases. Above all, thanks to the marine presence, the patrols actually did operate at night.

So that night I was walking in darkness with Vietnamese troops, a first in my experience. There were four other Americans in the squad walking along paddy dikes in the dark of the moon. We had been told at a briefing that ARVN intelligence had reported that five hundred Vietcong were crossing the area we were patrolling. That was not a casual piece of information or a common report, so we were very alert.

Sometime after midnight we settled into a paddy to spend several hours in an ambush. We were off the dike, sitting in water amid the rice leaves. (The rice paddies in Vietnam were fertilized with human excrement. When I came down with hepatitis a few weeks later, I remembered this night.) I was looking one way, and a Vietnamese squad member was just behind me, looking the other. We each seemed to feel confident that the other would stay awake and alert, guarding each other and the rest. It was a close feeling. For a while we even rested our backs against each other, a lot closer than American and Vietnamese troops usually got. Just before dawn we moved back to the base.

We hadn't made any contact, and it didn't seem likely that the report of a big Vietcong movement had been accurate. But the other CAP out that night had been shot up in an ambush as it moved through a hamlet. I went to talk with the Vietnamese squad leader, one of the wounded. He was lying on a canvas cot, heavily bandaged, but he could talk.

I had been well impressed with the rapport of the Vietnamese and Americans that night; Corson's theory seemed to me to work out very well. But this squad leader had a different story. He spoke in Vietnamese through an interpreter, but it was easy to hear bitterness in his voice. The Americans didn't really listen to the Vietnamese, he said. Apparently an American had been leading the patrol. When the squad leader tried to tell him something, the marine didn't pay any attention.

I asked him through the interpreter, "What did you try to tell him?" He raised himself up from the cot on an elbow and spoke some words to me. I couldn't make them out, though it didn't sound to me like Vietnamese. I asked him to repeat it, and he did, slowly and distinctly, but it was still gibberish to me. I asked the interpreter, "What language is he speaking?"

The interpreter said, "English."

I asked him if he had understood it, and he said no. I asked him to find out in Vietnamese what the man was saying and tell me. They exchanged sentences in Vietnamese. The interpreter, who spoke good English, translated for me: "We are walking into an ambush."

I said, "Hmm," and asked the squad leader how he had known that. He said, through the interpreter, that as they approached a hamlet, "No dogs were barking. And there was no light." At that time of night, he explained, they should have seen some lanterns or fires in the huts through doorways or windows, and some dogs should have been out chasing them and barking. The silence and darkness meant to him that the doors and windows were shut and someone was muzzling the dogs inside. Vietcong were waiting for them. But when he tried to tell the American sergeant that there was an ambush ahead, the marine just ignored him and went on ahead as if he hadn't said anything. That's the way the Americans always were, he said. So when the firing broke out, they had suffered three wounded, and they were lucky to get away alive.

I told the interpreter, and later I told Corson, that I thought I had identified a real problem. The language training needed work and perhaps more focus. There were certain phrases in particular they should really get down very reliably, and an interpreter should check everyone out for comprehension of them. "We are walking into an ambush" was one of these. It was especially important that the Vietnamese could say that with a good American accent, since they were the ones likely to use it. In fact, this incident illustrated the strength of Corson's concept, of Americans working closely with Vietnamese, if they could get on top of the communication problem. It was a rare case when I was able to praise a program, when I got back to MACV, though they weren't very anxious to hear it. They still had no interest in wasting U.S. troops alongside Vietnamese.

Within weeks of going out on night patrol I came down with hepatitis. It came on me when I was taking a week's leave at Pattaya, a beach in Thailand I'd visited with Patricia the year before. I lay on my back in a nursing home in Bangkok for a month, till I could be flown back to my own bed in Saigon, where I lay for another month. By that time pacification was being reorganized, put under MACV and Westmoreland at last, but with a civilian head, Bob Komer from the NSC. If I'd stayed on, I would probably have been a deputy or assistant to Komer, an old friend of mine from Rand days and Washington. But the need to recuperate would keep me out of the field for at least six months. In those circumstances I decided to return to research in the States. Harry Rowen had become president of Rand, and he was anxious to have me back.

Lying on my back with a typewriter perched on my stomach, I spent my time in bed writing long memos summing up what I'd learned about why we weren't going anywhere as things were and how we might conceivably do better. These were for the Mission Council, my civilian and military colleagues in Saigon, so I didn't suggest we just find a way out, what I had personally favored for almost a year. I was saving that advice for Washington, when I got back. People here couldn't decide that, couldn't effectively even suggest it. They'd been sent to do their best, to make the most of it, so I focused on ways we could do *better* than we'd been doing, reducing obstacles to improvement, without putting new ones in the way of getting out.

One long memo proposed a reorientation of the overall pacification priorities and effort for 1967. But my major effort was a thirty-eight-page, single-spaced paper on U.S. stakes in the coming elections in Vietnam and why our policy should change from exclusive backing for military candidates, Ky or Nguyen Van Thieu, to encouraging, or simply permitting, their replacement by respected civilian leaders. As an outstanding Vietnamese journalist, Ton That Thien, had put it to me, the leadership that the country needed had to have respect, and "for a government to be respected, it must be respectable." Air Force General Ky, currently serving as premier (by support of the other generals and the Americans), could hardly be further from meeting that criterion. Vietnamese saw him as immature, lacking in strong nationalistic instincts, a playboy, promiscuous, narrowly educated, undignified, impulsive, only sporadically "serious." And flamboyant (commonly visiting the countryside in a black nylon flying suit with a lavender scarf and a pearl-handled revolver, on which was engraved the name of his mistress). This in a Confucian culture giving highest values to age, dignity, maturity, education, and virtuous example. As Thien said, for America to favor or support a Ky—at the time I wrote this, the only choice of the mission for the presidency—as symbolic chief of state was seen by him and by a wide range of Vietnamese as an insult, a gesture of contempt.

But personality and appearance were the least of it. Ky was a northerner, a military man, a former French officer lacking any record of patriotic opposition to the French, widely believed to owe his position to American support. All in all, I suggested, "It is a challenging exercise to imagine just how one could change or add to this set of properties to invent a *less* acceptable, more alien figure for the role of national leader in Vietnam."

As for General Thieu, Ky's chief military rival for the candidacy, his liabilities were only marginally less than Ky's. He wasn't a northerner, but he was still from Central Vietnam, not the South, and he added to his list of liabilities by being a Catholic. He was more dignified, I acknowledged, more mature, more experienced and prudent than Ky, yet for other reasons these qualities didn't assure him more public confidence. "Where Ky fails to gain the instinctive trust and respect of the Vietnamese because he is so 'different' in Vietnamese cultural terms, Thieu fails their trust because he is simply regarded as untrustworthy": conspiratorial, sly, "too clever," an impression strengthened by his role in the coups that had displaced a number of his predecessors. "Above all, as he himself admits, Thieu shares with Ky the political burden of being a military man; as he is reported to have remarked some weeks ago, 'The Vietnamese people are weary of military rule.'" I quoted a young Constituent Assembly member: "Give us anything. Young, old, I don't care, Central, Southern, Northern: just as long as he's not military."

The next thirty single-spaced pages argued in detail why there would be no real prospect of any sort of lasting progress in South Vietnam, civil or military, without a drastic change in the character of government at the top. The upcoming election was the best opportunity in years to bring this about peacefully, if the generals could be induced by the United States to allow an election that did not guarantee the victory of one of them by coercion and manipulation.

Of the many Vietnamese I quoted anonymously in the paper, Tran Ngoc Chau had had the most influence on my thinking, partly by introducing me to others. I gave it to him to look over. A week later he mentioned that he had shown it to Thieu, who had been a friend of his for many years. I was lying in bed, not supposed to make sudden movements. That jerked me upright in horror. I said, "What? How could you do that?"

Chau said, "He loved it. I was sure he would. He read every word. He said he didn't know there was any American in Vietnam who understood Vietnamese attitudes so well."

"But good God, Chau, what I said about him!"

Chau said, "Oh, no problem. He was so happy at what you said about Ky he didn't mind what you said about him."

The morning Komer was due to arrive I went over to the embassy to greet him. I had just been up for a few days after two months in bed. I was in his office talking to some of the staff when his plane touched down at Tan Son Nhut, and we listened on Armed Forces Radio to his press conference just after he got off the plane. He was very assertive about the progress in Vietnam and pacification he had observed from Washington and spoke of how high his expectations were of continuing it to the point of success. It was the way McNamara talked, and LBJ and Westmoreland, but none with Komer's tone of exuberance. I knew from statements I had read in the press that he was always very aggressive and antagonistic with reporters, hammering down any doubters, but I had never heard his public manner live before. It worried me. He sounded as if he might actually believe he was telling the truth.

It was easy to tell when he'd arrived at the embassy; you could hear him barking greetings on the lower floor. He had earned a reputation for putting on pressure, getting things done, and he loved his nickname, Blowtorch. I could hear him as he came up the stairs and burst into his outer office. He shook hands and slapped the backs of people in the room. He sounded just as he had on the radio, loud and optimistic. He was whirling, filling the room with energy and enthusiasm. I told him I had come to say hello and good-bye, and he nodded and said, "Come on in, Dan," as he strode into the next room and shut the door behind us. He sat down behind the desk and leaned back, grinning.

I said, "Bob, did you believe any of that stuff you were saying at the airport?"

He leaned forward with his elbows on the desk and held his head in his hands. He looked down at the desk and closed his eyes. He seemed exhausted. He said softly, "Dan, do you think I'm crazy?"

After a silence I asked, "Bob, why did you take this job?"

He sat up. He said, "That's what my wife asks me. She keeps asking it: 'Why are you going over there now? Why don't you just refuse? Leave the government if you have to.' I keep telling her, 'When the president of the United States says he wants you to do something, you just don't say no to him. When he says you're the one who's got to do this, the one he wants, you've got to do it, no matter how hopeless it is.'"

A few days later I left Vietnam.

PART II

SECRETS

12

Jaundice

I had decided, on my return from Vietnam, to return to Rand rather than to the Pentagon. A major reason was that I wanted to be free again to tell what I knew and what I believed about our Vietnam policy to officials across the board in government agencies without having to worry if I was contradicting the position of a boss or a department. I had been closer to that in Vietnam, under the very loose supervision of Lansdale and Porter, than under McNaughton in Defense, where I'd had to be as circumspect as John himself in concealing my own views when they diverged from McNamara's. After three years of largely listening and learning, I believed that I knew things about the situation in Vietnam worth passing on in my own voice, as I had done on nuclear planning and command and control at Rand. Rand was the perfect institutional base for that. It wasn't the public at large I wanted to talk to. It was still people with clearances, people with responsibility for making or advising on national security policy. As a Rand analyst I could come into a variety of offices as a consultant and say what I thought in a way I could never have done as a government official representing a particular department or agency and its official views, with a boss I could embarrass by talking out of turn.

In the week I spent in Washington signing out of State, I made appointments with a number of people to express my thoughts on where we were in Vietnam and what we should do. I spent an hour with McNamara in his office in the Pentagon. Toward the end of that I handed him a short memo I'd written criticizing our current support for Thieu and Ky in the upcoming Vietnamese elections and raising the possibility of clearing the way for a civilian candidate who would be willing to seek peace by negotiating with the NLF, which he read in front of me.

McNamara said that he basically agreed with me but that political policy like this was really in Rusk's area, and he wasn't taking it on. He said he was concentrating on another issue. From the newspapers I knew that Senator John Stennis was scheduling public hearings to give the JCS a platform to press its case for an expansion of the war and particularly for taking restraints off the targets and scale of the bombing of the North. I said, "Putting a lid on the bombing?" He nodded. I said, well, nothing could be more important than that, and I wished him success as I left.

I didn't know it at the time, but two months earlier Robert McNamara had promoted a negotiated exit strategy. His draft memo to the president was marked "Top Secret-Sensitive," and even so, circulated to the JCS, it evoked a storm of protest that marked the beginning of the end of his influence with the president and of his tenure. I was not aware during our meeting of just how much our views were in sync, but I would not have been surprised.

The day before I had talked about negotiations with Chet Cooper, a CIA intelligence officer on the NSC staff who was now working as an aide to Ambassador Averell Harriman. Cooper had for some time been trying to set up negotiations with North Vietnam, and Harriman later served as the U.S. negotiator in the Paris talks. I was frank with Cooper, and he knew my views when he urged me to talk with Harriman the next day. That seemed to confirm my guess that Harriman, like Cooper, was on my wavelength. I was after all proposing a negotiation and an interim settlement much like that for Laos in 1962, and it had been Harriman who had conducted that negotiation for Kennedy and been a strong advocate of the coalition arrangement against Defense Department and CIA skeptics. So I was as frank with Harriman as with Cooper.

Maybe too frank. Kai Bird, the biographer of the Bundy brothers, came across Harriman's reaction to our meeting in his private files, in a transcribed excerpt of a telephone conversation between Harriman and Cooper on July 27: "H: 'I saw that fellow you wanted me to see. I was unimpressed. He is in a very sour mood. To him everything is black, no sun in anything. I think I brought out his innermost thoughts and they went so far that he himself came around to the other direction. I don't think he talks to many people bluntly enough. He went so far that he was about as far out in one direction as some of our friends are out in the other. You have to get some balance some place. He has had hepatitis so I think that contributes to his attitude.'"

Harriman was mistaken to think that I didn't speak as bluntly to everyone who asked to hear me as I had to him. But he wasn't the only one who regarded my observations as jaundiced, whether or not they attributed it to my liver disorder. A day or two later I gave my wrap-up to Murray Gell-Mann, who would later win the Nobel Prize in physics, and several of his fellow scientific advisers to the Defense Department. I was to be followed by George Carver, head of the Vietnam Task Force in the CIA, who for the last year had been singing in the same key as Walt Rostow. After hearing my comments, sitting next to me in a small room in the E-ring of the Pentagon, Carver started off defensively: "I don't know what *our* [CIA] men in the field may have been smoking, but they have a different story to tell from Dan's." He went through the litany of MACV's signs of encouragement in the latest developments. "The VC are scraping the bottom of the barrel in their recruiting, they're running out of manpower, they're recruiting fourteen-year-olds. . . ."

I got impatient listening to this. Gell-Mann turned to me when Carver was done and asked if I had any comments. I went down the list, pointing out that every piece of this good news had cheered up the French long ago. "They've been beating the U.S. and our allies with fourteen-year-olds as long as we've been there. . . ." I was mad. Maybe it *was* my liver. I said, "I don't know what your men in the field are smoking, but I know that horseshit like this has been the opiate of Washington for twenty years."

Somewhat embarrassed, the scientists got up to go to another meeting.

Over at State, Bill Bundy, who was in charge of Far East, seemed to agree with everything I was saying about our prospects in Vietnam. It was the end of the day, and he was friendly but very tired, low-energy. On my proposal to use the Vietnamese election that fall as a way of getting out gracefully, he said it was too late to change our policy on that. As for getting out of the war in general, he said, "I don't think we can have any movement till after the election." He was referring not to the election in Vietnam but to ours, in 1968.

I said, "But that's a year away!"

He sighed and shook his head sadly. "I know, but I just don't think Hanoi will get serious about negotiating till they see who they're dealing with after next November." We both knew, I didn't have to say it, that

Hanoi would get serious quickly enough if we started talking about our getting out rather than their giving up or about power sharing in Saigon.

I took for granted (perhaps mistakenly) that his talking about *Vietnamese* calculations as slowing the prospects up was just a euphemistic way of saying that LBJ wouldn't decide to lose Vietnam before he got reelected. An assistant secretary of state couldn't say that directly, even in private. In his tone of voice I also heard him say that he wasn't going to try to buck that; it just wasn't worth it for him. I could understand that, since he was probably right about LBJ. What bothered me, shocked me really, was how relaxed he seemed about his forecast, how easily resigned he was to the prospect of another year of war, along with the risk, always, that it would get even larger if it went on.

I knew I could expect a very different mood from Walt Rostow. Formerly head of the policy planning staff in State, he was now in the White House, McGeorge Bundy's successor as assistant to the president for national security. I'd last seen Rostow just before I left for Vietnam, in August 1965. The bombing of the North that he had proposed four years earlier had been under way since March, and a hundred thousand more U.S. troops, the first installment of the new open-ended troop commitment, had just set out for South Vietnam. Rostow had been ready to celebrate the capitulation of the NLF. He had told me then, "Dan, it looks very good. What we hear is that the Vietcong are already coming apart under the bombing. They're going to collapse within weeks. Not months, weeks."

Two years later I didn't plan to remind him of that, but others told me that his mood hadn't changed. I was determined not to argue pacification or progress in the field with him. From all I'd heard, he was impervious to bad news, or rather, he was buoyed up by it, by any news at all. I didn't even bother to bring my recent province reports with me.

I was hardly inside his office in the West Wing before Walt wanted to share with me his enthusiasm for the progress he was reporting to the president in pacification and in the military field. He said it was clear we had finally turned the corner. "The other side is near collapse. In my opinion, victory is very near." I said that I really wanted to talk with him about the political situation. He said, "But, Dan, you've got to see the latest charts. I've got them right here. The charts are very good, Dan. Victory is very near."

Even to be polite, even to get a hearing on other matters, I couldn't sit for that. I said, "Walt, I don't want to see your charts. I've just come back from Vietnam. Victory is *not* near. Victory is not on the way."

I don't recall how the discussion went after that. I didn't stalk out, he didn't show me the door, and I managed not to see the charts, but the session didn't last long. Still, it ended less abruptly than a meeting that John Vann had with Walt a year later, after the Tet offensive. An appointment to see the president had been arranged for him, but Rostow had asked to talk with him first. John at the time was expressing a lot more optimism than many other people, including me, but he wasn't talking about victory; he was talking about our ability to avoid defeat. He told me that very quickly Rostow began to get restive. Finally Walt said, "Look, I think the war will be over by the end of the year."

Feeling flippant, John said with a straight face, "Oh, no, I think we can hold out longer than that."

Rostow looked at him and got up and left the room. Vann waited for him to come back, but a little later an aide told John that the president wouldn't be able to see him after all.

By mid-1967, for most of a decade I had been primarily engaged, in my own mind, in learning about government decision making in hopes of helping the president, and the rest of the government, make *better,* less dangerous or misguided, decisions in situations of conflict and uncertainty. Vietnam was a preeminent example of the room—indeed the urgent need—for improvement. After two years there I thought I had identified at least part of the problem and a possible answer to it: a conscious effort by high officials to circumvent internal lying and deception. I saw two ways of doing that: to bypass it and to punish it.

What I saw as a major "lesson of Vietnam" was the impact on policy failures of internal practices of lying to superiors, tacitly encouraged by those superiors, but resulting in a cognitive failure at the presidential level to recognize realities. This was part of a broader cognitive failure of the bureaucracy I had come to suspect. There were situations—Vietnam was an example—in which the U.S. government, starting ignorant, did not, would not *learn.* There was in Vietnam a whole set of what amounted to institutional "antilearning" mechanisms working to preserve and guarantee unadaptive and unsuccessful behavior. There was the fast turnover in personnel and the lack of institutional memory at any level. Rach Kien was a perfect example: a battalion commander with no infantry experience who had scarcely met his company commanders when they went into combat together; an operation eight months later in the same paddies that was not even aware American troops had ever visited them before. As Tran Ngoc Chau said to me in 1968, "You Americans feel you have been fighting this war for seven years. You have not. You have been fighting it for one year, seven times." There was a general failure to study history or to analyze or even to record operational experience, especially mistakes. Above all, effective pressures for optimistically false reporting at every level, for describing "progress" rather than problems or failure, concealed the very need for change in approach or for learning.

When I returned to Washington in the summer of 1967, I found that McNamara had launched a historical study of Vietnam decision making. Mentioning a pioneering investigation for President Kennedy of a high-level policy-making fiasco as a guideline, the secretary of defense had assigned the project to John McNaughton in my old department, International Security Affairs, which Paul Warnke was scheduled to take over in July.

McNaughton had given the task to his deputy, Mort Halperin, who put his own deputy, Leslie Gelb, in charge of it. Gelb had been a graduate student under Henry Kissinger at Harvard and, like Halperin, had assisted Kissinger in courses. He had come to the Pentagon from being a legislative assistant to Jacob Javits, the Republican senior senator from New York.

The McNamara study had been launched with a series of questions to which the secretary wanted answers. In choosing researchers, Gelb had suggested the historical studies as a more comprehensive response. He and Halperin wanted people with analytical skills, an ability to see patterns and propose lessons learned. He also wanted people, if possible, who either had served in Vietnam (neither Halperin nor Gelb had visited the country) or had taken part in the decision process on Vietnam in Washington. I fit all three of those criteria, so I was among the first they approached. I agreed to help them draft one volume in hopes that would give me eventual access to the whole study for a comparative analysis and search for patterns, which was what really interested me.

Gelb showed me the work space he was organizing. A large room near the secretary's suite, with an array of desks for researchers, was being lined with four-drawer top secret file safes. They were already filled, or being filled, with cables and papers on Vietnam from a generation of officials in all parts of the government. Gelb told me I could choose any subject or period that I wanted to work on. To minimize my own effort in turning out a study, I could very naturally have chosen 1964–65, the period I had worked for McNaughton in Washington, where I had witnessed the decision making firsthand. Instead I chose the Kennedy decision making of 1961, a period of which I knew little and wanted to know more. As I've described earlier, my first visit to Saigon had been in the fall of 1961, shortly before the Taylor-Rostow mission. What we had heard then about the regime of President Ngo Dinh Diem seemed extremely unpromising as a basis for any greatly increased U.S. involvement. I was glad at that time to see that President Kennedy had shortly thereafter rejected proposals I had heard in Saigon to send American combat units, though he did, understandably, continue to provide support to a Catholic anti-Communist leader and to increase it in what seemed like moderate ways.

I wasn't really surprised by this back in 1961, though I thought it was moving us in the wrong direction. What did surprise me were the official reasons given for his choices. Kennedy said he was following closely the recommendations of Walt Rostow and Maxwell Taylor, two of his top advisers, whom he had sent to Saigon personally to assess the situation and in particular to judge the necessity of sending U.S. ground forces. Upon returning from the trip, General Taylor and his team had reportedly concluded that South Vietnam's military resources, with the addition of marginal American supplements, were adequate to deal with the insurgency. "I have great confidence in the military capability of South Vietnam to cope with anything within its border," Taylor said, and to "defend the country against conventional attack." On his return, the *New York Times* reported, "Officials said that it was correct to infer . . . that General Taylor did not look favorably on the sending of United States combat troops at this time. . . . While opposing the sending of American combat forces, General Taylor is understood to favor the dispatch of necessary military technicians. . . ."

From all that I'd heard in Saigon on my first visit, that was malarkey. I could understand it as a public rationale for not sending troops. But could the president really allow the public to be reassured like that about the situation he was getting deeper into if he'd heard anything like what I had? And had he or hadn't he? Taylor and Rostow must have been talking to exactly the same people in MAAG that I had spoken with only a few weeks earlier. His team had to have heard the same briefings, read the same reports. How could they have concluded, how could they have told the president, that advisers alone, with helicopters and specialists, would turn that situation around?

I don't think it occurred to me in 1961 that the White House might be lying about what the president had been told. From my own experience as a consultant in the Pentagon, it was easy for me to suppose that for some bureaucratic reasons the president's representatives had been misled. Or if not lied to, they must at least have heard from people of very different opinions from the ones I had talked to.

I too thought we shouldn't send troops, but not out of optimism, just the opposite. On whether an open-ended commitment of U.S. combat forces could ever ultimately win the war—if costs, risks, and casualties were no consideration—there was disagreement in Saigon. But one clear lesson I drew from what I'd heard was that military advisers and support units alone—just what Kennedy was sending—would definitely *not* be adequate. Why would the same majors and colonels who had just spoken so candidly to me have told an entirely different story to Maxwell Taylor? Could they have fooled him that badly even if they wanted to? Or could he have wanted to mislead the president?

The hypothesis I brought in the fall of 1967 to the data on 1961 was the familiar one from accounts of the whole period up till then, including those by David Halberstam and Arthur M. Schlesinger, Jr. This was essentially the quagmire model; that optimistic operational reporting plus ill-founded assurances from advisers in Washington, especially military ones, had confirmed for President Kennedy, mistakenly, the adequacy of the course he chose. Referring initially to the 1961 decision to send advisers, Schlesinger wrote: "This was the policy of 'one more step'—each new step always promising the success which the previous last step had also promised but had unaccountably failed to deliver." Extending this to subsequent years, Schlesinger asserted, "Each step in the deepening of the American commitment was reasonably regarded at the time as the last that would be necessary. Yet in retrospect, each step led only to the next, until we find ourselves entrapped today in that nightmare of American strategists, a land war in Asia—a war which no President, including President Johnson, desired or intended."

Before I had read these documents, this sounded plausible. It was the point of view with which I began my work on the McNamara study project—or, as it eventually became known, the Pentagon Papers. I knew from my own experience in the Pentagon that Schlesinger, like many others, was mistaken to rely on this same explanation for President Johnson's escalations in 1965. But I imagined as of 1967 that the 1964–65 period had been an exceptional crisis of pessimism.

After all, from my own field experience in the years immediately following, it was hard not to suppose that President Johnson was being misled by the wildly misleading, rose-colored reports of progress that I knew were being fed upward to Walt Rostow's and Bob Komer's White House offices, which would hardly have supplied a compensating filter for the president. The effect of this widely held inference was greatly to reduce the burden of responsibility, or blame, for an inadequate and failing policy attributed to each of the presidents and to place it on their advisers, particularly those in the military, and on their defective perceptions and reporting, a systemic cognitive failure. The solution seemed to be to find ways to get better information to the president ("If the czar only knew . . . !"), as I had already tried to do by my direct briefings and my advice on how to learn to McNamara and Komer and the ambassadors in Saigon.

I knew from journalistic accounts that reassuring operational reporting and optimistic military proposals of the sort I myself had witnessed in 1966–67 had likewise been characteristic of 1962–63, of the late 1950s, and of earlier in the French command in the period just before Dien Bien Phu. None of these happened to be years in which major decisions to escalate were taken, but like many other analysts, I assumed this pattern of optimistic deception or self-deception flowing upward to be true, as well, of our critical years of commitment (except for 1965). These included Truman's decision to support the French effort directly in 1950, Eisenhower's commitment to Diem in 1954, and Kennedy's decision to break through the Geneva ceiling on U.S. advisers in 1961.

Within a month of working from the files in the McNamara study offices, I had discovered that this assumption was mistaken. Every one of these crucial decisions was secretly associated with realistic internal pessimism, deliberately concealed from the public, just as in 1964–65.

I began by sifting through the Pentagon documents and the National Intelligence Estimates relating to Indochina, which I requested and received from the CIA, for the years 1950–60, before moving on to 1961. What was evident in each one of the years of major decision was that the president's choice was *not* founded upon optimistic reporting or on assurances of the success of his chosen course. Contrary to nearly all public accounts, neither of these elements was present for Truman in 1950 or for Eisenhower in 1954–55. Nor were they present for Kennedy in 1961, any more than for Johnson in 1965. There were indeed periods of wishful optimism before or *between* the years of decision. But they could never account for the subsequent escalation, which was always immediately preceded and accompanied by a breakthrough of gloomy realism, including an internal consensus that the new commitment the president was choosing would probably be inadequate for success. In this light, the actual pattern of escalation seemed all the more mysterious.

I chose to look at 1961 because I had always been puzzled about Kennedy's choice in Vietnam that fall. What was he led to believe? What was his understanding of what he was starting then? I was looking for an explanation of the apparent contradiction between what I had heard and seen in September 1961 and what Taylor and his team, according to the press accounts and official statements, had concluded in October: supposedly that the measures Kennedy approved in November would be adequate. That contradiction dissolved as soon as I held in my hands Taylor's actual, personal recommendations to the president and the judgments on which he based them. The press accounts of the time had simply been wrong. The official statements were lies.

Maxwell Taylor had not advised the president that the program he ended up approving would be adequate, even in the short run, even to avert defeat, let alone to win. Also, Taylor had not recommended against combat troops. Just the opposite. In a top secret cable "Eyes Only for the President," he not only recommended the introduction of a U.S. military force into South Vietnam "without delay" but also said that he had "reached the conclusion that this is an *essential* action if we are to reverse the present downward trend of events. . . . In fact, I do not believe that our program to save SVN will succeed without it."

He was recommending an initial force of six to eight thousand troops, but with a clear recognition that many more could follow: "Although U.S. prestige is already engaged in SVN, it will become more so by the sending of troops. If the first contingent is not enough to accomplish the necessary results, it will be difficult to resist the pressure to reinforce. If the ultimate result sought is the closing of the frontiers and the clean-up of the insurgents within SVN, there is no limit to our possible commitment (unless we attack the source in Hanoi)."

Nor was he alone in his recommendation of ground troops or his other judgments: that they were essential to avert victory of the Communists, that sending moderate forces initially might lead ultimately to engaging very large U.S. forces and even to war with China, but that without sending any combat units, all the other measures proposed (those that Kennedy adopted and announced) would be inadequate to prevent defeat. As Secretary of Defense McNamara wrote in a memo to the president a few days later, speaking for himself, his deputy, Roswell Gilpatric, and the Joint Chiefs of Staff: "The chances are against, probably sharply against, preventing [the fall of South Vietnam to communism] by any measures short of the introduction of U.S. forces on a substantial scale. We accept General Taylor's judgment that the various measures proposed by him short of this are useful but will not in themselves do the job of restoring confidence and setting Diem on the way to winning his fight."

Nor, according to McNamara and the JCS, would the initial eight thousand combat troops be enough to "tip the scales decisively." They recommended—as did Taylor and Rostow—that the United States "commit itself to the clear objective of preventing the fall of South Vietnam to Communism," and accompany this commitment and the initial troops with "a warning through some channel to Hanoi that continued support of the Viet Cong will lead to punitive retaliation against North Vietnam. If we act in this way, the ultimate possible extent of our military commitment must be faced. The struggle may be prolonged, and Hanoi and Peiping [Beijing] may intervene overtly. . . . I believe we can assume that the maximum U.S. forces required on the ground in Southeast Asia will not exceed 6 divisions, or about 205,000 men."

In retrospect, that was an underestimate—we had put that many in South Vietnam by early 1966, even though China had not intervened, and we still weren't winning two years later, when we had sent almost three times as many—but it was not a *small* figure.

The same recommendations, on the same grounds, had the support of McGeorge Bundy, special assistant to the president for national security, and his brother William Bundy, then acting assistant secretary of defense for international security affairs, who had dealt with the Geneva Conference and its aftermath when he was in the CIA. That was a consensus of every high-level national security official, with the single exception of Secretary of State Rusk.

Rusk's reservation about sending troops was not that they weren't necessary or that the decision could safely be postponed, but that under Diem at least, it wasn't clear that *even* U.S. troops would make the difference. In a cable from Japan, he warned Kennedy: "If Diem unwilling trust military commanders to get job done and take steps to consolidate non-communist elements into serious national effort, difficult to see how handful American troops can have decisive influence. While attaching greatest possible importance to security in SEA [Southeast Asia], I would be reluctant to see U.S. make major additional commitment American prestige to a losing horse."

Rusk's first sentence, in effect, specified (realistically, in retrospect) two more conditions that were essential to success. Also, Rusk was indicating that in the absence of these changes in the regime (which looked unlikely and were indeed unmet) Diem looked like a "losing horse" whatever the

United States did. Rusk's deputy, Undersecretary of State George Ball, argued the same point even more forcefully.

In sum, what I found in my search of the 1961 documents for the McNamara study was that not a single one of Kennedy's military or civilian advisers had told him that the program of advisers and support units he announced in mid-November would be adequate to stop the deteriorating trend in South Vietnam even in the short run, let alone to bring ultimate success.

Well, that answered one question. Taylor and his team had not heard in Saigon, and hadn't told the president, anything different from what I'd heard a few weeks earlier about the prevailing situation and prospects in Vietnam. The official statements and news stories about their judgments and recommendations, and about their view that advisers would be adequate, had simply been false. Why the administration had lied about these matters wasn't hard to explain either. If the president, rejecting the nearly unanimous advice of his senior officials, was going to send advisers and support units but no more than these, it wouldn't be helpful to tell the truth about the actual judgments he'd heard on the ineffectiveness of this program or the urgent recommendations he'd received to do more.

All this raised a new puzzle. Faced with these recommendations and judgments, how in the world could Kennedy have done just what he did, not more and not less? None of the documents I found answered this challenge; instead they posed it acutely. At the same time, they demolished Schlesinger's "quagmire" explanation described earlier. What these secret documents showed was that his explanation didn't fit Kennedy's 1961 decisions any better than Johnson's in 1965 or the Truman and Eisenhower escalations earlier.

Whatever it was each president thought privately he might achieve from what he had decided to do, it could not simply be the product of bureaucratic euphoria or deception. Indeed in each of those crisis years—in contrast with the years in between—there had been enough realistic intelligence analyses and even operational reporting available to the president that it was hard to imagine that *more* truth telling or even pessimism would have made any difference to his choices. Could it be, then, that none of the lying to the presidents had mattered to their decisions?

Thus the problem remained of explaining how and why the president had arrived at the choices he made. If each president had been told at the point of escalation that what he was choosing to do would probably *not* solve the problem, what then was he up to? Why did he not do more—or less? Moreover, why did each one mislead the public and Congress about what he was doing in Indochina and what he had been told?

Kennedy's decision to send advisers and not combat units did indeed look like a relatively small step compared with Johnson's later escalations, but as I learned from the documents, *no one* had promised it success. Nor was it "reasonably regarded at the time"—or even unreasonably regarded—by anyone at all inside the government as "the last step that would be necessary." The same was later true under Johnson. For Kennedy, as for Johnson, in fact, it was the president who was deceiving the public, not his subordinates who were deceiving him.

Kennedy had chosen to increase U.S. involvement and investment of prestige in Vietnam and to reaffirm our rhetorical commitment—not as much as his subordinates asked him to, but significantly—while rejecting an element, ground forces, that nearly all his own officials described as essential to success. In fact, at the same time he had rejected another element that all his advisers, including Rusk, had likewise described as essential: an explicit full commitment to defeating the Communists in South Vietnam. Why?

I soon got a crucial commentary on this Kennedy paradox, as I thought of it, from his brother. In the fall of 1967 I was invited to address a gathering of executives from local CBS affiliates from all over the country. I gave a talk along the same lines I had been delivering to other high-level groups since I'd returned from Vietnam that summer: the irrevocability of stalemate in Vietnam, the deceptions and illusions fostered by the government about "progress," and the need to end our involvement. By that time it was clear to me—and to most officials who had served in Vietnam, though not yet to the public—that the most pessimistic predictions I had heard in 1961 had been realistic. Not only had the advisers and support that JFK had sent been totally inadequate, but the open-ended commitment of combat troops that he had rejected and Johnson had accepted had proved no more successful.

Bobby Kennedy also spoke. He seemed to have a passionate concern for our predicament that I hadn't heard in any of the other officials I had talked with that summer. At the end of the lunch Kennedy's press aide, Frank Mankiewicz, told me Kennedy would like to talk with me further and suggested I drive back with him to his Senate office. In the car Kennedy told me he liked what I said, it confirmed what he had been thinking, and he wanted to hear more.

I'd met Bobby only once before, three years earlier, when he was in his last days as attorney general. He hadn't impressed me at that time, particularly as a potential secretary of state, a role he was said to want then. He seemed very young, not very sure of himself, and with a surprisingly uncertain memory for foreign events. I was interviewing him in his office at the Justice Department for a highly classified official study I was doing of the Cuban missile crisis of October 1962. At one point he said, "There was something else going on at the same time, very important, it had our attention . . . what was it?" He looked up at the ceiling, searched his memory for a moment, then looked at me and asked, "When was Vienna?"

He was referring to the Vienna summit with Khrushchev nearly a year and a half before the missile crisis. I said, "That was in June 1961."

He said, "Ah," and went on thinking for a moment looking at the ceiling, then gave up. He didn't seem embarrassed. I was thinking, "This is a secretary of state?"

But he was much more impressive now, more mature and sure of himself, independent. Being his own man in the Senate after losing his brother, and with his father disabled, must have had a lot to do with it. He asked me questions about my experience in Vietnam and what had led me to the conclusions I had just described. I was glad to have the chance to tell him what I had seen and what I thought should be done, but I also wanted to ask him about the period I was investigating for the McNamara study, the Kennedy decision making in 1961.

I told him briefly why I had picked that year to study and how I was now more puzzled than ever by the combination of decisions I found the president had made. In rejecting ground troops and a formal commitment to victory, he had been rejecting the urgent advice of every one of his top military and civilian officials. With hindsight, that didn't look foolish; it was the advice that looked bad. Yet he did proceed to deepen our involvement, in the face of a total consensus among his advisers that without the measures he was rejecting, in fact without adopting them immediately, our efforts were bound to fail.

I told Bobby it was hard to make sense out of that combination of decisions. Did he remember how it came out that way? I felt uneasy about describing the problem that way to the president's brother, but I knew it might be my only opportunity ever to get an answer, and his manner with me encouraged me to take the chance.

He thought about what I'd put to him for a moment and then said: "We didn't want to lose in Vietnam or get out. We wanted to win if we could. But my brother was determined *never* to send ground combat units to Vietnam." His brother was convinced, Bobby said, that if he did that, we'd be in the same spot as the French. The Vietnamese on our side would leave the fighting to the United States, and it would become our war against nationalism and self-determination, whites against Asians. That was a fight we couldn't win, any more than the French.

I pressed him for more. In late 1964 and early 1965 it looked to the same advisers as if U.S. ground combat involvement were now essential to avoid defeat *in the short run.* Yet at that point it would have been even harder politically to get out or to accept defeat than in 1961. What would Kennedy have done then if he had lived?

Bobby answered carefully, in a way that made what he said more credible: "Nobody can say for sure what my brother would actually have done, in the actual circumstances of 1964 or '65. I can't say that, and even he couldn't have said that in '61. Maybe things would have gone just the same as they did. But I do know what he *intended.* All I can say is that he was absolutely determined not to send ground units."

I went on to the hard question. Would JFK really have been willing to accept defeat, to see Saigon go Communist, as the alternative to sending troops? Again Bobby answered in an even tone. "We would have fuzzed it up. We would have gotten a government in that asked us out or that would have negotiated with the other side. We would have handled it like Laos."

In Laos, Kennedy had rejected military urging to put in ground troops and instead had entered into negotiations that led to a coalition government, including Communists. Most of his officials, and Kennedy himself in official discussions, had always ruled out the acceptability of treating Vietnam like Laos. Bobby's comment to me was the first and only time I ever heard that JFK had even entertained the possibility of a "Laotian solution" for South Vietnam. There is no evidence at all that Lyndon Johnson or Richard Nixon ever did so for a moment. Yet Bobby's statement had the ring of truth. For one thing, it was clear to me by 1967 that he was describing the only realistic way that the war could have been brought to an end. So it made sense that one American president, at least, might have considered this a serious contingency.

But what wasn't clear to me was how Kennedy could have been so prescient in 1961, or where he would have gotten such a strong personal commitment, as to draw an absolute line against American ground combat in Vietnam. Bobby had not said that his brother had already decided in 1961 to withdraw from Vietnam; he had simply told me that JFK preferred and intended to do that rather than to send ground troops, if it came to the point where those seemed the only two alternatives to imminent military defeat. I hadn't heard of any American—among those reluctant to get out of Vietnam, for cold war reasons—advancing that precise point of view before 1964 (though some, notably George Ball, didn't want to send even advisers). Obviously none of Kennedy's most senior advisers shared it. I also hadn't thought of JFK as having idiosyncratic opinions, let alone a conviction like that, about Indochina. I asked, a little impudently, "What made him so smart?"

Whap! His hand slapped down on the desk. I jumped in my chair. "Because *we were there!*" He slammed the desktop again. His face contorted in anger and pain. "We were there, in 1951. We saw what was happening to the French. *We saw it.* My brother was determined, determined, never to let that happen to us."

I saw Bobby Kennedy a number of times in the next few months, sometimes for fairly long discussions, but this was the only time I heard an outburst of emotion like this. It made a strong impression on me. I believed him, and still believe him, that his brother was strongly convinced that he should never send ground troops to Indochina, and that he was prepared to accept a "Laotian solution" if necessary to avoid that. If true, that subjective conviction and readiness would mark John F. Kennedy as significantly different in his attitude toward our stakes and appropriate strategy in Vietnam from both Lyndon Johnson and Richard Nixon, neither of whom shared this felt constraint or readiness to concede under some conditions. Whether President Kennedy, if he had survived, would have lived up to this conviction in the face of a crisis in 1965 is (as his brother acknowledged) another question, unanswered.

I wondered after listening to Bobby just what they had seen and heard in Vietnam that had shaped his thinking so strongly (and so well, as it looked to me by this time). How long had they been there? It was years before I learned the answer.

One day, it turns out. According to Richard Reeves, Kennedy recalled that day to Taylor and Rostow just before they left for Vietnam in October 1961.

> Kennedy told Taylor about his own experiences in Vietnam, which he had visited for a day in 1951 as a young congressman on an around-the-world tour. He had begun that day in Saigon with the commander of the 250,000 French troops fighting Viet Minh guerrillas. General Jean de Lattre de Tassigny had

assured him that his soldiers could not lose to these natives. He had ended the evening on top of the Caravelle Hotel with a young American consular officer named Edmund Gullion. The sky around the city flashed with the usual nighttime artillery and mortar bombardment by the Viet Minh.

"What have you learned here?" Kennedy asked the diplomat.

"That in twenty years there will be no more colonies," Gullion had said. "We're going nowhere out here. The French have lost. If we come in here and do the same thing we will lose, too, for the same reason. There's no will or support for this kind of war back in Paris. The home front is lost. The same thing would happen to us."

Ask the right person the right question, and you could get the picture pretty fast.

In the fall of 1967 I knew that Westmoreland and the Joint Chiefs had been pushing for an expanded war and that McNamara was opposing it. What we couldn't figure out was where the president stood. He claimed publicly to believe that we were progressing satisfactorily in Vietnam, but that told me nothing, since McNamara did the same. In mid-October I got a reading from a truly authoritative source, Johnson's press secretary, Bill Moyers. Scarcely anyone other than Lady Bird knew LBJ's mind better than he did. My notes of a meeting with him on October 17 in Cambridge show him judging "that the President is likely not only to continue roughly in the present approach to the war—in terms of aims and strategy—until the election, but that after the election, assuming that he wins (which Moyers thought likely, though not inevitable), he is more likely to move in the direction of escalating our strategy rather than to reduce U.S. objectives and adopt less ambitious tactics. For instance, he might well then yield to pressures and logic urging him to invade North Vietnam. That would probably be in stages: ground probes across the DMZ, a limited invasion across the infiltration routes just north of the DMZ, finally an Inchon-type landing."

Someone asked skeptically if it was conceivable that a politician like LBJ could possibly move so far in a direction away from the minds of the public at such sacrifice to all his domestic political goals. Moyers said that would depend on whether the president continued to believe, as he had come increasingly to do in the past year or more, that his place in history would be determined by the resolution of the Vietnam conflict. As Moyers saw it, Johnson had a strong tendency to see his role and problems in "Trumanesque" terms and to believe that it was his responsibility to make difficult decisions for the good of the country, at the cost of public support in the short run if need be, but with the expectation of being vindicated in the end, at least in the eye of history.

Moyers's own attitude was that even one or two years more of the conflict in its present form—with its moral ambiguities and consequent controversy, and with its lack of evident progress toward *any* U.S. objectives—would do irreparable harm to the unity, morale, institutions, and internal political balance of the country. Expansion would make it even worse, and he saw it as being of the highest importance for the United States either that the president's state of mind be changed, which he thought very unlikely, or that he be displaced in office. I asked him if he really meant what he seemed to be saying. He replied soberly: "I never thought the situation could arise when I would wish for the defeat of LBJ, and that makes my current state of mind all the more painful to me. I would have to say now: It would depend on who his opponent is."

Moyers was confirming for me that there was reality to my worst nightmare. Since we had invested our prestige in a military effort in the spring of 1965, I had worried that a frustrating stalemate there would push any president in the direction of breaking out of it by following the path to victory urged on him by the JCS. Now, as before, that path led into North Vietnam, right up to the border of China, and probably beyond it. It was the hope of averting that stalemate and this consequence that had encouraged me to try to find, perhaps from General Lansdale or John Vann, ways of achieving some sort of success that wouldn't demand expansion of the war. That effort was a failure. If there was such a way, the U.S. government wasn't up to finding it in time or acting on it.

I was still a cold warrior looking for lessons in our Vietnam experience that could help the United States defeat Communist insurgencies *elsewhere* in the world where circumstances were different and our chances of success were better. But I already saw it as urgent to avoid further escalation, and Moyers's judgments of the president made that seem even more likely than I'd feared. To avert that, I wasn't thinking about a new president; there wasn't even time for that solution. It was necessary to make people aware of the possibility of escalation, to build opposition to it, and to get the war over with somehow before circumstances made it unavoidable. As I would be for years to come, I was driven by the perception "This war isn't ending, *and it's likely to get much larger than it is now if the president's policy isn't changed.*"

13

The Power of Truth

On November 21, 1967, General Westmoreland had said in a major speech at the National Press Club that we were entering the final phase of our efforts in the war. The headline of the story in the *Washington Post* was WAR'S END IN VIEW—WESTMORELAND. Misleading as it was, I think he believed it; certainly he knew it was the message Johnson desperately wanted him to deliver. It was also a message many people desperately wanted to hear. Unfortunately for Westmoreland, it was to be refuted only two months later in a spectacular fashion—not by a skeptical press but by the actions of the Vietcong themselves when they launched a sweeping offensive on January 29, 1968, the start of Tet, the lunar new year celebration that was Vietnam's major holiday.

The scale and coordination of Tet, almost simultaneous attacks in nearly every province in South Vietnam as well as in Saigon itself, would have been astonishing at any time. But the immense impact of Tet on public consciousness and the attitude of Congress can be understood only against the background of the intense public lying over the preceding six months, climaxing only weeks before.

Soon I was called back to Washington to help staff a high-level working group evaluating the full range of Vietnam options for Clark Clifford, who was due on March 1 to succeed McNamara as secretary of defense. (McNamara had been "promoted" by President Johnson to be president of the World Bank, evidently as a result of his secret memo to LBJ on November 1, 1967, recommending an end to the bombing and negotiations with the

NLF and Hanoi.) Brought in as a consultant from Rand, I once again had access to the high-level memos and traffic that were circulating at the Pentagon.

My knowledge of JCS recommendations since 1964, but especially over the last year, led me to believe that Wheeler and Westmoreland would be pushing for major escalation. My fears were confirmed on February 27, when I saw a top secret report to the president that day by General Wheeler, chairman of the JCS. Wheeler reported Westmoreland's request for an additional 206,000 troops, almost exactly the same request that he had submitted the previous April. Wheeler's report presented a very dark picture of the war and presented the call for new troops as necessary to stave off collapse in South Vietnam. With this request by Wheeler and Westmoreland, it appeared that we were on the verge of another cycle of escalation, this one the most dangerous of all.

Although Wheeler's request was couched in terms of preserving the situation, I believed that such an increase in troops, which required mobilization of reserves, would inevitably lead to a *wider* war. The mobilization and continued high U.S. casualties would make the public and Congress receptive to the JCS for winning the war by expanding it. I suspected (correctly, it turned out) that the real reason Westmoreland and the JCS wanted those extra troops was not to ward off defeat but to carry out an expansion of operations, something Westmoreland had long advocated, to include Cambodia, Laos, and at least the southern part of North Vietnam. Already after his talks at the Press Club in November 1967 Westmoreland had been making statements to the press about supplies coming in through Cambodia, with definite hints in favor of expanding the war. All the more, I learned in the Pentagon, after the enemy had been weakened at Tet, Westmoreland believed, and was urging, that this was the opportunity to move decisively into North Vietnam. Down this path, I thought, lay certain ruin.

I didn't believe an invasion of North Vietnam would long stay limited to its southern region. Its failure to end the war would lead to military pressure for an Inchon type of landing near Haiphong to occupy Hanoi and fight throughout the North, "the source of the problem." But reproducing the French occupation would not merely double our problem; it would be much worse than that. From my discussions with Westmoreland's staff when I was in Vietnam, I had concluded he was not clear about the difference between the politics of North and South Vietnam. In South Vietnam we were not fighting all the population; even so, we were thoroughly stalemated with five hundred thousand U.S. troops. In North Vietnam we would be fighting every man, woman, and child. In that situation, we were almost sure to have military difficulty vastly greater than we had yet encountered, so much so that we might end up protecting our troops, eventually with tactical nuclear weapons. That would almost certainly come about if, as was likely, an expansion of the war up to the Chinese border brought Chinese forces into North Vietnam. That, above all, I wanted to avoid. Yet that is where I saw us heading.

In fact, the challenge to use U.S. tactical nuclear weapons could arise much sooner than that, in South Vietnam itself. On February 10, General Wheeler was quoted in the *Washington Post* as saying to several senators that the JCS would recommend their use if they were needed for the defense of the five thousand marines besieged at the outpost of Khe Sanh, though he didn't think they would be required. Senator Fulbright, chairman of the Senate Foreign Relations Committee, along with Senators Clark and Aiken, denounced the possibility of such use—which British Prime Minister Harold Wilson, on a visit to Washington during this debate, called "sheer lunacy"—after Secretary Rusk failed to rule it out in answer to Senate questions.

President Johnson stated in a press conference on February 16 that as far as he was aware the secretaries of state and defense and the JCS had "at no time even considered" the employment of nuclear weapons. I knew that was untrue. Mort Halperin in the Pentagon had already told me that it had been discussed at the regular Tuesday luncheon at the White House among the two secretaries, the president, and General Wheeler. The president had asked for a definite assurance from the JCS that Khe Sanh could be held without using nuclear weapons; General Wheeler, after consultation with General Westmoreland, was not able to give that categorical assurance, under bad weather conditions that hindered conventional air support.

Westmoreland later reported in his 1976 memoirs that he had had a more positive attitude about the possible benefits of using nuclear weapons at that time in the region around Khe Sanh, where "civilian casualties would be minimal."

> If Washington officials were so intent on "sending a message" to Hanoi, surely small tactical nuclear weapons would be a way to tell Hanoi something. . . . It could be that use of a few small tactical nuclear weapons in Vietnam—or even the threat of them—might have quickly brought the war there to an end. . . . Although I established a small secret group to study the subject, Washington so feared that some word of it might reach the press that I was told to desist. I

felt at the time and even more so now that to fail to consider this alternative was a mistake.

Indeed, the debate in Congress and the press throughout February and March about possible use of nuclear weapons had been started by a rumor leaked to the Senate Foreign Relations Committee on February 5 of the existence of just such a study on Vietnam. I didn't know specifically of Westmoreland's interest at the time; I simply took it for granted, under the circumstances. The word Wheeler brought back from Vietnam on February 27 was far from reassuring to me. Clearly, the likelihood of a major NVA assault on Khe Sanh, and the possibility of dealing with it decisively, were still uppermost in Westmoreland's mind.

After I read Wheeler's report, I got in touch with Frank Mankiewicz, Robert Kennedy's press person, who had arranged my previous meeting with Bobby in October. When I told Frank that I had information of great importance for the senator, he arranged for me to see Kennedy at his home in McLean, Virginia. On February 28, I handed Bobby the Wheeler report. He began reading it immediately in my presence.

This was the first time I can recall ever showing a classified document to somebody outside the executive branch, not to mention a top secret document intended for the eyes of the president. In this instance, though, I thought of Bobby Kennedy as being in a category of his own. I don't think I would have shown it to any other senator at that time. I associated him primarily with the executive branch; as JFK's brother he had in some respects been almost an assistant president. He certainly had had the clearances.

Soon after the twenty-eighth, there were a series of statements to the press by Senator Fulbright and other senators concerning rumors of a big request for troops from Westmoreland. No specific numbers were mentioned. The senators were also suggesting that any such request or other major change in policy should not occur without consultation with and authorization from Congress. The president had now been conducting the war on the basis of the Tonkin Gulf Resolution for three and a half years. Fulbright was in effect warning the president not to think about going further without input from Congress.

Despite this activity, as the Pentagon Papers disclose, and as I understood it at the time, all indications in the Pentagon were that the president was likely to go ahead with Wheeler's request. The expectation was that Secretary of Defense Clifford would in the end, under pressure from Westmoreland, Wheeler, and perhaps the president, recommend approving the requested deployment, including mobilization. But then on Sunday, March 10, the *New York Times* came out with a very accurate account of the request for the 206,000 troops. Someone—not I, I regret to say—had leaked the figure, along with much of the substance of the Wheeler report and the ongoing debate inside the Pentagon. The story by Neil Sheehan and Hedrick Smith was a bombshell. After having already, for several days, expressed concerns about rumors of just such a new deployment, Fulbright was now saying explicitly that in his view the Tonkin Gulf Resolution was effectively null and void. For the first time he expressed his belief that the resolution had been extorted from Congress by deception, and said that he regretted his sponsorship of the resolution more than anything he had ever done in public life.

This climate of opposition by no means sealed the president's decision against a troop increase. What was clear, though, after the March 10 leak was that LBJ could not make such a deployment *openly* without evoking enormous opposition. Previously this would have posed no problem for him, as he had never before openly and clearly announced his plans to escalate the war. He might well have supposed that in this case too, as in the past, he could succeed with escalating by stages, covertly, with no indication how far he was going. The unprecedented leak of the 206,000-troop request was the first indication that he might not be able to get away with this again.

Initially I was surprised by the shock the leak evoked from members of Congress and puzzled by their reaction. The request was virtually the same as Westmoreland's previous one in May 1967, and that was in the same range as his earlier requests. What was so startling about it? Then suddenly it sank in for me that the public had never actually heard one of the real requests before. They all had been kept secret; the requests had been publicly denied and lied about by the president. Those lies had then been tacitly confirmed by Westmoreland, who had not revealed that he had made larger requests than the president had announced. When Johnson said in May that Westmoreland had requested no more than about 40,000 troops, he could be sure that the general would not contradict his commander in chief.

In light of Tet, the JCS was clearly pressing for the president this time to make an open declaration of increased commitment, a troop increase that would surely require a general mobilization of the reserves. Yet the mood in Congress indicated that this was as politically inopportune a time as one could devise for LBJ to make such a declaration. He did have a tested alternative, though. He could once again conceal the real scope of the request and what he had granted. By all previous experience, that was what I expected President Johnson to do. I wanted to deter him from it. I feared that once he had sent even more troops and called up reserves, the public and Congress would demand an all-out attack against the North, up to and perhaps beyond the Chinese border, both to "protect the troops" and to vindicate the increased effort by seeking victory. That was what the JCS expected—I was sure that was a major reason it had wanted mobilization ever since 1965—and I thought its expectation was sound. Whether or not some of the chiefs actually wanted war with China and use of nuclear weapons—I'm not sure on that question to this day—that was what we would actually be risking.

The striking impact of the unauthorized disclosure of the troop request—at that time one of the more closely held secrets in the administration—suddenly opened my eyes to my responsibilities as a citizen. I had never considered up till that point leaking classified information to Congress, much less to the public through the press. I had just put my toe in the water by giving the top secret Wheeler report to Bobby Kennedy, but I hadn't consciously thought of this as a leak. I'd seen it as informing a former and probably future high executive official.

As I observed the effect of this leak, it was if clouds had suddenly opened. I realized something crucial: that the president's ability to escalate, his entire strategy throughout the war, had depended on secrecy and lying and thus on his ability to deter unauthorized disclosures—truth telling—by officials. That did not mean with certainty that he could not have carried out his plans openly or that he still could not do so. The fact was, however, that he had never chosen to test that possibility, and it was doubtful now, in the wake of Tet, that he was ready to give truth a chance. Under the circumstances, the idea of asking for more troops merely to continue the present strategy within South Vietnam, which was how General Wheeler chose to couch the request, would have seemed so bizarre to the public and Congress that Johnson almost had to use secrecy and lying if he was going to get that. That meant he had to rely on all informed subordinates to keep his secrets and conceal his lies from Congress. His experience over the past three years would give him confidence that he could do just that.

There might well have been support for more troops if he or the JCS had openly proposed what Westmoreland really advocated: a drastically new, expanded war strategy for which the military promised victory. But that would also have led to intense public controversy and probably to ultimate rejection. The JCS was more likely to get what it wanted in the form of a presidential fait accompli, *after* a troop increase the full dimensions of which were initially concealed, as usual. The very surprise of the public and Congress when they had just heard the size of the troop request focused me for the first time on the thin—yet almost impermeable—membrane that separated the executive branch from the legislative in terms of information. I had seen for years how effectively the president could lie about his policies, with the safe assumption that his lies would not be exposed. That assumption was based on his subordinates' loyalty to him, to their bosses, and to their own careers and on the effective strength of their promises and oaths to keep secrets, no matter what was concealed or what the evident impact of the concealment was.

Of course there were circumstances, such as diplomatic negotiations, certain intelligence sources and methods, or various time-sensitive military operational secrets, that warranted strict secrecy. But what I had just come to realize was that there were times when it was potentially a dangerous thing for a president to have too much confidence in his ability to keep secrets. It could encourage him to take, secretly, the first step in a process that he could not later control, a fatal misstep that public debate might well have prevented. August 1964 had been such a time, likewise March and July 1965. I now saw this as another.

I had never questioned the assumption of many students of presidential power that secrecy is vital to preserve a president's range of options. But I now saw how the system of secrecy and lying could give him options he would be better off without, or it could dangerously prejudice his choice. For one thing, it made it harder for the president to resist pressures from the military. Secrecy from the public averted countervailing pressure from that direction. Secrecy made it possible to give the JCS at least part of what it asked for in a way that would not cause the president disastrous political trouble at home. Thus he might feel irresistible pressure to comply at least partially with a request from the Joint Chiefs, indeed fearing that if he didn't meet their requests, they would leak their demands to hawks in Congress and cause him domestic trouble. This was something a president always feared (Lyndon Johnson in particular, for some reason): the charge that he was too cowardly, too weak or irresolute to do what the military thought had to be done. There was thus a strong incentive for the president to give the Joint Chiefs enough of what they wanted, with the hope of getting more, that they would be appeased. That was what I had seen Johnson do in July 1965.

Now I was confronting the specter of a very specific and imminent course of escalation in the form of Westmoreland's new troop request. I very much wanted to exclude from the options available to the president the course that past experience and his own inclinations would surely recommend to him: to comply with the request, in full or in part, under the cover of secrecy and lies. I wanted him to confront a new reality, the realization that he had lost his power reliably to keep secrets from the American public.

I still don't know who leaked the 206,000 figure. It may have just been someone's slip of the tongue. It could have come from a hawk, who favored the request, or more likely from someone who opposed it. Whatever the case, this hero, patriot, or perhaps merely careless person had just opened my eyes. In the past, I had instinctively accepted the ethos of my profession, the idea that leaking was always inherently bad, treacherous, or at best an unhelpful thing to do. I had been wrong. Obviously, leaking could be a patriotic and constructive act.

However, the aim I now conceived would not simply be to inform Congress about something that had already happened. My thought was to expose and subvert the very process of presidential lying about war policy. The ultimate target of the leaks I imagined would be not Congress but one person, the president himself, or advisers who would reach the appropriate conclusion and bring it to his attention. The relevant information for the president would be that his administration had become somehow a goldfish bowl, that there was at least one highly placed insider, someone with access to high-level information, who was ready to inform Congress of matters of grave importance. It might be someone in Defense or one of the other agencies, someone who had crossed the line and abandoned caution about his career.

What I had in mind was very simple: a leak a day of a closely held secret, something that showed high-level access. The content was much less important than the leak itself. The real meaning should be clear to the president: that if and when he made a decision to grant most or all of the Westmoreland request, it would be known publicly.

In mid-March I went for the first time to a newspaper office with classified reports and cables to give to a journalist. I chose Neil Sheehan, who was now covering the Pentagon for the *New York Times.* I gave him secret and top secret documents that had been made available to the working group addressing the appropriate response to Westmoreland's troop-level request. I knew this would narrow the search for the source of these leaks and could well lead to me. But I wanted the White House to infer that whoever was providing this information would be likely to know the president's decision on the troop request when he made it.

The first result of my project was a story in the *New York Times* by Sheehan that appeared on March 19, datelined from Washington the previous day. The headline was U.S. UNDERVALUED ENEMY'S STRENGTH BEFORE OFFENSIVE: CIA REPORTS FORCES WERE SIGNIFICANTLY LARGER THAN INTELLIGENCE ESTIMATES; GAP IS 50,000 TO 100,000. This brought to the surface the battle between CIA analysts and MACV over the previous six months about MACV's exclusion from the order of battle—the estimate of enemy strength—of the categories of political apparatus and part-time irregulars. In the wake of the Tet offensive, which had been very largely conducted in the cities by people in the very categories that Westmoreland had dropped from the enemy-strength figures, the CIA had abandoned its bureaucratic compromise with MACV. It added some hundred thousand to the total of enemy forces. It was now contradicting internally Westmoreland's deceptive claim at the National Press Club that enemy strength had declined in 1967.

Sheehan's article was extremely detailed and possibly confusing to the average reader. But the conclusion was crystal clear: Westmoreland had been either consciously misleading or dangerously wishful in his public accounts before the offensive. I hoped to convey to readers in the White House that the *Times*'s reporters were working directly from a high-level document they had acquired from a source within the administration. That message got through. On the day this appeared, Secretary of Defense Clifford received a memo from Richard Steadman, deputy assistant secretary of defense, ISA, classified top secret (emphasis added):

> The figures on enemy strength contained in the *New York Times* this morning are precisely the same as those in the last two columns of the attached table, Top Secret, Noforn [not to be shown to foreign nationals]. The CIA figures are from a March 1 memorandum prepared as part of the ongoing review of the situation in Vietnam. This document, copy attached, is classified secret. The last column of the table was added to demonstrate the accuracy of the figures Mr. Sheehan quotes from the NIE [National Intelligence Estimate]. This document is classified Top Secret. *Somewhere in the government there has obviously been a horrendous security violation,* and it is my personal belief that this should be investigated, with prosecution, if appropriate.

The next day, March 20, there appeared another story based on the same information that I'd given Sheehan, this one bylined by Charles Mohr and datelined Saigon. Helpfully it added to the impression that there were leaks all over the place. This one dealt with new figures and new assessments.

Then, on Thursday, March 21, there was another story from Sheehan, datelined Washington, March 20, which began:

> In a year-end report submitted 29 days before the communist offensive against South Vietnam cities and major towns, General William C. Westmoreland predicted that the allied war gains of last year would be increased many fold in 1968. The military commander in South Vietnam sent his report to Washington on January 1. Excerpts from the classified document have been obtained by *The New York Times.* They made clear that not only was the offensive unexpected but also that U.S. military planning did not envision the possibility of a setback on the scale of that inflicted by the enemy attacks at Tet, the lunar New Year holiday.

The essence of Westmoreland's report, cited by Sheehan in direct quotation (from the handwritten notes I had given him), was that "the destruction and neutralization" of enemy bases in South Vietnam "should force him to place greater reliance on sanctuaries in Cambodia, Laos and the Northern DMZ." But the story continued: "American intelligence specialists have since concluded, however, that the assaults on the cities and towns were mounted from bases within South Vietnam." As Sheehan wrote, Westmoreland's prediction "apparently reflected the belief expressed by General Westmoreland during his visit to the United States in November, that allied military pressure was forcing the enemy away from the population centers and denying the enemy the ability to mount major attacks from bases within South Vietnam. The enemy, he asserted, was becoming increasingly confined to staging frontier battles from bases across the border of Cambodia, Laos, and North Vietnam."

This last assertion of Westmoreland to the president (and earlier to the Press Club) was meant to indicate more than his success in South Vietnam. He was laying a basis for the importance of his being allowed, with the additional troops, to go across those borders into Laos, Cambodia, and North Vietnam. The essence of this message was that we had driven the enemy to the borders and that we ought to pursue them across those borders. That was precisely what Westmoreland was secretly recommending at that time. Now, of course, what was becoming increasingly clear was that the enemy had staged these operations to draw Westmoreland's forces away from the populated areas to allow themselves unimpeded access.

These excerpts from Westmoreland's year-end assurances to the president appeared in the *Times*'s morning edition of March 21. That evening General Wheeler was told unexpectedly by the White House that Westmoreland would be leaving Vietnam to become chief of staff of the army. Johnson made the announcement the next day, on the twenty-second. The following day, March 23, Wheeler flew out to see Westmoreland and told him there would be no mobilization and no change in strategy to expand the war.

On March 25, President Johnson told a gathering in the White House of former high officials, the "wise men":

> Our fiscal situation is abominable. . . . There has been a panic in the last three weeks. It was caused by Ted Kennedy's report on corruption and the ARVN and the GVN being no good and now a release that Westmoreland wants 206,000 men and a call up of 400,000. That would cost $15 billion. That would hurt the dollar and gold. The leaks to the *New York Times* hurt us. The country is demoralized. I will have overwhelming disapproval in the polls and elections. I will go down the drain. I don't want the whole alliance and military pulled in with it. . . . I wouldn't be surprised if they repealed the Tonkin Gulf Resolution. Senator Russell wants us to go in and take out Haiphong. Senator [Eugene] McCarthy and Senator Kennedy and the left wing has informers in the departments. The *Times* and the *Post* are all against us. Most of the press is against us. How can we get this job done? We need more money in an election year, more taxes in an election year, more troops in an election year, and more cuts in an election year. As yet, I cannot tell them what they expect to get in return. We have no support for the war. This is caused by the 206,000 troop request and the leaks, by Teddy Kennedy and Bobby Kennedy. I would have given Westy the 206,000 men if he said they needed them, and if we could get them.

On Tuesday, April 2, 1968, I was eating lunch at Princeton with other participants at the conference "America in a Revolutionary World." The meeting was, oddly, cosponsored by the Woodrow Wilson School at Princeton and the American Friends Service Committee (AFSC). Most of those at my table represented the AFSC sponsorship, to judge by their looks and the tales they were telling. They were the first activists I had ever met from the antinuclear movement of the fifties and the civil rights and antiwar movements of the sixties. A number of them had been to jail repeatedly for civil disobedience actions or for draft resistance going back to Korea or World War II.

Their lives and mine were parallel in some respects, intersecting in others, both in ironic ways. Like me, they abhorred nuclear weapons. But some of them had sailed in the mid-fifties into the prohibited Bikini test zone on the sailing ship *Golden Rule* to oppose nuclear testing. A few years later I was working on nuclear war plans, hoping to stave off a Soviet surprise attack during the period of the supposed missile gap.

Now we were all against the Vietnam War. Who wasn't, in April 1968? But Bob Eaton and others at this table, on the example of the *Golden Rule,* had sailed a similar vessel, the *Phoenix,* into Haiphong Harbor in North Vietnam with a load of medicine. From there they had sailed to South Vietnam, where the ship was turned away, at a time when I was working in the embassy in Saigon. It was amazing to find myself at the same table with them now.

With respect to the subject of the conference, it seemed safe to assume that they were sympathetic to a variety of revolutionary causes. My own interest in the conference stemmed from my past and current work on averting or defeating Communist-led revolutions. I was there in effect as a professional counterrevolutionary.

I had apprenticed at that trade in the Pentagon in 1964 and 1965. Then for two years in Vietnam I had worked on "pacification," which could have been defined—though it wasn't, by U.S. officials—as rural counterrevolution. Just one month before the Princeton conference, the Tet offensive had proved that everything that my colleagues and I had done had been totally unsuccessful. That was no surprise to me. My current research project at Rand was titled "Lessons of Rebellion and Insurgent Forces," and it was no secret that I was exploring almost entirely what I saw as lessons from failure. Nor was I looking to apply those lessons to better effect in Vietnam except to avert escalation and to get us out of that conflict. From the time of my return in the summer of 1967 the Vietnamese war of independence was one revolution I did not want to see my country try to counter anymore. Tet had simply confirmed, spectacularly, much of what I had been trying to tell the government since I returned. The war was an endless, hopeless bloody stalemate.

The president seemed finally to have gotten the message. Just two nights before, on Sunday, March 31, in the midst of packing to come to the Princeton conference, I had watched on television as Lyndon Johnson told the nation that he was halting the bombing of northern North Vietnam and calling for negotiations. He also announced he would not run for renomination as president. Now at Princeton Tom Hayden, a founder of SDS and one of the main speakers on the platform, announced, "We have just toppled a president or come as close to it as our system allows. We have ended a war."

"We." Hayden would not have had me in mind. Yet I as much as anyone there wanted to believe the war was over. (It was not, nor was it ending; Hayden was wrong about that. Nor had Lyndon Johnson gotten the message.) By leaking top secret documents just weeks before this meeting with the assorted peace activists, I had very consciously been risking arrest and imprisonment or, as I thought more likely, the loss of my clearances and the ending of my career in a way not unlike their own actions of civil disobedience. To be sure, I didn't think of what I had just done in those terms. I'm not sure that I had ever even heard the term. But for what I was about to hear, I realize in retrospect, I was unusually ready.

A young woman was sitting almost directly across the lunch table from me. From India, wearing a sari, she was dark, almost black. On her forehead was a dot of red dust. She was talking, in a lilting voice, to some friends on my side of the table. I wanted not to stare at her and didn't try to listen to her conversation. Then, in a moment of silence around us, as she responded to someone's remark about "enemies," I heard her say, "I come from a culture in which there is no concept of enemy."

A strange statement. Hardly comprehensible. No concept of enemy? How about concepts of sun and moon, friend, water? I came from a culture in which the concept of enemy was central, seemingly indispensable—the culture of Rand, the U.S. Marine Corps, the Defense and State departments, international and domestic politics, game theory and bargaining theory. Identifying enemies, understanding and predicting them so as to fight and control them better, analyzing the relations of abstract enemies: All that had been for years my daily bread and butter, part of the air I breathed. To try to operate in the world of men and nations without the concept of enemy would have seemed as difficult, as nearly inconceivable as doing arithmetic, like the Romans, without a zero.

If her overheard remark had come from someone less striking, I might have puzzled over it for a moment, then let it slip. But she was . . . beautiful, and her speech was like singing, so instead I looked hard at her and asked, "What do you mean by that?"

She answered briefly. What she said intrigued me. I wanted to hear more. We made a date to talk the next morning. After breakfast we talked through the morning session of the conference, missing it, had lunch, then talked through the afternoon session and into the night.

Her name was Janaki. She was from South India, the region of Madras. The red dust on her forehead was the "footprint of God"; she was a Shivaite Brahmin. Her parents were committed followers of Mahatma Gandhi, and she had worked for years in the *sarvodaya* movement, the Gandhian constructive action movement, which aimed at rural transformation and was led by Gandhi's disciple Vinoba Bhave, along with the Bhoodan movement seeking land gifts from the rich to villages and landless peasants. In 1963 she had marched with others across India to the Chinese border to protest India's role in the India-China War. They had done this, she said, to the dismay of Vinoba himself, whose sense of nationalism during wartime had overcome his pacifism. She ate no meat and wore nothing from animals that had been slaughtered. (I had, as it happened, a new leather briefcase, which I liked very much. "It's beautiful," she said at one point. "What was it?")

The sense of what she said in our protracted discussion was this. First, in answer to my question: In Gandhi's teaching, no human should be regarded or treated as being "an enemy," in the sense of someone you have a right to destroy, or to hate, or to regard as alien, from whom you cannot learn, for whom you can feel no understanding or concern. These are simply not appropriate attitudes toward another human being. No one should be regarded as being—in his or her essence or permanently—evil or as utterly antagonistic. No people should be seen as being evil persons, as if they were without good in them, a different, less human order of being, as if one could learn nothing from them or as if they were unchangeable, even if what they were *doing* in the moment was harmful and terrible, indeed evil, and needed to be opposed. Thus the whole notion of enemy was both unneeded and dangerously misleading.

This was so, said Janaki, even though what people do is often terribly wrong, in the extreme sense that it demands not merely to be condemned but to be resisted, nonviolently but militantly, at personal cost to oneself, even at the risk of one's own life. This was the very sense in which one could characterize certain ways of acting—though not the actors themselves—as "evil." Yet in opposing people's wrongdoing, even the worst sort, evildoing, in trying to change their hearts and their actions and, above all, to protect others from their harmful behavior, one need not, should not, attempt to destroy them or threaten them with physical harm.

What did that leave to force change? Noncooperation: withdrawal of resources, tax or draft refusal, boycott, general strike. Nonviolent obstruction: from the presence of the *Golden Rule* in the nuclear test zone to sit-down strikes and sit-ins at lunch counters. Exposure: truth telling, acting out the truth of one's sense of human rights, and wrongs, relinquishing silence that can be interpreted as, and amounts to, acceptance and support. All these went beyond "petition" to confront and undermine power with other forms of power, nonviolent, forceful opposition, what Gandhi called *satyagraha* (truth force).

Nearly all evildoing, she pointed out, like nearly all coercive power, legitimate and illegitimate, depends on the cooperation, on the obedience and support, on the assent or at least passive tolerance of many people. It relies on many more collaborators than are conscious of their roles; these include even many victims, along with passive bystanders, as in effect accomplices. Such cooperation could be withdrawn with powerful effect. Actions of individuals could ignite organized noncooperation, as the example of Rosa Parks led to the Montgomery bus boycott. Her refusal to obey a command, valid under the law in Alabama, to yield her seat on a bus to a white male passenger, her choice to suffer arrest instead, challenged the habits of obedience of all black people in Montgomery. Recalling his college reading of Thoreau's essay on civil disobedience, in light of Parks's action and arrest, Martin Luther King, Jr., reflected, as Janaki quoted to me: "Something began to say to me, 'He who passively accepts evil is as much involved in it as he who helps to perpetrate it. He who accepts evil without protesting against it is really cooperating with it.' . . . From this moment on I conceived of our movement [the bus boycott] as an act of massive noncooperation."

As I listened to Janaki, I found myself hearing a surprisingly coherent doctrine and a relevant body of experience supporting it, all new to me. It was intellectually challenging, plausible, a new way of understanding problems and possibilities. Apparently there was an arithmetic of power you could do without a zero, at least without the starting point familiar to me. Yet if it did without an "enemy" and the threat of violence, it didn't forgo the notions of adversarial conflict, opposition, struggle, resistance, and moral judgment. On the contrary, as I came to understand, all these were essential to Gandhi's way of thinking and acting. But Janaki was describing a new way of reasoning about them and of relating to them. It wasn't the only way to think—it didn't displace everything I had learned—but I saw that it was, for me, a genuinely new way, one that made sense. Something like that didn't turn up very often. It seemed as though it might even offer something that familiar ways of thinking had never delivered, a chance of bringing about real change *away* from violence and revenge.

She spoke a good deal of Martin Luther King and urged me to read his *Stride Toward Freedom,* which she had just quoted to me. I had never thought much about King, and I certainly hadn't known his concept of militant nonviolent action. I had scarcely been aware of the strength of King's opposition to the Vietnam War since 1965. I was impressed by her description of the stand he had taken at the Riverside Church in New York City almost exactly a year before, April 4, 1967. Against the urging of many of his allies, black and white, he had risked losing support for the civil rights movement and sacrificed his access to the White House by denouncing the war uncompromisingly because, he began by quoting, "There comes a time when silence is betrayal." (When I read the full speech much later, I found he had in 1967 a grasp of the real history of the conflict that I didn't come to for two more years. In addition, his concrete proposals for extrication—ending the bombing of North and South, setting a date for the unilateral withdrawal of U.S. troops, accepting that the NLF must play a role in negotiations and in any future Vietnam government—went well beyond the public proposals of any other major figure in 1967–68. His program could and should have been the basis for ending the conflict in any month of the next five years.) Janaki urged me to meet with him—she thought she could arrange it—and I decided I must. Her account gave me a sense of hope for what might come to happen in America that I had also found, just in the last few months and in a different way, in Robert Kennedy.

We didn't go back to the conference. We stayed together and talked through the next day as well. Late that afternoon, April 4, 1968, we turned on the evening news and learned that Martin Luther King, Jr., had been killed. Washington was burning.

14

Campaign '68

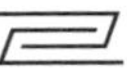

With the president's speech of March 31, 1968, it was taken for granted by the general public and most commentators that he had decided to end the war promptly on the best terms he could get expediently, whatever they were. Evidently the Hanoi leaders thought so too, initially, for to the surprise of Johnson and Rusk, they agreed for the first time to hold direct discussions even though bombing was still going on. Why else would he have dropped out of the campaign so dramatically and halted most of the bombing of the North? But I wasn't so sure, as weeks went by and there was still no agreement even on a place for the two sides to meet, let alone on an agenda.

One day in April in his office in the Pentagon, Mort Halperin remarked to me, apropos of the bombing that was still going on, more intensely than before below the nineteenth parallel and in Laos, "There are exactly three people in this government who believe in what we're doing: Walt Rostow, Dean Rusk, and the president." That was an unusually precise estimate. Yet it had the ring of plausibility. On opposite sides of his desk, we sat for a few minutes and ran through a list of players, partly in our heads and partly aloud, to see if the generalization stood up or if we could enlarge his list by a name or two. Each of us moved to an unusual extent among different agencies in Washington dealing with Vietnam, so we knew a very wide range of participants in policy matters, but we couldn't think of anyone else. Not in the JCS or the team drafting the Pentagon Papers, not anyone we knew at the CIA or State or the White House.

As Mort has reminded me recently, recalling the estimate, that didn't mean that everyone we could think of was a dove, determined to withdraw. There were those, especially in the air force, who still believed that we ought to be pursuing a much more aggressive bombing campaign. The point was that they no longer believed that what we were doing was a "second best" approach or minimally acceptable, even as a possible precursor to doing more. It no longer made any sense to them, as an alternative either to pounding the North very much harder than we were or to withdrawing or negotiating our way out. In effect these officials shared the attitude that was still widespread in the public: Win or get out.

Strikingly, in our own estimate, there was a much *lower* proportion of officials or military men with a preference for escalation over withdrawal by this time—even before Tet and more so after it—than in the general population. Even among relatively conservative military officers, a number of whom were on the Pentagon Papers task force, and especially among officers who had served in Vietnam, there was more readiness for simple withdrawal by late 1967 than there was in the public even after Tet. Nevertheless, the orders to bomb were still coming down, and the orders were being executed. In the ten months after McNamara left the Pentagon, Clark Clifford, under the president, dropped a greater tonnage of bombs on Indochina than had been expended in the previous three years: 1.7 million tons compared with 1.5. If Halperin was right, and I believe he was, orders that led to the doubling in ten months of the total tonnage dropped were obediently carried out by men who, from Clifford on down to flight crews, believed it served no national purpose whatever. I have spent a lot of time in the last thirty years seeking to comprehend and, in some sense, to come to terms as an American with that phenomenon.

As the election year got under way, I was anxious to share my perceptions and views with any political figure who wanted to hear them. My reputation from Vietnam and the Pentagon, among insiders, was such that quite a few wanted to listen, in both parties. As I heard responses from advisers or representatives of a field of presidential candidates from Romney and Rockefeller to Kennedy and Humphrey, I found that they all seemed to share my priorities. Persuasive effort by me didn't seem as needed or as urgent as it had at the start of the year, but I could still serve to reassure skeptical outsiders about their intuitive inclinations to get out. Regrettably I didn't know anyone in touch with George Wallace, who had picked General Curtis LeMay as his running mate. As for Nixon, his purported "secret plan to end the war" sounded to most observers (wishfully and, as it turned out, mistakenly) like some scheme for a disguised withdrawal. In fact, columnists Walter Lippmann and Joseph Kraft both guessed that the "new Nixon" was actually more likely to end the war expeditiously than was Humphrey, with his ties to the Johnson policy. That sounded plausible to me. My highest hope was that there might emerge a consensus among all the candidates—except probably Wallace—on a course along these lines that would extricate us.

Early in his campaign, Robert Kennedy phoned me in California to ask me to be "his man on Vietnam" for the campaign. It would mean leaving Rand, setting up an office in Washington or New York, and coordinating material for all speeches, statements, and position papers on the war. I was strongly tempted. But I preferred to stay free at least till the conventions to contribute to a consensus, if I could, rather than to press differences between the candidates in the course of working for one of them. And I had a personal reason for declining as well at that particular moment: I was just getting started in psychoanalysis, four sessions a week, and I didn't want to leave Los Angeles.

But all my sympathies were with Kennedy. Like a number of other people, I had come to feel more attached to Robert Kennedy than to any other person in public life I have ever met. Since my return from Vietnam, no other American had so impressed me with the depth and urgency of his concern, even anguish, about the war. I liked him. A lot.

From my talks with him going back to October 1967, I had concluded that RFK was the single major candidate (McCarthy being highly unlikely to win the nomination) who could be counted on to bring about early and decisive U.S. extrication from Vietnam. I'd heard that Humphrey had been an early skeptic about our involvement, but it was hard to respect the degree to which he had knuckled under to Johnson's policy and was still doing so. I assumed that he would get out of Vietnam too, but much more tentatively and slowly, raggedly, perhaps with some backsliding, as he tried to avoid embarrassing or enraging his former boss or criticizing the policy of the past eight years. That impression wasn't contradicted by my first meeting with him.

I was invited to a luncheon at the Waldorf-Astoria on the day Humphrey addressed a major rally in New York. A number of guests, including Zbigniew Brzezinski of Columbia University and Sam Huntington of Harvard, had been invited there to "advise" him, though really, it turned out, they were there to be looked over or encouraged to serve as prospective staffers for the campaign. During the meal Humphrey made a remark about a theme common among McCarthy and Kennedy supporters. Looking around the table, he said, "I'm really very worried about this simplistic slogan 'No More Vietnams.' That's very dangerous." He was addressing the group, but I was sitting almost directly across from him, and I thought some comment was called for. After a slight silence, with no one else volunteering, I said, "Well, it's better than a slogan '*More Vietnams.*'" Another short silence ensued.

As we were leaving an hour later, I pressed the point again. I was hoping to discourage him from staking out his "worry" on this point as a campaign position. "If 'No More Vietnams' means 'no more unilateral U.S. military interventions without authorization by Congress,' that's really a pretty good policy." He nodded noncommittally.

There was another problem with the proposition "No More Vietnams": It suggested that the Vietnam War itself was over or at least was on the way to ending, with no further need for attention or pressure from the electorate. In reality, neither was true in 1968 or for seven more years. Yet one or the other of these beliefs, both denying a need for antiwar activism, was held by a large majority of the electorate—the media and establishment in particular—for most of the whole period in question.

In late May I had been working with Kennedy's aides Adam Walinsky and Jeff Greenfield on the policy line on Vietnam for Kennedy's last speech before the California primary. It was to be given at the Commonwealth Club of San Francisco on May 31. I didn't try to supply the actual words; as a speechwriter Walinsky was in a class by himself. But for some speeches they were asking my advice on what substantive points needed to be made at that juncture. I stayed fairly late one night in their office at the Ambassador Hotel, going over Walinsky's final draft. The campaign had most of the rooms on an upper floor in the hotel, as bedrooms and offices for the staff. Kennedy slept in one of the suites.

The next morning I woke with some last-minute thoughts on a couple of points. I wrote them out and my friend Yvonne, who was driving me to the airport, took me first by the hotel. It was still very early, and hardly anyone was in the lobby. The elevator we took opened on the hall the campaign was using. It was nearly deserted. There had been a lot of coming and going and people talking in the hall when I had left late the night before, but now we both were struck by the absence of any security guards. There was one person walking down the hall toward us, in a bathrobe. It was Bobby. He hadn't shaved, his hair was tousled, and he had a cup of coffee in his hand. He looked great. He said, "Hello, Yvonne," which blew her away, since we'd spent only one evening together several months earlier.

We talked for a couple of minutes. I didn't bother him with the issues I was going to raise with Adam, but I waved the piece of paper I was carrying with my suggestions, hoping, I suppose, to get a little credit for bringing it so early in the morning. He continued down the hall as I went in to see Walinsky, who was already hard at work. I mentioned to Adam that it was surprising that nobody had stopped us on the way up, no one had asked for identification, and no guards were in the hall. He said that Kennedy had refused to have Secret Service protection (which at that time wasn't automatic for candidates before the conventions) because he believed they were spying for the White House, reporting on everyone he saw and where he went. He'd also turned down Mayor Sam Yorty's offer of L.A. police, for similar reasons. Still, we had an odd feeling, going back into the deserted hall, now empty of Bobby. It was a kick for Yvonne to run into him like that and to have him remember her in the midst of the campaign, but it was a little unnerving. As she said while we went down alone in the elevator, "We could have been anybody."

She drove me to the airport. On the way we were laughing about an exchange between Bobby and Ethel when we had had dinner with them in Washington, at network correspondent Sander Vanocur's. As dinner was ending, Vanocur asked if we all would mind watching a show on drug abuse he had taped earlier that was just about to go on. We went into a small room next to the dining room to watch, and at one point, as Vanocur on the screen was talking about acid, Ethel asserted, "LSD is just as bad as heroin."

Bobby, dryly: "No, Ethel, it's not."

"It is, I know it is, it's just as bad as heroin!"

"Ethel, I'm the attorney general, and I say it's not."

In 1964 that was a pretty funny line, delivered in his flat, nasal Boston-Harvard twang.

His timing was always very good. It had struck me when I had interviewed him while I was researching the Cuban missile crisis. Initially he hadn't made a very strong impression on me. But his timing and deadpan delivery on a comment about Soviet Ambassador Anatoly Dobrynin made me take another look at him. He said that Dobrynin had told them early in the crisis that there were no Soviet missiles in Cuba, and none would be sent there. Measuring his words, almost pedantically, he said that after the missiles, which were already there as Dobrynin spoke, had been removed, "My brother and I thought that he should go. Because either he had knowingly lied to us, in which case his usefulness was at an end, or his authorities hadn't trusted him with the information, in which case too his usefulness was at an end."

I waited for him to continue, but he didn't. I said, "But he didn't go."

"No." Pause. "And his usefulness was not at an end."

I was in Chicago for a conference on Vietnam on Tuesday, June 4, the day of the California primary. I spent the evening with Susan Bellow, a friend. We watched the primary returns together. Kennedy had swept South Dakota and seemed to be winning by a good margin in California, which most people were saying made him the odds-on candidate for the nomination. It had been a long day, and I was tired. I didn't wait up to hear his victory speech at the Ambassador, which would be after midnight in California. I took a taxi to my hotel.

The next morning there was a knock on my door as I was shaving. It was Susan, who was crying. I asked her what was the matter, and she said, "Don't you know? Turn on your television. Bobby's been shot." I stopped breathing. On the TV we saw the end of Bobby's speech. Then he was going through a crowd. Then he was lying on the floor of the kitchen, eyes stricken, silhouetted figures hovering over him. A commentator was saying he was in a coma in a hospital and wasn't expected to recover. I was dizzy. I was saying, "What! What? What is this?" I was pacing back and forth between the beds in the small hotel room. It was the only time I ever wanted to beat my head against a wall. I began to cry, then to sob. I sat on the bed, chest heaving, out of control. Susan watched me and didn't try to say anything.

I knew now as I wept, though I hadn't thought about it before, that I loved Bobby. He was the only politician I ever felt that way about. I realized at this moment that all my hopes had been on him. Not just for Vietnam, but for my country. I had a sudden vision that the war wasn't going to end. I was thinking: Maybe there's no way, no way, to change this country.

After almost half an hour I stopped crying. I washed the tears and shaving cream off my face and finished dressing. Susan drove me to the conference. Several of the people there were in the same state as I was; it seemed few had stayed up long enough to see the news the night before. We went on with the conference, in a subdued way, in shock. I found myself speaking that day with unusual vehemence about an American addiction to a particular kind of violence, strategic bombing. On Thursday, after the conference had ended, some of the participants flew to New York for the funeral service on Friday morning at St. Patrick's Cathedral. I flew back to Los Angeles.

Saturday in Malibu was a bright day. When I turned on the television in my house, the funeral train was moving along the East Coast, past crowds of mourners at little towns. I had no desire to be on it or anywhere. I wanted to be on the moon. I walked up and down the beach, then sat and watched the waves hit the rocks offshore for a long time. When I went back to my house, the black train was still moving slowly down the other coast. I was glad to be far away from it.

Meanwhile the bombing was still going on heavily in the North up to the nineteenth parallel. On August 1 it was reported that American planes had dropped 2,581,876 tons of bombs and rockets in Indochina since 1965. That was 1 million tons added to the total on March 1—when it had been 1.5 million tons, or as much as we had dropped on Europe during World War II—just since Clifford had replaced McNamara at the Pentagon. In those five months, four of them after Johnson had stopped the bombing of most of North Vietnam and called for negotiations, we had dropped half the total tonnage of World War II, which was 2 million tons. There were, it turned out, nearly three World War IIs to go.

While that persisted, the Hanoi participants in the Paris talks wouldn't discuss anything but the unconditional and permanent cessation of the attacks on the North, and Johnson wouldn't stop those without assurance, and perhaps evidence, of some "reciprocation" by the North Vietnamese. This the Vietnamese refused, on the grounds that the attacks had no legitimate basis and Americans had no right to demand anything in return for stopping them. Ho Chi Minh had even reached back to the same American analogy I had used in explaining Vietcong terrorism in speeches I drafted for McNaughton and McNamara in 1965; he said the United States was acting like a Chicago mobster who offers not to shoot if his target will pay him "protection money." Hanoi did offer a "reciprocal" assurance that it would not bomb or invade North America, which had a good deal of logic but was treated by the U.S. negotiators as flippant.

McCarthy was still in the race, but curiously passive—perhaps depressed—after the murder of the rival he hated. Humphrey's position might not be set in stone; a platform fight lay ahead at the convention. During this interval I had another discussion with him. At the suggestion of one of his aides I went to a fund-raiser for him in Los Angeles and then rode with them in their limousine to the following appointment, to discuss next steps in Vietnam. Humphrey wanted to come out for an unconditional bombing halt, but he expressed great concern that a halt, if it occurred, might be followed by another wave of attacks, for which he would then be blamed. I couldn't tell him this was impossible. The best I could tell him was that it seemed to me not very likely, and much less likely than if there was *not* a halt. I strongly thought the political risk for him was worth taking. He listened, but as we shook hands and parted, he didn't look any less worried about the prospect than when he brought it up.

The threat to Humphrey didn't really come from the NVA; he faced danger on both sides at home. He might not get the nomination, and he was still less likely to have the party unity that could bring him an election victory, if he didn't separate himself from Johnson's position on the war, at a minimum on the bombing (he wasn't about to call for a coalition in Saigon, the truly important issue). But if he did declare some independence, ever so slightly, he faced a variety of forms of retribution from an enraged president.

Meanwhile the Hanoi regime wasn't acting as if it were in a great hurry, either, to get our bombing stopped or to end the war by making concessions. Indeed, it was not a bluff for either side. Neither party was ready to make any significant concession, and the leaderships weren't hurting from the continued war, no matter how bloody it was for some of their citizens and how sad for their bereft families. So the way to bet was that even if one or both of them had changed their tactics, met the other's conditions for talking, and started "negotiating," there would have been no result. Nothing would have changed.

Eventually, in November, both sides did do that. They did get into direct, formal talks, and that was what happened: nothing. The war went on. More than ten thousand Americans were killed in 1969, as many as in 1967, with negotiations going on both publicly and on a secret track; ten thousand-plus also died during the next three years of negotiations. Thus, by itself, "stopping the bombing" of the North altogether, unconditionally, permanently, was something of a false issue, almost a distraction, when it came to ending the war. So, for that matter, was "getting into talks," for which stopping the bombing was seemingly a precondition. Either made sense only as part of a package of policies designed to resolve the conflict or to end U.S. involvement in it.

Given our past investment of rhetoric, effort, and lives, a policy that could be described as simply cutting and running didn't look remotely feasible politically. There was little public support in polls or from well-known voices for immediate, unilateral withdrawal of all U.S. ground forces. That policy was proposed by exactly one candidate running for the presidency in

1968, Eldridge Cleaver, the Black Panther and former convicted rapist who was running underage on the Peace and Freedom party ticket in New York and California. It was not a mainstream position.

The Kennedy, McCarthy, and Humphrey strategists worked out a peace plank for the convention, proposing a total bombing halt and mutual withdrawal of U.S. and North Vietnamese forces and urging the Saigon regime to negotiate directly with the NLF toward a coalition government. The first two points by themselves would have gotten nowhere, but in combination they offered a negotiable basis for ending the war. Humphrey accepted the plan, but when President Johnson bitterly rejected it, Humphrey abandoned it (to his later expressed regret).

So the Vietnam issue went to a bitter and divisive floor fight at the convention. I watched the three-hour debate on TV in Malibu. There was a long demonstration on the floor when Pierre Salinger said that Robert Kennedy would have supported the peace plank if he had lived. But the administration plank, described by Ted Sorensen as one "on which Richard Nixon or even Barry Goldwater could run with pleasure," was rammed through by Johnson's representatives, 1,527 votes to 1,041.

I didn't want to watch Humphrey being nominated on that platform. After the vote on the Vietnam plank, I turned off the TV. So it wasn't till the next morning that I saw the film clips of the police riot in Chicago that night, with McCarthy organizers like Dave Mixner pushed through the plate-glass windows of the Hilton Hotel and pursued inside by club-swinging cops; clouds of tear gas drifting up to the McCarthy and Humphrey suites and the improvised first-aid stations for beaten demonstrators, staffers, and journalists on the upper floors of the Hilton; chaos on the floor of the convention, during the voting, as delegates denounced the outside mayhem they were watching on TV screens throughout the hall. I remember that the news portions of the *Today* show the next morning showed film of demonstrators being tossed through the air into paddy wagons. The film was in slow motion so that it looked like a ballet, and, unusually, the producers had added a sound track; it was Frank Sinatra singing slowly in the background, "Chicago, Chicago." I turned off the TV again, tuned off on the campaign, and dropped out.

I didn't watch another moment of the campaign on television till Johnson actually stopped the bombing on October 31, five days before the vote. I wasn't very absorbed in my project at Rand either; "the lessons to be learned from Vietnam" were too depressing. I didn't spend a lot of time at the office and didn't care much if I was fired. I didn't care much about anything. It was a depressing time for many Americans. Looking back on that summer and fall, I thought we had been in a kind of political depression not unlike an economic depression: The majority of people were out of work politically. There seemed nothing useful to do if you wanted to end the war. We had two major candidates going around the country not talking about ending the bombing. That was not an incentive to help either of them win or even to pay much attention to them.

In retrospect, there really *was* a great difference between the two candidates. There wasn't much difference between Nixon and Johnson in their perspectives on Vietnam, and there really was a big difference, in secret, between Johnson and his vice president. Thus, there was actually a large difference between Nixon and Humphrey in their private views on Vietnam. But neither of them made it possible for most people to know that. Certainly I didn't, and I also didn't know anyone else who did. In hindsight, timely support from a lot of us for Humphrey, tipping a razor-close election to him, could have made an enormous difference to Vietnam, sparing it, and America, five or six more years of war.

Yet I can't strongly reproach myself or the many others who withheld effort or support that might have made the difference. That included McCarthy, who refused to endorse Humphrey till the last days of the campaign and then did so only halfheartedly, or the antiwar activists, starting with the demonstrators in Chicago, who acted on the assumption that there was no difference between the candidates, didn't worry if their actions hurt the Democrats or helped Nixon, and denounced anyone who did endorse Humphrey. These choices turned out to be consequential, even tragic, but given the information available, I can't find much to blame. Throughout this story I do hold myself accountable for various sins of omission or commission, times when I didn't act on what I knew or felt. This was a time when I, like others, couldn't act on what I didn't know. In particular, Nixon successfully concealed his intentions, except to a select few who he knew would support them. If I had even guessed that fall about what I came to know—almost alone, outside the White House—of those intentions one year later, I would have been acting desperately to prevent his election. As it was, those ten weeks were almost the only period in eleven years when my thoughts were not focused obsessively on Vietnam policy. Most of my energy went instead, obsessively, into a bachelor private life.

When Johnson announced on October 31 that he was halting all bombing of the North, I woke up to the campaign. I remember the first Humphrey-Muskie paid ad I watched on TV. It was informal footage, a home movie depicting Humphrey and Muskie, in shirtsleeves, bowling together in some private two-lane recreation room, and the pinsetter jammed on them. They had to walk down the alley together and fix it. A voice-over said, "It was that kind of a campaign. . . ." In Nixon's ads, I found, he was typically buttoned down, tight ass. The contrast gave me some enthusiasm for voting after all. Anyway, it was obvious that Humphrey would be much better on *domestic* issues. I stopped at the campaign office in Santa Monica and got a Humphrey-Muskie poster, which I taped to the hood of my Spitfire. It wasn't a big contribution to the campaign—though the tape did take paint off my hood when I removed it a few days later—but it symbolized to me that I cared again who won.

The race was a dead heat at that point, with some polls showing Humphrey slightly ahead. He had managed to come up from being fifteen points behind Nixon after he had finally brought himself, in late September, to say that he would end the bombing of North Vietnam. The decisive spurt came in the last few days when the president in effect joined that position; it halted abruptly the day before the vote, when President Thieu announced his refusal to join negotiations in Paris.

Humphrey got about 31,270,000 votes (including mine) on November 5, or 42.7 percent of the total. Wallace had approximately 9,906,000 votes, 13.5 percent, sharply down from the 20 percent support he had been showing in polls before he introduced his running mate General LeMay in a press conference in which the former chief of the Strategic Air Command gave a surrealistic imitation of General Jack D. Ripper in *Dr. Strangelove.* The winner got about 31,770,000 votes, 500,000 more than Humphrey, a winning margin of less than seven-tenths of 1 percent.

Richard Nixon was elected president with 43.4 percent of the vote. Not much of a mandate for anything specific. Still, it was clear that most voters—not just those who had voted for him—expected him to end the war. He had promised an ending "with honor." Many Americans liked the sound of that. But how did he intend to get there? And what did "with honor" mean to him? The answer, as I learned nearly a year later, was that it meant more to him than almost anyone else guessed. It meant that the war would not end in his first term or, if he had had his way, in his second.

15

To the Hotel Pierre

For two years after Lyndon Johnson's decision not to run again for president, from his announcement on March 31, 1968, to Nixon's invasion of Cambodia on April 30, 1970, the Vietnam War more or less disappeared from the mainstream of American political debate as a major issue. In that whole period, which included the Democratic primaries, the fall election campaign, and the first sixteen months of the Nixon administration, it surfaced as a debate, briefly, only twice: during the Chicago convention and in some six weeks of tumultuous protest in the fall of 1969.

The lack of public controversy (except for these brief eruptions) reflected a tenacious belief underlying American political discussion: that Johnson's March 31 announcement, which included his decision to end the bombing of the northern part of North Vietnam and to seek public negotiations with Hanoi, constituted a conscious and decisive turning point toward the prompt ending of major American involvement in the war in Indochina.

The Pentagon Papers themselves—the top secret "History of U.S. Decision-making in Vietnam, 1945–68"—reflect in their closing pages and in their very title this same interpretation. The study, when launched by McNamara in mid-1967, was formally open-ended in terms of content and time period, and work on it continued into early 1969; but its authors and its supervisors decided to end it with Johnson's speech of March 31, 1968. The choice of this cutoff date for the history of U.S. decision making in Vietnam clearly reflected the fact that those in charge of the study (Morton

H. Halperin and Leslie Gelb, under Paul Warnke) shared the public's belief that the decisions announced on that date meant a decisive shift toward U.S. disengagement. A three-page "Epilogue" at the end of the study begins with the April 3 announcement by Hanoi that it would negotiate with the United States and goes on: "The first step on what would undoubtedly be a long and tortuous road to peace apparently had been taken. In one dramatic action, President Johnson had for a time removed the issue of Vietnam from domestic political contention."

"For a time" turned out to be for most of the next two years.

What was remarkable about this prolonged period of misguided public confidence that peace was at hand was that although some form of talks and eventually formal negotiations were proceeding throughout the interval, so was the war, and at much the same scale of violence as before, especially in the air. After March 1968, U.S. planes were no longer bombing above the twentieth parallel in North Vietnam. After November they were not bombing North Vietnam at all. But they simply shifted their targets to South Vietnam and Laos (and secretly, in early 1969, to Cambodia as well), while dropping a higher total tonnage than before.

For an interval from November 1968 to August 1969, I was as (mistakenly) hopeful as anyone else about the prospects for a negotiated settlement. But I seemed to be among a very small minority who kept the reality of continued large-scale war in mind, along with the possibility that the war might actually go on for a very long time and the recurrent possibility that it might escalate, by deliberate decision in Washington or Hanoi.

By November 6, 1968, the day after the election, I was back to my regular obsession with Vietnam after ten weeks of determinedly not thinking about it. To read that morning that Hubert Humphrey had lost was not a cause for consternation for me. I'd voted for Humphrey for every reason *but* Vietnam, and that was still my main concern. I knew no reason to think that Nixon would prolong the Democrats' failed war longer than Humphrey; if anything, as a Republican, he might do the contrary. The bombing of the North had stopped, opening the prospect for real negotiations, and Nixon had supported that publicly. He'd even offered to go to Saigon, just before the election, to urge Thieu to end his refusal to join the Paris talks.

In fact the worst comment I heard on Nixon came from Harvard's Henry Kissinger, the long-time protégé and adviser of Nelson Rockefeller. He visited Rand on Friday, November 8, three days after the election, at the invitation of Fred Iklé, head of the Social Science Department. In a talk that day Kissinger repeated in his deep, somber Germanic drawl a statement he was reported to have made at the Republican National Convention: "Richard Nixon is not fit to be president."

It seemed an indiscreet remark for someone who was active in Republican politics, especially now that Nixon had been elected president. Anyway, it didn't stop Kissinger from accepting Nixon's invitation a few weeks later to be his special assistant for national security.

This was one of Kissinger's first visits to Rand, after a long period of coldness that had begun in the late 1950s because of Rand's critique of his advocacy of limited nuclear wars as instruments of U.S. policy in his 1957 book *Nuclear Weapons and Foreign Policy.* The theme had drawn more favorable attention from Nixon, then vice president. A photograph on the front page of the *New York Times* showed Nixon holding the book under his arm with the title clearly displayed as he entered a meeting of the National Security Council. I remember thinking it was an unusual book promotion.

But neither Nixon nor Kissinger had made positive public comments about nuclear weapons for years. In recent years Iklé had befriended Kissinger and patched up his relationship with Rand. And on the subject of Vietnam, I had quite a favorable impression of him, going back to discussions in Saigon in 1965, when he'd visited as a consultant to Ambassador Lodge.

He seemed to return the feeling. In that talk in November 1968 he told the Rand audience, of which I was a member, "I have learned more from Dan Ellsberg than from any other person in Vietnam." It was a nice thing to hear in front of my colleagues; Kissinger has an engaging habit of saying very flattering things about a person in his or her presence. I guessed what he might be referring to. It was not so much specific information I had given him in our talk in Saigon in October 1965—I had been no expert on Vietnam at that point, having arrived only a couple of months before—as it was some useful advice on how to learn in Vietnam that I had passed on to him. He had started by asking a good question: how to inform himself quickly.

I had told him to avoid wasting his time at official briefings or in talking to anyone in the presence of his boss or agency head. Instead he should seek out individuals who had spent a long time in Vietnam, who were known to be savvy about the situation—in particular, people who spoke Vietnamese, had knowledgeable Vietnamese friends, and moved in the countryside as well as the cities. He should talk to them privately, ask them for the names of others they respected, and then talk to those people separately. He should especially ask them for the names of Vietnamese to talk to. I'd been lucky enough to get that advice when I arrived, and it was working for me. I gave him a list of Americans and Vietnamese to start him off.

I had told him that so far as I'd heard, McNamara never did any of these things on his frequent trips to Vietnam. The defense secretary got elaborate briefings and talked to the top officials, and when he met with advisers or lower commanders, it was always in the presence of their commanding generals. He never seemed to realize—so I'd been told—how much these practices cost him, how they enabled the embassy and MACV to manipulate him, or how much he was being misled. The same applied to virtually all other high-level visitors.

I was impressed that Kissinger actually acted on my advice, unlike other visitors to whom I said the same things. He did see the people I suggested, and in a couple of brief visits he learned a lot. He's an incisive questioner and a very good listener, who takes notes. Before long he had become realistically skeptical and pessimistic, especially about the character and prospects of the Saigon regime.

In 1967 and 1968 I had been with him in conferences on Vietnam, where he was expressing a point of view that was well in advance of that of any other mainstream political figure at that point. He argued that our only objective in Vietnam should be to get some sort of assurance of what he called a "decent interval" between our departure and a Communist takeover, so that we could withdraw without the humiliation of an abrupt, naked collapse of our earlier objectives. He didn't spell out how long such an interval might be; most discussions seemed to assume something between six months and two years. Few imagined that the Communists would wait any longer than that or that a government including them could hold together longer once our troops had departed.

How would we get a delay even that long? Kissinger's premise was that the North Vietnamese would be induced to remove their troops in a negotiated mutual withdrawal. That would leave the GVN and ARVN confronting only the NLF. With our continued material and financial aid, they should be able to delay a Communist victory for a year or two or make a deal with them that would hold up that long. Meanwhile they would have time to prepare for the new regime coming, by either emigrating or finding some way to accommodate to it.

Would Hanoi agree to mutual withdrawal? In 1969 and later the answer turned out to be no; over the next six years the North never came close to accepting it. But that answer wasn't obvious, either to me or to others, in 1968. The proposal hadn't yet been put forward in negotiations—in fact there hadn't yet been any serious talks at all—and it seemed to offer enough to the North Vietnamese that there was at least a chance they would accept it. So this proposal seemed to be the right place to start in negotiations. As in 1967, calls for total unilateral U.S. withdrawal, either gradual or immediate, were still left mainly to radical intellectuals like Howard Zinn and Noam Chomsky (whom I was just beginning to read), peace activists and agitators like Abbie Hoffman and Dave Dellinger, and the Peace and Freedom candidate Eldridge Cleaver. The only major public figure who had proposed this, I later realized, was Martin Luther King, Jr.

The Republican platform for the 1968 campaign was very close to the Johnson-supported plank of the Democrats. Nixon's people had joined forces with representatives of Nelson Rockefeller, notably Henry Kissinger, to resist the more hawkish position of Governor Ronald Reagan. However, Kissinger's personal views seemed closer to the peace plank of the Democratic dissenters than to either party's official platform. In particular, his practical objective of a decent interval seemed less ambitious and more realistic than what anyone else in the mainstream was willing to state publicly. It went well beyond encouragement of a coalition government—the compromise plank that Humphrey had accepted but that Johnson and his forces had shot down—to stipulate acceptance of a Communist government in Saigon, not immediately but within a couple of years. No other major figure was saying that publicly.

Of course Kissinger hadn't yet made his proposals publicly either, but he was presumably already pressing them on his Republican candidate, Nelson Rockefeller. Although mainstream critics calling for an end to the bombing and to U.S. involvement hinted at an acceptance of an eventual Communist government in South Vietnam, they weren't saying that explicitly, even in private discussion. Kissinger's willingness to speak of that as an acceptable outcome in the fairly short run was unusual for those circles.

Altogether, then, to a wide circle of nonhawkish insiders and academics who knew what Kissinger had been saying in 1968, it was reassuring when Nixon surprisingly picked him for his national security assistant after the election. The heartening inference was that Nixon's own inclination to "get out of Vietnam" was at least as great as Humphrey's. This presumption was strengthened when Kissinger's *Foreign Affairs* article "The Vietnam Negotiations" appeared in January 1969. It finally spelled out in public and in some detail his formerly private arguments for seeking no more than a "decent interval" before a Communist takeover. It was in many respects a valuable contribution to the mainstream debate on Vietnam. But given the timing and context, it seemed to be much more than that. Appearing simultaneously with the inauguration of the new administration, to which his own appointment had been announced two months earlier, the article looked unmistakably like a presentation of newly official views. It was taken for granted that the incoming president must have read the text, or at least known its substance, before making the appointment and that he must have approved its publication. An indelible impression was created that President Nixon endorsed Kissinger's published ideas.

This impression was greatly mistaken and very misleading. So long as he was in office, and even afterward, Nixon never accepted that Saigon should become Ho Chi Minh City under a Communist regime after a "decent interval," or ever, and he was prepared not only to prolong the war indefinitely but to expand it to prevent that. Kissinger had almost certainly been informed of this by his new boss before his article appeared. But it was a secret, which he kept very well, from everyone outside the White House and most within.

Soon after his appointment by President-elect Nixon, Kissinger asked Harry Rowen, president of Rand, for a study of Vietnam "options" to prepare for his first National Security Council meeting in January. He made the request through Fred Iklé. Harry proposed that I head this project; it was a natural choice, given my background. Kissinger approved, though with one reservation, which Iklé came to me to pass on. He told me that Kissinger was happy to have me do the study, but he had one worry about me, my "discretion."

I was astonished. No one had ever raised such a question before, over the last decade. My whole career was based on a well-founded trust in my discretion. (I didn't believe that Kissinger, or anyone else outside the *New York Times,* knew about my onetime leaks to Neil Sheehan the previous March.) What could have raised this concern?

Fred answered, "Henry said that he had benefited greatly from your frankness in speaking with him in Vietnam. But now that he was on the other side of the fence, he saw things differently," meaning his memory of my candor in Saigon—the very basis of his flattering comment weeks before—worried him when it came to taking me on as a consultant. I said to Fred, "But when I was speaking with him then, he was an official consultant to my boss, the ambassador!" No matter; the message was that standards of discretion were going to be higher now. It turned out Kissinger was sensitive about letting it be known that he had turned for help to Rand, an outside group regarded as relatively dovish (by Republican standards) within the defense community. He particularly didn't want it known that I was associated with the study, since by that time I was known by insiders to be a critic of our involvement. It was a sign of his respect for me that he was willing to have me direct the project anyway. I reassured Fred that Henry needn't worry.

Personally, however, I had some misgivings about doing staff work like this on Vietnam at this stage of the game. It was obvious that from Kissinger's point of view, introducing himself both to the president and to the bureaucracy, his presentation would have to be "balanced," "objective," just presenting "alternative options" without arguing strongly for one over another. Necessary as that was for him, I didn't feel easy at this point about suppressing my own hard-won views about various matters on which I felt strongly, in a presentation to be made to the president. If a new president, whether it was Nixon or Wallace, wanted to know what I or someone else at Rand with experience on Vietnam actually thought—or even if he hadn't asked for it, if there was some way to get our views in front of him—that was fine, nothing could be better. But that wasn't exactly what was being asked for here.

However, Rand had wanted for years to operate at a higher level of policy than the air force or even the Defense Department. This was the first real chance it had ever had to work directly for the White House. Being helpful to Kissinger might open doors for Rand. I also wanted to be helpful to Harry, despite my misgivings about presenting "fairly"—as if I thought they were reasonable—some approaches that I had come to believe were dangerous traps. Besides, it occurred to me that even if I had to be more evenhanded in my presentation of pros and cons than I really wanted, there were advantages to being in charge of the project. I could ensure that the cons of escalation and the pros of more dovish alternatives were presented more adequately, more fully and forcefully than others—say, a working group including military officers responsive to service or JCS superiors—were likely to do.

Defining strategic alternatives reflecting various objectives and points of view—in ways that would be accepted by their respective advocates as expressing their perspectives accurately—had long been a professional specialty of mine, at Rand and in the government. It was another reason, along with my experience in Vietnam and Washington, that made me a logical coordinator of this project.

But on one point, when it came to defining the "whole range of options," I did take a strong stand. One person, in one of the initial exploratory meetings I chaired, said that for completeness there should at least be mention of the possible use of nuclear weapons. I said, not if I were to have anything to do with the project. I wouldn't be party to a paper that suggested in any way that nuclear weapons deserved consideration in any conceivable circumstances in Vietnam. No one raised the issue again, and the word "nuclear" didn't occur in any of the drafts.

There was about to be a new administration, a new party in power after eight years. The Tet offensive had demolished the underpinnings of the Westmoreland strategy, and Secretary Clifford had put a ceiling on troop levels. Formal negotiations were about to get under way. The country was ready for, was demanding and expecting, a change in course. Overwhelmingly what was wanted was to move in the direction of withdrawal. But how, how fast, with what rationale?

I went to Washington for over a week to check my contacts in the Pentagon and State. I read cables and estimates and talked at length with Mort Halperin, Les Gelb, and a number of others to get their ideas on what information a new president most required. I concluded that what he needed above all else was to be alerted to a split in thinking within official circles that was sharper and more systematic than had existed for years.

In the afternoon of Christmas Eve 1968, I gave the last draft of the options paper to the secretaries at Rand to type up. By arrangement with my former wife, I spent Christmas Eve with my children; I gave them their presents that night in Malibu. The next morning, Christmas Day, I dropped them off at their mother's, picked up the copies of the paper at Rand, and drove to the airport with Harry Rowen and Fred Iklé. That evening in New York we checked into the Hotel Pierre, which Nixon and Kissinger were using as their office quarters during the transition. We gave the study to Kissinger for him to read overnight. I was scheduled to discuss it with him the next day.

The next morning in the hotel room Henry was using as his office, I went over the twenty-seven-page draft with him page by page. Fred and Harry weren't present, but Kissinger had invited Tom Schelling to come to New York to sit in for this. Schelling, an economics professor at Harvard, had been a key influence on my thinking about bargaining theory. He had been the official adviser on my Harvard Ph.D. thesis on uncertainty. Now also a Rand consultant, he had become my close friend. I hadn't realized how close Kissinger and Schelling were too.

As it turned out, Schelling raised more questions than Kissinger. One of his first comments was: "Dan, you don't have a win strategy here, one that you yourself think would win." Actually, the first three military strategies offered were described as aiming at a "Communist 'Fade Away' or Negotiated Victory," and the beliefs of their advocates that these would succeed, within varying estimates of time, were spelled out explicitly. But it was obvious that I had no faith at all in these predictions, or their underlying assumptions, or the respective strategies.

Tom said, "It seems to me that when you're confronting a new president with a full range of alternatives, you ought to lay out for him a strategy that you think would win, even if you wouldn't recommend it because you think it would cost too much or would be too dangerous, or for some other reason. You'd say, 'Here's what you'd have to do for victory,' even if you don't think he should do it."

I said, "But I don't believe that there *is* a way to win. It doesn't exist. Some people think they know how to do it, and I've laid out their approaches, but I think they're all kidding themselves. I'm not convinced that any of their hopes are more than illusions."

There was a short silence. As far as I knew, Kissinger had reached that same conclusion himself years earlier. I went on: "You could put a million troops into South Vietnam, or maybe two million, and you could keep the place quiet as long as they stayed there. Till they left.

"You can invade North Vietnam, like the French, and have a war five times worse than what we've had. You can chase the Communists across the borders, into Laos and China, and pursue them there. How far are you prepared to follow them, and for how long?

"And you could kill all the people, with nuclear weapons. I wouldn't call that winning." In fact, I added, if anything survived at all, it would probably be the control apparatus of the Lao Dong (Vietnamese Communist) party, which could operate from Laos or China, if necessary.

Schelling didn't press the point. But he came up with another, more telling criticism: "You haven't said anything in here about threats. You don't have a threat tactic."

I was taken aback. Schelling and I both were analysts of bargaining theory and threats, and he was my mentor. For him to have to be the one to point this omission out to me was embarrassing. I said, "You're right." Then

I added, "It's hard for me to believe that new threats of escalation could have any effect on them. We actually bombed them for three years, and that didn't give us any bargaining power." Nevertheless, I had included other options preferred by the Pentagon that I didn't think would work.

Kissinger finally spoke, in his gravelly accent: "How can you conduct diplomacy without a threat of escalation? Without that there is no basis for negotiations."

I said, "Well, Henry, a lot of negotiation, a lot of bargaining, does go on in the world without a threat of bombing."

But I took Tom's point; I said I would include a threat option in the next draft. I worked on that the rest of the day and into the next and handed it in that afternoon.

In a second meeting with Kissinger at the Pierre on December 27, I discussed the purpose behind the set of questions I'd included as an appendix to the options paper. I told him about the questions McNamara had addressed to various parts of the Department of Defense when he had come into the Pentagon and about another set of questions that I had later drafted on the JCS plans for general nuclear war, which the deputy secretary of defense had sent to the Joint Chiefs in the spring of 1961. In both cases, their value wasn't just for getting information; the questions themselves had great impact. They helped establish McNamara's authority in the building, early. For one thing, they showed that he and his deputy had advisers who were very familiar with bureaucratic controversies within the building. So it would be dangerous to try to snow him or mislead him with a united front that papered over disputed issues because—the very nature of the questions revealed—he evidently had people at his right hand who already knew "where the bodies were buried." He had either current sources within their agencies or advisers whose knowledge of such sources and agency disputes was quite recent. Either way, the recipients of these questions could foresee, he would know if he were being bamboozled, and he presumably would respond accordingly.

Moreover, in the case of Vietnam it was important for the president to learn just how much uncertainty and controversy there was about many important matters. He wouldn't find that out if he followed the usual practice of addressing a question only to the agency that had primary responsibility for a given matter. Other agencies that were normally forbidden, by rules of the bureaucratic game, from kibitzing on that matter or forwarding their own views directly to the president might have information or judgments that were not only different (signaling an area of uncertainty) but actually more convincing, objective, and reliable than the sole opinion the president ordinarily sought.

An example was the dispute between the generals in Vietnam and the CIA on just how strong the Vietcong forces were during the previous year. Normally no civilian intelligence agency was called on or even allowed to make an estimate of enemy forces independently from the JCS or the field commander, though the CIA's estimates (before it caved in to MACV in 1967) had been more relevant and accurate. But there were a dozen such disputes right now—for example, the performance of ARVN or the possibility of stopping infiltration by mining Haiphong or bombing the North. Civilian agencies like the CIA or the intelligence branch of State (INR) or the civilians in the Defense Department (International Security Affairs and Systems Analysis) wouldn't normally be called on to give direct opinions on "military" subjects to the president. If they presumed to do that, the military, the JCS and MACV, would be outraged and claim that "these civilians" were exceeding their authority and their expertise.

As for expertise, including objectivity and veracity, that accusation was often flat wrong, in terms of relative information, regional experience, and analytical ability. For that matter, many of the experts in these civilian agencies were also highly competent military officers. Their judgments on these matters at the moment weren't just different and more pessimistic than those of their parent services; they were a lot more reliable. But the military, defending its turf, could normally keep the president from hearing these "unqualified" or "renegade" opinions.

What Nixon could do once in office, I suggested, was address certain questions—chosen precisely in awareness of, and designed to expose, such controversies—to the whole set of interested agencies and to call for separate, parallel responses from them without coordination. You couldn't forbid coordination as a general practice—it was of the essence of the bureaucratic process—but on a onetime basis, with a short deadline for response to make coordination more difficult, you could legitimize presentation to the president of divergent and well-informed "rogue" opinions that wouldn't normally ever make it to the top.

This process would guard the new president against two current problems at once. First, the answers he would otherwise get from the principal agency would often be wrong or less reliable than he could get elsewhere. Second, right or wrong, these opinions would be presented with a degree of certainty that was unwarranted and misleading. A onetime collection of contradictory judgments on the same issue might be disconcerting to the White House, but it would be a valuable warning of the uncertainties.

Moreover, the very revelation of controversies and the extremely unconvincing positions of some of the primary agencies (in light of the unaccustomed challenges and rebuttals alongside their own answers) would be embarrassing to the bureaucracy as a whole. It would put the bureaucrats off-balance and on the defensive relative to the source of the questions—that is, Kissinger.

Kissinger liked the sound of that. It had a special attraction for him that I didn't know at the time: Nixon intended, with his help, to concentrate the control of foreign policy, including Vietnam, in the White House, and my last point would serve Kissinger's moves to that end. Moreover, he had Morton Halperin drafting for him at that very moment new procedures for coordinating interagency planning under his chairmanship at the NSC. In the month ahead, the questions that I was to draft for him and that he issued kept the various agencies distracted and preoccupied while he got these new arrangements into place; he may have foreseen this potential effect as I talked to him.

In any case, at the end of my discussion, Kissinger told me to separate my list of questions from the options paper and to make it considerably larger (my original set was presented only as examples), and he would issue it as a separate research directive, a National Security Study Memorandum (NSSM). (This became NSSM-1, the first of hundreds of studies he was later to request.) He asked me to work full-time on that starting immediately. Preparing a final version of the options paper should be left to Fred Iklé.

Kissinger was not rushing to end our conversation that morning, and I had one more message to give him. "Henry, there's something I would like to tell you, for what it's worth, something I wish I had been told years ago. You've been a consultant for a long time, and you've dealt a great deal with top secret information. But you're about to receive a whole slew of special clearances, maybe fifteen or twenty of them, that are higher than top secret.

"I've had a number of these myself, and I've known other people who have just acquired them, and I have a pretty good sense of what the effects of receiving these clearances are on a person who didn't previously know they even *existed.* And the effects of reading the information that they will make available to you.

"First, you'll be exhilarated by some of this new information, and by having it all—so much! incredible!—suddenly available to you. But second, almost as fast, you will feel like a fool for having studied, written, talked about these subjects, criticized and analyzed decisions made by presidents for years without having known of the existence of all this information, which presidents and others had and you didn't, and which must have influenced their decisions in ways you couldn't even guess. In particular, you'll feel foolish for having literally rubbed shoulders for over a decade with some officials and consultants who did have access to all this information you didn't know about and didn't know they had, and you'll be stunned that they kept that secret from you so well.

"You will feel like a fool, and that will last for about two weeks. Then, after you've started reading all this daily intelligence input and become used to using what amounts to whole libraries of hidden information, which is much more closely held than mere top secret data, you will forget there ever was a time when you didn't have it, and you'll be aware only of the fact that you have it now and most others don't . . . and that all those *other* people are fools.

"Over a longer period of time—not too long, but a matter of two or three years—you'll eventually become aware of the limitations of this information. There is a great deal that it doesn't tell you, it's often inaccurate, and it can lead you astray just as much as the *New York Times* can. But that takes a while to learn.

"In the meantime it will have become very hard for you to *learn* from anybody who doesn't have these clearances. Because you'll be thinking as you listen to them: 'What would this man be telling me if he knew what I know? Would he be giving me the same advice, or would it totally change his predictions and recommendations?' And *that* mental exercise is so torturous that after a while you give it up and just stop listening. I've seen this with my superiors, my colleagues . . . and with myself.

"You will deal with a person who doesn't have those clearances only from the point of view of what you want him to believe and what impression you want him to go away with, since you'll have to lie carefully to him about what you know. In effect, you will have to manipulate him. You'll give up trying to assess what he has to say. The danger is, you'll become something like a moron. You'll become incapable of learning from most people in the world, no matter how much experience they may have in their particular areas that may be much greater than yours."

It was a speech I had thought through before, one I'd wished someone had once given me, and I'd long hoped to be able to give it to someone who was just about to enter the world of "real" executive secrecy. I ended by saying that I'd long thought of this kind of secret information as something like the potion Circe gave to the wanderers and shipwrecked men who happened on her island, which turned them into swine. They became incapable of human speech and couldn't help one another to find their way home.

Kissinger hadn't interrupted this long warning. As I've said, he could be a good listener, and he listened soberly. He seemed to understand that it was heartfelt, and he didn't take it as patronizing, as I'd feared. But I knew it was too soon for him to appreciate fully what I was saying. He didn't have the clearances yet.

In mid-February Halperin called me to Washington to read through the agency replies to NSSM-1, more than five hundred pages in all. His assistant, Winston Lord, a young Foreign Service officer, was coordinating the answers, farming out different sections to parts of the NSC staff to compare and summarize them for the president. Since I'd written almost all the questions with an eye to the likely controversies, Halperin wanted me to be the one to read the entire batch of answers and check that the partial summaries caught the most important agreements or disagreements. I also helped Lord draft the final summary, though he did most of the writing, based on the sections from the working group he established.

The split of opinion did show up as I'd predicted in my draft of the options paper. One coalition consisting of the JCS, MACV, CINCPAC, and Saigon embassy, often joined by the East Asia bureau of State, took a consistently optimistic line, though without coming close to assuring victory in any time frame. Their views were sharply counterbalanced by the other group, made up of the CIA, the Office of the Secretary of Defense (ISA and Systems Analysis), INR (State Department intelligence), and the civilian analysts in Washington, who were far more conservative or pessimistic than the first group in their views of progress in pacification (they saw none), of the effects of bombing in Laos and Vietnam on the war in the South (likewise), and of VC influence in the countryside and overall strength. The latter seemed far more realistic to me, but in any case I was glad to see their estimates presented to the president, on matters in which otherwise the MACV and JCS estimates would have stood unchallenged. Even the average of the optimistic (first group, military) estimates of GVN control and pacification progress implied that it would take 8.3 years to pacify the 4.15 million contested and VC population of December 1968. The more pessimistic estimates implied success (if ever) in 13.4 years. The practical significance of that difference was not great.

More important, the NSSM-1 exercise finally put to rest the attrition strategy, for good. MACV, along with the JCS, had to concede that even the huge losses suffered by the NVA and NLF during 1968 were not beyond their ability easily to recoup, from the recruiting pools open to them both in the South and the North. Moreover, without more Tet-like offensives, that rate of attrition could not be forced on them. "Three fourths of the battles are at the enemy's choice of time, place, type and duration. CIA notes that less than one percent of nearly two million Allied small unit operations conducted in the last two years resulted in contact with the enemy and when ARVN is surveyed, the percentage drops to one tenth of one percent." Thus, all respondents agreed (at last), "Under current rules of engagement [limiting ground combat to South Vietnam] the enemy's manpower pool and infiltration capabilities can outlast allied attrition efforts indefinitely. The enemy basically controls both sides' casualty rates."

Some of the points of general agreement were more significant than the disagreements. We reported consensus to the president:

> —The GVN has improved its political position, but it is not certain that the GVN and other non-communist groups will be able to survive a peaceful competition with the NLF for political power in South Vietnam.
>
> —The RVNAF [all forms of Saigon military forces, including ARVN] alone cannot now, or in the foreseeable future, stand up to the current North Vietnamese–Viet Cong forces.
>
> —The enemy have suffered some reverses but they have not changed their essential objectives and they have sufficient strength to pursue these objectives. We are not attriting his forces faster than he can recruit or infiltrate.

All agreed that the soon-to-be-announced Vietnamization policy enlarging, reequipping, and modernizing the ARVN and non-Communist militia forces to take over a larger combat role would never make them adequate to stand up to a sizable number of NVA (North Vietnamese regular) forces without "U.S. combat support in the form of air, helicopters, artillery, logistics and some ground forces." In fact the JCS, MACV, and CINCPAC believed that it would take three years, at least, before the RVNAF alone could cope even with the southern Vietcong insurgency, without that U.S. combat support. The Defense Department didn't think that goal would be met even by 1972, or ever, without major and unlikely reforms in the ARVN.

After Winston Lord and I had finished the summary of the answers to NSSM-1 for the president, I decided to suggest some subjects for further studies, including a study of the actual extent of civilian damage from our artillery and bombing in Vietnam. Another alluded to the most recent National Intelligence Estimate (NIE 50-68), which had downgraded the domino theory, concluding that such a development would bring Cambodia and Laos into Hanoi's orbit but would "not necessarily unhinge the rest of Asia." All the agencies answering NSSM-1, as Lord and I reported, "reject the view that an unfavorable settlement in Vietnam will inevitably be followed by Communist takeovers outside Indochina." Some were more pessimistic, but "phrasing the adverse results in terms such as 'pragmatic adjustments' by the Thais and 'some means of accommodation'" did not make it clear how injurious they would be to U.S. security. After fifteen years of dire internal warnings of "accommodations" and "adjustments," never defined, throughout Southeast Asia and beyond if Vietnam became Communist, I proposed an interagency study at last be undertaken of what these terms might mean concretely and of why and how much we should care.

When Mort Halperin presented my proposed studies to Kissinger for his possible signature, Kissinger told him, "We've had enough questions for now." That didn't sound unreasonable to me as a matter of timing after the two dozen questions of NSSM-1 we had just sent out, but of course none of these studies was ever performed.

As I prepared to leave, it was obvious to me that the five hundred pages or so of answers from all the different agencies to the questions of NSSM-1 would be of extreme interest to my colleagues at Rand who were working on various research projects on Vietnam. In fact, there was really nothing like them—parallel answers by a variety of agencies to the same questions without coordination. This was the sort of data that any Rand employee participating in a working group in Washington would try to get back to one or more colleagues in Santa Monica for their benefit. Mort Halperin knew that, of course. So he took me aside in the Executive Office Building offices one morning and said, "I'm going to ask you not to show any of this material to anybody at Rand or to take any copies back with you." There was a certain plausibility to this request, since this was material in the possession of the NSC, which would not normally be accessible to a contractor. In fact, so far as I was aware, there were very few precedents, if any, for a Rand researcher, such as myself, to participate in an NSC study or to have any access to such material.

I took it for granted from Mort's unemphatic, pro forma tone that what he meant was simply to go on the record as telling me not to do this, thereby signaling that it should not get back to the White House that Rand had his material and indicating definitely that he, Mort Halperin, had not authorized its transfer or was aware of it.

It was obvious to me that this information was not that sensitive. The bulk of it was communication from the agencies to the NSC, not memos between the NSC staff members and the president. Also, it did not reflect views of the president or Henry Kissinger personally. The summary was for the eyes of the president and Kissinger, but it merely summarized the views of a subordinate agency. Anyway, if Mort had really been serious about keeping me from sending this back to Rand, he could have conveyed that very reliably, and he knew it, by his tone of voice and the look in his eyes as he said something to the effect of "Dan, this *really* can't go back. I mean it. I'm counting on you not to do it; and that means not to Harry Rowen, not to Fred Iklé, not to anybody."

So having registered Mort's warning and agreeing with him, I took care to copy all the documents myself in the copying alcove of the NSC, rather than hand them to a secretary to copy, as I would otherwise have done. When I took them back to Rand, I convened a rather large meeting of perhaps a dozen people working on Vietnam. Having made and passed out a number of copies, I repeated the warning that Halperin had given me that I not copy any of the documents and give them to people at Rand. I said this was presumably so he could disclaim responsibility for having given them to me and that it was important that no word should reach the White House that we had them. I said that if anyone was talking to Halperin or anybody else at the White House, he shouldn't indicate that he knew the contents of the papers or even that they existed at Rand, because I was sure that Halperin would not want to be put on notice that I had violated his instructions.

This wasn't an unfamiliar kind of warning to Rand analysts, though it had perhaps never involved the White House before. Documents that were obtained "under the counter" were always being brought back. If they were entered into the Rand records at all, they would be under a disguised description.

Some months later, to make sure for future reference that I was understanding communications from my friend and colleague Mort Halperin

John T. McNaughton, assistant secretary of defense, international security affairs, and my boss at the Pentagon.

An evening at Ed Lansdale's house in Saigon. *Left to right:* Lansdale, Ambassador Henry Cabot Lodge, and Lowell Kelso, team secretary.

Operations in Rach Kien district, December 1966 to January 1967.

Peter Arnett snapped this picture of the AP photographer Horst Faas and me at the end of the "long day" in Rach Kien.

Christmas Eve dinner 1966 in Rach Kien, with a U.S. Army adviser, an ARVN battalion commander, and, with his back to the camera, the major who spent much of the rest of the night trying to shoot the adviser and me.

Patricia and me in the Ganges River, Benares, India. The photo was taken by our boatman just after I proposed and she accepted, in January 1966.

General William Westmoreland shaking hands with Prime Minister Nguyen Cao Ky. Between them is Lansdale team member Colonel Napoleon Valeriano, U.S. Army. I look on at left.

Press conference at Andrews Air Force Base, October 1966. Secretary of Defense Robert McNamara, with General Earl Wheeler, chairman of the JCS, is telling the press about the progress he has just witnessed in Vietnam, minutes after telling me that everything was much worse than the year before. John McNaughton is at far left.

My knack for magic tricks always worked with kids in Vietnam.

John Paul Vann, my mentor, friend, and driving partner in Vietnam, in 1967.

Ed Lansdale and Tran Ngoc Chau seeing me off at Ton Son Nhut airport, June 1967.

Randy Kehler giving the talk at Haverford College on August 28, 1969, that opened my eyes to the possibilities of resisting war.

A break in the War Resisters' International Conference at Haverford. Janaki is standing behind us.

Robert, thirteen, Mary, ten, and me in Malibu, in the summer of 1969, just before we started copying the Pentagon Papers.

Patricia's and my wedding ceremony, August 8, 1970, in North Salem, New York. My brother and best man, Harry, is at left, partially obscured.

"All the News That's Fit to Print"

The New York Times

LATE CITY EDITION

Weather: Partly cloudy, chance of showers today, tonight, tomorrow. Temp. range: today 69-83; Saturday 65-85. Temp.-Hum. Index yesterday 78. Full U.S. report on Page 111.

SECTION ONE

VOL. CXX . . No. 41,413 — © 1971 The New York Times Company. — NEW YORK, SUNDAY, JUNE 13, 1971 — BQLI — 50 CENTS

Tricia Nixon Takes Vows In Garden at White House

CITY TO DISCLOSE BUDGETARY TRIMS FOR DEPARTMENTS

Mayor's Aides Make Decision on Final Figures Scheduled to Be Announced Today

By MAURICE CARROLL

Mayor Lindsay has summoned his supercabinet, the heads of all major city departments, to Gracie Mansion this morning to tell them the cuts that their departments face in his revised budget.

"All of them made their pitch to the Mayor within the last 48 hours," a mayoral aide said yesterday. "Sunday they get the word."

The $9.13-billion budget originally made public by the Mayor must be trimmed by a few hundred million dollars to reflect the revenue package he extracted from Albany, which provides for less than the $1.1-billion gap that Mr. Lindsay had said existed between projected income and spending.

No Details on Cuts

The Mayor's advisers were not saying precisely yesterday how much the budget would have to be cut, or where.

Vietnam Archive: Pentagon Study Traces 3 Decades of Growing U. S. Involvement

By NEIL SHEEHAN

A massive study of how the United States went to war in Indochina, conducted by the Pentagon three years ago, demonstrates that four administrations progressively developed a sense of commitment to a non-Communist Vietnam, a readiness to fight the North to protect the South, and an ultimate frustration with this effort—to a much greater extent than their public statements acknowledged at the time.

The 3,000-page analysis, to which 4,000 pages of official documents are appended, was commissioned by Secretary of Defense Robert S. McNamara and covers the American involvement in Southeast Asia from World War II to mid-1968—the start of the peace talks in Paris after President Lyndon B. Johnson had set a limit on further military commitments and revealed his intention to retire. Most of the study and many of the appended documents have been obtained by The New York Times and will be described and presented in a series of articles beginning today.

> Three pages of documentary material from the Pentagon study begin on Page 35.

Though far from a complete history, even at 2.5 million words, the study forms a great archive of government decision-making on Indochina over three decades. The study led its 30 to 40 authors and researchers to many broad conclusions and specific findings, including the following:

¶That the Truman Administration's decision to give military aid to France in her colonial war against the Communist-led Vietminh "directly involved" the United States in Vietnam and "set" the course of American policy.

¶That the Eisenhower Administration's decision to rescue a fledgling South Vietnam from a Communist takeover and attempt to undermine the new Communist regime of North Vietnam gave the Administration a "direct role in the ultimate breakdown of the Geneva settlement" for Indochina in 1954.

¶That the Kennedy Administration, though ultimately spared from major escalation decisions by the death of its leader, transformed a policy of "limited-risk gamble," which it inherited, into a "broad commitment" that left President Johnson with a choice between more war and withdrawal.

¶That the Johnson Administration, though the President was reluctant and hesitant to take the final decisions, intensified the covert warfare against North Vietnam and began planning in the spring of 1964 to wage overt war, a full year before it publicly revealed the depth of its involvement and its fear of defeat.

¶That this campaign of growing clandestine military pressure through 1964 and the expanding program of bombing North Vietnam in 1965 were begun despite the judgment of the Government's intelligence community that the measures would not cause Hanoi to cease its support of the Vietcong insurgency in the South, and that the bombing was

Continued on Page [illegible], Col. 1

NIXON CRITICIZED AS MAYORS MEET

Housing and War Policies

Vast Review of War Took . Year

By HEDRICK SMITH

In June, 1967, at a time of great personal disenchantment with the Indochina war and rising frustration among his colleagues bombing of North Vietnam and announced his plan to retire, and while the peace talks began in Paris, the study group burrowed through Government files mentary record, which the researchers did not supplement with personal interviews, partly because they were pressed for time.

The study emerged as a mid-

U.S. URGES INDIANS AND PAKISTANIS TO USE RESTRAINT

Calls for 'Peaceful Political Accommodation' to End Crisis in East Pakistan

FIRST PUBLIC APPEAL

Statement Is Said to Reflect Fear of Warfare if Flow of Refugees Continues

By TAD SZULC
Special to The New York Times

WASHINGTON, June 12—The United States appealed today to India and Pakistan to exercise restraint and urged the Pakistanis to restore normal conditions in East Pakistan through "peaceful political accommodation."

It was the first public statement by the United States on the situation in the subcontinent since the Pakistani Army last March 25 began quelling the East Pakistani movement for autonomy and later for independence. The statement reflected the increasing concern here that hostilities may erupt

The *New York Times* publishes the Pentagon Papers, June 13, 1971.

On June 28, 1971, after two weeks underground, Patricia and I arrived at the U.S. Courthouse and Post Office Building in Boston. I'm giving my statement to the press shortly before being placed under arrest. The Supreme Court voided the injunctions two days later, allowing the press to resume publication of the Pentagon Papers.

Anthony Russo, who copied the papers with me and, like me, was indicted and tried for that act.

Case dismissed, May 11, 1973.

correctly, I told him what I had done and what I had said at Rand. I asked him if I had been right in thinking that he had assumed I would do exactly this and that it was OK with him so long as he was not told about it by me or anyone else. Halperin said, "Of course."

In contrast, the warnings he gave me that same week, as I prepared to take some volumes of the McNamara study from Washington to Santa Monica, about sharing them or even the fact of my possession with anyone else at Rand, were entirely different. On these, the instructions for handling couldn't have been more explicit or restrictive. I had occasionally read drafts of some of the McNamara study when I was in the Pentagon in 1968. The last parts of the study, mainly dealing with the events of early 1968 and negotiations, had been completed late that year. Les Gelb had stayed on in ISA for a few months in the new administration, largely to finish up the editing and production of the study, before he moved to the Brookings Institution. In December he and his bosses Paul Warnke and Halperin had made a written agreement with Harry Rowen that two sets of the complete study, one belonging to Warnke and one to Halperin and Gelb, would be stored as classified materials at the Rand Washington office. (Brookings did no classified research and had no classified storage facilities.)

They made the unusual but not unique arrangement that the material, though stored, guarded, and handled as top secret, would not be entered in the formal top secret control system, which entailed its being logged in by the TS control officer, given a TS number, and entered in the records of TS materials. My assumption when I heard this was that it was their desire to have access to it, even though their TS clearances might have lapsed between government jobs. Evidently, as I learned later, that was not the reason. Halperin, in particular, was still concerned that Walt Rostow or someone else would come to worry about the existence of such a record and make an effort to hunt down all copies and destroy them. They wanted to assure that one or two copies of such a historical record survived. They didn't want it to show up in any official inventories, open to the air force, the Department of Defense, or the White House. For the same reason, they wanted knowledge of its presence at Rand limited to the utmost degree, preferably to Harry himself, lest word trickle back eventually to Rostow or others. Since that would have eliminated its usefulness to Rand as research material, they provided in the written agreement for others to be given access on an individual basis, but only with the consent of two of the three donors.

Harry and I urged that I be included, since I had looked forward to a comparative study of the volumes from the beginning of the project; I saw it potentially as the main basis for my project "Lessons of Vietnam." Gelb denied that he had made any such agreement with me—that was true—and had no memory of having encouraged me to think I might have complete access eventually. He and Halperin were initially reluctant to include me. I take it their concern was not that I would reveal the contents or existence of the study to anyone without a clearance but that I might let either slip to some colleagues, who would in turn want access. But after Harry pressed the point that my research depended on this—I may have been the only researcher on government contract anywhere at that particular point studying lessons from Vietnam, which notably was not a governmental obsession at the time—they agreed to add my name.

In March 1969 the issue arose again over transporting some of the volumes to Santa Monica so I could read them there. Again, Gelb worried this would lead to broader knowledge of their whereabouts and would make it less convenient for him to consult them himself. However, I promised to bring them back on short notice if he needed them. I would have to handle transport both ways personally; if they were carried by an air force officer or shipped on an air force plane, as most classified material was sent from Washington, they would have to be entered formally into the TS system and delivered to the TS control officer. So, on March 4, I was sworn in at the Rand Washington office as a top secret courier. Two big packages of double-wrapped volumes filled two large briefcases—courier pouches, with flaps and combination locks—that I was to have with me at all times on the way home; they couldn't be checked into luggage. On a speakerphone in the Washington office of Rand Vice President Larry Henderson, I got my marching orders from Rowen: When I got back to Santa Monica, the packages were to go into my safe. Jan Butler, the top secret control officer, and her boss, Dick Best, the security officer, were not to know of their arrival.

No one at Rand ever did learn from me that the study was there. A number of people who had heard about the study, including Fred Iklé and Bob Komer, asked me if I was aware that a copy existed at Rand. I lied to them. But I usually followed that by urging Harry to get Gelb and Halperin to extend the distribution list. It wasn't that I minded lying to close friends—that was slightly uncomfortable, but it was part of the job, and they were bound to understand that if they found out—but that the people I really wanted to share this material with were the researchers who had been chosen to work on the project and had written part of the material themselves, as well as some other gifted analysts at Rand. I found some of the patterns revealed in the written record to be puzzling (and still do), and I wanted others to have the chance to formulate and test hypotheses. It was frustrating for me to state unfamiliar, implausible-sounding generalizations about decision making in meetings or memos without being able to respond to challenges by citing the study's analyses I was really drawing upon. But every time Rowen, at my urging, raised the question with Halperin and Gelb that one or another specific researcher be added to the list, he was rebuffed. Somewhat later two others who had worked on the project were added, Rand researcher Richard Moorsteen and Ernie May, a professor of government at Harvard. But Gelb and Halperin held the line at that point.

16

The Morality of Continuing the War

The "Lessons of Vietnam" study, to which I returned after my Washington trip in the spring of 1969, addressed, among other things, "criteria for nonintervention," warning indications of involvements we should avoid or terminate. It had long been obvious to most Americans that Vietnam was one of these, given the way we were likely to perform, and had performed, and the unlikelihood of any kind of success. Nevertheless, as late as that summer the question "How could we have won in Vietnam?" still held an intellectual attraction for me. So did its counterparts: What might the United States have done to improve the odds of success? If certain goals were infeasible—at least, after some point—to what lesser aims might the presidents reasonably have aspired?

These were among the questions I addressed in a working paper that I wrote in July and August 1969, the ninth in a series of internal Rand documents that I turned out, titled "Infeasible Aims and the Politics of Stalemate." The questions were of more than academic interest; they obviously had a bearing on effective policy in other regions where American counterinsurgency programs might be more appropriate. I suppose they still revealed in me, at that date, what Richard Barnet has described as an American preoccupation: "The American national purpose is to win." My perspective was about to change drastically—in part, because I was about to read, in September, the earliest portions of the Pentagon Papers—so the concerns reflected in this draft paper marked the end of a period for me. It was to be the last month that my writings expressed a concern with how we might have won in Vietnam.

Reading a few years later my analyses written before mid-1969, I was struck by their tacit, unquestioned belief that we had had a *right* to "win," in ways defined by us (that is, by the president). The same is true of the writings of that time by virtually all other strategic analysts, as well as all official government statements, both public and internal. That unspoken premise underlay another one, also unspoken, held by the large and growing number of officials, former officials, and liberal members of the establishment who no longer believed in the practical feasibility of "winning" at acceptable cost. This was the assumption that we had nevertheless a right to prolong an unwinnable war to postpone defeat or, at the very worst, to lose only gracefully, covertly, slowly, at the cost of an uncounted number of Asian lives, a toll on which they and our policy set no real limit.

Already in the late spring of 1969 I had begun to reject the latter presumption, as I began to question the *relevance* of a political estimate that underlay—for most American officials, including me—our sense that both the original intervention and its continuation were legitimate. My rethinking began just after I had lectured on the politics of South Vietnam to a class at the University of Ohio in May 1969. By asking a question of the students, I had brought out a difference of opinion that, I suspected, underlay a reserve they seemed to feel about my views. I asked for a show of hands from those who believed that the great majority of South Vietnamese supported a victory by the NLF. As I expected, almost all raised their hands. I said they could be right, but I didn't think so. The truth of the situation, I believed, was not the opposite of what they thought, but it was somewhat different. Drawing on a distinction familiar among Vietnamese, though not in this country, I remarked that the great majority of the South Vietnamese people were best described as non-Communists but not as anti-Communists. That meant that unlike, say, the Catholics, landlords, functionaries, and military men who supported the GVN wholeheartedly—perhaps 10 to 15 percent of the population—the non-Communist majority would not actively participate in or support, by free choice, a violent campaign to exclude Communists from power or to destroy them as a political force, let alone to exterminate them. Still less was the majority willing to see its country destroyed under the weight of American firepower in pursuit of such aims.

"Right now," I went on, "the main political aspiration of this largest grouping is probably for the war to end. I suspect that for some time now most of the people of South Vietnam have preferred that the war be over—with a victory by *either* side—than that it should continue at anything like the present scale."

Later that evening a new thought began to emerge for me as I replayed in my mind what I had heard myself saying during the lecture. Contrary to the belief of most younger members of the antiwar movement—including most students in this class—the majority of the people of South Vietnam were not enthusiastic, committed supporters of the VC or of their Communist leaders (other than Ho himself). We were not in that sense battling, illegitimately, against majority opinion in South Vietnam.

Not in that sense. But what of the other judgment I had expressed, in my effort to define Vietnamese political opinion? What was the implication of saying that the majority of South Vietnamese wanted the war to be over no matter who won? What did that say about the legitimacy of imposing our will to continue the war?

I pondered that question late that night. The next morning, before I flew home to California, I called Mort Halperin, who was working for Henry Kissinger in the White House on Vietnam.

I said to him, "Let me put a question to you, Mort. What would be your best guess on the proportion of Vietnamese, by now, who would rather see the war over, no matter who won?"

He said, not to my surprise, "I suppose about eighty or ninety percent."

"What do you think your boss would say?" I was referring to Kissinger.

"I've never discussed it with him. But I would guess he would say about the same."

I said, "Those guesses sound about right. But here's a question that's new for me. It's starting to bother me a lot. If it were true that most of the South Vietnamese wanted the war to be over, whether that was at the cost of either a Communist victory or a GVN victory, how could we be justified in prolonging the war inside their country? Why would we have the right to keep it going even one more day?"

There was a long silence. Then Mort said, "That's a very good question. I don't have an answer. Let me think about it."

On the flight home and afterward, my moral perceptions and feelings began to shift with something of the effect of a Zen koan. The result was not entirely logical; it came from a different perspective, different considerations. I didn't share the students' beliefs—demonstrated in a show of hands—that the great majority of South Vietnamese actively or tacitly supported the NLF. Yet I came to realize that what I did believe about South Vietnamese lack of support *for the war* did not suggest that our own policy was less outrageous or criminal than the class clearly thought. I understood in a different way the students' reserve I had sensed during my lecture, their evident feeling of distance from the attitudes they had heard from me. I began to feel that distance myself.

For purposes of our own, involving both external and domestic politics, we were carrying on a war in someone else's country, a country in no way implicated in attacking our own or anyone else's. To continue to do that against the intense wishes of most of the inhabitants of that country began to seem to me morally wrong.

That sense was strongly reinforced in the next few months, as I finally turned to reading on the origins of the war. Nearly a year before I had begun to read standard historical accounts, some in French. These in turn led me at the end of August to bring back to Rand from Washington the early volumes of the Pentagon Papers, covering the years 1945–60. The belief that we had *ever* had a right to try to "win" in Vietnam, to impose our political preferences by military means, died for me in August and September 1969 as I read these volumes.

In the spring of 1969, Hoang Van Chi, now a friend consulting at Rand, had told me, "You must understand that in the eyes of all Vietnamese we gained our independence in March 1945, and the French set out to reconquer us in the North almost two years later." I scarcely knew then what he was talking about, nor would, I suspect, almost any U.S. official I had worked with. He was referring to the facts that the Japanese had interned the French occupying force on March 9, 1945, proclaiming Vietnam independent of France, and that the emperor Bao Dai had reasserted independence five months later and abdicated formally to Ho Chi Minh. Between that time and November–December 1946, when the French began their violent campaign of colonial reconquest, the French purported to regard at least Tonkin, the northern third of Vietnam, as an independent state within the French Union, with Ho Chi Minh as its president. Ho's repeated urgent pleas to the United States during that period to recognize Vietnam as a fully independent state were ignored by the State Department under Truman.

The internal documents make clear that the fact that Ho himself was a Communist—though head of a mainly non-Communist coalition governing the North—was far from critical in the decision in 1945 not to reply to his appeals. Rather, our nonresponse reflected a policy decision, made by President Roosevelt with some reluctance but firmly asserted, to assure the

French that we recognized French "ownership" of Vietnam as a colony, despite the wartime hiatus and any postwar local claims of independence. That decision, sustained under President Truman, contradicted the American tradition of anticolonialism (and FDR's personal feelings that the French had exploited and abused this particular colony) and the promises of self-determination in the Atlantic Charter, to both of which Ho appealed in his letters to Truman. It was adopted entirely in the interest of good relations with France in Europe as well as with Britain, which, despite having joined in the Atlantic Charter, had no wish or intention to see it applied to its own colonial authority in India and Malaya.

In France in the spring and summer of 1946, in negotiations over the future of Cochin-China, the southern region including Saigon, Ho Chi Minh, I learned with some astonishment, was accorded the honors of a head of state and negotiated with the French on that basis. Jean Sainteny, former chief representative of France in Vietnam, had signed an agreement in March that the decision on whether to include the South in that independent state would be settled by a popular referendum. But the French government had no intention of carrying out that agreement. Its failure to do so, and its clear intention to return Tonkin as well to quasi-colonial status by force, led to the outbreak of hostilities on both sides at the end of 1946. In five years as an American official or consultant dealing with Vietnam, I had remained ignorant of this history or at least of its clear import. By the end of the summer I knew the story from the works I've cited (see note to p. 249), which I can still recommend to American readers. What was more impressive to me was to find the same appreciation of the situation in the McNamara study's top secret history and documents of that period.

I already knew from my research in 1967 for the McNamara study on the 1950–61 period that Ho and his colleagues had every reason to feel betrayed in the fifties by France, the United States, and the international community—perhaps above all by their Communist allies, the Soviets and Chinese—because of their failure to enforce the exactly comparable agreement in the Geneva Accords in 1954. These had explicitly *denied* that the demilitarized zone (DMZ) was an international border separating two independent states. They had called for an internationally supervised election in 1956 to determine the government of a unified Vietnam. I hadn't known this as a Pentagon official. I believed then the State Department sophistries I was reading even in classified memoranda about the accords and the failure to hold elections. Both internally and to the public Secretary of State Rusk and his subordinates proclaimed over and over that "all we ask is that

North Vietnam leave its neighbors alone" and that it observe the provisions of the 1954 accords. The implicit and often explicit premise was that the accords had created two separate, independent sovereign states, the two "neighbors," North and South Vietnam. That was, I found from reading the accords at last, a brazen reversal of the letter and spirit of the accords as written. Equally brazen, I now realized, was the frequently repeated demand by the United States throughout the sixties for a "return to observance of the 1954 Accords" when the United States had never intended, did not support, and would never permit observance of the central political provision of the accords, which called for nationwide elections for a unified regime.

But it was clear from the documents I read in 1967 in the Pentagon that the head of my department had known better. In March 1964 Secretary McNamara had told President Johnson that de Gaulle's proposal for "neutralization" of South Vietnam would include total U.S. withdrawal and that "To negotiate on this basis—indeed without specifically rejecting it—would simply mean a Communist takeover in South Vietnam. Only the U.S. presence after 1954 held the South together under far more favorable circumstances, and enabled Diem to refuse to go through with the 1954 provision calling for nationwide 'free' elections in 1956." What I read in 1969 was that an exactly comparable written accord had been violated eight years earlier, in 1946, by the French. The consequences of that earlier violation, so parallel to the consequences of the later one, were, I found, seen with amazing precision by both sides. In my reading of that autumn, one quotation stood out as an epigraph to the whole history of the conflict. It was Ho Chi Minh's somber plea to Jean Sainteny in September 1946 in France, at the close of his abortive negotiations: "Don't let me leave this way; arm me against those who seek to surpass me." (In Vietnam, Ho's colleagues and rivals were bitterly criticizing his concessions in negotiations that he had made in the interests of avoiding a settlement by war.) "You will not regret it. . . . If we must fight, we will fight. You will kill ten of our men, but we will kill one of yours. And in the end it is you that will tire."

The uncanny foresight in this warning was not confined to the leader of the Vietnamese. From the time I first read it, in September 1969 in the earliest volume of the Pentagon Papers, I have been equally haunted by an internal U.S. memorandum written a few months later after Ho's warning. On December 19, 1946, a month after an "incident" in which French warships, planes, and artillery had punitively shelled and bombed civilian quarters of Haiphong, killing more than six thousand civilians, fighting had broken out in Hanoi. The French then began their attempt—almost unique among former colonial powers in the postwar world—to reconquer militarily their former colony. Four days later, on December 23, 1946, John Carter Vincent, director of the Bureau of Far Eastern Affairs, sent a memo to Undersecretary of State Dean Acheson, which made this assessment (emphasis added):

> Although the French in Indochina have made far-reaching paper-concessions to the Vietnamese desire for autonomy, French actions on the scene have been directed toward whittling down the powers and the territorial extent of the Vietnam "free state." *This process the Vietnamese have continued to resist.* At the same time, the French themselves admit that they lack the military strength to reconquer the country. In brief, with inadequate forces, with public opinion sharply at odds, with a government rendered largely ineffective through internal division, the French have tried to accomplish in Indochina what a strong and united Britain has found it unwise to attempt in Burma. *Given the present elements in the situation, guerrilla warfare may continue indefinitely.*

Reading on, at Rand in September 1969, in the early volumes I had just brought back from Washington, I found Vincent's initial appreciation of the situation was never contradicted in subsequent years. Nor did the discussions show ignorance of the political facts of life that underlay these unwelcome estimates, even certain "unpleasant" facts. That term occurs in a striking passage in the State Department's secret Policy Statement on Indochina, September 27, 1948, a year and a half before we took up—for the next generation—what it calls the "onus of intervention" (emphasis added):

> We have not urged the French to negotiate with Ho Chi Minh, even *though he probably is now supported by a considerable majority of the Vietnamese people,* because of his record as a Communist and the Communist background of many of the influential figures in and about his government.
>
> . . . Our greatest difficulty in talking with the French and in stressing what should and what should not be done has been our inability to suggest any practicable solution of the Indochina problem, as we are all too well aware of the *unpleasant fact* that Communist Ho Chi Minh is the strongest and perhaps the ablest figure in Indochina and any suggested solution which *excludes* him is an expedient of uncertain outcome. We are naturally hesitant to press the French too strongly or to become deeply involved so long as we are not in

a position to suggest a solution or until we are prepared to accept the onus of intervention.

This clear awareness that if we should support the French directly (as we were readying ourselves to do a year later, while China was in the process of "falling"), we would be opposing a nationalist movement whose Communist leader had the support of a considerable majority of the Vietnamese people cast a new light for me on the "nobility," the "altruism," of our original, and continuing, involvement in Vietnam. Vincent's estimate was an enduring appraisal of the probable indecisiveness of the French colonial campaign we were about to join. This policy statement, while scarcely seeming to notice it, went far toward disposing of the legitimacy, by American standards, of our indirect and potentially direct intervention. The moral implications of a president's choices could hardly stand out more clearly, or in a harsher light, than in such documents of the earliest period, from 1945 to 1950, when the Vietnamese had just begun their struggle to retain their newly proclaimed independence. But in subsequent years, I now saw from my new reading, American policy had followed a continuous arc, in which neither the practical nor the moral dimensions had ever really changed.

In late 1949, with Communist victory in China—and with the rise of Senator Joseph McCarthy in early 1950, charging with others that it was Democratic malfeasance or worse that had led to the "fall of China"—the U.S. administration suddenly saw preventing Communist control of Indochina as an American interest. More realistically, it saw protecting the Democrats from the charge of losing another area to communism as vitally important, justifying direct aid and support to France's transparently colonial effort.

Ironically, as Vu Van Thai pointed out to me at Rand, it was just at this time that the French effort at reconquest had become, in Thai's term, "Sisyphean." When Communist forces reached the border of Vietnam in late 1949, the border became open to Chinese Communist aid to the Vietminh independence movement. As Thai put it, "From that time on it became impossible for the French to defeat the Vietminh forces." The French had become disheartened (realistic) about their prospects about the same time and wanted out. But at the same time, and for the same reason—refracted through U.S. domestic politics—it became politically "impossible" for a U.S. administration to allow the French to be defeated or to withdraw (since the United States was not anxious to send its own troops). It was the beginning of what I later termed the stalemate machine. From then on, the French were more U.S. instruments than allies in this struggle, with the United States urging and demanding that they continue and providing, eventually, 85 percent of the funding. The United States, often accused at home and abroad of exporting its "values" insensitively, was not here exporting "democracy, self-determination, independence, freedom" (under French colonial rule?). The American values it was helping impose on the Vietnamese were: Better French than Red. Some Vietnamese agreed with that, but most did not, and the United States was funding a French effort to jail or kill all those who disagreed. So the United States was also expressing in its aid the values, for Vietnamese: Better at War—or Better Dead—than Red. The slogan was familiar in America in that precise period, but it didn't translate well in a country where the Reds were leading an almost universally popular independence movement.

As I knew well from the later period, American officials were sincere in their belief that these values really were best for the Vietnamese, as well as for the United States. Better for them the French, better the Diem regime, better the generals (the former French lieutenants) than Communist rule. There was some realistic basis for the belief that many Vietnamese were naive and misled in their notions of what a Communist-led victory would do for them. But as I now realized, we American officials were no less ignorant or self-deceptive, in turn, about the nature of French rule or of the various Saigon regimes we supported or imposed later or the incentives that would lead people to take up and persist in armed struggle against greatly superior forces—and above all, about the burden of the war on the rural population. In any case, to presume to judge what was best for them, with life and death at stake, was the height of imperial arrogance, the "arrogance of power," as Senator Fulbright later called it.

Where earlier I had read only intelligence estimates for the decade preceding 1961, I now finally read the full analyses in the McNamara study, with documents, of the decision making throughout the fifties, both during the "French war" and the ensuing years of American "support" to a "South Vietnamese" political struggle and resumed guerrilla conflict. I had left these to read last because I had presumed they were least relevant to an understanding of the sixties. I could not have been more mistaken.

Here are some things I understood, in a way I had not just months before, when I had finished reading the full Pentagon Papers toward the end of September 1969:

- There had been no First and Second Indochina Wars, just one continuous conflict for almost a quarter of a century.
- In practical terms, on one side, it had been an American war almost from its beginning: at first French-American, eventually wholly American. In both cases it was a struggle of Vietnamese—not all of them but enough to persist—against American policy and American financing, proxies, technicians, firepower, and finally, troops and pilots.
- Since at least the late 1940s there had probably never been a year when political violence in Vietnam would have reached or stayed at the scale of a "war" had not the U.S. president, Congress, and citizens fueled it with money, weapons, and ultimately manpower: first through the French, then funneled to wholly owned client regimes, and at last directly. Indeed there would have been no war after 1954 if the United States and its Vietnamese collaborators, wholly financed by the United States, had not been determined to frustrate and overturn the process of political resolution by election negotiated at Geneva.
- It was no more a "civil war" after 1955 or 1960 than it had been during the U.S.-supported French attempt at colonial reconquest. A war in which one side was *entirely* equipped and paid by a foreign power—which dictated the nature of the local regime in its own interest—was not a civil war. To say that we had "interfered" in what is "really a civil war," as most American academic writers and even liberal critics of the war do to this day, simply screened a more painful reality and was as much a myth as the earlier official one of "aggression from the North." In terms of the UN Charter and of our own avowed ideals, it was a war of foreign aggression, American aggression.

The last judgment was not one I came to lightly or easily. It was the kind of charge I associated with antiwar rallies. I had never been to one of these (since the first one, with Patricia in 1965), but I had read references to such claims before and dismissed them, as my colleagues did, as overblown rhetoric. It was what "extreme" critics, radicals, and most international lawyers, though I didn't know that, had been saying about the nature of our involvement for years. I had not believed them. Now I had to.

Five years earlier, in December 1964, my boss John McNaughton had commented to Rand researchers briefing him on "Viet Cong Motivation and Morale": "If what you say is true [of the nationalistic motivation, the patriotism, the discipline and lack of corruption, the attitudes toward the peasants of the Vietcong], we're fighting on the wrong side." I now saw that that way of putting it missed the reality since 1954. We *were* the wrong side.

In the end it wasn't categories of international law, controverted definitions that were never enforced against great powers anyway, that really concerned me. It was a more fundamental sense that there never had been any legitimacy in our involvement or our war in Vietnam, or any legitimate claim to authority for any of the regimes we backed, either under the French or later. Not in Vietnamese eyes; nor should there have been in our own eyes if we had been informed and realistic about our role in past and present. Realistically seen, it was *never* a "just cause."

For some years I had seen the war as an involvement that should be ended and that above all must not be escalated. That attitude I shared, as far as I knew, with most of my colleagues in the government with experience of the war in Washington or Saigon. But, beginning in the summer of 1969, and definitively by the end of September, when I had read these early volumes, I no longer shared their view of the war as a worthy effort gone wrong or gone too far, as a case of good intentions that failed of their legitimate, though perhaps infeasible, aims. It was impossible to see in that light the history I had now read of our nine years of diplomatic support of the French claims of sovereign ownership of a former colony that had proclaimed independence with full popular support; above all, the last five years of the French effort at military reconquest, in which we had urgently pressed the French to continue their military struggle against the independence movement and funded it almost entirely. Nor did the nature of the conflict change in 1954, when the American paymasters of the indigenous colonial administration and colonial army ceased delivering their funds through the French and directly paid their former collaborators. Nothing after that had changed it fundamentally either.

For me as an American to read, in our own official secret documents, about the origins of the conflict and of our participation in it was to see our involvement—and the killing we had done and were still doing—naked of any shred of legitimacy from the beginning. That strengthened and extended backward in time the conclusion I had drawn in May, in Ohio: the immorality of our deliberately prolonging the killing by a single additional day, or bomb, or death.

Already that summer, since my talk in Ohio, I had come to see as morally wrong our prolongation of the war against the wishes of most of Vietnam's inhabitants, who would gladly have accepted terms to end it that we refused to consider. Now I realized that it was not just the *continuation* of the locally devastating, hopelessly stalemated war that was unjustified; it had been wrong from the start. In that light our prolongation of it seemed to me a wrong of the highest degree imaginable. A crime. An evil.

If the war was unjust, as I now regarded it, that meant that every Vietnamese killed by Americans or by the proxies we had financed since 1950 had been killed by us without justification. I could think of no other word for that but murder. Mass murder. Could it ever be precipitate to end a policy of murder?

That was not a perspective I intended to press to my colleagues or the public. I couldn't reasonably expect them to agree, or to convince them of it, while they remained ignorant of the history in the classified reading I had just done. I was hardly one to blame other officials, or the general public, for such ignorance. I had shared it myself till that summer, after five years of intense involvement in Vietnam affairs. Like me, they accepted official government accounts, both public and classified, whose relation, I now realized, to the historical realities hidden in the government's own long-unexamined secret files was that of a photographic negative to a print. Nor could I expect many of them anytime soon—even if they could be given access to it—to read even hundreds of these thousands of pages that had just changed my own thinking.

The difference these private perceptions made for me was in my personal sense of obligation and urgency, of moral imperative, when it came to ending the war altogether, not just to avert escalation. I now regarded our involvement not as something to be terminated as soon as it could be done "gracefully," without harming other American significant objectives, as I had thought over the last two or three years, but as something that ought to cease, that we *must* cease, as quickly as possible.

That is what I had concluded by mid-September 1969. But a month earlier, in mid-August, when I was already most of the way to this conclusion, I had learned that it was not about to end.

Talking on the phone, elliptically, in midsummer, Morton Halperin told me, "Nixon's staying in; he's not getting out." That almost surely meant that the war would eventually get even larger. It was very bad news, in fact horrible. Yet to someone who had read most of the McNamara study by this time, it was not terribly surprising. It meant simply that a new president was following in the footsteps of his four predecessors. I didn't question Mort further in this call. I didn't expect him to say more over the phone, and he didn't. When I stayed at his home later that summer, he told me more.

Nixon had no readiness at all to see Saigon under a Vietcong flag after a "decent interval" of two or three years—or ever. Not, at least, while he was in office. That meant not through 1976, if he could help it, as he believed he could. That didn't mean he expected the VC or DRV to give up, permanently, its aim of unifying the country under its control. And so it meant that the war would essentially never end. His campaign promise of ending the war was a hoax. But he believed that an eventual end *to the U.S. ground combat role* would be seen and accepted by the American public as amounting to the same thing. Could that be done without "losing" Saigon? Nixon believed that it could, in one of two ways. The first, and preferred, way would be if the North would after all agree to mutual withdrawal of North Vietnamese along with U.S. troops. In that case the United States would continue to provide the GVN and ARVN with full financial and material support. In addition, U.S. air support to ARVN would continue indefinitely, with the threat and intention of returning to full-scale attack on the North if there were a later NVA offensive. With U.S. air support an enlarged and enhanced ARVN could handle the remaining NLF forces on its own, without U.S. ground troops. That was Nixon's primary hope.

Nixon meanwhile was also pursuing a separate track. In this second scenario U.S. forces would be reduced unilaterally, but slowly, in relatively small increments, so that large numbers would remain over the next several years while Vietnamization built up ARVN. But there would be no plan for them to be removed altogether so long as Hanoi rejected mutual withdrawal. There would be a fairly high floor to the number of U.S. troops remaining in the country as long as sizable NVA forces remained, perhaps two hundred thousand U.S. troops or more, almost surely no fewer than fifty to one hundred thousand, remaining indefinitely. This part of Nixon's planning was also reported to me by John Vann, on visits home later that summer. He had learned it from his friend General Bruce Palmer, then deputy chief of staff of the army. As Vann had long been saying, there were at the moment vastly more U.S. troops in the South than were needed to maintain reliable control over the densely populated areas and even to keep most of the "contested" areas from being thoroughly controlled by the NLF, even with NVA forces remaining in the South. So Nixon could afford to send home, over time, several hundred thousand American troops (almost immediately, Vann thought, but that was heresy to MACV) and still keep reliable control over Saigon and the major cities and populated areas, through 1976 and beyond.

How would this be made palatable to the American public—either the slow rate of withdrawal or the large residual force? By assuring that the rate of American casualties would go down sharply, eventually close to zero; this was to be achieved by threatening the North that otherwise it would be burned to the ground. Mort told me that Hanoi had already been told, through its ally the Soviet Union, that the North would suffer that fate not only if it launched a new offensive but if it failed to meet the reasonable U.S. terms for a settlement—that is, if it failed to agree soon to mutual withdrawal. But after Hanoi's rejection of mutual withdrawal, Mort suspected that Nixon had drawn back from this specific threat. (In this, we learned years later, Halperin was mistaken.)

But Mort didn't believe that Nixon was bluffing when he threatened to expand the war again in the event of an NVA/NLF offensive against residual U.S. forces and even to prevent or deter intense attacks on ARVN and residual forces. He saw Nixon as intending and expecting by his threats to keep South Vietnam safe for the indefinite presence of large numbers of U.S. troops—from fifty thousand, at a minimum, to two hundred thousand—in a permanent conflict, a stalemated war at reduced costs to American taxpayers with very low U.S. casualties. Alternatively, Nixon hoped, as the DRV recognized it couldn't use NVA units in South Vietnam without suffering inordinately in the North, this might change its position on mutual withdrawal and it might seek a formal settlement on U.S. terms. Under either track, total U.S. withdrawal of combat troops, *ever,* was strictly conditional on *mutual* withdrawal by the North Vietnamese; without that, Nixon intended to keep sizable residual U.S. forces in South Vietnam indefinitely, as in Korea. And even if mutual withdrawal of ground troops took place, U.S. air support for ARVN was to continue independently as needed.

In other ways, in addition to verbal warnings, Mort told me, Nixon intended to underline his threats that he was prepared to carry out the full-scale, all-out attack on the North from which Johnson had always drawn back: mining harbors and blockading, hitting dikes, population bombing, even nuclear weapons. Eight months earlier I had posed the question rhetorically to Schelling, with respect to such a threat strategy: "Why would a threat of escalation work when the actual practice of bombing the North had not?" Nixon's answer to this challenge, Mort now explained to me, was in effect: "I'll carry out, if necessary, heavier destruction than the North has ever actually experienced before. And I'll *demonstrate* that meanwhile by expanding the war in ways that Lyndon Johnson didn't dare." That was the meaning, Mort said, of the ongoing secret bombing of Cambodia that Nixon had begun in February. It was still "secret" despite a front-page story in the *New York Times* in May, because the Pentagon had simply denied it the same day, and no journalist had followed up on it. Mort had made me aware of it earlier simply by referring me to the William Beecher story in the *New York Times* and telling me, "It's right." (He had not been the source; he believed the leak came from the Pentagon.)

The main point of the ongoing bombing, Mort said, was to demonstrate to the North that Nixon would not be bound by the constraints that had applied under Johnson if the Communists challenged a permanent U.S. presence in the South by attacks that maintained high U.S. casualties. Nixon was also prepared to carry out other such demonstrations. There had already been a secret incursion by marines into Laos (Operation Dewey Canyon).

What I was hearing was not just that the war was going to go on, indefinitely, but that it would again get larger, eventually larger than it had ever been. That was not, apparently, what Nixon actually wanted or expected. He expected, Halperin said, that his threats would work, given his demonstrations: Hanoi would pull back, hold down the level of violence permanently, or agree to mutual withdrawal and a settlement. But I didn't believe that, and neither did Halperin. At the same time, unhappily, I was able to believe that Nixon did; I had been reading the McNamara study. It was what Nixon's boss Eisenhower had believed throughout the fifties; what Johnson and McNamara and Walt Rostow had believed, or acted as if they did, in 1965; what the JCS had been urging as an article of faith since 1961.

If I hadn't been immersed in that history, I might have reacted to Mort's account as, he told me years later, others did to whom he told the same story in subsequent months and years: "Nixon can't still believe that; you can't be right," they said. But Mort by this time had read that history too, and he was now convinced that the continuities revealed in the McNamara study hadn't ended in March 1968. Knowing him, I found that good enough for me. He didn't tell me just how he had learned this, and I didn't press him further till later that fall. But what he did tell me was concrete enough. He said, in August 1969, "This administration will not go into the election of 1972 without having mined Haiphong and bombed Hanoi." (He was wrong about Hanoi. It wasn't bombed till six weeks after the election.)

That prediction presumed that the threats would fail and that Nixon, rather than lose face, would carry them out. We both believed the first, from our experience of the last five years (and what we had read of the last twenty-four). Halperin believed the second, from his experience of Nixon in the last six months. It wasn't hard to persuade me that would be true, once the president had become publicly committed to this course, once he saw his own credibility and honor as being at stake. But I still thought it might not be too late to deflect him from such an essentially foolish course. No commitment was final till it was acted on publicly. What Halperin was telling me was still a secret decision. It wasn't at all what the public expected from him, the opposite really. If Nixon could be induced to think again, to postpone decision or even announce a different policy, no one would know the difference. Halperin didn't seem to think there was any prospect of doing this from within the NSC staff (he was leaving anyway, and this was among the reasons), and he didn't suggest any alternative. But that was what was in my mind, urgently, as I left Washington for a meeting in Haverford, Pennsylvania.

17

War Resisters

In the last week of August 1969 I went to the campus of Haverford, a Quaker college near Philadelphia, to attend the triennial conference of the War Resisters' International (WRI). The theme of the meeting, "Liberation and Revolution," was not unlike that of the Princeton conference "America in a Revolutionary World," sixteen months earlier. But this gathering of war resisters had no Ivy League cosponsor. And I was no longer coming as a committed counterrevolutionary.

Neither was I, on the other hand, a Gandhian nonviolent revolutionary or a pacifist, as many of the other participants thought of themselves. But after a year of reading along lines Janaki had suggested, I had reached a point where I wanted to meet people who did see themselves that way. So far Janaki was the only such person I had really come to know or had even met more than briefly. Since Princeton she had visited me in Malibu, and we had spent a few days together in London. She had made a profound impression on me. I could say she was a hero of mine, like one I had only read about, Rosa Parks. Fifteen years earlier one of my heroes was John Wayne, who had helped recruit me, and a lot of others, into the Marine Corps with *Sands of Iwo Jima.* Something had happened to me, I noticed about this time. My heroes had changed color and sex. But I wanted to meet some others on this path, preferably some whose life experience was closer than Janaki's to my own and who were living daily the Gandhian principles that I had been reading about. I was ready to be challenged and even changed by them.

In the last year I had read books Janaki had recommended to me, among others, King's *Stride Toward Freedom; The Conquest of Violence,* by Joan Bondurant, on the philosophy and practice of Gandhian nonviolent direct action; and *Revolution and Equilibrium,* by Barbara Deming, whose essays on the need for nonviolent resistance to the Vietnam War I read over and over. I did the same with another essay on what seemed the same subject, though it was written a century earlier during a different American war, Henry David Thoreau's "On the Duty of Civil Disobedience." The original, equally subversive title was "Resistance to Civil Government."

Disobedience to civil authority a "duty"? Was it even a legitimate choice? In certain circumstances, yes, according to Thoreau, as when "a whole country is unjustly overrun and conquered by a foreign army," when "ours is the invading army." In such a case, he said, obedience to leaders in an unjust cause was itself a choice, the wrong choice. He himself went to jail for refusing to pay a poll tax, in protest against the Mexican War (to which he was referring above). It was just for one night because, against his wishes, "someone interfered, and paid the tax." Thoreau was as nonviolent as Gandhi or King, but against the evils of slavery and of a wrongful war his essay was a call to mutiny, to nonviolent rebellion. By his example he urged, like Rosa Parks, something beyond verbal dissent and protest: withdrawal of cooperation, militant disobedience by a *civilian,* akin to that of a "soldier . . . who refuses to serve in an unjust war." In his state of Massachusetts, he claimed, such a soldier was applauded by many, but not imitated, out of the "thousands who are *in opinion* opposed to slavery and to the war, who yet in effect do nothing to put an end to them. . . . They hesitate, and they regret, and sometimes they petition; but they do nothing in earnest and with effect. They will wait, well disposed, for others to remedy the evil, that they may no longer have it to regret. At most, they give only a cheap vote. . . ."

To a century of readers (Tolstoy quoted him against conscription; Gandhi distributed his words in India before several mass actions) Thoreau proclaimed: "Cast your whole vote, not a strip of paper merely, but your whole influence. A minority is powerless while it conforms to the majority; it is not even a minority then; but it is irresistible when it clogs by its whole weight."

I read that passage first in the summer of 1968. A year later, after voters casting strips of paper had failed once again to end a war that most of them wanted over, it was reverberating in my mind. *Cast your whole vote . . . your whole influence.* I had come to Haverford in hopes of finding out what that might mean.

Many things had happened during those sixteen months that should have made a difference and had not: a presidential election campaign that had begun with the war as the central issue; a complete change of party and administration; at the onset of the new administration, a thorough reexamination of alternative options and a questioning of the bureaucracy; the opening of negotiations with Hanoi. Not one of these, or any other aspect of normal politics, seemed to have brought extrication any closer, despite an electorate that expected it and was obviously anxious for it. If I was ready to change my own relation to the situation, ready even to change my life, there was reason for it.

Janaki had invited me to the conference, of which she was one of the organizers. She had urged me to be a speaker, to raise the questions about pacifism I had been posing to her from the reading she had suggested to me. I turned that down quickly. I was too new at this subject, and my thoughts were too tentative, for me to be sounding off from a platform. My usual credentials, from Harvard, Rand, the Defense and State departments, and Vietnam, would not impress this crowd favorably, and I didn't have much else to qualify me as a speaker in their eyes. I told her I wanted to listen, not to debate.

At the conference I saw little of Janaki. She was too busy as one of the organizers. But I did begin to meet, as I had hoped, the sort of activist who had shared a lunch table with us at Princeton the day I met her. In fact, all those same people were here. One of them, Bob Eaton, who had sailed to North and South Vietnam on the *Phoenix,* was scheduled to be sentenced to prison on the third morning of the conference, in the federal courtroom in the Post Office Building in downtown Philadelphia. He expected a three-year sentence.

Eaton was the first draft resister I had ever met. That was probably one more than any of my associates in Washington or Santa Monica. Looking back, I find it striking how isolated my colleagues and I were, as late as 1969 and even after many of us had become deeply critical of the war, from the active antiwar movement or the broader and older peace movement. My knowledge of such people still came almost exclusively from media accounts, overwhelmingly negative, in which they were presented as being, in varying degree, extremist, simplistic, pro-Communist or pro-NLF, fanatic, anti-American, dogmatic. I went to Haverford in part to find out if these labels were accurate. None of these was a trait I wanted to be associated with. (In coming years, as a price of joining in nonviolent resistance to the war, I heard all these terms applied to me.)

But no such problems arose with the real people I was now meeting and hearing. The four days of intense, articulate discussion I encountered, including much controversy over principles and broad strategy as well as tactics, refuted each of the stereotypes above. To mention just one, the anarchist-pacifist critique of state power and violence that nearly all the participants shared provided little basis for an admiring or uncritical view of the Soviet Union, the Hanoi regime, or the NLF. The people in this gathering opposed the war without romanticizing the Vietcong, third world violent revolutionaries, or socialist states any more than they did their own states.

Just as in opposing the war, so in confronting abuses of state power they went beyond criticism from the sidelines. A number of those present, including Michael Randle, chairman of War Resisters' International, and Devi Prasad, WRI general secretary, had taken nonviolent direct action to Eastern Europe in September 1968, leafleting a number of capitals in protest against the Soviet and Warsaw Pact invasion of Czechoslovakia. This meant demonstrating in city squares where such protest was illegal and led to instant arrests. In most cases they had been detained and risked long imprisonment.

I had misgivings about the dogmatic commitment to absolute pacifism I presumed they shared. The War Resisters' International, of which the War Resisters League (WRL) was the American branch, had begun after World War I as an association of conscientious objectors, at a time when few countries formally recognized that status. In the twenties it had adopted a Gandhian perspective and now furthered a broad range of nonviolent liberation struggles, but it had kept its pacifist premises. I told Randall Kehler, head of the San Francisco WRL branch and one of the conference organizers, that I believed I couldn't join WRL because, as I understood it, that involved signing a pledge to refuse participation in all wars, all of which were regarded as crimes against humanity. Despite Vietnam, and my increasing tendency to look skeptically at the claims of any particular war to be "just," I told Kehler, I still thought (as I do today) that violent self-defense was justified against aggression, like Hitler's. Kehler told me he shared similar reservations. "I've never signed that pledge," he said. He asked others standing around us and found that most of them hadn't either. Their pacifism was nondogmatic, evolving and exploring, with a considerable recognition of uncertainties and dilemmas.

A striking aspect of the conference was that the Vietnam War was by no means in the forefront of attention, either on the agenda or in the discussions. This despite the facts that virtually everyone present, from the United States or elsewhere, was a committed and active opponent of the war and that the war was continuing just as violently as before. True, U.S. planes were no longer bombing North Vietnam, but they had simply shifted their targets to Laos and to South Vietnam and secretly to Cambodia. Altogether they were dropping a somewhat higher total tonnage than before, at a rate of one million tons of bombs a year or half the total tonnage of World War II. Yet the transcript of the conference shows that only one of the ten background papers and one of the twenty speakers focused directly on the war, which all the speakers clearly regarded as being on the way to ending.

These antiwar activists shared an assumption accepted by nearly all segments of American society over the sixteen months since Hanoi had accepted Johnson's proposal for open negotiations on April 3, 1968. The assumption was that the Tet offensive and Johnson's offer of negotiations had permanently settled, in the affirmative, the issue of whether the United States would ever withdraw from Vietnam and end the war. Supposedly the only question that remained was what one speaker described as "the tempo of withdrawal . . . in this fag end of a long and beastly war."

But I knew the assumption was wrong. I had just learned, in Washington the week before the conference, the closely guarded secret that Nixon himself did not accept that assumption. Nixon was no more ready than Johnson to accept U.S. failure to determine the politics of South Vietnam, failure to preclude Communist predominance in Saigon and elsewhere. In my head as I went to Haverford was Halperin's flat prediction to me in Washington: "This administration will not go into the election of 1972 without having mined Haiphong and bombed Hanoi." And Vann's disclosure that there would still be tens of thousands, at the least, of U.S. troops in South Vietnam at the end of 1972. I could not reveal at the conference what I knew. It had been revealed to me on an unusually confidential basis. There was little I could say about it without seriously compromising my sources, John Paul Vann and Morton Halperin, who were themselves not supposed to be privy to the information and had learned it confidentially. In any case I was still trying to sort out its implications. I had put aside for the four days of the conference addressing the specifics of what I ought to try to do about it.

On Tuesday evening, I finally had a chance to talk with Bob Eaton, the night before he was to go to prison two years after telling his draft board that he would no longer cooperate with the Selective Service System. Since then, in addition to his voyage on the *Phoenix* to North and South Vietnam, he had worked on the pacifist networks AQAG (A Quaker Action Group) and The Resistance, supporting noncooperation with the draft. In September 1968 he had been one of the members of the WRI who had risked imprisonment in Eastern Europe, conducting protests against the invasion of Czechoslovakia.

A troublemaker. Yet given the prevailing belief that the war was in the process of ending, Eaton's impending prison sentence probably seemed to many of those present almost an anachronism. He had alluded to this attitude in his talk on the first day. It addressed resistance to militarism in the large rather than to the Vietnam War, because, as he said, "The basis of GI organizing now is, no one wants to be the last guy shot in a war. . . . That's also a problem for the Resistance, because I think no guy wants to be the last guy to go into prison resisting a particular war."

He seemed unnaturally calm about the thought that he might be doing just that. That day before his sentencing, August 26, he had attended all the sessions, including one that had gone on till ten-thirty that evening, till it gave way to a beer party and dance. I found him in a side room away from the party, with a beer in his hand but still talking long-range strategy, tactics for transforming America. I suggested to him that wouldn't be the way I'd spend my last evening before going to prison. He said offhandedly, "Oh, this is what I do. I'm an organizer. I'll organize in prison, same as on the outside."

The conference was holding no meetings the next morning, Wednesday, so that members could go into Philadelphia to circle the Post Office Building in a vigil while Eaton was being sentenced inside. Buses and cars had been arranged to take us all in. I tried to think of an excuse to get out of it that the others could accept, but it wasn't easy. I was embarrassed by my own reservations. What was the problem? A man I admired was being sentenced to prison for an act of conscience. He and his friends wanted a show of solidarity for straightforward political reasons and perhaps because it would make him feel better. There was an invitation to join that in the company of one of the heroes of the century, Pastor Martin Niemöller, and others I admired no less. How could I not go?

The fact is, it was a problem for me. It was a combination of the small risk of my being discovered and an undeniable feeling I had that there was something demeaning about the whole thing. What if the press or the police or the FBI took pictures of us? What if my name was mentioned in the media and got back to Washington or Santa Monica? I knew what my associates in either place would think: that I had gone out of my mind. They would see it as a total sacrifice of dignity and of elite insider status, for nothing, for an action of no consequence, no effectiveness, nothing worth taking the smallest risk of losing access to secret information and to people of influence. It could be explained in no other way than a fit of madness. I could hear their reaction in my head, and I couldn't really argue with it. This was hardly the place, or the way, to announce to Rand, the Pentagon, and the White House that I was joining the public opposition to the war. To their war.

But Bob Eaton was going to prison, and I couldn't think of a reason I could give his friends for refusing to see him off. I thought of saying I was sick, but the conference had two days to go, and I couldn't keep that up plausibly. So, on an August morning in 1969, while Martin Niemöller and Devi Prasad were inside with Bob, making statements to the court on his behalf, I found myself on a sidewalk in downtown Philadelphia in a line of variously dressed peaceniks, some of them carrying placards, others handing out leaflets. I walked along with them, at first with great misgivings. The sidewalk outside the Post Office Building in Philadelphia that morning was a long way from the Executive Office Building in Washington, where I had spent February that same year writing memos for the president. Both were places perhaps for "speaking truth to power," the Quaker phrase for vigils and acts of "witness to peace" of the kinds we were engaged in that morning. But you could not do that in both places, not if you wanted to be welcomed back to the NSC. You could not have the opportunity to draft top secret commentaries for the president on Vietnam options, or give his national security assistant confidential advice, if you were the sort of person who spent days off from work demonstrating in support of draft resisters on street corners in Philadelphia.

You could not have the confidence of powerful men and be trusted with their confidences if there was any prospect that you would challenge their policies in public in any forum at all. That was the unbreakable rule of the executive branch. It was the sacred code of the insider, both the men of power and those, like me, privileged to advise and help them. I knew that as well as anyone. I had lived by that code for the last decade; it was in my skin. I was, it seems, in the process of shedding that skin on that morning. Before I had grown a new one.

I felt naked—and raw. My memory is of feeling chilled on a gray, wintry day; I have to remind myself that it was Philadelphia in August. But no one after all was noticing me. There was no press, no police. People passed by incuriously, mostly without pausing to read our placards. Some accepted the leaflets we handed to them; others didn't or handed them back. Passersby looked briefly at us or kept their eyes straight ahead, as they would glance, or not, at panhandlers or nowadays at the homeless.

As a form of political communication this seemed one step below standing on a soapbox in Hyde Park. Without even saying very much, you were making a spectacle of yourself, being a public nuisance, in front of people who didn't count for much themselves and felt free to ignore you. If you were going to confront the state with a public stand, it seemed hard to imagine a lower-status or less effective way to do it. The views of my fellow officials or consultants were mine as well. If you had nothing better to do with several hours of your time than to try to change the minds of a few dozen random pedestrians by handing them leaflets, you must be very powerless indeed. The thoughts "Why are we doing this? What am I doing here?" seemed at first as visible on my forehead as the signboards my neighbors were carrying. I felt ridiculous.

That passed. After all, no one was paying much attention one way or the other. My companions seemed at ease. They all had probably done this before. I wanted to be helpful. I took a bunch of leaflets and began offering them to the people walking by. There seemed to be some technique to getting them to accept one. I experimented with different expressions, all pleasant, and various verbal formulas. Some worked; some didn't. I started to get into it. Before the morning was over, I was offering leaflets, with some success, to cars stopped momentarily in the adjacent intersections. My mood had changed. I was feeling unaccountably lighthearted. Around noon the word was passed that Eaton had been sentenced and had been taken off to a cell. The judge had listened respectfully to the statements by Pastor Niemöller and the others and had then given Bob the three-year sentence he had expected. We went back to the conference.

Something very important had happened to me. I felt liberated. I doubt if I could have explained that at the time. But by now I have seen this exhilaration often enough in others, in particular people who have just gone through their first action of civil disobedience, whether or not they have been taken to jail. This simple vigil, my first public action, had freed me from a nearly universal fear whose inhibiting force, I think, is very widely underestimated. I had become free of the fear of appearing absurd, of looking foolish, for stepping out of line.

One other thing had happened, though again I didn't fully recognize it till later. By stepping into that particular vigil line, in solidarity with Bob Eaton and in company with others whose views I shared and whose lives of commitment I respected, I had stepped across another line, an invisible one of the kind that recruiters mark out on the floor of an induction center. I had joined a movement.

On the next day, August 28, 1969, the final day of the conference, I heard a talk by Randy Kehler during the last session in the afternoon. Alone out of all the presentations at the conference, Randy's talk was personal. He said he wanted just to share some things on his mind.

I hadn't had a chance to talk with Kehler at any length earlier, but he had made a good impression on me. He listened carefully, responded thoughtfully and with good sense. Of the many younger American activists I had met at the conference, he was one I wanted to see more of; I had decided to arrange to visit him in San Francisco soon. He had a very simple and direct manner, along with warmth and humor. He was a very appealing person. I was somewhat surprised, when he began, to hear that we had gone to the same college, that he was, like me, a transplant from Cambridge to California. I remember thinking, Well, here's a credit to Harvard! And one who learned some things after he left. I then heard for the first time about the path that had led him to head the War Resisters League office in San Francisco.

"When I finished Harvard College and three weeks of graduate school at Stanford, I was out on the West Coast. I was involved in a demonstration in which hundreds of men and women were sitting in the doorways of the [Oakland] induction center trying to pose a question to all those going through the doors, to be inducted or to take their physicals. We wanted that question to be very real, and not just a matter of words, so we actually placed our bodies in those doorways.

"Well, that was a very new experience for me and one that really changed the whole course of my life. Before I knew it, I was behind bars with that same couple of hundred people, and I found a community of people for the first time that not only . . . were committed to each other, but a community of people that were committed to something larger than themselves, something probably more noble, more ideal, than anything I had been involved in after twenty-two years of public education. And it was as a result of that demonstration and that time I spent in jail with those people that I saw a very real alternative to the kind of life I was leading, which made me leave school and go to work for the WRL in San Francisco."

He talked about nonviolence as a way of life, about hope, about two worlds both existing just now, a waning world dominated by fear, an emerging world becoming more and more like a family. What I remember most vividly is not the content of what he had said so far but the impression he made on me as he spoke without preparation from the platform. Listening to him was like looking into clear water. I was experiencing a feeling I don't remember having had in any other circumstances. I was feeling proud of him as an American. I was proud, at the end of this conference, that this man on the platform was American. As a matter of fact, it was hard to imagine anyone whose looks, manners, and virtues were more American than Randy Kehler's. That was what was recalling to me a sense, not so familiar lately, of national pride. The auditorium was filled with people from all over the world. I was thinking as he spoke, I'm glad these foreign visitors are having a chance to hear this. He's as good as we have.

At that moment he brought me out of my reverie by saying something with a catch in his voice. He had just said, "Yesterday our friend Bob went to jail." He had to pause for a moment. He cleared his throat. Evidently he had tears in his eyes. He smiled and said, "This is getting to be like a wedding we had a month ago, when Jane and I were married on the beach in San Francisco, because I always cry a lot." After a moment he went on, in a steady voice. "Last month David Harris went to jail. Our friends Warren and John and Terry and many others are already in jail, and I'm really not as sad about that as it may seem. There's something really beautiful about it, and I'm very excited that I'll be invited to join them very soon."

Again he had to pause. The audience seemed taken by surprise. A scattering of applause began, then suddenly swelled, and people began to stand up. But he was going on, and people stopped applauding, continuing to rise, in silence. "Right now I'm the only man left in the San Francisco WRL office because all the others have gone to prison already, and soon, when I go, it will be all women in the office. And that will be all right. . . . I think I know that, and I think Bob and David know that, but there's one other reason why I guess I can look forward to jail, without any remorse or fear, and that's because I know that everyone here and lots of people around the world like you will carry on."

The whole audience was standing. They clapped and cheered for a long time. I stood up for a moment with the rest, but I fell back into my seat, breathing hard, dizzy, swaying. I was crying, a lot of people must have been crying, but then I began to sob silently, grimacing under the tears, shoulders shaking. Janaki was to talk next, but I couldn't stay. I got up—I was sitting in the very last row in the amphitheater—and made my way down the back corridor till I came to a men's room. I went inside and turned on the light.

It was a small room, with two sinks. I staggered over to the wall and slid down to the tile floor. I began to sob convulsively, uncontrollably. I wasn't silent anymore. My sobbing sounded like laughing, at other times like moaning. My chest was heaving. I had to gasp for breath.

I sat there alone for more than an hour without getting up, my head sometimes tilted back against the wall, sometimes in my hands, without stopping to shake from my sobbing. I had never cried like this before except, more briefly, when I learned that Bobby Kennedy was dead. A line kept repeating itself in my head: We are eating our young.

I had not been ready to hear what Randy had said. I had not been braced for it. When he mentioned his friends who were in prison and remarked that he would soon be joining them, it had taken me several moments to grasp what he had just said. Then it was as though an ax had split my head, and my heart broke open. But what had really happened was that my life had split in two.

We are eating our young, I thought again, sitting on the floor of the men's room in the second part of my life. On both sides of the barricades we are using them, using them up, "wasting" them. This is what my country has come to. We have come to this. The best thing that the best young men of our country can do with their lives is to go to prison. My son, Robert, was thirteen. This war would still be going on when he turned eighteen. (It was.) My son was born to face prison. Another line kept repeating itself in my head, a refrain from a song by Leonard Cohen: "That's right, it's come to this, yes, it's come to this. And wasn't it a long way down, ah, wasn't it a strange way down?"

After about an hour I stopped sobbing. I stared blankly at the sinks across from me, thinking, not crying, exhausted, breathing deeply. Finally I got up and washed my face. I gripped the sink and stared at the mirror. Then I sat down on the floor again to think some more. I cried again, a couple of times more, briefly, not so violently. What I had just heard from Randy had put the question in my mind, What could I do, what should I be doing, to help end the war now that I was ready to go to prison for it?

No transition period occurred, during which I asked if I was willing to go to prison to help end the war. That didn't come up as a question; it would have answered itself. I knew myself from Vietnam. I had risked my life or, worse, my body, my legs, a thousand times driving the roads there or walking in combat. If I could do that when I believed in the war, and even after I didn't, it followed self-evidently that I was capable of going to prison to help end it.

Might some action that risked prison help shorten the war? Obviously Randy thought so. That came close to being a good enough answer. Besides, I could have little doubt, from my own experience in the moment, that he was right. I had just felt the power of his action on my heart. As of this evening, I realized that I had the power and the freedom to act the same way.

18

Extrication

I returned from Haverford by way of Washington, where I stopped to pick up another eight volumes of the McNamara study from the Washington Rand office to bring home to Santa Monica. I had postponed reading the earliest studies covering the years 1945 to 1960, assuming initially that they weren't very relevant to the current situation. That was a mistake, for me as a reader. Now I read them as confirming—with official, classified U.S. government internal documents—what I had just read in accounts by French journalists and historians. No other volumes of the papers—the later ones held few surprises for me—had so great an impact on my perspective toward the war.

But for me, in addition to the moral conclusions I've explained, there were also conceptual and tactical conclusions to be drawn from this new reading in September. These not only complemented my earlier research but led to a new conviction on how this steady course of history might be changed in the months ahead. On the one hand, these findings closed the book for me on the quagmire myth, the notion that presidents had been misled at critical turning points by unrealistic optimism in their civil and military advisers. It was clear that Harry Truman, in his decision to support the French directly in May 1950 (after years of knowingly allowing American aid to be used indirectly to support the war), must, like each of his four successors, in similar situations, take heavy personal responsibility for the ensuing bloody stalemate punctuated by "crises."

Likewise, Eisenhower's support after 1954 of a police state dedicated to silencing, jailing, or exterminating every political figure in Vietnam, Communist and others, who called for observance of the provisions of the Geneva Accords for elections and unification ensured that armed struggle would resume. We had no more right to win that struggle than the French had had, and that was zero. Moreover, though like the French with U.S. assistance, we could prolong it year by year, we had no better prospect of winning that struggle than the French had had. Again, zero.

That last point, on prospects, had been presented by authoritative advisers to every president from Truman on. Each had been told of the likelihood that his chosen approach (and, as some advisers told each of them, any approach) would be stalemated and would at best postpone departure and defeat. That had been my own message at intermediate levels each year since 1966, but every president since 1946 had heard it personally from sources far more authoritative than I. Yet each of them had chosen to "soldier on," deceiving the public on what he was doing and what he had been told its prospects were.

Better internal forecasts at moments of decision would not reliably have made a difference to presidential choices. As I had hoped and expected, in March 1969 President Nixon had gotten a ration of realism from the uncoordinated answers to NSSM-1 perfectly adequate for him to have chosen a different course from the one Halperin had revealed to me in August. On the basis of the record ever since 1946, "telling truth to presidents" privately, confidentially—what I and my colleagues regarded as the highest calling and greatest opportunity we could imagine to serve our country—looked entirely unpromising as a way to end our war in and on Vietnam.

That conclusion challenged the premises that had guided my entire professional career. To read the continuous record of intelligence assessments and forecasts for Vietnam from 1946 on was finally to lose the delusion that informing the executive branch better was the key to ending the war—or to fulfilling one's responsibilities as a citizen. It appeared that only if power were brought to bear upon the executive branch from outside it, with the important secondary effect of sharing responsibility for later events more broadly, might the presidential preference for endless, escalating stalemate rather than "failure" in Vietnam be overruled. "Inside" consulting and advice, as in the Rand mode, or the normal practices of the broader "establishment" withheld from Congress and the public the facts and authoritative judgments needed for the self-confident exercise of such a power. By that very silence—no matter how frank or wise the "private" counsel—it supported and participated in the structure of inordinate, unchallenged executive power that led directly in circumstances like Vietnam to its rigid, desperate, outlaw behavior. To absorb and act on that perception looked inconsistent with remaining long at Rand, to which I'd returned with the desire and expectation of staying the rest of my professional life.

That wasn't all. Along with their implications of the illegitimacy of our policy and thus the urgency of changing it, the early volumes of the Pentagon Papers confirmed for me what I had begun to suspect with my reading of the subsequent volumes over the last two years: *The president was part of the problem.* This was clearly a matter of his role, not of his personality or party. As I was beginning to see it, the concentration of power within the executive branch since World War II had focused nearly all responsibility for policy "failure" upon one man, the president. At the same time, it gave him enormous capability to avert or postpone or conceal such personal failure by means of force and fraud. Confronted by resolute external resistance, as in Vietnam, that power could not fail to corrupt the human who held it.

The only way to change the president's course was to bring pressure on him from outside, from Congress and the public. The best chance of mobilizing that was to give outsiders knowledge of Nixon's preferred course. Unfortunately I didn't have documents to prove what that was, to contradict the deceptive gloss the White House could be expected to give it, presenting it as a path toward total U.S. withdrawal with no prospect of escalation. Without those documents, my account could only seem implausible, even incredible. Halperin and Vann knew the truth, but it didn't even occur to me to urge them to go public with what they had told me. They didn't have documents, either, to back up such testimony, and indeed (like me) they weren't supposed to know it and wouldn't want to compromise their confidential sources. For the same reason it didn't enter my mind to reveal them as sources, ending their careers. There were those who, knowing my own general access, would give my views great credit, though as I expected (and discovered) even they found what I was claiming "extreme," alarmist, almost impossible to believe: that Nixon could be following a course so evidently unrealistic, so foreseeably unpopular, in the post-1968 circumstances. None of them of course had read the Pentagon Papers.

If the American people couldn't be shown documents that proved what the president was about to do or hear accounts from current members of the administration, a next best approach seemed to be to present them with public recommendations by former officials with great authority or second-level analysts who could claim access to classified information, even if not to current highest-level plans. In the first category were the sorts of notables that the Carnegie Endowment had gathered together in Bermuda two years earlier. In the second were those among my Rand colleagues who had for more than a year been pressing for extrication. Perhaps by going public with our "expert" and "informed" views, we could get the first group to join us, specifically, to get former Democratic officials to call for extrication. By doing that openly, before Nixon had committed himself in public to his own secretly preferred course, they could not only pressure him but assure him credibly that they would share responsibility for the withdrawal. It was especially after completing my reading, that September, of the entire twenty-three years covered by the McNamara study that I had come to see such an assurance by potentially rival politicians as essential to a president's willingness to face charges of "losing a war."

Leaders within the Democratic opposition, including former officials, would have to accept, against their instincts, both that extrication was now the appropriate course and of overriding interest and that their own public dissent from impending presidential policy was essential and worthwhile. Even harder for them, they would have to take most of the blame for the predicament that forced such a choice on the new president and convince him of their willingness to share responsibility for shifting course and for its consequences. This would not be easy to bring about. But it seemed to me to be the task that most needed doing right now, and it was the one to which I set myself.

Organizing pressure on the current president, in part by encouraging the self-condemnation of his opposition, was inconsistent with the life of a Rand analyst. It also looked designed to incur for me the hostility of the leaders of two political parties, the Democratic and the Republican. After my visit to Haverford, both these concerns appeared petty. It was beginning to seem unlikely that I would ever be able to consult for a president of either party again, up till now my highest ambition. But reading the Pentagon Papers on the disastrous behavior of four presidents in Vietnam, and reflecting on my own experience with the fourth and now a fifth, suddenly made that easy to accept. It had burned out of me the desire to work for presidents, to be in any sense a "president's man."

That might sound pretentious, considering the lowly levels at which I had served. I had never, after all, so much as met a president (except once in a receiving line, in 1967, when my friend and Saigon housemate Frank Scotton got a medal from President Johnson for his innovative work with the USIA). But even as a lieutenant in the Marine Corps I'd thought of myself as serving in a presidential guard, ready to fight wherever and whomever the president should decide. I think some sense of responsibility directly to the president, of working for him, is characteristic of most, or very many, members of the executive branch. But that satisfaction died for me that month, after what I had learned of five presidents' behavior in this particular generation-long war. I no longer identified with presidents, no longer saw serving a president as the most desirable, or best, or most effective way to influence policy or to serve the public welfare.

However, with this disillusionment also came a new freedom. I would no longer be awaiting a call from the White House or from any official serving at the president's pleasure. That was as liberating, as expanding of options of resistance, as my newfound willingness to go to prison if necessary. I now found it easy to contemplate forms of opposition to present policy that were likely to bar me from future employment in the executive branch. Fear of that particular penalty, not jail, was the ultimate deterrent that kept most of my colleagues, past and present, from considering political actions that went beyond a certain point. I was no longer held in line by that fear. From their point of view, I was about to become dangerous to know.

In mid-September I told my colleague Konrad Kellen that I was now ready to join with those at Rand who had been pressing for two years for a strategy of unilateral extrication from Vietnam. I suggested we meet to discuss what we should do, and he brought four others together in his office one afternoon: Mel Gurtov, Paul Langer, Arnold Horelick, and Oleg Hoeffding. Gurtov was an expert on China and Southeast Asia, Langer on Japan, and Horelick and Hoeffding on Russia.

I told them what I had learned from Halperin and Vann about Nixon's policy. The president had tried the approach of proposing mutual withdrawal in negotiations, and that had failed. He seemed to be hoping that this could still happen if we stayed long enough, but I didn't expect this, and I didn't want to go on bombing and fighting while we waited for it. I now accepted the group's argument that the only way for us to get out of Vietnam was to get out unilaterally. Because Nixon hadn't spoken much about his policy since he had announced his hopes for mutual withdrawal in the spring, I thought there was still a chance to encourage him to take a different path before the passage of time, more U.S. casualties, and his own public pronouncements made him feel so personally responsible for the outcome of the war that he couldn't accept less than success.

That was likely to happen, we all agreed, even with Clark Clifford's July

1969 proposal in *Foreign Affairs* (he was now out of office) to withdraw all U.S. ground combat troops from Vietnam by the end of 1970, leaving the eventual withdrawal of logistics, airlift, and air support units to be determined by later developments. Though it was in the right direction compared with current strategy and went further than what any other public figure had so far proposed, it wouldn't end the war, nor would it end direct U.S. combat participation—with airpower—by any definite or foreseeable time. However, Clifford was right to propose that the United States should set a course toward disengagement that was independent of the wishes or the adaptations of either Saigon or Hanoi. But the others at the meeting had wanted for the last two years to go further than he was proposing, and I now agreed with them.

Thus far since King's death the only public figures who had been willing to say to the government, "Get out," get all the way out, had been counterculture activists like Abbie Hoffman, radicals perceived as supporters of North Vietnam, and advocates of direct action and civil disobedience. What they called for was ignored or discounted. In fact their advocacy of complete withdrawal served to tar it and to threaten mainstream figures who might have been tempted to discuss it favorably with the stigma of association with them. The single closely reasoned and eloquent expression of this approach had been a pamphlet by the historian and civil rights activist Howard Zinn, *Vietnam: The Logic of Withdrawal.* But Zinn's powerful argument, which was endorsed by Noam Chomsky in a review, didn't recruit any allies among mainstream academics and intellectuals.

Former LBJ advisers who had become public critics of his policy, like Arthur Schlesinger, Jr., Richard Goodwin, and John Kenneth Galbraith, had called in Johnson's last year for reducing our involvement, ending bombing, and negotiations. But they chose to distance themselves from and denigrate more "extreme" proposals; they all took pains to say that they were not proposing, in fact *opposed,* simple "withdrawal." The same was true for politicians like Eugene McCarthy, George McGovern, Frank Church, and even Bobby Kennedy before his death. None of these had gone beyond this so far in 1969; not much had been heard from them at all. When they called for negotiations, they didn't say what their subject should be or what outcome we should be prepared to accept. An earlier exception had been a statement by Bobby Kennedy in early 1966 that we should deal with the NLF in negotiations and that it should have a role in the future government, but the reaction from both the administration and the establishment had been so fierce that he backed off and didn't bring it up again in public. In early 1967 Bobby had urged this same proposal on President Johnson in private, as had Robert McNamara a month later, but neither of them had ever made their advice known to the American people or to Congress after the president had dismissed it.

In this climate, if the new president were to do what I thought he ought to do—for example, what Kennedy and McNamara had proposed privately, in the context of a plan to withdraw—he would have to get out publicly *in front* of those establishment figures who had been most critical of the war, risking that even they would attack him for taking too simplistic and extreme an approach. It would be the most dangerous kind of leadership, a sharp change in policy and a repudiation of near-sacred premises of the cold war without his having identified any allies with authoritative credentials. That seemed the last thing any president was likely to do.

The beauty, the power, and the purpose of the Rand analysts' making a public statement along the same lines as the antiwar activists was that it demonstrated that you didn't have to be a radical or a hippie, you didn't have to be unpatriotic or a fan of Hanoi, and above all, you didn't have to be ignorant of classified information to advocate total and prompt U.S. disengagement from the Vietnam War. Zinn and Chomsky could be written off not only as "radicals" but as uninformed of the secret information available to the president and his advisers. Rand "defense intellectuals," with clearances and government contracts as Vietnam researchers and consultants, could not.

We hoped our public statement would encourage opinion leaders in the media and Congress who intuitively agreed with this approach but were not Vietnam specialists to feel confident enough of its soundness to support it openly. In the face of foreseeable charges by their colleagues that it was simplistic and extreme and reflected innocence of the real considerations at high policy levels, they could point to us for protection. Together with us, they would give the same kind of confidence to members of the general public and to their representatives in Congress. At a minimum, we could aim to expand the range of respectable, responsible debate to include total extrication as a legitimate option or position.

Even if Nixon didn't accept this approach in the next year, serious discussion and advocacy of it could help influence him to a much faster drawdown of U.S. forces in Vietnam than he was now secretly planning, maybe a schedule closer to what Clark Clifford had proposed in July (withdrawal of all U.S. combat troops by the end of 1970). That wouldn't get us out, and it was very much worse in our eyes than what we were proposing, but it was a lot better than Nixon's current policy and more likely than ours to be adopted.

I was happy to join in any such effort. Speed was important. We needed to get our views into the public domain within weeks, before Nixon took a public stand. Another consideration was that major demonstrations against the war were planned for October 15. They were scheduled to take place all across the country on the same weekday, cutting into the workday, in a form of general strike. In lieu of that provocative description, the campaign was being called the Moratorium. If these pressures were powerful, Nixon would be reacting to them in the fall, either positively or negatively. We should try to affect the positions expressed in the Moratorium, just weeks away, as well as influence Nixon's response to them. We discussed a variety of options, internal and external, formal and informal, to get our thoughts out.

"We can only do it in a letter," someone in the group finally said. That was the only way we could publish something outside Rand without going through a formal clearance process. Even written comments we intended to read at outside conferences were supposed to be cleared. According to corporate rules, only spontaneous, unplanned remarks at such a conference or a letter to a newspaper or journal (an odd loophole in the rules) could bypass clearance. I was dubious that a letter would be adequate for our purpose. I thought we needed a study that would lay out the facts as we saw them and present our argument more exhaustively than a brief letter could do. A letter just wouldn't be convincing to anyone who didn't already agree with us.

"It's a letter or nothing," the others said. If we invited a process of security clearance, the argument would be made that we were indirectly basing our position on classified data to which we had had access. To a certain extent this was true. We even wanted it to be understood that we had indeed seen such official data. But ironically, the realities from which we were drawing our conclusions were known to most people in the world. They were hidden only from those who believed the public lies of the U.S. government. The secret we were exposing, that we wanted to expose, was that the data privately available to the government did not invalidate the realistic knowledge and conclusions that most people outside our government already shared, about the folly of our hopelessly stalemated involvement.

What needed revealing was that it was possible to have pursued a career as a sophisticated, expert, informed, responsible government researcher and consultant with access to the same estimates and plans and inside dope that high government officials relied on, and also to have reached the same conclusion as Abbie Hoffman and a growing number of observers around the world without special information: that the place for the United States to be, relative to Vietnam, was out.

A letter could do that. It didn't need a lot of argument; it didn't need to convince people who were resistant to the conclusion. It would serve an important function if it just gave some confidence to the many who already agreed with it and if it got the notion at last onto the agenda of the public debate as a serious, "responsible" alternative. Gurtov and Kellen volunteered to work on a first draft, and we made a date to meet again and go over it.

Meanwhile I started work on a second letter of my own, not for publication but to the Carnegie Endowment for International Peace, which had called together a group of consultants and former officials to try to influence President Johnson's policy two years before. I wanted the group or one much like it to meet again, to the same end, extrication, as our letter from Rand (though not to be bound to our same proposal). I called Joe Johnson, the head of the Carnegie Endowment. He sounded encouraging and told me to write a letter with my proposal to Charles Bolté, the executive director.

This was a much longer and more analytical letter, because I actually wanted to persuade these readers, all former (and, they mostly hoped, future) high-level insiders, to do something that was strongly against their instincts: to bring public pressure to bear on an incumbent president. Nevertheless, I took the chance of using language in my closing appeal that I knew risked putting them off, because I wanted to convey the sense of an unusual sort of challenge and urgency. I proposed that a group be convened to declare a policy "aimed unconditionally at U.S. extrication," and that discussion within the group should be limited to proposals that had that clear character. I ended:

> There should by now be an extreme burden of proof upon any proposal that might compromise the certainty of ceasing the—to use precise, necessary words—bloody, hopeless, uncompelled, hence surely immoral prolongation of U.S. involvement in this war.

The wording of that final sentence of the letter, especially the adjective "immoral," was anything but casual, and it did not go unnoticed at the other end. Bolté told me later that Joe Johnson had read the letter carefully and brought it back to him, pointing at the word "immoral." He said to

Bolté, "We can't invite Ellsberg to any more of our meetings. He's lost his objectivity."

I sent many copies of my letter to past members of Carnegie study groups and to other high officials of the Johnson administration and Democratic members of Congress. The response from all was essentially that of Carnegie's executive committee, which was that it was "hard to see anything useful" the endowment could contribute at this moment. The other establishment individuals agreed that there was nothing to do just now; it wasn't the time.

My own feeling was that there clearly was something they could usefully do and that time was running out. I wanted "clear, uncompromising, conscientious statements of dissent to the present course of Administration policy" before the president, any day now, committed himself publicly to that course. For the effect I wanted, some of these statements had to come precisely from *Democrats,* above all former Johnson officials who would thereby be providing Nixon with protective, bipartisan cover. They needed to give the Republican administration as strong assurance as possible against attack by their opposition party for a change in course that might otherwise be challenged as an abandonment of a Kennedy-Johnson "commitment."

For that they needed to go beyond dissent. What they could "usefully do," in fact what was essential if the policy was to change, was to acknowledge, at last, before the American people, their own responsibility for the misguided and failed policy of the past and present. They had to show readiness to share with the new president responsibility for changing it and for any consequences that might follow.

I decided to make this argument directly to the two Democrats, former officials in the Johnson administration, I thought most likely to respond to my appeal. I knew they both wanted strongly to see the United States out of Vietnam. They were both on the Democratic Policy Advisory Committee, a key group formulating the party's platform and policy, so they were in a position to line up top Democrats for what I had in mind if they agreed. To the one I called first, I outlined what I thought had to be addressed to Nixon, in a public statement by former officials who had in fact shared responsibility for the Vietnam involvement that Nixon had inherited, if he was to be induced to end it.

I told him what I'd come to believe from a tactical point of view. I didn't think any president who expected to be held solely accountable for the outcome of a war would be willing to end it with less than success. That was why public demonstration of an effective readiness to share responsibility with him for a shift in course couldn't be delayed any longer. Before long the continuation of the war would be so identified with his own term in office that he couldn't reasonably hope to escape primary responsibility for the outcome. I knew that what I was asking was very hard to do, or even to contemplate, and that was why there was probably no precedent for it. I would be happy to join in the statement myself, but what was really needed was a declaration by people of much higher status, like him. I said, "You don't have to use these words, but this is the real substance of what has to be said: 'Mr. President, this is not your war. This is our war. Don't make it yours. We made the mistakes that got us in. Don't make those same mistakes. Get us out. We will stand with you if you do.' "

There was a silence on the other end of the phone. Then he said, "Dan, we can't do that. Not now. It would mean the destruction of the Democratic party. The Republicans would say, 'You got us in, and now you're pulling the rug out.' We'd be blamed for starting the war and then for losing it. It would be another stab-in-the-back legend."

I argued a little further. I pointed out that there was a good deal of truth to the charge that we had gotten the country in; didn't that give us an obligation to take unusual steps to help get us out? But he was firm. He didn't dismiss my logic, but the cost to the party would be just too great, and that wouldn't be good for the country either. This wasn't the time. It was too soon after these same officials had left office; it would sound like sour grapes. (That was how the French had sounded to us in 1964: "What we couldn't win, you can't win." But the French had been right!) What he was really responding to, I think, was a sense that I was proposing that Democrats take all the responsibility for an unwinnable war and most of the responsibility for losing it. That *was* pretty much what I was proposing. He couldn't go along. Maybe at some later time, he said. As we hung up, I was thinking, *Later?* Later would be too late.

It was beginning to occur to me, from the reactions I was getting, that there were Democrats who actually had some willingness, even preference, to see the war go on for a while under Nixon until it did become "Nixon's war." I suspected they were secretly looking forward to that, to the time when the failure was no longer their sole responsibility. *Then*—they might be telling themselves—they could work with him to end it or, better yet, follow his lead when he decided to seek their support in giving up. The initiative would come from him, from his own bitter experience, rather than be triggered by their guilty admission. The trouble was, as I saw it, that an appeal to them from Nixon to share responsibility for a change in policy would never come later. Once it had become Nixon's war he wouldn't be willing to give up his hopes of some sort of success, whatever the Democrats might be willing to say then. It would be too late. The war would go on for years.

These somewhat bitter thoughts were confirmed when I called the second person, who had been a White House aide to Lyndon Johnson. I had talked with him several times when I came back from Vietnam, and we seemed to be totally on the same wavelength. In early 1968 he had worked closely with the first and with Clark Clifford to try to persuade President Johnson to end the bombing of the North in order to get negotiations started. I knew he was well wired into Democratic politics. I gave him the same pitch and got the same reaction as before, almost the same words. He ended dramatically: "Dan, if we did what you suggest, there'd be a political bloodbath such as you've never seen. And that means you and me, Dan."

I was shocked by his last words. I said, as evenly as I could, that he might well be right about that. That would be a hard time for us. But I thought we would just have to deal with that, as best we could. I said I wasn't willing to protect my own political future, or the Democratic party's, at the cost of more lives of American soldiers or Vietnamese. There was a bloodbath going on right now, in Vietnam. I wouldn't want to think we'd prolonged that for a day, or a month, or a year, just to save my political skin or his.

He made no reply. We said our good-byes and hung up.

19

Murder and the Lying Machine

On the morning of September 30 I got out of bed, opened my front door to the Pacific Coast Highway, and picked up the *Los Angeles Times.* As I usually did, I went back to the bedroom overlooking the beach and got back into bed to read the paper.

The main story that day concerned what had become known as the Green Berets, or Special Forces, murder case in Vietnam. I had been following this story for weeks, and it had appeared on the cover of every newsmagazine. Since July the colonel in command of Special Forces in Vietnam, Robert Rheault, and five intelligence officers assigned to him had been charged with premeditated murder and conspiracy to commit murder. A sergeant and a warrant officer were being held with charges held in abeyance.

The lead story by Ted Sell summarized the charges: "The victim in the case was reported to be Thai Khac Chuyen, 31, a native of North Vietnam, who had been employed by the Special Forces since December 1963. . . . Information reportedly became available that Chuyen had taken part in meetings with communist intelligence officers. After interrogation—both with lie detectors and under the so-called truth serum sodium pentothal—these charges were allegedly considered confirmed by Special Forces officers. On June 20, Chuyen was reported to have been shot, his body placed in a weighted bag and the bag sunk in the South China Sea."

The headline on Sell's story in the middle of the front page was MURDER CHARGES AGAINST GREEN BERETS DROPPED BY ARMY. The story read:

> The Army Monday overruled its field commander in Vietnam and dismissed murder charges against eight Green Berets suspected of killing a Vietnamese double agent.
>
> The surprise action was ordered by Secretary of the Army Stanley R. Resor, who only 11 days earlier had indicated he strongly felt the case should be brought to trial.
>
> Resor said he took the action on grounds the soldiers could not receive a fair trial because the Central Intelligence Agency had refused to make witnesses available. But it was apparent the decision involved soul-searching at higher levels. . . .

Sell explored two theories of the case: the first, that CIA operatives in the field may have approved and then disapproved of the killing; the second, that testimony by clandestine CIA operatives might reveal that the murder of agents suspected of also working for the enemy was not uncommon, hence singling out the soldiers was unfair.

On the first point, Sell reported later in the story: "Local CIA officials reportedly told the Army group to 'terminate with extreme prejudice'—a phrase said to mean death. Then, according to other reports, the CIA rescinded that direction and urged that Chuyen not be killed. But by then, according to the report, Chuyen was already dead."

Sell wrote that Resor appeared to be saying that "if the CIA refused to present information regarding the alleged crime," the soldiers could not receive a fair trial, so charges had to be dropped. He didn't say, but it appeared self-evident, that the CIA could not "refuse" to produce witnesses without the backing of the president. Both Pentagon and White House spokesmen denied any White House involvement in the process or the decision, but this story (and all others) took it for granted that these denials were false. (The diary of Nixon chief of staff H. R. Haldeman has recently confirmed that all decisions were made by Nixon and Kissinger.)

Why had the unprecedented trial been brought by the army in the first place? According to Resor: "I want to make it clear that the acts which were charged, but not proven, represent a fundamental violation of Army regulations, orders and principles. The Army will not and cannot condone unlawful acts of the kind alleged." As Resor repeatedly put it, "The Army cannot condone murder." General Creighton Abrams, commander of U.S. forces in Vietnam, who ordered the court-martial, took the same position:

that he had no choice but to bring charges, given the evidence of murder. There was some tension between this position and the assumption that the White House had chosen to drop the unpopular charges; it appeared that although the army could not condone murder, apparently the president could.

Yet if it were true that such murders were not uncommon but had never before been brought to trial, the question remained, "Why had these charges been brought at all?" Why this trial, in particular, when it seemed especially likely to prove embarrassing to the administration and its war policy? Resor's and Abrams's accounts of the motivations for prosecution appeared inadequate—that is, untrue.

Later in his account Sell commented that "Abrams's motive in approving a trial that would almost certainly focus attention on unseemly aspects of the war in Vietnam was reported to be rage at having been told a lie. According to these reports, Rheault, or others, queried by Abrams's headquarters about Chuyen, said that he was on a sensitive secret mission outside South Vietnam when he was already dead."

An accompanying analysis by reporter Robert Donovan added that Rheault himself had been initially misled on what had happened by intelligence operatives under his command, including Captain Robert F. Marasco, the alleged triggerman, and other captains, who had ordered subordinates down to the sergeant and warrant officer to participate in a false cover story.

I lay on my bed and listened to the ocean and the gulls and thought about what I had read. One aspect of it was the outrage by Democrats and Republicans in the House and the Senate that American officers should ever have been put under criminal charges, risking imprisonment, just for killing one Vietnamese civilian in cold blood. And there was a sense of unfairness, of selective prosecution, in singling out these particular soldiers for a kind of killing that was "not uncommon."

Donovan's report cited statements of approval of the dismissal by many leading members of Congress. "I think this action by the secretary," said Representative George Bush, "is a correct one and should prove significant in helping the morale of our combat troops."

Nevertheless, Donovan noted, "It raised a serious moral question about the right of soldiers to kill a prisoner in cold blood without a trial, if that is indeed what happened, as has been charged. . . ."

Could killing under orders, in wartime, be murder? My infantry training said yes. Killing prisoners or civilians in your custody? For sure. It so happened that I had just come to a much broader answer to that question, to cover all killing in an unjust war like our war in Vietnam. I didn't expect Army Secretary Resor or General Abrams to agree with me on that, but in narrow circumstances like these, they had to. Yet if they didn't personally condone an individual murder, they were taking part in a lot of lying about the bringing and dismissing of charges of it. A vision forming in my mind was what seemed to be the skeleton of the two stories I had just read: a ladder of lies about a murder case.

Actually the only time the word "lie" occurred in either story was in connection with General Abrams's rage at being deceived, he thought, by Colonel Rheault. But neither writer attempted to conceal his belief that official untruth was not confined to this one incident. Following journalistic practice, neither reporter attached the words "lie" or "untrue" to statements by officials. They simply followed most of these statements with a contradictory account, headed by locutions like "The fact that . . . suggests . . ."; "Hence, it appeared . . ."; "What appeared to have happened . . ."; "But it was apparent. . . ." However, these euphemisms didn't conceal their judgment on the truth value of official pronouncements. At the same time, it was striking how nonjudgmental, how matter-of-fact the journalists were about the existence of all these discrepancies, how much they took them for granted, at every single level of the bureaucracy.

General Abrams himself, in Sell's and Donovan's accounts, was committed to a deceptive cover story; so were the secretary of the army and the president. Not only Colonel Rheault, but below him several majors, captains, a warrant officer, and a sergeant had constructed the false cover story given to Abrams. That was pretty much the whole chain of command, civilian and military.

I lay in bed that Tuesday morning and thought: This is the system that I have been working for, the system I have been part of, for a dozen years—fifteen, including the Marine Corps. It's a system that lies automatically, at every level from bottom to top—from sergeant to commander in chief—to conceal murder.

That described, as I had come to realize from my reading that month, what that system had been doing in Vietnam, on an infinitely larger scale, continuously for a third of a century. And it was still going on. I thought: I'm not going to be part of it anymore. I'm not going to be part of this lying machine, this cover-up, this murder, anymore.

It occurred to me that what I had in my safe at Rand was seven thousand pages of documentary evidence of lying, by four presidents and their administrations over twenty-three years, to conceal plans and actions of mass murder. I decided I would stop concealing that myself. I would get it out somehow.

It would have to be copied. I couldn't do that at Rand or at a copy shop. Maybe it was possible to lease a machine. I got out of bed and picked up the phone in my living room and called a close friend, my former Rand colleague Tony Russo. I said there was something I would like to discuss with him. I'd be over shortly.

Tony had been part of the Rand VC Prisoner and Defector Interrogation Study in Vietnam. I'd first met him briefly when I arrived in Saigon in 1965. When we were back together in Santa Monica in 1968, he had often discussed with me, in his office just down the hall from mine, what he'd learned from his interviews. He showed me a number of the transcripts, some of them sixty single-spaced pages. Many of those he had talked to, through interpreters, had impressed him very much by their patriotism and dedication, their conviction of the rightness of their cause. Even the defectors, nearly all of whom had left for personal reasons or because of the hardships of guerrilla life, had nothing negative to say about the cause or their national leaders. (Konrad Kellen, who had dealt with prisoner interrogation material in World War II and Korea and defectors from Eastern Europe, read hundreds of these transcripts for the Rand project and told me he had never seen any like these. "Prisoners and defectors tell you what they think you want to hear. These people, you can't get them to say anything critical of their regime." His conclusion, which he urged me to pass on to Kissinger, was that this was one adversary whose leadership and population simply "could not be coerced." They could be annihilated but not coerced.)

Tony had a degree in aeronautical engineering and had worked for NASA before studying political science at Princeton. He had started out as a cold warrior like me, but meeting the North Vietnamese and Vietcong and hearing their stories had changed him. He had come not only to admire them as people but to believe they were right about the justice of their cause. I remained focused on the injustice of ours, as I had come to see it by mid-1969. I hadn't had his face-to-face experience—I never knowingly encountered an actual member of the NLF—and I remained skeptical that their hopes would be fulfilled if their well-justified nationalist struggle led to a Stalinist regime, as I thought likely.

In any case, it wasn't nominally for his political views that Tony had been dropped from the Rand Economics Department, in effect fired. I had seen only hints of his sympathy for the VC in our talks while he was still at Rand; he didn't make it public or put it in writing. But it was what he did put in writing, I was sure, that got him in trouble with our hawkish department chairman, Charlie Wolf. He had written a careful statistical study of the effects on the population of our herbicide program, which was supposedly addressed to denying food to the VC but had a much wider impact. Also, from his personal observations of prisoners in custody, he had exposed, in a classified study, the widespread practice of beatings and torture of VC prisoners by ARVN captors and jailers, often with American advisers observing. Wolf didn't like these or another study Russo did on the relation of VC control to land tenure policies, and others at Rand worried about the reception of these studies by our air force sponsors. I didn't yet know Tony on a personal basis when he told me that Wolf was firing him, but I had been impressed by his work, and I told Charlie that I thought it was a mistake and a real loss for the department. Charlie insisted that the decision was only for budgetary reasons, though Tony seemed the only one affected.

After Tony left Rand, I started seeing him after work. I came to like him more and more. He was funny, and he had a very original and creative mind, and not just about the war. We became close friends. He had begun reading radical analyses that presented our Vietnam policy not as an aberration or misadventure but as being in line with unacknowledged U.S. objectives and covert activities elsewhere in the third world. Again, I wasn't there yet; I hadn't done that reading (and didn't get to it till after the war). But on September 30 I didn't have any doubt that this was one friend, the only one, I could tell what I wanted to do.

As I got dressed, I was thinking about what was in the minds of the people I'd just read about, the ones who'd done the lying and helped the killing. So many of them had lied (and some of them may have helped kill) for no other reason than that they'd been told to. They were ordered to lie, or kill, by a boss. They were told it was for the good of the service, or the war, or the administration, or the Special Forces, or their bosses, or to keep their jobs. That was good enough for them; it was all they needed to know. I understood that. I'd been there, and I'd worked in those same offices. But they'd been mistaken to have acted like that, just as I'd often been. Too long, no longer.

A thought came into my head in the form of a rule: No one is ever going to tell me again that I have to lie, that I have a duty to lie, that it's all right just because someone's telling me to do it. No one is going to say that and have me believe him, or think I have to obey him. I'm not going to listen to that anymore. It no longer has any authority for me.

Lying to the public, about anything, but above all on issues of life and death, war and peace, was a serious matter; it wasn't something you could shift responsibility for. I wasn't going to do it anymore.

It came to me that the same thing applied to violence. No one else was going to tell me ever again that I (or anyone else) "had" to kill someone, that I had no choice, that I had a right or a duty to do it that someone else had decided for me.

This new principle, as I already thought of it, didn't answer all questions about whether one should ever use violence or when, the questions I'd been wrestling with ever since I met Janaki and began reading Gandhian and Christian pacifists, but it did answer some. For example, about whether unquestioningly to accept being drafted. That wouldn't face me again, but it might face my son Robert. I would tell my kids, I thought, that no one could make it all right for them to carry a gun or shoot anyone just by telling them they had to. That would have to be their choice, their entire responsibility. If I ever did it again—I would tell them, as I now told myself—it would be because I chose to do it or chose to follow such orders as the right thing to do, not just because someone gave me an order. I would also examine very critically my own reasoning for it. I would have to have better reasons, which stood up better under a skeptical look, than I had in Vietnam. Responsibility for killing or being ready to kill was not something you could delegate to someone else, even a president.

Meanwhile, as I drove over to Tony's house, I was thinking how this would fit in with what I was trying to do this month. Sickened, at last, as I was by the lying machine, the simple act of exposing it wasn't an urgent priority. My concern was what the current lies (like the old ones, in this history) were about: what they were concealing, what they were facilitating. It was bad that they indicated past killings to have been murder, but I personally had no interest in putting anyone on trial or behind bars. I certainly wouldn't have courted trial or a life behind bars myself to accomplish retribution or just to set straight the historical record of Vietnam. My interest was in stopping the ongoing killing, preventing murders in the months and years ahead.

At first it wasn't obvious that revealing the McNamara study to the public would contribute to that at all, however educational it might be for the longer run. But from the moment that morning I had decided to do it anyway, I had begun to have new thoughts that suggested that it might be useful even in the short run.

It was true that the study didn't prove what needed to be exposed about Nixon's secret strategy: what Halperin had told me, what I'd passed on to my Rand colleagues and to the establishment figures I had written recently. But at the same time, it did strengthen the case for it, more than a little. It showed that what I was claiming Nixon was doing was essentially what his predecessor had done. When I claimed he was prepared to mislead Congress and the American people on what he was doing, what he was ready to do, and what his real aims were, the study demonstrated that *four* of his predecessors had done exactly that. Granted, he implied he had given up the aims and priorities that they all had acted on, but the continuity the study revealed raised questions about that, to say the least, questions Congress might be persuaded to pursue.

Simply revealing the McNamara study would not end the war or come close to it. But it could help, and in my present mood that was justification enough. If I could get this out—ideally, if there were hearings in Congress based on it, with witnesses under subpoena and oath, or if it could be published otherwise—Nixon would have to worry that his secret policy couldn't be protected from debate and skeptical challenge. In effect, I could hope for the same effect I'd sought eighteen months earlier, with my leaks to the *New York Times.* It would warn a president that his policy had lost the assurance of invisibility. He might be induced to give it up.

Now that I was thinking positively about this project, it occurred to me there was another way these studies could be helpful. They would make it much easier for Nixon, the new president, the Republican, to blame the war on the Democrats. After all, the Democrats pretty much deserved the blame (even if their motive had been largely to avoid domestic attacks by right-wingers like Nixon himself!). He wouldn't have to change course, to disown his own prior support of the war, as vice president and when out of office. He could say that the Democrats had screwed it up irrevocably, beyond repair; it was now too late to do anything but clear the decks of their mess. That wasn't far from the truth (though I felt sure that the mess would have been even worse if Nixon had won in 1960 and had done what he'd recommended all these years), and if that's what it took to get him off his present intentions, that was fine with me. I knew some Democrats who wouldn't thank me for this, but as far as I was concerned, it was a matter of priorities. I had made a serious effort to get some of them to volunteer to share the responsibility for getting out by taking the blame for getting in. So far, no volunteers. Nixon wouldn't thank me either. But if the hidden history in the McNamara study could make the American people even more disgusted with the war than they already were, and at the same time make it easier for Nixon to claim that he was cutting losses that the Democrats had incurred, it might tip the balance for him toward accepting a "disguised defeat" rather than prolonging the war.

I'd told Tony before that I'd worked on a study in Washington about Vietnam decision making, but I hadn't talked about what was in it until, as it happened, just a couple of weeks earlier, one afternoon on the beach behind my house. He had been describing a pattern of lying about the defector project by some of his superiors and about the nature of the war at low levels in the government, and I'd said that the study I was reading in Washington revealed the same thing at the highest levels. I didn't tell him, and he didn't guess, that it was the McNamara study or that I had access to it in Santa Monica. Tony said: "You ought to put that out."

It was an unusual thing for him to say and for me to hear. People who had had clearances didn't tell other people with clearances that they ought to leak something. Tony didn't know of my leaks to the *Times* a year and a half earlier; I hadn't told anyone. But I wasn't shocked at his suggestion. In his present situation, away from Rand, it was natural for him to think of it (just as it was natural for him earlier not to have thought of taking his own classified reports with him when he left Rand). He knew that now I shared his state of mind about the war, which was that it was a time for acts of resistance.

Compared in effectiveness even with the Rand letter I was helping draft, and my other overtures to Democrats, Tony's comment had scarcely struck me as worth considering. The McNamara studies hadn't seemed sufficiently relevant to this crisis. They said nothing about the "new" Nixon as president, and they ended on March 31, 1968, under LBJ. Nixon had just won an election precisely on the claim that he had grown during his years out of office and, more plausibly, that he had no intention of following the obviously failed policies of the past. What I needed, and lacked, were documents that disproved that. If Mort had given me, in Washington in late August, a document demonstrating what he believed about Nixon's policy, I would have put it in the hands of Senator Fulbright or the *New York Times,* or both, before I ever went to Haverford. I didn't have that proof, and the McNamara study wasn't a substitute.

But two weeks later the overtures to Democrats had gone nowhere, and our letter might or might not ever get out. Meanwhile in those two weeks I had finished reading the earliest sections of the study, on the origins of the war. The *L.A. Times* story that morning, on top of all the influences of the past month, had tipped me over the edge. I felt ready to go to prison just to expose lies about murder. Once I began really to think about it, I started to see that it might actually be useful to make this history public—if it could be done fast, before the president made it Nixon's war. Within weeks, by all signs, the president would go one way or another. These documents weren't as good as I might have wished for the job of influencing that choice, but along with the letter from Rand, they were what I had. It was time to cast my whole vote.

When I got to Tony's apartment, I said to him, "You know the study I told you about a couple of weeks ago? I've got it at Rand, in my safe, and I'm going to put it out." As I expected, Tony didn't need to be asked to help. He said, "Great! Let's do it." He didn't wait to hear the reasoning I'd just come through on the way over. I'm not sure I ever did discuss it with him; it wasn't necessary. I told him the study was very long and would take a lot of work to copy. I wanted to give a copy to the Senate or maybe the newspapers. Did he happen to know where we could get hold of a Xerox machine? He said he did. He had a girlfriend, Lynda Sinay, who owned a small advertising company. He called her while I was there, and she said it would be fine for us to use her machine after hours. We could start the next night.

PART III

SECRETS

20

Copying the Papers

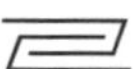

In the early evening of October 1, 1969, I opened the top secret safe in the corner of my office and started to pick out volumes of the McNamara study to copy that night. The forty-seven volumes filled two drawers, about eight feet. I thought I'd better start with the highest-priority studies. I didn't know how long it would take to copy a volume, and I didn't know how much I'd be able to copy before it was time to go public. I hadn't thought through yet just how I would release them or when that would be. I wanted to do it on or before the October 15 Moratorium. That didn't leave much time.

I might also get caught before that. In fact, that might happen in about ten minutes. I didn't think that was too likely; I didn't remember the guards ever asking to look in my briefcase as I left the building. But I didn't remember whether I'd ever seen them do it or if in fact they never did. I'd never had occasion to think about it or notice it. I'd never taken any classified papers home with me from Rand. Washington was entirely different. I hadn't taken classified papers home there either, but I had traveled between the Pentagon, the State Department, and the White House with top secret cables all the time. When I left my cubicle within the suite of offices in International Security Affairs, my door had usually been left open, with my desk piled high with top secret documents. There was usually a secretary or two sitting outside, but not always, and the doors to the ISA suites weren't locked either.

But Rand was a different world. You would rarely walk down the hall with a top secret document in your hand, except to or from the Top Secret Control Office. You couldn't leave it on your desk or even locked up in your secret file safe when you left the room. You couldn't let it out of your sight at all unless you had a top secret safe to lock it up in, and not many people had. Those who didn't had to read top secret documents in the Top Secret Control Office or return them there when they left their offices. That was a drag if you dealt with top secret papers more than occasionally, but most people didn't; if they did, they tried to get their own top secret safes. These were heavier than the secret safes and had a different kind of combination lock. There weren't enough for all those who wanted them. A top secret safe was something of a status symbol; it could be spotted immediately in someone's office because it was black instead of gray. Most of them were two-drawer. Mine had four drawers, all full.

I chose the volumes on 1964–65 to start with. They had the most relevance to the current moment. That was the history I was trying to keep from recurring: a president making secret threats of escalation, and secret plans to carry them out if they didn't work, as was almost certain; a war on the way to getting much larger and longer, with the public wholly unaware. Those volumes alone would tell the main story that needed telling, as background to the claims I would be making about Nixon's policy. They would prove, at least, it had all happened before. The truth was, it had happened again and again, over twenty-four years. The proof of that was in my safe too; it was the whole study, but that would take a lot of copying. In just a few nights, I hoped, I could have a copy of the 1964–65 period somewhere so I could arrange to get it out even if I were caught before I could do the rest.

These were thick volumes. The set I had in my safe consisted of the ones I had never logged into the system. They had blue cardboard covers, without sign-out sheets. The covers, front and back, were marked "Top Secret" in large black print on the tops and bottoms. I put the volumes into my brown leather briefcase and started down the hall. I was very conscious of what I was carrying. I had never tried to walk past the guards in the lobby with classified documents in my briefcase before.

I opened the doors to the lobby. There were two guards behind the desk as usual. I was wearing my badge, but they knew everyone by sight. They said, "Good night, Dan," friendly as usual, and I waved my free hand good night as I passed the desk, where one of them was checking my name off on a list and noting the time. I walked past the posters on tripods that had World War II security reminders on them: "Loose Lips Sink Ships"; "What You See Here, What You Say Here, Let It Be Here, Let It Stay Here." A cartoon showed a man being interrogated in a cell by a team of security guards: "Want to Meet New Friends, Visit Interesting Places? Leave Your Safe Unlocked." I pushed open the glass doors and went out into the parking lot.

I went over directly to Tony Russo's apartment. Lynda Sinay was with him. She was pretty, in her twenties, and, as I soon noticed, very smart. She was very young to be running an ad agency. We drove to her office at the corner of Melrose and Crescent. It was on the second floor, above a flower shop, up an outside staircase with iron railings. Lynda showed us how to turn off the alarm system with a special key, though she wasn't sure if we were supposed to turn it to the right or left; she said she would find out and tell us the next day.

The Xerox machine was just inside the glass door at the top of the stairway, on the left in the reception room. There were two other rooms with desks, a larger area with drafting tables, a small kitchen, and a bathroom. Lynda showed us around and then showed me how to use the copy machine. It was a big one, advanced for its time, but very slow by today's standards. It could do only one page at a time, and it took several seconds to do each page. I tried pressing the book down on the glass to do two pages at a time, but the middle section was faint and uneven. Fortunately the books were bound with metal tapes through holes so they could be taken apart. I tried to open them as carefully as I could so it wouldn't be obvious they'd been undone. I decided at first to make two copies, though it would take longer. The machine didn't collate, and the bar had to come back and travel just as slowly for each copy. Tony and Lynda were talking in the next room. I handed a bunch of copied pages to Tony and asked him to separate them. I went back to the machine and pressed down another page.

There were a couple of sharp knocks on the glass door to my left. Two uniformed policemen were standing there, at the top of the stairs. One of them had just rapped the door with his nightstick. He gestured to me to open the door. I closed the lid of the machine on the top secret page lying on the glass. As I turned to let them in, I dropped a piece of blank paper casually on top of the pile of pages with their top secret markings. I thought: Jesus Christ! These guys are fantastic! How did they do this? I said, "What's the problem, Officers?"

One of them gave a wave and said, "Your alarm has gone off."

I called into the next room, "Lynda, there are some people here to see you." I hoped Tony would cover up the pages. He had, as the police trooped in.

One of them said, "Hi, Lynda. You've done it again, huh?"

Lynda said, "Oh, God, I'm so sorry. I'm hopeless with that damned key."

The policeman said, "Oh, no problem." They hadn't come over very fast, and they had obviously been there a number of times before. They looked around casually. "You've got to get a lesson on that thing," one of them said.

"I will, I will," Lynda replied. They waved good-bye and left. We looked at one another for a moment, and I went back to work.

Tony took a turn at copying, and I collated. After a while Tony and Lynda left. I wanted to get as much done as I could. I worked all night. To speed up, I tried to program my motions. One hand picked up a page, the other fit it on the glass, top down, push the button, wait . . . lift, move the original to the right while picking another page from the pile. . . . This is all very familiar now, but it was a new technology then. It took a little extra time to put the top down and up, and I didn't know why it had to be done. Did it have to do with the copying quality, or was the light bad for the eyes? Was it dangerously bright? How did it work, anyway? Was that peculiar green color some kind of radiation? To save time, I finally started to copy with the top up—the copies seemed to look all right—hoping that I wouldn't get a headache or go blind. I tried not to look at the light, or I shut my eyes. But my vision seemed OK, so I stopped worrying.

By five-thirty it was light outside, and I was ready to quit. I put the binders back together again, carefully, so that it wouldn't be too noticeable that they'd been tampered with. I finished collating the copies, and I made a separate pile of the pages that had been blurred or spoiled one way or another. They all were marked "Top Secret," and Lynda's office didn't have a shredder. I put them in my briefcase to dispose of them at Rand. In the Pentagon you put classified wastepaper in big burn bags, to be collected at the end of the day and burned. At Rand there were slots in the halls like mail chutes for it; it went down to a bin in the basement to be shredded.

It was too early to go to the office. I often worked very late, but the guards weren't used to seeing me come *in* before eight in the morning. On the way back I stopped at Zucky's delicatessen and had a big breakfast. I waited till eight, then walked into the lobby with my briefcase, past the guards, who said hello and checked me in. It was no problem. I dumped the volumes in my safe, locked it, and left the building by a different lobby, past different guards. I drove home to get some sleep, up the Pacific Coast Highway to Malibu. I wasn't used to driving in that direction at that hour; the light came at a different angle, the sun rising above the hills was on my right instead of left. The morning was clear and bright; the sky was blue. Before I went to bed, I went into the water and rode some waves to shore. I had bodysurfed every day I'd lived at the beach for the last two years; there was nothing in the world I liked better. I wondered how many more mornings I would be able to do that.

In the afternoon, after I had slept a few hours, I went back to the office and dealt with Rand business. There was a meeting of our group to work over the draft of the letter. Around seven that night I loaded up my briefcase again with volumes of the study and went past the guards. Again, no problem. I drove to Lynda's office and spent the night copying. Over the next days this became a pattern. I wasn't getting much sleep. It was a long, tiring job. But there were things that kept it from being routine.

The top secret markings on the top and bottom of every page reminded me constantly of the stakes. I didn't know yet how I was going to get this information to the public, but however that happened, it was going to change my life very drastically and suddenly. It was also going to happen very soon, maybe even in two weeks—at the Moratorium on October 15 or maybe the one after that, November 15. In a month or so I might be behind bars, probably for the rest of my life.

I took it for granted that what I was doing violated some law, perhaps several. In the course of my career, going back to the Marines Corps, I must have signed a dozen secrecy agreements. Every time I'd glanced at sheets of warnings that specified federal statutes under which I would be subject to prosecution and imprisonment if I violated the agreement by giving "information relating to the national security" to unauthorized persons. I'd never read those sections carefully—though I'd often initialed a box on the form stating that I had—because I had never contemplated the possibility of doing anything that would invoke them. So I couldn't have identified the statutes in question or how exactly they might apply. But you didn't need to have seen or signed such an agreement to suppose that publishing top secret documents without authorization must be a serious crime. That was obvious.

At the same time, I had a vague sense that "leaks" to the press, which seemed to happen every other day, hadn't been prosecuted very often. In fact I couldn't remember ever hearing of a prosecution, even though many of the leaks had inspired rage and denunciation in the executive branch and there were reports of intensive investigation. In at least a few of those cases the investigation must have identified a source beyond doubt. If even those cases hadn't led to indictments, I figured there must exist political or bureaucratic reasons—it wasn't hard to imagine some—that could result in a deliberate decision not to prosecute. There seemed some possibility that could happen in this case. Fine with me. But the chance seemed pretty small, maybe one or two in a hundred. As far as I knew, no one had ever leaked thousands of pages of top secret documents before. I didn't see how the authorities could ignore a challenge to the system like that if they could find the source. And in this case that wouldn't be hard. Probably the main obstacle to prosecution in past cases, I figured, was that it was hard to pin down the origin of the leak enough for a conviction. There were usually lots of potential suspects, all of them denying it, and the journalist wouldn't talk. But that wasn't going to apply this time. Unless for some unlikely reason that I couldn't guess in advance the administration was determined not to prosecute the case, it was certain to launch a criminal investigation. As soon as it did that, it would know the source. I would tell it.

Just a dozen people had possession of the McNamara study outside the Pentagon, and a handful of others had access to it. Every one of them, as it happened, was probably seen by the administration as opposing continuation of the war and for that reason as suspect. But every one of them was a former boss or colleague of mine; I respected them all, and some were my closest friends. I had no intention of letting them stay under suspicion if I could help it. I wanted to protect them from legal liability or the toils or consequences of investigation as far as I could. That meant that at the first signs of such a criminal investigation, I would declare that I was the sole source of the publication. (I wouldn't do it earlier; I wasn't taking this action in order to get prosecuted, and I didn't want to taunt the authorities into it.) I would say that I had acted on my own, not only without any collaboration from any of these specific people but without having given them any reason to suspect that I might do such a thing. I also wanted that to be true. I wanted them to be able to pass lie detector tests on that. I didn't kid myself that they would owe me much thanks for this courtesy. Once I identified myself, they all would pay some price professionally for their past association with me and for letting me have access to the study. For the very ones I was closest to, the burden might be heavy. I didn't know any way to avoid that and still do what needed to be done. All I could do for them was to try my best to get them off the hook legally.

If I hadn't expected that what I was doing would probably land me in prison and that the situation made that worth accepting, I probably would have been more concerned than I was about what it would mean for my colleagues' careers. But once I'd decided that I had this job to do, I focused on doing it. I didn't dwell on what the future held for me, or for them. The people who were actually helping me, starting with Tony and Lynda, were obviously taking a legal risk, but they were doing it voluntarily. I didn't think the risk was very great for them. (I was wrong.) They could plead ignorance about the contents. At least, I urged them not to read the documents, though of course that didn't stop Tony. Even Lynda read a little.

What I did worry about was what my children would hear about what I had done. They were used to my being away, in Washington or Vietnam, though this time it would be forever. They'd be able to visit me, briefly, but I had an image of the visiting booths in a maximum-security prison, where I would see them, for the rest of my life, only through glass, talking on a monitored telephone. I'd never been in a jail; my notion of these things was from movies. I knew there were country club prisons, but I didn't think lifers qualified for those, or people who copied seven thousand pages of top secret documents. In fact I didn't expect to be granted bail prior to my trial. So within a couple of weeks I would lose the chance to talk to my children face-to-face, ever again, except through glass. They would see me brought into the visitors' booths in handcuffs, wearing prisoner's clothes.

They would read right away, and hear on television, that their father was a traitor. That I had gone mad, done something bizarre. I wanted them to have a memory they could hold on to that would counter those stories. If they could spend an evening with me while we copied the papers, they could see that I wasn't acting weird, wasn't crazy. I was working, with friends, in a matter-of-fact way, doing something that I was confident had to be done. They might not be old enough to judge for themselves yet whether what I had done was right, but I could let them see for themselves, and remember, that I had been acting normally, calmly, doing what I thought was necessary and right.

That was the main thing, but there was one other thing. I wouldn't be able to do much for them the rest of my life, not even help put them through college; but I could give them one piece of knowledge that wasn't easy to come by. It was what I had gotten from Bob Eaton and Randy Kehler; I was grateful for that, and it was something I could pass on to them, maybe the only thing. They would learn that they might have to do something like this themselves someday. Remembering my everyday mood as we worked, and reflecting on the whole story as they grew up and perhaps read the McNamara study themselves, they would know that it might be necessary, it might be the right thing to do, in some circumstances to take an action that would send them to jail. Then when that situation came around, they would recognize it, sooner than I had done. They wouldn't need to meet another Randy.

I wanted this for both of them, but I knew their mother would have a fit at the thought of involving Mary in it. She would feel the same about Robert, but he was almost fourteen (Mary was just under eleven), and I felt determined to give him the chance to be part of this if he was willing. I also believed I had to give my former wife some warning that my income and hence her alimony and child support were about to be cut off, but I wanted to talk to Robert first.

On Saturday, October 4, three days after I started, I took Robert to lunch at the Brentwood Country Market. It was a favorite place for the kids (and for Rand lunches). When they were little, we would bicycle there down San Vicente, about a mile from our house on Carmelina, Robert on his bike, Mary on a seat behind me. There was a little courtyard surrounded by shops, with wooden picnic tables. We would eat barbecued chicken and french fries and drink mixtures of pineapple and coconut juice or apple and grape juice from a juice bar.

Over lunch I told Robert about the McNamara study. I said that it told the truth about what the presidents had planned to do in Vietnam, contrary to what they led the public to believe. I told him that it was happening again and that the war was likely to keep going and get larger, but that it might help to head that off if people finally learned how they'd been misled in the past. So I was planning to get that information out somehow. But since it was classified, I would have to go to prison for that, like the draft resisters. I had told him about Bob Eaton and Randy Kehler. I would probably have to go for a longer time.

I had brought back from the War Resisters' International Conference at Haverford College, a month earlier, a bunch of pamphlets for him, including Thoreau's *On the Duty of Civil Disobedience* and *Revolution and Equilibrium* by Barbara Deming. He had already read the Thoreau, and we'd talked about it. I told him this was going to be an act of civil disobedience. I asked him if he would like to help me. He said he would. I had picked up some volumes from Rand that morning, and we went off to Lynda's office that afternoon. Lynda was there, working, but she had said the rest of her staff would be away over the weekend. I showed Robert how to use the Xerox machine and let him do the copying while I collated. We all went out to an early dinner, then came back and did some more.

Robert was working the Xerox machine when the police came again. He let them in. There were three this time, suddenly appearing in Lynda's office, where I was sitting on the floor cutting top secret markings off the tops and bottoms of pages. There wasn't much time to cover anything up, and their attention could have been caught by the scraps of paper marked "Top

Secret" on the floor. But it was a reassuring scene, I guess, with Lynda at her desk and a thirteen-year-old doing something on the copier, a family Saturday afternoon. They left almost immediately. Robert's memory is that police came *twice* that day while he was there. That could be true. I have a vague sense of two different teams responding to the same alarm. Two years later, when Lynda was in front of the grand jury, the prosecutor was pressing her for an exact date when she had been present while I was copying. She said he could get it from the records of the police station the days the alarm went off. The prosecutor said, "Lynda, do you have any idea how many times you triggered the alarm that year?" It was something like seventeen.

It was the first visit by the police several nights earlier that had given me the idea of cutting off the top secret markings on the pages. They were stamped on with thick black letters above and below the text. You could see them across the room. I knew for someone who wasn't used to seeing that stamp, as I had become in Washington, that the effect was startling. I could still remember the feeling I had the first time I was reading something I wasn't supposed to see, stamped "Top Secret"—the JCS general war plan, which a colonel had given me to read in a basement room in the Pentagon—my heart beginning to pound, my breath coming short, the notion that someone was looking over my shoulder. Now, although I'd covered up the markings in time when the police first appeared, after they left, I looked at the classification marks from their perspective. If we were going to be carrying these pages around over a period of time, I thought something had to be done to make them a little less eye-catching.

The same interruption had made me aware that our whole process could be terminated at any moment by the police or FBI before I was ready to reveal the documents. They would confiscate what they found with me and any other copies they could locate. So it was essential that there be enough copies, hidden in different places, that they couldn't get them all. Then I could get the word out from jail, some way, to someone who could recover a set of the papers and publish them. But it meant that at some point I'd need to get the documents copied commercially; I couldn't make enough copies myself on a slow machine like this. And I couldn't come in off the street and hand documents marked "Top Secret" to a clerk in a copy shop to duplicate. I had to make them look like an ordinary manuscript. Hence the efforts to "declassify" them.

Of course short pages with the tops and bottoms unevenly cut off weren't entirely reassuring in appearance either. So I ran them through the copier again to get full-page copies that looked ordinary. At some point Tony Russo suggested to me the next technical improvement in the process. He measured pieces of cardboard to fit over the margins at the tops and bottoms of the pages where "Top Secret" was normally stamped. He taped these on the glass of the Xerox machine at the right locations, fit a top secret page on top of them, pushed the button, and . . . presto! Instant declassification. It was a big step forward; it seemed to promise an end to scissoring, which was the slowest step in the process. As someone who wasn't generally very handy, I was impressed.

Unfortunately, it wasn't foolproof. I didn't notice it for a while, but it turned out that the markings, which had originally been stamped by hand, weren't always at the same location on the margins. Some were in line with or below the page numbers. Tony's original cardboard strips had missed quite a few of these. If the copy shop attendant was paying attention—in those days, many commercial machines did not yet have automatic feeding—every twenty or thirty pages he would find himself looking at a page of information marked "Top Secret." Not good. Back to the scissors for those, with occasionally the problem of losing a line or two of text in order to sterilize the page. Oddly, though this should have been easy enough to catch on one run-through, it seemed that every time I looked through a copied volume over the next year and a half I came across top secret marks, or legible fragments of stamps, that we had somehow missed earlier.

The first night of copying, I took the copies home with me, but I wanted to change that quickly. It would be the first place the FBI would search, along with Tony's or Lynda's. I dropped in on a friend who owned a condominium a mile south of me on the Pacific Coast Highway. (I knew enough already not to leave a phone record. I hadn't called her for quite a while, and I didn't after this.) I told her I had a bunch of documents that I needed to store somewhere, away from my house, and there would be more coming. They had to do with the war, with trying to stop it, and there would be some real risk in keeping them for me. She wasn't very political, but when it came to ending the war, she was political enough, even for this. That was true for a lot of people in those days, nearly everyone I asked for help. She said yes right away. She had space on a shelf in a closet in her bedroom, next to the windows looking out over the ocean. Mornings driving north from Rand after that, I would stop at her apartment on my way home and deliver another batch of documents for her closet.

I had to face my ex-wife. I thought I had to give her as much warning as I could—it might not be much, only days or weeks—that her income was about to be cut down abruptly to her own earnings. That discussion was hard, as I'd expected. We had been gradually getting on better since I'd come back from Vietnam; she had been skeptical of the war from the start. But this tore it, for quite a while. Robert hadn't told her what he had done with me on Saturday, but Sunday afternoon I told her what I was doing, and why, and where it was likely to lead for me. She asked right away what that meant for my obligations to the family. I said I expected to be in jail as soon as the documents came out, and I hoped they would be out within weeks. I would be without income from the time I was indicted and perhaps for the rest of my life. It was just possible I wouldn't be prosecuted; I told her that I knew of no earlier prosecutions for leaks, though that didn't give much assurance in this case. Even without prosecution, or after I got out of prison, my income, perhaps from teaching at some obscure college, wouldn't be much. I could give her my savings, but they were only a few thousand dollars. She and the children would be without alimony or child support.

She said flatly, "You can't do that. You're obligated. You're under a court order!" I said I wouldn't be able to obey it; I would be in prison. I didn't look forward to that, but the issues were very large, larger than me, or even my own family. I simply wouldn't be able to do anything for them. She asked about the children's education. I said they would have to make their own way. Fortunately they both were very smart; I hoped they could get scholarships. Probably they all would have to move out of this neighborhood, to a much cheaper house, away from their friends. She might need to start thinking about this right away; that was why I was telling her. I hoped the children would understand all this someday. I told her about Robert's help and said I had asked him not to mention it to her till I'd had a chance to speak with her. She was very angry that I had involved him and was not in a mood to hear my explanation. She didn't want him to do any more.

Then I went over to Rand to fill my briefcase again and drive out to Melrose. But I didn't work late that night. The group writing the letter to the *New York Times* was meeting early Monday morning to go over the latest draft.

21

The Rand Letter

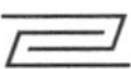

The six of us in the drafting sessions had agreed early on that we would run the letter by Harry Rowen, the president of Rand, before we sent it. We didn't think he could formally forbid us from sending a letter as private individuals; we didn't intend to use the Rand letterhead or even identify that we worked for the corporation. On the other hand, he could raise questions of our past access to classified information, which we meant to hint at ourselves; he could even cut off our access, or threaten to fire us.

Konrad Kellen thought that if Harry didn't approve its going out, we couldn't send it, and the others agreed. If he approved our sending it, we would then show it to our respective department heads, Fred Iklé of Social Sciences and Charlie Wolf of Economics. They would certainly hate it, but if Harry had approved, they couldn't block it. Our bosses could show their displeasure other ways, but we agreed that wouldn't stop us, so long as Harry had cleared it from the point of view of Rand.

I was the only one who knew Harry personally. I was pretty sure he would sympathize privately with our proposal, whether or not he thought it was the best way of getting out. I suspected he was as opposed to continuing the war as any of us. Yet it was hard to imagine his actually OK'ing the letter, in his capacity as president of Rand. So the agreement to rely on his approval made this approach look fairly dubious, not real, at least to me. Yet I could see why the others had reached that agreement. They weren't where I was when it came to losing their jobs or their clearances. I was rather detached from these discussions of whether and how to slip this letter past the Rand hierarchy. In fact after October 1 I wasn't even a very active participant in the group discussions on the substance of the drafting. I was too tired, from spending every night copying the Pentagon Papers. I did get a few hours' sleep in the morning, and with the help of a lot of coffee I managed to sit in on the afternoon meetings, but I didn't have much to say. But that wasn't because I thought the letter was less important than the papers, if it really was possible to get the letter out. On the contrary, I still tended to think that authoritative public statements opposing current policy and pressing an alternative held *more* promise of helping change policy than the historical documents in the papers, however dramatic those revelations would be. However, I wasn't relying on any one thing to head Nixon off. No single approach I could think of looked more promising than the others. Still, I was working to get a large stack of top secret documents into the hands of Congress or the public by October 15, the first Moratorium Day, about ten days off. I figured I would be in jail by late October. That prospect freed me from an active concern with the job-related considerations that naturally interested the others.

Finally on Wednesday, October 8, we had a letter, on plain paper, no letterhead, not mentioning Rand but identifying us as professional researchers and analysts on Vietnam, by implication working for the government. We made an appointment with Harry's office and took it down to him as a group. He read it carefully and nodded. He didn't seem to dislike it. He commented that it was going to cause a good deal of trouble for Rand from its sponsors, and he may have said that he preferred we not send it. (His later statement to the Rand staff indicated this, though I don't specifically remember it.) But he didn't press the point. Holding the letter in his hand, he raised his head, looked at us through his professorial glasses, and asked, "Why isn't this on Rand letterhead?" We explained that we hadn't wanted to associate Rand with it. He said, "No, there'll be stories on this; it'll come out that you're at Rand anyway. It would look as though we were trying to hide it. Retype this on Rand letterhead. We'll get heat for this, but there's a good side to it too; it will show we encourage a diversity of views here. Just put in a disclaimer that you're speaking as individuals, not for Rand or for other employees of Rand."

That was the only comment he made. We were excited when we left his office to redraft the first paragraph and have it retyped on a Rand Corporation letterhead. Addressed to the editors of the *New York Times,* it now read (in part):

> Dear Sirs:
> Now that the American people are once again debating the issue of Vietnam, we desire to contribute to that discussion by presenting our own views, which reflect both personal judgments and years of professional research on the Vietnam war and related matters. We are expressing here our views as individuals, not speaking for Rand, of which we are staff members; there is a considerable diversity of views on this subject, as on other issues, among our Rand colleagues.
>
> We believe that the United States should decide now to end its participation in the Vietnam war, completing the total withdrawal of our forces within one year at the most. Such U.S. disengagement should not be conditioned upon agreement or performance by Hanoi or Saigon—i.e., it should not be subject to veto by either side.
>
> It is our view that, apart from persuasive moral arguments that could lead to the same conclusion, there are four objections to continued U.S. efforts in the war:
>
> 1. Short of destroying the entire country and its people, we cannot eliminate the enemy forces in Vietnam by military means; in fact "military victory" is no longer the U.S. objective. What should now also be recognized is that the opposing leadership cannot be coerced by the present or by any other available U.S. strategy into making the kinds of concessions currently demanded.
> 2. Past U.S. promises to the Vietnamese people are not served by prolonging our inconclusive and highly destructive military activity in Vietnam. This activity must not be prolonged merely on demand of the Saigon government, whose capacity to survive on its own must finally be tested, regardless of outcome.
> 3. The importance to the U.S. national interest of the future political complexion of South Vietnam has been greatly exaggerated, as has the negative international impact of a unilateral U.S. military withdrawal.
> 4. Above all, the human, political, and material costs of continuing our part in the war far outweigh any prospective benefits, and are greater than the foreseeable costs and risks of disengagement. . . .

We do not predict that only good consequences will follow for Southeast Asia or South Vietnam (or even the United States) from our withdrawal. What we do say is that the risks will not be less after another year or more of American involvement, and the human costs will surely be greater.

Daniel Ellsberg, Melvin Gurtov, Oleg Hoeffding, Arnold Horelick, Konrad Kellen, Paul F. Langer

The Rand Corporation

We sent a copy to Fred Iklé and made an appointment to see him after he'd read it. I must have also shown it to Charlie Wolf, but I have no specific memory of that. Meanwhile I called the Los Angeles office of the *New York Times* and talked to Steve Roberts, the bureau chief, to find out how best to get the letter into the paper. He was sure that there was a news story in this and that I should give the letter directly to him. I told him to wait for me in the Rand parking lot.

The meeting with Iklé was hard. Four of the signers worked directly for him, and they said almost nothing; they let me respond to him. We had signed the letter in alphabetical order, and my name came first. Like most readers of the letter, Fred mistakenly assumed that I was its principal drafter, as well as its catalyst, which was less far off. Fred mainly ignored the others and directed his challenges to me.

We had been friendly colleagues for a decade, though I didn't know him intimately, if anyone did. He was Swiss, very reserved in manner and speech, not an easy person to get close to. He spoke with a strong accent in a low monotone that put some people off, but I liked and respected him, and he did me.

Fred didn't spend any time arguing with the substance of the letter; he probably didn't disagree with it all that much. Like most others at Rand later, he was not concerned with that. He started off with dismissive, rather patronizing comments. Our approach just didn't make any sense. A letter to the newspaper! How could that possibly accomplish anything? He didn't need to remind us of our privileged alternative: direct access both to staffs and to high government officials on a classified basis. We didn't have to communicate with them through a letters to the editor column, open to anyone, which they probably didn't even read. And what other audience really mattered, by comparison? All this went without saying;

it was implicit in the contemptuous tone of his reference to "a letter to the editor."

He said it was very unlikely that it would get any attention at all. There he was not on strong ground. I said we had reason to believe that it would get at least a news story in the *Times.* He stopped being condescending and began to get agitated. That would be really bad! It still wouldn't accomplish anything, but it would be seriously damaging for Rand. Here he was up against the fact that Harry had OK'd the letter, but that didn't mean Rowen was right. I told him I didn't agree with his estimates of impact. We would have to see.

He was getting distraught. His hair was short, but he began almost pulling at it. He said, "What I can't understand about your doing this, what gets me about it, is that it's so—so *ineffective.* So counterproductive!" He turned to one of the others and took a more collaborative tone. "There are so many other things you could do that would be more effective. For example, look, you could do a classified study of the budget costs of the war, and you could send a letter to the commander of SAC, top secret, pointing out how the continuation of the war is cutting into his budget for modernization!" He was getting wild. He turned back to me and said, in a more controlled voice, "This letter is no way to operate in Washington."

I wouldn't take that. I said, "Fred, which of us knows more about operating in Washington, you or me?"

He said, "You."

I said, "I think this is worth doing." He looked very unhappy as we left his office, and it was twenty-two years before he spoke to me again.

In the hall I checked with others. "Are we going ahead with this? Are we all still on this?" Each nodded and said yes, though several who worked for Fred looked glum. I took the letter outside to the Rand parking lot and found Steve Roberts waiting in his car. I told him, "Send this in, and then stay away from your phone for a while, OK? Everybody's in on this, as of now, but some of them are under a lot of pressure, and that could change. How soon can this appear?" He said New York was expecting it. He thought it would come out the next day. It was midafternoon. I went home, turned the phone off, and went to sleep, to prepare for more copying that night.

The next morning, Thursday, October 9, there was a one-column story in the *New York Times,* on an inside page, with the heading SIX RAND EXPERTS SUPPORT PULLOUT: BACK UNILATERAL STEP WITHIN ONE YEAR IN VIETNAM. It was bylined "Steven V. Roberts," from Santa Monica, October 8.

The lead repeated the headline, adding that all of us had done research on Vietnam for the federal government. "The six said that they were acting as individuals, not as employees of Rand . . . [which] still does 76 percent of its work for the Defense Department. The letter, written by men of considerable expertise who normally shun publicity, provided new impetus to the growing public demand for swift disengagement from Vietnam."

Under the subhead "Two Years in Saigon," the story continued: "Under contract to the Pentagon, the six have studied subjects ranging from the effectiveness of bombing North Vietnam to the interrogation of enemy prisoners. One of them, Daniel Ellsberg, spent two years working for the State Department in Saigon before joining Rand. The group includes experts on Russia, China and Japan. One signatory, Melvin Gurtov, is the author of a forthcoming book on the future of American policy in Southeast Asia." Roberts quoted an unnamed member of the group as commenting, "Unilateral withdrawal is now respectable." The story went on to quote directly from the letter, reproducing about half of it and paraphrasing—not entirely accurately—the rest. A few points I thought important were left out, and since it was treated as a news story, the whole letter didn't appear on the editorial page. Nevertheless, the essence of our position was there, and the story ended with our final sentence.

Because the *Times* hadn't carried our letter in full, we offered it to the *Washington Post* as well, and it printed the whole letter prominently in the center of its editorial page on Sunday, October 12, with the heading A CASE AGAINST STAYING IN VIETNAM. It was sandwiched between denunciations of our position. To its right was an op-ed piece by Henry Owen, former head of the policy planning staff in the State Department, who dismissed the proposal for a one-year deadline or total withdrawal as extreme and unrealistic. To the left was a long editorial on the Moratorium, also directly attacking our letter. (We were described three times as "hard-core critics," once as "extreme critics." These were not, then as now, neutral terms.)

The editorial writers clearly shared Owen's belief, as he put it on the same page, that the administration itself was "moving toward withdrawal, visibly and probably irreversibly." They and Owen almost surely understood the term "withdrawal" to mean total withdrawal (eventually), not merely partial reduction; it was to "bring our combat participation" in the war "to an end." In other words, they clearly believed that the president's public declarations of endless loyalty to the GVN did not express his real intentions. His real operational strategy, they thought, was to stop the war or at least to bring our participation in it *gradually* but—contrary to what he said—*unconditionally,* totally, unilaterally, irreversibly, to an end. Basically, just what we were asking him to do!

So what did they see as the difference between the president's strategy and that of his "extreme," "hard-core critics" like us? Timing. Nixon's withdrawal would be "gradual," longer than the twelve months we specified and without an explicit, announced timetable, "in hopes that some part of our original purpose might be achieved." They clearly sympathized with the president's "effort to save something," hence with his tactics, as they understood them.

But exactly what part of our original purpose was the president striving to save? How likely was he to get it, ever? Just how long—beyond twelve months—would he keep American troops, or beyond that, American airpower, in combat to pursue it? Did the editors of the *Post* ever imagine? Four years, at least? Over twenty thousand more Americans dead, and hundreds of thousands of Vietnamese? We did, and that was what happened, in Nixon's Ahab-like pursuit of keeping General Thieu in power in Saigon indefinitely. U.S. bombing ended when it did in 1973 only by an act of Congress, not by Nixon's choice, in the context of a constitutional crisis that led to a near impeachment and to the end of his presidency.

In the same issue of the *Washington Post* there was a column by Joe Kraft, datelined Santa Monica, where he had gone to interview me and some of the other letter writers. Headed BREACHING THE CODE: RAND ANALYSTS' PROTEST ON VIETNAM POLICY RAISES BASIC QUESTION OF RESPONSIBILITY, it began: "When six analysts from the Rand Corp. drop their slide rules and open their mouths to protest about Vietnam, something important has happened. For the Rand protest . . . goes beyond the issue of Vietnam to the central moral problem of American public life. It raises the question of the responsibility borne by officials and analysts for the actions and policies they serve."

Kraft observed that Rand's "existence depends on having funds from, and good relations with, the federal government. In the past, Rand analysts have repeatedly questioned prevailing government policies behind closed doors. . . . But the six men involved in the present letter . . . go way beyond the tradition. For they speak out as a group in direct opposition to a government policy which they had not before challenged. They published their letter over strong opposition from some of Rand's chief executives. And they did so at some risk to their future careers. . . ."

After paraphrasing the substance of our letter, the column continued:

> There is nothing shocking in these views. They are shared by many high officials in this and previous administrations. What is remarkable is that only a handful of those who have come to believe these ideas have said so in public.
>
> Most have suppressed their true beliefs. They have preferred to play inside politics. They have subscribed to the basic Washington mystique that fidelity to a President transcends fidelity to convictions on even the most critical issues. They have followed the code of the apparatchik.
>
> The Rand letter is chiefly important as a repudiation of the apparatchik code. The public protest breaches the bureaucratic tradition of mute service even when policy conflicts with conscience.

There never was a better statement than that of one lesson I hoped officials might draw from the example of our letter (and my later release of the Pentagon Papers).

From the day the *Times*'s story appeared, memos began coming at us from our colleagues, each addressed to the six cosigners and usually to a long list of others as well. Out of roughly five hundred professional employees at Rand, I recall getting about seventy responses, some brief, some three or four single-spaced pages. It was easy to circulate memos within Rand, but I don't recall any other instance of a corporation-wide flood of responses like this.

It couldn't be called a controversy, because nearly all of them were on the same side, against our action, making the same points. With two or three exceptions, every one of them was negative, often very hostile, angry, reproachful, disdainful, accusatory. Moreover—this is what most surprised me, what I was least prepared for—hardly one took issue with the substance of our letter or even addressed it, unless in a sentence or two, dismissing our argument as shallow or unsupported. More commonly, each memo writer indicated that he (these were virtually all men, as were nearly all the professionals at Rand then) opposed the continuation of the war as much as we did, before going on to say, as one put it, that our action showed "a sense of almost complete irresponsibility toward your colleagues at Rand, the corporation itself, and quite possibly, the welfare of the country."

Somehow the word had gotten out that we had written the letter on the Rand letterhead, though this wasn't in the *Times* story, and it drove people wild, into a frenzy of memo writing condemning our "lack of professional ethics" and our "reprehensible" behavior. They attacked, in tones ranging from cold to furious, our heedlessness of the security of their jobs and what that rested on, Rand's contractual and confidential relationship with the Defense Department. One writer began like several others by saying, "I, too, agree with your conclusions, but not with your right to express these publicly as a member of the Rand staff." He closed his letter: "You may become famous for your act, but I think the word is 'infamous.'" In between he summed up what many expressed less concisely: "On the lowest level, while you may well feel strongly enough to lay your own jobs on the line, you do not have the right to lay mine there as well."

I was startled that this expression of self-interest was so frequently a theme of our colleagues' responses and that it was so explicit. I had expected this particular concern to be tacit behind a critique of our policy position or a charge that by our open dissent we were endangering Rand's ability to contribute to the national security through a confidential relationship with the executive branch. But it was striking how much the reverse was true: The latter theme, when expressed at all, seemed secondary to the dangers our statement posed to the Rand contracts and the writers' incomes. As one expressed it pungently, "I am simply appalled to learn that professional researchers, acting in concert and using the corporate name and apparent prearrangements with interviewers to assure notoriety for their views, would unleash a torpedo so unerringly as to strike at least glancing blows on your largest and most faithful clients, your employer, and your fellow researchers simultaneously."

My surprise at this focus might seem naive, but Rand after all was not a profit-seeking corporation. Its initial grant from the Ford Foundation specified that its work was to be in the national interest, and it was taken for granted that this applied to all our contractual work. Most of its employees were engineers who could have earned higher salaries in private corporations in the aerospace industry. I myself had gone into the government, temporarily, at a considerably higher salary than I had received at Rand, and that was true for several colleagues. Very few of us, I would have thought, were at Rand for the money. A major incentive was the relative freedom of thought and speech within Rand and with our clients, compared with the constraints of hierarchical structures within the government bureaucracy. But just how free was our thought at Rand, after all, in the light of these outpourings of anxiety?

Like most of my colleagues, I had accepted the mystique of Rand's fearlessness and independence, its willingness to tell the air force and other patrons conclusions and recommendations that were in some cases strongly unwelcome, very much what the client did not want to hear. Indeed there were important, undeniable instances of this, above all, Rand's prolonged skepticism about the need for what was to Chief of Staff General LeMay and others the air force's highest priority, acquiring the high-flying supersonic B-70 bomber (which later became the B-1). I was proud of this tradition. For me, as for many others, it was the source of strong loyalty to Rand, as a collection of people and an institution that could truly be described as bold, freethinking, independent-minded, courageously candid in the public interest. But could this self-image really be accurate, among analysts who were panicked to this extent by six of their colleagues writing a letter to a newspaper, endorsing a proposal that many of them supported privately along with major members of Congress and the majority of the American public!

At one point Konrad Kellen relayed to me a conversation he had just had with an unnamed "high Rand official" (a vice president, it turned out). "He said that if one Rand secretary lost her job because of this letter [through a budget cut], we didn't have a right to send it." Ironically, the *only* Rand employees who were going out of their way to congratulate me on the letter were secretaries, all women. They didn't write memos, but unlike the men who had started cutting me in the hallways or frowning angrily when they saw me, the secretaries would nod warmly or stop me to shake hands in the hall, whispering, "Good job! Great letter!" More than one said, "It makes me proud to be at Rand." One of the two or three memos that defended both our right and our decision to send the letter was by one of the few women professionals at Rand, Kathy Archibald.

The other was from a two-year guest consultant, Ben Bagdikian, on leave from the *Washington Post.* In a rather biting memo expressing "shock" at some of the other memos, he pointed out that a number of influential staff members of the sort that was now attacking the propriety of our getting our views into print had in the past sought his advice and help in doing the same for them. "It so happened that they were almost always expressing approval of weapons development. . . ." He noted, "I can understand the worry that contractors' retaliation for independent opinions might cost jobs. But the proposition that what is good for my personal income is automatically good for Rand and for my country is hardly a high ethical principle."

One of our colleagues had taken part in the earlier discussions of the extrication option as a friendly critic, though apparently it hadn't occurred to any of my cosigners to ask him to join us. He may have spoken for a number of other employees when he explained to me, unasked, why he would not have. I was having dinner with him alone that week in his house in Pacific Palisades—his wife was out—when he said to me, "Dan, the fact is you can't work for the government and publish a letter like that. You can't operate both ways; you just can't do it."

I said, "Well, what do you mean, you *can't*? Aren't you stating that a little too strongly? The six of us all work for the government, and we've just done it."

He said, "It isn't right. Anyway, you can't do it and get away with it."

I said, "Well, I guess that remains to be seen."

He gestured around his well-furnished two-story living room and said, "Dan, if I were willing to give up all this . . . if I were willing to renege on my divorce agreement from my earlier marriage, on my commitment to send my son to Groton . . . if I were willing to sell my house and use the money to buy a Colonel Sanders franchise . . . I would have signed that letter."

I admit that in finding all these concerns a little overdrawn at the time, I may have underestimated somewhat the realities. Because of the letter, someone in Congress did introduce a resolution to delete the Rand contract from the defense budget as a line item. That didn't go anywhere. As for my cosigners, Konrad told me years later that "the rest of us held on to our jobs by our fingernails after that. They tried to get rid of all of us." Mel Gurtov told me recently that Iklé called him into his office soon after the letter appeared and told him that he had no future in the department, he should look elsewhere. I knew that he had left Rand to teach at Irvine a year and a half later, but I hadn't known it was connected with our letter.

On the other side of the ledger, the day after our letter was published in the *Washington Post,* Monday, October 13, Senator William Fulbright sent me a letter inviting me, as the first listed signer of the letter, and two of my cosigners ("unfortunately" there would not be "time to hear all six"), to testify before the Foreign Relations Committee on various Vietnam resolutions introduced by members of Congress, in hearings scheduled to begin October 27. We would probably be testifying on the thirtieth or thirty-first. On the same Monday, Senator George McGovern quoted from our letter in a speech in the Senate and entered the whole letter into the *Congressional Record.*

When my boss, Charlie Wolf, head of the Economics Department, heard that I had accepted an invitation to testify in two weeks before the Senate Foreign Relations Committee, he called me into his office and asked me to resign from Rand before I appeared. I said I wouldn't. He said, "You're only being asked because you're from Rand. You're exploiting the name of Rand, its reputation for objectivity and high-level access. You should dissociate yourself from Rand by resigning, so you can speak as an individual. Otherwise, you're using the name of Rand to give your opinions an authority they wouldn't have otherwise."

I said, "But I *am* a Rand analyst. I won't be speaking for Rand, but I've earned the right to be presented to the committee as speaking *from* Rand as much as anyone in this building. How does Rand get its reputation, anyway? From the work of people like me. Who's exploiting whom? Rand uses *our* objectivity, our honesty, our names, or rather our work. Yes, they called me because they wanted a Rand researcher who had signed this letter, and as far as I'm concerned, that's what they're going to get."

I said, "You can fire me, Charlie. But I'm not going to resign. You'll have to fire me if you feel that strongly."

Charlie looked black, and I left his office. I was determined to appear before the committee with all the authority I could command—as a past official of Defense and State, with two years' service in Vietnam, and a past and current Rand analyst—which after all I had earned. So I didn't want to be separated from Rand before I appeared, now that I'd been invited. One hidden effect of that invitation was that I had to change my priorities and my schedule on getting out the papers I was copying every night. I realized I could never make the deadline of the Moratorium, now only days away, *and* appear in front of the Senate committee as a Rand employee at the end of the month. So I had to put off leaking the papers. That gave me more time to copy. Moreover, the Senate hearings themselves would give me an ideal location and opportunity to hand over all the documents I could copy by then.

Later that day I told Harry that Charlie had asked me to resign. Harry said quickly, "Well, I'm not asking you to do that. In fact I don't want you to do that. That would look bad for us." We had a long talk in his office. It was late in the day. I remember him sitting on a low sofa, his arm stretched out along the back, while I told him in more detail than I had before what I thought Nixon's strategy was and where it was heading. I said that part of the policy was to reduce our ground presence to a point where U.S. casualties, and budget costs, were down to a level that the American public could accept indefinitely. I acknowledged that contrary to what most people supposed, Nixon might actually be able to achieve that over time—by the permanent use of American airpower in support of ARVN and against the North—though it would never cause the NLF or Hanoi to give up or end the war.

Harry looked reflective. He said, "Well, if he really can get the costs and casualties down that low, and the American public would find that acceptable . . . what's so bad about it?"

I said, "It would mean our bombing Vietnam forever. And that's not acceptable to *me.*" Later, as I was leaving, Harry said again not to worry about Charlie. I said, "It won't be just Charlie. I know this is giving you trouble, but this isn't the end of it. I'm not going to resign. You may have to think about firing me yourself. I'll be giving you a lot more trouble."

He said, "Really?" He was laughing. "Just what do you have in mind?"

I said, "I haven't decided yet."

That was untrue or certainly misleading. But there was a reason for my not giving him more warning. I knew I really was going to cause him terrible trouble. (Our letter didn't get him fired as president of Rand, despite the best efforts of some of his internal critics, but my later release of the Pentagon Papers, coming on top of the letter, essentially did.) The thought that I was going to do this to my closest friend was the most anguishing consideration I faced throughout the process of getting out the papers. The one way I could help him get through it, I thought, was to give him no indication at all that I might do such a thing. I wanted him to be able to say to interrogators with the utmost conviction that he had no basis for foreseeing it or forestalling it. I did the same thing, for the same reason, with Mort Halperin and Les Gelb, and anyone else who would probably come under suspicion when the papers came out. But in the case of Harry, it meant prolonged concealment from the one person I would normally have confided in. If I departed from that discipline of silence ever, it was in this one exchange. It seemed vague enough. But I supposed he would think back to this conversation, perhaps before very long.

22

Capitol Hill

When the White House announced that the president would make a major speech on Vietnam on November 3, Fulbright postponed his scheduled hearings to await its contents and the public response to it. I still expected to testify, and I continued to copy the McNamara study at night in preparation for that. The October 15 Moratorium demonstrations against the war had been unprecedentedly large, and the November 15 Moratorium was to be accompanied by a major march in Washington, though the president claimed that he would pay no attention to these protests.

After three years apart Patricia and I had gotten together briefly in May and again in the summer. We had arranged to spend a week together at my home in Malibu starting November 2. In the late afternoon of that day I was waiting for her to arrive from the airport when the phone rang. Sam Brown, one of the four people coordinating the Moratorium, was calling from Washington. We'd never spoken before. He wanted me to come to Washington that night or the next morning to join a strategy session of the Moratorium Committee to help it figure out a response to Nixon's speech that evening and then to lobby Congress on it. They would pay for my travel and accommodations. As we were speaking, there was a knock on the door, and I opened it to let Patricia in from the Pacific Coast Highway where the taxi had dropped her off. I gestured to her that I was on the phone and that she should come in and sit down. While she paid the taxi and brought in her bag, I continued talking with Brown. What he was describing sounded important. I told him I would come.

It was a touchy situation. This was to have been the longest Patricia and I had been together in three years, but we had arranged it before I started copying the papers. I hadn't wanted to call her off, but I also didn't want to stop—or to refuse Brown's request. Among other things, I thought it would be a chance for me to offer the papers to Fulbright.

When I got off the phone, I told Patricia about the call and said that I would have to go to Washington the next morning. I was afraid it sounded awfully similar to the time in 1965 when I told her I had just volunteered to go to Vietnam. At least this time I said I'd be happy if she could go with me to Washington. Actually, Patricia took this surprisingly calmly and agreed at once. So early the next morning we left for the airport, she with the suitcase she hadn't bothered to unpack, and I with the first thousand pages of the McNamara study packed underneath the shirts in my suitcase.

Nixon's Vietnam speech was scheduled for seven that evening, and since our plane didn't get in till after five, we'd arranged to go straight to the Moratorium headquarters from Dulles. The president was just about to start as we came into the offices with our bags. We paused to shake hands before joining everyone in front of the television set. It was taken for granted that Nixon would try to undercut our demonstration of November 15, in response to the huge turnout in October. People in the room were making last-minute bets on how big a troop withdrawal he would announce. Twenty-five thousand? That was probably too small, good for us. Fifty thousand? A hundred? We all were listening closely for that announcement. When the speech was over, we couldn't believe it. He hadn't announced any further withdrawal!

Given that we never expected to hear what we really wanted, an end to the war, he seemed to be playing right into our hands, by not even pretending to be getting out with a token reduction at this time. On the contrary, he named tough conditions that had to be met before the United States would get out altogether. Either Hanoi had to give up its aim to unify Vietnam and to expel foreign presence and control, or the Saigon regime had to become capable of meeting the challenge on its own. It seemed obvious that neither of those would ever be met. Confronted by the largest antiwar movement any American president had ever faced, he had chosen to challenge us as bluntly as possible, offering us nothing at all.

It seemed reckless of him, puzzlingly so. He didn't seem to be in touch with the public mood, and that gave us a lot to work with in calling for opposition to his policy. Nixon himself, we thought, had just doubled the size of the upcoming demonstration.

The next morning I went to a meeting that had been arranged with ten liberal members of Congress, headed by Abner Mikva, Robert Kastenmaier, and Don Edwards, who worked together and called themselves the Group. They had seen the Rand letter, and I gave them copies of the long letter I had sent out. After I had spoken to them about Nixon's speech, Mikva asked me to draft a statement for them along the lines of my comments, and I found an office with a typewriter and went to work. In the early afternoon, I handed Mikva's aide a four-page single-spaced memo headed "Nixon's War." It began: "Monday night the President picked up a fallen standard and proclaimed Nixon's War. On a closer look, the war he proposes to continue is dismayingly close to Johnson's War: A commitment to the pursuit in Vietnam of unattainable ends, open-ended in time, cost, and the use of American firepower against Vietnamese."

The next day, November 5, Representative Don Fraser used my whole memo as the text of his own speech in the House. Meanwhile all ten of the Group signed a "Dear Colleague" letter calling for more cosponsors for a resolution to be introduced shortly. The statement accompanying the resolution began with the opening paragraph of my memo and went on to paraphrase it closely: "The fundamental flaw is in the narrowing of the choice to two positions: 'precipitate' withdrawal or an indefinite commitment to prop up militarily the present government in Saigon (with the pious hope of transferring the ground war ultimately to the South Vietnamese forces). We do not propose either, and we find the President's Vietnam policy tragically ill-conceived for three principal reasons."

The next three paragraphs were taken verbatim from the Rand letter. The statement ended, "It is for these reasons that we conclude" that it should be "resolved that it is the sense of Congress that United States forces in South Vietnam should be systematically withdrawn on an orderly and fixed schedule—neither precipitate nor contingent on factors beyond our control—to extend only over such period of time as shall be necessary to (a) provide for the safety of U.S. forces, (b) secure the release of American prisoners of war, (c) assist any Vietnamese desiring asylum, and (d) enable the U.S. to make an orderly disposition of its facilities in South Vietnam."

It was the first time in my life that I had consulted with members of Congress on a proposed piece of legislation or helped draft it, as well as the first time, a week earlier, that I had in effect drafted a speech for one of them. Rand people had occasionally done this for projects that had the blessing of at least some high officials in the air force. But to work directly with opponents in Congress of the president's policy, explicitly criticizing and challenging that policy, without even tacit support of anyone in the executive branch, that was another boundary breached.

The next afternoon I met with Jim Lowenstein, the Fulbright aide who had invited me to the hearings before they were postponed, and Norvil Jones, Fulbright's legislative assistant. For the first time, I told them what the McNamara study was and how it could be used as the basis for hearings. They decided that Fulbright had better hear this himself.

It was late afternoon, but it was dark in Fulbright's office, which was lit by lamps. I had the Pentagon Papers with me, all that I had copied so far, transferred from the suitcase into a couple of briefcases. I sat on a sofa, the briefcases beside me. I told them the background of the McNamara study and why I thought Congress and the public ought to have it. The studies were classified top secret, but much of the information had been wrongfully withheld from Congress and was highly relevant to what was going on now. I gave them my understanding of Nixon's policy and what I thought it would mean—the war going on and getting bigger. Fulbright agreed with me, though he said that the initial reaction to Nixon's speech suggested that many people, including some on his own committee, were being fooled into believing what they wanted to believe, that Nixon was getting out.

I told them that I didn't have documents on Nixon proving otherwise, but that this history showed a pattern of the same sort of deception, the same secret threats and plans to escalate, the same pessimistic internal estimates, and the same public reassurances, over four previous presidents. Bringing that out, proving it with internal documents, would prepare the public to recognize that it was happening again with a fifth president. Instead of living with the escalation as a fait accompli, Congress could act in time to stop it.

I said that I had considered taking these documents to the press, and I was prepared to do that, but it seemed to me that congressional hearings were the best place to reveal them. The documents didn't tell the whole story, by any means. There were crucial aspects of the policy that had never been written down, that only participants could reveal. Congress could subpoena witnesses, in both closed and open sessions, and force them to explain the discrepancies between these documents and what they had told the public. In the course of that process the senators and their staffs could get truths out of some of those witnesses that could never have been hoped for without this documentary evidence, which could be the basis for an unprecedented kind of questioning.

I told him of my own knowledge in 1964 that Fulbright himself had been deceived when he was handling the Tonkin Gulf Resolution. As late as his hearings of February 1968 on those incidents, I said, he was still being lied to in McNamara's testimony. Fulbright broke in to say that they had heard of a study by Joseph Ponturo on the Tonkin Gulf, done for the operations staff of the JCS, which the Defense Department had refused to make available to them. I said that I had copied my own notes, largely verbatim, from that study and had them with me.

Fulbright was enthusiastic about what he was hearing. He said I should give the material to Jones, and they would move ahead on preparing for hearings. I said that it was obvious that what I had done in copying these papers exposed me to prosecution. I said I wasn't eager to go to prison and that if it was possible to use the documents without revealing me as the source or calling me to testify, I would prefer that, but what mattered was using them to the best effect. I was prepared for whatever came out of that. For example, if they needed me to testify to the authenticity of the studies or how they had come to be prepared or into the committee's possession, they should call on me.

Fulbright said, "I don't think any of that would be necessary. There's a number of ways we could handle this. I don't think we would even have to associate you with our acquiring these papers. For one thing, we should be able to get them officially from the administration if we ask. If they hold back on the studies, we could ask for specific documents, now that we know what to ask for. We wouldn't need to call you at all."

I said that was fine with me. I just wanted it understood that I didn't want the risk to me to be the dominant consideration in making choices on these things. It wasn't unimportant to me, but given the stakes, it wasn't what mattered most, either. I was in this all the way. Whatever got the job done best, that was the way it should be done. I was ready to go to prison; that was what I was expecting when I began copying these a month earlier. Fulbright said he admired my attitude; he was grateful for what I was doing. But he didn't think it would come to that. Congress had a right to this information, indeed it should have had it long before, and he didn't think a former official could be put in prison for coming forward and giving it to them.

He stood up, and we all stood and got ready to leave, but I had one last thing to do. I wanted to be able to say in court, whatever happened later, that I had made an effort to give this material to the chairman of the Senate Foreign Relations Committee. I wanted to hand him at least one piece of paper from the study personally, in the presence of others.

I had made an extra copy of the volume on Tonkin Gulf for him, along with my notes on the Ponturo study. Would he like to look at them? "Indeed I would!" he replied. He had a smile on his face as broad as his southern drawl. He reached out for the papers I was holding and took them in front of everyone. He said he would read those right away, and I could believe that he would.

I knew that volume was less candid than almost any other, although the subject matter was more dramatic than most. It was being written right during and after Fulbright's 1968 hearings on the same subject by an active-duty air force officer who, working for McNamara on the study, was prudent enough not to spell out in explicit detail the contradictions in his analysis to McNamara's sworn testimony during those concurrent hearings. As far as I had seen, it was the only volume that had been subject to a degree of self-censorship. But I knew it was still revealing enough to make Fulbright mad.

We left Fulbright in his office, and in the next room I emptied out my briefcases on Norvil Jones's desk and promised him that I would send him the rest of the study as I finished copying it.

After we got back from Washington on November 6, Patricia went to Seattle to spend a few days with a close friend of hers who was about to be married. I went back to the nightly routine of taking out a briefcase full of McNamara study volumes from Rand late in the evening and driving to Lynda Sinay's office in Hollywood to copy them. I still wasn't getting a lot of sleep. As before, I would go to bed at nine or ten in the morning and sleep till three or four in the afternoon, then work at Rand till eight or nine, when I left for the night's work on Melrose Avenue. I was still hoping for Fulbright to hold hearings of the Senate Foreign Relations Committee on extrication from Vietnam, though he hadn't rescheduled them yet. I wanted to get as much of the study copied as possible before that, as well as do a lot of it while Patricia was away. I hadn't yet told her anything about what I was doing with the papers. I didn't want to implicate her or anyone else who wasn't actually helping me copy. The only other person I had told, by phone, was Janaki. For the same reason, I had meant to tell Randy Kehler too before he went to prison in December. I wanted them to know how much influence they had had on me. I wanted them to know that I had joined them in the way they were using their lives.

The copying was drudgery by now, and I was doing it alone. Lynda and Tony didn't come anymore. I worked all night, making copies and collating, and reappeared at Rand around eight. I dropped the copies off at my friend's apartment as before.

I drove home along the Pacific Coast Highway, against the morning traffic, and went into the ocean before I went to bed. It was beginning to get cold, and I couldn't stay in the water too long, but even riding a few waves was a kind of ecstasy for me, and I didn't know how much longer I would be able to do it. Given that, there was no better place in the world for me to live than Las Tunas Beach in Malibu, a narrow strip of sand where the water hit the cottage at high tide in the winter and great waves to ride were never more than a few yards from the house. Throughout October till mid-November, while I thought the papers would be coming out in days or weeks and I expected to go to prison at that point, I often came out of a wave in front of my house in the morning after a night of copying, looked around at the sky and the waves coming in and the hills on the other side, and thought, How *can* I be giving this up?

23

Leaving Rand

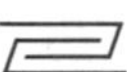

By the end of 1969 I figured I'd have to stay at Rand for perhaps a year and a half more. Nixon would be reducing force levels slowly, I thought, and the North Vietnamese would be inclined to let him do so without disturbing his schedule. Eventually, when he reached a plateau and slowed down or stopped withdrawals, and U.S. casualties were way down because U.S. units were no longer engaging in major offensive actions, the North Vietnamese were likely to turn the heat up in the hope that this would increase public pressure on him to keep withdrawing or to get out entirely. It was at that point that I feared, from what Mort had told me, that Nixon would escalate by resuming heavy air strikes against the North. But that probably lay a year and a half or two years into the future. During that time the public probably wouldn't respond much to criticism of his policy, in their belief that he was on his way out altogether.

Nixon meant to demonstrate to Hanoi in action and not by words alone how far he was prepared to go, further than Johnson ever had, if and when they launched a major attack on remaining U.S. forces or ARVN. Halperin understood the secret Cambodian bombing in that light, and he thought there could be more such demonstrations. But Nixon was still keeping that bombing secret.

That's an ironic description of the state of affairs, since, as I've already mentioned, there had been a front-page story on that bombing in the *New York Times,* by William Beecher in March 1969. But when the Pentagon simply denied the story, the press, Congress, and the public all had accepted the denials and let the matter drop. There were no further stories, though the bombing continued unabated, with dual reporting to deceive Congress with false top secret reports of the targets. In those days a government denial was all it took to make a reality disappear. LBJ had come to be widely perceived as a liar, yet the press and public still had no real awareness of just how much they had been lied to, even by LBJ, let alone by his predecessors and now by his successor.

The Pentagon Papers, as history, no longer seemed to me an effective vehicle of resistance to Nixon's policy. They ended in March 1968, well before Nixon came into office. He had persuaded the American people that he had a new policy. The Pentagon Papers weren't likely to change that misunderstanding. If they were to be revealed publicly at this point, they would be seen, in Fulbright's words, as "only history," without much bearing on the new course Nixon was supposedly taking toward extrication. If I were to argue that the consistent pattern of deception by four previous presidents suggested that Nixon again might be misleading the country on his intentions, my warning would be heard as unduly cynical, short of some alarming escalation or a prolongation of the conflict by years. I expected both of those over time, but meanwhile there seemed little urgency about making the papers public in the short run. Nor was there any longer the incentive of supporting the Moratorium. In the aftermath of Nixon's November 3 speech and the apparent lack of effect of two enormous demonstrations, that campaign seemed to have fizzled.

Still, the Pentagon Papers might eventually help the country get out of the war. They might someday help a majority in Congress get up the nerve to challenge the president and end the war by ending funding. That would be at the point when enough members were ready to recognize that the history in the papers was repeating itself yet again. In readiness for that, but no longer with a sense of urgency, I continued to copy the rest of the study and to send shipments of it to Fulbright.

I brought them with me on a trip to New York, in case I went down to Washington. I had about three thousand pages left. I called Fulbright's aide Norvil Jones to tell him what I had, and he suggested that I send them by airfreight, for speed and security, when I went to the airport en route back to L.A. I wasn't sure I had another copy of everything I had with me, so I looked in the yellow pages for a cheap copy shop in the neighborhood of my hotel. I called one, and it said it could do the job right away if I brought it over.

The copy shop was a crowded room upstairs in a large office building. I filled out the order form, and the clerk said it would take several hours. Just before I handed the papers over, I decided to riffle through them to make sure they were in the right order. Within seconds I was looking at a page clearly stamped "Top Secret." I flipped past it quickly and kept going. A few pages down I saw another, this one with the tops of the letters missing but still legible. My cardboard declassifiers hadn't removed them; some of the markings were too low on the page for the strips to catch them. I closed the papers up, took them off the counter, and stuffed them back in the briefcase. I didn't know how the copying staffers would react if they saw those stamps, but I didn't want to find out.

I told the woman behind the counter that I would be back shortly, and I left. I bought large scissors at an office supply store. Nearby was a nearly deserted coffee shop. I took a table in the middle of the shop, put my briefcase on the chair next to me, and ordered a cup of coffee and a sweet roll. The breakfast rush was over, and I was the only customer in the place. I put a pile of pages in front of me and began to go through them one by one, turning them facedown. After only a few pages I came to one with "Top Secret" running across the page number. With the scissors I cut off the top margin of the page and put the strip of paper in the pocket of my raincoat. Every half hour or so I bought another cup of coffee or juice and kept going.

The people behind the counter didn't pay any attention to me, but gradually the tables began to fill up. All of a sudden a flood of people came in, filled every seat, and stood at the counter for takeout. It was noon, lunchtime for the offices nearby. To hold my table, I ordered lunch, which didn't leave room for my piles of papers on the tabletop. I had more than a thousand pages left to go through. I took out a handful at a time from my briefcase, tilted them in my lap, and edged open the corners one at a time to see if a top secret marking was showing at the top or bottom of the page.

Every forty or fifty pages I found one. Trying not to let anyone see it, I would slip that page to the front, close to my chest, cut a strip off the top or bottom with the scissors, and stuff the slip of paper in my pocket. Fortunately everyone around me was busy eating. There was a lot of noise. It was an unusual performance I was going through, but I tried to act matter-of-fact, and New Yorkers didn't seem inclined to pay much attention. Every once in a while I took a few bites of lunch. Finally the place emptied as abruptly as it had filled up, and I had it to myself again. I didn't have to go through the last hundred pages quite so close to my chest. When I finished, the pocket of my raincoat was jammed with wadded-up strips of top secret markings. I emptied them into a trash can on the street.

I took the briefcase back to the copy shop and handed the papers over to be copied. It took quite a while—even the big machines weren't very fast in those days—and the bill was about three hundred dollars. At the airport I took the package to airfreight and shipped it off to Norvil Jones at the Senate Foreign Relations Committee, another forty-five dollars. I called Norvil and told him it was on the way. He said, "That's great! We can't wait to get it! Of course, we'll be happy to cover your expense."

I was surprised. He hadn't said anything about that before, and I was very glad to hear it. At ten cents a page, a full copy of the study cost seven hundred dollars. I'd already spent several thousand dollars on copying. But that wasn't all for Fulbright, and I decided not to mention past costs just then. I said, "Wonderful! I wasn't going to ask, but that will really be helpful. What I'm sending you today cost three hundred and forty-five dollars to copy and send."

He sounded shocked. He said, "Oh, my goodness, we don't have that kind of money."

I said, "What was it you were offering just now?"

"To pay postage."

I said, "Oh, forget it."

On my birthday, April 7, 1970, I got a call from my former wife. That was very unusual. Carol said that FBI agents had been to see her six weeks earlier, asking her to talk with them about top secret documents her former husband had copied. They said I'd given them to Senators Fulbright and Goodell. She had refused to talk with them without her lawyer present, a demand they rejected. Instead they had gone to her lawyer on this issue, and he had told Carol that I should be informed. Patricia and I had a lot to think about after I hung up, as we celebrated my thirty-ninth birthday.

The next day Carol and her lawyer declined to talk with the FBI. But I presumed that the next step for the FBI would be to come see me at Rand or to ask to talk to Harry Rowen. Apparently the jig was up. I didn't want to be arrested at Rand. I wanted to spare Harry. I had to separate myself from Rand before the FBI came down on me, and that might be at any moment.

Early the next morning I called Everett Hagen, a professor of economics who was running the Center for International Studies at MIT. He had called me a month or two earlier with an offer to spend a year as a senior research fellow at the center, work on a book if I wanted. He had mentioned that Bill Bundy was a fellow at the center writing a book on Vietnam, and that there was some student unrest at the fact that there were no critics of the war on a comparable basis. He told me frankly that he was interested in having me there in part as a perceived counterbalance to Bundy. (Bundy later mentioned in a book that he himself had suggested my name to Hagen in this connection.) At the time I'd turned him down. I thought I could write as well at Rand as anywhere else. But the sheriff would soon be at my door, and I didn't want the door to be Rand's.

I asked Hagen if the offer still stood and if I would be able to write anything I wanted. He said that he would be happy to have me start immediately and that no one would even look at what I wrote before I published it. He offered me the same salary as Bill Bundy's, the highest salary MIT was able to offer. It was half what I was earning at Rand, but that wasn't an issue for me. I accepted immediately and arranged to go to MIT the following week to sign the contract.

Upon my return to the office I went to see Harry Rowen, and I told him that I thought the time had come for me to leave Rand. He made no counterargument at all. I said it matter-of-factly, and he agreed in the same tone, that yes, that would be best. Understatement was his normal manner anyway. But I drew from the prompt acceptance of my announcement that it must have been a great relief for him, after the last few months. He said, simply, "It's too bad it has to end like this."

My department head, Charlie Wolf, contained his disappointment even more effectively. I had been invited, again, to testify before the Fulbright committee on May 13, and his first thought was that I should be away from Rand as soon as possible before that, so he asked that my departure become effective by April 15. That fitted my own concerns. I expected the FBI to call any day. He did want me to remain a Rand consultant so that I could finish the paper I was working on, "Revolutionary Judo." I was reluctant to retain that tie, for Rand's sake. It contradicted my very purpose in leaving. But I couldn't give him a good reason for refusing, so I said yes.

On Monday, April 13, I flew to Boston, went straight from the airport to the center at MIT, and signed my contract. Janaki, who was doing graduate work at Harvard, picked me up there and we drove down Memorial Highway next to the Charles River toward her home. Under the hood of her Volkswagen, though I hadn't told her yet, was a suitcase with an almost complete set of the Pentagon Papers that I meant to leave with her. As we came near Harvard, we could see a crowd flowing across one of the bridges, and we heard shouting and sirens. In the evening darkness we pulled off into a side street next to one of the Harvard houses and walked over to Mass. Ave. to see what was happening. It was an amazing sight. We were in the midst of a throbbing mass of demonstrators that was being held from entering the square by what appeared to be a full battalion of riot police with long batons and plastic shields down over their faces. I'd never seen so many police massed in one formation.

There was a space between the police and the throng on Mass. Ave. next to the Harvard Yard, filled with clouds of tear gas, drifting toward one side, then the other. Apparently, we were told, an antiwar rally on the other side of the river had spilled out as it ended over the bridge and into the square, from which it had been expelled by the busloads of police just before we arrived. The crowd was surging back and forth, very excited, and some windows of shops along Mass. Ave. were being broken. It was my hometown, the place I felt most at home in the world, and I'd known every one of those shops for more than twenty years. This was a dizzying return to Cambridge. The country, including the neighborhood most familiar to me, seemed to be spinning out of control.

There was still no word from the FBI. It had spent six weeks negotiating with Carol; I didn't know how long its investigation might proceed before its agents came to me, and I still didn't know how much they knew—or how they knew it. I couldn't stay on the East Coast indefinitely. All my belongings and files were in California. I went back home to Malibu the last week in April to finish up a Rand paper and prepare my testimony for the Fulbright committee in May. I rarely went into Rand, and only briefly. I was edgy about it, since the whole point of my quitting Rand as a full-time employee was to avoid being apprehended at the office or while I had a Rand connection. But Charlie Wolf, who didn't know any of these problems, was leaning on me to get my paper done by June, later extended to July. The FBI didn't seem to be lurking, and gradually, as the days and then weeks went by, I thought less and less about the problem.

On April 30 I watched President Nixon's address to the nation on TV announcing the invasion of Cambodia. The country, in particular the campus world, erupted. On May 4, the day of the National Guard shootings at a demonstration at Kent State, Howard Miller of *The Advocates,* the program on public television, called me to help him on the Cambodian invasion.

The Advocates was run like a trial, with opposing attorneys and witnesses and cross-examination. The next day I flew to Washington with Miller to help him find witnesses.

I had had a long session with Clark Clifford toward the end of 1969. Miller had never met him, and he was counting on my briefing of Clifford to serve as an entrée, but Clifford made it clear that he didn't want to go public with criticism of the president's initiative on Cambodia or even to discuss his own views with us in private. How he did that, after Howard had introduced himself and his program and begun to describe what he wanted, was to go off into a long, unstoppable set of reflections on the virtues of the TV program *Sesame Street,* how wonderful it was in educating children while entertaining them, how he liked to watch it with his grandchildren, what a wonderful character Big Bird was, and so on. I think the connection was that *Sesame Street* was also on public television, like *The Advocates,* and he felt moved to express his appreciation to Miller for public television. We tried to get him onto the subject of the Cambodian invasion, perhaps to suggest other guests that we might ask or angles of argument, but he went on talking, with a chuckle, about Oscar the Grouch, with the fingertips of his two hands pressed lightly together, his elbows on the arms of his leather chair. Howard and I looked at each other. We said our good-byes and left in a cloud of well-wishing from Clifford.

I learned later that Clifford's proclivity to filibuster, when he didn't want to discuss something, was well known. But his reluctance to be on the program turned out in the next few days to be widely shared, at least among the former military and government officials we approached. No takers.

On Friday, May 8, I flew to St. Louis to take part in my first public teach-in against the war, at Washington University. I had been invited by a navy captain, in charge of the NROTC unit there, who had worked with me in ISA. Under my direction, he had coordinated in the spring of 1965 a study on mining Haiphong that had persuaded McNamara to stop recommending it at that time. Another speaker against the war that evening was Senator Charles Mathias. The big event on that campus, just before our talks, had been the burning of the ROTC building. In the question period a student referred to this, with much applause and cheering from the audience, and asked me challengingly what I thought of it. The implication was that my questioner had taken part in the burning, though he didn't say that, and it was clear that it had been a popular act among the students.

I said that I had been trained in the Marine Corps to do violence and that I had seen a lot of it in Vietnam. Its effectiveness, which was ultimately its justification, wasn't just a hypothetical question for me. I had had a good deal of experience on which to judge that, and I was no longer so impressed with it, and I knew much more about how it could go wrong than when I had been a marine. I very well understood, and shared, the frustration of the students at their inability to stop the war. But it seemed to have a lot in common with the frustration of the troops in Vietnam, who were the same age as the students in this audience, at their inability to win the war. And the response I had seen in Vietnam was very similar. As I spoke, the memory seemed very fresh to me, as if I had just come back, though three years of war had passed since I'd returned from Vietnam. I told them of the soldiers in Rach Kien, burning down every hut they came to, for no real reason than to leave some mark that they had passed that way, that they were not just plowing the sea. It was understandable, but it didn't really help anything, it didn't change the situation.

It was very American, I said, to think that to be willing to use violence was to show seriousness and to be effective, but that was not what I'd learned in Vietnam. I said I could see that many people in the audience felt proud of what had just happened on their campus but that I couldn't tell them I believed that burning down ROTC buildings would be any more productive for ending the war than burning down villages in Vietnam. It would take commitment, and courage, and tenacity to end this war, but not an imitation of the government's own destructive tactics.

Many applauded, but there were some boos, and many were silent. It was in fact a very challenging question facing the antiwar movement and the nation at that moment: What did it take, what should be done, what might work to stop this government, this president, from prolonging and expanding the war? No one, including myself, could be confident of the answer to that. Nothing, neither violence (of which there hadn't been very much) nor massive peaceful protest and civil disobedience, *had* worked. I could say only what was in my heart at this moment, based on my recent reading on nonviolence in the light of my own experience. But I couldn't be sure I was right. (After thirty more years of experience, watching the world, I've become much more sure that I *was* right. But I was new to these thoughts then.)

Four students lay dead at Kent State, and more than five hundred colleges were on strike. The senator and I flew back to Washington together Saturday morning, and we landed in a capital city that by the next day was clouded in tear gas. We drove into town through streets that were filling with more than a hundred thousand students coming from shut-down campuses all over the country.

We had become friendly on the flight, and Mathias told me something striking. He had known Nixon for a long time, and as the Republican senator from Maryland (Vice President Agnew's state) he had been to the White House a number of times. He said that in recent months he had been disturbed by an increasing sense that the president was becoming "unbalanced." One example was Nixon's choice of new uniforms for the White House guards, which seemed to have been designed for an operetta set in nineteenth-century Central Europe. Mathias was not the only one to have had this reaction to the uniforms; there had been a good deal of similar comment in the newspapers. But what capped his concern was an evening he had spent at the White House recently when he and his wife had been the Nixons' only guests for a quiet dinner. They had been waiting alone in the dining room, near a banquet table set for four, when they heard a fanfare of trumpets, followed by a section of the Marine Band playing "Hail to the Chief." The president and Pat Nixon, arm in arm, were proceeding slowly down a staircase to meet their two guests, while the band played. Mathias was very unnerved by the sight. The word he used for the impression the chief executive had made on him was "insane."

On the Saturday I arrived back in Washington, Howard Miller decided that I should be the one to oppose the war on *The Advocates,* though we'd been aiming higher up till then. I would be joined by Senator Goodell. It would be my first public appearance on television as a war critic, except for some brief clips on local stations about the Rand letter. During Sunday I walked through downtown Washington with Patricia, who had come to Washington to join me. We saw hundreds of demonstrators sitting down spontaneously on streets leading to the White House, which was ringed by parked buses. Tear gas canisters were being fired into the streets, apparently from the White House lawn. But it wasn't tear gas, or police, that was keeping the protesters from blockading the White House. It was young protesters with official-looking armbands who were moving among those sitting or lying down, grabbing them by their elbows, and pulling them to their feet, saying "We're not doing civil disobedience today." These, it turned out, were mostly Socialist Workers party members, who had volunteered to be marshals for the demonstration scheduled for that afternoon. Their Trotskyist party was ideologically opposed to civil disobedience as a tactic, on the ground that workers were alienated by it. A bitter conflict was in progress that day among the demonstration organizers over that issue.

As Patricia and I watched this process on Fourteenth Street, I was thinking that a big mistake was being made. For once there were so many people in town ready to do civil disobedience that they could have shut the city down. Also, for the first and last time in the war, the mood of Congress was so angry at the president—for the insult of invading another country without any pretense of consulting Congress—that such an effort would have had the tacit or even open sympathy of much of Congress, with a number of members, I suspected, actually participating. I believed then, and still do, that this was the time when sustained, committed public protest over days or weeks might well have convinced both houses of Congress to end the war, by passing the McGovern-Hatfield bill to cut off its funding. A cloud of tear gas came up the street from the direction of the White House, and our eyes were stinging. Back at our hotel, I washed the tear gas out of my hair in the shower and put on my best suit to be on television that evening.

The program was broadcast live that evening from the National Press Club. Some of the protesters who had left the legal rally of a hundred thousand or who had been dispersed from sitting in by tear gas (and SWP marshals) were in the audience. The topic was: "Should Congress resolve that the president immediately withdraw all troops, aid, and advisers from Cambodia and commit no further forces outside Vietnam?" A mild proposal at the moment. The president, the day after Kent State, had already promised Congress that U.S. troops would be withdrawn from Cambodia by the end of June, and then made that a public commitment at a news conference. Kissinger calls it in his memoir a "panicky decision . . . one concrete result of public pressures."

The debate proposal was thus essentially on the Church-Cooper resolution, which cut off funding for operations in Cambodia, giving legislative "teeth" to the president's commitment. It was not on the McGovern-Hatfield bill, which cut off all funds for the war in Indochina by the end of 1971. (That was voted down in September, 55–39, the uproar over Cambodia having dissipated.)

But I was there to speak for the McGovern-Hatfield bill, as Advocate Howard Miller made clear in introducing me as "here to tell us why Congress must mandate withdrawal from Cambodia and Southeast Asia." So, presumably, was my fellow "witness" in favor of the proposal, Senator Charles Goodell. To honor Charlie Wolf's wishes, no mention was made in my background description of my association till recently with Rand. I was described as being at the Center for International Studies, MIT, and a former "adviser" (official, actually) in the Defense and State departments.

Opposing us and the proposal were conservative advocate William T. King and witnesses Senator Robert Dole and William H. Sullivan, deputy assistant secretary of state for East Asian and Pacific affairs and a former U.S. ambassador to Laos, who, according to Miller, had been directed by the administration to participate. Given the mood within the government, many might have resigned before they would have spoken on TV for the invasion. Sullivan was not one of these, but that didn't mean he really approved of the action. Several cabinet members had publicly opposed it, and a large number of Foreign Service officers had signed an unprecedented petition denouncing it. Miller said Dole, who was head of the Republican National Committee, was the only Republican senator he had been able to find to take the position supporting the administration.

My most vivid memory of the program was an exchange between Miller and Dole, who said at one point, as I remember: "The life of a single American boy is worth more than any imaginary line on a map." He was referring to the Cambodian border, which our invading tanks had just crossed, allegedly—by the administration's rather obscure logic—in order to protect the lives of American troops. Miller, as the opposing advocate cross-examining him, exclaimed, "That line, Senator, is an international frontier!"

Dole replied, "I don't care what you call it, it's not worth the life of a single American boy."

A later exchange I had with my cross-examiner:

King: You feel that the President of the United States has been brainwashed?

Ellsberg: Presidential candidates have admitted to that in the past. [George Romney, governor of Michigan, finished himself off as a rival to Nixon in the Republican primaries in 1968 with that candid remark.] I believe, as a matter of fact, sir, that five Presidents have brainwashed themselves, brainwashed their own staffs, and brainwashed the American public for a number of administrations. We have had a generation of that.

King: You don't like the government in South Vietnam, do you?

[Pause]

Ellsberg: That seems to me a strange question, Mr. King. I am not—

Moderator: I don't think he meant it as a point of personal affection, asking you whether in fact you are antipathetic to the Government of South Vietnam.

[Pause]

Ellsberg: I believe the Government of South Vietnam is a narrow, unrepresentative, corrupt, military dictatorship. [Laughter and applause.]

If I may add, what is more relevant to its association with the United

States . . . I believe it consists of a narrow group in South Vietnam that alone prefers to see this war continue indefinitely than to see it end with American withdrawal.

King: Well, let me ask you how you feel about the Government of North Vietnam?

Ellsberg: The Government of North Vietnam is in many respects [pause] not any better than the Government of South Vietnam.

King: In other words, you don't care which government wins; is that right?

Ellsberg: The notion that it is for an American, whether it is me or you or the president of the United States, to determine the Government of South Vietnam, is a tragic mistake that has led to tragedy for both countries.

On May 13 I testified before the Senate Foreign Relations Committee. My session, in Fulbright's opening words, called for "testimony concerning the historical, political, and economic impact of U.S. policy on Vietnam and Southeast Asia." The hearings were originally planned to be educational and uncontroversial, reflecting the mood of the Senate and public, but within these limits I had decided to comment frankly on the nature of the U.S.-supported Saigon regime.

In this context I went on to review the efforts of our government to prevent true "self-determination" in Vietnam, the stated object of our intervention. The reality was that "not one of the regimes we have supported, from the Bao Dai regime controlled by the French, through Ngo Dinh Diem, to the military junta that rules today behind a constitutional facade, could have resulted from a process of public choice that was truly free, or free of our own outside influence."

In my testimony I related the history of U.S. efforts to maintain a series of governments with little or no popular support, simply on the basis of their reliability in maintaining our dominant interest, preventing eventual Communist domination. I spoke at length about the specific case of my friend Tran Ngoc Chau, who had been arrested in Saigon and whose illegal trial had taken place in March. Chau had allegedly been arrested because of his secret contacts with his North Vietnamese brother. In fact these contacts had been encouraged by Ambassador Lodge and were well known in the embassy. The real reasons Thieu was pursuing Chau, John Vann had told me, were that Chau had been denouncing the corrupt dealings of Thieu's bagman in the Assembly and that he had been calling for negotiations with the NLF.

Fulbright took the opportunity to question me at length about my knowledge relating to the Tonkin Gulf incident, a topic in which he maintained a keen interest.

I noted that in previous hearings Fulbright had said that he felt "shame" for his part in obtaining the congressional resolution after this incident. I said that the word had leaped out at me "because I had not remembered seeing an American official use such a word or in any way imply a sense of personal responsibility to that degree." I said that as unusual as such sentiments were, they were appropriate. I regretted only that such sentiments had not been expressed by any of those who had misled him, and the country, at the time.

24

Kissinger

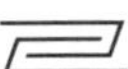

In August 1970 my friend Lloyd Shearer, an editor of *Parade* magazine, mentioned that he had a date to interview Kissinger at San Clemente and asked if I would like to come along. I said sure. I thought I would encourage Kissinger to read the Pentagon Papers, at least parts of them, so that he might discover that escalations like Cambodia had been talked through in earlier years in terms that would probably now look very fresh to him. He would read that all the earlier hopes before the escalations were actually threatened and carried out had been disappointed. Maybe he could learn from that.

Also, I believed that his policy, as I understood it, depended for its viability on being invisible to the American public. I wanted him to know that the outlines of the policy really were visible, at least to some people, including me, who were telling other people about it. (For one thing, someone from the White House must have told *me.*) In effect, I had the idea of leaking information *into* the White House about what was actually visible from the outside, where I was now. I wanted Kissinger to worry that the trend of his policy was foreseeable, so that it might seem less viable to him. That was much the same effect I'd aimed to have on President Johnson with my leaks to the press in March 1968.

We drove down to San Clemente. I remember driving into a parking lot through a gateway and hearing a loud voice out of nowhere like the voice of God, telling us where to park. There seemed to be an unseen eye controlling our movements; I finally realized we were hearing a loudspeaker on top of the guardhouse. We sat in an outer waiting office like a dentist's waiting room, with large color photographs of Nixon lining the wall. The official photographer himself chatted with us in the lobby till he dashed out the door as a pink golf cart went by in the driveway outside. There was one person aboard driving it at about seven miles an hour like a little electric Disneyland car. It was Nixon. He was scowling, looking very grim, with his shoulders hunched over, piloting the cart like a driver of a bumper car. Right behind him was another pink golf cart being driven by Bebe Rebozo, and behind that, a third pink cart with two Secret Service men. A pink convoy.

Finally we were taken to a small patio for lunch with Kissinger. His aide Alexander Haig, now a general, was at the table. As we all said hello, Kissinger turned to Lloyd and said, in his ingratiating manner, "You know, I have learned more from Dan Ellsberg than from any other person—" I assumed he was about to repeat what he'd said about me at Rand two years earlier: "in Vietnam." But instead he said, "—about bargaining."

I was taken aback. Bargaining? For a moment I didn't have any idea what he was referring to. Then I remembered the talks I had given to his seminar at Harvard in 1959, from my Lowell Lecture series, "The Art of Coercion." That had been eleven years earlier. I said, "You have a very good memory."

Guttural drawl: "They were very good lectures."

Nice. Except that when I thought about it later, it made the hair on the back of my neck stand up. The lectures I had given to his class had had to do with Hitler's blackmail of Austria and Czechoslovakia in the late thirties that had allowed him to take over those countries just by threatening their destruction. One of the talks was titled "The Theory and Practice of Blackmail," and the other was "The Political Uses of Madness." Hitler had deliberately cultivated among his adversaries the impression of his own irrational unpredictability. He couldn't be counted on not to carry out a threat to do something crazy, mutually destructive. It worked for him, up to a point, because he *was* crazy, madly aggressive, and reckless. But after a certain point it brought the world down around him. It wasn't a tactic I was recommending for the United States, or anyone else, for that matter. Far from it. For someone to imitate Hitler in this respect was to cultivate madness and court disaster.

News leaks about the Cambodian invasion the previous April, coming from backgrounders with unidentified administration officials, had in fact asserted that a major motive for the invasion was to convince the Soviets, the Chinese, and the North Vietnamese that our decision making at the highest levels was unpredictable and that since we could do something so evidently erratic and crazy as to invade Cambodia at this stage of the war, they could not count on our reasonableness or prudence in a crisis. When I read those, I had wondered if the "high official" sources with that ill-conceived strategy could possibly have been Kissinger and Nixon themselves. I hoped not.

Kissinger's little compliment answered that question. It was chilling to realize that the memory of Hitler's tactic, as such, was in the mind of the top White House adviser three months after Cambodia.

The four of us sat down to lunch on a terrace outside the house. Just as it was beginning to be served, Lloyd raised the subject of Vietnam, taking advantage of my presence, and Kissinger said, "Well, we are not here to talk about Vietnam." What then? I thought. He looked at me nervously and made it clear that he didn't want to talk in front of me. I assumed it was because he wanted to lie to Shearer about Vietnam in ways that wouldn't have been easy in my presence. It was after all to keep him honest on Vietnam that Lloyd had wanted me to be present for the discussion.

But it turned out, Lloyd told me later, that what Kissinger really wanted to discuss with him was his sex life and how it was being presented in the media. Lloyd wrote the "Personality Parade" column, under the pseudonym Walter Scott, for the inside cover of the Sunday supplement *Parade*. It was "the most widely read page in American journalism," Lloyd said proudly. He was in effect the premier gossip columnist in the country. He frequently ran items, supposedly in answer to reader queries, about Kissinger's bachelor life with Jill St. John and other starlets. This PR was generally approved by the administration as a humanizing touch for the Nixon White House, but it had some obvious risks. Kissinger wanted to encourage it, to get advice from Lloyd, and to manage the spin on it.

This wasn't something he wanted to do in front of me. He began drumming his fingertips on the table and then suddenly said, "Tell you what, Dan, why don't you and General Haig have lunch together while we talk on other matters? Then we will all get together." So he did after all get rid of me. Haig and I went off to the other side of the house and had lunch. Haig was very affable, and I decided that I would try my tactic on him of "leaking in" the Nixon strategy on Vietnam. He listened and nodded. I took this just as acknowledging that he was following my argument, not that he was confirming it, which I didn't expect him to do. He certainly didn't reject it or try to correct me, although the policy I was describing was very different from what the public was choosing to believe.

After an hour Kissinger joined us. He said, to my surprise, that he wanted to talk with me, and we set up a meeting for his next trip to California. Patricia and I had set a wedding date in August, and the date he wanted was in the middle of our scheduled honeymoon in Maui. Strange as it seems to me now—I was obsessed, I remember that—I accepted it. I wasn't passing up any chance to get through to Nixon, perhaps avoid more Cambodias and help shorten the war. I was sure Patricia would agree (and she did). We cut short the honeymoon so I could make the appointment.

On the drive back to Santa Monica, Lloyd told me about his conversation with Kissinger. He had asked him one question that I'd suggested: Could he imagine any circumstances under which he would leave his position and oppose the president's policy? Kissinger's first answer was no, none at all. But when Lloyd pressed him, he said, "Well, I suppose, if there were plans for gas chambers . . ."

I said, "Of course plans for using nuclear weapons wouldn't count." It was a random shot; I didn't know yet that Kissinger was sitting on just such contingency plans. "Look, Lloyd, for Henry Kissinger there is exactly one crime against humanity that he can recognize as such, and it's happened already, it's in the past. It was done by Germans, against Jews. That's the only political act he can conceive as being unquestionably immoral."

Lloyd was a little shocked. He said, "Dan, that's a pretty harsh thing to say. Do you really believe that?" I said yes, and I didn't think it applied only to Kissinger.

On August 8, 1970, Patricia and I exchanged wedding vows in a marriage ceremony with our families and many friends. We wrote our own vows. Mine began, "I will love you, Patricia, and cherish you, honor and respect you . . . through all the days of our lives." That vow I have kept, as she has hers.

At the end of August, after our scheduled meeting was once postponed, I met with Kissinger again in his office at San Clemente. He said he had only half an hour, but he started out by saying, "I'm very worried about the Middle East situation." There had been a number of leaks in the papers recently, apparently from Kissinger, about his criticisms of Secretary of State William Rogers's handling of the Middle East negotiations, which Kissinger was not at that point allowed into. "I'm afraid that that situation may blow up."

I had only half an hour to pursue my own agenda, so I said, "Well, Henry, I want to talk to you about your Indochina policy. I think *that* may blow up." The night before I had worked to reduce my understanding of the Nixon strategy to a single dense page, which I laid out orally: the ambitious (publicly undeclared) objectives, the meaning of "peace with honor"; the slow, drawn-out reduction of U.S. forces, down to a sizable residual force; threats of escalation, which I felt sure would fail to deter or coerce despite demonstrative actions like Cambodia; probable future invasions, Laos, perhaps the southern part of North Vietnam, and renewed bombing; the ultimate mining of Haiphong; and throughout, deliberate deception of the public. What lay ahead, as I saw it: an endless, expanding war.

As I recited all this, he looked at me with narrowed eyes, frowning, lips pursed, in a way that told me I was not on the wrong track. But he made no response. He drummed his fingers on the table, then said abruptly, "Well, I do not want to discuss our policy; let us turn to another subject."

I asked if he knew about the McNamara study on Vietnam, and he said yes. (I didn't know then that he had actually been a consultant in the first month of the study.) "Do you have a copy of it in the White House?" He said that he did.

I was encouraged to hear it. I asked, "Have you read it?"

"No, should I?"

I said that I thought strongly that he should, at least to read the summaries, which were only a few single-spaced pages at the start of each volume. He could have an assistant read the texts and pick out passages that seemed especially pertinent. But the summaries alone added up to about sixty pages. "They make a very readable story. You really should make the effort."

"But do we really have anything to learn from this study?"

My heart sank. I thought: My God! He's in the same state of mind as the rest of them all along. They each thought that history started with his administration and that they had nothing to learn from earlier ones. Yet in fact each administration, including this one, repeated the same patterns in decision making and pretty much the same (hopeless) policy as its predecessor, without even knowing it. *That* was what there was to learn from the study, and Kissinger obviously needed it. The Pentagon Papers offered a chance to break this pattern, but its mere existence evidently hadn't done it.

I was suddenly depressed, but I went on to answer, "Well, I certainly do think so. It's twenty years of history, and there's a great deal to be learned from it."

He said, "But after all, we make decisions very differently now."

My depression deepened. I said, "Cambodia didn't look all that different."

Kissinger looked uncomfortable, and fidgeted in his chair. He said, "You must understand, Cambodia was undertaken for very complicated reasons."

I said, "Henry, there hasn't been a rotten decision in this area for twenty years which wasn't undertaken for very complicated reasons. And they were usually the same sort of complicated reasons."

That wasn't the way you talked to a high official if you wanted to get another visit to his office. But I was a year into copying, and I wasn't giving much weight to preserving my access to Henry Kissinger. I'd done what I wanted to do with him without much evidence of success. I would have been glad to spell out for him what I meant if he had picked up on it, but he didn't. Nevertheless, my tone didn't end the interview or even keep him from urging me to return. Instead he referred to his irritation at the group of Harvard scholars—most of them past colleagues of both of us, including Tom Schelling—who had visited him to resign en bloc as consultants in protest against Cambodia. (Their finest hour, as I saw it.) He was contemptuous of their presumption that they could judge a policy when they knew so little about policy making from the inside. He said dismissively, "They never had the clearances."

That was what he said. He had drunk deep of Circe's potion. So much for my experiment two years earlier in trying to inoculate him against it. To remind him of that conversation and to escape being dismissed in the same terms, I said, "But that's not true of me."

He said hastily and emphatically, "Oh, no, of course not, I didn't have you in mind at all."

I went on provocatively. "And it's not true of Walt Rostow." The main point I was trying to communicate in this visit was that Kissinger's current secret policy could be seen—by someone who knew what it was and who had read the Pentagon Papers—as strikingly similar to that of Walt Rostow, who had preceded him in that office, and before him, McGeorge Bundy. It was still the same policy; that was the secret I was trying to leak into the White House. But I couldn't make that point effectively by mentioning Rostow.

Kissinger said, "Walt Rostow is a fool."

I said, "That may be. But McGeorge Bundy is no fool."

He said, "No, McGeorge Bundy is not a fool. . . . But . . . he has no sense of policy."

In short, the strategy's not *really* the same, and even if it were, those guys didn't do it right; they didn't know how to threaten, they couldn't make it work. This conversation was confirming my sense of the year before.

This wasn't a policy, or a pattern of decision making, that was going to be changed from the inside, from "speaking truth to power" as a consultant. Cambridge professors come to power couldn't learn from the failure of a former close colleague any more than Republicans could learn from Democrats or the Americans from the French.

But for some reason, which I never did learn, Kissinger expressed some urgency about seeing me again, and pressed me for a date. I said I would call him from Cambridge; we were in the midst of a move.

I did call him, and a date was set. Then, just an hour before I was due to fly to Washington, I got a call from his secretary that it was postponed, and she set another date. That was postponed in turn, and she suggested a third date. I said, "Look, it's obvious that he's very busy. I don't want to keep planning to come down when it's clear that he doesn't have time to see me." She said, "No, he wants to see you very much." The next time I called to check half an hour before I left and learned that it would be postponed again. She asked me to set another date, but I said he should call when he knew he would be free. I didn't hear again. I never did learn what all this had been about. At the time I let the matter drop because I concluded from the cancellations that his interest was minimal, that he wanted to see me only so he could say he was listening "to everyone, the whole range of opinion—Dan Ellsberg, for example."

The next time I heard from him, indirectly, seemed to confirm my suspicion. I was in Minneapolis in mid-January 1971 to testify at the trial of two of the so-called Minnesota Eight, who had been caught destroying files in a draft board office. I had a large batch of the Pentagon Papers with me in a briefcase, which I intended to introduce into the record of the trial. I hoped that I would be able to give a kind of testimony, as an expert witness, that would enable me to offer these papers as evidence. Then perhaps the defense could subpoena the whole study from me and get them into the court record.

The night before the trial, the lawyer defending the Eight questioned me on my background to establish me as an expert witness in court. He asked if I had ever worked for this administration. I said that I had, but I couldn't talk about that in court. For two years I had kept quiet about that because Henry Kissinger hadn't wanted known his reliance on Rand, and particularly on me, for that help. I wasn't at Rand any longer, but I didn't want to embarrass it in its relations with Kissinger by mentioning my past work now, even though the lawyer believed it would add greatly to my authority in court.

The next morning, January 14, Patricia mentioned on the phone that I'd received a call from Don Oberdorfer of the *Washington Post.* I had an hour before I went to court, so I called Oberdorfer. He said he was doing a two-year wrap-up on Nixon's policies, including Vietnam, and he had asked Kissinger what the origin of the current policy had been. Kissinger had said, "Ironically, certain people who are now great critics of the administration had been crucial in the development of the policy," in particular, Oberdorfer said, "a guy named Ellsberg."

I was astonished. I said, "Kissinger mentioned me?"

"Yes, definitely. That's where I got your name. He also mentioned Halperin and Schelling. But he said that you had been involved in the study of alternative policies and questions."

As far as I knew, this was the first time that Kissinger had mentioned any outside help on those options to any journalist. I asked, "What did Kissinger say the policy *was*?"

Oberdorfer said, "It's the policy of negotiating with Hanoi while withdrawing the troops from Vietnam."

I said, "Look, if that summed up the policy, I would still be at Rand and Mort Halperin would still be in the White House. This guy is still concealing what their policy really is, and he's smearing us as being implicated in *his* rotten policy." I asked him if Kissinger had said anything to him about threats of escalation, demonstrative actions, mutual withdrawal as an absolute demand, or plans to keep a large residual force. Kissinger had not, and Oberdorfer was surprised to hear my account of the role of these elements. He went on to talk to other people and to conclude that I was right, that he had been misled by Kissinger. He was one of the first journalists I succeeded in reaching with this interpretation.

The immediate result of this talk was that I did feel free to mention my work for the first time in public when I went into court a couple of hours later. When I was asked on the stand if I had ever worked for this administration, I said that I had just learned that Henry Kissinger had revealed it on the record, so that I was free to acknowledge it.

I didn't succeed, however, in getting the Pentagon Papers into the trial. I had described the papers to the defense lawyer the night before. We had worked out an approach for getting them accepted as part of the court record as evidence. He would ask me to comment on some (false) statement by Kennedy or Johnson; I picked out a good candidate for him later that night. I would say on the stand: "That statement is false." He would say: "That's a very serious charge; you're accusing the president of the United States of lying. Do you have any evidence to back up that charge?" I would say: "Yes, I do. I have a great deal of documentation here that constitutes proof of it." He would then move to have these documents entered into the court record as defense exhibits, available to prosecution, judge, and jury. The judge could decide, as I understood it, whether or not to make the documents public or even to submit them to the jury. But in any case he would have a chance to read them, and they would be part of the court record even if he sealed them. They could be seen by an appellate court, and they might, somehow, evoke a judicial reaction on the war.

I took the briefcase with me when I took the witness stand the next day. When the lawyer asked me the leading question, to comment as an expert on the statement I'd picked by President Johnson, I said, "That statement is a lie." Everything stopped. The judge rapped his gavel sharply to interrupt the proceedings and ordered the lawyers to approach his bench. He spoke out of the hearing of the jurors, but from my seat on the witness stand, next to him, I heard what he said. He was very angry. He told the defense lawyer, "I warned you earlier that I would not allow any testimony in this courtroom critical of the government."

I was thinking: Critical of the government? What is this trial about? There are two people at the defense table facing long prison sentences for acts they acknowledge taking as expressions of criticism of a president's policy. They think he's conducting an immoral, criminal war; that's pretty critical all right! That's their motive. Can testimony or evidence on the reasonableness of their "criticism" really be ruled out summarily? As if he were reading my thoughts, the judge answered them by saying further at the bench: "The government and its policy are not on trial here. I'm warning you for the last time: If you try again to put on testimony that the government has lied, I will find both you and your witness in contempt."

The judge instructed the jury to disregard the last question and my answer. My testimony continued, but my briefcase stayed shut.

Apparently Don Oberdorfer told Kissinger my displeasure at his use of my name, because the next, and last, time I saw him, two weeks later, he came across the crowded room to offer his hand. He said, as we shook hands, "I must apologize if I embarrassed you at all with Don Oberdorfer."

I said, "Oh, no, Henry, no problem at all." I meant it, since I was glad that I'd had the occasion to set Oberdorfer straight on the policy.

This was at a reception opening a conference of MIT students and businessmen, many of them parents of the students, who were critical of the war. The idea of the conference, January 29–31, was to bridge the generation gap between the students and the businessmen, many of whom were liberal Republicans, in joint opposition to the war. The conference was called "Runnymede," after the field where the English barons had forced the Magna Carta on King John. An interesting choice of title; it more than suggested that the MIT students, as well as the businessmen, had an elite sense of themselves as barons in their confrontation with the king. It was going to lead off with a backgrounder by Henry Kissinger.

Kissinger's talk revealed to me why he was so enormously effective as a PR man. He was extremely smooth and persuasive. Aiming apparently at the students in the audience, he spoke about the "tragedy" of revolutionary movements having unfortunate destabilizing consequences and the "tragic" need to deal with them forcefully. In the question period he seemed equally self-assured and responsive. At one point he expressed some irritation, in a convincing way. Several questioners asked why the rate of withdrawal had not been faster, and he finally burst out after one of these: "You're questioning me as if our policy was to stay in Vietnam. But our policy is to get *out* of Vietnam. We are trending down the war in Vietnam, and I assure you that the war will continue to trend down." He pointed to troop reductions and declining U.S. casualties.

One question he turned aside, but again in a manner that strengthened his credibility. One of the student organizers of the conference, Mark Gerzon, asked him a probing question about developments in his life, growing up, that had affected his values and his perception of the world. It seemed to call for personal revelations that Kissinger declined to give. He said with some dignity, "You would not respect me if I attempted to psychoanalyze myself in public."

After a number of other questions, which he handled convincingly and with great poise, I got up, and he recognized me. I said that I had one question, but that I wanted to make one comment first, to respond to something he had just said.

"You have said that the White House is not a place for moral philosophizing. But in fact the White House does educate the people by everything that it does and everything it says and does not say. Specifically, tonight you *are* expressing moral values when you tell us that the war is trending down and will continue to trend down, and then in that connection you mention only U.S. troop presence and U.S. casualties. You failed to mention Indochinese casualties, or refugees, or bombing tonnages, which in fact are trending *up*. By your omission, you are telling the American people that they need not and ought not care about our impact on the Indochinese people, and you encourage them to support decisions that ignore that impact.

"So I have one question for you. What is your best estimate of the number of Indochinese that we will kill, pursuing your policy in the next twelve months?"

He was completely and obviously stunned. This was startling to the audience because it was the first time he'd shown any break in his composure at all. He lowered his head, frowned, and half turned away from the audience. He turned back, gave me a very penetrating look with narrowed eyes—I thought of him drumming the table with his fingertips at San Clemente—and said in an accusatory tone, "That is a very cleverly worded question. . . . I answer even if I don't answer."

I said, "I'm not trying to be clever. That is a very fundamental issue. Can you give an answer?"

He thought silently for a minute, then said, "You are accusing us of a racist policy."

It was illogical. But he was still fighting my wording, fighting for time. I said, "Race is not the issue here. Let me put it: How many human beings will we kill under your policy in the next twelve months?"

There was another pause. He paced. He was making no pretense of being in command of this exchange. The audience was very quiet. Then he burst out, "What are your alternatives?"

I said, "Dr. Kissinger, I know the language of alternatives and options very well, and that has nothing to do with this question. I'm asking you for an estimate of the consequences of your own policy in the next twelve months, if you know them. Do you have an estimate or not?"

There was another silence. Then the student who was moderating the evening got up and said, "Well, it's been a long evening, and I think we've had enough questions now. Perhaps we should let Dr. Kissinger go back to Washington." The meeting broke up. A few students crowded around Kissinger to ask him some last questions. I didn't try to approach him before he left.

The next morning I was in a workshop session in which I described what I believed to be the Nixon strategy to a small group that included Osborne Elliott, the editor of *Newsweek.* I talked about the likelihood that the next move would be, at best, the invasion of Laos; at worst, the invasion of southern North Vietnam. Elliott was extremely skeptical. He said that at *Newsweek* they'd had no indication of any such threat of escalation, of any kind. But after a midmorning break he came over to me and said, "Ellsberg, apparently there may be something in what you were saying. I've talked to my New York office. They just heard from our Saigon bureau that a total embargo has been put on news from South Vietnam. Something unusual is up."

By the next day the news was out that ARVN had invaded Laos, with U.S. combat support. It turned out that at the very moment Henry Kissinger was telling us that "we are trending down the war in Vietnam, and I assure you that the war will continue to trend down," the pre-invasion bombardment of Laos had begun. After taking the time from his busy schedule to give that assurance to this small, elite audience in Massachusetts, he had had to fly back to monitor the invasion. He must have been up most of the night.

On my return from the MIT conference, with the Laos invasion in full swing (not yet the ARVN debacle it became), I published an analysis and critique of Nixon's policy as I understood it. I called it "Laos: What Nixon Is Up To," but the editors of the *New York Review of Books* gave it the title on the cover "Murder in Laos." Three months later, Kissinger alluded to it by that title in the Oval Office, as evidence of my imbalance since he had known me in 1968. Skipping over my consultations with him in 1969 and 1970, he told the president, Ehrlichman, and Haldeman on June 17, 1971, that I had denounced him as a "murderer" at the MIT conference earlier that year. Actually, I had not used that word either at Runnymede or in the article, nor made any personal accusations whatever; but he was not, perhaps, oversensitive to hear it in my questions and comments. Drawing on our exchange at Runnymede, I posed the query in the *New York Review:*

> How many will die in Laos?
>
> What is Richard Nixon's best estimate of the number of Laotian people—"enemy" and "non-enemy"—that U.S. firepower will kill in the next twelve months? *He does not have an estimate.* He has not asked Henry Kissinger for one, and Kissinger has not asked the Pentagon . . . and none of these officials differs in this from his predecessors. . . .

I cited calculations made by Senator Edward Kennedy's Subcommittee on Refugees:

> At least 300,000 civilians have been killed in South Vietnam—mostly by U.S. firepower—between 1965 and 1970, out of at least one million casualties. Of

these . . . about 50,000 civilians were killed in Nixon's first year in office, about 35,000 in his second.

The article, which appeared at the end of February 1971, concluded:

. . . Americans must look past options, briefings, pros and cons, to see what is being done in their name, and to refuse to be accomplices. They must recognize, and force the Congress and President to act upon, the *moral* proposition that the U.S. must stop killing people in Indochina: that neither the lives we have lost, nor the lives we have taken, give the U.S. any right to determine by fire and airpower who shall govern or who shall die in Vietnam, Cambodia, or Laos.

25

Congress

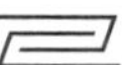

In late December 1970 I had what turned out to be my next-to-last talk with Senator Fulbright, in his office, about what to do with the Pentagon Papers. He now had nearly everything I had, including NSSM-1 and my notes on the Ponturo study of Tonkin Gulf. Norvil Jones had made it clear that there would be no public hearings on the war of the sort he'd envisioned back in May, during the Cambodian invasion. The public concern just wasn't there anymore, nor was there support for such hearings on the Foreign Relations Committee itself. The war had scarcely been an issue in the November congressional elections. Fulbright himself didn't disagree with my own urgent concern, after the failed Son Tay raid to rescue American prisoners of war, and the renewed bombing of North Vietnam, that the war would soon be getting larger, but he didn't see much possibility of mobilizing opposition in Congress until that happened.

As for the Pentagon Papers, Fulbright seemed sympathetic to my desire to find some way, apart from immediate hearings, to bring them to bear on the continuing war. He mentioned a number of ways in which it would still be possible to get the papers out with relatively little damage to me, though that wasn't my major concern. He raised the possibility of issuing a subpoena to Secretary of Defense Melvin Laird for the papers. He didn't have to limit himself, he said, to requesting them from Laird, as he had done several times so far. He could demand them.

At this point Norvil revealed what I take it had been his real worry from the beginning. He thought that the committee, even if it got the papers from Laird by request or subpoena, couldn't put them out to the public on its own, without administration approval. Even more, the chairman couldn't do it on his own because he and the committee were supposed to safeguard for the Senate as a whole classified material, which they got all the time and for which they had storage facilities. If Fulbright leaked the papers or went ahead and distributed or published them, he could be charged with having jeopardized the ability to get classified material from the executive, not only for the committee or himself but for the entire Senate. Jones also mentioned that the committee members, and in particular its staff members, were often accused of leaking. It was easy for me to guess that Jones himself didn't want to be accused of this. He had often shown great concern that I not reveal to anyone that I had given the papers to Fulbright.

Fulbright told me that he had asked Laird several times now for the study, but it seemed unlikely that he was going to get it. It was becoming clear to me that Jones was not going to encourage Fulbright to stick his neck out by releasing or using what I'd given him. Fulbright himself said to me, "Isn't it after all only history?" I said, well, yes, but it seemed to me quite important history. It was also a history that wasn't over yet. He said, "But does it really matter? Is there much in there that we don't know?" He asked if I would give him an example of a revelation that would make a big splash.

I said that it was not any individual page or revelation, or even a small set of them, that was very important. It was the overall detailed documentation of our involvement over the years and the repetitive patterns of internal pessimism and of desperate escalation and deception of the public in the face of what was, realistically, hopeless stalemate. It was the total lack of a good reason for what we were doing anywhere in the whole story. You had to read a lot of it, perhaps a thousand pages, covering a number of periods, to get the full effect. Moreover, it was still going on. That was the point. It was hard to believe that could be true unless you were exposed to a very long segment of this record.

After my talk with Fulbright in his office, Jones and I moved to Jones's office next door and continued the discussion. It was at this point that he suggested that I might just give the study to the *New York Times*. I said that I had already considered this possibility. It was considerably more risky for me legally, though I was prepared to do it if I had to. I asked Jones if he could think of any other senators who might be willing to release the study. He pulled out an extension board from his desk; taped to it was a list of all the senators' offices and telephone numbers. He went down the list with his finger, one by one, fairly quickly, looking for a probable candidate. He didn't spot one. I put the name McGovern to him. Jones thought not, though he agreed that McGovern was the most likely to do it. I mentioned Mathias and others. Jones really thought that no senator was likely to do it, but that a House member was more possible, having less to risk in some sense. The trouble was that a representative could not conduct a filibuster. He or she couldn't set out to read it into the record and might not even be able to have it inserted into the *Congressional Record.* It was much too long. Moreover, a House member wouldn't give me the same degree of protection, given the Senate's responsibility in foreign policy. However, he thought that Pete McCloskey, a Republican representative from California and a decorated war hero from Korea, was my best bet for using it. So I set out to check with McGovern and McCloskey.

In Cambridge in January I happened to talk with Sandy Gottlieb, executive director of SANE (Committee for a Sane Nuclear Policy), and we discussed filibusters and other out-of-the-way maneuvers. Gottlieb thought Gaylord Nelson was the most likely senator to do something like this. At the time of the Tonkin Gulf Resolution he had raised the sharpest questions on the floor about the dangers of giving the president a blank check, and he had even proposed an amendment to the resolution, drafted by his aide Gar Alperovitz, who was pressing him to force the issue, that ruled out expansion of the war without further action by Congress. But Fulbright had persuaded him that to force the joint resolution into a conference with the House to resolve the wording would defeat the purpose of sending a clear message of unanimity and determination to North Vietnam in the wake of the (supposed) attack on our ships and the president's "response." Nelson had not, at the end of the day, joined Senators Morse and Gruening in voting against the resolution. But as a later protest he was almost alone in voting against the defense appropriations bill because of the war. I mentally added him to my short list of prospects.

McGovern seemed to be the best of these, so in late January 1971 I called Arthur Schlesinger, Jr., and asked him to arrange a meeting for me. McGovern was running late by the time I got into his office and had to go off for lunch in a little less than an hour. I spent the time talking in general terms about Vietnam policy—he seemed interested in what I was saying about Nixon's aims—and political tactics. He made a very good impression on me with his views on what needed to be done and the importance of doing something radical. He said, when I asked, that he believed in filibusters and was definitely prepared to undertake one on the war (though he never did). He said he wanted to talk more, and we made a date for later that afternoon.

I went to the Senate cafeteria, where I happened to notice I. F. Stone eating alone. I'd never met him, but I recognized him from pictures. I had long wanted to tell him how right he had been about the war from the beginning in his remarkable newsletter. I introduced myself and asked if I could speak with him. He waved me down, peering at me from behind thick lenses, and we spoke for most of an hour as we were eating. He was so upset at the way things were going in Vietnam that at one point his eyes filled with tears. He said that when he talked to students, he just didn't know what to tell them about what could be done, things seemed so hopeless.

I began to tell him what I was trying to do, partly to cheer him up a little but also to get his opinions. Impulsively I told him what I was doing with the Pentagon Papers. I wanted his advice, but that wasn't the only reason I was taking such a chance. I was telling him because he was a hero of mine, speaking in the same spirit in which I'd sought out and told Janaki and Randy Kehler what I was doing, to let them know that they had inspired me and that I was joining their effort and, surely, to gain their respect.

His feeling was that McGovern was really the only bet, though he thought I should try Gaylord Nelson too. Stone offered to help any way that he could. He asked if I was ready to pay the consequences, and I said that I was. At the very end as I got up, he grabbed my arm tightly and told me, "Bless you for what you're doing, I admire you." Behind the thick lenses (he was soon to go blind) he again had tears in his eyes. It meant a lot to me to hear that from him.

I had more than an hour before I was supposed to see McGovern again, so I called Nelson's office, saying that Stone had suggested it. He happened to be free to see me right away. We talked in a leisurely way for about an hour.

I had a large batch of the Pentagon Papers with me in my briefcase, and I was prepared to tell him about them and offer them to him, but I needed to feel him out first on whether he was really prepared to do something unconventional or daring. His annual vote against the defense appropriations bill was already an example. I congratulated him on that, but he didn't seem to want to take much credit for it. Since he had so little company doing it, he thought of it as a purely symbolic gesture. But to my disappointment, after what Sandy Gottlieb had told me, it didn't appear from our discussion that he was ready to add anything to that gesture. When I raised the possibility of a filibuster—I thought of that as a litmus test for a senator's possible willingness to do something like reveal classified documents—he brushed it off with a shrug. He'd already raised objections to several other initiatives I'd mentioned—voting against appropriations aside from defense, discussing impeachment, obstructing various pieces of legislation or appointments the administration wanted, committing in advance to votes against appropriations, anything that hadn't yet been tried—dismissing them mainly on the obvious lines that they weren't very likely to work.

Finally I asked him what his own proposal was for ending the war. He said, "Well, picking up supporters one by one for the McGovern-Hatfield bill." I asked if he believed that could pass in the House, and the answer was "No, not really." I said that approach was fine if it ended the war before we destroyed Vietnam. He didn't seem to disagree with my description of the urgency of the situation, but that didn't appear to make him feel very desperate. He seemed oddly passive, even resigned about the impossibility of doing anything from the Senate to block further escalation. Of course his own experience with the issue justified a good deal of cynicism about his fellow senators, but I was beginning to wonder if by this point he was really all that different from them.

He didn't seem in a hurry to end our discussion, but his cool dismissal of one tactic after another as impractical or naive suddenly got under my skin, and I abruptly got up to leave. He looked surprised. I said, "You know, Senator, a few years ago when I was in the Pentagon, there were some things I could have done to stop this war, and now I'm sorry that I didn't do them. I hope a year from now you won't have to be sorry that you didn't try any of these things."

It was not a warm note to end on, and I didn't try to pretend that it was. I thanked him for giving me the time and left. I went to McGovern's office and waited for him. When he came back, we picked up our discussion where we'd left off in the morning, and as I heard his anguish about the war, I became more and more confident that the "messenger" that morning, the voice in my ear on the shuttle, was right: He was the man. He was desperate to see the war ended. He wanted to help end it. I wanted to help him.

I decided to lay it out for him. In his first speech announcing his candidacy for president, he had said that he wanted to tell the truth to the American people. I now told him, if that was what he really wanted to do, I could give him so much truth that he wouldn't be able to tell it all between now and November 1972. I described the McNamara study in some detail. I said

I'd copied it, told him about Fulbright and where that stood, said that I had parts of it with me, and offered to let him have it.

He agreed, enthusiastically. He wanted it, wanted to put it in the record from the floor of the Senate. He would filibuster with it. It was exactly what he needed. He mentioned that there was no legal risk for him to reveal this information on the floor of the Senate. Nor would he ever have to tell where he got it.

I told him what I'd told Fulbright, that I wasn't eager to go to prison but that I was ready to take any necessary risk. He said, more emphatically than Fulbright, that there wasn't any need for that. There was no way he could be compelled to reveal his source. He got up, went over to a tall bookcase in an alcove, and brought down a thick volume that contained the Constitution. He looked for a passage and read it to me. As a senator he could "not be questioned" about anything he said on the floor of the Senate. Couldn't be questioned, he emphasized, not by the FBI, the Justice Department, the executive branch, a judge, a grand jury, or his fellow senators.

I took that ringing reassurance mainly as a token of his own commitment to the project. It didn't really go very far to protect me, since I would be an obvious suspect and all of them could question *me,* all right. I had no intention of lying if I was asked directly under oath or by an authority, nor, after the experience of the McCarthy era, was I willing to take the Fifth Amendment. In fact, if I ended up, under investigation, acknowledging myself as his source, I would want him to confirm that I was telling the truth. But I liked the tone of his assertions and the energy he gave to them; it signified that we were in this together and that he would do all he could to protect me.

I did think I had a degree more protection giving the papers to a senator (or, if I had to, a member of the House) than to a newspaper, even if the applicable law didn't recognize a distinction. At a minimum I'd lose my clearances and my career, in any case, but there might be some hesitation to prosecute me if a prominent senator was championing the rightness of my giving the information to him and the public. Also, even if I was prosecuted, that might affect the verdict or at least the sentence. Still, what was more important to me was that the papers would be introduced in the Senate chamber, with every prospect that this would lead to hearings. McGovern was a member of the Foreign Relations Committee and could call for hearings, and presumably if Fulbright didn't have to fear executive retaliation for exposing the classified documents—since McGovern would already have taken personal responsibility for doing that—he wouldn't feel inhibited any longer about scheduling hearings and calling witnesses. Listening to McGovern's initial reaction, I felt as if I were on the way at last to getting these papers off my back and into the public consciousness.

In fact McGovern was sounding so unreservedly enthusiastic that I wasn't sure he was facing up to the political risks of this for himself. I didn't want to think that I was taking advantage of him, leading him into something that he hadn't fully calculated. I took the role of devil's advocate, confronting him with some of the challenges he might face. For example, he might be accused of using this as a campaign ploy. He said he thought that would not be a serious problem. His position on the war was long held and well known, and revealing this history would be very consistent with it, so he wouldn't be accused of electioneering. I asked, "What about the fact that these revelations would seriously embarrass former Democratic officials?" Wouldn't he be accused of undermining the party, and wouldn't that hurt his campaign funding? He answered that without hesitation on the most practical level. He said, "My sources of funding, for my campaign, are different from those of most of the others, like Muskie. The people who are backing me would like my doing this. It wouldn't hurt me."

I asked, "What about the accusation that you are running to be president, to be in charge of the whole secrecy system, and here you are playing fast and loose with it by disclosing all this classified material on your own initiative?" He said that would be the most serious charge. He would simply have to say that this was a special circumstance. We were in a bad war with no other way to bring it to an end, and it was necessary under the circumstances to reveal this information to the public. Indeed, from what I'd told him about the contents of the study, it would mainly be confirming charges and evaluations he had already been making for years. It was obviously information that the public deserved to have and Congress needed to have, which had been wrongly withheld. It was an abuse of the classification system to have concealed it.

He had the message, words, and music; I didn't need to help him with it. He sounded both sober and confident. He said, "I want to do it. I will do it." He told me to give the material I had with me to his assistant John Holum. Then he sounded a note that seemed prudent and responsible. He said, "That's the way I feel right now. But I don't want to give the final word today. I think I should let it sit in my mind for a few days. I won't speak to anyone else about it. I'll just live with it, to make sure I feel the same way a week from now. I'll call you in a week." That sounded more than reasonable to me. If anything, it was reassuring that he was taking this with the seriousness it deserved. We shook hands, and he introduced me to Holum, to whom I gave the contents of my briefcase.

I flew back to Cambridge and told Patricia the good news. Of course I had heard this once before; Fulbright had been just as enthusiastic and reassuring at first. But I really was feeling hopeful. I would even say that I was confident after our conversation that McGovern wouldn't change his mind. Yet when he called me in Cambridge just a week later to say, "I'm sorry, I can't do it," I reacted with a calm that seems surprising to look back on. I simply said, "I understand," and I believed that I did understand. I really did sympathize with his position as a presidential candidate. I wanted him to run a strong campaign, and my own reaction to his disappointing decision indicated that I must have had misgivings, more than I'd acknowledged to myself, about whether what I was proposing was really the right course for him. Still, I hoped that he might be an ally, an adviser, now that I'd shared the story with him. I didn't want to talk about it over the phone. I asked him if we could discuss the matter a little more when I was back in Washington—but not to reconsider his decision—and he said, "Certainly." We made a date for the following week.

After Senator Fulbright had said to me in December 1970, "Isn't it after all only history?" and after Senator McGovern too had backed off, Patricia asked me how sure I was that it was worth putting out the papers, worth the likelihood of prison for me. She said, "These senators don't seem to think it's worth the risk. Why are you so sure that they're wrong about that and you're right?"

I said, "Well, I can't be sure about that. They might be right. No one can say, and I don't know, what the effect will be. The problem is, I'm the only one who's read these documents. They haven't. So I can't go by their judgment. I have to rely on my own."

But now that we were married, the prospect of my going to prison didn't affect me alone. Patricia deserved to have a voice in that decision, and she couldn't really do that when she didn't know what was in the papers. Up till now I had deliberately kept her from reading them. I wanted her to be able to say that she hadn't known what was in them. But if she was to keep going through this with me now, she needed to have a better understanding of what it was about. The only way to get that was for her to read some of this material even if that increased her own risk. I thought the time had come for her to read some of the studies. She agreed.

I picked out some of the memos that I remembered from my own time in the Pentagon, 1964–65, about the pros and cons of various bombing strategies. I thought they would reveal to her how much the public had been misled in the 1964 campaign and afterward, with no knowledge that this Goldwater-like strategy had been advocated, taken for granted really, within the Johnson administration. The memos were by colleagues of mine like John McNaughton and Bill Bundy, one level above me in the bureaucracy, people I worked with and knew well.

Our third-floor apartment was a converted attic, with one large room that combined a kitchen and living room and a small bedroom just big enough for our bed. Patricia took the volume into the bedroom to read and closed the door, in case I had to use the phone. While she was in there, I sat at my desk in the living room, which was covered with piles of papers, and looked through other volumes of the study to see what else I should show her. After about an hour she came back into the living room, holding the volume I had given her. She had seen something in those pages that I hadn't seen when I first held them in 1964–65 or even when I reread them in the McNamara study. She pointed out to me that passages about alternative bombing programs were filled with phrases about "a need to reach their threshold of pain"; "We all accept the will of the DRV as the real target"; "Judging by experience during the last war, the resumption of bombing after a pause would be even more painful to the population of North Vietnam than a fairly steady rate of bombing"; "'water-drip' technique"; "DRV pain in the North"; "VC pain in the South"; "It is important not to 'kill the hostage' by destroying the North Vietnamese assets inside the 'Hanoi donut'"; "Fast/full squeeze" option versus "Progressive squeeze-and-talk"; "the 'hot-cold' treatment . . . the objective of 'persuading' Hanoi, which would dictate a program of painful surgical strikes separated by fairly long gaps"; "our 'salami-slice' bombing program"; "ratchet"; "one more turn of the screw" . . .

Patricia said, "This is the language of torturers." Her eyes were filled with tears. She said, "These have to be exposed. You've got to do it."

26

To the *New York Times*

On February 28, 1971, I was in Washington on a Sunday night to take part in a panel the next day at the National War College. I had dinner with Dick Barnet, Mark Raskin, and Ralph Stavins of the Institute for Policy Studies, a left-wing think tank. They were working on a book analyzing U.S. involvement in Vietnam in relation to war crimes. As background for their research I had actually given them parts of the Pentagon study, including my own draft of the 1961 decisions, and they had followed my efforts to get it out through Congress.

When they pressed me now on how I was doing, I told them about striking out with Fulbright and McGovern. They said that they thought it was very important that I get it out. They wanted their book out by June, and they were counting on being able to refer to the documentation in the study.

They told me I ought to take it to the *New York Times,* the same thing Fulbright and McGovern had mentioned. I had always thought of this choice as a backup, though it seemed unlikely that a newspaper would do more than publish some excerpts. But at this point it was looking as though Congress was closed off. Among newspapers, the *Times* was the obvious choice. It was the only journal of record, the only paper that printed long accounts, such as speeches and press conferences, in their entirety. No other paper would do that. Only the *Times* might publish the entire study, and it had the prestige to carry it through.

They asked me if I knew anybody at the *Times.* I told them I knew Neil Sheehan from Vietnam. I didn't mention that I had also given him top secret leaks in 1968. For that very reason I had tended to stay away from him in recent years. But now all the signs seemed to be pointing me in his direction.

On Tuesday, March 2, I was back in McGovern's office. He told me that though he knew he'd said he wouldn't discuss it with anyone else, he had decided he had to have legal advice, so he had gone to his close friend Gaylord Nelson, who was a lawyer. I kept a poker face as I heard this, but I could see where it was heading. I asked, "Did you mention my name?"

"I wasn't going to, I didn't say who had given me the material. But strangely enough, when I mentioned that it was a former official, Gaylord asked, 'Was it Dan Ellsberg?' So I said yes."

So much for the vows of silence the week before. I asked if Nelson had mentioned that he had met with me, and he said no, just that Gaylord said he, McGovern, was a presidential candidate and just couldn't do a thing like this. "He felt very strongly about it, and he convinced me."

I didn't argue. I wished him well on his campaign and left his office with no hard feelings. I really did understand. It was funny to hear that he had received his advice from Gaylord Nelson. I didn't think the advice was payback for my parting shot to Nelson; it was consistent with what I'd heard from him earlier in our conversation. The truth was, I thought, McGovern would have heard the same advice eventually from almost anyone he asked. I couldn't even say it was wrong. I didn't want to derail his campaign, which was obviously a very important medium for opposing the war. In some other year McGovern would have been the most promising member of Congress for my purposes, as his own first reaction had indicated. But it was plausible that if it was going to be a senator to deal with this year, it would have to be one who wasn't running for president. I had Senator Mathias in mind, and Senator Mike Gravel, who had replaced Senator Gruening and written me a letter congratulating me on my *New York Review of Books* article. I went over to Mathias's Senate office that same day.

Mathias and I hadn't talked for almost a year, since our plane ride back from St. Louis to a capital city filled with tear gas during the Cambodian invasion. But we'd both formed a good impression of each other during that trip, from our speeches and our talk on the plane, and we started our conversation that afternoon on a tone of mutual trust. Very quickly he was telling me in confidence that he was ready, as a Republican senator, to lead a movement against the war.

"That was the way Joe McCarthy had to be brought down," Mathias said. It had to be from the right, or rather, from the center, by another senator, and it had to be a senator from his own party, Senator Flanders. That was the way it had to be done. That's what we need now, on the war. And I'm ready to do it."

I was impressed, and I congratulated Mathias on his resolve. To take on an incumbent president from one's own party on any issue—an ongoing war, to boot—took guts. Senator Goodell had just been drummed out of that party and, in the midterm election the previous fall, lost his seat for his challenge to the White House on the war. Mathias was proposing to step into those shoes.

Well, I had something that might help him. After I'd told him about the study and what might be done with it, his response was that the historical study I was describing wasn't challenging *enough* to do the job. (I feared that myself of course by 1971.)

"That's history. It's the Democrats. I need revelations about *Nixon's* policy. Don't you have anything on Nixon directly?"

I did, as it happened. Not as much as I wanted, but better than nothing. I told him about the options paper and NSSM-1. I explained that the NSC documents I had didn't prove the case, but they did foreshadow Nixon's secret strategy, by showing interest in invasion of Cambodia from the very beginning of the administration and by showing that the White House had been warned at the outset of the limits of Vietnamization and the need for prolonged U.S. ground troops and indefinite U.S. air support.

Mathias was excited. He wanted the documents I was describing right away. Even if they didn't prove anything definitively, the drama of revealing them would lay down a challenge to the White House and open the debate on a strong note. I went through the usual discussion of the legal implications for me and my willingness to go to jail on this—if anything, NSSM-1, as a relatively current document from the incumbent administration rather than "history," seemed more certain to provoke a prosecution—and at this point, exactly like McGovern, he brought out the Constitution and read me the same passage: He could not be questioned. So the administration would not learn the source of his documents from *him.*

I hadn't brought a copy of either the options or NSSM-1 with me to Washington, but I remembered that I had given a copy to Norvil Jones for Fulbright. At the end of our discussion, I went over to the Foreign Relations Committee and told Jones that I needed to retrieve it. It was in a large manila envelope in a safe; Jones gave it to me. I took it right back to Mathias's office and handed it over to him and his assistant. It was a fairly bulky package, about five hundred pages. Mathias glanced through it and was very enthusiastic and appreciative. He said he and his aide would read through it and decide how to proceed. I repeated my offer of the Pentagon Papers as well, but he didn't even want to deal with them. They weren't as relevant; what I was now handing him was just along the lines of what he needed.

However, over the next couple of months I called Mathias's aide twice, to hear what was happening. He said they were still strategizing and laying the foundations for the campaign. It sounded good, but after my experience with Fulbright and McGovern, my hopes were not high.

In the late evening of Tuesday, March 2, 1971, after my afternoon talk with Mathias, I called Neil Sheehan at his home in Washington, D.C., and asked him if he could put me up for the night. He said he had a den in the basement with a sofa bed I could use. When I came over, he showed me downstairs, and I helped him make the bed up with blankets and sheets. But I didn't use it until dawn. We talked all night.

We started on an article he had just written on war crimes for the *New York Times Book Review.* But what came through was his passionate involvement with the war, his feeling that it had been a terrible mistake and a waste of lives on both sides, his intense desire to see it over. I hadn't run into this kind of urgency among journalists before, except for David Halberstam, or in many people outside the active antiwar movement. Sheehan's very readiness to entertain the notion that Americans might have committed war crimes, and that the war itself might be a crime, already stamped him as having one foot in that movement.

Before the night was over, I had described to him the McNamara study and told him that I had it, all of it. I told him of giving it to Fulbright, and where that stood, and that McGovern had agreed to use it, then changed his mind. (I didn't mention that Mathias had rejected it just that afternoon in favor of NSSM-1.) He was eager to see the study. He couldn't promise that the *Times* would use it, but if it was all that I said it was, he believed it would. I said I would show it to him in Cambridge, and we made a date for him to come up.

A week earlier, back in Cambridge, I had received a call from a reporter on the *Boston Globe,* Tom Oliphant. My article in the *New York Review of*

Books had caught his attention, and he asked to come over for an interview. I went over my analysis of Nixon's strategy and my concerns about where the policy was heading. I described to Oliphant how Nixon's secret threats fitted into a pattern of failed threats and escalations that had lasted over twenty years, and I told him—what I hadn't mentioned in the article or anywhere else—of the secret study of that whole period I had worked on and later read in its entirety. I'd never mentioned this to a reporter before, and I didn't intend to say much about it in this conversation. I didn't, of course, say that I'd copied it or had access to it. I just wanted to indicate that my warnings about the war were based on more than intuition. Oliphant seemed struck by a comment I made that the other two people who had read this whole history had drawn much the same policy conclusions from it as I had. He asked me who they were, and I told him Gelb and Halperin (since both of them were now out of the government). This exchange took only five or ten minutes out of a discussion that lasted well over an hour, and I didn't think much about it till I saw his story the following Sunday, five days after talking to Sheehan.

The headline on Oliphant's story on March 7, 1971, was: ONLY 3 HAVE READ SECRET INDOCHINA REPORT; ALL URGE SWIFT PULLOUT. In his lead he described the secret review of the history of the war ordered by McNamara and said, "Several individuals in the government at the time read parts of it, but as far as can be determined, only three men read every word of it. Significantly, every one of them today is of the opinion that the United States should withdraw from Indochina unilaterally and swiftly. Moreover, every one of them, before deciding to leave government service . . . held sensitive jobs during the formative months of the Nixon Administration."

After talking to me in Cambridge, Oliphant had gone to Washington to interview Halperin and Gelb. In the article he described their jobs under Nixon in 1969 and said that the following year, after the invasion of Cambodia, they had coauthored "a widely quoted article for the *Washington Post,* entitled 'Only a Timetable Can Extricate Nixon.'" He added: "Last month . . . [Halperin] signed on to run the 'peace office' at Common Cause, the citizens' lobby established by John Gardner, which two weeks ago announced its intention to join the fight for a unilateral withdrawal from Indochina." He quoted Halperin as telling him, "I think the President is not getting out. I think the present policy runs grave risks of further escalation, and I think it's splitting the country apart. Read that recent State of the World message. It's all there. I believe the President. He means what he says, namely, that we're not getting out."

Oliphant quoted me as saying that the study had had "an enormous effect" on my views. When I had started working on it, "I viewed the war as a well-intentioned effort, reasonable, though in retrospect, mistaken. But it soon became completely clear that American [decisions] were really a series of desperate gambles actually perceived as such by those who made them at the time."

"Looking back on his involvement," Oliphant wrote of me, "he said quietly during an interview, 'I was participating in a criminal conspiracy to wage aggressive war.'" He ended his piece with my comment on Nixon's current strategy: "'In my opinion, it is a criminal policy.'"

When I read this article, I suspected that it might draw the attention of the White House. Sure enough, Oliphant told me that the day it appeared Kissinger had called the Washington office of the *Globe* with inquiries about the article. Oddly, he had wanted to emphasize that Dan Ellsberg had never been a member of the NSC staff (the article didn't say I was). I also realized that it was the first time, as far as I knew, that the McNamara study had been mentioned in print. (It turned out later there had been two brief references to it earlier—one by Lloyd Shearer—but this was the first article on it.) It presented me with something of a crisis.

I'd discussed the study with Kissinger the previous August at San Clemente. He could quickly infer that if I were describing it in public now, along with my interpretation of its bearing on Nixon's secret policy, I might be about to release it myself, if by any chance I still possessed a copy after leaving Rand. The same applied to the FBI, which for some reason hadn't sought to interview me after approaching Carol a year ago. I didn't know then that a year earlier the FBI had discussed with Rand a report that I had copied the study and given it to Fulbright and Goodell; I still don't know whether the FBI had informed Kissinger in 1970 of this report or its discussions with Harry Rowen. But even without knowing this, I guessed that this story would be a red flag both to the White House and to the FBI. That meant that my apartment might be visited any minute by the FBI, with a search warrant or perhaps without one. For a year and a half my greatest fear had been that the FBI would swoop down and collect all my copies of the papers before they had been released by the Senate or elsewhere. Now, thanks to this article, that might happen within days.

I'd made at most three copies of large parts of the study, only two of some parts. After giving a complete set to Fulbright, I had just one or two copies left. I no longer had access to a private Xerox machine. I had put off, again and again, making more copies at a commercial shop because I had a feeling that the day I did it might be a day or two before the FBI turned up. I was afraid that a stray remaining top secret marking or a casual reading of the documents might result in a call to the police from the copy shop.

I showed the article to Patricia and told her what might be coming shortly. She said, more pungently than usual for her, "You've been talking about making more copies of those papers for months; now you'd better get off your ass and do it." She offered to help. We went immediately to her younger brother Spencer's apartment, where I'd stored the box of papers. It was going to be a job just to put them in order. I pulled out a section to leaf through. Just as I'd found in New York, on one of the first pages I looked at I found a top secret mark that had escaped my "instant declassification" techniques. There was nothing to do but go through every page once again, seven thousand of them.

Patricia took them over to a copying service in Harvard Square while I kept at it. It took all night and into the next morning. If there was a need to do this at all, it had to be done fast, before the FBI reacted to the article or to the White House or to a call from a copying service.

Big commercial machines were faster than the ones I'd used, but not nearly as fast as they are today, and multiple copies of thousands of pages took time. We needed to spread the work around to get it done quickly. Fortunately there were a number of shops near the square, and several of them stayed open all night. It was exhausting work. We would take turns lying down for an hour in the bedroom while the other kept going through the pages and occasionally scissoring. Every hour or two Patricia would take a load of papers over to one or another of the copy shops or go to pick up the copies.

The premise of this immediate effort was that the FBI, which I knew had known of my copying for a whole year, might well be triggered into tight surveillance of me by the Oliphant story. Catching us in the very act of copying would be a coup for its case. This possibility kept it interesting for Patricia to pick up the copies. Each time she came back to a shop there was the chance that the FBI would be waiting in the back room. By this time we had probably taken care of the markings or nearly all of them, but a lot of the content was unusual enough to attract the notice of anyone who bothered to read it. There were many references to plans and recommendations of the Joint Chiefs of Staff or Special National Intelligence Estimates by the CIA. What if somebody happened to read a little of what he was copying and got nervous about it? That was really why I'd hung back so long from having extra copies made. The top secret markings alone I could take care of, but there was no way to assure that documents with headings like these wouldn't ring an alarm bell for someone who took a look at it. So the pick-ups involved a good deal of suspense for Patricia.

Once we had our copies back, sorted them out, and put them in order in separate boxes, I had to find places to store them. One box went to my brother in New York. Others went to friends' attics or basements in the area; almost none of them was told what was in the box, just that they were papers I needed stored.

When Neil Sheehan came back to see me in Cambridge on March 12, I was sleepless from the nights spent making extra copies. Oliphant's article had significantly heightened my sense of anxiety—from the fear not of going to jail but of losing control of my copies before they could be released.

I took Neil over to Spencer's apartment, where I was storing copies, and showed him into the study. He had taken a room at a motel off Harvard Square. He could see at once, leafing through the pages, that the papers lived up to my description. To promote them to the *Times,* he said, he had to go through most of them, which would obviously take time. He asked to make a copy, but I didn't want that to happen—not yet.

There were two key considerations in my mind. On the one hand, I was determined, one way or another, that a large mass of the documents themselves should become available to the public. I was skeptical about whether the *Times* would be willing to do that. At the same time, I was afraid that if the papers went to the *Times* before the management had made any commitment or even had developed an inclination to publish them, someone there would inform the FBI, or the bureau would somehow get wind of it and come after my other copies.

If the newspaper was (1) committed to publishing and (2) planning to publish large sections of the study, with actual documents, then the loss of my other copies (and my own indictment) would be no great problem as far as I was concerned. But if it was not the case that both these conditions obtained, then the loss of the other copies, and surveillance of me by the police, would mean that the game would be over as far as publication outside Congress was concerned. The longer the documents were there, without a decision, the more people would learn about them and see them, and the bigger the chance that one of them would inform the government. The upshot of these calculations was that I didn't want any large amount of these papers to go to the Times Building unless and until someone high up there had decided the newspaper was ready to publish, and to publish large quantities of them.

I was counting on Neil to serve as the *Times*'s representative on this. I was ready to let him see the documents as much as he wanted and to take notes. But I wouldn't let him make a copy to take back to the newspaper.

It seemed obvious that he couldn't give me a commitment on this right away, as he pointed out. He would have to give his editors a good picture of what there was, and there would have to be high-level discussions of what it meant for the *Times.* Moreover, I told him, I knew that a guarantee could never be absolute. On something like this, I understood that however surely they promised and actually intended to carry it out, they could always change their minds at the last moment. That was a risk I would accept at the point I gave them the papers.

I told him, "When I let you copy these and take them off, I'll be resigned to the fact that I've lost any control over them. That copy is out of my hands. For practical purposes, they'll be yours [i.e., the *Times*'s], to do with as you choose. I can't affect that; that's the way I'll look at it. I couldn't keep you from printing, in whatever form, and I couldn't make you print. So my giving you a copy will be my agreement to letting the *Times* have them and print them, as it chooses. In effect, it will mean giving my OK in advance to whatever you do."

I knew I couldn't make "conditions" in the sense of written, contractual guarantees that could be enforced by any sanctions. But on two points, before I agreed to giving the *Times* a copy of the study, I wanted assurances as strong as I could get: first, that the paper did intend to publish something; second, that it would be a "big story," with a great deal of space allotted to it—that it would not be just a single day's story, large or small, but a multipart project that could do justice to the text and documents, pages and pages of print. In a later meeting Neil assured me that if the *Times* did go ahead and print, it would be as "big" as I could want. He even went beyond that to assure me that it would print the documents verbatim. I hadn't made that a condition on the same level as the others, but he knew it was something I wanted very much, and he agreed with me. I also asked that the *Times* give "serious consideration" to publishing the entire study eventually through a book-publishing arrangement.

We didn't talk about protecting me as the source. I took it for granted that it would do that, up to a point, and I didn't ask for any special measures if it came to the paper's facing legal pressures. I didn't want credit either as a source or as a participant in the study, but I didn't make any requests on how the *Times* handled that. I assumed that the government would know, or assume, that I was the source. But I told Neil what I had told the senators: that I didn't want to taunt the government into prosecuting me if otherwise they were inclined not to prosecute, whether for political or legal reasons.

Neil's response to all this was entirely to reassure me about the *Times* as the best channel for this information—which he obviously thought must be delivered to the American people—and the likelihood, though not certainty, that he would convince his bosses of this. Meanwhile he had to read through the material and take notes. After a while we left him to it. I couldn't stand over him the whole time. I told him I was counting on him not to go against my wishes, not to take the material over to the square and get it copied. I told Patricia that I really didn't think he would do it after that. It was a chance I would just have to take. We dropped in on him frequently, and he was always tired but increasingly excited and enthusiastic. He continued to press for the need to copy volumes to convince his editors, but he seemed to accept my limiting him to a few sample pages. After a couple of days he left, with the understanding that he would return soon for a longer stay.

When he did, he brought back the news that his editors were definitely interested, but that—unsurprisingly—there was a lot of debate, uncertainty, and qualms about the project. They needed to know more about the content. That still wasn't good enough to make me willing to hand over the whole study or even volumes of it. He settled down to read more, take more notes, and prepare himself better to sell them on it. His own attitude wasn't in question. He never complained about the length or the dry parts. Neil's obsession with the war was on a par with mine, and for such a person—above all, for a journalist who knew he had been lied to but, like all his colleagues, could never have dreamed just how much—this material was endlessly fascinating.

By the time Neil left again, he was more committed than ever to convincing his bosses that this story deserved unique play, but in several telephone calls from New York over the next few weeks the word he gave me was not very encouraging. They were having trouble deciding and not moving very fast toward a resolution. He still hoped, and in fact expected, that they would eventually move to publish it, but it wasn't clear how long it might take before they got really serious about it. Neil himself, he told me, had been assigned to work on other stories. (All this turned out to be false.)

In April he called to say that although his editors were still dallying on a decision and he was working on another project, he wanted to keep working on the study in preparation for their eventual decision to use it. He would have to work nights and weekends on it, and he could do that only if he had a copy in New York. Was I ready to let him have one? By this time the continuing escalation of the war had made me feel even more pressed to get the papers out. I had become increasingly doubtful of getting anywhere with Congress. I didn't count on the *Times*'s going ahead, after this much delay, but I didn't have much of an alternative, and by this time I was ready to take a bigger risk. On that basis, I said yes.

In agreeing to hand over a copy, even in the absence of any assurances that the *Times* planned to run the story, I was aware, as presumably Neil was, that I was signaling my trust in him to use the material as he saw fit. It was my consent for the *Times* to publish at its discretion. But in fact, as I learned later, he did not need my consent, or my copy for that matter. What I did not know, what he chose not to tell me, was that the *Times* had already rented several suites in the New York Hilton, where a team was working over the Pentagon Papers on a crash basis, writing commentaries and selecting parts of the text and documents for inclusion. They had had a full copy of what I had shown to Neil for more than a month.

Parts of this story came out over the next two years (though major parts remain obscure or puzzling to me to this day). Near the end of my trial, on belated discovery, we got the contents of Howard Hunt's White House safe, which included a chronology by Hunt indicating that Neil and Susan Sheehan in March had checked in under assumed names at hotels in Cambridge and had taken thousands of pages, eventually the entire study, to local copying establishments in Medford and Boston.

One weekend, when he knew I would be out of town with Patricia, Neil had come secretly to Cambridge and used a key to Spencer's apartment that I had given him. He removed the whole study, and he and his wife took it to a copy shop in Medford.

Meanwhile, unaware of these behind-the-scenes developments, I proceeded with my efforts to raise awareness of Nixon's policies, while seeking out any promising avenues for getting the papers out.

27

May Day 1971

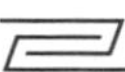

The antiwar organizer Rennie Davis had called for a big demonstration in Washington on May Day, enough people to shut down the streets. The slogan was "If They Won't Stop the War, We'll Stop the Government." A group of us in Cambridge who got together to consider what to do next, an affinity group, wondered if we should endorse this in Boston and encourage people to go down to Washington. What did it mean, "stop the government"? Were they planning violence, like the Weathermen? Was it well planned? Was it likely to get out of control? There was talk in the movement press that there would be "mobile tactics." What did that mean, beyond not sitting still, waiting to be arrested? Did it mean overturning cars, putting barrels in the streets, throwing things?

No one wanted violence, but it didn't seem very well organized. It was hard for us to decide whether we wanted to go down ourselves. We didn't want to take part in a replay of the melee at the Democratic National Convention in Chicago in 1968. As of a couple of days before May Day, when I attended a rally at Brandeis at which I was scheduled to speak, I still hadn't decided whether I wanted to go. The fate of the Pentagon Papers was still undecided, as far as I knew. I was still looking for members of Congress who might make them public, while otherwise trying to find other things worth doing. Nothing looked very promising.

The auditorium in Brandeis was packed; people were sitting in all the aisles and stairways; there was very high energy. I never planned what I was going to say beforehand, and as I got near the end of my comments, I started talking about the possible usefulness of nonviolent civil disobedience. The thought came into my mind of a line in the recent film *Little Big Man,* in which Dustin Hoffman plays an old man reminiscing about his long life among the Indians, which included surviving the Battle of the Little Bighorn and the massacre at Wounded Knee. The analogies to Vietnam were on everyone's mind. I said, "You remember the line that goes through the movie, a saying of the Lakota, the Sioux, just before they go into a battle: 'Come, brothers, this is a good day to die.' Well, the truth is, it's never really a good day to die. But I think that May first is a good day to get arrested in Washington."

There was a wild response. They all got up to their feet and applauded and hollered. I went home and said to Patricia, "Well, it seems that I'm going to Washington."

Our affinity group,* which had independently come to the same decision, got to Washington late in the evening. The organizers had been working to find places for thousands of people to stay, in schools, churches, and homes. We were directed to someone's house, where we found scores of people already trying to sleep on every available surface. All the beds and couches were taken, and many people were just lying on the floor, some in sleeping bags, others on rugs or the bare floor. We found space on the floor of a basement recreation room and slept for a few hours. By about four-thirty everyone was up, getting ready. The light was still dim; there was only one orangy lamp in the basement room. Young people, mostly in their late teens or early twenties, were filling water bottles and putting food in small packs, brushing their teeth, writing on the backs of their hands numbers of lawyers to call when they got arrested. They were quiet and businesslike, focused.

It reminded me very much of the dim lights in the hold of a troopship, at four in the morning on the day of an amphibious landing exercise, the troops in the narrow aisles between the four high bunks adjusting their web gear and packs and getting ready to go over the side. I suspected that, underneath, the young people in Washington felt very much the way the young soldiers did before they went down the cargo nets on the side of a ship into a heaving landing boat. Apprehensive, excited. None of them had ever been arrested before, any more than I had, and they didn't know how

*Howard Zinn, Marilyn Young, Fred Branfman, Mitchell Goodman, Noam Chomsky, Zelda Gamson, Cindy Frederick, and Mark Ptashne.

they were going to do or how the police were going to act. But none of this showed.

It was still dark when we went outside, and we were prepared to walk downtown if we had to. But as soon as we got to the corner a taxi stopped for us. A black woman was driving, and she asked if we were going to the demonstration. When we said we were, she offered us a lift free of charge. She'd read about the event in the papers, and this was the second load she'd ferried over. We heard later that all over town taxis were doing this, especially ones with black drivers. Many ordinary drivers on their way to work were also giving rides when they saw groups of young people heading downtown.

It was light by now, overcast and gray. On the other side of the Washington Monument we could see troops in field gear and wearing helmets. They looked to me like marines, and I went up by myself to see who they were. I talked to a couple of them, and I was shocked to learn that they were Fleet Marine Force troops from my old division, the Second Marine Division, brought up from Camp Lejeune, North Carolina. I looked around and saw how young they were, even the platoon leaders, like the people I had woken up with that morning. They looked familiar to me, family. I didn't think it was right to give marines this kind of duty. Apparently some of them felt the same way. They were holding rifles with one hand and giving us the peace sign with the other.

Back at Fourteenth Street, knots of people were standing on the grass in front of the monument, and it seemed time to get started, whatever we were going to do. Cars were going past toward the Fourteenth Street bridge, not in a steady stream, but one at a time. They were going at a pretty good clip, but we figured they could see us ahead, and they wouldn't want to hit us. They were going in the general direction of the Pentagon, in Arlington across the Potomac, so this seemed like a logical spot to stop traffic. Our affinity group moved off the sidewalk and sat down in the middle of the street, in a circle facing outward, shoulders touching. A couple of cars went around us, slowing down. We could see police a block or two away, pushing people back onto the sidewalks. Clouds of tear gas were drifting toward us from somewhere down the street where other people had been sitting.

Then we saw a policeman in full gear just across from us on the monument side pull down a long plastic mask in front of his face and start for us. He was drawing a can of Mace from his belt. At the same time another policeman was coming at us from the direction of the bridge, this one holding a long club. His plastic mask was tilted back on top of his helmet, and he was raising the club as he approached. They both were coming at us at right angles to each other. We looked at one another, and apparently we all had the same thought, that it was too early in the morning to get arrested. We scrambled up and moved out of the way, just as the two cops converged on us.

What happened then was like a beautifully choreographed scene from the Keystone Kops. I can still see it in my mind in slow motion, as if it had been perfectly rehearsed. The policeman coming up from the south was leaning forward with his club raised high above his head, and the policeman with the mask on sprayed his Mace at us, only we weren't there anymore, so the spray hit the other cop, square in the left side of his unmasked face. I watched him as he staggered, dropped his club, and knocked his helmet off as he clutched his face in his hands. The cop who had Maced him put his arm around him to hold him up, no longer paying attention to us as we began moving back onto the Mall.

Now that we all had discovered the meaning of "mobile tactics," we looked for the next place to do the same thing again. We did it a couple more times, of course never again with such spectacular results. We sat on narrower streets, where the cars tended to stop in front of us instead of trying to go around. When policemen drew near, we got up and moved off. The police concentrated on moving the traffic instead of chasing after us. If they had, we wouldn't have run or resisted arrest. We were, after all, academics of one sort or another.

This being a company town, most of the people in these cars were on their way to doing the normal business of the government, which among other things meant pursuing the war in Vietnam, even if the people in the particular cars we were stopping weren't working directly on that. We weren't stopping the government, for sure, but for the drivers it wasn't business as usual. We were giving them a little pause on their way to work, a moment to think, conceivably, about the work they were trying to be on time for and why some people would behave this way to try to stop it. Doubtless many of them were simply thinking about how irritating this was and that we were wasting their time. But not all of them, surely. Quite a few honked and smiled and flashed peace signs out their windows.

On one side street, in front of a ramp that funneled traffic to an underpass beneath some buildings, we actually stopped a line of cars for quite a while before a policeman found us. By that time we weren't expecting to be pursued or arrested, and we just got up when he came up to us and went over to the corner and began walking up the street. This one seemed to be following us because I could hear Fred Branfman behind me saying something to him. I turned around to hear what they were talking about. The policeman was a middle-aged man wearing an ordinary uniform, no helmet or mask, with a noncommittal expression. Just as I looked around and as Fred was talking to him, he calmly held up a can of Mace and shot it at me. He hit me directly in the eyes, as I presume was his intention.

I had been tear-gassed before, that morning in fact, and in marine training I had spent minutes in a tear gas chamber without a mask, but this was a different experience. I couldn't see anything, and I was totally disoriented. I didn't know where I was. Someone was holding on to me, holding me upright. It was the kind of effect with Mace I'd read about. When I could talk, what I said was, "God, that's good Mace!" As if I were a connoisseur. What I meant was that this was a product that really worked as advertised.

By that time in the morning we were all ready to get arrested, but the police didn't seem interested in obliging us. They had pretty well scattered the demonstrators, so traffic was flowing fairly normally on the main streets. The demonstration seemed to be over. As far as we had seen, no one had been arrested at all. We sat and talked for a while in Lafayette Park, across from the White House. No other groups were in sight. Someone called up I. F. Stone from a pay phone and arranged for us to meet him at a Chinese restaurant for lunch. Afterward we decided to disperse, some to engagements we had planned to miss, expecting we would be in jail. Noam flew off to Texas to an event at a GI coffeehouse, one of the centers supporting resistance to the war within the army.

I took the shuttle to New York to go to a lecture at the Council on Foreign Relations by McGeorge Bundy. It was the first of three lectures he was scheduled to give there, supposed to be published later as a book. Someone said it was his bid to be considered for secretary of state in the next Democratic administration, after he left the Ford Foundation. However, Bundy's lectures were never published. The publication of the Pentagon Papers six weeks later, covering the same period he was talking about, exposed his account as rather misleading. His brother's memoir on Vietnam, on which Bill Bundy had been working for two years at MIT, suffered the same fate.

I went from La Guardia to Patricia's apartment in New York, where I had some clothes in the closet and could take a shower and put on a suit. I had to scrub down more than usual. My hair, like all the clothes I'd been wearing, was saturated with the smell of tear gas and Mace. After washing that out of my hair and putting on clean clothes, I turned up at the Council on Foreign Relations late that afternoon, along with a crowd of former bosses and colleagues from the Pentagon, the State Department, and the embassy in Saigon. The whole Vietnam establishment, all the former ambassadors and cabinet officials, was there to listen to Bundy. It looked to me like the defense dock at Nuremberg. The difference was that none of us had yet been indicted. (In the end I was the only one who was.)

In Washington, after breaking up the demonstration by late morning and restoring the flow of traffic without arresting many people, the police had started making mass arrests about the time we were having lunch. It no longer had anything to do with the morning's demonstration, which was over. The police made no effort to find out if the people they were grabbing had had anything to do with the demonstration, and most of them hadn't. If you were young and had long hair, all you had to do to get arrested in Washington that afternoon was to walk down the street in Georgetown. Tourists, students between classes, shoppers, the children of some members of Congress all got swept up.

Thirteen thousand people were arrested in Washington that afternoon and evening. There were too many to put in jail, so they were held in Robert F. Kennedy Stadium. The police had no evidence that any of them had even been in an antiwar protest or done anything illegal, except those they knew, like Abbie Hoffman, who had his nose bashed in again by a two-by-four in the course of his arrest. Most of them probably hadn't been protesters at all, though the night in RFK Stadium might have planted the seeds of rebellion. Many years later they got a small settlement for false arrest after a class-action suit.

But I didn't know any of this was happening as I listened to Bundy in New York, saying there had been "no intent to mislead Congress" in connection with the passage of the Tonkin Gulf Resolution; the resolution "was not meant to be [in Nicholas Katzenbach's phrase in 1967] a 'functional equivalent of a declaration of war.'" I remember thinking, Oh, man, Bundy, don't do this. Don't keep saying things like this in public. It's too late; this stuff is going to be coming out soon.

It was a surreal experience, after a morning of mobile tactics on Fourteenth Street, to be sitting in a room surrounded by my fellow war criminals, listening to Johnson's assistant for national security tell lies about the war.

28

Approaching June 13

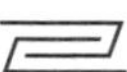

Although the Laos invasion had ended in a debacle, Nixon showed no signs of scaling down his objectives or his strategy, which I felt pointed toward still further escalation. In fact there had been disquieting talk of expanding the ground war into North Vietnam in connection with that invasion. Prime Minister Ky had openly called for it. I'd been concerned about the prospects and pace of escalation ever since the Son Tay raid in November; the Laos invasion hadn't surprised me. I was hoping the release of the papers might lend momentum to the McGovern-Hatfield bill in the Senate cutting off U.S. funding for the war. The approach to the *Times* didn't seem to be catching hold.

I'd heard Pete McCloskey speak against the war on a couple of occasions and had been very impressed by him. He had a very quiet way of speaking, which underscored the unusually powerful and uncompromising things he was saying. He was an especially valuable member of an antiwar panel because he gave it a bipartisan nature; he was one of the few Republicans willing to criticize a president of his own party. He even spoke of intending to challenge Nixon for the nomination on the issue of the war if it was still going on in 1972.

After we both spoke at a panel at Princeton, I asked to see him privately. It seemed hard to arrange a time. He was just about to fly back to his district in California, and he suggested that I go with him. It would give us several hours together. It seems strange, in retrospect, that I would take a cross-country flight at my own expense just for this opportunity, but that was what I did. I brought a full briefcase with me and handed him several volumes of the Pentagon Papers to read when we were on the plane.

He agreed fully with the importance of getting the study out. He said he would do it on the floor of the House, if necessary. But first he felt he owed it to his committee to try to get it officially. I told him that Defense Secretary Laird had several times refused to give it to the Senate Foreign Relations Committee, but he thought he had at least to go through the motions of trying to get it through channels. I gave him the rest of what I had brought, for him to read in California.

When he got back to Washington, he did get his committee chairman to request the study, and he mentioned the study in testimony before the Senate committee, leading Fulbright to complain in open session at his inability to get it and to request it once again from Laird. McCloskey told me that he wasn't really expecting to get it, but that he had to give the administration some time to respond.

It looked as though I would need a lawyer soon. I made an appointment for the last week in May 1971 to see Jim Vorenberg, who was teaching at the Harvard Law School. Patricia knew him slightly because he had been a Harvard Law classmate and friend of her brother-in-law's. We both went over to his large house in Cambridge in the evening and started with small talk about her sister and brother-in-law. Patricia and I were in easy chairs facing him, in a corner of the living room. I told him my background and of my work on the McNamara study, which I described in some detail. I explained how the history related to Nixon's policy as I understood it, why it was important for Congress and the public to know it, what I had done so far, and what was in progress. But I hadn't gotten very far in that last part before he suddenly held up his hand and said, "I have to stop you right now. I'm afraid I can't take part in this discussion any further."

"Pardon me?"

"You seem to be describing plans to commit a crime. I don't want to hear any more about it. As a lawyer I can't be a party to it."

The top of my head blew off. I got up out of my chair and said in a low, tense voice, getting faster as I went along, looking down at him: "I've been talking to you about seven thousand pages of documentation of crimes: war crimes, crimes against the peace, mass murder. Twenty years of crime under four presidents. And every one of those presidents had a Harvard professor at his side, telling him how to do it and how to get away with it. Thank you, good night."

I decided to turn to someone else I had met briefly a year earlier, Leonard

Boudin, who was also in Cambridge that year, as a guest lecturer at Harvard Law. We had been introduced by the radical lawyer Peter Weiss, who had said flatly, "Leonard Boudin is the most distinguished constitutional lawyer in the country." He had argued, and won, many civil liberties cases before the Supreme Court. I called him the day after I had talked to his colleague at the law school. We talked in the basement office of the house he was renting in Cambridge. I liked him very much. He heard me out, and at the end he said, "You know, I'm not a hero or a martyr. I'm a lawyer. But I've represented people like that. I'll be happy to represent you."

Soon after this I read in the newspaper that Senator Mike Gravel was planning to filibuster the bill extending the draft when it came up in June. He didn't yet have any colleagues willing to join him, but he was willing to do it alone. As I said, that was a kind of litmus test of senatorial initiative, as I had come to see it. Southern senators almost routinely, reflexively filibustered civil rights bills, alone, if necessary, yet not one filibuster had ever been conducted against the war. Gaylord Nelson had brushed aside my suggestion, and Senators Harold Hughes and Charles Goodell had told me they would consider it only if they could round up others to join them, as was unlikely. With only one or two speakers, not only was it certain to fail, but it would look obviously futile and grandstanding, absurd. "And, Dan," Goodell explained to me, "that is the one thing you cannot afford to do in this chamber: look ridiculous, be a laughingstock." So here was a new senator, perhaps less socialized in the ways of the Senate, willing to stand up alone and look silly. And on a good issue to protest. What could these old and middle-aged men be thinking of, raising their hands when the draft required their positive assent to be extended, to send more young men to this war in its seventh year?

I'd heard nothing for several weeks from Neil Sheehan about the possibility that the *Times* might bring out the papers, and before that, only vague optimism on his part. Senator Mathias hadn't decided yet when or how he would use the copy of NSSM-1 I'd given him. Gravel sounded like the best bet in the near future. I thought I might have to fly to Washington with a set of the papers to give him on Monday. In preparation for that, I got a set from Spencer's apartment. It was the first time since we'd made copies that I had allowed a set to be in our own apartment at 10 Hilliard Street.

Saturday night, June 12, we had a date with Howard and Roz Zinn to see *Butch Cassidy and the Sundance Kid* at the University Theater on Harvard

Square. I'd seen it twice before; it was one of my favorite films. That morning I got a phone call from Tony Austin, an editor of the *New York Times.* He had come up to Cambridge sometime during the previous fall to interview me for a book he was writing on the Tonkin Gulf incidents and their aftermath. He had impressed me with his energy, insight, and determination to solve the mystery of the "second attack" on August 4. On this last point I told him that I doubted if he could fully succeed in dispelling all uncertainty. Despite my skepticism I had decided to help him by giving him what I had. I described the McNamara study to him, and without telling him that I had a copy of the entire study, I had let him read an excerpt from it, the volume on the Tonkin Gulf incidents. To my astonishment, he was eventually able to provide conclusive evidence that dispelled any remaining possibility that the North Vietnamese had launched a second attack on our destroyers on August 4. Had he published this in the *Times* I thought it would certainly deserve a Pulitzer Prize. But he had wanted to save his conclusions for his book *The President's War.*

Now on the phone Austin was almost in tears. He said in despair, "Dan, my book is ruined! It's coming out in a couple of weeks, but my book is sunk. It's a disaster!"

I told him I didn't see how that could be. What had happened?

He said, "That study you showed me part of, the *Times* has the whole study, including that part; they're starting to bring it out today. The building is shut down tight. They're checking everybody who wants to come in or out. They're afraid the FBI will come after them before they can print. They're expecting an injunction."

I said that was very interesting. I said I guessed it was a good thing the *Times* was bringing out the study. But why would that ruin his book? After all, all it would have on the Tonkin Gulf was the volume I'd shown him. He'd gone far beyond that even before his big discovery. If the newspaper printed the whole study, it would raise interest in the history of the war and specifically in the subject of his own book. It would raise questions about the Tonkin Gulf that only he could answer. Maybe the timing was perfect for him.

I was speaking soothingly, trying to reassure him, but he was distraught. He was sure that the *Times*'s series on the whole war would outweigh his narrow book and smother any attention it might have gotten. I asked him casually if he knew how the *Times* had gotten hold of the study, but he didn't. I said, well, let's hope for the best and see how it comes out, and he hung up.

My heart was pounding. I dialed Neil's number at the *Times.* While I waited for him to answer, I was thinking: So they're worried about an injunction, are they? They're expecting the FBI any moment, and Neil hasn't mentioned that to *me;* he hasn't given me any warning over the last week or the last month or, for Christ's sake, *this morning*! When was he going to tell me? And I had a full copy in my living room at this moment, for the first time in months!

Neil didn't answer his phone. Half an hour later, after giving Patricia the news, I called him again. No answer. I called his desk at the paper and left word for him to phone me. I didn't hear from him that day (or the next).

I had to get the documents out of our apartment. I called the Zinns, who had been planning to come by our apartment later to join us for the movie, and asked if we could come by their place in Newton instead. I took the papers in a box in the trunk of our car. They weren't the ideal people to avoid attracting the attention of the FBI. Howard had been in charge of managing antiwar activist Daniel Berrigan's movements underground while he was eluding the FBI for months (so from that practical point of view he *was* an ideal person to hide something from them), and it could be assumed that his phone was tapped, even if he wasn't under regular surveillance. However, I didn't know whom else to turn to that Saturday afternoon. Anyway, I had given Howard a large section of the study already, to read as a historian; he'd kept it in his office at Boston University. As I expected, they said yes immediately. Howard helped me bring up the box from the car.

We drove back to Harvard Square for the movie. The Zinns had never seen *Butch Cassidy* before. It held up for all of us. Afterward we bought ice-cream cones at Brigham's and went back to our apartment. Finally Howard and Roz went home before it was time for the early edition of the Sunday *New York Times* to arrive at the subway kiosk below the square. Around midnight Patricia and I went over to the square and bought a couple of copies. We came up the stairs into Harvard Square reading the front page, with the three-column story about the secret archive, feeling very good.

29

Going Underground

On Monday evening, June 14, 1971, we went to a dinner party at the house of Peter Edelman and Marian Wright Edelman. It was jammed with people sitting on the floor and sofas with plates in their laps, and there were two topics of conversation: What the Pentagon Papers were revealing, and who had given them to the *New York Times*. Patricia and I listened without contributing much. Jim Vorenberg was eating, on the floor, in one corner of the room. Our eyes didn't meet.

Tuesday morning the third installment appeared. Attorney General John Mitchell sent a letter to the *New York Times* asking it to suspend publication and to hand over its copy of the study. The *Times* declined, and that afternoon the Justice Department filed a demand, the first in our country's history, for an injunction in federal district court in New York. The judge granted a temporary restraining order while he considered the injunction. For the first time since the Revolution, the presses of an American newspaper were stopped from printing a scheduled story by federal court order. The First Amendment, saying "Congress shall pass no law . . . abridging the freedom of speech, or of the press," had always been held above all to forbid "prior restraint" of newspaper or book publication by federal or state government, including courts and the executive branch. The Nixon Justice Department was making a pioneering experiment, asking federal courts to violate or ignore the Constitution or in effect to abrogate the First Amendment. It was the boldest assertion during the cold war that "national security" overrode the constitutional guarantees of the Bill of Rights.

I got a call from Dunn Gifford, a friend of Neil Sheehan's, whom I had met a month earlier. He had told me then that Neil had asked him, as a former naval intelligence officer, if publishing cables of the sort in the study might lead to compromising U.S. codes. He had said, correctly, no. In telling me this, he had also remarked cryptically that I should realize Neil would follow his own priorities as a journalist, not mine.

In his phone call Tuesday morning Gifford followed up his earlier warning by urging me strongly to give the papers to the *Washington Post,* now that the *Times* was enjoined from continuing publication. The idea hadn't occurred to me, and my first reaction was to say, "I wouldn't do that!" Already by Saturday night, when I saw the first installment in the *Times,* I had gotten over my irritation at Neil and the *Times* for keeping me in the dark the previous three months. When I saw how they were handling it and the impact they were achieving, I was nothing but happy over their treatment of the story, and I already felt a warm sense of obligation toward Neil and the *Times,* whatever distance they had decided to keep from me. It seemed almost certain that Neil or the *Times,* or both, would win a Pulitzer Prize, which would be well deserved. For me to give the study now to the *Post* might undercut that or force them to share the prize. Or the *Times* might lose its incentive to keep on with the publication, at the planned length, if parts were being published elsewhere.

Neil and I had never discussed exclusive rights to the story for the *Times,* but I had taken it for granted that the editors would demand that if they met my conditions for giving it to them, and that was fine with me. He may have been less than certain that I would abide by such an agreement. It seems that a major, perhaps crucial consideration pushing the *Times* toward publication, despite its lawyers' reservations, was a concern, fueled in part by Neil, that otherwise I would go elsewhere and it would be scooped by the *Post.* Oddly, he was raising that likelihood by pretending for so long that the *Times* was still on the fence. But in fact I never considered telling another paper about it once I started talking with Neil, and I told Gifford I felt a loyalty to Neil by now, and I couldn't compromise it by giving "their" scoop to the *Post.*

Gifford pointed out that what was at stake here was much larger than how much credit the *Times* or Neil got. He believed it was essential to keep the momentum going, to maintain a continuity of public interest in the contents of the papers. Who knew how long it would be before the *Times* could resume publication? We couldn't even be sure that the injunction would be denied! This could be the end of the revelations—unless other newspapers were prepared to pick up the torch, in defiance of the Justice Department and the administration.

His arguments were powerful. I had to think about them, though I continued to have a strong sense of uneasiness about crossing Neil and the *Times.* The commitment and risk they had taken on in deciding to publish were now apparent. In view of the unprecedented injunction, the possibility that they would face criminal indictments no longer looked small. (In fact the Justice Department was making serious preparations for this, to follow my own trial, before very long.) They may not have treated me as a partner, but I admired their courage, and I felt grateful to them, as a citizen and an activist.

On the other hand, I had to take seriously Gifford's warning that the whole process might stop for good unless I moved it forward. Thanks precisely to the administration's decision to treat the publication as a national crisis, justifying unprecedented efforts to censor the press, the contents of the Pentagon Papers were getting amazing attention. Newspaper readers had to assume that the history that the executive branch was so anxious to suppress was unusually worth their reading. I had always believed that the full impact of this story depended on the full sweep of the history being available. It wasn't any one page or volume or individual revelation that was so dramatic; it was the tenacity and nature of the patterns of deceit and recklessness and cynicism that were ultimately stunning. For that to register on any one reader or the country as a whole, much more had to come out.

The first three installments in the *Times* had dealt with the Johnson administration, but a teaser in Tuesday's paper had indicated that the next installment would focus on Eisenhower. I didn't want the history course to be short-circuited just there. The more I thought about it, the more Gifford's proposal appealed to me.

The *Times* considered printing Wednesday morning's paper with dramatic pages of white space instead of the planned installment. White space by reason of government injunction would be a first in any American newspaper, and, one hoped, the last. But it ran other stories instead. There was plenty of news and analyses to fill the space, since the injunction itself triggered one of the greatest constitutional confrontations of the last two centuries. Television, which had almost entirely ignored the low-key first installment of the papers on Sunday, was now devoting at least the first fifteen minutes of the half hour nightly national program on each of the three major networks to the Pentagon Papers and the court cases.

Late Tuesday night someone called me from *Newsweek* to set up a meeting with a bunch of editors the next morning. I met for breakfast off Harvard Square with Lloyd Norman, the newsmagazine's Pentagon correspondent, whom I'd known for years, and Joel Blocker, a senior editor. They started off by informing me that their cover story for next week would be the release of the Pentagon Papers and that they planned to name me as its source. I said, "I'm not going to comment on who the source may have been. But I'll comment all you want on the contents of the papers and what I think they mean. I had access to the whole study, and I've read it all."

Blocker said, "We're convinced you're the source, but we can't go ahead unless you're willing to confirm it."

I said that I wasn't going to speculate about that, but that I had no doubt, as someone who had worked on the study and who knew it well, that it was a good thing it was being published. The public needed and deserved to know everything that was in it. Likewise, Congress. In my opinion, every word of the study should be published in some fashion. There could be no harm to national security in that, only benefit. I should be happy to go into specifics of the contents, at any length they wanted.

The senior editor said, "Look, it comes down to this. There won't be a cover story unless we have your confirmation on the source."

"Too bad. You're missing a big story on the contents of these papers if that's true."

We talked for more than three hours, ending up at my office at MIT. In his account of the interview (appearing June 21), in which he said I "flatly refused to comment on whether he had, in fact, turned the classified papers over to the *Times,*" Blocker quoted me as saying: "I'm glad it's out. . . . I wish it had been available to the Congress and the public two or three years ago. The documents show that Presidential assistants and other officials had virtually unlimited license to lie to the public. But now, those responsible for the escalation of the war will be held to account for the papers they signed."

Blocker reported I had told them of my fruitless efforts to get high government officials like Henry Kissinger and Undersecretary of State John Irwin to read the study or at least the summaries and learn from them. With no hint from me, *Newsweek* had later interviewed John Holum, Senator McGovern's legislative aide, and Pete McCloskey, both of whom said that I had offered them classified documents. According to Holum, "He said he'd make them public even if it meant he had to go to jail." (This from the Senate office that had said it would never mention my name, in an issue appearing more than a week before I was indicted.) "On [Holum's] advice, McGovern turned down the offer."

But it wasn't my opinions on the contents of the study or on the war that the *Newsweek* editors wanted to report, eager as I was to offer those. "Ellsberg, 40, proved to be an intense, almost a compulsive, talker. . . . With an insistence close to obsession, Ellsberg kept returning to the salutary effects of the documents' publication. They were, he said, 'the best we have—a good starting point for a real understanding of the war, the U.S. equivalent of the Nuremberg war-crimes documents.'"

They were unhappy as we parted. But I wasn't tempted to give the confirmation that they wanted at this point. As yet there had been no indication that the Justice Department had decided to seek criminal indictments in addition to the injunction. I wasn't surprised that *Newsweek* had been led to me as the probable source so quickly—the last line of its story on the interview was that I had said with a smile, "I am flattered to be suspected of having leaked it"—and I was sure that Justice was in little doubt by this point. But I was determined not to goad the administration into an unprecedented criminal prosecution by taunting it publicly, if it had any inhibitions about indicting me. A cover story would have been a good forum—God knows the *Times* hadn't asked me my opinions about anything—but I didn't think my contribution was essential. The thousands of pages of documents could speak for themselves—if they got out. And as it turned out, *Newsweek* did do a cover story, as I'd hoped, not on me but on "The Secret History of Vietnam" (June 28, 1971, appearing June 21).

As soon as Blocker and Norman left, I went to a pay phone and made arrangements through a friend to call Ben Bagdikian at the *Washington Post.* Bagdikian had left Rand to return to the *Post* as an editor the year before. I took it for granted he would be hunting for a way to get a piece of the papers; I guessed, correctly, that he would already suspect that I was the source and was probably trying to find me. But it wasn't a call I could take at home. Through the intermediary, "Mr. Boston," Ben got directions to call a number in Cambridge from a "secure phone." It was a 617 number, and Ben read this message as coming from "Mr. Boston in Boston." He figured it was a pseudonym and decided he'd better make the call. He went across the street to the Statler Hilton and phoned from a coin telephone. Mr. Boston said he had a message from an old friend, but Ben would have to give the number of a pay phone where he could be reached. Ben gave the number of the phone next to his.

When I called Bagdikian a few minutes later, he recognized my voice. I asked him if the *Post* would print "the papers" if it could get them. He said yes. I asked if he could commit the *Post.* He said he would have to call back.

We arranged that if he got assurance, he should make a reservation at a Boston or Cambridge hotel, call a different number with an answering machine, and leave the message where we could meet. He suggested the message "Mr. Medford from Providence [where he used to work] will wait for you at the hotel." I told him to make the reservation quickly because most hotels were full for commencement week. He should bring a large suitcase.

Ben got the go-ahead from his managing editor, Ben Bradlee, who added, when Bagdikian called him from the airport, that if he got the goods and they weren't in the next day's newspaper, the *Washington Post* would have a new executive editor. Bagdikian checked into his Boston motel under the name Medford and, as he told me later, was dismayed when the clerk said he had a message for a Mr. Bagdikian, who was expected about the same time from Washington. Did that have anything to do with him? Apparently I had forgotten the cover name; I didn't have my friend's instincts. Ben identified himself, saying that he wrote under the name Medford. As he got to his room, he got a call from me to go to a Cambridge address to pick up the material and to tell the clerk to let some friends into his room while he was out.

When he came back in a taxi with one of two identical cardboard boxes he'd been shown in a Cambridge cellar, he found Patricia and me waiting for him in his motel room. I had meant for him to bring the second box as well; I had to call Cambridge, and before long someone delivered it to his room. Meanwhile we had been going through the first messy box of papers. It had nearly a full set of volumes, but they were out of sequence, and because of our several stages of "declassifying" with cardboard strips, scissors, and paper cutter, there were very few page numbers. Most of the numbers had coincided with a top secret marking that we'd removed. The second box, when it arrived, had the same contents. It reflected a condition I wanted to make on giving the material to him, which at first Bagdikian was very reluctant to accept. I wanted him to give the second box to Mike Gravel if the senator from Alaska was willing to use them. Ben's sense of professionalism conflicted with his acting as any kind of intermediary to Congress. As a layman I wasn't very sympathetic about that problem, under the unusual circumstances. The *Post* obviously wanted what I had to give it, and it seemed to me it could do me this favor. I couldn't see any other way to get the papers to Washington quickly. Finally he agreed.

I had, as he recalls, two other conditions. The *Post* wouldn't reveal my identity—that he took for granted—and it would not print the date-time groups or message numbers of any cables it reproduced. Already various people were charging that the *Times* publications had compromised secret codes. I was sure that wasn't true, but I wasn't sure that the government would admit that in court. We spent much of the night at the motel with him, cutting out footnotes with date-time groups and trying to sort out the various volumes. Patricia went home to get some rest while we kept working. Ben made reservations back to Washington, first-class reservations for "Mr. Medford and one." He meant to take the suitcase with the papers on the seat next to him. Early the next morning we realized that the suitcase Ben had brought wasn't nearly big enough. He decided he had to take them to Washington in the large cardboard boxes they came in, but we didn't have string or tape to close up the second one. In the early morning he went down to the desk to get a piece of rope. The desk clerk couldn't find any, but he suggested that Ben look outside where guests sometimes tied their dogs. He came back with six feet of rope from the fence next to the swimming pool. Ben packed up the box and left for the airport. I called Patricia and told her to come back and get me. I rested on one of the beds till she arrived.

Before we left the motel room, we turned on the TV to catch the local morning news. We saw our own porch at 10 Hilliard Street on the screen, with two men identified as FBI agents knocking on the door. The announcer explained that they were seeking to question Daniel Ellsberg for possible help in their investigation of the leak of the Pentagon Papers. After a few moments of knocking without an answer, the two men were photographed leaving. Patricia and I had a feeling they might not have gone very far. We hadn't come expecting to spend the night, let alone a second one—we hadn't brought so much as a toothbrush—but it didn't seem a good time to go home. Nor did it seem a good idea to stay in a room checked out to Mr. Bagdikian of the *Washington Post.* We checked into a hotel on the Cambridge side of the Charles River under assumed names. The next morning we moved to another. For the next several days we moved through various motels in Cambridge. Later, hideouts in apartments and houses in Cambridge were found for us. It was twelve days before we got back to our apartment.

Watching the news on the morning of Thursday, June 17, we soon learned why the FBI had chosen that day to call on our apartment. Late the night before, while we were working away in the motel trying to put the papers in some sequence, a journalist named Sidney Zion had appeared on the Barry Gray talk show in New York and announced that he had discovered that I was the source to the *Times* of the Pentagon Papers. As I'd expected, both the White House and the FBI had already, on the basis of initial interviews, identified me as the prime suspect, but my FBI file reveals that it was Zion's announcement that triggered instructions from Washington FBI headquarters to the Boston office to interview me immediately. The New York office was instructed to interview Zion. In both places, thanks to the publicity the night before, the FBI agents encountered hordes of press and cameramen staked out at the residences. Zion refused to say anything further, and we weren't found at home, since we'd spent the night with Bagdikian. But if Zion hadn't made his announcement, there wouldn't have been any TV cameras outside 10 Hilliard Street to record the visit of the FBI agents, and we wouldn't have seen the scene on live television. Instead we would have been in the scene when the agents met us as we returned or found us there that afternoon. Things worked out extraordinarily well, though it wasn't obvious right away that Zion had been particularly helpful.

The main secret to avoid being found by the FBI (in the 1970s) seemed to be: Don't use your home or office phone. The people who helped us find places to stay and who distributed the papers for us communicated face-to-face or on randomly chosen pay phones. Not one has ever been questioned by any official or grand jury or identified in the press from that day to this. (After thirty years of anonymity they all seem to want to keep it that way. I haven't been able, yet, to persuade any of them to come out publicly or to let me express our gratitude to them by name.)

For thirteen days we were subject to what was described in the press as "the largest FBI manhunt since the Lindbergh kidnapping." FBI agents were reported interviewing people in so many parts of the world that I began to suspect that some were abusing the opportunity to take junkets. We were in Cambridge the whole time, in five different locations, moving sometimes after one night. The arrangements were made by several key friends, who drew on their own friends among graduate students and others in the neighborhood. It's notable that all these people cooperated in the face of widespread publicity that the FBI was hunting for me. In theory, they just wanted to question me, but it was clear that at any moment a warrant could be issued for my arrest, and our hosts could have been indicted for harboring a fugitive. It was a time in our country's history when you could reach out to almost any young person and say, "I'm doing an action against the war. It may help, it may be important, but it could be dangerous for you. Can you help?" One friend told us later that she simply called acquaintances from antiwar rallies and other activities and told them, "I need your apartment for a few days. We'll take good care of it. Please don't ask me any questions." No one asked, and no one turned her down. To this day I've never known their names.

On one occasion, "Mr. Boston" went downstairs and across the street to a phone booth on the corner, about fifty yards from the apartment building where we were staying that afternoon. He talked for about ten minutes to my friend Lloyd Shearer in Los Angeles, relaying some questions I had for Shearer, who was giving me advice on whom to deal with in the media. We happened to be looking out the front window when he left the booth and came back. Just as he entered the front door, perhaps twelve minutes from the time he placed the call, four police cars converged on the phone booth from two directions. Brakes screeched, and police jumped out with guns drawn, though the booth was now empty. Evidently Shearer's line was tapped. We all dropped to the bare floor below the level of the windows, which had no curtains, as the police began looking up and down the street. When they left, we arranged to spend the night somewhere else.

Sometimes we stayed in one apartment for two or three days. Except when we moved, mostly at night, Patricia and I were alone together most of the time. Looking back, I realize it was the quietest, least stressful two weeks we were to have at a stretch for the next two years. There wasn't much we had to do, except to decide which newspaper to deal with next and what parts of the study to give it. The actual arrangements all were handled by our helpers, since we couldn't even use the phones or go out to use pay phones or do any errands. I told people where they could pick up documents to deliver, but they took it from there; generally they didn't even tell me how they were doing it.

Our friend "Mr. Boston" turned out to be very talented at clandestine operations. When he had first contacted Ben Bagdikian for me, some of his arrangements for communicating or passing on the documents struck some editors as being more elaborate than necessary, but they worked. The FBI wasn't able to intercept one transfer, as parts of the papers turned up in one spot after another across the country. It was also his idea to parcel out subsequent portions to one paper at a time. He recalls that my own first inclination, after the second injunction, was to dump the rest of it out to a number of papers at once, to make sure it all got out before I was stopped. He quickly persuaded me, from his own earlier experience working for a member of Congress, that it would be better to keep the story going by approaching one at a time, which he undertook to arrange. He deferred to me to pick the next outlet each day, and he made the contact and arranged the handover.

What made all this somewhat easier was that no one had to do a lot of negotiating to get a newspaper to agree. Nearly every major paper wanted to get in on the action—impressively, given the unprecedented legal actions and evident fury of the administration—and not one we approached turned down the opportunity. After the *Washington Post* was enjoined, the *Boston Globe* was an obvious choice for the next recipient, not so much because it was our local paper as because it had been one of the first and strongest to oppose the war. That was also true of the *St. Louis Post-Dispatch,* which I thought had earned the right to invite an injunction. (It received one, along with the *Globe.*) As Sanford Ungar has noted, it may be a coincidence that the only four newspapers that were enjoined, out of twenty that printed sections of the papers, were all strong critics of the Nixon administration and skeptical about the war. Others I picked on more idiosyncratic grounds. The *L.A. Times,* which I thought had also done good reporting on the war, was my former hometown newspaper; the Knight chain of eleven newspapers included my father's town of Detroit; and the *Christian Science Monitor* was my father's main paper (he sent me subscriptions to it for many years).

Our friends brought us food and newspapers and toilet articles, shirts and underwear and socks. Patricia and I spent the days together reading the newspapers and watching the news on TV. I remember in particular one program we watched on the last day of our quiet time together, Sunday, June 27, the day before I surrendered to arrest at the federal courthouse. General Maxwell Taylor was being interviewed by Martin Agronsky, in a program that had been taped earlier. He was describing his recommendations to President Kennedy in November 1961. He was telling Agronsky and the American public ten years later: "I did not recommend combat forces. I stressed we would bring in engineer forces, logistic forces, that could work on logistics and help in the very serious flood problem in 1961. So this was not a combat force. . . . I did not recommend anything other than three battalions of infantry. Pardon me, three battalions of engineers."

A decade had passed since his actual recommendations, and the president to whom he had given them was dead. I recall thinking two things as I listened to him: The president's men think they have a license to lie that never expires, and "Watch what you say, General. Your cables are coming out any day now."

Two days after this interview was aired, the Supreme Court lifted the injunctions, and the *Times* resumed publication the next day with the Kennedy era. Among the documents it printed on Wednesday were Taylor's eyes-only cables to the president in late October 1961, describing the immediate introduction of U.S. ground combat forces as "an essential action if we are to reverse the current downward trend of events. . . . In fact, I do not believe that our program to save South Vietnam will succeed without it," and describing the "engineer" role as a cover story that would not long be plausible.

An exactly contradictory impression of Taylor's recommendation had been given at the time, in 1961, and had persisted for years. A decade of deception ended on the eve of my arraignment. If this history still mattered enough to be lied about, it mattered enough to be worth revealing, even at a personal price.

Time magazine got word to me through Charlie Nesson, a Harvard law professor who had agreed to join our legal team, that it was going to do a cover story on me but needed to spend time with me for interviews. Derek Shearer, working with us, discussed this with his father, Lloyd, who urged me strongly not to do it. He said the daily press reporters would be furious if I gave an exclusive like that, especially to *Time,* which they looked down on (the managing editor at *Time,* Henry Grunwald, had consistently muzzled and overruled his reporters on the war; several had resigned). They would look on me as just seeking personal publicity. I should continue to try to keep the focus on the war and the contents of the papers, not on me. I sent word to *Time* that an interview would be impossible; I didn't have time for it. It continued to press. It said it couldn't do a cover without an interview; it had a rule about that. I said, too bad then. It offered me three pages to say whatever I wanted, with no editing, as part of the piece. That was tempting, and I felt a little guilty about turning down the chance. But I knew it really would take my attention away from what we were doing, and I should stay focused on what was happening. In the end *Time* did the story anyway. It was the first cover it had done without a personal interview, I was told, since the one on Adolf Hitler in 1943. At the last minute the editors got through to me with just one question. Were my eyes brown or blue? We told them blue. That was all they asked. It did make a difference, though. Later someone from *Time* gave me an earlier proof copy of the issue with my portrait on the cover, with brown eyes.

Time had gotten photographs of me (not in color) from my father in Detroit, as had *Life.* He had boxes of photos of me. A number of them showed me in Vietnam, mainly when I was in Rach Kien, wearing field gear and carrying a Swedish K submachine gun. *Life* had a big picture of me lying in a rice paddy with the K to my shoulder. Another showed me in my marine blues. I used to think that those pictures from Dad probably helped me out, discouraging the White House from pressing the notion that I was unpatriotic. Instead it had to fall back on the spin that I was erratic, flaky, a little nuts, as shown by my radical change; though this raised the question of why I had been trusted so long with so many secrets and consulted at high levels, and by Republicans as well as Democrats. Even sympathetic stories exploited the drama of the supposed extremity of my shift in views. The headline in *Life* was FROM HAWK TO VIOLENT DOVE. I thought the adjective for my present state was interesting, since it was for the previous period that its pictures showed me carrying a machine gun.

Dad's testimony about me in Detroit was very helpful too. I read it in AP dispatches and saw him a couple of times on television. It warmed my heart. He was after all a Republican. My radical brother couldn't stand to talk with him about politics. Dad (who was eighty-two years old) had voted for Richard Nixon *twice.* Yet when he was interviewed about me, he wasn't just sympathetic; he was eloquent in total support of what he assumed I was doing. When he was interviewed by the *Detroit News,* he said, "Daniel gave up everything to devote himself to ending that foolish slaughter. . . . If he did give them that report, and if the government accuses him of some crime . . . well, he might be saving some boys they'd have sent there otherwise." The article went on: "Ellsberg said his son 'gives me so damn many things to read about the war that we don't waste time talking about it when we're together. We know where we stand—and it's in the same corner.'"

I hadn't given him any clue to what I was planning or doing and no warning (I didn't have any myself) about what was about to happen. I wasn't able to call him while I was hiding. But in other interviews he laid out the issues as well as I could have written the words for him. Really better. He spoke of the Constitution and the role of free speech in our democracy; the terrible, hopeless, wrongful war; the men who had been lied to death by the deceit of our presidents; the lives I was trying to save. It was thrilling for me to hear this from him. A week after we went underground, at my request Tom Oliphant conveyed the message, in his story about me in the *Globe,* that "he wanted his father Harry Ellsberg . . . to know that he is deeply grateful for the expressions of support he made to the press last week." Where had all this come from? He told me later, "It was from you. I started out supporting the war, but your letters from Vietnam opened my eyes."

What was happening in the country was astonishing, unprecedented. A newspaper industry that for thirty years and more had been living happily—when it came to foreign policy and defense matters—on government handouts was suddenly in widespread revolt. One paper after another was clamoring for its chance, not just to get a piece of a story but to step across the line into radical civil disobedience. There had never been an injunction that had stopped the presses before in our history. Before the Supreme Court ruled, there had been four, and there could just as easily have been twenty.

Every paper that published after the initial temporary restraining order against the *Times* was defying a solemn White House and Justice Department proclamation that they were causing irreparable harm to national security. The people and institutions doing this were justly known as pillars of the establishment. For any one of them to contemplate challenging to this degree in action the urgent judgment of the president and commander in chief in wartime would have been in the most literal sense unthinkable, before it happened. Reading about it and watching on TV in our various hideouts, I thought it was marvelous. They were going through the same process I had, learning the need to think for themselves, to use their own judgments about what was right for them to do in a crisis, discovering their own readiness to risk recrimination and face heavy penalties when they had to. I felt an obligation, while this situation lasted, to spread that opportunity as widely as I could. That meant that television networks too should have the chance to join the mutiny.

The TV news programs were already devoting half and more of their nightly news programs to the confrontation with the government, but that reporting didn't put them in the position of the press that was actually publishing the papers. The networks so far were just reporting on a revolt, not participating in it. But now that their counterparts in the press had risen to the challenge of showing some real courage, I thought the national networks should be given the opportunity to stand with them.

We started with NBC because I'd seen a picture of its president, Julian Goodman, on its nightly news, supporting the *Times*'s publication of the secret study. One of our friends got through to the high executive levels at NBC with a message of congratulations from me to Goodman, and my offer to help him join the *Times* by releasing a large so far unpublished segment of the Pentagon Papers on his own network. Within half an hour Goodman had turned this down. ABC declined even faster, immediately on hearing the offer. But CBS showed real interest, over a matter of days.

The decision was finally negative, but that was made only reluctantly after a full day of soul-searching by the highest brass. A major consideration was that CBS was just at that moment involved in a legal confrontation over its documentary on military public relations, *The Selling of the Pentagon.* A congressional committee had recommended that CBS be charged with contempt of Congress for refusing to turn over its outtakes (film that was not used in the final version) to an investigation. The House of Representatives was just about to vote on the recommendation, and Frank Stanton of CBS and most of his subordinates thought that it would prejudice that vote, and would be taking on too much at one time, to defy the Pentagon's classification policy in the same week. I could understand that, and I respected the fact that in contrast with the other two networks, CBS had really wrestled with the issue. For that reason, a few days later, when all three networks, through intermediaries, were asking to interview me while I was underground, I found it easy to pick CBS.

I hoped it would choose as the interviewer Walter Cronkite, the anchorman for the evening news, described as "the most trusted man in America." It was Cronkite who, on his return from Vietnam just after the Tet offensive in 1968, had said to his audience that we were mired in a "stalemate," using the word the White House had dreaded for a year. President Johnson, watching that, said to an associate, "I've lost Middle America." Weeks later he withdrew from the presidential campaign.

In the late afternoon of June 23, Cronkite and his crew arrived at a large house in Cambridge, where I was waiting for him. Parts of the interview were shown on the early evening news, with a late, half-hour version from ten-thirty to eleven that same night. In the body of the interview I had an opportunity to present at some length to a prime-time national audience an understanding of Nixon's secret strategy and how it resembled what I had done in the Pentagon in 1964.

Some of the passages, including the opening and end of the program:

Cronkite [opening]: During the controversy, a single name has been mentioned most prominently as the possible source of the *Times'* documents. Daniel Ellsberg, a former State Department and Pentagon planner, and of late something of a phantom figure, agreed today to be interviewed at a secret location, but he refused to discuss his role, if any, in the release of the documents. I asked him what he considers the most important revelations to date from the Pentagon documents.

Ellsberg: I think the lesson is that the people of this country can't afford to let the President run the country by himself, even foreign affairs, any more than domestic affairs, without the help of the Congress, without the help of the public. . . .

Cronkite: Isn't this correcting of this problem of public information more in the character of the leaders in Washington than it is in anything that can be legislated? . . .

Ellsberg: I would disagree with that. It seems to me that the "leaders"—by whom, I think, you're referring to the executive officials, the Executive Branch of government—have fostered an impression that I think the rest of us have been too willing to accept over the last generation, and that is that the Executive Branch *is* the government, and that indeed they are leaders in a sense that may not be entirely healthy, if we're to still think of ourselves as a democracy. I was struck, in fact, by President Johnson's reaction to these revelations as "close to treason," because it reflected to me this sense that what was damaging to the reputation of a particular administration, a particular individual, was in effect treason, which is very close to saying "I am the state." And I think that quite sincerely many Presidents, not only Lyndon Johnson, have come to feel that. What these studies tell me is we must remember this is a self-governing country. We are the government. And in terms of institutions, the Constitution provides for separation of powers, for Congress, for the courts, informally for the press, protected by the First Amendment. . . . I think we cannot let the officials of the Executive Branch determine for us what it is that the public needs to know about how well and how they are discharging their functions. . . .

Cronkite: How was [this study] kept a secret from the White House?

Ellsberg: The fact is that secrets can be held by men in the government whose careers have been spent learning how to keep their mouths shut. I was one of those.

Cronkite: The documentation being somewhat incomplete, "flawed history" is what some have said of it.

Ellsberg: It's a start. It's a beginning toward history. I would say it's an essential beginning, but it's only a beginning. . . . In the seven thousand pages of this study, I don't think there is a line in them that contains an estimate of the likely impact of our policy on the overall casualties among the Vietnamese or the refugees to be caused, the effects of defoliation in an ecological sense. There's neither an estimate nor a calculation of past effects, ever. And the documents simply reflect the internal concerns of our officials. That says nothing more nor less than that our officials never did concern themselves with the effect of our policies on the Vietnamese.

Cronkite: How would you describe the men who do not have the same emotional reaction to reading this, to knowing these, being privy to these secrets, as you? Are they cold? Are they heartless? Are they villainous?

Ellsberg: The usual assumption, of course, the usual description of them is that they are among the most decent and respectable and responsible men that our society has to offer. It's a very plausible judgment, in terms of their background. And yet, having read the history, and I think others will join this, I can't help but feel that their decency, their humane feelings, are to be judged in part by the decisions they brought themselves to make, the reasons for which they did them, and the consequences. I'm not going to judge them. The evidence is here.

I'm sure this story is more painful for many people at this moment than for me, because of course it is familiar to me, having read it several times, but it must be painful for the American people now to read these papers—and there's a lot more to come—and to discover that the men to whom they gave so much respect and trust, as well as power, regarded them as contemptuously as they regarded our Vietnamese allies.

Cronkite: What about the immediate effect [of these revelations] on the war as of these days in June, 1971?

Ellsberg: Yes, the war is going on. . . . I hope the Senate will go much further. I hope that they discover that their responsibilities to their citizens, the citizens of this country and to the voters, do go beyond getting reelected, and that they're men, they're free men who can accept the responsibility of ending this war.

My father had a favorite line from the Bible, which I used to hear a great deal when I was a kid: "The truth shall make you free." And I hope that the truth that's out now—it's out in the press, it's out in homes, where it should be, where voters can discuss it—it's out of the safes, and there is no way, no way to get it back into the safes—I hope that truth will free us of this war. I hope that we will put this war behind us . . . in such a way that the history of the next 20 years will read nothing like the history of the last 20 years.

In its brief before the District of Columbia Circuit Court on Tuesday, June 22, the *Washington Post* in effect acknowledged the legal impact of the efforts of our underground team to keep spreading the papers around. "The newspaper also warned the appellate court that 'the government's efforts will ultimately prove futile'; with more and more newspapers breaking the story, 'one thing is certain: public revelation of the contents will soon become available to the American public.'" The "certainty" of this of course depended on our network's not being penetrated by the FBI and rolled up and on the supply of copies' holding out. All the releases were coming directly or indirectly from us. The timing and urgency of Patricia's pressure to make those copies had serendipitously proved to be indispensable, though no one had foreseen these particular circumstances that made them so valuable.

A Nixon appointee, Judge Roger Robb, raised the issue of further disclosures in other newspapers, wondering if the government was "asking us to ride herd on a swarm of bees." He was presumably referring to the newspapers, but "a swarm of bees" was a nice description of our pickup team of clandestine operators.

On Thursday, June 24, the metaphor of a swarm of bees was overtaken by that of the breaking of a dam. Across the country the eleven papers of the Knight chain—Detroit, Miami, Tallahassee, Akron, Boca Raton, and two each in Philadelphia, Charlotte, and Macon—came out simultaneously with new revelations, along with the *Los Angeles Times.* On that day the *New York Times* appealed to the Supreme Court to review the Second Circuit decision in favor of the government. Among other things, Alexander Bickel on behalf of the *Times* asked for an immediate hearing because "not only has the public's right to know been infringed for over a week but the *Times,* which courageously initiated the publication of the documents, is being preempted by other newspapers."

Presumably it was essentially for the same reason—the continued hemorrhaging of information from the papers in the face of its efforts—that the Justice Department seemed to give up on seeking further injunctions, for a space, after it got a restraint on the *Boston Globe.* No legal process was started against the *Chicago Sun-Times,* the *L.A. Times,* or any of the Knight papers, though in principle they all posed the same danger of immediate and irreparable damage to the nation that the government claimed in the earlier cases.

On Friday morning, June 25, five justices of the Supreme Court voted to take up the newspaper cases of the *Times* and the *Post* on an emergency, expedited basis. They agreed to hear oral arguments the next day in an unprecedented Saturday morning session.

Four justices—Hugo Black, William Douglas, William Brennan, and Thurgood Marshall—had dissented from the decision to hear oral arguments, "saying they would have refused the cases, and immediately lifted all restraints against the *Times* and the *Post.*" To lift the injunctions, it was clear that at least one of the remaining justices remained to be persuaded. So for two reasons, I wanted to keep adding newspapers to the list of rebels: At worst, if the Court upheld the injunction shortly, I wanted as much as possible of the contents of the papers out on the streets before that happened. Furthermore, the wider the flood spread over the land, the more chance that one or more of the swing justices would be impressed, like Robb and the majority of the D.C. Circuit, that the issue of injunction had become moot. I wanted to provide the justices, as they deliberated, with even more evidence that the judicial system had already proved decisively incapable of preventing the free flow of this information (a job for which, under our First Amendment, it had never been intended or designed).

The Justice Department of course had opposite motives. I doubt if it believed there was any way it could really stanch the flow, but evidently it thought it would help its argument before the Supreme Court if it underlined the view it had been pressing for almost two weeks of the urgency and gravity of the revelations by pursuing the source of them as a criminal. News stories indicated that the department was working hard to get an indictment and an arrest order out on me before the Supreme Court met on Saturday morning. The problem presumably was that no one from within any of the newspapers had testified (or ever did, so far as I know) that I had provided the papers, nor had I yet announced this. As late as the Cronkite interview on the twenty-third, I declined to comment on my role, since there had still been no clear indication that the administration intended to prosecute. It had strong circumstantial evidence, in particular press statements by McGovern and McCloskey confirming that I had given the papers to them and that I had asserted my readiness to go to jail to get the information out. But without a statement by me (or a journalist who had received the papers from me) this fell well short of demonstrating that I had provided the documents to the press.

On the copying, my former wife provided an affidavit on what the children and I had told her. Tony Russo refused to testify, but given a grant of immunity, and facing jail for contempt if she then refused, Lynda Sinay did provide testimony. With such evidence, U.S. Magistrate Venetta S. Tassopoulos issued a warrant for my arrest on Friday night, June 25. That was just in time for the Supreme Court justices to read about it in their Saturday morning papers.

When my lawyer Charlie Nesson got through to me with this, he told me I would have to present myself to an arresting officer immediately. I said, "I can't do that. I still have some more copies of the papers to distribute."

Charlie said I had no choice. "If you don't turn yourself in, you'll be a fugitive."

"Too bad. I'm not finished."

Charlie chewed that over and left to confer with Boudin. When he came back, he asked, "How long will it take you to get rid of the rest of the papers?"

"A couple of days."

They called the Justice Department and tried out the idea, after checking it with me, that I would turn myself in immediately if Justice would guarantee that I would be released without bail over the weekend. As we expected, they did not get very far. Charlie called me and asked, "When can you come in?"

"Monday morning."

Charlie called the U.S. attorney in Boston and told him that I would be surrendering on Monday morning, not till then. The attorney said, "You know he can't do that."

Charlie said, "Well, that's what he's going to do."

There was a pause. The U.S. attorney said, "Oh, well, the FBI couldn't find him by then anyway."

Charlie said to him, "You know, you're talking over a tapped line." That was the assumption my lawyers were going on, though they didn't actually know it.

"You're kidding."

"No."

The Justice Department official said, "Oh, God," and hung up.

Charlie relayed all this to me and said, "You've got two days." I looked over what we had left and decided whom to ship it to. Of course I wasn't really essential for that. I could very well have surrendered myself and left this to someone else, but I'd been on top of the process so far and I wanted to stay with it to the end. After working toward this action for twenty months, and after the last two glorious weeks of open and successful defiance, I wasn't in a mood to jump when the authorities told me to. My attorneys were in a more awkward position, edging into an area of some legal jeopardy for themselves, but they shouldered this without complaint. They announced at a press conference in Boston, as the Supreme Court was hearing arguments in Washington, that I would surrender myself at the office of the U.S. attorney in Boston at 10:00 A.M. on Monday, June 28. They were vague about the reasons for the delay.

On Saturday I divided up the last of the copies we had pulled together, and over the weekend our team got them to the *Christian Science Monitor* and *Newsday.* By Sunday night the cupboard was bare. We got ready to surface the next morning. I didn't know what would happen in terms of bail; these extra two days as a fugitive might not have disposed a judge to let me walk out of court. In the last of our borrowed rooms, we thought it might be our last night together for a while. But in face of the government's desperate urging on Saturday that the Court continue to withhold this information from the American public, it seemed to me worthwhile to demonstrate, as the justices deliberated, the practical futility of their trying to do that, so long as there were newspapers *willing* to act as if they were free.

On Monday morning, June 28, Charlie Nesson came over to our last hideout to accompany us to the federal court for arraignment. He said to expect a lot of press there. I put on my best suit, which someone had smuggled out of our apartment. It was a wedding present from my brother-in-law, the only tailor-made suit I ever owned. I wore it throughout the trial. In those days, before Watergate, it seemed plausible that someone in a good suit and tie would look innocent to a jury.

Charlie passed on a tip from a reporter that the FBI was desperate to pick me up off the streets somehow before I reported to the courthouse. The bureau was embarrassed by its inability to find me over the last two weeks, while I was distributing the papers and appearing on national TV, and wanted last-minute vindication. I had been struck myself by its failure to find us or to intercept any of the copies of the papers before they appeared. A couple of days later I asked my lawyer Leonard Boudin, "What is the FBI really good at?"

Leonard said: "Taking surrenders."

From past experience, Boudin believed that the Justice Department was eager to present me to the cameras as a criminal in custody, in handcuffs, if not chains. I had no desire to be a willing participant in this drama. Charlie said I should expect a lot of police cars on the streets leading to the courthouse. He thought the government would be happy to nab me even if it was at the last minute, just before we got into Post Office Square. He had brought a taxi over to take us there. He got the driver to follow a very circuitous route along back streets. We went fairly far out of the way to cross the Charles on a little-used bridge.

That morning I had thought through a short statement I wanted to make to the press if I had the opportunity before I was arrested. It would be my first chance to take sole responsibility for the release of the papers. So long as I was underground and not yet openly acknowledging myself as the source, I couldn't corroborate what I assumed my former colleagues were telling the FBI in order to help get themselves off the hook. Now I wanted to start saying as convincingly and as often as I could that I had done this on my own responsibility and "alone," so far as any other government insider, anyone with a clearance, was concerned. (Obviously, once I made my decision, I was far from alone when it came to crucial help from friends, family, and antiwar resisters.) That was the main point of what I wanted to say, but it would also be the first statement directly from me on my motives and hopes.

While we were driving our roundabout route, it occurred to me that Patricia ought to have a copy of what I wanted said, so that if I was arrested in the midst of making my statement or before I could start it, she could take over for me. In the backseat of the cab, with Patricia beside me, I wrote out my statement on some notepaper and gave her the pages. I told her that if the police got us before we arrived or took me away before I could say anything or before I was finished, she should step to the microphones and finish it for me.

Charlie was in the front seat with the driver, and all of us—including me, out of the corner of my eye as I was scribbling my notes—were watching for patrol cars and waiting to hear sirens. But the streets the cabbie chose were almost deserted, even on a Monday morning. Just as I finished writing and handed the pages to Patricia, the taxi turned a corner and stopped at the entrance to Post Office Square. It was jammed from one side to the other with people, some of them holding up signs of support for me. We got out of the cab, and a great cheer went up as the crowd pressed in around us.

At first glance the crowd seemed to be made up entirely of people we knew, none from my long stay in the government and Rand but from before and after that, especially from Boston and Cambridge and all over the East Coast. It was like a surprise birthday party, or *This Is Your Life,* or the near-death experiences that people report after a coma, when, walking through a tunnel toward a blue light, they encounter everyone they cared about in life.

At one end of the small square was the Post Office Building, with the federal court and the U.S. attorney's office inside. I could see official-looking people, with police, standing on the steps. But they didn't seem to be coming after me. They were acting like good sports. Evidently, since I had gotten this far without being handcuffed, they were ready to give up the game and let me come to them. They waited while we hugged friends, shook hands with supporters in the crowd, and became engulfed in a tide of press. There was the biggest array of reporters, press photographers, and TV cameras I'd ever seen. They were all around us; there was no front line to address. But I spoke into a tangle of microphones that was held up somehow to my face, and I gave my statement. Patricia, pushed close to me by the crowd, didn't have to take over. I said:

> In the fall of 1969 I took the responsibility, on my own initiative, of delivering to the chairman of the Senate Foreign Relations Committee the information in the so-called Pentagon Papers, including the studies of U.S. negotiations, which have not been revealed to any newspaper. Until that time these studies were accessible only to me and to a few dozen other individuals. By this spring—two invasions later—after some nine thousand more Americans and several hundred thousand Indochinese had died, I could only regret that I had not, at that same time, revealed this history to the American people through the newspapers. I have now done so: again, on my sole initiative.
>
> All these acts contradicted the secrecy regulations and, even more, the information practice of the Department of Defense. However, as a responsible citizen I felt I could no longer cooperate in concealing this information from the American public. I acted of course at my own jeopardy, and I am ready to answer to all the consequences of my decisions. That includes personal consequences to me and my family; whatever these may be, they cannot after all be more serious than the ones that I, along with millions of Americans, have gladly risked before in serving this country.
>
> This has been for me an act of hope and of trust. Hope that the truth will free us of this war. Trust that informed Americans will direct their public servants to stop lying and to stop the killing and dying by Americans in Indochina.

At the end, as we made our way through the crowd toward the federal building, a reporter asked me, "How do you feel about going to prison?"

I said: "Wouldn't you go to jail to help end the war?"

We walked up the steps where the officials were waiting. Some of them were smiling. They didn't bother to put on cuffs; the moment for that picture had passed. They waved us inside, and the doors closed on the crowd cheering outside. The people were still waiting, and they cheered again as I came out two hours later, released on $50,000 bail without surety to await further arraignment and trial.

On Tuesday morning, June 29, while the Supreme Court was considering the Pentagon Papers cases, the *Monitor* published its own story based on the study, billed as the first in a series of three. I knew that Dad would be very happy to see his Christian Science paper, in effect, endorsing my action.

Tuesday night, June 29, Senator Mike Gravel of Alaska cast his whole vote, twice: first on the Senate floor, where he was the only senator to attempt a filibuster against the war and finally the only one to accept the Pentagon Papers from me and try to read them into the record; second, later that night, in a hearing of the Subcommittee on Buildings and Grounds of the Senate Public Works Committee that he had hastily called.

He had rushed up from the Senate gym on Friday, June 18, to take a phone call that his aide suspected was from me. (The *Washington Post* published its first story that morning and was clearly about to be enjoined.) Without introducing myself, I asked him from a pay phone whether he was serious about conducting a filibuster, and if he would like to use the Pentagon Papers for this purpose. He said yes to both questions firmly. On June 24, Ben Bagdikian, despite his qualms as a journalist, carried out his promise to me to transfer the box with a second set of the papers to Gravel (from one car to another in front of the Mayflower Hotel on Connecticut Avenue).

At 5:55 P.M. on Tuesday, June 29, Senator Gravel was blocked by a Republican parliamentary maneuver from launching a one-man filibuster in the Senate chamber that he meant to last till the draft expired thirty hours later on Wednesday midnight. He proceeded to use his whole influence, as no other senator had dared. He called a night hearing of the obscure subcommittee of which he was chairman and, as the only senator present, began reading the Pentagon Papers into the hearing record at 9:45 P.M. in front of television cameras. He inserted the rest of the papers that Bagdikian had conveyed to him into the record as he adjourned the one-man hearing at 1 A.M. Then, with the help of his staff, he distributed great bundles of previously unpublished top secret documents to a crowd of newsmen and to the Associated Press, which put them on its news wire across the country. He did this without the assurance of congressional immunity for these actions, and with a strong prospect (partly realized) of ostracism by his colleagues, with possible censure or loss of his seat. As the Supreme Court justices prepared to rule that morning, news bureaus all over Washington and elsewhere were readying stories based on the classified material the senator had handed out.

That same Wednesday morning, June 30, as the *Monitor* published its second installment, the Long Island afternoon paper *Newsday* published new revelations we had given it over the weekend. It became the last newspaper to risk Justice Department action, just as the Supreme Court that afternoon—by a 6–3 vote (both Potter Stewart and Byron White joining the majority)—voided all the injunctions on constitutional grounds and cleared further publication of the Pentagon Papers, which began the next day.

PART IV

SECRETS

30

The War Goes On

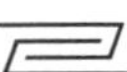

H. R. Haldeman to President Nixon, Oval Office tapes, June 14, 1971, on the impact of the Pentagon Papers:

To the ordinary guy, all this is a bunch of gobbledygook. But out of the gobbledygook comes a very clear thing: you can't trust the government; you can't believe what they say; and you can't rely on their judgment. And the implicit infallibility of presidents, which has been an accepted thing in America, is badly hurt by this, because it shows that people do things the president wants to do even though it's wrong, and the president can be wrong.

As a general proposition that message got through to the public. Thanks to the drama of Nixon's injunctions and their defiance by a large part of the press of America, there had been more attention to the contents of the papers than I could ever have dreamed: fifty full pages in the *New York Times;* half the nightly newscasts for a month; daily front-page stories not just in the nineteen newspapers to which we'd given copies but in virtually every paper in the country. Also, nearly every headline and editorial, every day for a month, hammered home the message that Haldeman had summarized cogently and early. Unfamiliar and painful as it was, no one really challenged it; the documentation was irrefutable. That was a change in American consciousness, reinforced two years later by the Watergate revelations, a change that could be only to the good, if we were to remain a Republic.

Yet as I was soon to learn, there remained enormous resistance in the minds of voters and commentators to believing that these generalizations applied to an incumbent president. At least they were resistant in the absence of documentation comparable to what I had provided for past administrations. That was what I had to conclude over the next two years, after ample opportunity to test it. The Justice Department decision to indict me, after a highly publicized, unsuccessful two-week manhunt, gave me that opportunity. It gave me as much prominence as I could possibly use to relate my major message: that the pattern of executive deception, abuse of war powers, and the hopeless strategy of secret threats and secret and overt escalation that was revealed in the Pentagon Papers over a twenty-three-year period was *continuing* in the Nixon administration, in its third year and beyond.

Almost no one believed me. I didn't have documents to prove what I was saying about Nixon's secret policy, and no one from within the administration stepped forward to provide them. My indictment on three federal felony charges, raised by the end of the year to a dozen for a possible total sentence of 115 years—with Anthony Russo, who joined me in the superseding indictment, facing 25 years—was certainly intended to deter such unauthorized disclosures in imitation of ours, and it may well have had that effect. Understandably, few in the public wanted to believe what I was saying about the prospects for continued war and further escalation, and lacking stronger evidence than I could provide, they didn't feel compelled to. So far as I could tell, I didn't convince anyone who wasn't already active in the antiwar movement. Mainstream interviewers and most commentators listened to me and treated me with respect. But neither these people nor the public at large could take seriously the warning I was trying to convey: This war isn't over, and it's not in the process of ending; it will almost surely get larger again.

Unfortunately, events proved me right, but in the fall of 1971, in the immediate glow of Nixon's announcement in mid-July of the opening to China, the public grasped at the idea that the war itself had become old news, mere history, and my message seemed especially unconvincing and untimely. People read between the lines of Nixon's spectacular announcement of his forthcoming trip to China that a successful deal on Indochina was in the making. President Nixon and Henry Kissinger may have believed that themselves. I did not.

I saw no sign that Nixon had given up his secret aims: to coerce the North into withdrawing its troops from the South along with ours or to accept a cease-fire in place that left the Thieu regime permanently in exclusive power in Saigon. Nor did I see any sign that these terms had become remotely acceptable to Hanoi. For North Vietnam to agree to stop fighting on the promise of elections that would be prepared and managed by the anti-Communist Saigon regime would be for it to buy essentially the same empty settlement package it had been sold by the French in 1946 and by the "guarantors" of the Geneva Accords in 1954. However, that was exactly what Richard Nixon had in mind; he didn't even bother to change the wrapping.

His memories of 1954 to 1960 were just as vivid as theirs; he had been vice president at the time. He had no more intention in 1972 or 1973 of allowing elections that might lead to power sharing in Saigon or Communist domination in the South than Dwight Eisenhower or John Foster Dulles had had in 1954 or 1956. Indeed, I suspect that he hoped precisely for the replay of Geneva that Hanoi was determined to resist: that the Soviet Union and China would again force a similar settlement on their small ally for the same reason as before, to improve their relations with the United States. However, despite Nixon's scheduled trips to Beijing and Moscow, I believed that rivalry between China and the Soviet Union would continue, as in the last decade, to assure Hanoi of their adequate support to resist that outcome. Sooner or later, next year or the year after that, there would be another offensive to which Nixon would respond with increased bombing and perhaps still-stronger measures.

Meanwhile, he was increasing deceptively labeled "protective reaction strikes" against the North to a level that amounted to the resumption of Johnson's bombing. Starting the day after Christmas 1971, he launched a thousand U.S. bombers during five days of bombing against North Vietnam, in the heaviest raids since 1968. Thus, six months after the publication of the Pentagon Papers, when people asked me at the end of the year what I thought it had accomplished, I said, "Nothing." Nothing in regard to the war, my overriding concern. It wasn't public opinion I had been ultimately seeking to change: It was the bombing, the war, Nixon's policy. None of those had been influenced by American public opinion since the start of his term in office, as far as I could see, or by the release of the papers.

Most Americans in truth had wanted out of the war long before the papers were published; a majority had even come to regard it as immoral. Perhaps the majorities in both cases were larger now, after the publicity and the headlines about the papers and whatever they had read in them. But to what effect? In the face of that majority sentiment, the president had kept the war going by reducing ground troops, while he increased the bombing, and by recurrently convincing the public that he was on the verge of a settlement. He did that again in the next few months, unveiling in January 1972 the secret talks and a deceptively "generous" offer that he knew was unacceptable to Hanoi.

I was spending my time, in the months before our trial was scheduled to begin in May, writing commentaries on a collection of my writings about Vietnam, *Papers on the War.* As I finished the introduction to the book in late March, I was compelled to write the melancholy observation that "the war goes on, still endlessly 'ending,' while bombing persists at the steady rate of World War II." Days after I wrote that, on March 31, the North launched the blitzkrieg that for three years Mort Halperin and I had expected and Nixon and Kissinger had hoped to avert with their threats, their bombing, their demonstrative invasions of Cambodia and Laos, their triangular diplomacy with China and the Soviet Union. An unfounded faith in the power of these earlier threats and escalations, at the very least to deter or prevent an offensive on that scale, had been at the heart of their strategy for the previous three years. The very occurrence of this attack, in an election year, represented the total failure of their earlier policy. As Halperin and I had also expected, they responded with long-planned, unprecedented escalation.

From the beginning of April I foresaw the imminent mining of Haiphong and with it, I was sure, virtually unrestricted bombing of North Vietnam, including by B-52s. There was little I could do to add to my earlier warnings. For what it was worth, it was time to publish the last documents I had bearing on the war, NSSM-1 and the options paper. I had wanted to do this the previous fall as soon as the publication of the Pentagon Papers had run its course, but Patricia had argued that in the aftermath of the China opening and with Congress about to adjourn, it would have little effect. Now at least it would demonstrate that Nixon had contemplated the mining of Haiphong as early as the spring of 1969 and that its military ineffectiveness had been forecast by all civilian intelligence analysts at that time.

My lawyers felt sure, as they had in the fall of 1971, that this new release would lead to new counts in my indictment, if not to another, separate trial. Moreover, since it involved secret NSC documents from the current administration, documents that could not easily be described as "history," an acquittal would be much less likely. However, they put no pressure at all on me in making this call. As we approached the all-out attacks I had been working to avert for seven years, Patricia agreed that this was the time for us to do whatever we could. The one concession my lawyers asked was that I not wave a red flag to the Justice Department by releasing the five hundred pages of secret documents at a press conference or by announcing myself as the source.

Again Senator Mike Gravel offered himself as the channel to the Senate *Congressional Record* and this time to the media. Although trying to defend his aides against prosecution for their role in his publication of the Pentagon Papers by the Beacon Press—he had just fought a case up to the Supreme Court—he had urged me in December to give him anything else I had. I had turned over NSSM-1 to him to await the right moment. As in June, he was blocked by parliamentary objections in his attempt to introduce the documents into the *Congressional Record* via a speech in the Senate. Anticipating this, he had already given them to Jack Anderson and *Newsweek,* and major stories appeared in the *Washington Post* and the *Washington Star,* starting on April 25, the day the Senate declined to allow Gravel to read from them on the Senate floor.

Eight days later, on May 3, 1972, I took advantage of the presence of Senator Gravel and Representative Ron Dellums at a rally I was addressing on the Capitol steps to arrange—at the suggestion of Dellums's legislative aide, Mike Duberstein—for Gravel to transfer the documents to Dellums. After removing stray classification markings with a scissors, Duberstein put five hundred pages of secret documents in the hopper for extended remarks for the House *Congressional Record,* in which they were published on May 10 and 11. So the senators who were in the middle of closed sessions debating if they had the right to receive classified documents from Gravel or to defy in any way a classification decision by an executive official were able to read them in full after all.

However, the administration too had learned some lessons. This time there were no demands for restraint by the press or injunctions by a court, no charges or complaints, no new counts to my indictment, though the president, along with his attorney general, knew perfectly well the source of this new massive leak of classified studies. Shrewdly administration figures did not respond or comment at all on the publication. As a result, the disclosure of five hundred pages of secret Nixon administration documents got only a brief flurry of stories, to no perceptible effect.

My fears of what might lie ahead for the people of North Vietnam were not exaggerated, as the latest tapes of White House discussions to become available (April 2002) have recently revealed. On April 25, 1972, the morning that the *Washington Post* first published accounts of NSSM-1 and its

1969 analyses of mining Haiphong, these exchanges were taking place in the Oval Office:

President Nixon: We've got to quit thinking in terms of a three-day strike [in the Hanoi-Haiphong area]. We've got to be thinking in terms of an all-out bombing attack—which will continue until they— Now by all-out bombing attack, I am thinking about things that go far beyond . . . I'm thinking of the dikes, I'm thinking of the railroad, I'm thinking, of course, the docks. . . .

Kissinger: . . . I agree with you.

President Nixon: . . . we've got to use massive force. . . .

Two hours later, at noon, H. R. Haldeman and Ron Ziegler joined Kissinger and Nixon:

President: How many did we kill in Laos?

Ziegler: Maybe ten thousand—fifteen?

Kissinger: In the Laotian thing, we killed about ten, fifteen. . . .

President: See, the attack in the North that we have in mind . . . power plants, whatever's left—POL [petroleum], the docks . . . And, I still think we ought to take the dikes out now. Will that drown people?

Kissinger: About two hundred thousand people.

President: No, no, no . . . I'd rather use the nuclear bomb. Have you got that, Henry?

Kissinger: That, I think, would just be too much.

President: The nuclear bomb, does that bother you? . . . I just want you to think big, Henry, for Christsakes.

One week later, on May 2, after hearing from Kissinger and Haig the merits of combining bombing and blockade, the president agreed to do both. As he concluded, "[B]lockade plus surgical bombing will inevitably achieve our objective—bring the North Vietnamese to their knees." Thus, even "if the South Vietnamese collapse" in the meantime, a possibility according to Kissinger, the North, under the dual pressure, had "got to give us back our prisoners; *America* is not defeated. We must not lose in Vietnam. . . . So—we must draw the sword. So—the blockade is on. And I must say . . . that I like it. . . . And I want this clearly understood. The surgical operation theory is all right, but I want that place bombed to *smithereens.* If we draw the sword, we're gonna bomb those bastards all over the place. Let it fly, *let it fly.*"

On May 4, discussing his decision with Kissinger, Al Haig, and John Connally, Nixon put the confrontation with Vietnam in perspective. Heard on the Oval Office tape, he thumped his desk as he pointed to an imaginary or perhaps a real map on it:

> Vietnam: Here's those little cocksuckers right in there, here they are. (Thump) Here's the United States (thump). Here's Western (thump) Europe, that *cocky* little place that's caused so much devastation. . . . Here's the Soviet Union (thump), here's the (thump) Mid-East. . . . Here's the (thump) silly Africans. . . . And (thump) the not-quite-so-silly Latin Americans. Here *we* are. They're taking on the United States. Now, goddamit, we're gonna *do* it. We're going to *cream* them. This is not in anger or anything. This old business, that I'm "petulant," that's all bullshit. I should have done it long ago, I just didn't follow my instincts.
>
> . . . I'll see that the United States does not lose. I'm putting it quite bluntly. I'll be quite precise. South Vietnam may lose. But the United States *cannot* lose. Which means, basically, I have made the decision. Whatever happens to South Vietnam, we are going to *cream* North Vietnam.
>
> . . . For once, we've got to use the maximum power of this country . . . against this *shit-ass* little country: to win the war. We can't use the word, "win." But others can.

In a later exchange Nixon observed to Kissinger: "The only place where you and I disagree . . . is with regard to the bombing. You're so goddamned concerned about the civilians and I don't give a damn. I don't care."

Kissinger responded: "I'm concerned about the civilians because I don't want the world to be mobilized against you as a butcher. . . ."

At the Capitol rally on May 3, I predicted the imminent mining of Haiphong. It turned out that the president had secretly made the decision the day before. It was executed six days later, on May 8. Richard Nixon had looked forward to that specific operation, out of office and in, for most of a decade. I had opposed it and feared what it might lead to, in the form of massive bombing, for almost as long. I remember feeling that afternoon, and telling Patricia, that it was the darkest day of my life.

Later, as we prepared for our trial to begin in Los Angeles, I said to Mort Halperin, who had joined our defense team as a consultant, "Well, we've come to the end of the predictions you gave me three years ago."

He said: "No. Hanoi hasn't been bombed yet."

In July, after hearings on motions and selection of a jury, our legal proceedings were suspended following the revelation by the Justice Department of the electronic overhearing of one of our lawyers. During the lengthy suspension I spent the campaign season of 1972 warning every audience I could find of the possibility of further escalation. That included virtually the entire press corps covering the president's renomination at the Republican National Convention, at a press conference in Miami sponsored by Representative McCloskey. There and elsewhere my listeners were polite but totally incredulous. They found it much easier to believe Kissinger's announcement in late October that "peace is at hand," which contributed the next week to the president's reelection in the second-largest landslide in American history. In some respects his margin surpassed that of Lyndon Johnson in 1964, which was won on the slogan "We seek no wider war" three months before he began the bombing of North and South Vietnam.

Six weeks after the election, a week before Christmas 1972, President Nixon sent B-52s over Hanoi for the first time ever. In the next eleven days and nights—with Christmas off—American planes dropped on North Vietnam 20,000 tons of bombs (the explosive equivalent of the Nagasaki A-bomb). That added to the 150,000 tons on North Vietnam between April and October. Since the Pentagon Papers had been published a year and a half earlier—well after a majority of Americans polled had regarded our continued combat involvement in the war as "immoral"—President Nixon had launched 1.5 million tons of bombs on Indochina. That was the total tonnage of U.S. bombs dropped on Europe in World War II.

In Christmas week of 1972 I was asked frequently what I thought the release of the Pentagon Papers had accomplished with respect to the war. I gave essentially the same answer that I had given a year earlier. "Nothing. No effect. That's true for the entire peace movement, of which the publication of the papers was just one part. And not just the peace movement, the whole antiwar majority has had no influence. Nor the electorate."

During the most concentrated weeks of bombing in history, six weeks after the landslide votes cast on the assurance that "peace is at hand," I went on to say: "The American people had as much influence over what is happening over Hanoi and Haiphong this week as the Soviet people had over the invasion of Czechoslovakia. Unlike the Soviet Union, we have democracy, in important respects. What we don't have, at this time, is democratic control of American foreign policy."

At the end of January 1973, with the signing of the "Paris Peace Accords," American bombing in Indochina halted, except for Cambodia, where it increased. However, as I anticipated—along with the White House, it turns out—the official title, "The Agreement on Ending the War and Restoring

Peace in Vietnam," proved Orwellian. The agreement failed to bring a moment's peace or cease-fire to South Vietnam and held no real promise of an end to the war. What Kissinger and his boss had in hand in October and renegotiated, essentially unchanged, in January was not, in their eyes or in reality, a settlement of the war. It was basically an agreement with Hanoi to withdraw U.S. ground troops unilaterally in exchange for the return of American POWs, along with a hollow pledge to prepare and run open elections in South Vietnam with the participation of the NLF.

Since leaders in both Washington and Saigon quickly made clear they had no intention to fulfill the latter provision, the arrangement left unchanged the exclusion of the NLF from open political participation in South Vietnam, where with the support of America the Thieu regime claimed sole legitimacy and a monopoly of power. Thus there was no prospect of a cease-fire acceptable to the NLF or DRV or, for that matter, to the GVN. With hostilities continuing between ARVN and the NLF/NVA, I expected American bombing to resume indefinitely in North and South Vietnam and Laos after a two-month pause while American ground troops left the country. Larry Berman's *No Peace, No Honor* (2001), the first account of Nixon's policy and negotiation to reflect near-adequate documentation and interviews on both sides, makes it clear that Nixon held the same expectation. He had repeatedly given, in secret, "absolute" assurances to President Thieu that he would resume large-scale bombing as soon as necessary. He had every intention of carrying out those promises, as did Henry Kissinger. As Berman reveals, Kissinger strongly urged air strikes, on the scale of the Christmas bombing, against Laos and Vietnam in March 1973, even before all U.S. troops had been withdrawn.

Yet that bombing, fully intended by the White House, did not happen, for reasons, after all, that had everything to do with American democracy and the rule of law. The prosecution of Tony Russo and me, with courtroom proceedings beginning again in January, represented the public face of Nixon's response to release of the Pentagon Papers. But it was not the only response. That unauthorized disclosure turned out to have set in motion a hidden train of reactions in the administration that, over the next several years, proved crucial to curtailing President Nixon's usurpation of war powers, preventing the resumption of American bombing in Vietnam and Laos, and shortening the war.

31

The Road to Watergate

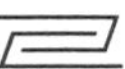

White House tapes and transcripts now available reveal two different and somewhat contradictory White House reactions to the publication of the Pentagon Papers starting on June 13, 1971. On the one hand, Nixon's private reaction to the contents of the first installments of the Pentagon Papers—with their unflattering revelations about his Democratic predecessors—becoming known to the public was entirely positive. On the other hand, he was very concerned lest this revelation be a precedent for exposure of his own past and present secret actions and policies in Indochina. Both these attitudes prompted actions by the president and his subordinates that led to the political debacle known as Watergate.

Both reactions could be heard in the tape of his first conversation with Henry Kissinger on the subject that Sunday afternoon. As Kissinger, phoning from California to the Oval Office, saw it:

> In public opinion, it actually, if anything, will help us a little bit, because this is a gold mine of showing how the previous administration got us in there. . . . I think they outsmarted themselves, because . . . they had sort of tried to make it Nixon's war, and what this . . . proves is that, if it's anybody's war, it's Kennedy's and Johnson's. . . . So that these Democrats now bleating about . . . what we're doing wrong, this graphically shows . . . who's responsible for the basic mess. . . . This is an indictment of the previous administration.

By the next day the president had adopted this interpretation enthusiastically. But in this very first conversation he raised his concern that files on

"Laos and Cambodia," the secret bombing campaigns that typified his still secret aims and strategy, might leak from the State or Defense Department.

Thus, Nixon's anxiety about leaks was limited to unauthorized disclosures of his own policies. He was so little worried that revelations about past presidents would undermine his ability to conduct a secret foreign policy that he favored more leaks of secrets that would demonstrate the fallibility of Democratic presidents, Kennedy in particular. He saw Ted Kennedy as his most formidable potential rival in 1972. Nixon was anxious for the series of revelations to continue at least long enough to undermine the Kennedys further.

On Monday, June 14, after two installments had appeared in the *Times,* Nixon had this exchange with his domestic counsel, John Ehrlichman, at 7:13 P.M.:

Ehrlichman: Hello, Mr. President, the Attorney General [Mitchell] has called a couple times about these *New York Times* stories; and he's advised by his people that unless he puts the *Times* on notice, he's probably gonna waive any right of prosecution against the newspaper; and he is calling now to see if you would approve his putting them on notice before their first edition for tomorrow comes out.

President: Hmmn.

Ehrlichman: I realize there are negatives to this in terms of the vote on the Hill [Wednesday's scheduled vote on the McGovern-Hatfield bill cutting off funding for the war by December 1971].

President: You mean to prosecute the *Times*?

Ehrlichman: Right.

President: Hell, I wouldn't prosecute the *Times.* My view is to prosecute the goddamn pricks that gave it to 'em.

Ehrlichman: Yeah, if you can find out who that is.

President: Yeah, I know . . . I mean . . . uh, could the *Times* be prosecuted?

Ehrlichman: Apparently so.

President: Wait a minute—wait a minute—they, on the other hand, they're gonna run another story tomorrow.

Ehrlichman: Right.

President: Why not just wait until after that one?

Ehrlichman: Well, his point is that he feels he has to give them some sort of advance notice, and then if they go ahead in disregard, when there's no danger of waiver; but if he doesn't give them notice then it's almost like entrapment—we sit here and let them go ahead on a course of conduct and don't raise any objection.

President: Well, could he wait one more day? —They have—they have one more day after that . . . I don't know . . . I don't know.

Neither in this call nor in Nixon's phone conversation immediately following with Mitchell, in which the president agreed to the attorney general's issuing a "low key" warning to the *Times* that afternoon, was there any mention of the possibility of injunction, as distinct from possible prosecution of the *Times* and its sources. Not once during the first three days of publication, in any of the transcripts available, did the president or any White House aide, including Kissinger, show any interest in stopping publication by injunction; the impetus for this seems to have come exclusively from Mitchell and the Justice Department. On Tuesday, after Mitchell had gone to court seeking an injunction on the ground that further publication of the papers would constitute an immediate and irreparable injury to national security, the president told Haldeman that it would be good to get the Kennedy chapters of the Pentagon Papers to the public. He asked, "The injunction was only to the *Times,* Bob. Right?" Shortly after being assured on this point, in a discussion with Haldeman and Kissinger in the Oval Office, the president said, "Stuff on Kennedy I'm gonna leak. We'll just leak it out. . . . Now that it's being leaked, we'll leak out the parts we want."

Part of Nixon's concern about Ted Kennedy as a rival was that the president was trying to court the Catholic swing vote away from the Democrats. (The front-runner for the Democratic nomination at the time, Senator Edmund Muskie, was also a Catholic.) Nixon was particularly impatient to see the volume of the papers dealing with the assassination of President Ngo Dinh Diem in print. With the *Times*'s appeal of the restraining order working its way toward the Supreme Court, which might issue a permanent injunction, time was short to make public the still top secret evidence on the murder of a friendly Catholic head of state in a coup sponsored by President Kennedy, Ted's Catholic brother.

On Wednesday, the president told Henry Kissinger: "I want to get out the stuff on the murder of Diem. Get one of the little boys over in your office to get it out." After a pause, during which his adviser for national security was silent, Nixon said, "All right then, I'm gonna get it out."

Kissinger commented, "My guy shouldn't put out classified papers."

The president repeated, "I'm gonna put it out."

After Kissinger had left the room, the president on the phone gave the task to White House Counsel Charles Colson, who assured him it would be done (despite his having told the president on Monday, "You simply cannot allow a newspaper to publish classified documents").

In the next few days the *Washington Post* and the *Boston Globe* were also put out of the running by successive restraining orders requested by Mitchell. I had asked Bagdikian that the *Post* start with something other than material from the Johnson administration—I wanted to show a pattern, not to have lying appear to be solely a Johnson characteristic—and it did so with a story on Eisenhower's determination to avoid an election in Vietnam from 1954 to 1956. But the editor of the *Globe,* Tom Winship, had asked for something on the Kennedy administration, there being special interest in the Kennedys in Boston. That evening, when Nixon was informed that the *Boston Globe* evening edition "has a large picture of John F. Kennedy and then four different stories . . . that just burned Kennedy," the president asked, "Did they get Diem? Great!"

Actually, they hadn't, and Mitchell had already called the editor to tell him, as Winship recalled, "I just have to do this to you [request an injunction] because if I didn't, the other papers would be upset; it wouldn't be fair to the *Times* and the *Post.*" While the *Globe* was in the process of being enjoined, the *Chicago Sun-Times* printed documents on the Diem coup that same night, June 22. It was the fourth paper to defy the government's general warning about the threat to national security and the first to be allowed to publish, that day and for successive days, without being threatened with injunction.

Meanwhile, the president was getting increasingly excited by the thought of searching the files of classified materials for documents embarrassing to President Kennedy and his brothers and leaking them. The litany of cases to be examined for good leaks was a recurrent theme over the next months and even years: the Bay of Pigs, the Cuban missile crisis, the Berlin Wall, as well as the Diem coup. This was clearly a massive research task, which needed to be headed by someone with a sense of history, among other credentials. Going over possible candidates with Haldeman and Ziegler on June 24, while the FBI was searching for me, Nixon observed: "It will be very good to have somebody who knew the subject. I mean, what you really need is an Ellsberg, an Ellsberg who's on our side; in other words, an intellectual who knows the history of the times, who knows what he's looking for."

There was of course another side to the president's attitude toward me and what I had done. He was appreciative of the precedent I set for instant declassification and leaking of the history of earlier Democratic administrations but very concerned at the thought that it might be a precedent for unauthorized disclosures about his own, as indicated by his worry about "Laos and Cambodia" in his first discussion of the *Times* publication of the papers with Kissinger on June 13. To deter such revelations, criminal prosecution of the sources to the *Times*—"the goddamn pricks that gave it to 'em"—seemed an automatic and obvious answer.

Whoever was involved, the president was anxious to prosecute them to put "the fear of God into other people in this government." On Tuesday, June 15, he was pounding his desk: "[G]oddamn it, *somebody has got to go to jail!* . . . [T]hat's all there is to it!" He asked Mitchell that day, "Incidentally, could you—can you haul in that son-of-a-bitch Ellsberg right away? Ells—what's his name?"

"Ellsberg."

Nixon, sarcastically: "*Ellstein* . . . Well, we don't know. It's either Ellstein or Halperin or Gelb. All three of them had access to the papers."

Two days later, on June 17, he was getting impatient. When Haldeman mentioned me, he asked, "Why doesn't the FBI pick him up, throw him in the can? That's the next move, isn't it?" (We had gone underground that morning.)

The need to keep others from following my example was particularly urgent in this administration precisely because Nixon and Kissinger shared my sense that their real Vietnam policy had to be kept secret if it were to be politically viable. They were pursuing a policy that was very vulnerable if it was exposed to questioning and debate, as they were well aware. They didn't regard their course as foolish, reckless, hopeless, and wrong, as I did, but they did understand that many others would see it that way if by virtue of new leaks, especially with documents, it ceased to be secret from and misunderstood by the American public.

In that first phone conversation on the *Times* publication on Sunday, June 13, 1971, the president was particularly concerned that the bombing of Cambodia in early 1969 and later (code-named Menu, for a series of raids initially code-named Breakfast, Lunch, and Dinner) might be about to be revealed. Likewise, on Tuesday, June 15, in urging prosecution of those responsible, Kissinger told Nixon: "The reason you have to be so tough, also, Mr. President, is because if this thing flies on the *New York Times,* they're gonna do the same to you next year. They're just gonna move file cabinets out during the [1972] campaign. I mean, these guys . . ."

Nixon replied: "Yeah. They'll have the whole story of the Menu series."

I suspect that both men understood better than most that documentation was crucial to the impact of such revelations. William Beecher's detailed story in the *Times* in March 1969 on the secret bombing of Cambodia had triggered such rage in them that they instituted highly secret, warrantless (illegal) wiretaps by the FBI on a number of NSC staffers and journalists, seeking its source. But the Beecher story, lacking documents, had been a one-day affair and totally ignored by the rest of the press after the Pentagon had blandly denied it. The possibility raised by the Pentagon Papers precedent of a well-documented exposé, even two or three years later, was a different matter.

There were special reasons for the sensitivity of the Menu operation against Cambodia. Beecher's story had been particularly embarrassing to the White House because it revealed details on the operation that the White House had meant to keep secret from Secretary of Defense Mel Laird and Secretary of State William Rogers, both of whom strongly disapproved of this widening of the war. Nixon and Kissinger regarded the two cabinet secretaries almost as adversaries with respect to Vietnam policy, to be kept in the dark as much and as long as possible lest they raise objections forcefully or even, in the case of Laird, leak to Congress or the press. When the president brought them in on it at all, it was only sketchily and at the last moment. Nevertheless, in the first conversation with Kissinger on the thirteenth, and frequently afterward, Nixon was concerned that the two secretaries might after all have more documents than he intended them to have, or perhaps memoranda of conversations with him. "Whenever I've had to call Rogers and Mel [Laird] in on some of these, on Laos and Cambodia, . . . those guys will have made their own records . . . they'll indicate what I've ordered, you know."

Kissinger was reassuring. "Oh, they'll indicate what you have ordered, but they weren't in on the reasons," which he and the president took care not to tell them, especially in writing.

It remained true through 1971 that bombing "pressures" on North Vietnam and in Laos were being run directly by Nixon and Kissinger, in a "direct channel" to Admiral Thomas H. Moorer, chairman of the JCS, secretly bypassing Laird for the same reason of his disagreement with their strategy. A particularly sensitive secret was that the FBI was wiretapping for the White House the office and home of Laird's military assistant, General Robert E. Pursley, to monitor how much the secretary of defense knew about these operations and whether he was leaking anything to Congress, which he had left to join the administration.

Moreover, Congress, which had to appropriate the money for these operations, had been given false top secret documentation on what country they were paying to bomb. Hundreds of military staffers in MACV and CINCPAC headquarters were kept busy faking classified flight plans and after-action reports of the bombing raids, falsifying the coordinates of the actual targets to indicate that they were in South Vietnam rather than in Cambodia. When in 1970 Nixon ordered secret bombing of the Plain of Jars in Laos (which had no relation to infiltration routes), he used the same system of dual bookkeeping he had used to conceal the bombing of Cambodia. In some cases the pilots themselves were misled on the countries in which their target coordinates were located, but generally the purpose was to deceive Congress and the public (and to some extent, on the scale and frequency of the operations, Laird and Rogers). There was no intent or effect of deceiving the targeted Communists or their allies; the people on the ground were not in doubt, nor meant to be, about who was bombing them from B-52s.

The secrecy of this system within the administration was effective for almost four years—until a single sergeant (one of hundreds involved in the falsification), worried that the president might be unaware of the true targeting, revealed documents to Senator Harold E. Hughes. A modern president's practical ability to drop secretly several hundred thousand tons of bombs on a country with which we were not at war was a considerable tribute to the effectiveness of the postwar secrecy system. It gives our presidents a capability to initiate and escalate war in secret that was scarcely possessed by monarchs of the past.

At the time of these discussions, after all, this bombing had been going on in secret for more than two years, both before and after the overt invasion of Cambodia (and it continued in secret for almost two more). But the need for its being hidden from the public reflected the fact that it was part of a policy of covert threats—again, kept undisclosed from the American electorate, not from the Communist recipients of the threats or their allies—that had not yet been fully carried out. Attacks on the Red River dikes, which Hanoi charged, and observers confirmed, as happening deliberately on a piecemeal basis in the spring of 1972, and B-52s over Haiphong and Hanoi still lay a year in the future, though contingency plans had come close to execution several times since 1969. All these past, current, and likely future actions were still unrevealed in mid-1971; they were pillars of Nixon's secret policy that Congress might act to remove by budgetary constraints if they were exposed. Hence the special urgency of steps to deter or prevent any leaks from his own administration even while promoting them about earlier ones. Hence the unprecedented injunctions, and the need to move to unprecedented actions beyond them.

Yet it wasn't at all clear whether we would be convicted at our trial. There would be little controversy about the facts of the case. I readily acknowledged, and testified to, all the acts of which I was accused. But Congress had never passed any law that provided criminal sanctions against what I had done: copying and giving official "classified" information without authorization to newspapers, to Congress, and to what our constitutional principles regard as our "sovereign public." Most countries—not only authoritarian ones like China but our mother democracy, Great Britain—have such laws. They don't have constitutions with our First Amendment, which prevents Congress from passing such a law. There is no explicit or intended statutory basis at all for the classification system that has existed through a succession of executive orders since World War II. The regulations governing documents classified confidential, secret, and top secret constitute an administrative system under which employees of the executive branch who have signed secrecy oaths or agreements are subject to *administrative* penalties for unauthorized disclosures, from losing access to such information to being fired. A simple constitutional principle of our form of government is that the president cannot make criminal law for civilians, by executive order or otherwise; only Congress can do that, by statute. And except for some specialized, narrowly defined categories of secrets not relevant to the top secret Pentagon Papers documents—nuclear weapons data, communications intelligence, and, more recently, covert agents' identities—Congress, in light of the First Amendment, had never done that.

Although almost no one recognized it at the time or later, the criminal prosecution of Tony Russo and myself for copying government information—with the intention not of transmitting it secretly to a foreign power (espionage) but of revealing ("leaking") it to the American press and public—was just as unprecedented, as historically unique, as the prior restraint and attempts at permanent injunctions that led to the Supreme Court Pentagon Papers case.

The simple fact was that there had never before in this country been a prosecution for a leak. I had been warned of the prospect of prosecution for any unauthorized disclosure many times while working in the government—every time I got a secrecy briefing or signed a secrecy agreement for a clearance. Those written warnings always made explicit reference to the very provisions of the Espionage Act under which I was the first to be indicted for unauthorized disclosure, rather than for espionage. In effect, those warnings were a threat to use parts of the espionage statutes as if they constituted an official secrets act, like Britain's. Yet even though leaks of classified information (on a smaller scale than that of the Pentagon Papers) are commonplace, indeed almost daily, events, and though the small minority of them that are not in fact authorized by high officials have often caused these officials to feel rage and a desire for punishment, prosecution had never before followed. Department legal counsel or the Justice Department had often noted to those officials urging prosecution the absence of an intended official secrets act or its equivalent. Counsel sometimes went on to point out that since congressional debate during the passage of the Espionage Act had explicitly disclaimed any legislative intent to use it against unauthorized disclosures to the press, any attempt to use parts of it as an official secrets act could well result in those sections' being thrown out as unconstitutional violations of the First Amendment. The government would then be without any law to cite in its warnings to the millions of government employees signing secrecy agreements; in effect, its bluff would be called.

None of this was known to me at the time I copied and released the Pentagon Papers, or to my lawyers, or, as far as I know, to any of the newspapers that printed them. All of us assumed—along with Nixon, Kissinger, Mitchell, and nearly everyone else—that there *was* some equivalent of an official secrets act in the United States. In other words, we believed that there was a law that I, and presumably the newspapers, were violating. I saw what we were doing as an act of deliberate civil disobedience. So how could the president justify directing subordinates to leak top secret documents to the press and how could they justify doing it—when that was precisely what he was indicting me for?

I think I know the answer to that, from my own experience in the Pentagon. The issue of justification simply didn't arise. As a consultant or an official, I had never given any particular thought to the First Amendment or, for that matter, to the Constitution, or to possible constraints of domestic law on our work. I worked in the executive branch for the president, on military and foreign policy. I didn't think that the Constitution or congressional laws applied to me in what we were doing. In that respect I was exactly like the various White House officials who testified later during the Watergate hearings that they had believed—in the words of their boss, President Nixon—that "when the president does it, it is not illegal." It was in that spirit, I'm sure, that Nixon directed Colson and others to perform acts of leaking that he sincerely, though mistakenly, regarded as criminal and even treasonous for others (along with acts of burglary and cover-up that are universally regarded as criminal).

In other words, they assumed that the president, and they in working for him, were above any domestic law. Along with my colleagues working on foreign policy and military matters, I certainly believed that to be true in the area of national security. Regrettably, so do many members of Congress and the public. Along with that belief in exclusive, untrammeled presidential jurisdiction and freedom in these fields goes the assumption of unlimited right to control what the public will know about executive decision making in these matters. As I had belatedly come to see it, that way lay monarchy and more Vietnams, or worse. I found that lesson summed up in words that I read during our trial and proceeded to learn by heart, words written by James Madison, drafter of the First Amendment:

> A popular government, without popular information or the means of acquiring it, is but a prologue to a farce or a tragedy; or, perhaps, both. Knowledge will forever govern ignorance: And a people who mean to be their own governors, must arm themselves with the power knowledge gives.

My first hint of the startling conclusion that what Tony and I had done was *not,* in our country, illegal came from my lawyer Leonard Boudin in late 1972, about a year after my second indictment. Boudin told me briefly of the study of case law, the legislative history of the statutes cited in our indictment, and the research our legal team had been conducting over the past year, including a search for possibly unrecorded prior cases. As he summed it up, "As far as we can tell, Dan, you haven't violated any law."

I said, "That's great! So I'm home free!"

But Boudin said, "I'm afraid it's not as simple as that. When the U.S. government goes into a courtroom and says to a jury, 'The government of the United States versus Daniel Ellsberg,' and presents twelve felony counts . . . you can't be sure you will walk out of that courtroom a free man."

I chewed that over. Then I asked, "Well, what are my odds?"

"Fifty-fifty."

"*Fifty-fifty?* And I haven't broken any law?"

Leonard said, "Well, let's face it, Dan. Copying seven thousand pages of top secret documents and giving them to the *New York Times* has a bad ring to it."

On June 22, 1971, with the Supreme Court decision lifting the prior restraint on publication still more than a week away, the president said to Ehrlichman, Ziegler, and others, "Get the injunction procedures over with. We're going to lose that. . . . And that's it. . . . We lose, we move immediately to the criminal prosecution . . . of Ellsberg." On the afternoon of the thirtieth, just after the Supreme Court announced its decision—I had been indicted on federal felony charges the day before—the president asked Attorney General Mitchell, in the presence of Henry Kissinger in the Oval Office, "Don't you agree that we have to pursue the Ellsberg case now?"

Mitchell: No question about it. . . . This is the one sanction we have, is to get at the individuals. . . .
President: . . . Let's get the son-of-a-bitch into jail.
Kissinger: We've *got* to get him.
President: We've got to get him. . . . Don't worry about his trial. Just get everything out. Try him in the press. Try him in the press. Everything, John, that there is on the investigation, get it out, leak it out. We want to destroy him in the press. Press. Is that clear?
Kissinger and Mitchell: Yes.

However, minutes earlier in this same conversation, just before Mitchell entered, and again immediately after this exchange, Kissinger brought up a new piece of information from Laird that transformed the situation they were facing. Up to this point the tapes show no real worry about what I had revealed or might reveal, which was assumed to be limited to the period of the Democrats. The need to prosecute me and discredit me was just to set an example to deter others, past and present officials of the current administration, who might reveal its secret policies. This concern was confined mainly to leaks from State and Defense, and even there Kissinger had been reassuring that the danger was minimal because no one there, from the secretaries on down, had anything very significant in writing if anyone knew anything at all. Real policy was made in the White House, and the NSC was very trustworthy and secure. Still, what Kissinger had just heard from Laird that morning was that Senator Mathias had "a bundle of documents" that he had gotten from Ellsberg. "They are just memos to us—and our replies can't be much because all we ever said was, 'The President has decided that . . .'" Nixon asked about the source of the information. Then:

President: And they have some NSC documents?
Kissinger: Well, they have some NSC . . . Yeah.
President: We don't have anything on Cambodia in there, in the NSC, do we? Goddamn it . . .
Kissinger: (a) It's from '69. (b) Our whole system is different. I don't know what it is. . . . We can certainly have some silly memos from Rogers. . . .

When Kissinger raised this issue with Mitchell, just after the discussion of prosecuting me, the attorney general confirmed that he had learned of this from Mathias himself, who had called him "earlier." (On June 13, I learned later, though Mitchell didn't acknowledge this in the Oval Office. In late 1971, Senator Mathias told former senator Charles Goodell, then acting as one of my attorneys, that on Sunday, June 13, the day that the *Times* began publication of the Pentagon Papers, he had felt compelled as a Republican senator to phone Attorney General Mitchell at home and tell him, "John, there's something I think you ought to know about. . . .") Mitchell added, "Why he never came forward about this Ellsberg I don't know. I chewed him out for that. Ellsberg's been talking to Mathias."

The questions were obvious: Where in the bureaucracy had I obtained these documents; what exactly were they; what else did I have; who were my sources; what else might come from them, and from me?

President: . . . The shit's going to hit the fan now . . . there must be more stuff than these documents, isn't that right?
Mitchell: Very much so.
Kissinger: That would be right, but of course now, if this leads to a situation where all our enemies in the bureaucracy can leak all of the documents of *our* administration and force us into defenses . . .
Mitchell: They're going to look at the fact that Mr. Ellsberg is under indictment.

This last thought was indeed the purpose of putting me under indictment, but it was beginning to look inadequate to the problem. I might have more material on the current administration, and I might continue to serve as a safe channel for others, such as those who had presumably given me the documents I had given to Mathias on March 2, 1971. I had clearly shown that I was not deterred by the prospect of prosecution or prison. According to Colson, Kissinger had said in the Oval Office in front of him, the president, and others, "Daniel Ellsberg is the most dangerous man in America. He must be stopped at all costs."

Whatever dangers Kissinger saw in me when he made that statement, just days after publication of the Pentagon Papers began, they obviously did not rest on that publication at all. The president saw mainly opportunity in further publication of the dirty linen of past presidents, by himself, if necessary. Whether or not Kissinger had already learned that Mathias had received NSC documents from me—Mitchell already knew it, and so did the FBI—he knew from my direct contacts with him in 1970 and my letters and writings since then, plus my wiretapped phone conversations with Halperin, that I understood their secret policy. For example, the FBI wiretap logs, which were read by Kissinger's assistant Al Haig and some of which went directly to Kissinger and Nixon, showed Halperin and me agreeing on November 22, 1970, within days of the Son Tay raid and the bombing near Hanoi and Haiphong: "This is the time to act, to get people activated; that if this doesn't move people nothing will until the holocaust—the destruction of Hanoi or the invasion of Laos." Now it appeared that I could have documents to back up such predictions. They could have come to me not only from Halperin but from Tony Lake, Larry Lynn, or others who had left the NSC staff in protest over Cambodia, or from still others who had never left.

Kissinger continued to express confidence that his NSC operations were safe from leaks, but his assurances now had to be taken with some skepticism. Nixon began to talk about the need to have a special clearance for conversations with the president.

Kissinger: But you're pretty secure here. We have nothing into the bureaucracy of *our* memos. There isn't anything floating around like Bundy's stuff. I've never shown any cabinet member, except occasionally to John [Connally], memos I've written to you . . . Rogers, Laird, nobody has ever seen. . . .

President: . . . My point is . . . that we have a new classification . . . for any conversation with the President . . . goddamn it, it's got to be classified. . . . There're a million people that have top secret clearances in this government. *One million.* For Christsakes . . .

Kissinger: But I'm thinking, Mr. President, that after—if, if this doesn't blow up our various schemes now . . . that we might consider, you might consider, going to a joint session of Congress and say this has gone too far now and ask for some laws and get a tough battle going.

Two hours later on June 30, in another discussion with Kissinger and Haldeman on the implications of the Mathias revelation, Nixon came back to the immediate challenge:

> My point is, Henry, my point is, Henry, the reason this is terribly important, of course, is that we have been saying consistently that this, these documents do not involve this administration. This appears—it appears now that we were wrong. . . .

From this point on, the taped discussions suggest that the president had lost his personal interest in the legal proceedings against me, which had begun just the day before. Extralegal proceedings seemed to hold more promise. The next day, July 1, the president said to Haldeman, Colson, and Ehrlichman,

> The difficulty is that all the good lawyers around here . . . they're always saying, well, we've got to win the court case through the court. We're *through* with this sort of court case. It's our position—I don't want that fellow Ellsberg to be brought up until after the election. I mean, just let—convict the son of a bitch *in the press. That's the way it's done. . . .*

It had a crucial impact on the White House response to the word from Mathias, and thenceforth to its response to me, that no one in the administration knew what it was that I had given the senator, except that it was of the Nixon era, dealt with Vietnam, and was from the NSC. Mathias hadn't told Mitchell or Laird more than that. Kissinger expected to see the documents on the afternoon of June 30, but Mathias didn't show them to him or anyone else in the executive branch throughout July. According to Mitchell on July 6, Justice and Defense hoped to see them on the eighth (it didn't happen), but "Mathias is playing a little cat and mouse game. . . ." As late as July 20 Ehrlichman was proposing to the president that someone, perhaps Elliot Richardson or Richard Kleindienst, be deputized to take off the "kid gloves" with Mathias and force him to show exactly what he had. So there was no awareness throughout that period that what I had given Mathias was (simply) NSSM-1. Moreover, it's clear from numerous taped discussions that Kissinger never did reveal to Nixon the embarrassing information that I had worked directly for him in February and March of 1969, in the NSC offices in the Executive Office Building, specifically on NSSM-1. Since no one knew both those pieces of data, Mitchell's conclusion on July 6, agreeing with the president that there must be a conspiracy, was inescapable:

With respect to Ellsberg and the papers that Mathias has, obviously, there's somebody else other than Ellsberg who is taking them out of the government and, uh, we may have some problems finding that guy, but hopefully we will be able to. That guy or guys.

That came in an hourlong discussion among Nixon, Mitchell, Haldeman, and Ehrlichman (Kissinger was not present) of what the president called "the Mathias thing . . . the rest of the papers."

President: . . . the problem that we have on those is . . . these are papers from the NSC, is that correct? Y'see—that's what I'm concerned about. . . .

Mitchell: They are . . . the Nixon papers. As far as I know he has not described them.

Haldeman: How did they get—

President: How did they get out of the NSC file, that's my point . . . that's the investigation that's got to be given the highest priority immediately now. . . .

Nixon: Well, in any event, when you say Nixon papers— Are these papers—not apparently *from me,* or, or are they? . . . I don't see how they could be . . . because I, I've scared Henry within an inch of his life from the time he's been here. He's never going to get anything from me out on anything.

Ehrlichman: Well, I gather these are to or from you—one or the other. And—

Nixon: It wouldn't be *from* me. They're not from me, John, because they're written from Henry. You know what I mean. The NSC—that's the way it's done.

Mitchell: I understood it as being during the Nixon Administration. . . . That's as much information as I have on it.

Nixon: We'll know in a couple of days. . . . If he makes good on it. But in case, if Ellsberg's sources are *contemporary* . . .

Mitchell: I believe that.

Nixon: . . . I think we've got to get at the conspiracy angle here. Ellsberg is not a lone operator. Ellsberg is a, he's a—I don't know who's in it. . . . But we have got to get at the people who are conspirators in it. . . . This has to be tried in the papers, in the newspapers, you understand what I mean? . . .

And in this instance, these fellows have all put themselves above the law and, including apparently, including two or three of Henry's staff and by God we're going to go after 'em because there's just too much stuff in there now that I don't want another one of his boys to leak it out. That's why— John, you cannot assume that Henry's staff didn't do this. Because we've got to find out whether people *currently* . . . still in the government.

You've got the Ellsberg case. I'm not so interested in getting out and indicting people and then having our mouths shut. I'm more interested in, frankly, getting the story out, see the point? That's even on the Ellsberg thing. I'm not so sure that I would, that I'd want him tried, convicted—we had to do that because he's admitted . . .

And the other thing is, I think right now I have a feeling you're in an excellent position to go forward letting the leaks and everything else out which would indicate that these bastards are guilty as hell and, I . . . cannot wait for, uh, the conviction of Ellsberg and so forth.

Mitchell: No, I quite agree.

The president was not really confident, however, that his attorney general or the Justice Department was fit to do what needed to be done. On July 1, the day after the Supreme Court lifted the restraints against publishing classified history and the day after the White House had learned that I still presented a problem that couldn't be handled by a trial, the president said to Haldeman:

> Actually, when Mitchell leaves as Attorney General [to run the campaign], we're going to be better off in my view. . . . John is just too damn good a lawyer, you know. He's a good strong lawyer. It just repels him to do these horrible things, but they've got to be done. We have to fight this. . . .

Earlier that day Nixon had laid out to Haldeman, Colson, and Ehrlichman his requirements for "a man in this White House staff who's full time on the two things." The two things were, first, leaking against previous Democratic administrations, especially Kennedy's but going back to FDR and Pearl Harbor ("You know, how he knew what was happening, and he did it deliberately"). "Let's have a little fun. . . . It takes the eyes off of Vietnam. It gets them thinking about the past rather than our present problems." The second thing was leaking against me.

President: . . . we won the [Alger] Hiss case in the papers. We did. I had to leak stuff all over the place. . . . It was won in the papers. John Mitchell doesn't understand that sort of thing. He's a good lawyer. It's hard to him. John Ehrlichman will have difficulty.

But what I mean is we have to develop now a program, a program for leaking out information. We're destroying these people in the papers. . . .

This is a game. It's got to be played in the press. That's why Mitchell can't do this. It isn't possible for him.

Haldeman: It's got to be a guy you can really trust, because it's got to be—

President: Run from the White House without being caught . . .

In the course of these conversations Colson pressed the candidacy of "one guy on the outside that has the capacity and ideological bent who might be able to do all of this. . . . He's hard as nails. . . . He just got out of the CIA. . . . His name is Howard Hunt." He added, on the basis of a phone conversation with Hunt he had surreptitiously taped and transcribed earlier that day, "Ideologically, he is already convinced this is a big conspiracy." In that call, Colson had asked Hunt about me, "Do you think this guy is a lone wolf?"

Hunt had replied, "Yes, I do: with the exception of the Eastern establishment, which certainly aided and abetted him." On the question of prosecuting me, Hunt had said, "I want to see the guy hung if it can be done to the advantage of the administration."

In a memo to Haldeman recommending Hunt, Colson mentioned, "I had forgotten when I talked to you that he was the CIA mastermind on the Bay of Pigs." An unusual job recommendation—uncannily prescient, as it turned out—but evidently effective. Hunt got the job on July 7, though perhaps what was critical to his hiring, in the eyes of Haldeman's boss, was Colson's next sentence: "He told me a long time ago that if the truth were ever known, Kennedy would be destroyed."

The *Times* had covered the volume on the Diem coup in its first issue after the Supreme Court had lifted the injunctions, but that didn't go far enough, as the president saw it, in exposing the Kennedy White House. Hunt was assigned to search State Department and CIA files for highly secret back-channel cables not included in that study that would, in Colson's words, "indicate direct complicity" of President Kennedy in the murder of President Diem. Unable to find any—he suspected that the files had been purged—Hunt was encouraged by Colson to "improve" on the files available by forging cables that would be more incriminating to the former president. Using his CIA tradecraft, he produced two cables that Colson arranged for him to show to a journalist from *Life,* who was excited by them and wanted to reproduce them in the magazine. Hunt warned Colson that the forgeries wouldn't stand up to scrutiny. Hunt hadn't been able to reproduce the right White House typefaces for the period, and "after the Alger Hiss case, everyone was typewriter conscious." So the article didn't appear, and the forgeries rested in Hunt's White House safe until the Watergate break-in.

Though Hunt remained on Colson's White House staff payroll, he had been lent on July 17 to a special investigative unit (SIU) set up in the White House by the president who assigned responsibility for it to his domestic counsel, John Ehrlichman. It was directed by Egil Krogh, an Ehrlichman aide, and David Young, an aide to Henry Kissinger, who supervised the activities of Hunt and a former FBI agent, G. Gordon Liddy. The group came to be known to history as the White House Plumbers because of an in-joke in the team. A relative of David Young's had read in the *Times* that he was working on leaks in the White House. She told him, "Your grandfather would be proud of you . . . he was a plumber." Young subsequently hung a sign outside room 16 in the basement of the Executive Office Building, their otherwise-unmarked, highly secure office suite, reading MR. YOUNG: PLUMBER.

The irony of calling themselves "plumbers" was that a major function of the group was to support the dual program of *leaking* that the president had called for. Thus Hunt's first job was to leak secret cables—actually, "improved" or fake secret cables—on President Kennedy and Diem. His first use of the disguises and false identification he had been given by the CIA was in a surreptitious investigation of Ted Kennedy's role in Chappaquiddick, the results of which of course were to be leaked or used to manipulate or blackmail Kennedy. The second part of the job was to gather information, partly surreptitiously, on me, to be leaked.

These were the objectives of a Hunt memo to Colson on July 28, 1971, which came out almost two years later as a result of an inquiry launched in our courtroom. The subject heading was "Neutralization of Ellsberg." It began: "I am proposing a skeletal operations plan aimed at building a file on Ellsberg that will contain all available overt, covert and derogatory information. This basic tool is essential to determining how to destroy his public image and credibility."

There followed a list of eight "items" that represented "desiderata," identifying potentially useful sources of information to this end, ranging from clearance materials to interviews with my former wife and former colleagues at Rand and ISA. Two of these items were: "Request CIA to perform a covert psychological assessment/evaluation on Ellsberg" and, fatefully, "Obtain Ellsberg's files from his psychiatric analysis."

The last proposal, which led to the burglary of the office of my former psychoanalyst in Beverly Hills, Dr. Lewis Fielding, and the hiring of Howard Hunt have commonly been seen, with reason, as a beginning of the undoing of the Nixon administration. The motives that lay behind both of these have scarcely been guessed at, however, and the guesses have been wide of the mark. The most authoritative statement of the aims both of the SIU and of the Fielding break-in is by the man in charge of the unit, Egil Krogh, who is at the same time the only one who has been thoroughly candid. In his statement to Judge Gerhart Gesell at his sentencing, after a guilty plea for approving the Fielding break-in, he laid out both the aims of the burglary and the intended uses of the information sought from it. "The aims of the operation were many." One of these aims was "to ascertain if prosecution of Dr. Ellsberg would induce him to make further disclosures that he otherwise would not."

That has an odd ring, except in the context of a discussion between Kissinger and the president on July 27, the day before Hunt drafted his proposals for an extralegal investigation to "neutralize Ellsberg":

Kissinger: I think Mitchell ought to go easy trying Ellsberg until we've broken the Vietnam War one way or the other. Because that son-of-a-bitch— First of all, I would expect—I know him well. . . . I am sure he has some more information. . . . I would bet that he has more information that he's saving for the trial. Examples of American war crimes that triggered him into it. I don't know, but it would be my instincts.

President: Uh, huh.

Kissinger: It's the way he'd operate.

President: [indistinct: Postpone?] Ellsberg prosecution . . .

Kissinger: Secondly, once we've broken the war in Vietnam, then we can say, this son-of-a-bitch nearly blew it. Then we have, then we're in strong shape—then no one will give a damn about war crimes.

. . . Because he is a despicable bastard.

In his January 1974 statement to Judge Gesell, Krogh described the "potential uses" of the information to be gained from the burglary as "multiple":

> Primary, of course, was preventing further disclosures by Dr. Ellsberg and putting an end to whatever machinery for disclosure might have been developed. It was also thought, particularly by E. Howard Hunt, that the sought information could be useful in causing Dr. Ellsberg himself to disclose his true intentions. Finally, there is the point that has been most stressed in the current investigative process—the potential use of the information in discrediting Dr. Ellsberg as an anti-war spokesman.

Krogh expanded on the last function—which, in contrast to the presumption in virtually all accounts since, he did not regard as "primary"—in another part of the statement:

> To discredit Dr. Ellsberg would serve to discourage others who might be tempted to emulate him in disclosing information. It would also make him less able to mobilize opposition to President Nixon's chosen Vietnam policy. The freedom of the President to pursue his chosen foreign policy was seen as the essence of national security.

Thus, one of the goals of the SIU and the proposed break-in was to gather the sort of information that would serve the task Nixon laid on Mitchell, Colson, and Hunt: to "convict [me] in the press" by leaking it out. However, in the eyes of Egil Krogh (as he has since confirmed to me), that was not the *main* function either of the overall effort aimed at me or of the specific raid on my psychoanalyst's office. According to Krogh's 1974 statement (emphasis added):

> My best recollection is that I focused on the *prevention of further leaks* of Dr. Ellsberg and the termination of any machinery he may have established for such disclosures. That was the use most central to the assignment of the unit as I understood it.

There was nothing paranoid in the suspicion of President Nixon and Henry Kissinger that I might well put out further classified documents that would threaten their Vietnam policy. Given what Senator Mathias had told them—but not yet shown them—they knew that I had secret documents on Vietnam from their own National Security Council, documents that I had not yet released to the public. Not knowing that these were documents I myself had worked on (for Kissinger), copied, and brought back to Rand, they could only assume that they had been given to me by someone who had been on the NSC staff in 1969, and perhaps was still there, still in a position to give me other documents. Even if my source had left the NSC at some point, plans had already been laid in 1969 for every one of the escalations that had been the basis for secret threats to Hanoi and for escalations actual and pending, from 1969 through 1971. The contingency plans, threats, and some of the actual escalations in Cambodia and Laos were kept secret—not from Hanoi or its Communist allies but from the American public and Congress—precisely because to make them public would, in Egil Krogh's unusually insightful formulation, threaten what the White House saw as the very "essence of national security": "[t]he freedom of the President to pursue his chosen foreign policy."

I suspect that President Nixon was entirely sincere in asserting later that he saw me as a threat to national security, if you define national security in that precise sense. I threatened, to the best of my ability, to make public a strategy that our democratic system was not likely to permit him to pursue freely, if it was correctly understood.

That leaves the question, How was information to be gained from a psychoanalyst's office to contribute to "preventing further disclosures" by me? That was obscure to me until I heard an answer in 1975 from Taylor Branch, journalist and, more recently, Pulitzer Prize–winning biographer of Martin Luther King, Jr. In that year Branch and his fellow journalist George Crile interviewed the Cubans involved with Howard Hunt in a number of ventures beginning with the Bay of Pigs. These included Eugenio Martinez and Bernard Barker, who participated both in the burglary of the office of Dr. Fielding, my former psychoanalyst, and later in Watergate (and also in an attempted assault on me in 1972, which I will describe in the next chapter). Branch had learned from them that in 1971 they were seeking information on me that I would strongly not want revealed, information with which I could be blackmailed out of revealing any other secrets affecting national security I might possess. They knew nothing of what those secrets might be; they knew only that I was a "traitor."

To this end, Branch said, they were equally interested in finding information on Dr. Fielding himself in his files, in order to induce him to change his refusal to talk to the FBI about me. When I heard it, that made more sense to me than anyone's naive supposition that they would find the kind of information the SIU wanted in a psychoanalyst's written files. To somehow induce the analyst to talk about his patient would produce a great deal more information. Indeed, Barker told an interviewer for *Harper's* that he had looked at Fielding's income tax reports in his files and "got the impression that the good doctor was not paying all his income taxes." They told

Branch they were also interested in anything they could find out about my children or my wife, as much as anything on me, for this purpose of manipulating me.

None of this excluded simply leaking the information that might be gained from Dr. Fielding or his files, perhaps by Colson (as one of the SIU's memos suggested at the time). In terms of the objectives of the SIU as Krogh understood them, however, the prospect not of actually leaking it but of *threatening* to reveal something they had discovered made great sense. According to Branch, some rather specific objectives were discussed. Faced with some sufficiently shaming exposure, I might at a minimum be induced to refrain from further disclosures. I might even be led to flee the country for asylum in Cuba or Algeria, like Eldridge Cleaver or Timothy Leary, or possibly induced to commit suicide (the maximum hope of some in the FBI in sending Martin Luther King, Jr., tapes of his alleged sexual adventures). I feel sure, knowing myself at that time, that nothing could have induced me to do any of those things. But it wasn't irrational to hope otherwise. And there was a lot at stake, as the White House understood the threat posed to its secret war policy by possible disclosure of it.

32

End of a Trial

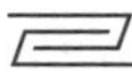

On April 27, 1973, at the opening of the eightieth court day of the trial of Anthony Russo and myself, Judge Matthew Byrne turned over to the defense a memo he had received the day before from the Justice Department. Dated April 16, it was from the Watergate prosecutor Earl Silbert to Assistant Attorney General Henry E. Petersen. It began:

> This is to inform you that on Sunday, April 15, 1973, I received information that at a date unspecified, Gordon Liddy and Howard Hunt burglarized the offices of a psychiatrist of Daniel Ellsberg to obtain the psychiatrist's files relating to Ellsberg.

When this was released, out of the presence of the jury, to members of the press in our courtroom, they rushed to the phones in the hallway. It was the first time we'd seen them acting like trial reporters in an old movie, racing competitively to file stories. They were envisioning, as one journalist put it, front-page headlines: WATERGATE MEETS THE PENTAGON PAPERS TRIAL.

Hunt and Liddy were already known to the press and public, though not as well as they became in the final two weeks of our trial and thereafter, for their role in the Watergate break-in. The same was true of the three Cuban-Americans, all Bay of Pigs veterans and "assets" of the CIA since then, who were soon to be named as having broken into my psychoanalyst's office, under Hunt and Liddy's direction. Two of them, Bernard Barker and Eugenio Martinez, had been arrested inside the Watergate offices of the

Democratic National Committee on June 17, 1972. (The third, Felipe de Diego, had participated in an earlier break-in at the Watergate, in May.) Hunt, Barker, and Martinez had pleaded guilty, and Liddy had been convicted for the Watergate break-in in a Washington court in March 1973, the month before Judge Byrne's announcement in our trial. The White House had repeatedly denied any connection to this "third-rate burglary" of the Watergate, and none of the defendants had acknowledged any links to higher-ups or knowledge of any other crimes, even when given immunity and questioned under oath before a grand jury after their conviction.

Silbert had argued the Watergate case on the theory that Liddy—an ex-FBI agent, now the legal counsel of CREEP, the Committee to Reelect the President (Nixon)—had been off on a "private caper," in which he had enlisted Hunt and the four men arrested in the Watergate offices. Judge John Sirica had been openly skeptical of this explanation, since Hunt, whose White House office number in the Executive Office Building had been found in the burglars' effects, and all the other participants except Liddy had been employees or contract agents of the CIA. But the judge had not been able to break it down until one defendant, James McCord, a former high security officer in the CIA now working for CREEP, sent him a message before sentencing that there had been perjury during the trial and that others had been involved in ordering the operation. However, McCord was unaware of any White House connection.

After reading Silbert's letter, Judge Byrne demanded that the prosecutor provide quick answers from the government on a number of questions, such as "Were Hunt and Liddy acting as agents of the government at the time of the burglary, and at whose direction had it been committed?" On Monday, April 30, Judge Byrne received, and passed to our defense, an FBI report of a new interview with John Ehrlichman on April 27. This introduced to the public the prior existence of the special investigative unit, the Plumbers, supervised by Ehrlichman for the president. It answered Byrne's first question: As employees of the White House pursuing a project focused particularly on me, launched by order of the president soon after my indictment, Hunt and Liddy had directed the burglary of the Beverly Hills office of my former psychoanalyst, Dr. Lewis Fielding, on September 3, 1971, over the Labor Day weekend. This was the first public acknowledgment by Nixon administration officials—specifically, Ehrlichman and White House Counsel John Dean, who had made the disclosure to the prosecutors on April 15—of the White House direction of a clear-cut domestic crime. Clear-cut, at least, to all those who (unlike Ehrlichman and Nixon) rejected the notion that a claim of national security precluded any question of criminality of any action undertaken in the administration's name.

That evening, April 30, President Nixon announced the resignations of Ehrlichman and White House Chief of Staff H. R. Haldeman—"two of the finest public servants I have ever known"—and of Richard Kleindienst as acting attorney general, along with the departure of John Dean.

Evidence of other White House illegalities and criminal obstructions of justice followed in quick succession. Hunt was brought back before the grand jury, and his new testimony, recanting his earlier perjury, was released in our courtroom by our prosecutor or judge as our trial continued. Hunt revealed that in response to requests by Ehrlichman, the CIA had (illegally) furnished logistic support for a domestic covert operation, including false identification, a voice-altering device, a gait-altering shoe insert, clandestine cameras, fake glasses, and wigs, and had prepared for the White House two "psychological profiles" on me. The Fielding break-in, which Hunt had suggested, had been in part for the purpose of furnishing data for the second of these profiles. All this was in violation of the statutory charter of the CIA, forbidding it to engage in domestic covert or police or intelligence activities, including counterespionage, which at the federal level were the exclusive province of the FBI. The agency had never constructed a psychological profile on an American citizen before (believing itself forbidden by law from so doing). With internal misgivings in the staff and following a specific plea from Director Richard Helms that its role be concealed with unusual discretion, the CIA had fulfilled the White House requests that Hunt had suggested from his knowledge of past profiles on such foreign targets as Indonesia's President Sukarno and Castro.

Asked before the grand jury about other crimes for the White House project, Hunt mentioned the two cables he had fabricated, at Colson's urging, implicating President Kennedy in President Diem's murder. Along with his revelation to prosecutors on April 15 of the Fielding break-in, White House Counsel Dean, who was plea-bargaining with the prosecutors for immunity from prosecution for running the White House cover-up of Watergate and other White House crimes, had revealed the probable destruction of these cables. When Dean had gone through the contents of Hunt's White House safe a few days after the Watergate break-in, he had found the two forged cables, along with folders on me, including the two CIA psychological profiles, and memos to Colson on his White House activities. (The latter had also included the clandestine investigation of Ted Kennedy for which Hunt had first used the disguise materials provided by the CIA.) Ehrlichman had told Dean to shred all these documents, which looked especially sensitive in an election year (and implicated White House staffers, including him). Larger items from the safe, such as a briefcase filled with apparatus for bugging, Dean could "deep-six" by tossing them over a bridge on his way home. Dean had concerns about doing any of this, for two reasons: It was illegal, and a number of people had witnessed him in possession of these materials. He had pointed out that Ehrlichman passed over the same bridge on the way to his home; he could toss the briefcase himself if that seemed appropriate. Finally they agreed that if anyone were going to destroy potential evidence in a criminal trial, they preferred it to be the acting director of the FBI, Nixon loyalist L. Patrick Gray.

According to Gray, they called him to Ehrlichman's office, handed him two sealed envelopes from Hunt's safe (containing the folders above), which Dean described as "highly sensitive and very secret files" from Hunt's safe that were "political dynamite" but had nothing to do with the Watergate case. He told Gray, "They should not be put in the FBI files and they should never see the light of day. Here, you take them." Gray later testified that he had to infer from these admonitions by Dean, speaking as a representative of the president in the presence of the president's assistant, that he was meant to destroy them, and he did. He variously said that he had shredded them in his office and put them in his burn bag or that he had stored them at home and much later burned them with holiday wrapping paper a few days after Christmas.

All this figured in discussions in our courtroom among the judge, the prosecutor, and our lawyers, since materials relating to me, the nature and bearing of which were now beyond discovery, had been among those destroyed by the FBI chief. Dean revealed his transaction with Gray in the discussion he held with the prosecutors on April 15, when he told them of the Fielding break-in. After Gray acknowledged to Acting Attorney General Kleindienst that he had indeed destroyed the documents, he was forced to resign as acting director of the FBI. He did so on the same day, April 27, that Judge Byrne disclosed the Fielding break-in. The news of his reason for resigning was the first administration revelation of obstruction of justice encouraged by the White House.

Others followed quickly. Among other things, Judge Byrne asked the prosecution on April 27 why the memo from Silbert about the break-in, dated April 16, had taken ten days to reach his courtroom. It turned out that the president had personally directed Assistant Attorney General Petersen not to send it off to the judge in our criminal trial, though it was the legal obligation of the Justice Department to do so, on the ground that it was a "national security" matter and on his assertion that the burglary had been a "dry hole," discovering nothing that could have affected the trial. Since Petersen and his boss, Kleindienst, knew that was a question for the judge to determine, they grew increasingly anxious—as our trial proceeded without benefit of this information—that they, along with the president, could be charged with obstruction of justice.

On April 25 Kleindienst told Nixon that the Silbert memo "must" be sent to the judge in Los Angeles. The judge would have the option of holding the information in camera (undisclosed to the press and public) and having an in camera hearing on whether the evidence affected the trial. He could also order the Ellsberg attorneys to make no public reference to the information or the in camera procedure. Nixon told Kleindienst that it was important to let the judge know, as the information was passed on, that the Fielding break-in was "a national security investigation of very great sensitivity." Kleindienst reported an hour later that the prosecutors hoped to persuade Byrne to hold off on disclosure and hearings entirely until after the trial, then to proceed only in case it ended with a guilty verdict. Nixon responded: "That's good. Let me say one other thing. I don't know how you can get this to the judge, but I think it's very important for him to know that this is a national security investigation of the highest importance. It really is, you see . . . you know that and I know it." He repeated that he wanted the prosecutor to know it too. He went on, in the transcript of the phone call: "Okay. Well, sleep well, boy . . ."

Kleindienst: Hang in there, Mr. President.

President: Good luck. What the hell, you know. People say impeach the President. Well, then they get Agnew. What the hell? [Laughter] Is that all right? Is that all right?

Kleindienst: There's not going to be anything like that.

President: All right, boy. Fine . . .

This may be the first mention of the possibility of impeachment on the White House tapes. The president phoned Kleindienst several times on the twenty-sixth to ask about the judge's decision. Petersen informed Nixon on the twenty-seventh that Judge Byrne had read the report given him by the prosecutor the previous evening "and was inclined to the view that disclosure to him was sufficient. And then apparently overnight he changed his position."

Actually, over the objection of the prosecutor, Judge Byrne had in effect left it up to me. On the afternoon of April 26, he had called all the lawyers and defendants in and told David R. Nissen, the chief prosecutor, that he had looked at the contents of the sealed envelope Nissen had given him earlier and had concluded it was not information he could receive privately. He asked Nissen if he was willing to turn it over to the defense. Nissen said he would have to check with his Justice Department superiors. The next morning he told the judge that they had decided not to reveal the contents of the memo. Byrne then called Tony and me and the attorneys on both sides up to the bench, out of hearing of the press, and ordered Nissen to give the document to the defense. He told us that we were entitled to this information and to a hearing if we requested it.

I remember the moment well, in particular because it was the first time in two years since my proceedings in his courtroom began that the judge looked me in the face and addressed me directly. All his communications to our defense team had been addressed to my lawyers; I don't recall his ever having looked at me eye to eye till that moment. He said to me, "Mr. Ellsberg, I don't need to reveal this information publicly. I can keep it in camera if you wish." I took it he meant that I might not wish it revealed that I had been in psychoanalysis (a fact *Time* magazine had already revealed—to Howard Hunt, among others—two years earlier). I said, "Are you kidding? Put it out!" They were my own first words directly to the judge since my not-guilty plea. The press rush to the phones followed shortly.

Our trial continued, with a fascinating surprise nearly every day, such as the departures from the White House of Haldeman, Ehrlichman, Kleindienst, and Dean on the evening of April 30, Gray, the acting head of the FBI, having resigned on the twenty-seventh. As Kissinger noted in his memoirs, the impression was unavoidable that the president was "no longer in control of events." But that was true not just of Nixon. Early the same day my lawyer Charlie Nesson got a phone message from Mort Halperin, who was in Washington, that the morning edition of the *Washington Star* reported that Judge Byrne had met some weeks earlier with the president and Ehrlichman at the Western White House at San Clemente to be offered the job of director of the FBI.

Having been notified by Nesson that this report would be introduced in court, Judge Byrne read a hastily drafted statement that he had had such a meeting, though he had not discussed the case and had told Ehrlichman that he could not discuss the job offer till the case was over. On April 30 our defense lawyers had argued for an immediate hearing on the Fielding break-in for the next day, with John Dean (who had been named in *Newsweek* as the source to Silbert), Patrick Gray (who had admitted destroying documents that might have related to my case), Hunt, and Liddy to testify in our court. However, the next day, May 1, our defense lawyers changed our position to a motion for dismissal of the indictment. Leonard Boudin emphasized the grounds of the FBI report on Ehrlichman we had just received that morning. Leonard Weinglass, Tony Russo's lawyer, also pointed out that at the time "Ehrlichman met with your honor on April 5," Ehrlichman knew both that "he was part of an investigation into the break-in" and "that your honor was trying a case involving Dr. Ellsberg. . . . It raises the question of what was in Mr. Ehrlichman's mind when he had the meeting with your honor." He suggested that Ehrlichman's actions "make the issue of what was obtained from Fielding's office insignificant."

Judge Byrne denied the motion for dismissal, while saying that it could be renewed later. He specifically rejected as grounds for dismissal that part of the defense motion referring to the job offer, asserting that he had in no way been influenced by it. He mentioned that he had met only briefly with the president and that there had been no discussion of the case with either Nixon or Ehrlichman.

A few days later in May the press, not Judge Byrne, disclosed that he had phoned Ehrlichman to ask for a second meeting, which had been held on April 7 in Santa Monica. The judge acknowledged the second meeting, which he said he had requested in order to reiterate that he could not discuss the offer till the end of the trial. Ehrlichman claimed that Byrne had expressed great interest in the job on both occasions and shared his thoughts on how the FBI should be run. Weinglass remarked to a journalist, "If one of us had offered Judge Byrne a job during this trial, we'd all be in jail."

White House tapes later showed that Byrne's name entered the White House discussions of candidates for this post in late March, when Hunt was expected to go before the grand jury with immunity after his recent Watergate conviction. (Byrne was unaware of this, of course.) Despite the president's recent decision to pay Hunt for his continued silence (discussed below), it was feared that news of the Fielding break-in might shortly be on its way to Byrne's courtroom, where the judge would have discretion whether to reveal it to us and the public. Press reports after April 27 quoted unnamed high officials in the Justice Department as being furious with the judge for turning over the Silbert memorandum to the defense, and there were later conjectures that this was the motive for the leak to the *Star*.

Why this personal obstruction of justice on Nixon's part? For the same reason—it can now be inferred, from the White House tapes and the totality of evidence—that he had involved himself in the cover-up and obstruction of justice, including payments to criminal defendants for their perjury and silence to maintain the cover-up, from the earliest days after the Watergate arrests. That was not from a need to protect himself from direct implication in the Watergate break-in itself. None of those arrested in connection with it, including Hunt and Liddy, were able to link the president or anyone in the White House to that break-in. Indeed, to this day no testimony or evidence has ever emerged showing foreknowledge of the Watergate burglary on June 17, 1972 (or an earlier one on May 23), by Nixon or any other White House official.

The reason for Nixon's direct involvement, as early as June 23, 1972, and continuing, has turned out to be his concern to keep Howard Hunt from revealing the earlier Fielding break-in and other illegal actions of the Plumbers. As I learned later, the burglary of my psychoanalyst's office in September 1971, though best known, was not the last or most dramatic of these. Eight months later, on May 3, 1972, on orders from Colson to Liddy and Hunt, the White House secretly flew a dozen Cuban-American CIA "assets" from Miami to Washington to disrupt a rally that I and others were addressing on the steps of the Capitol and to assault me physically.

This was the rally described earlier, five days before the mining of Haiphong and eight days after Senator Gravel had released NSSM-1 to the press. The purpose of the planned assault on me remains obscure. However, an Oval Office tape of May 2 reveals that Nixon was aware that I had chosen this moment to reveal NSSM-1 at last. Whatever else I had from NSC files could be presumed to be on the verge of disclosure. According to Nick Akerman, the attorney on the Watergate Special Prosecution Task Force (WSPTF) who investigated this incident (with over one hundred interviews), some members of the team from Miami had orders "to incapacitate [me] totally." Different members of the team had different perspectives on their functions. All of them reported that Hunt and Liddy had shown them my picture (and that of Bill Kunstler, also at the rally) and told them I was the "target." Several told the FBI or WSPTF that, as one put it to *Time,* "We were to call him 'traitor' and punch him in the nose." Bernard Barker (who with Eugenio Martinez recruited the team in Miami) told the journalist Lloyd Shearer later that his orders had been to "break both [my] legs." (The team found the crowd too friendly to me to make it safe to carry out their mission. Some of them instead assaulted young participants on the edge of the crowd and were led away by police, who released them to two men showing government credentials. Several of them were driven that night by Hunt and Liddy to reconnoiter "their next objective," the Watergate offices of the Democratic National Committee.)

Just weeks after this, several who had participated in both of these criminal efforts directed by the White House—the Fielding burglary and the roughing up of demonstrators on May 3—were arrested in connection with the Watergate break-in. To keep them from pointing prosecutors to earlier crimes, including those against me, that could be traced directly to the Oval Office, Nixon had to direct a cover-up personally. For most actions of Hunt and Liddy when they were working for the Campaign to Reelect the President (except for the May 3 operation) the buck stopped with John Mitchell, who had left the cabinet to head the campaign. Neither Hunt, Liddy, nor McCord, let alone the Cubans arrested in Watergate, had any knowledge of any superiors higher than Mitchell in the penetration of the Watergate. But in 1971 and on May 3, 1972, Hunt and Liddy were ultimately, and unmistakably, working for the man in the Oval Office and directly for his close White House aides Ehrlichman and Colson. From the moment that arrests in the Watergate appeared likely to lead prosecutors to Hunt and Liddy, there was an implicit threat to the president that one or both of them would be tempted or forced to reveal to prosecutors earlier crimes they had committed for the White House. That danger focused on Hunt, since Liddy was known to adhere to a Mafia-like code of silence that Nixon thought "crazy" but reliable.

As early as June 23, 1972, six days after the original arrests—at Mitchell and Dean's suggestion—Nixon directed Haldeman and Ehrlichman to use CIA officials to induce the FBI to halt its investigation of Watergate short of Hunt and Liddy. Nixon wanted to limit indictments to those actually arrested at the scene, who did not include Hunt and Liddy; thus these two would be spared pressure from prosecutors to reveal *other* crimes. The tape of that conversation plotting an obstruction of an FBI criminal investigation was finally turned over to the impeachment committee in Congress in August 1974, after a thirteen-month battle by Nixon to keep it out of its hands. It proved to be the "smoking gun" that tilted even Nixon loyalists toward certain impeachment and conviction and led to his resignation. But the threat Nixon was defending against was made absolutely explicit on the tape of his March 21, 1973, "cancer on the presidency" discussion with John Dean. Dean informed him that Hunt was demanding $120,000 for "expenses," threatening explicitly that if he didn't get it, he would expose "the seamy things he had done for the White House." The president asked, and

Dean confirmed, that this referred to "Ellsberg" and "Kennedy." Nixon, overriding Dean's objections, then emphasized that there was no choice but to give Hunt money, immediately. That night $75,000 in campaign funds was found and delivered to Hunt's lawyer. Hunt was frustrated that it wasn't more, but he did continue, for the moment, to commit perjury before the grand jury.

On May 10, 1973, after daily revelations along the above lines in our trial and in Washington (though not yet the tape evidence above), the House, for the first time, voted to cut off all funding for the U.S. combat operations in Indochina, including any renewal of bombing. This was vetoed by the president. But knowing privately that he would eventually be facing a fight against impeachment (though the Ervin Committee had not yet even begun its public hearings), Nixon knew that he could not much longer sustain a veto on the bombing issue. Those who believe in retrospect that he "could not have" carried out a bombing campaign in support of his secret promises to Thieu and his own intentions to preserve the GVN, because "Congress would not have let him, even without Watergate," are thinking that a majority in Congress would have voted to cut off funds, which is probably true. But that itself would not have ended the bombing, nor would its prospect have averted it. To override his predictable veto of such a measure, the foes of bombing needed not just a simple majority but a two-thirds majority. Mort Halperin has pointed out to me that without the challenge of Watergate hanging over him, Nixon could almost surely have mustered the one-third-plus-one votes he needed to defeat a congressional attempt to override his veto, in a situation in which he could claim to be "enforcing a signed agreement" by bombing. As Larry Berman shows, that was precisely his argument for getting Thieu to sign the Paris Accords, which the South Vietnamese president otherwise detested; it would give Nixon a basis for renewed bombing that Congress could not reject. But with the Ervin hearings approaching, and Dean's testimony on Nixon's own obstruction of justice impending, Nixon could not afford to use up political capital peeling off votes against bombing when he would need every vote he could get to fight off impeachment.

Therefore, in June Nixon reluctantly reached a deal with both houses whereby all bombing would be ended on August 15. Probably most members of Congress thought of this as affecting only the bombing of Cambodia, which went on openly until that deadline. They were unaware how close the president had been to resuming the bombing of Laos and North Vietnam, which Kissinger had secretly been recommending since late

March, even before all the U.S. troops were out. Berman's book makes clear that Nixon had every intention to carry that out no later than April. According to *Time* magazine ("The Watergate Connection," May 5, 1975), the president had actually given "final, formal approval" to the order to resume bombing in April but rescinded it on hearing that Dean was talking to the prosecutors because he was "loath to deal with simultaneous severe criticism on two major fronts."

If that was so, it would have been specifically Dean's revelation to the prosecutors on April 15 of the Fielding break-in that would have posed an acute danger, enough to derail plans to present Congress with renewed bombing as a fait accompli. On May 10, two weeks after Dean's disclosure reached our courtroom on April 26, the House voted to cut off the funds. Since our courtroom was the essential forum for the public disclosure of the White House–ordered Fielding burglary aimed at me, the desire by Nixon and Kissinger that our trial be delayed till after both the election and the Vietnam War had been "wrapped up" proved fatal from their point of view.

Also that same day, May 10, the new acting director of the FBI, William Ruckelshaus, informed the court that despite many formal denials to the judge, there had been FBI electronic overhearing of me. When Judge Byrne demanded reports of the overhearing, Ruckelshaus replied on the morning of May 11 that the files were missing from the FBI and the Justice Department. (It turned out they had been removed from J. Edgar Hoover's personal files by his deputy William Sullivan on order of the president at the onset of my case. The reports included transcripts of fifteen conversations in which I had been overheard on Mort Halperin's secretly tapped home phone. These were sure to be requested on discovery by my lawyers. Since they were evidence of illegal wiretaps requested by the president and Kissinger, Nixon wanted them out of Hoover's hands lest he blackmail the White House in various ways by threatening to reveal them to Judge Byrne.)

On May 11 our defense lawyers asked the judge to rule on their motion for dismissal of the indictment with prejudice (meaning that the defendants could not be tried again on the same charges), based on "the totality of governmental misconduct, including the suppression of evidence, the invasion of the physician-patient relationship, the illegal wiretapping, the destruction of relevant documents and the disobedience to judicial orders." After the morning recess on May 11, Judge Byrne stated that his ruling was based "in that scope that Mr. Boudin has just stated. It is not based solely on the wiretap, nor is it based solely on the break-in and the information that has been presented over the last several days." He went on:

> Commencing on April 26, the government has made an extraordinary series of disclosures regarding the conduct of several governmental agencies regarding the defendants in this case. . . . Much information has been developed, but new information has produced new questions, and there remain more questions than answers.
>
> The disclosures made by the government demonstrate that governmental agencies have taken an unprecedented series of actions with respect to these defendants. After the original indictment, at a time when the government's rights to investigate the defendants are narrowly circumscribed, White House officials established a special unit to investigate one of the defendants in this case. We have been given only a glimpse of what this special unit did regarding this case, but what we have seen is more than disquieting.

He reviewed the break-in at the psychiatrist's office; the action by the CIA—"presumably acting beyond its statutory authority"—at the request of the White House, to provide disguises, photographic equipment, and other paraphernalia for covert operations and two psychological profiles; the fact that government officials who were aware of the illegal activities of this unit directed at the defendant did not make the court or apparently even the prosecution aware of them until Silbert's memorandum, "and then not for some ten days after it was written"; even earlier, the government's repeated withholding of exculpatory material; "the recent revelation of interception by electronic interception of one or more conversations of defendant Ellsberg" (after repeated denials by the FBI and the Justice Department), with the records of such surveillance having been removed from both the Justice Department and FBI files and missing since mid-1971. He exluded from his list mention of the offers to him of the FBI directorship on April 5 and 7, having earlier rejected these as grounds for dismissal. He went on:

> A continuation of the government's investigation is no solution with reference to this case . . . each passing day indicates that the investigation is further from completion as the jury waits. Moreover, no investigation is likely to provide satisfactory answers where improper government conduct has been shielded so long from public view and where the government advises the Court that pertinent files and records are missing or destroyed. . . .

> . . . The charges against these defendants raise serious factual and legal issues that I would certainly prefer to have litigated to completion. . . . However . . . the conduct of the government has placed the case in such a posture that it precludes the fair dispassionate resolution of these issues by a jury. I have concluded that a mistrial alone would not be fair. Under all the circumstances, I believe that the defendants should not have to run the risk, present under existing authorities, that they might be tried again before a different jury.
>
> The totality of the circumstances of this case which I have only briefly sketched offend "a sense of justice." The bizarre events have incurably infected the prosecution of this case. . . . I am of the opinion, in the present status of the case, that the only remedy available that would assure due process and the fair administration of justice is that this trial be terminated and the defendants' motion for dismissal be granted and the jury discharged.
>
> The order of dismissal will be entered, the jurors will be advised of the dismissal, and the case is terminated. Thank you very much, gentlemen, for your efforts.

In the courtroom, pandemonium. Cheers, hugging, crying, wild laughter. It started with a roar as soon as the judge finished his statement—in a place in which any hint of feeling from the spectators had been silenced peremptorily from the bench over the past four months—and he made little effort to stop it. He asked that the jurors be allowed to leave through the back. Then he turned around in his black robes and followed them out. The press ran to the phones; the prosecution team packed up wordlessly and left the courtroom to us. It seemed to be spinning, tilting. Patricia and I came to each other and kissed.

When we all poured out into the sunlight on the steps of the federal courthouse, to the sea of TV cameras and flashbulbs, someone held up the headline on the morning's paper: MITCHELL INDICTED.

John Mitchell, the man who had indicted me. The first of my attorney generals to face prison, soon to be joined by Kleindienst, who had presided over my prosecution until his resignation nearly two weeks earlier. Presently Haldeman and Ehrlichman and Colson were indicted too. And the White House aides assigned to neutralize me, and the CIA contract agents and other Cuban-Americans ordered to incapacitate me.

The Senate's Watergate hearings started one week later. They were to lead to the discovery of the White House tapes, which confirmed Dean's testimony that the president had directed the payment of hush money to Howard Hunt to keep him from carrying out his threat to reveal the "seamy things he had done for the White House," specifically "Ellsberg." (The "smoking gun" tape of June 23, 1972, which precipitated Nixon's resignation, revealed his effort to use the CIA to prevent Hunt from being investigated and indicted, for the same reason.) He was replaced by a president, Gerald Ford, who was unwilling, till the war ended on May 1, 1975, to act in violation of the congressional ban on further U.S. combat action in Indochina, passed by the House the day before our trial ended and by the full Congress in June 1973.

The taping system, which was closed down after Alex Butterfield revealed it to Watergate investigators on Friday, July 13, was still in secret operation on May 11, 1973, the day our trial was ended. A long conversation between the president and his former chief of staff H. R. Haldeman neared its close at 2:00 P.M., 11:00 A.M. on the West Coast. As Judge Byrne in Los Angeles was issuing his dismissal of our indictment, which had been anticipated all morning in the Oval Office discussions, the president addressed the situation in anguish and perplexity:

> For example, on this national security thing, we have the rocky situation where the sonofabitching thief is made a national hero and is going to get off on a mistrial. And the *New York Times* gets a Pulitzer Prize for stealing documents. . . . They're trying to get at us with *thieves. What in the name of God have we come to?*

What we had come back to was a democratic republic—not an elected monarchy—a government under law, with Congress, the courts, and the press functioning to curtail executive abuses, as our Constitution envisioned. Moreover, for the first time in this or any country the legislature was casting its whole vote against an ongoing presidential war. It was reclaiming, through its control of the purse, the war power it had fecklessly delegated nine years earlier. Congress was stopping the bombing, and the war was going to end.

ACKNOWLEDGMENTS

I have often read an author's acknowledgment that "without this person, this book could not have come about" as polite hyperbole. Never again. For this book I know that statement is unequivocally true—I say it with a grateful heart—about a whole set of friends and relatives. The list starts with my two sons: Robert, steadily from beginning to end, and Michael, in recurrent crises as we faced publishing deadlines. There was no way in the world that I alone would have met these deadlines, one after another, without the selfless, loving readiness of both sons to stay up with me nights on end, attached to each other by phone, e-mail, and fax lines, conferring, editing, and cutting.

Without the work of both of them—including Michael's ruthless cutting, meticulous copyediting, and insights on structure—Viking would have been presented with a manuscript several times this length, a year or two later (if ever). Every aspect of this text shows the wise judgment and moral vision of Robert—editor in chief of Orbis Books—who, working after hours and usually late at night (in crises, along with Michael, all night), has given me years of patient, reliable, and gifted counsel. Indeed, I owe a special thanks to Robert's wife, Peggy, and to his children, for uncomplainingly lending me so many hours of his family time. Robert—whose participation in this tale and project, like that of my daughter, Mary, goes back thirty-three years to the copying of the Pentagon Papers—is a saint among editors, and sons. And Patricia Ellsberg is a saint among wives of writers. I can't wish anyone greater happiness than the demonstration of caring, devotion, and real support from children and a spouse such as I have experienced in the last several years.

Yet in meeting the reasonable time and space constraints set by the publisher, the category of "indispensable" is not limited to my family. I have also been blessed with the generous help of friends who are either professional editors—Barbara Koeppel—or who have, like Michael and Patricia, a striking talent for editorial judgments, including Linda Burstyn, Julia Lieblich, Elizabeth Tomlinson, and Daidie Donnelley. Many others have read parts of the manuscript and made valuable suggestions or corrections, offered advice on process, or given me much-welcomed encouragement, including Mary Ellsberg, Sy and Liz Hersh, Margaret Brenman-Gibson, Peter Dale Scott and Ronna Kabatznick, Harry and Sophie Ellsberg, Joanna and Fran Macy, Patrice Wynne, Fred Branfman, Lynda Resnick, Bob Eaton, Randy Kehler, Mel Gurtov, Konrad Kellen, Rudi Gresham, Ron Kovic, Ruth Rosen, Janice Kruger, Floyd Galler, Ruth Garbus, Jeffrey Masson, and Stanley K. Sheinbaum. (Special mention to Edie Hartshorne, whose Feldenkrais skills saved my back at crucial times when I couldn't otherwise have kept typing.)

Countless people have contributed to my education and evolution in ways that are inadequately, or not at all, described within this book, but there is no space to remedy that here. However, because our long trial, except for its last weeks, is not covered here at all, one immense debt must not go unacknowledged. To Stanley K. Sheinbaum and

Morton H. Halperin, along with all the members of our defense team—the late Leonard Boudin, Charles Nesson, Leonard Weinglass, Dolores Donovan, Mark Rosenbaum, Peter Young, and their volunteer assistants—I owe special thanks for not having to write this book in jail. (With good behavior, I could have been out in 2008.) I'm also happy to acknowledge at last the timely pro bono legal advice I received during the first year after I began copying the papers from my friend and classmate Bob Herzstein. To Tony Russo, my permanent respect and gratitude, for many things: for eagerly sharing the full risks of unauthorized disclosure from the first day; for his principled refusal of immunity (and his consequent jail time); for seeing certain realities of our policy in Vietnam and elsewhere well before I did and patiently mentoring me on them; and for his comradeship before and, despite differences and frustrations, during our trial.

I have particularly benefited from insights and in many cases documents, both generously shared, from friends who are historians of this period: Larry Berman, Fred Logevall, Kai Bird, John Prados, Jack Langguth, Gareth Porter, Roger Morris, Arthur Schlesinger, Jr., Roger Hilsman, Jon Persoff, Gar Alperovitz, Allen Smith, and Peter Kuznick. To express my full appreciation to all of these for their own books and research, and for their contributions to my thinking, would take an entire essay.

Two more who were indispensable in crises were Jason Newman, indefatigable (all-night) research assistant and stenographer, and Tom Reifer, long-term friend and intellectual comrade. Dan Garcia helped greatly as a research assistant at an earlier stage, as did Jan Thomas. Douglas Weaver spent many hours listening to tapes of Richard Nixon and others from the Oval Office and selecting or transcribing them for me. Ken Hughes first alerted me to the relevance of these tapes and generously provided me with his own transcriptions of some of the references to me and the Pentagon Papers. WSPTF attorney Nick Akerman kindly made important files available to me.

As often over the last thirty-seven years, I had many long and particularly rewarding conversations with two of my oldest, most valued and respected friends, Morton Halperin and Tran Ngoc Chau. It will be obvious to readers of this book that—along with Janaki Natarajan and Randy Kehler (and, I could add, Noam Chomsky, Howard Zinn, and Peter Dale Scott)—no other living people have had more intellectual and moral influence on me.

Others who gave generously of their time, sharing memories of these events, include Neil Sheehan, Senator Mike Gravel, Representative Pete McCloskey, Charles Cooke, John Dean, Ben Bagdikian, Lynda Resnick, Howard Margolis, Tom Hughes, Norvil Jones, Richard Falk, Fred Branfman, Martin Garbus, Kevin Buckley, Nick Akerman, Frank Mankiewicz, Dunn Gifford, Hedrick Smith, Mark Raskin, Thomas Schelling, Douglas Dowd, Donald Hall, Len Rodberg, Senator Mike Mansfield, General Nguyen Khanh, and Egil Krogh.

Bert Schneider, my close friend since he coproduced *Hearts and Minds* with Peter Davis during our trial, deserves to be recognized as the godfather of this book. His belief in what I had to tell led him to loan me support for two years of writing, and to put me in touch with his friend, superagent John Brockman, who with his wife, Katinka Matson, has been all that agents should be. My deep appreciation goes to Wendy Wolf, who has overseen and moved this project along from beginning to end, and who in addition to making crucial judgments on the tone and nature of the book was a taskmaster of exactly the requisite sternness. I am also grateful to Wendy's assistant, Cliff Corcoran, and to Bruce Giffords for his patient and meticulous copyediting.

Finally: in a book I wrote thirty years ago, I acknowledged Patricia Ellsberg as my lover, partner, and closest friend. The greatest blessing of my life is that those words remain true to this day.

NOTES

Chapter 1. The Tonkin Gulf: August 1964

page

7 "Am under continuous torpedo attack": quoted in "The Phantom Battle That Led to War," 62.

8 "any further unprovoked offensive military action": quoted in Austin, 27.

8 9:42 P.M. in the Tonkin Gulf: Different accounts give different times for messages, reflecting varying time zones in Southeast Asia—in navy terms, Golf, Hotel, and India time. I use Golf time here for Herrick's command ship, off North Vietnam, eleven hours ahead of Washington, D.C. (EDT). (Saigon is on Hotel time, twelve hours ahead; many accounts use this, for convenience of description.) On time zones, see Moise, 63–64.

9 "Torpedoes missed": quoted in "The Phantom Battle That Led to War," 62.

9 "Review of action makes many reported contacts": quoted in Moise, 143.

10 "Entire action leaves many doubts": quoted ibid.

10 Herrick cabled: *Pentagon Papers* (hereafter *PP*), Gravel ed., vol. 3, 185. Scheer, 22. See also Moise, 177.

11 Would they be picked up immediately on radar: Moise, 215.

12 "air action is now in execution": quoted in Austin, 47.

12 *"routine patrol in international waters":* quoted in Siff, 117.

13 *"Unprovoked":* ibid., 119.

15 "our government which supplied these boats": quoted in *PP,* Bantam ed., 266.

15 "In the larger sense, that is so": ibid.

15 "Two junk capture missions": *PP,* Gravel ed., vol. 3, 553–54.

16 the president personally approved the next: Moise, 103–4.

16 "Do they want war by attacking our ships": quoted in Kahin, 224.

16 "Congress approves and supports": quoted in Siff, 115.

17 "no doubt": quoted in Austin, 88.

17 "U.S. public and official patience": Herring, 22.

17 "the greatest devastation": ibid., 7.

18 "D-Day" air assault: *PP,* Gravel ed., vol. 3, 167–68.

18 they recommended to him: ibid., 170.

18 "If prior to the Canadian's trip": quoted in Herring, 17.

19 "That the events of the past few days": *PP,* Gravel ed., vol. 3, 519.

20 *"sans issue":* quoted in Herring, 32.

20 "it is necessary": quoted ibid., 8.

Chapter 2. Cold Warrior, Secret Keeper

page

26 "[I]f the government cannot avoid it": quoted in Mann, 158.

27 "I am against sending American GI's into the mud": quoted ibid., 159.

29 senior economics honors thesis: Ellsberg. "Theories of Rational Choice . . . ," published partially in Ellsberg, "Classic and Current Notions . . ."; Ellsberg, "Theory of the Reluctant Duelist."

29 Ph.D. thesis: Ellsberg, *Risk, Ambiguity and Decision.*

30 uncertain of the consequences: Ellsberg, "Theories of Rational Choice . . ."; *Risk, Ambiguity and Decision.*

30 bargaining theory: "The Theory and Practice of Blackmail."

30 Even before . . . top secret Rand studies: Rand Report R-266, *Selection and Use of Strategic Air Bases,* April 2, 1954; Rand Report R-290, *Protecting U.S. Power to Strike Back in the 1950's and 1960's,* September 1, 1956. Wohlstetter, 1958.

31 the transcendent . . . decision . . . by a national leader: see Ellsberg, "The Crude Analysis . . ."

46 as recently released White House tapes reveal: Beschloss, 87.

Chapter 3. The Road to Escalation

48 "We still seek no wider war": quoted in Siff, 114.

48 Except for their chairman, Maxwell Taylor: *PP,* Gravel ed., vol. 3, 172–73, 179, 193, 550–51; McMaster, 139–47.

49 "the President who saw Southeast Asia go the way": quoted in Dallek, 99.

50 "those that say"; "Some of our people": quoted in Mann, 374.

50 "We seek no wider war": quoted in Dallek, 154–56.

52 In a memoir written years later: Cooper, 223.

53 "the Rostow thesis": quoted in *PP,* Gravel ed., vol. 3, 200: see also McMaster, 156–58.

53 "Given present attitudes": quoted in *PP,* Gravel ed., vol. 3, 201.

54 "graduated pressure on the DRV": ibid., 558–89.

54 "Plan for Action for South Vietnam": ibid., 556–59.

55 "The timing and crescendo": ibid., 558.

55 "would be designed to give the U.S.": ibid., 602.

57 I had recently drafted: Draft Memo to the Joint Chiefs of Staff from the Secretary and Deputy Secretary of Defense: Policy Guidance on Plans for Central War, May 1961, unpublished paper.

59 McNamara revealed in his memoir: McNamara, 345.

61 "hard knock": quoted in McMaster, 92–93, 147, 192.

62 threatening a million deaths from famine: *PP,* Gravel ed., vol. 4, 43.

63 "[W]e are not going to take on the masses": quoted in *PP,* Gravel ed., vol. 3, 163

63 General Taylor spoke of the real possibility: ibid., 174–75.

63 "a serious question": quoted ibid., 175.

64 "U.S. would never again get involved": quoted in *PP,* Gravel ed., vol. 2, 322.

Chapter 4. Planning Provocation

page

65 "to provoke a military DRV response": *PP,* Gravel ed., vol. 3, 193, 559.
65 "The main further question": ibid.
66 an attack on U.S. forces; Bien Hoa air base: ibid., 208.
66 "to use our military power": McNamara, 168.
66 with the mission of provoking: McMaster, 213–14.
66 like waiting for a streetcar: Karnow, 411.
67 "appropriate reprisal action"; "We seek no wider war": *PP,* Gravel ed., vol. 3, 305.
67 "created an ideal opportunity": ibid., 214.
67 "acts of relatively high visibility": ibid., 312.
67 "Once a program of reprisals": ibid.
71 my list of VC incidents; "continued acts"; "further direct provocations": ibid.
72 "We should develop"; ibid., 315.
73 "The President desires": ibid., 703.
79 "it is important not to 'kill the hostage' "; "as much or more": ibid., 706.
82 "My first reaction": quoted in Berman, *Planning a Tragedy,* 187.
82 "The South Vietnamese are losing the war": quoted ibid., 192–93.
83 "I don't believe we can win": quoted ibid., 121.

Chapter 5. "Off the Diving Board": July 1965

88 president's "current intention": quoted in McNamara, 204; *PP,* Gravel ed., vol. 3, 476.
89 "it should be understood": quoted in Berman, 103.
89 "re-establish the military balance": "it will not per se cause": "maintain the military initiative": quoted ibid., 180.
89 "twenty-four more battalions": Westmoreland, 140, 142.
90 "an important change in mission": Berman, 102.
90 "to take the offensive": Kahin, 363.
90 "the vicinity of 500 a month": Berman, 102.
90 A final draft was completed: Ellsberg, Draft speech on Vietnam for Secretary McNamara, unpublished paper.
91 talks I had given at teach-ins: Ellsberg, speech at Antioch College, unpublished paper.
91 On the day my draft: Ellsberg, Draft speech on Vietnam for Secretary McNamara, unpublished paper.
91 "Doesn't it really mean"; "This is a major change": quoted in Kahin, 382.
91 "Are we starting": quoted ibid., 383.
91 "How long will it take?": quoted ibid., 384.
92 General Harold K. Johnson: McNamara, 177.
92 "if we come in"; "what we need": quoted in Kahin, 384.
92 "It all depends"; In a discussion with Clark Clifford: quoted in Halberstam, *The Best and the Brightest,* 596.
92 "until we or our Vietnamese military allies"; "we are talking": quoted in Kahin, 349–50.

93 "In my opinion": quoted in Mann, 452.
93 "inconclusive outcome": *PP,* Gravel ed., vol. 4, 620.
93 "Do all of you think"; "Gallup poll"; "But if you make": quoted in Kahin, 385.
94 "We did not choose": quoted in *PP,* Gravel ed., vol. 3, 476–77.
94 "troubled by a difficult decision": Murphy, 180.
94 "First, we intend": quoted in *PP,* Gravel ed., vol. 3, 477.
95 "Does the fact"; "It does not imply": ibid.
95 "approved for deployment": ibid.
97 "At the Pentagon": Perry, 156.

Chapter 6. Joining the Foreign Legion

page
99 "The Communists have let loose": Lansdale, 176.

Chapter 7. Vietnam: The Lansdale Team

106 I sat in for Lansdale: Ellsberg, memo to Lansdale, July 25, 1966, unpublished paper.

Chapter 8. Travels with Vann

110 David Halberstam on Vann: Halberstam, *The Making of a Quagmire,* 147–49.
111 Here are my notes: Ellsberg, Memo for the Record: Visit to an Insecure Province, Hau Nghia, unpublished paper.

Chapter 9. Losing Hope

126 "In most of III Corps": Ellsberg, memo to Deputy Ambassador Porter, unpublished paper.
139 I gave her a book to read: Hoang Van Chi.
139 interagency study group: on the study and results, see *PP,* Gravel ed., vol. 2, 584–87; for part of my contribution, Ellsberg, *Papers on the War,* 156–70.
139 After meeting the journalist Frances . . . an article together: FitzGerald, 59–67.

Chapter 11. Leaving Vietnam

169 Corruption, he went on: see Ellsberg, memo to Lansdale, The Challenge of Corruption in South Vietnam, November 23, 1965, unpublished paper.
176 But my major effort: Ellsberg, Memo for the Record: Ky's Candidacy and U.S. Stakes in the Coming Election, unpublished paper.

Chapter 12. Jaundice

182 His draft memo: *PP,* Gravel ed., vol. 4, 12.
187 "I have great confidence": quoted in *New York Times,* October 26, 1961.

187 "Officials said": ibid., November 4, 1961.
188 "This was the policy": Schlesinger, 39.
188 "Each step in the deepening": ibid., 47.
190 "without delay"; "reached the conclusion": *PP,* Gravel ed., vol. 2, 90–92.
190 The chances are against": ibid., 108.
191 "tip the scales": ibid.
191 "commit itself": ibid., 109.
191 "a warning through some channel": ibid., 108.
191 "If Diem unwilling": ibid., 105.
196 "Kennedy told Taylor": Reeves, 244–55.

Chapter 13. The Power of Truth

page
199 WAR'S END IN VIEW: *Washington Post,* November 22, 1967.
200 Westmoreland's request: *PP,* Gravel ed., vol. 4, 441–43.
200 I suspected (correctly): Westmoreland, 355; Henry, 17–18.
201 Senators Fulbright, Clark, Aiken: *Washington Post,* February 16, 1968.
201 "at no time even considered": quoted in *New York Times,* February 17, 1968.
201 The president had asked: Schandler, 87–91.
201 "civilian casualties would be minimal"; "If Washington officials": Westmoreland, 338.
202 Indeed, the debate in Congress: See among others, "Rumors on Use of Atomic Arms Stirred by Expert's Asian Trips," *New York Times,* February 11, 1968; "Anonymous Call Set Off Rumors of Nuclear Arms for Vietnam," *New York Times,* February 13; "Wheeler Doubts Khesanh Will Need Atom Weapons," *New York Times,* February 15; "Fulbright and Rusk Clash on Atom Talk," *Washington Post,* February 16; "A-Weapon Report Merits Inquiry, McCarthy Says," *Washington Post,* February 17; "SANE Bids the U.S. Uphold Atom Bomb," *New York Times,* March 3; "Use of Nuclear Weapons Is an Invitation to Disaster," *Washington Post,* March 9.
207 "The figures on enemy strength": Steadman, Memorandum for the Secretary of Defense.
209 "Our fiscal situation": quoted in Gardner, 454–56; Clifford, 515–16.
213 "Something began to say to me": King, 51–52.

Chapter 14. Campaign '68

221 On August 1: Witcover, 309.
223 Robert Kennedy would have supported the peace plank: ibid., 322.
223 "on which Richard Nixon": quoted ibid., 333.

Chapter 15. To the Hotel Pierre

227 "The first step": *PP,* Gravel ed., vol. 4, 603.
233 The next morning . . . the twenty-seven-page draft: Ellsberg, Draft Paper on

Vietnam Options for Henry Kissinger and President Nixon, unpublished paper.
239 In mid-February Halperin: NSSM-1.
240 "Three fourths of the battles": Ellsberg and Lord, Report to President Nixon: Summary of Agency Responses to NSSM-1, unpublished paper.
240 We reported consensus; "U.S. combat support": ibid.
241 "reject the view": ibid.

Chapter 16. The Morality of Continuing the War

page
246 These were . . . a series of internal Rand documents: Ellsberg, U.S. Aims and Leverage in Vietnam, June 1969; Critical Postures on U.S. Decision-Making in Vietnam, June 1969; Vu Van Thai on U.S. Aims and Intervention in Vietnam, July 1969; Confucians and Communists, July 1969; U.S. Support of Diem, July 1969; On Pacification, July 1969; U.S. Policy and the Politics of Others, July 1969; Infeasible Aims and the Politics of Stalemate, August 1969; Communists and Vietnamese, August 1969; Revolutionary Judo, July 1970, unpublished papers.
249 standard historical accounts: Devillers, McAlister, Lacouture and Devillers, Lancaster.
251 "To negotiate on this basis": *PP,* Gravel ed., vol. 3, 502.
251 "Don't let me leave": quoted in Sainteny, 210.
252 "Although the French": *PP,* Gravel ed., vol. 1, 29.
252 "We have not urged": *PP,* GPO ed., vol. 8, 143–49.

Chapter 17. War Resisters

263 "a whole country is unjustly overrun": Thoreau, 229. See also Schlesinger, *The Imperial Presidency,* 42–43.
263 "ours is the invading army": ibid.
263 "someone interfered": ibid., 240.
263 "soldier . . . who refuses": ibid., 232.
263 "thousands who are *in opinion* opposed": ibid., 230, emphasis in original.
263 "Cast your vote": ibid., 235.
266 The assumption was that the Tet offensive: see, for example (as late as 1988), Sheehan, 722: "[After March 31, 1968,] John Vann could not accept the death of the war. He could not admit that Tet had written a finis to it."
272 "That's right, it's come": "Dress Rehearsal Rag," Leonard Cohen, 1967.

Chapter 18. Extrication

274 these findings closed the book for me on the quagmire myth: Ellsberg, Escalating in a Quagmire, unpublished paper; Ellsberg, "The Quagmire Myth and the Stalemate Machine."
279 Chomsky review of Zinn: Chomsky, 221–94 (first written July 1967).
282 "There should by now be": Ellsberg, Letter to Charles Bolté, unpublished paper.

Chapter 19. Murder and the Lying Machine

page

287 Haldeman diary: Haldeman, 86, 88, 90, 91.

Chapter 21. The Rand Letter

312 "Dear Sirs: Now that the American people": Ellsberg et al., letter to *New York Times,* unpublished paper.

Chapter 22. Capitol Hill

325 The next day, November 5: Fraser.

Chapter 23. Leaving Rand

330 Nixon would be reducing force levels slowly: Ellsberg, Notes on the President's Speech of November 3, 1969, and Memo to Senator Eugene McCarthy, unpublished papers.

334 He did want me to remain a Rand consultant: Ellsberg, Revolutionary Judo, unpublished paper.

341 On May 13 I testified: Ellsberg, *Papers on the War,* 197–233.

Chapter 24. Kissinger

344 One of the talks: Ellsberg, "The Theory and Practice of Blackmail."

354 "How many will die"; "At least 300,000": Ellsberg, *Papers on the War,* 271.

355 ". . . Americans must look past": ibid., 274.

Chapter 25. Congress

364 She pointed out to me . . . filled with phrases about: respectively, *PP,* Gravel ed., vol. 3, 649; vol. 4, 35; vol. 3, 650; ibid., 706; ibid., 410; ibid., 706; ibid., 509; vol. 4, 45–46; ibid., 44; ibid., 33; ibid., 65.

Chapter 29. Going Underground

396 "I did not recommend": quoted in Ellsberg, *Papers on the War,* 113.

398 "Daniel gave up everything": quoted in *Detroit News,* June 18, 1971.

398 "he wanted his father Harry Ellsberg": *Boston Globe,* June 22, 1971.

400 "During the controversy": Ellsberg, interview by Walter Cronkite, June 23, 1971.

402 "The newspaper also warned": Ungar, 209.

403 "asking us to ride herd": ibid., 210.

403 Four justices: Rudenstine, 263.

Chapter 30. The War Goes On

page

413 "To the ordinary guy": the President and Haldeman, 3:09 P.M., June 14, 1971, Oval Office. National Security Archive. See transcription by National Security Archive, George Washington University, www.gwu.edu/~nsarchiv/NSAEBB.

418 "We've got to quit thinking": the President and Kissinger, 8:53 A.M., April 25, 1972, Executive Office Building conversation 332-22.

418 "How many did we kill": the President and Kissinger, 10:45 A.M., April 25, 1972, Executive Office Building.

418 "blockade plus surgical bombing": the President and Haig, 12:42 P.M., May 2, 1972, Oval Office conversation 717-20.

419 "Vietnam: Here's those little cocksuckers": the President, Kissinger, Haig, Connally, 3:04 P.M., May 4, 1972, Executive Office Building conversation 334-44.

419 "The only place where": ibid. See also Deb Reichmann, "Tapes: Nixon Wanted to Use Nuke Bomb." *Washington Post,* February 28, 2002.

421 Since leaders in both Washington and Saigon: Berman, *No Peace, No Honor,* 234.

421 As Berman reveals: ibid., 254–58.

Chapter 31. The Road to Watergate

422 "In public opinion, it actually": the President and Kissinger, 3:09 P.M., June 13, 1971, Oval Office. National Security Archive.

423 "Laos and Cambodia": ibid.

423 "Hello, Mr. President, the Attorney General": the President and Ehrlichman, 7:13 P.M., June 14, 1971, Oval Office telephone conversation. National Security Archive.

424 a "low key" warning: the President and Mitchell, 7:19 P.M., June 14, 1971, Oval Office telephone conversation. National Security Archive.

424 "The injunction was only": the President, Haldeman, and Ziegler, 10:39 A.M., June 16, 1971, Oval Office conversation 522-2.

424 "Stuff on Kennedy": the President and Ziegler, 12:59 P.M., June 16, 1971, Oval Office conversation 522-7.

424 "I want to get out the stuff": the President, Kissinger, Ehrlichman, and Haldeman, 5:15 P.M., June 17, 1971, Oval Office conversation 525-1.

424 After Kissinger had left the room: the President to Colson, June 17, 1971, White House Telephone Transcripts, Oval Office 525-1.

425 "You simply cannot allow": the President and Colson, 6:21 P.M., June 15, 1971, Oval Office telephone conversation. National Security Archive.

425 "has a large picture": the President, Haldeman, Ehrlichman, and Mitchell, 5:09 P.M., June 22, 1971, Oval Office.

425 "I just have to do this": quoted in Ungar, 186.

425 "It will be very good": the President, Haldeman, and Ziegler, 9:38 A.M., June 24, 1971, Oval Office. Kutler, 5.

426 "[G]oddamn it, *somebody has got to go to jail!*": the President and Haldeman, 9:56 A.M., June 15, 1971, Oval Office.

426 "Incidentally, could you": the President, Mitchell, and Ziegler, 3:45 P.M., June 15, 1971, Oval Office conversation 521-9.

426 "Why doesn't the FBI": the President, Ziegler, and Haldeman, 2:42 P.M., June 17, 1971, Oval Office.

426 "The reason you have to be": the President, Kissinger, and Ziegler, 10:39 P.M., June 15, 1971, Oval Office conversation 520-4.

427 There were special reasons: For concern about leaks relating to Cambodia, Laos, or Menu, the President, Haig, and Kissinger, June 14, 1971, Oval Office; the President and Haldeman, 11:04 P.M., June 23, Oval Office; the President and Kissinger, June 30, Oval Office; the President and Haldeman, 8:45 A.M., July 1, Oval Office; the President and Ehrlichman, 10:58 A.M., October 8, Oval Office.

427 "Whenever I've had to call": the President and Kissinger, 3:09 P.M., June 23, 1971, Oval Office telephone conversation.

431 "A popular government": Foerstel, p. 11, citing *Writings of James Madison,* 9, ed. Gaillard Hunt (New York: Putnam, 1900–1910), p. 103.

432 "Don't you agree": the President, Mitchell, and Kissinger, 2:55 P.M., June 30, 1971, Oval Office. Kutler, 6.

432 "a bundle of documents": the President and Kissinger, 2:31 P.M., June 23, 1971, Oval Office.

433 "earlier"; "Why he never came forward": the President, Mitchell, and Kissinger, 2:55 P.M., June 30, 1971, Oval Office.

433 ". . . The shit's going to hit the fan": ibid.

434 "Daniel Ellsberg is the most dangerous man": quoted in Hersh, 385.

434 "This is the time to act": quoted ibid., 330.

434 "But you're pretty secure here": the President and Kissinger, 2:31 P.M., June 23, 1971, Oval Office.

435 "The difficulty is that": the President, Haldeman, Colson, and Ehrlichman, 10:28 A.M., July 1, 1971, Oval Office. Kutler, 10.

435 "Mathias is playing a little cat and mouse game": the President, Mitchell, Ehrlichman, and Haldeman, 11:47 A.M., July 6, 1971, Oval Office (Watergate Special Prosecution Force file segment, conversation no. 538-015, White House tapes).

435 "kid gloves": the President and Ehrlichman, 11:09 A.M., July 20, 1971, Oval Office.

436 "With respect to Ellsberg": the President, Mitchell, Ehrlichman, and Haldeman, 11:47 A.M., July 6, 1971.

436 "the Mathias thing": ibid.

437 "Actually, when Mitchell leaves": the President, Haldeman, and Colson, 9:15 A.M., July 2, 1971, Oval Office. Kutler, 5.

437 "a man in this White House": the President, Haldeman, Colson, and Ehrlichman, 10:28 A.M., July 1, 1971, Oval Office. Kutler, 10.

437 "You know, how he knew": the President and Haldeman, 3:09 P.M., June 14, 1971, Oval Office. National Security Archive.

437 ". . . we won the [Alger] Hiss case": the President, Haldeman, and Kissinger, 8:45 A.M., July 1, 1971, Oval Office. Kutler, 7.

438 "one guy on the outside": the President, Haldeman, Colson, and Ehrlichman, 10:28 A.M., July 1, 1971, Oval Office. Kutler, 13.

438 "Do you think this guy": Charles Colson's transcript of his phone conversation with Howard Hunt, July 1, 1971, Watergate documents, author's files.

438 "I had forgotten": memo to H. R. Haldeman from Charles Colson. Re: Howard Hunt, July 2, 1971, ibid.

438 "indicate direct complicity": transcript of E. Howard Hunt grand jury testimony, May 2, 1973, ibid.

439 "Your grandfather would be proud": quoted in Lukas, 101–2.

440 In his statement to Judge Gerhart Gesell: Statement to Court Prior to Sentencing, January 22, 1974. Furnished to me by Nathaniel Akerman.

440 "I think Mitchell ought": the President and Kissinger, 2:20 P.M., July 27, 1971, Oval Office.

441 "Primary, of course": "To discredit Dr. Ellsberg"; "My best recollection": Statement to Court Prior to Sentencing.

442 For concern about leaks of contingency plans, including the mining and blockade of Haiphong, and the taking out of the dikes: the President and Kissinger, June 13, June 15, June 30, 1971; the President, Kissinger, and Haldeman, June 30, 1971.

Chapter 32. End of a Trial

page

448 "That's good. Let me say": the President and Kleindienst, 8:20 A.M., April 25, 1973, White House telephone conversation. Kutler, 335.

448 "Okay. Well, sleep well, boy": ibid.

448 "and was inclined to the view": the President and Petersen, 4:31 P.M., April 27, 1973, White House telephone conversation. Kutler, 347.

450 Ehrlichman claimed that Byrne: Lukas, 448–49.

450 White House tapes later showed: ibid., 448.

452 "crazy": the President and Petersen, 5:37 P.M., April 25, 1973, Executive Office Building. Kutler, 337.

452 "cancer on the presidency": Kutler, 247.

452 "expenses"; "the seamy things": the President, Haldeman, and Dean, 10:12 A.M., March 21, 1973, Oval Office. Kutler, 253.

453 As Larry Berman shows: Berman, 195, 199, 218.

453 They were unaware . . . which Kissinger had secretly been recommending: ibid., 254–60.

454 "in that scope that Mr. Boudin": Ginger, 160–63.

457 "For example, on this national security thing": the President, Haldeman, and Haig, 12:53 P.M., May 11, 1973, Oval Office. Kutler, 473.

Author's Note: I encourage readers to send corrections and comments on this book to me at daniel@ellsberg.net. I may not be able to respond individually to all queries or comments. Unless otherwise requested, some may be posted on www.ellsberg.net, which will also present additional references to documentation, along with past and current files by me extending my discussion of various subjects addressed here.

WORKS CITED

Austin, Anthony. *The President's War.* Philadelphia: Lippincott, 1971.

Bagdikian, Ben H. *Double Vision.* Boston: Beacon Press, 1995.

Berman, Larry. *Planning a Tragedy: The Americanization of the War in Vietnam.* New York: W. W. Norton, 1982.

———. *No Peace, No Honor: Nixon, Kissinger, and Betrayal in Vietnam.* New York: The Free Press, 2001.

Beschloss, Michael. *Reaching for Glory: Lyndon Johnson's Secret White House Tapes, 1964–65.* New York: Simon and Schuster, 2001.

Bird, Kai. *The Color of Truth: McGeorge Bundy and William Bundy: Brothers in Arms.* New York: Simon and Schuster, 1998.

Bondurant, Joan V. *Conquest of Violence: The Gandhian Philosophy of Conflict.* Berkeley: University of California Press, 1965.

Bundy, William P. *A Tangled Web: The Making of Foreign Policy in the Nixon Presidency.* New York: Hill and Wang, 1998.

Chomsky, Noam. *American Power and the New Mandarins.* New York: Pantheon, 1969.

Cooper, Chester L. *The Lost Crusade: America in Vietnam.* New York: Dodd, Mead, 1970.

Dallek, Robert. *Flawed Giant: Lyndon Johnson and His Times, 1961–1973.* New York: Oxford University Press, 1998.

Deming, Barbara. *Revolution and Equilibrium.* New York: Grossman, 1971.

Devillers, Philippe. *Histoire du Viet-Nam de 1940 à 1952.* Paris: Éditions du Seuil, 1952.

Ellsberg, Daniel. "Theories of Rational Choice Under Uncertainty: The Contributions of von Neumann and Morgenstern." Senior honors thesis, Harvard University, 1952.

———. "Classic and Current Notions of 'Measurable Utility.'" *Economic Journal* 64:255 (September 1954), 528–56.

———. "Theory of the Reluctant Duelist." *American Economic Review* 45:5 (December 1956), 910–23.

———. "The Theory and Practice of Blackmail." In *Bargaining: Formal Theories of Negotiation,* ed. Oran R. Young. Urbana: University of Illinois Press, 1959, 1975.

———. "The Crude Analysis of Strategic Choice." *American Economic Review* 6:2 (May 1961), 472–78.

———. "Risk, Ambiguity, and the Savage Axioms." *Quarterly Journal of Economics* 75:4 (November 1961), 643–69.

———. "Vietnam Diary—Notes from the Journal of a Young American in Saigon." *Reporter* (January 13, 1966).

———. "Statement and Testimony of Daniel Ellsberg, Senior Research Associate, Center of International Studies, MIT." Hearings Before the Committee on Foreign Relations United States Senate, 91st Congress, Second Session: *The Impact of the War in Southeast Asia on the U.S. Economy. Part 1: May 13, 1970,* 257–346. Excerpts in Ellsberg, *Papers on the War,* 91–233.

———. "Laos: What Nixon Is Up To." *New York Review of Books* (March 11, 1971). Reprinted in Ellsberg, *Papers on the War,* 259–74.

———. "The Quagmire Myth and the Stalemate Machine." *Public Policy* (Spring 1971). Revised version in Ellsberg, *Papers on the War,* 42–135.

———. Interview by Walter Cronkite. *CBS News Special Report,* June 23, 1971. For transcript, see: www.ellsberg.net.

———. *Papers on the War.* New York: Simon and Schuster, 1972.

———. *Risk, Ambiguity and Decision.* New York: Garland, 2001. Ph.D. thesis, Harvard University, 1962.

———, Melvin Gurtov, Oleg Hoeffding, Arnold Horelick, Konrad Kellen, and Paul F. Langer. Letter to the Editor: A Case Against Staying in Vietnam. October 12, 1969.

FitzGerald, Frances. "The Tragedy of Saigon." *Atlantic Monthly* (December 1966), 59–67.

Foerstel, Herbert N. *Freedom of Information and the Right to Know.* Westport, Conn.: Greenwood Press, 1999.

Fraser, Don. Speech, November 5, 1969. *Congressional Record*—House, H10598–99.

Gardner, Lloyd C. *Pay Any Price: Lyndon Johnson and the Wars for Vietnam.* Chicago: Ivan R. Dee, 1995.

Ginger, Ann Fagan. *Pentagon Papers Case Collection.* Berkeley, Calif., and Dobbs Ferry, N.Y.: Oceana Publications, 1975.

Halberstam, David. *The Making of a Quagmire:* New York: Random House, 1965.

———. *The Best and the Brightest.* New York: Random House, 1992.

Haldeman, H. R. *The Haldeman Diaries: Inside the Nixon White House.* New York: Putnam, 1994.

Henry, John B., II. "February 1968," *Foreign Policy* 4 (Fall 1971), 3–33.

Herring, George C., ed. *The Secret Diplomacy of the Vietnam War: The Negotiating Volumes of the Pentagon Papers.* Austin: University of Texas Press, 1983.

Hersh, Seymour M., *The Price of Power.* New York: Summit Books, 1983.

Hoang Van Chi. *From Colonialism to Communism.* New York: Allied Publishers, 1964.

Hoffman, Paul. *Moratorium: An American Protest.* New York: Tower Publications, 1970.

Kahin, George McTurnin. *Intervention.* New York: Knopf, 1986.

Karnow, Stanley. *Vietnam: A History.* New York: Viking, 1983.

King, Martin Luther, Jr. *Stride Toward Freedom.* New York: Harper and Row, 1958.

Kutler, Stanley I. *Abuse of Power.* New York: The Free Press, 1997.

Lacouture, Jean, and Philippe Devillers. *La Fin d'une guerre.* Paris: Éditions du Seuil, 1960.

Lancaster, Donald. *The Emancipation of French Indochina.* New York: Oxford University Press, 1961.

Lansdale, Edward G. "Viet Nam: Do We Understand Revolution?" *Foreign Affairs* 4:1 (October 1964).

Logevall, Fredrik. *Choosing War.* Berkeley: University of California Press, 1999.

Lukas, J. Anthony. *Nightmare: The Underside of the Nixon Years.* New York: Bantam, 1977.

McAlister, John T., Jr. *Vietnam: The Origins of Revolution.* New York: Doubleday Anchor Books, 1971.

McMaster, H. R. *Dereliction of Duty: Lyndon Johnson, Robert McNamara, the Joint Chiefs of Staff, and the Lies That Led to Vietnam.* New York: HarperCollins, 1997.

McNamara, Robert S. *In Retrospect: The Tragedy and Lessons of Vietnam.* New York: Times Books, 1995.

Moise, Edwin E. *Tonkin Gulf and the Escalation of the Vietnam War.* Chapel Hill: University of North Carolina Press, 1996.

Murphy, Bruce Allen. *Fortas: The Rise and Ruin of a Supreme Court Justice.* New York: Morrow, 1988.

National Security Archive, George Washington University: www.gwu.edu/~nsarchiv.

NSSM-1. *Congressional Record,* May 10, 1972, E 4975–5066.

The Pentagon Papers: The Defense Department History of United States Decision-making on Vietnam, vols. 1–4. Boston: Beacon Press, 1971. (Senator Gravel edition.)

The Pentagon Papers: The Secret History of the Vietnam War, ed. *New York Times.* New York: Bantam, 1971. (*NYT*-Bantam edition.)

Perry, Mark. *Four Stars.* Boston: Houghton Mifflin, 1989.

"The Phantom Battle That Led to War." *U.S. News & World Report* (July 23, 1984), 356–67.

Rand Report R-266. *Selection and Use of Strategic Air Bases.* Santa Monica: Rand Corporation, April 2, 1954.

Rand Report R-290. *Protecting U.S. Power to Strike Back in the 1950's and 1960's.* Santa Monica: Rand Corporation, September 1, 1956.

Reeves, Richard. *President Kennedy: Profile of Power.* New York: Simon and Schuster, 1993.

Rudenstine, David. *The Day the Presses Stopped: A History of the Pentagon Papers Case.* Berkeley: University of California Press, 1996.

Sainteny, Jean. *Histoire d'une paix manquée: Indochine 1945–1947.* Paris: A. Fayard, 1967.

Schandler, Herbert Y. *The Unmaking of a President: Lyndon Johnson and Vietnam.* Princeton: Princeton University Press, 1977.

Scheer, Robert. "Tonkin—Dubious Premise for a War." *Los Angeles Times,* April 29, 1985.

Schlesinger, Arthur M., Jr. *The Bitter Heritage: Vietnam and American Democracy, 1941–1966.* Greenwich, Conn: Fawcett, 1968.

———. *The Imperial Presidency.* Boston: Houghton Mifflin, 1973.

Sheehan, Neil. *A Bright Shining Lie: John Paul Vann and America in Vietnam.* New York: Random House, 1988.

Siff, Ezra. *Why the Senate Slept.* Westport, Conn.: Praeger, 1999.

Steadman, Richard C. Memorandum for the Secretary of Defense [Clark Clifford]. Subject: Enemy Strength in South Vietnam. March 19, 1968. Courtesy of John Prados.

Thoreau, Henry D. *Walden and Resistance to Civil Authority.* 2nd ed. Ed. William Rossi. New York: Norton, 1992.

Ungar, Sanford J. *The Papers and the Papers.* New York: Dutton, 1972.

VanDeMark, Brian. *Into the Quagmire.* New York: Oxford University Press, 1991.

Westmoreland, General William C. *A Soldier Reports.* Garden City, N.Y.: Doubleday, 1976.

Witcover, Jules. *The Year the Dream Died: Revisiting in America.* New York: Warner, 1997.

Wohlstetter, Albert. "The Delicate Balance of Terror." *Foreign Affairs* 37:21 (January 1958).

Zinn, Howard. *Vietnam: The Logic of Withdrawal.* Boston: Beacon Press, 1967.

Unpublished papers by Daniel Ellsberg, accessible on www.ellsberg.net

Draft Memo to the Joint Chiefs of Staff from the Secretary and Deputy Secretary of Defense: Policy Guidance on Plans for Central War (draft of a section of the proposed new Basic National Security Policy). May, 1961.

Fishnet Report: Viet Cong Acts of Violence, February 11–15, 1965.

Speech at Antioch College, Vietnam Colloquium, April 25, 1965.

Draft Speech on Vietnam for Secretary McNamara. July 22, 1965.

Memo for the Record: Visit to an Insecure Province, Hau Nghia. October 1965.

Memo to Lansdale: The Challenge of Corruption in South Vietnam. November 23, 1965.

Memo to Deputy Ambassador Porter. Evaluation of 1966 Prospects for Revolutionary Development in III Corps National Priority Area. March 31, 1966.

Memo to Lansdale, Mission Council Meeting. July 25, 1966.

Memo for the Record: Ky's Candidacy and U.S. Stakes in the Coming Election. May 4, 1967.

Some Prospects and Problems in Vietnam. February 15, 1968.

Draft Paper on Vietnam Options for Henry Kissinger and President Nixon. December 27, 1968.

———. Vietnam Questions: NSSM-1.

Report to President Nixon: Summary of Agency Responses to NSSM-1. Coauthored with Winston Lord. February 1969.

U.S. Aims and Leverage in Vietnam, 1950–1965. June 1969.

Critical Postures on U.S. Decision-Making in Vietnam: Multiple Choice. June 1969.

U.S. Policy and the Politics of Others. July 1969.

Vu Van Thai on U.S. Aims and Intervention in Vietnam. July 1969.

Confucians and Communists: Hoang Van Chi on the Relation of Marxist to Confucian Concepts, and Cultural Susceptibility to Communism. July 1969.

On Pacification: Comments by Thai and Ellsberg. July 1969.

U.S. Support of Diem: Comments by Vu Van Thai. July 1969.
Some Lessons from Failure in Vietnam. Rand P-4036. July 1969.
Communists and Vietnamese: Comments by Hoang Van Chi. August 1969.
Infeasible Aims and the Politics of Stalemate. August 1969.
Letter to Charles Bolté. September 23, 1969.
Reflections on Vietnam Policy. November 1969.
Memo to Senator Eugene McCarthy: Notes on Vietnam Policy: A Strategy for Dissent. January 21, 1970.
Revolutionary Judo. July 1970.
Escalating in a Quagmire. Presented to American Political Science Association Annual Meeting. September 1970.
Coercive Diplomacy in the Light of Vietnam: Some Preliminary Notes. November 9, 1970.

INDEX